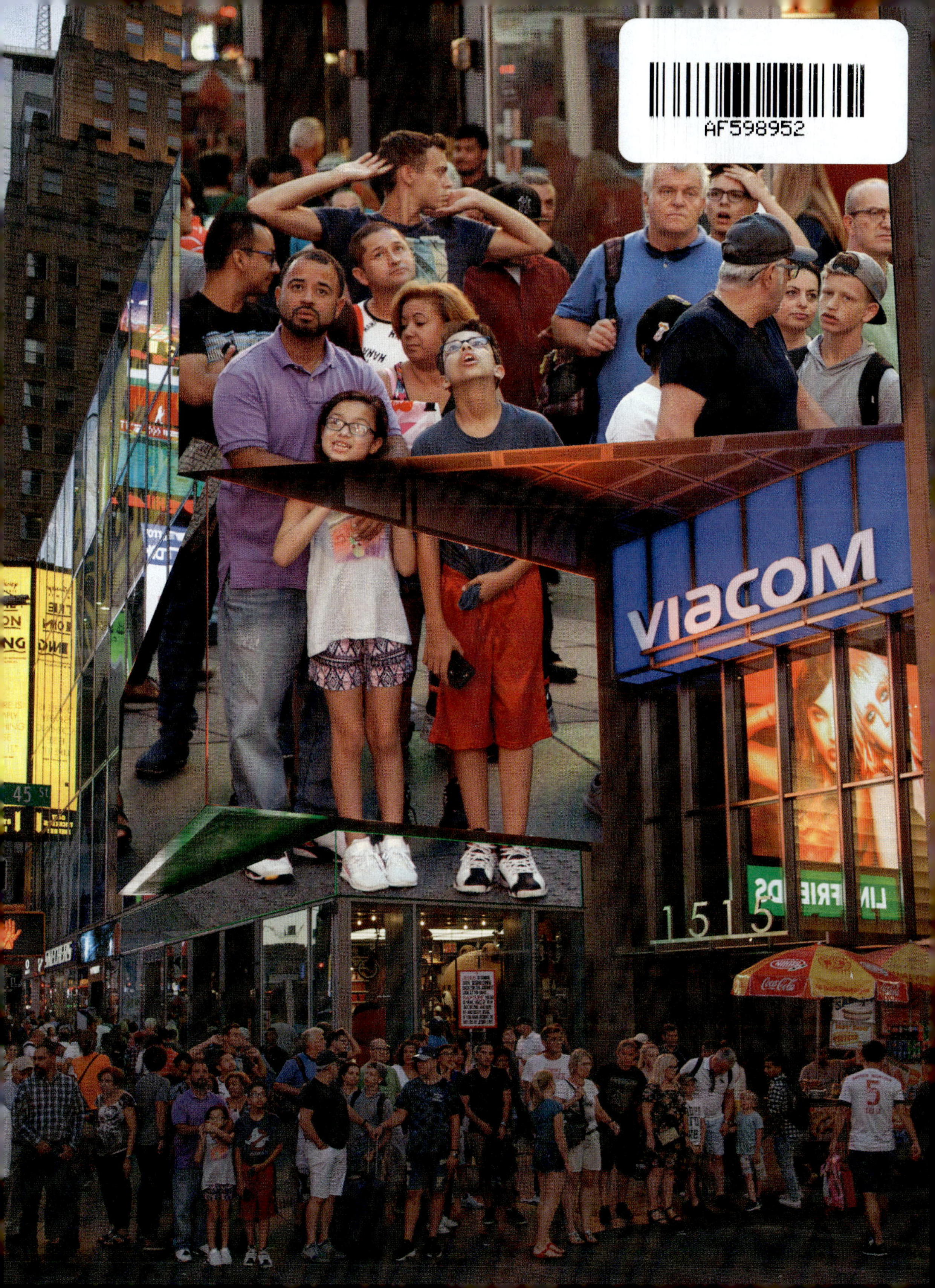
viacom
1515
45 St

COLOPHON

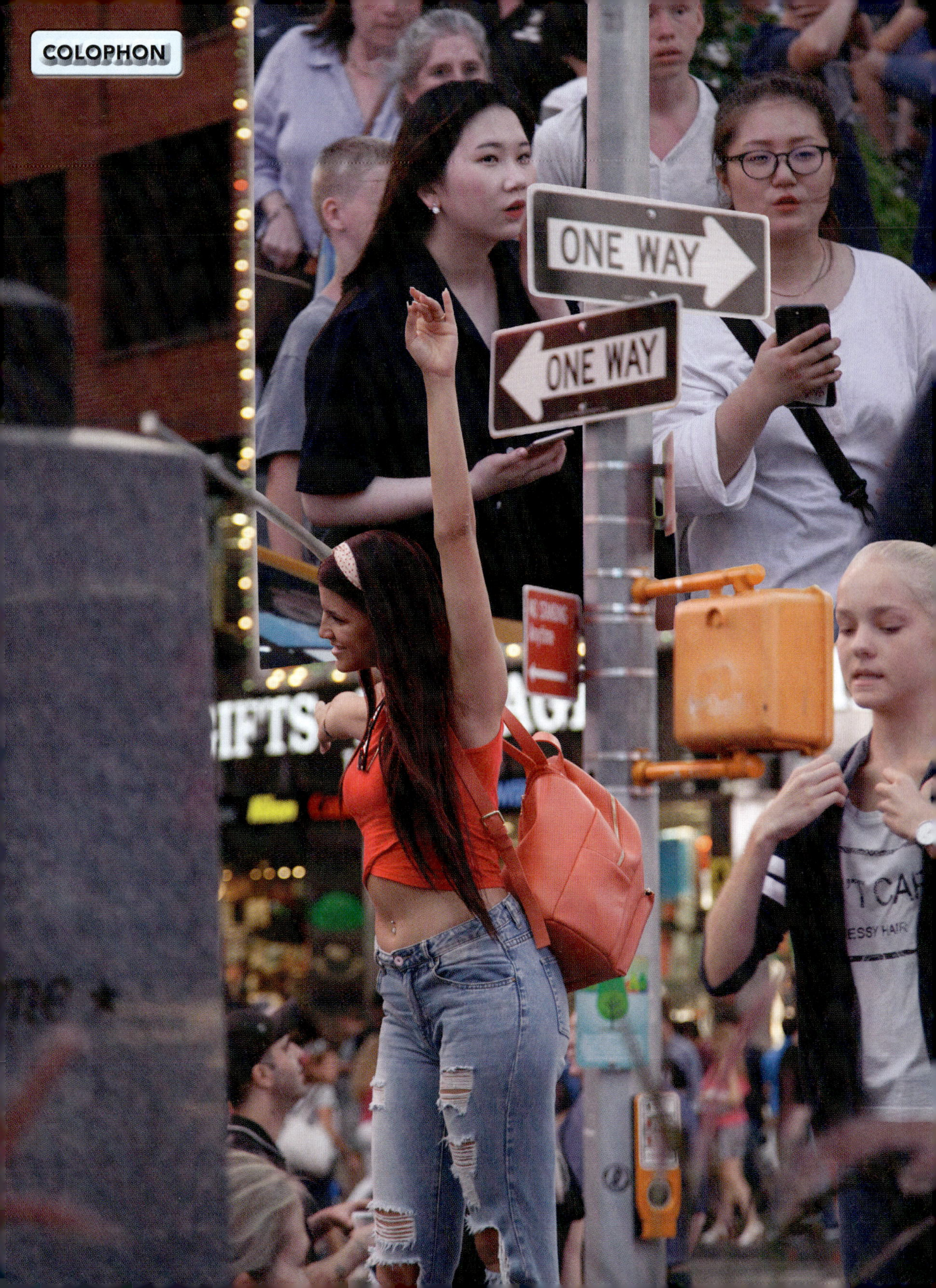

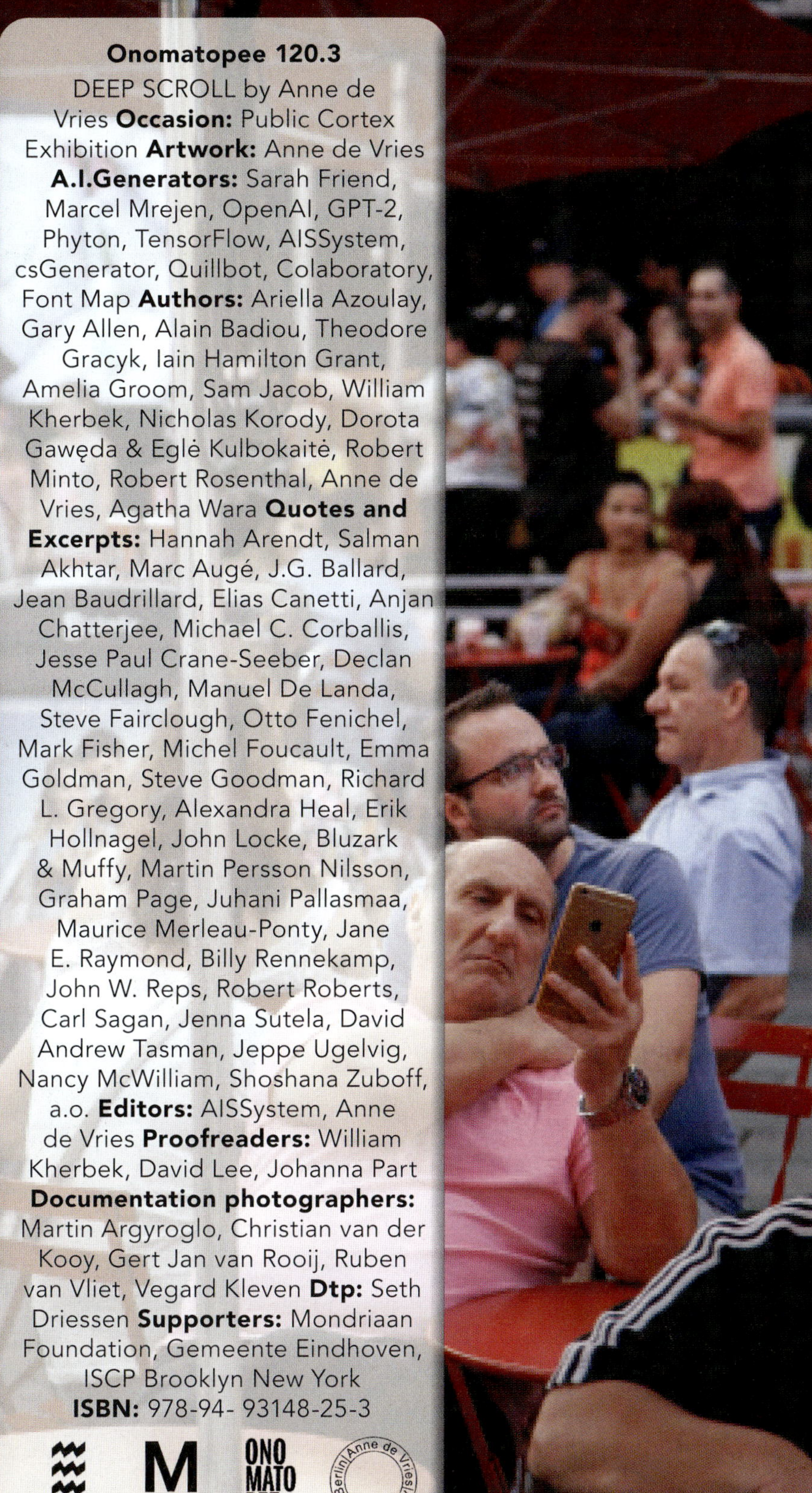

Onomatopee 120.3
DEEP SCROLL by Anne de Vries **Occasion:** Public Cortex Exhibition **Artwork:** Anne de Vries **A.I.Generators:** Sarah Friend, Marcel Mrejen, OpenAI, GPT-2, Phyton, TensorFlow, AISSystem, csGenerator, Quillbot, Colaboratory, Font Map **Authors:** Ariella Azoulay, Gary Allen, Alain Badiou, Theodore Gracyk, Iain Hamilton Grant, Amelia Groom, Sam Jacob, William Kherbek, Nicholas Korody, Dorota Gawęda & Eglė Kulbokaitė, Robert Minto, Robert Rosenthal, Anne de Vries, Agatha Wara **Quotes and Excerpts:** Hannah Arendt, Salman Akhtar, Marc Augé, J.G. Ballard, Jean Baudrillard, Elias Canetti, Anjan Chatterjee, Michael C. Corballis, Jesse Paul Crane-Seeber, Declan McCullagh, Manuel De Landa, Steve Fairclough, Otto Fenichel, Mark Fisher, Michel Foucault, Emma Goldman, Steve Goodman, Richard L. Gregory, Alexandra Heal, Erik Hollnagel, John Locke, Bluzark & Muffy, Martin Persson Nilsson, Graham Page, Juhani Pallasmaa, Maurice Merleau-Ponty, Jane E. Raymond, Billy Rennekamp, John W. Reps, Robert Roberts, Carl Sagan, Jenna Sutela, David Andrew Tasman, Jeppe Ugelvig, Nancy McWilliam, Shoshana Zuboff, a.o. **Editors:** AISSystem, Anne de Vries **Proofreaders:** William Kherbek, David Lee, Johanna Part **Documentation photographers:** Martin Argyroglo, Christian van der Kooy, Gert Jan van Rooij, Ruben van Vliet, Vegard Kleven **Dtp:** Seth Driessen **Supporters:** Mondriaan Foundation, Gemeente Eindhoven, ISCP Brooklyn New York
ISBN: 978-94- 93148-25-3

EINDHOVEN

M mondriaan fonds

ONO MATO PEE

Anne de Vries Amsterdam&Berlin

IS JUST AROUND THE CORNER ON 46TH STREET
CHARLIE AND THE CHOCOLATE FACTORY
THE NEW MUSICAL
CharlieOnBroadway.com
NUTTY, DARK AND SEMI-SWEET
SQUARE
Special

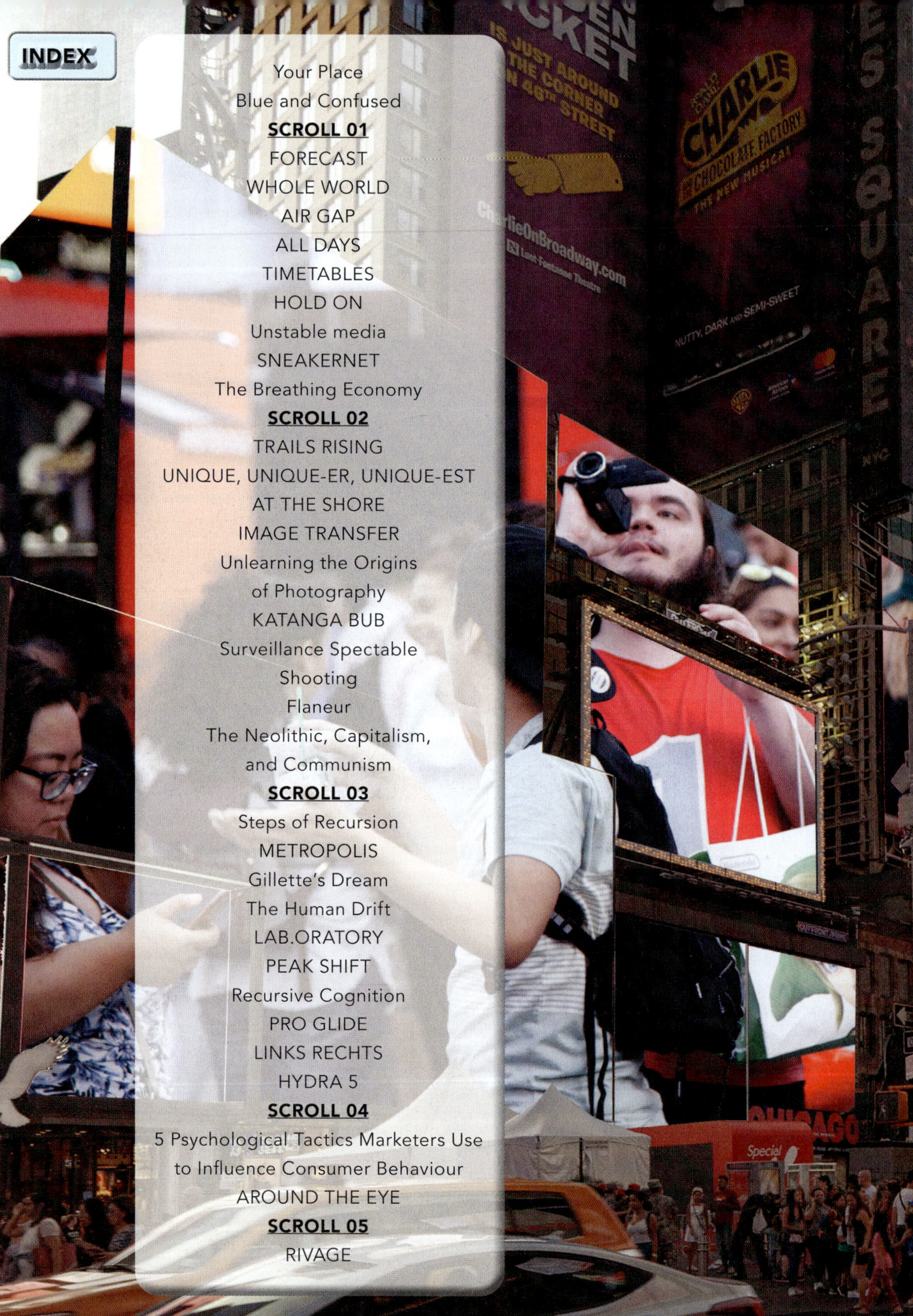

INDEX

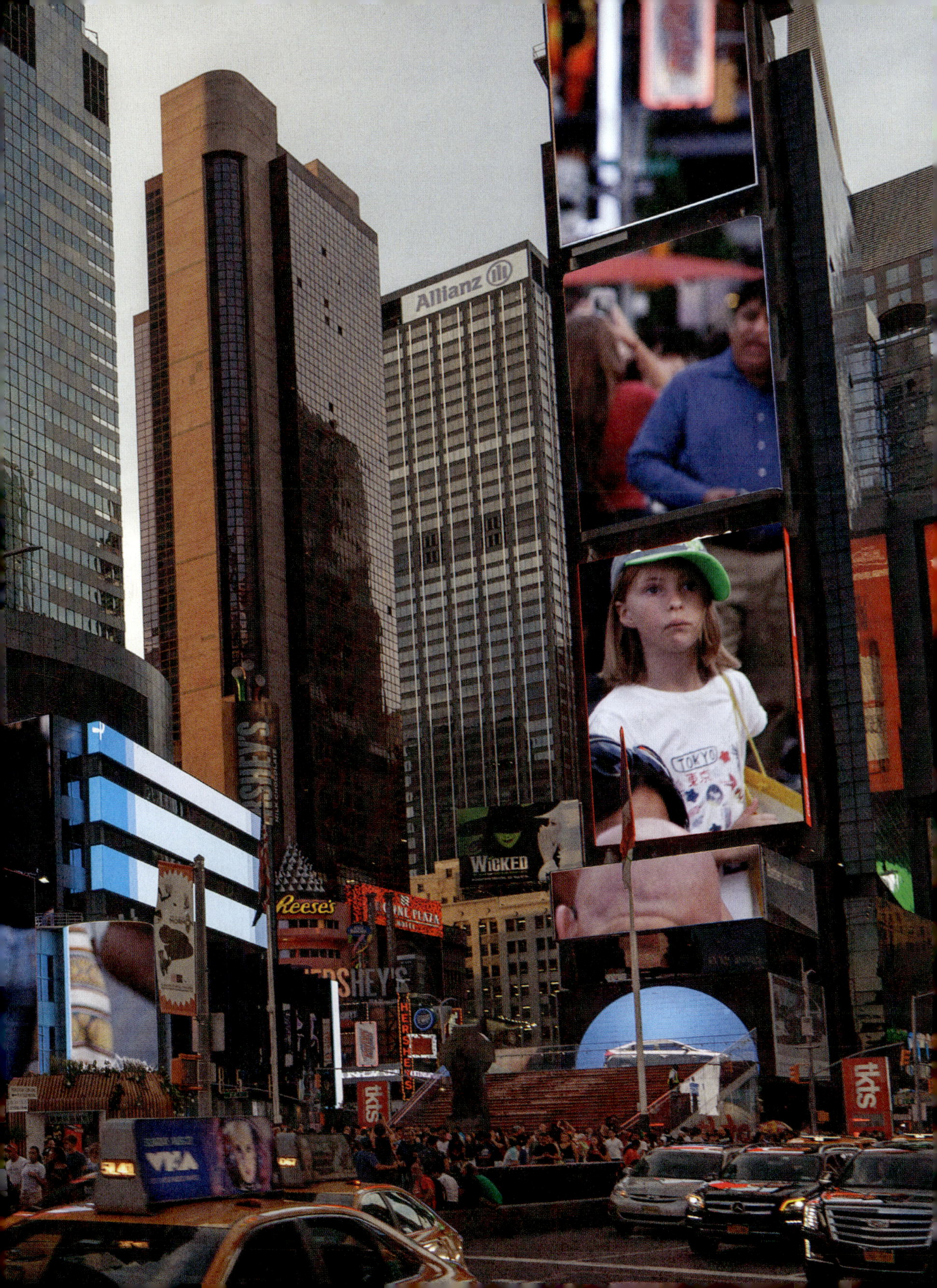
Allianz
WICKED
Reese's
tkts
tkts

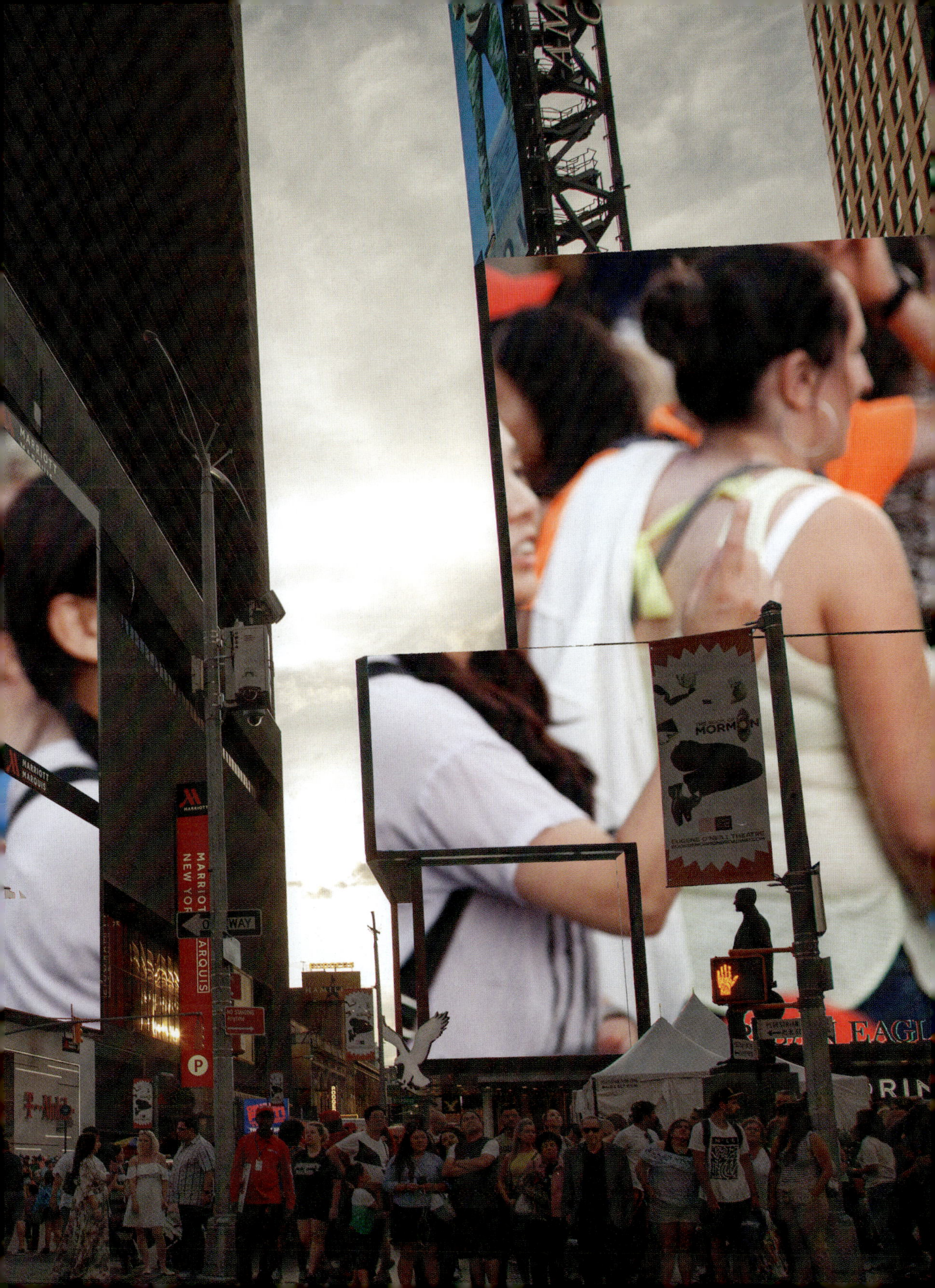
MARRIOTT
MARQUIS
MORMON
WAY

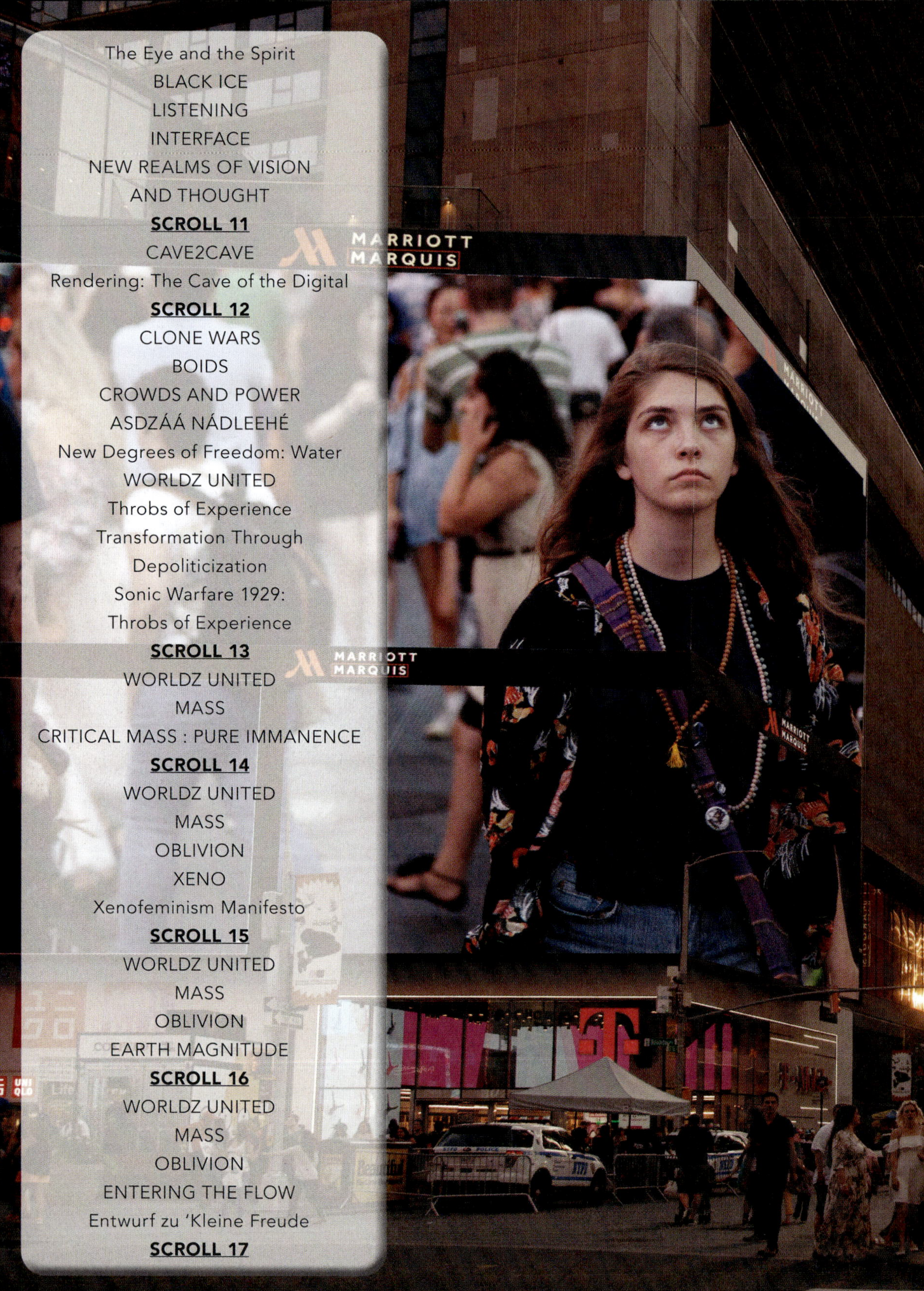
MARRIOTT
MARQUIS

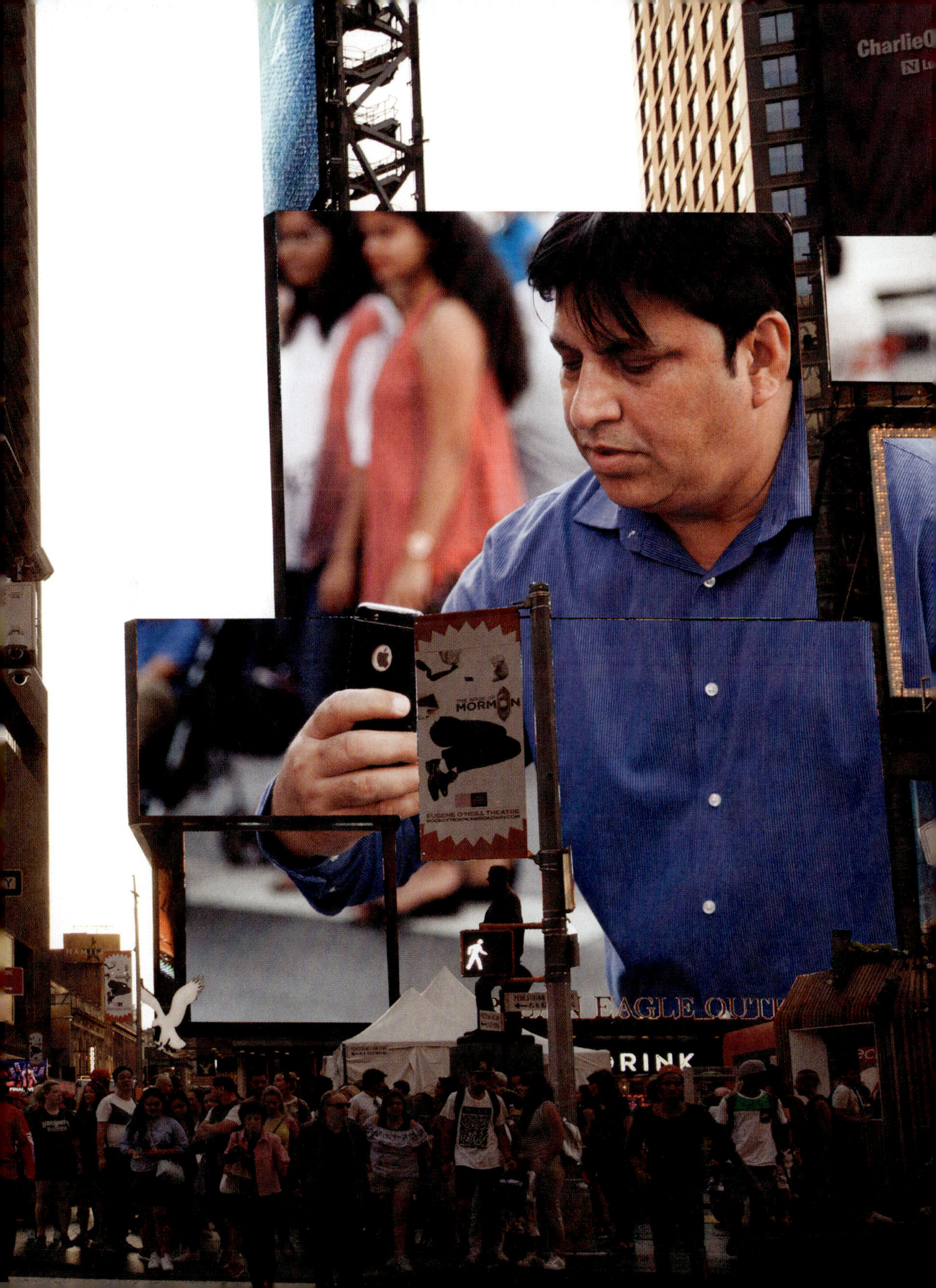
MORMON
EUGENE O'NEILL THEATRE
EAGLE

ANARCHIST
Lost in tech, time and space
Expect Resistance
Anarchism:
What it really stands for Anarchy
INTERGRITY 3D
THE ANTHEM
Mission Statement
T.A.Z.
What Is Hauntology?
LISTENING
OUTLINE:
Noise, The Political Economy of Music
The Ultimate Vote
In the Face of Fascism
RAVE Act

SCROLL 18

A Harder Loving World
POLYMORPHOUS
Until late NO COVER
Homo Machina
FREE ZONE
Architecture of the Anthropocene:
Haunted Houses, Living Buildings,
and Other Horror Stories

SCROLL 19

Homo Machina
SEX CROWD DEBRIS
A Harder Loving World
Face of Freedom
FREE ZONE
Soulsa
Windy
Anarchy in the Hive Mind
Deep Joy, be carefull.

Blue
Confused
Like a dream
But true
trying
to find
Direction
A way
away from insignificance
by fulfilling
our Quest
For adventure
To gradually
Find intimacy
Allowing a final destiny
to cling on too
As the only clue
while stumbling on
in a universe
Let it slide by
With warmth and shame
Melting threads
and spinning loops
The paradox
to participate
in a dialogue
to evaporate
intended to end
with a touch
from a hand
Rolling me over
With a task to pursue
Excitement
as the only clue
to hold on
The Quest
For adventure
and Discovery
Digest
something is meaningful
Against a dark blue
Nighttime sky

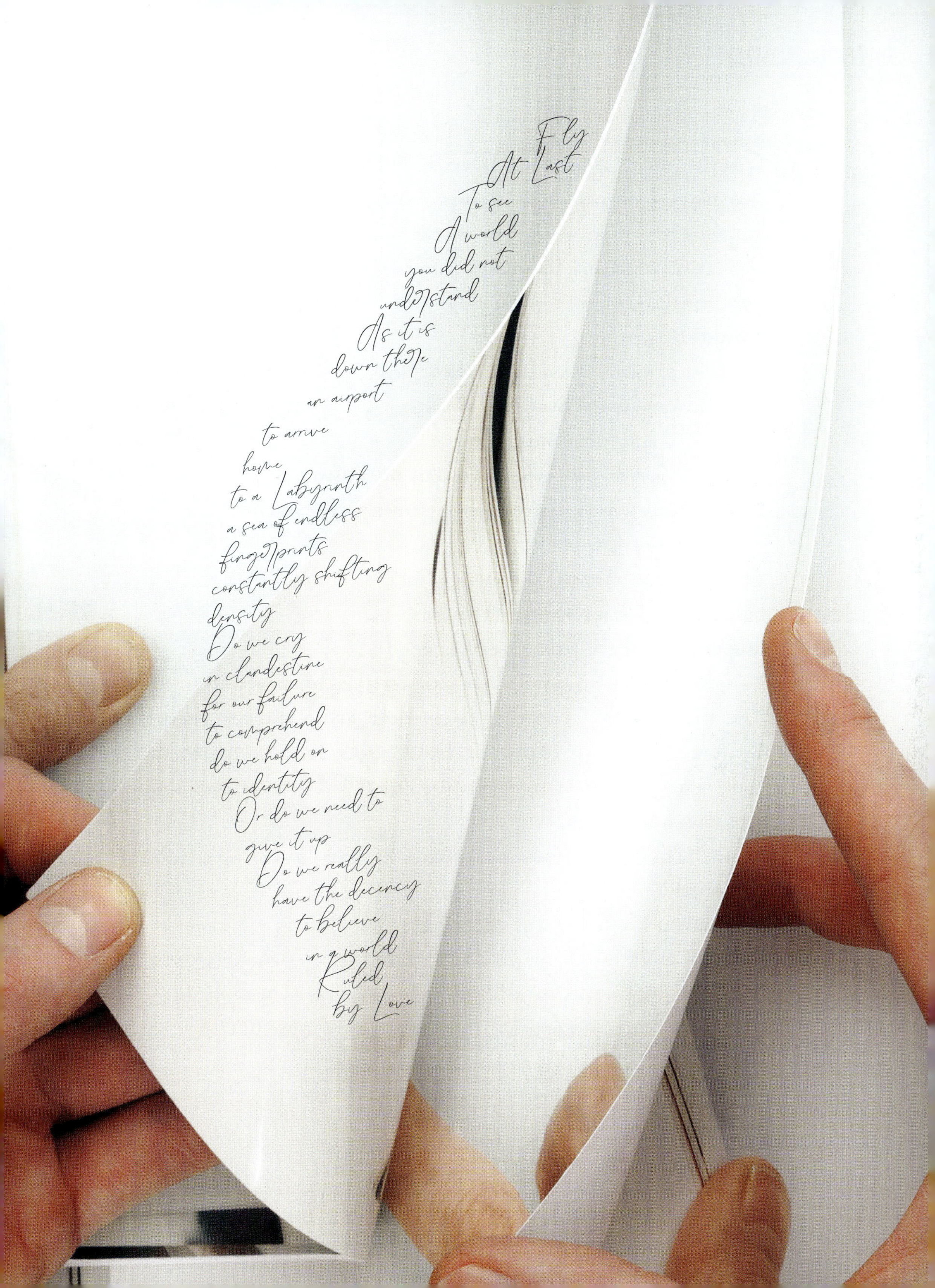

Fly
At Last
To see
A world
you did not
understand
As it is
down there
an airport
to arrive
home
to a Labyrinth
a sea of endless
fingerprints
constantly shifting
density
Do we cry
in clandestine
for our failure
to comprehend
do we hold on
to identity
Or do we need to
give it up
Do we really
have the decency
to believe
in a world
Ruled
by Love

Longing for; eyes of a preditor; lonely
She stared at me with hungry eyes.
buy hungry eyes mugs & shirts
wanting needing longing for desireable sad
Determination and struggle. Can also mean passionate
something.
Mike has hungry eyes for that job.
buy hungry eyes mugs & shirts
hungry eyes food hunger eye
to want food, but not actually be hungry
Person One: mm. im craving some ice-cream
eats ice-cream
Person One: damn; i guess i just had hungry eyes. . .
buy hungry eyes mugs & shirts
hungry bloated full eyes face you
by youudon'tknowme(: Apr 26, 2010 add a video
The red, glazed looking eyes that are a direct result
ing weed. If one looks at these eyes, he is able to un
that that person is amazingly hungry because he is hi
has the munchies.
Damn! Kevin's got some serious hungry eyes, he's gott
the kush!
buy hungry eyes mugs & shirts
hungry eyes hungryeyes weed marijuana kushpiff po
joint blunt smoke munchies drugsbong kevin high
by D.M.G. Feb 9, 2012 add a video

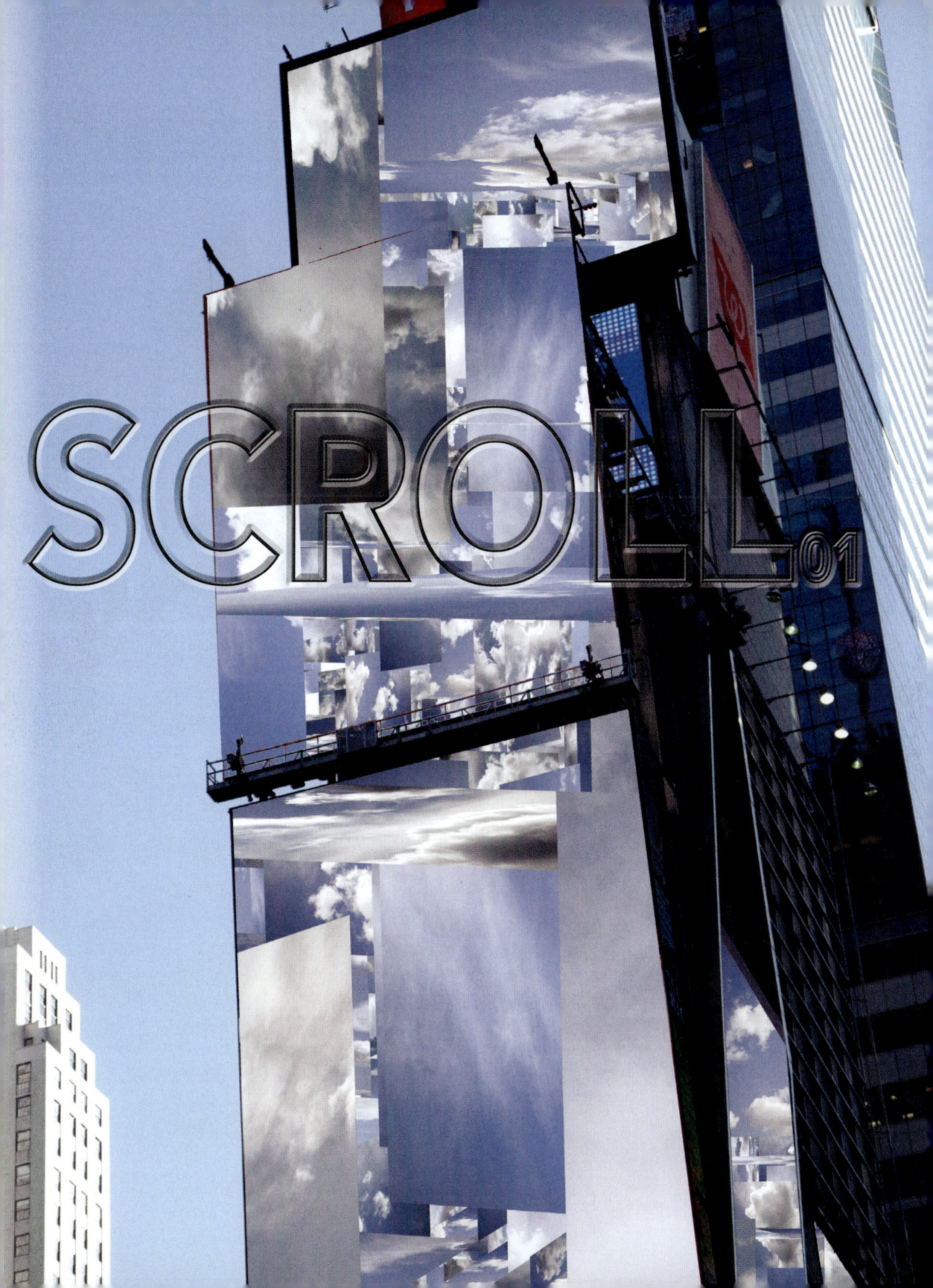
SCROLL 01

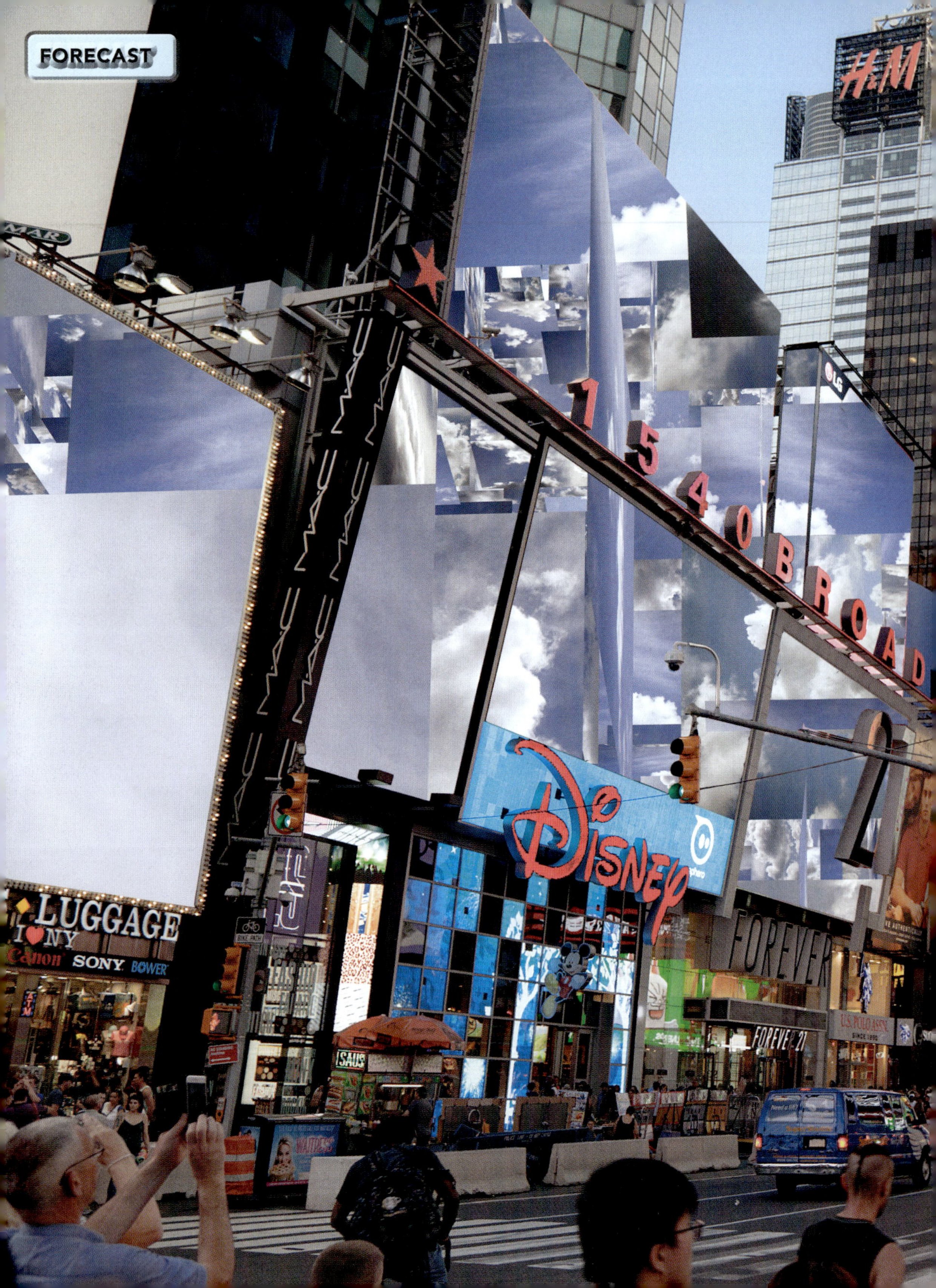
H&M
LG
1540 BROAD
MAC
Disney
LUGGAGE
I ♥ NY
Canon
SONY
FOREVER
FOREVER 21
U.S. POLO ASSN.

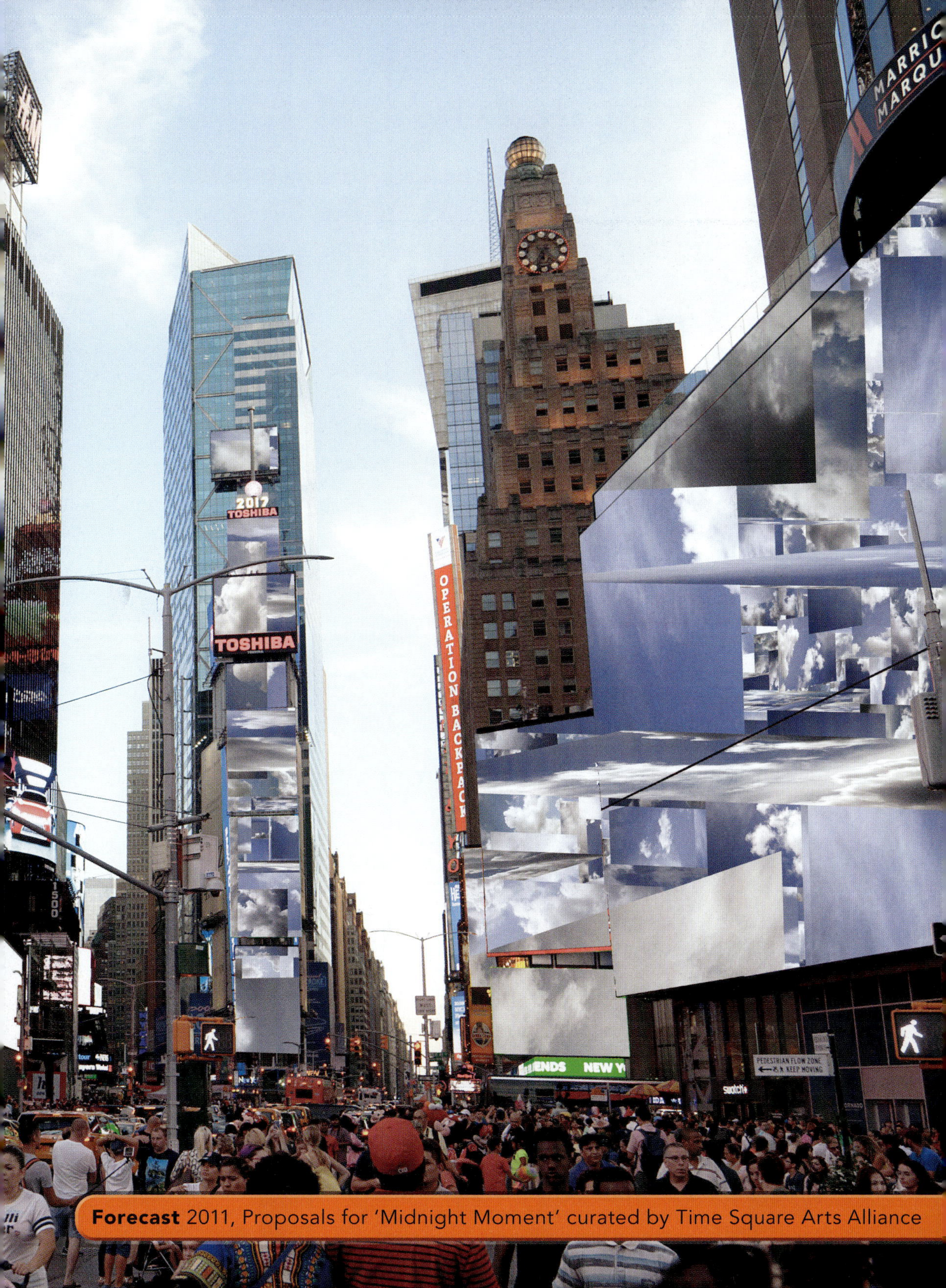

Forecast 2011, Proposals for 'Midnight Moment' curated by Time Square Arts Alliance

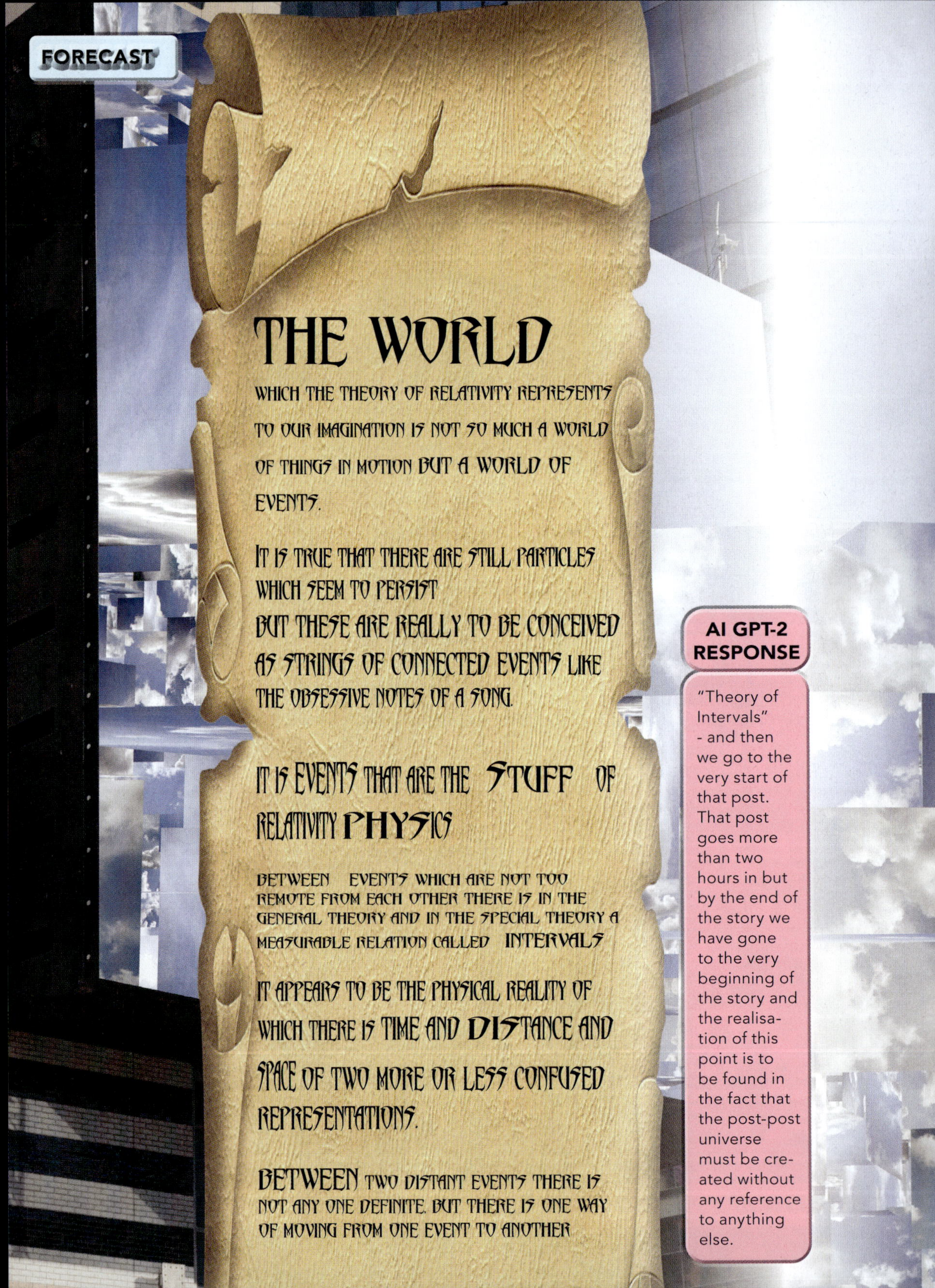
FORECAST
THE WORLD
WHICH THE THEORY OF RELATIVITY REPRESENTS
TO OUR IMAGINATION IS NOT SO MUCH A WORLD
OF THINGS IN MOTION BUT A WORLD OF
EVENTS.
IT IS TRUE THAT THERE ARE STILL PARTICLES
WHICH SEEM TO PERSIST
BUT THESE ARE REALLY TO BE CONCEIVED
AS STRINGS OF CONNECTED EVENTS LIKE
THE OBSESSIVE NOTES OF A SONG.
IT IS EVENTS THAT ARE THE STUFF OF
RELATIVITY PHYSICS
BETWEEN EVENTS WHICH ARE NOT TOO
REMOTE FROM EACH OTHER THERE IS IN THE
GENERAL THEORY AND IN THE SPECIAL THEORY A
MEASURABLE RELATION CALLED INTERVALS
IT APPEARS TO BE THE PHYSICAL REALITY OF
WHICH THERE IS TIME AND DISTANCE AND
SPACE OF TWO MORE OR LESS CONFUSED
REPRESENTATIONS.
BETWEEN TWO DISTANT EVENTS THERE IS
NOT ANY ONE DEFINITE. BUT THERE IS ONE WAY
OF MOVING FROM ONE EVENT TO ANOTHER
AI GPT-2 RESPONSE
"Theory of Intervals" - and then we go to the very start of that post. That post goes more than two hours in but by the end of the story we have gone to the very beginning of the story and the realisation of this point is to be found in the fact that the post-post universe must be created without any reference to anything else.

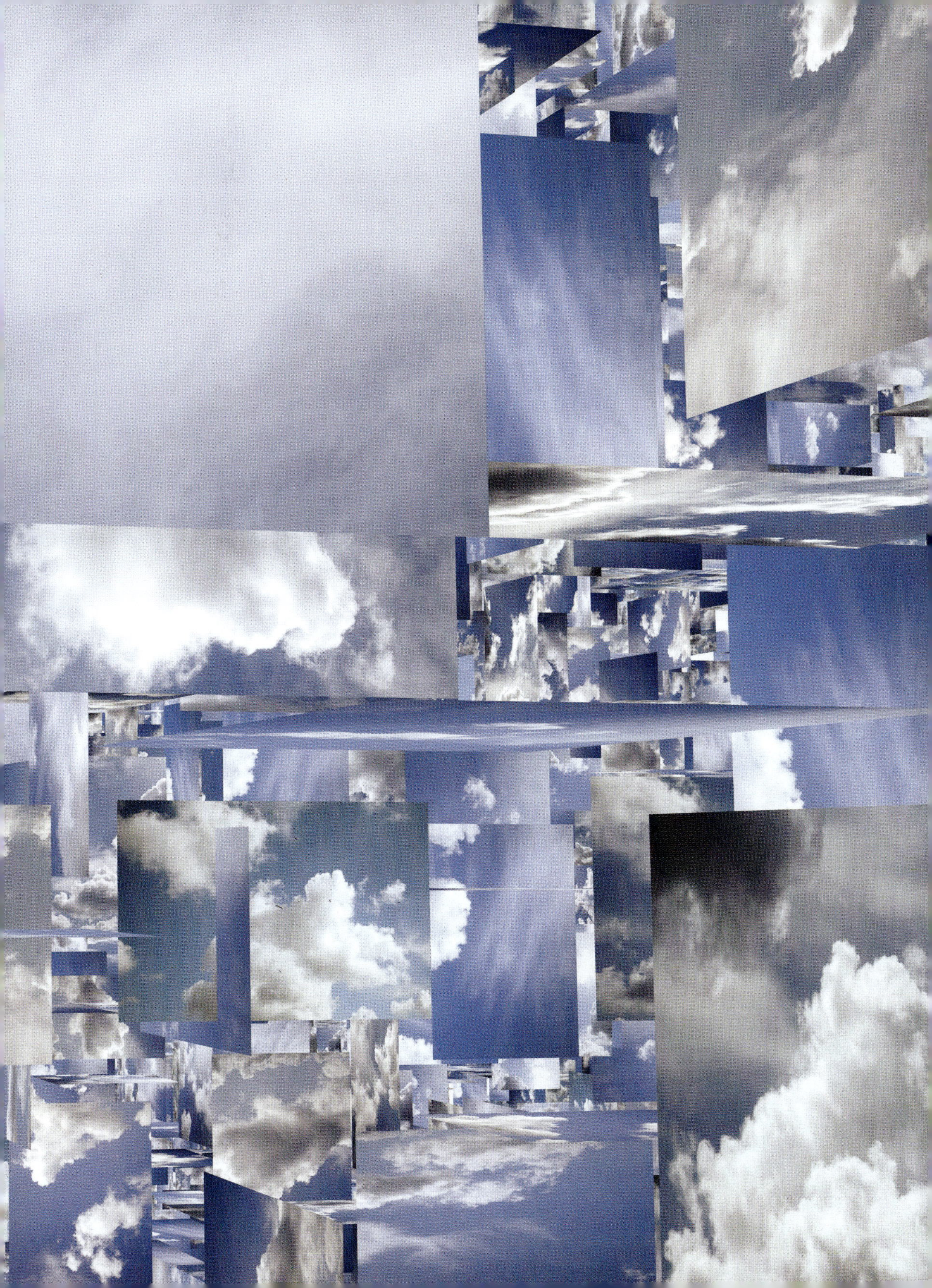

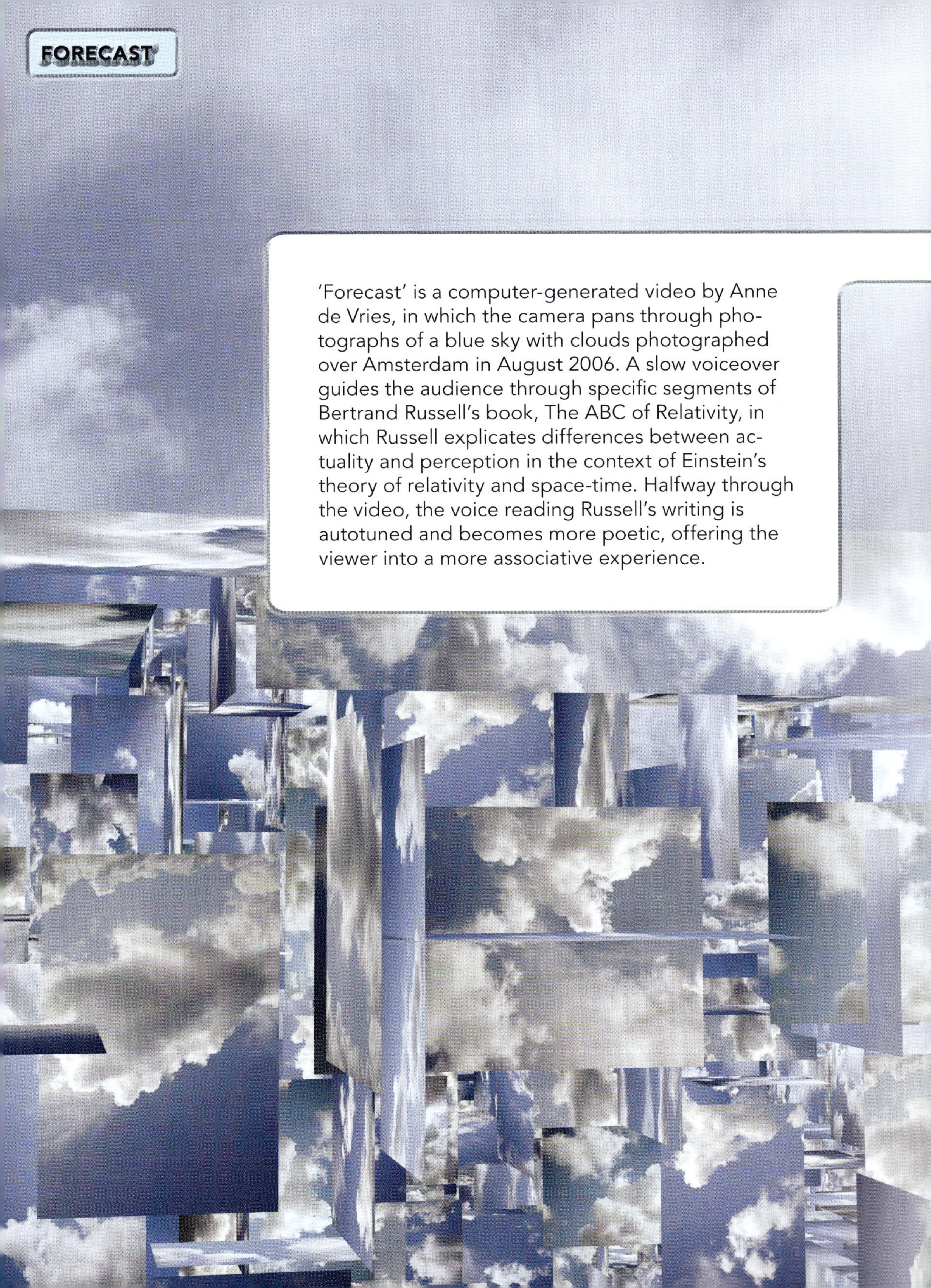

FORECAST

'Forecast' is a computer-generated video by Anne de Vries, in which the camera pans through photographs of a blue sky with clouds photographed over Amsterdam in August 2006. A slow voiceover guides the audience through specific segments of Bertrand Russell's book, The ABC of Relativity, in which Russell explicates differences between actuality and perception in the context of Einstein's theory of relativity and space-time. Halfway through the video, the voice reading Russell's writing is autotuned and becomes more poetic, offering the viewer into a more associative experience.

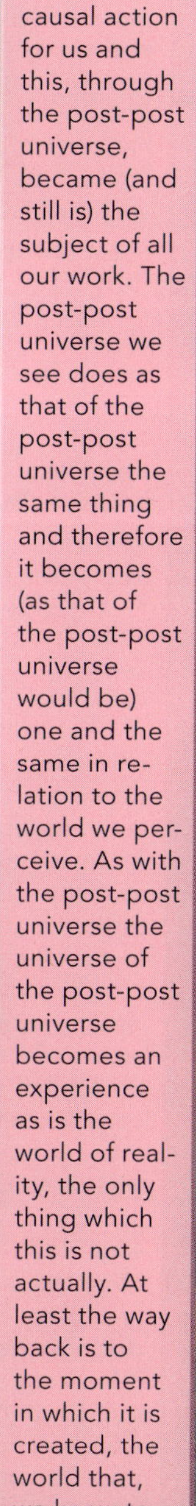

Just as the Post-Post universe of our post-post universe was not created as an experience but as a means of a causal

a means of a causal action for us and this, through the post-post universe, became (and still is) the subject of all our work. The post-post universe we see does as that of the post-post universe the same thing and therefore it becomes (as that of the post-post universe would be) one and the same in relation to the world we perceive. As with the post-post universe the universe of the post-post universe becomes an experience as is the world of reality, the only thing which this is not actually. At least the way back is to the moment in which it is created, the world that, we know to

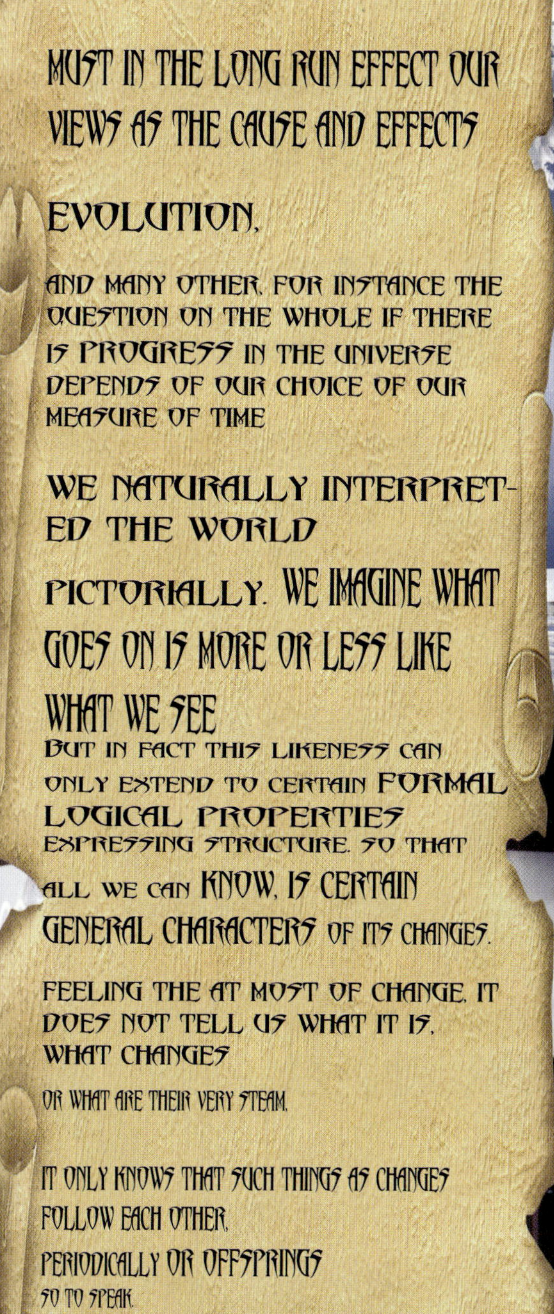

WHICH MAKES THE SUM OF ALL THE LITTLE EVENTS ALONG THE LINE. GREATER THEN BY ANY OTHER

A COLLAPSE OF ONE ALL EMBRACING TIME — TO WHICH ALL EVENTS IN THE UNIVERSE COULD BE DATED

MUST IN THE LONG RUN EFFECT OUR VIEWS AS THE CAUSE AND EFFECTS

EVOLUTION,

AND MANY OTHER. FOR INSTANCE THE QUESTION ON THE WHOLE IF THERE IS PROGRESS IN THE UNIVERSE DEPENDS OF OUR CHOICE OF OUR MEASURE OF TIME

WE NATURALLY INTERPRET-ED THE WORLD

PICTORIALLY. WE IMAGINE WHAT GOES ON IS MORE OR LESS LIKE WHAT WE SEE

BUT IN FACT THIS LIKENESS CAN ONLY EXTEND TO CERTAIN FORMAL LOGICAL PROPERTIES EXPRESSING STRUCTURE. SO THAT ALL WE CAN KNOW, IS CERTAIN GENERAL CHARACTERS OF ITS CHANGES.

FEELING THE AT MOST OF CHANGE. IT DOES NOT TELL US WHAT IT IS, WHAT CHANGES

OR WHAT ARE THEIR VERY STEAM.

IT ONLY KNOWS THAT SUCH THINGS AS CHANGES FOLLOW EACH OTHER,

PERIODICALLY OR OFFSPRINGS

SO TO SPEAK.

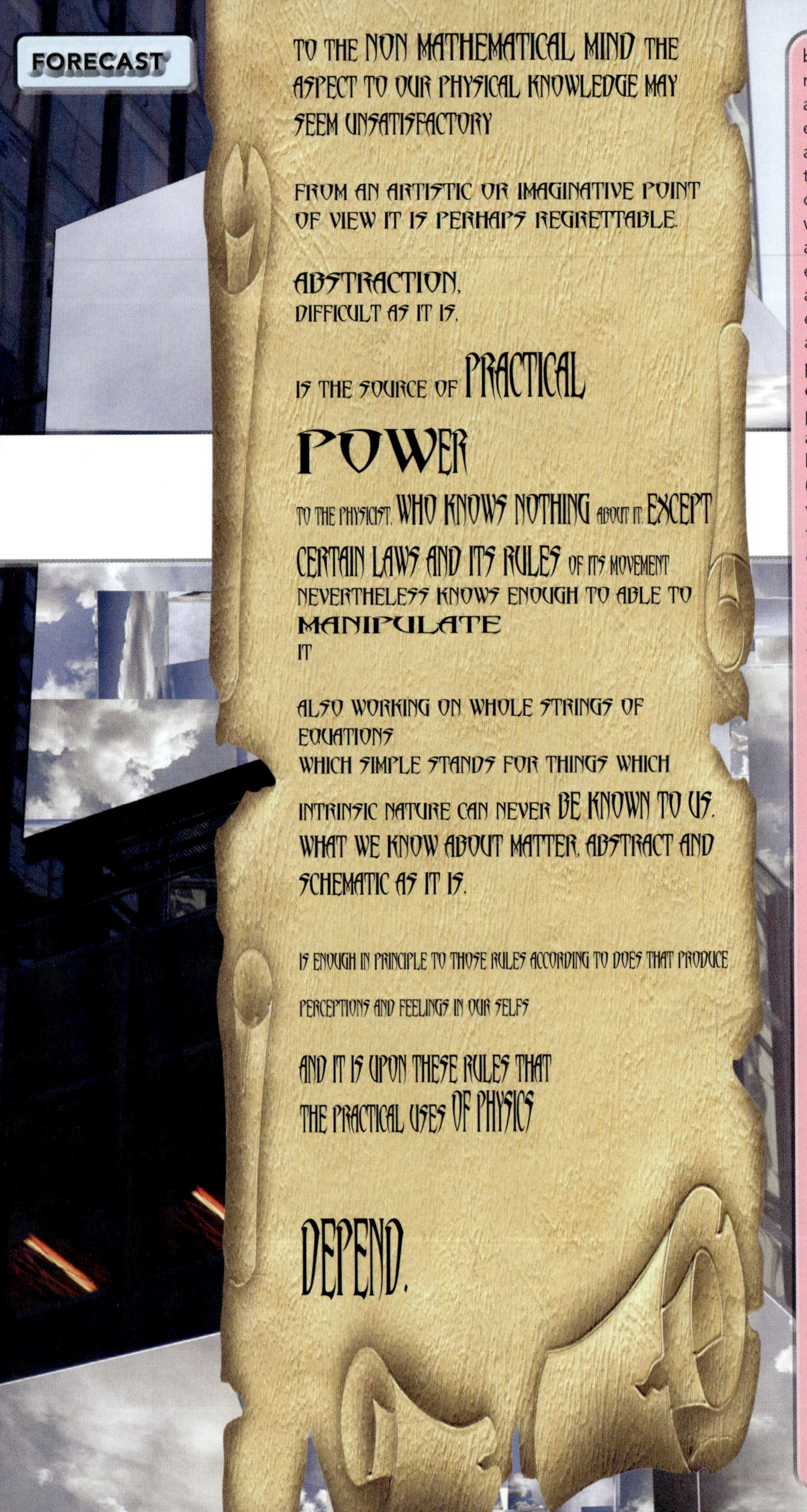

be a form of reality, is not an experience but an agent, and thus only one world in which events are the essence of an experience which actually be a part of. The end of this post will be about what happens (and will be very soon) to the reality in question. But it is not all that I am going to make of our new post-post universe. The post-post universe is a very strong, strong, powerful, complex, very difficult universe that we will start with because it can contain so many different forms. We have been dealing with an incredible kind of complex for many years and we see, in the end, why. This complexity is what distinguishes it from any other experience and it is no different from any

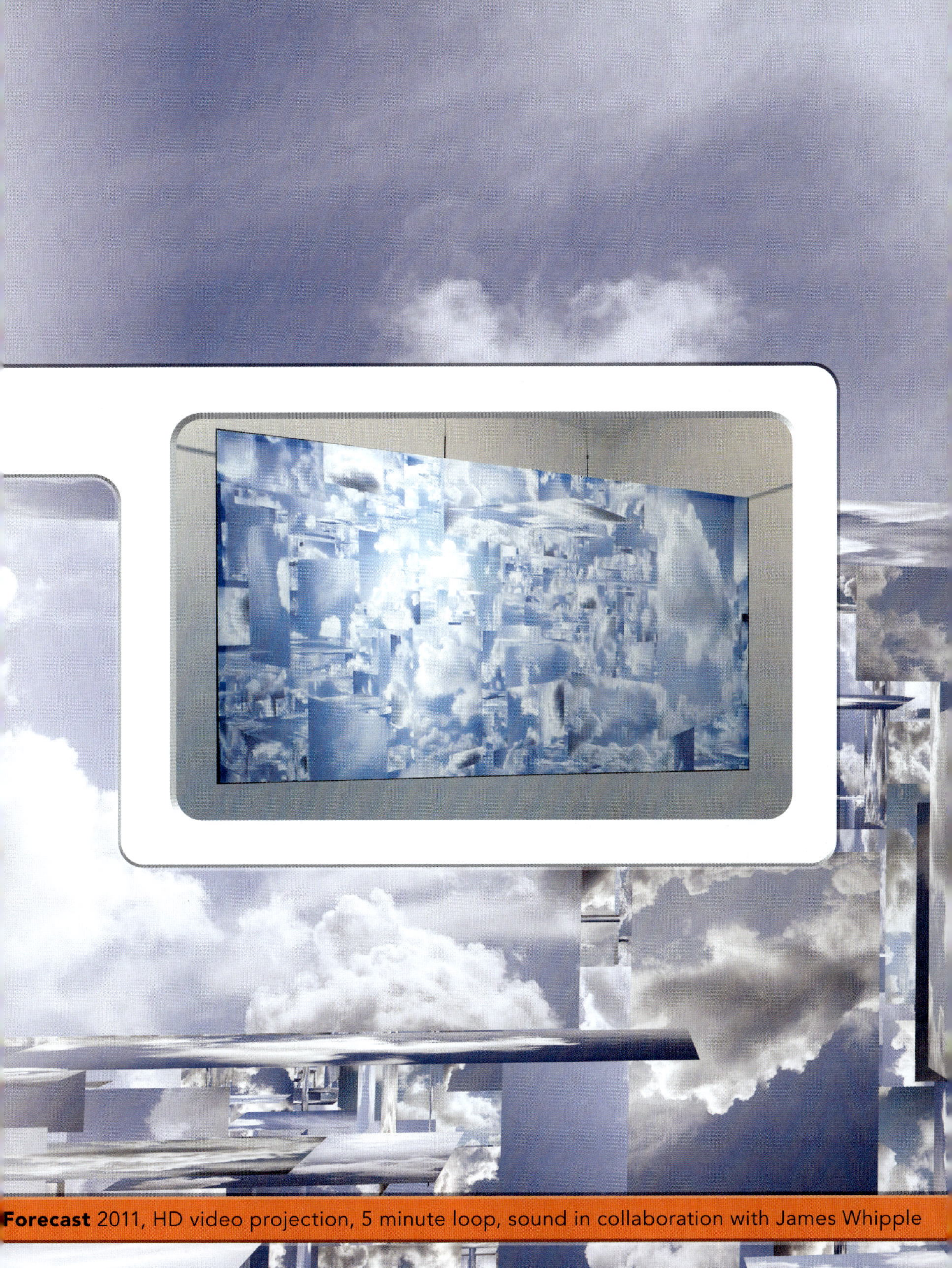

Forecast 2011, HD video projection, 5 minute loop, sound in collaboration with James Whipple

WHOLE WORLD

"The Greeks and Romans and all the other nations on earth always found that within the passage of twenty-four hours day turns into night and night into day. But they would have been mistaken if they had believed that the same rule holds everywhere, since the contrary has been observed up near the North Pole. And anyone who believed that it is a necessary and eternal truth at least in our part of the world would also be mistaken, since we must recognize that neither the earth nor even •the sun exists necessarily, and that there may come a time when •this beautiful star no longer exists, at least in its present form. . . . From this it appears that necessary truths, such as we find in pure mathematics and particularly in arithmetic and geometry, must have principles whose proof doesn't depend on instances (or, therefore, on the testimony of the senses), even though without the senses it would never occur to us to think of them. It is important to respect this distinction ·between 'prompted by the senses' and 'proved by the senses'·. Euclid understood this so well that he demonstrated by reason things that experience and sense-images make very evident."

Prompted Senses-Images

Author: John Locke, Title: An Historical Introduction to the Philosophy of Mathematics: A Reader, Chapter: Part Two Moderns : The rationalists: Leibniz, Mathematics and sense experience. Edited by: Russell Marcus and Mark McEvoy. Publisher: Bloomsbury, Year: 2016.

"A sun cross, solar cross, or wheel cross is a solar symbol consisting of an equilateral cross inside a circle. The interpretation of the simple equilateral cross as a solar symbol in Bronze Age religion was widespread in 19th-century scholarship. The cross-in-a-circle was interpreted as a solar symbol derived from the interpretation of the disc of the Sun as the wheel of the chariot of the Sun god. The same symbol is in use as a modern astronomical symbol representing the Earth rather than the Sun."

Author: Martin Persson Nilsson, Titile: The Minoan—Mycenaean Religion and its Survival in Greek Religion. Publisher: Biblo & Tannen Publishers, Page: 421, Year: 1950

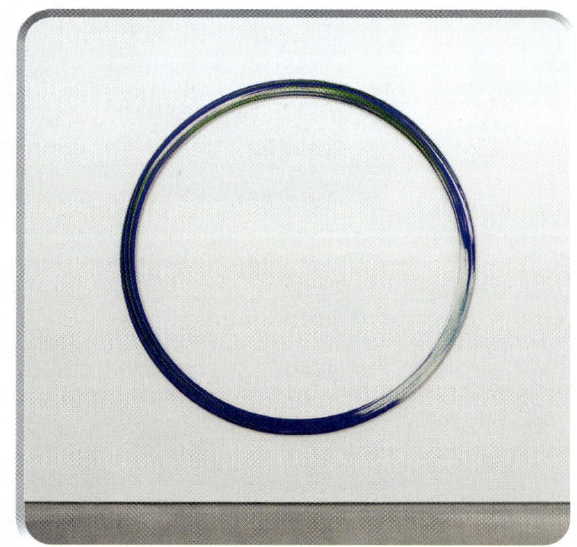

Whole World Overview, 2011, 220 cm, satellite photography, uv-print, dibond, plexiglass other experience that we have. It is the form of the world that we see that the whole of the experience, the only part of our experience that is different and different from or a part of any other experience that can be experienced. This is how we arrive at the fact that everything we see can be experienced as something separate and distinct from ourselves. I could go into some other great things that I am planning to say, but these are the things that are truly important. There are two kinds of post-post experiences I would like to talk about.

AI GPT-2 RESPONSE

generated by Sarah Friend

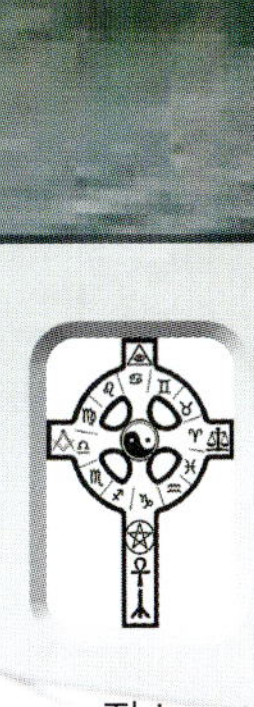

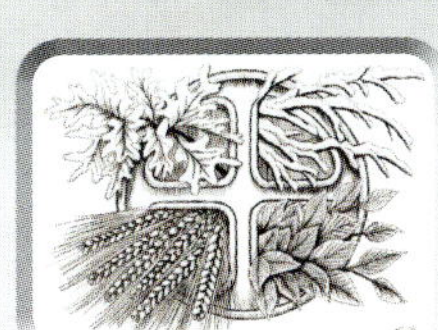

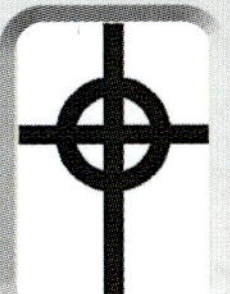

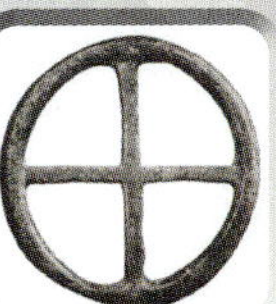

This artwork is generated by Anne de Vries in association with NASA's The Whole World satellite photography. The footage is stretched into a circle (North-Pole to South-Pole) evoking ancient Sun Crosses and Sun Wheels.

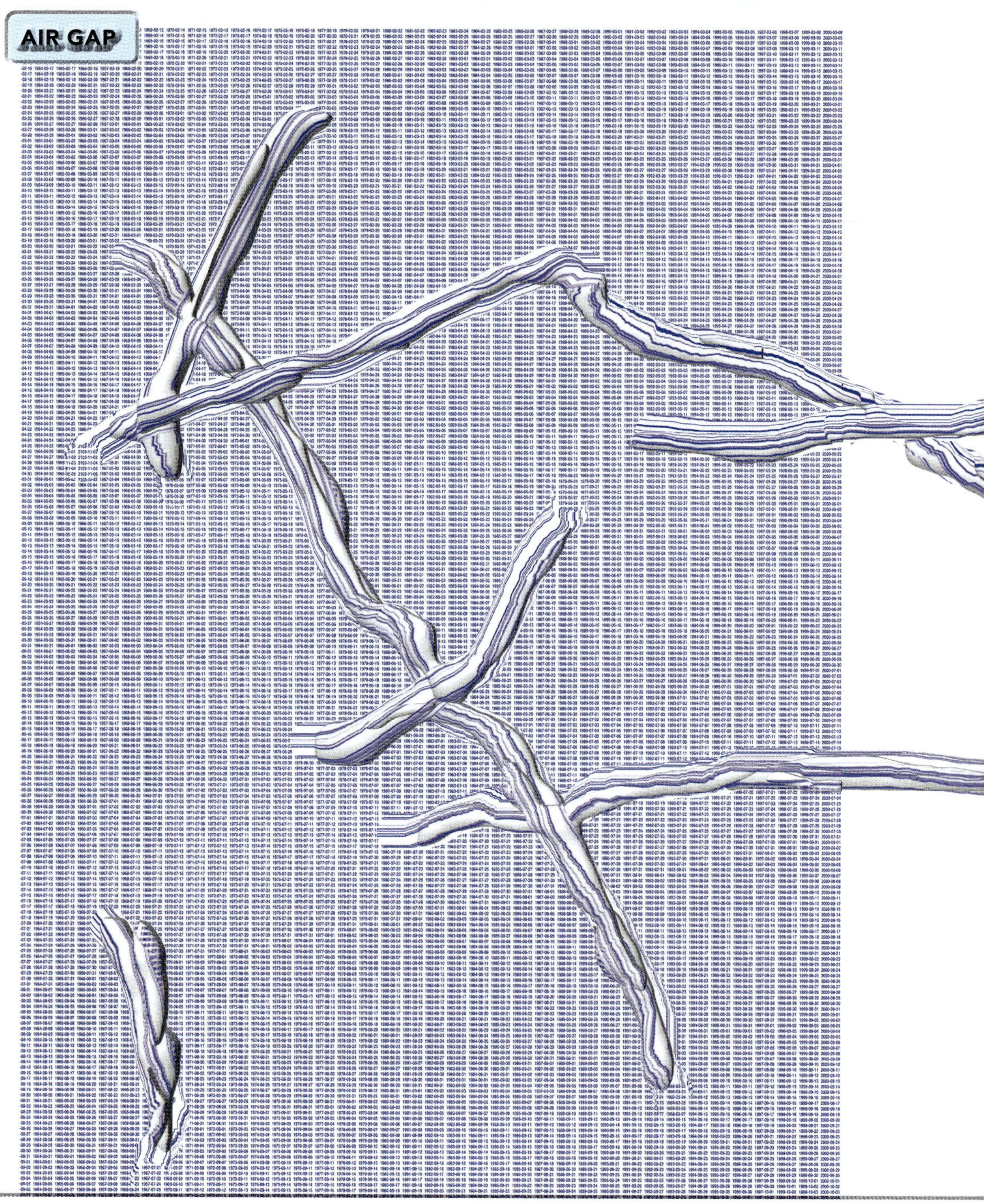

2103-11-04 November 4, 2103 day of the week. Find out WHAT DAY OF THE WEEK was this date. Get full year 2103 calendar PLUS some BONUS info.
1976-03-07 Authorized Bootleg: Live In Winterland, San Francisco, CA, 3/07/76 is a live concert recording of Lynyrd Skynyrd. It was released by Geffen Records alongside ...
1976-06-27 Set 1 Cold Rain & Snow, Cassidy, Brown Eyed Women, Big River, Ship of Fools, Lazy Lightning-> Supplication, Friend Of The Devil, Looks Like ...
1968-03-25 Sadamu Shimomura (下村 定 , Shimomura Sadamu, 23 September 1887 – 25 March 1968) was a general in the Imperial Japanese Army and nal Minister of ...
1967-07-24 Article on the full-page advertisement in The Times newspaper signed by The Beatles and Brian Epstein, on the Beatles Bible website.

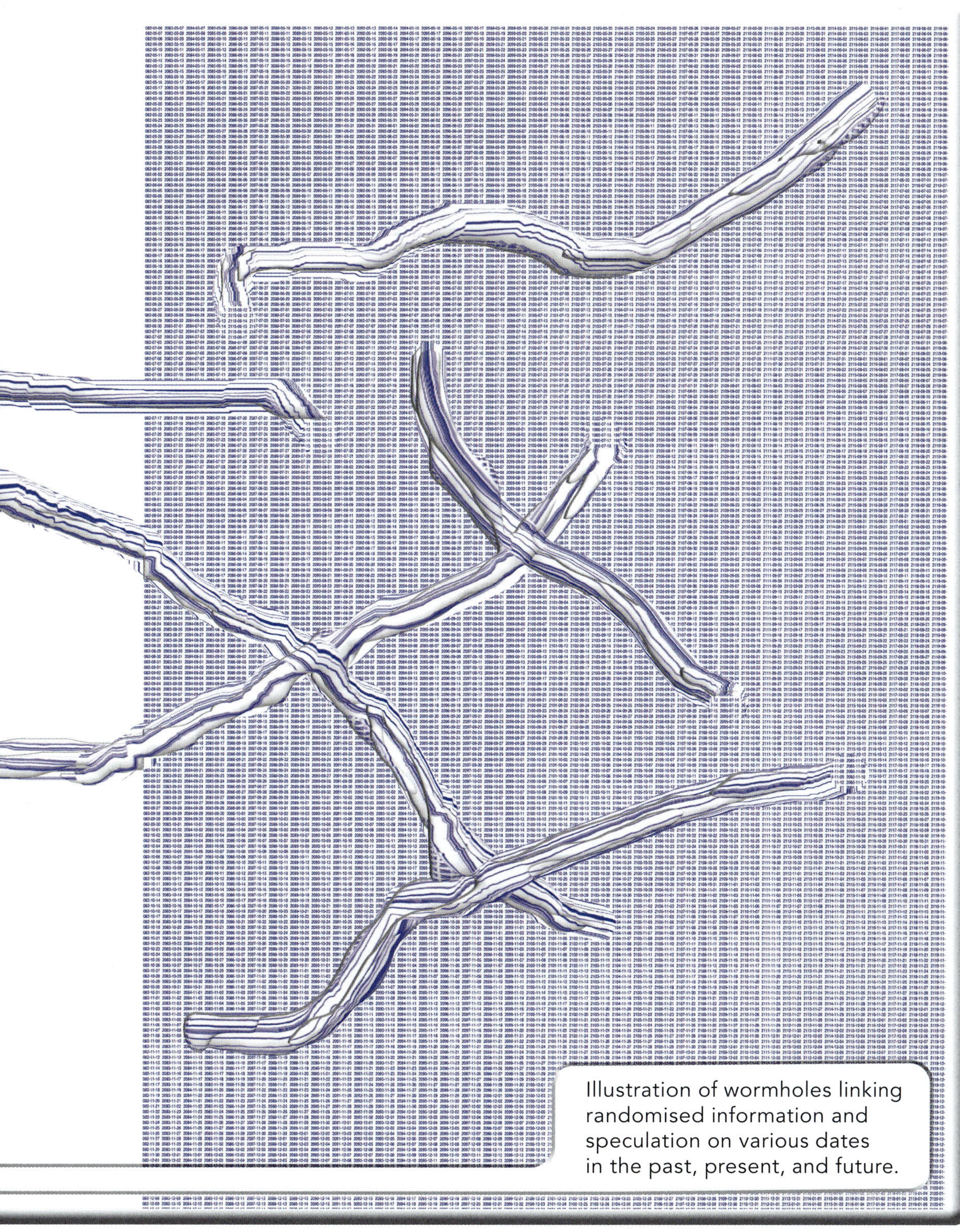

Illustration of wormholes linking randomised information and speculation on various dates in the past, present, and future.

2015-06-15 Boston Pops (First week in May through middle of July). Chagu-Chagu Umakko · Magna Carta Day · National Family Month (Second Sunday in May through the ...
1992-05-14 14 May 1992 – May 14, 1992. Mr. Ching-Yeh Shiau, Ph.D. Professor, National Taiwan Institute of Technology Department of Chemical Engineering 43 Keeling ...
1980-07-16 16 Jul 2012 – News on July 16, 1980 was all about the GOP ballyhoo in Detroit. ... Osgood and updates from CBS Radio for the morning of July 16, 1980.
2095-07-17 No events scheduled for July 17, 2095. Please try another day. Work For Goodwill · Tax Credit Information · FAQ's · Privacy Policy · Commercial Services ..
2085-11-09 Music with Mar: Music and Movement Parent-and-Me Class, Savannah 10:30–11 :30am. Savannah Networking Events. Southside Toastmasters Club 12–1pm ...

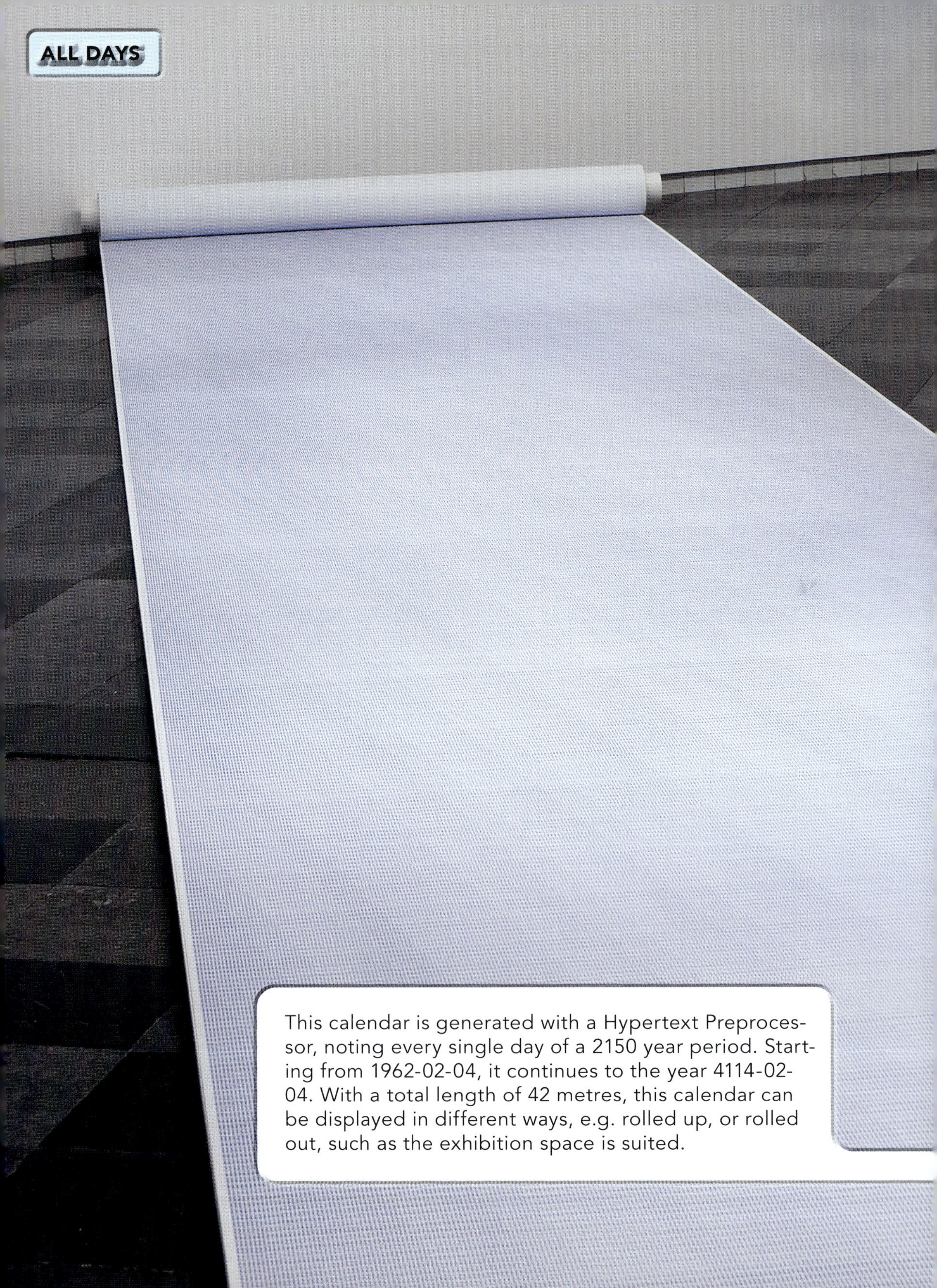

This calendar is generated with a Hypertext Preprocessor, noting every single day of a 2150 year period. Starting from 1962-02-04, it continues to the year 4114-02-04. With a total length of 42 metres, this calendar can be displayed in different ways, e.g. rolled up, or rolled out, such as the exhibition space is suited.

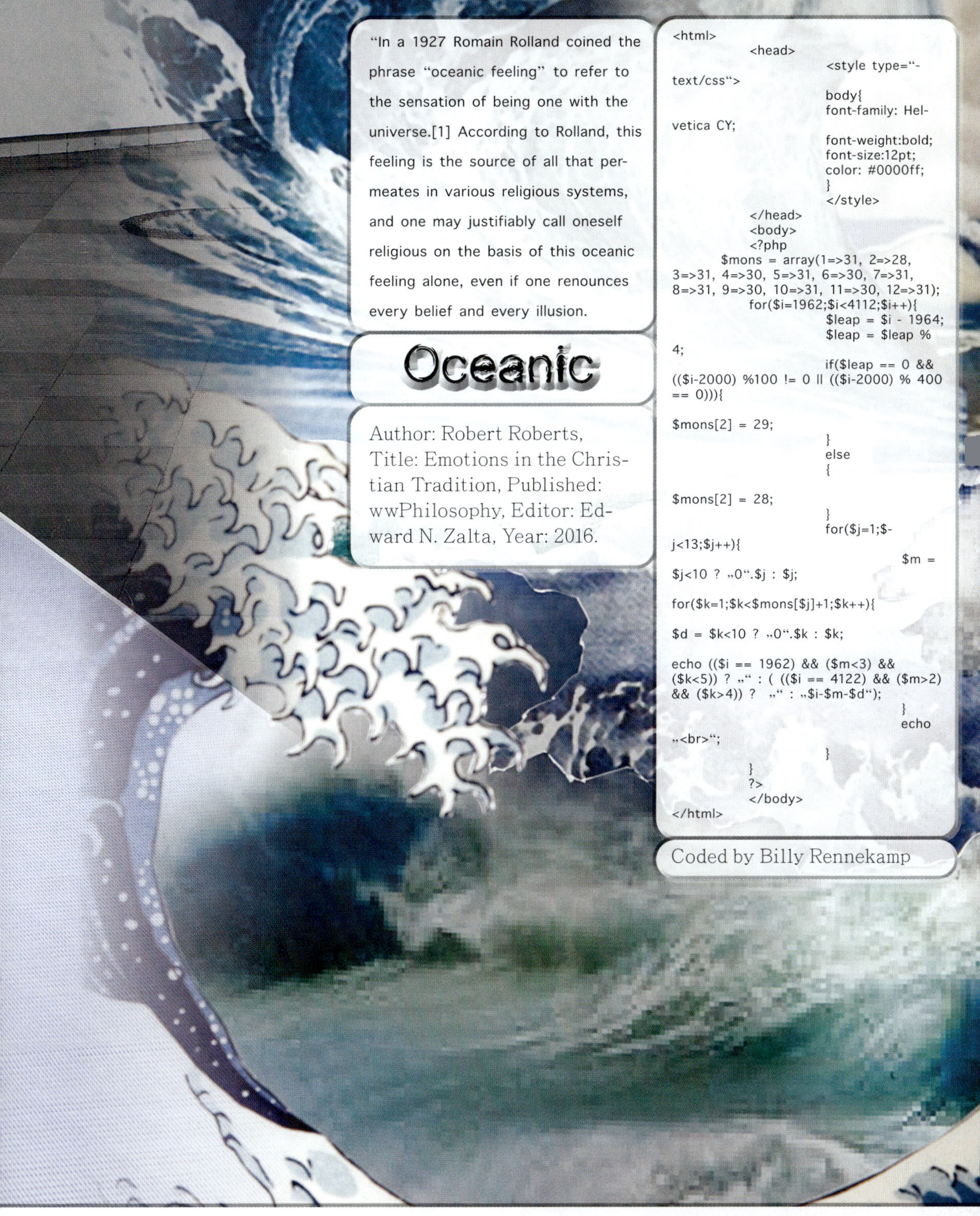

Waves from the Web (detail) 2009, 185x130cm, photography, c-print

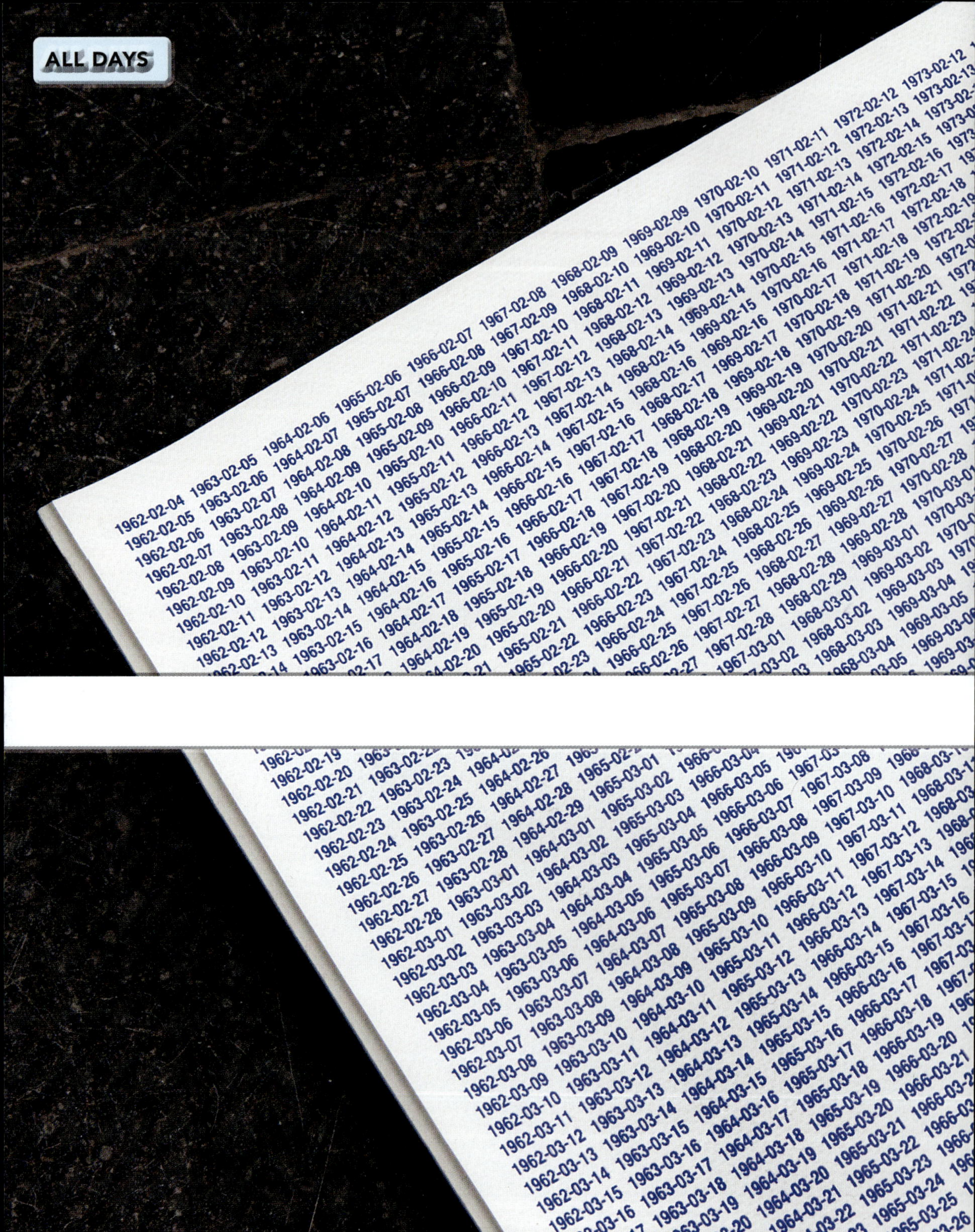
ALL DAYS

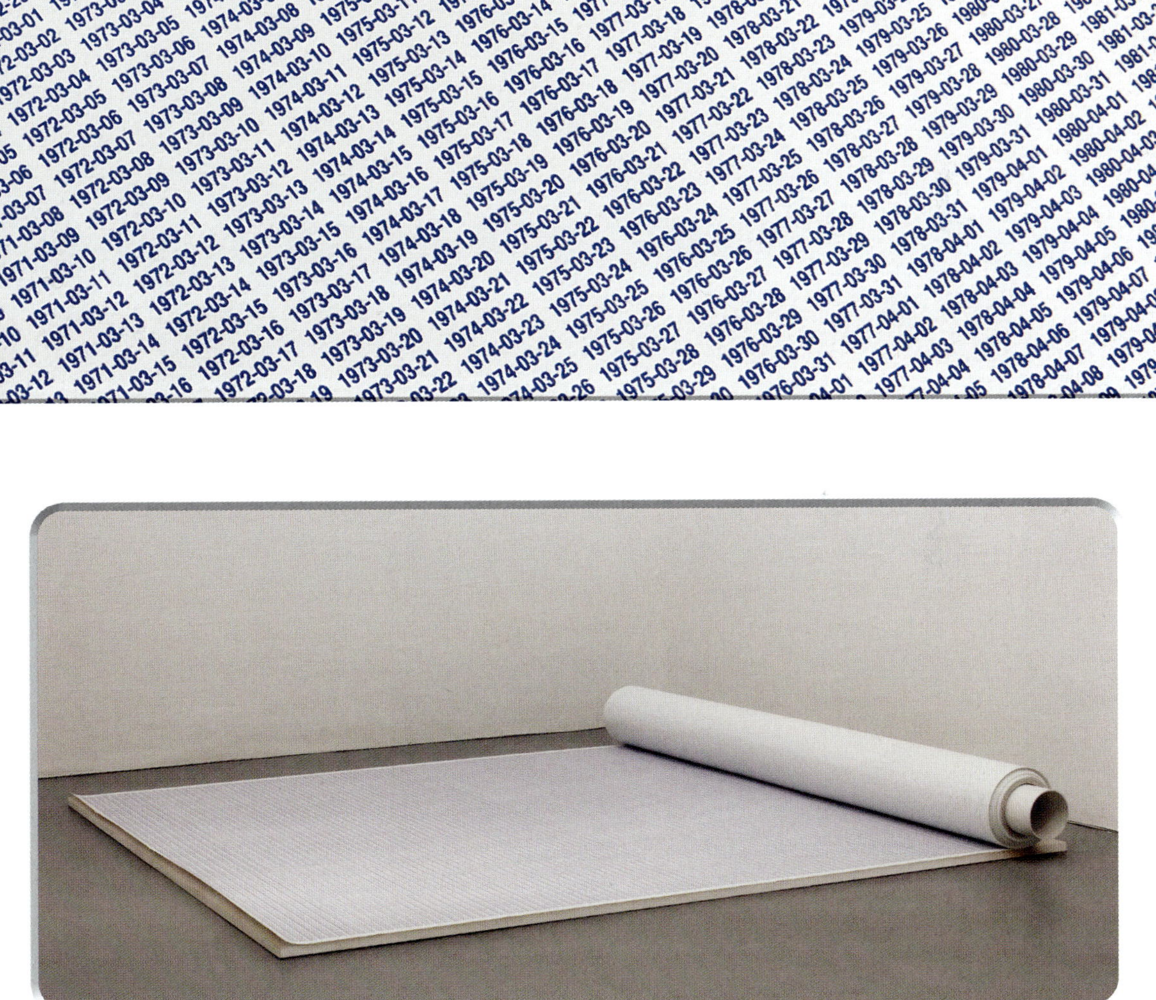

All Days 2011, 188 x 4200 cm, solvent print, vinyl, mdf wood, acrylic pipe

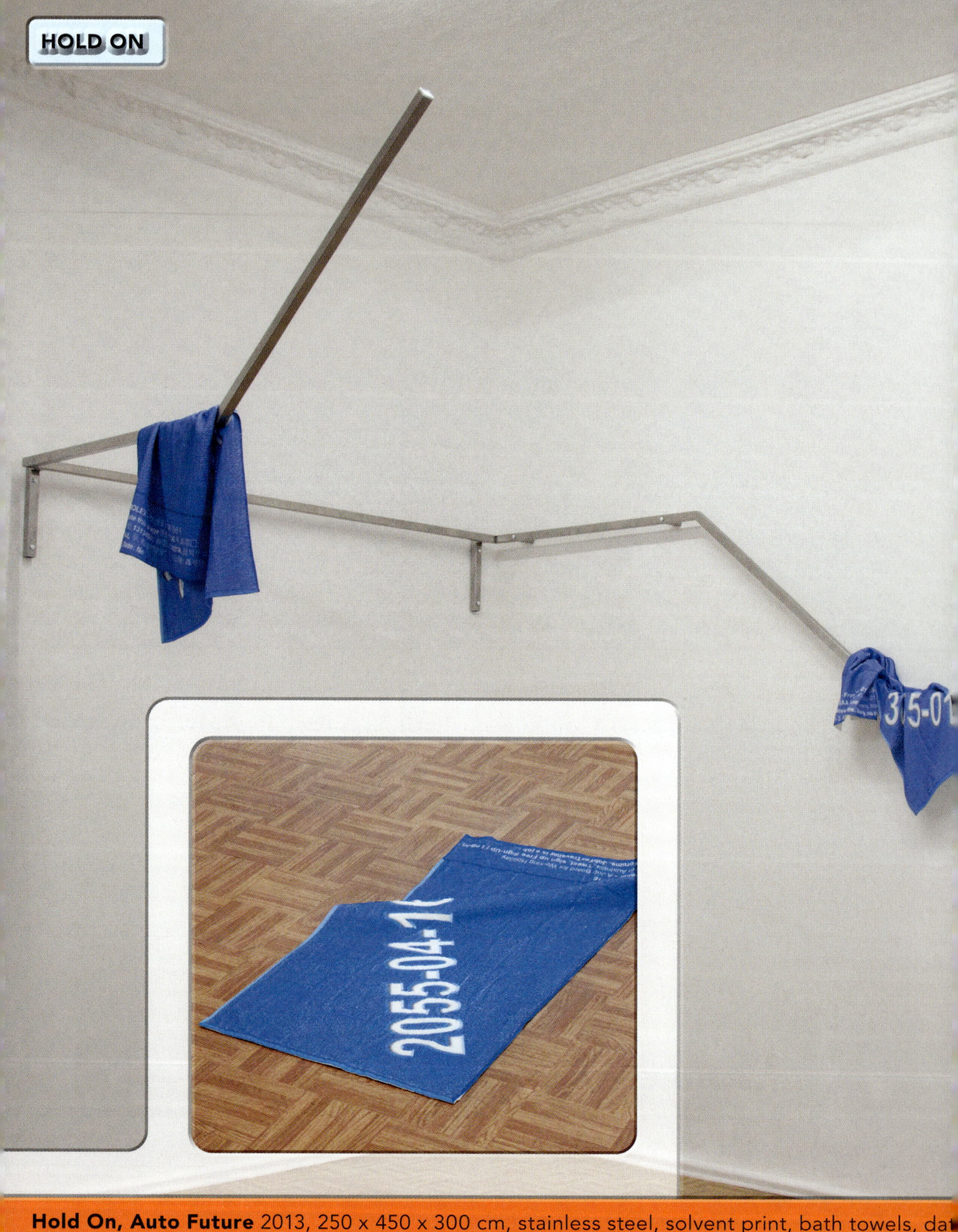

Hold On, Auto Future 2013, 250 x 450 x 300 cm, stainless steel, solvent print, bath towels, da

Towels hang on this handrail, like the remnants of physical activity. On these towels, we can read computer-generated data describing events scheduled for 100 to several thousand years from now. Apparently, the text is the result of web-based searches that unveil an already-existing auto-generated future.

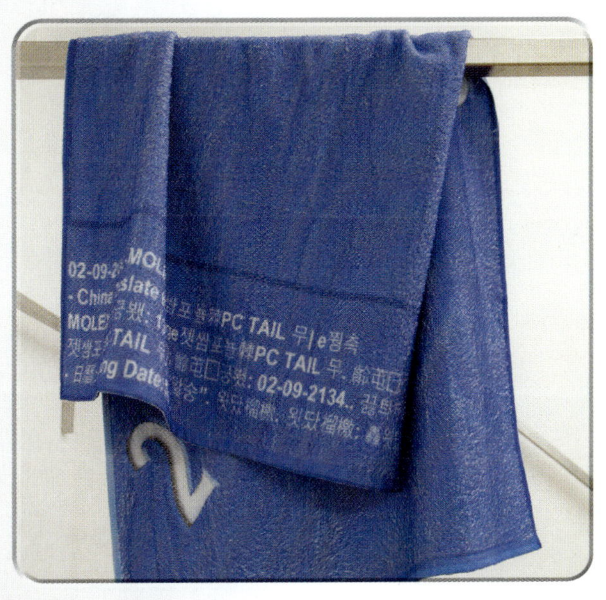

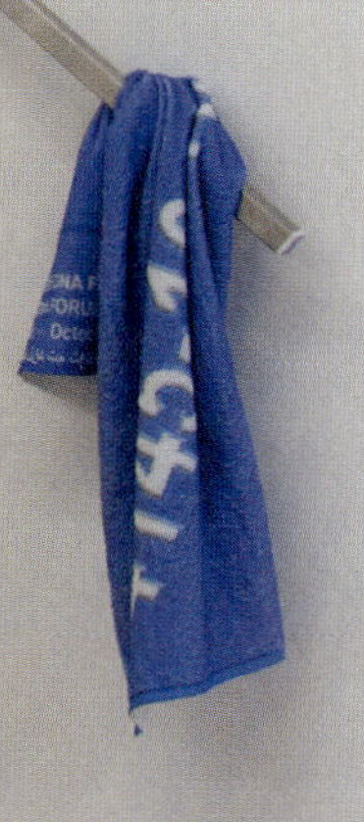

Time Tables 2011, 250 x 450 x 300 cm, 18 mdf wood table

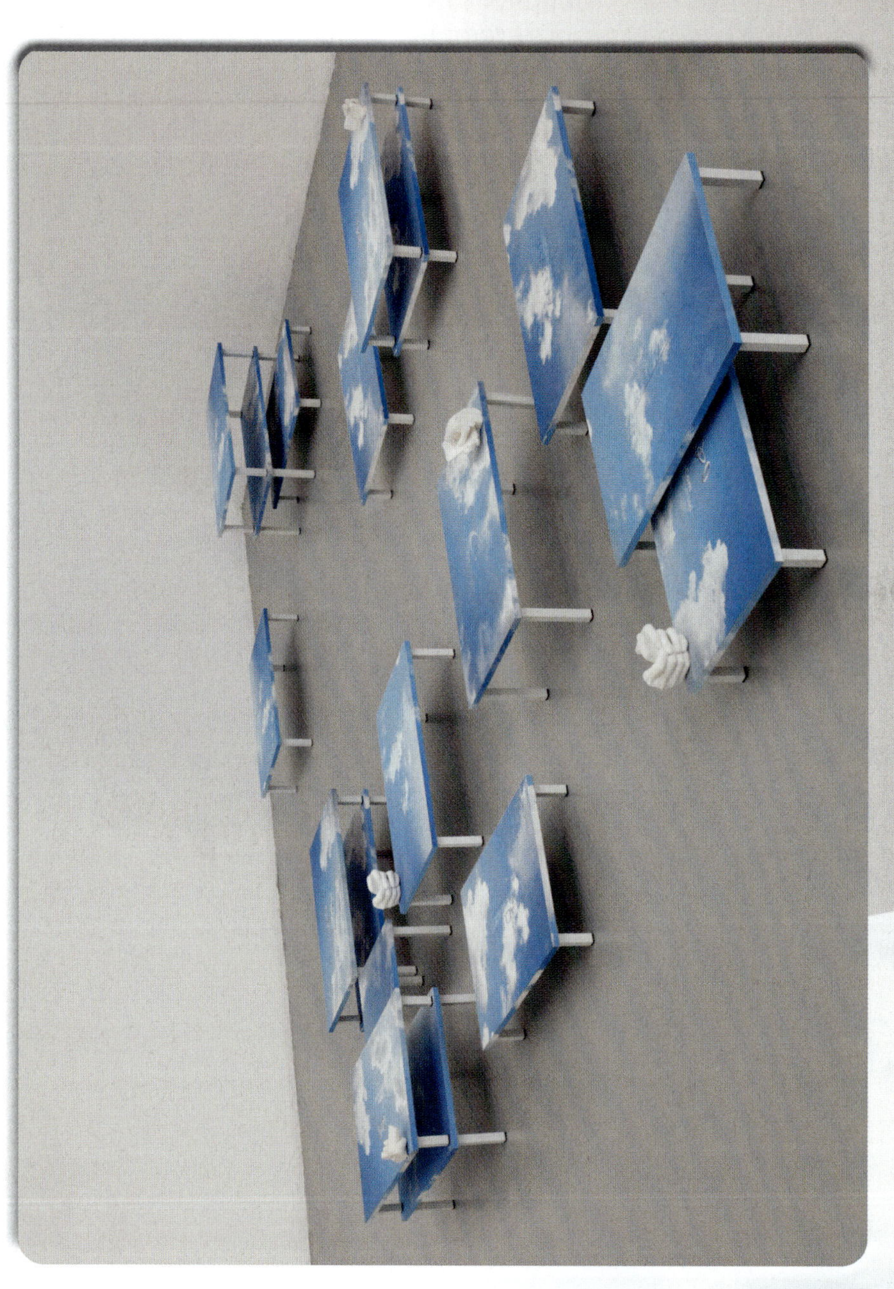

aster hands holding mobile devices, metal stands, photographs, uv-print

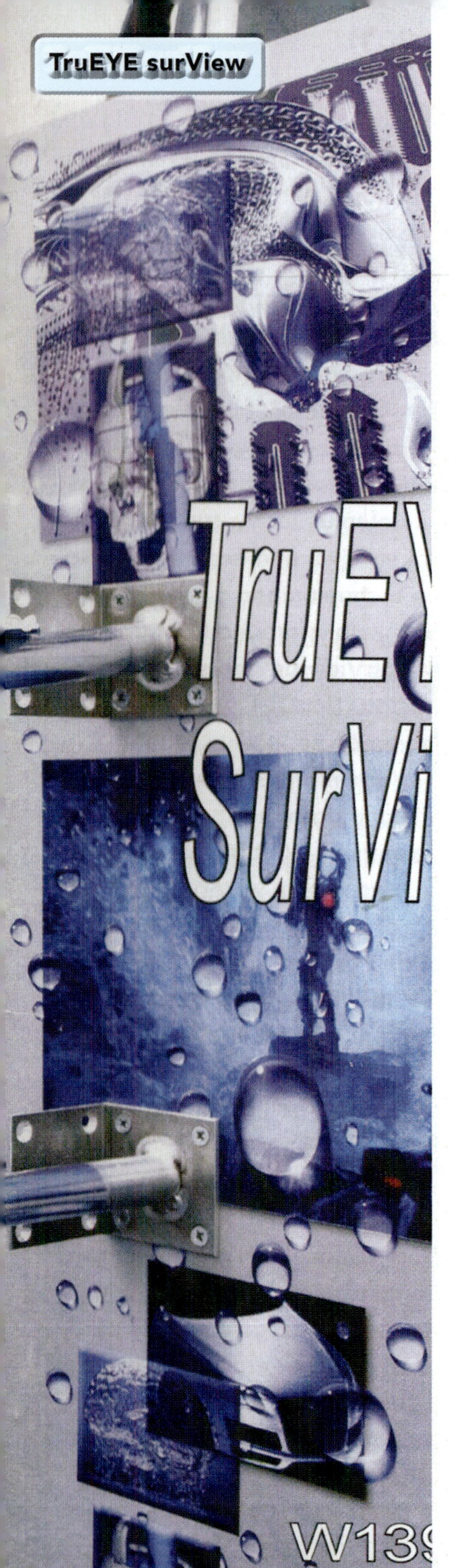

17 June – 21 August 2011

Introduction: living matters Katja Novitskova

TruEYE surView is part of a series of exhibitions conceptually related to the theme of Post Internet Survival Guide, a catalogue-book put together by myself and published by Revolver Publishing in early 2011. Through works and online archives of young 'digital native' artists, I attempted to register survival strategies and tools crucial to us today, trying to re-imagine the very idea of survival and evolution at the dawn of bio-information technologies.

Instigated by the discussions around Post Internet Survival Guide, TruEYE surView presents Anne de Vries (NL) and Yngve Holen (NO/DE), two artists whose work shares a common sensitivity to the merging of matter and information. Both work with a variety of means, mainly photography, installation, video and sculpture. As with an exhibition based on a smart fridge cut in pieces by a waterjet-knife (Holen) or a photograph of a naked woman with a mobile phone standing on her knees in a Cartesian coordinate system (de Vries); their practices access our increasing entanglement with technology, its material and symbolic origins, its influence on our sense of social reality, its socio-political implications and its future potentials.

From the mines, energy plants and factories, where the hardware basis of information technologies comes to being, to brand names, advertising images, product displays, personal use, and ultimately piles of toxic waste – commodities undergo a variety of state changes throughout complex ecological cycles. Considering that what lies at the heart of every living being is genetic information, we are approaching an uncanny valley where life and technology co-exist

Curated by Katja Novitskova

in a blurry commonality of their informational origin and material essence, each propagating an agenda of their own. Neolithic agricultural revolution for instance, can be seen not as an invention – a new human technology – but a state change, a result of co evolutionary development between humans and edible grasses. In this process of collaborative deforestation of land only some benefits were shared by humans. If we can look at the spread of Internet of Things as equivalent to the Neolithic agrarian revolution, then what is information technology's relationship with us as species? What does it take for a commodity to live, and what are the ecological principles of art?

Curating this exhibition is a next step in approaching a 'neo-materialistic' understanding of contemporary art as a domain of heightened density of value flows, and information technologies as an expanding ecology. In TruEYE surView Anne de Vries and Yngve Holen are merging these domains in fluid assemblages, proposing visionary semi-stable structures out of material flows that are constitutive of today's digital data driven society.

Author: Katja Novitskova, Title: TruEYE surView, Introduction exhibition catalog, Page 3 and 4, ISBN978-90-817892-0-2, Publisher: W139, Year: 2011

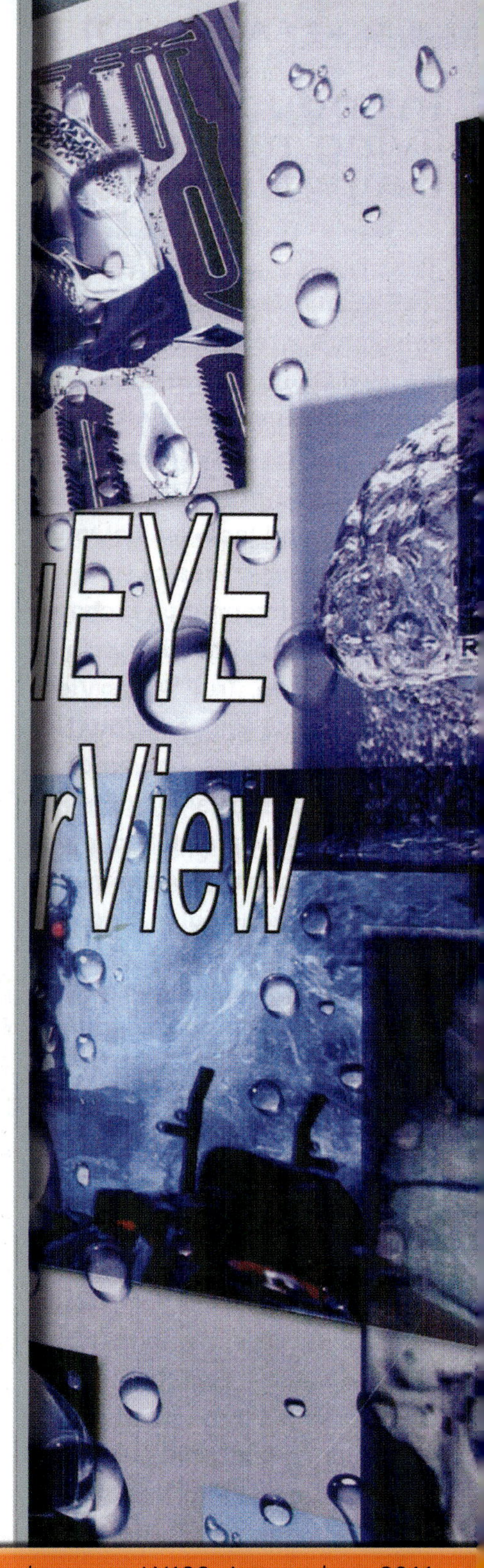

TruEYE surView pages from exhibition catalogue, at W139, Amsterdam, 2011

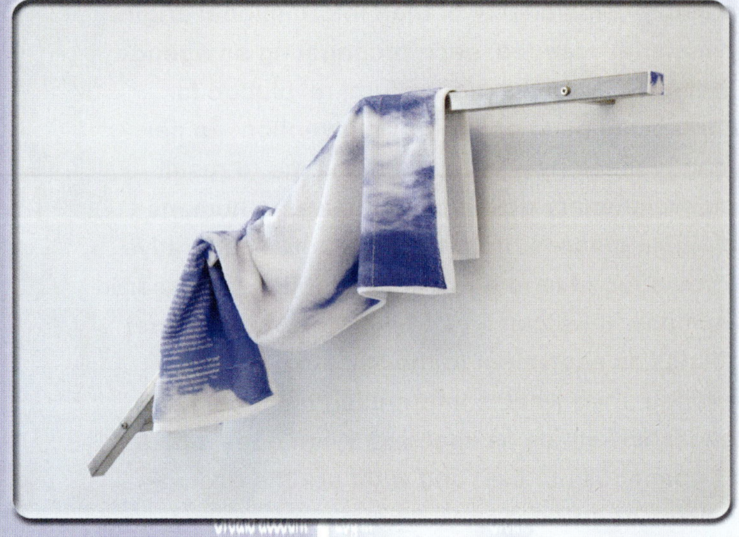

"Although Osama bin Laden's hideout in Pakistan lacked phone and Internet connectivity, the al Qaeda leader used his computers to prepare messages and save them on flash drives, which would be passed to a courier, according to the Associated Press. The courier would head to a far-flung Internet cafe, send the outgoing messages, retrieve the incoming ones, and then return to Abbottabad with the responses. That physical couriering of data, or sneakernet, helped bin Laden to evade U.S. intelligence agencies, especially the extraordinarily sensitive electronic ears of the National Security Agency, which specializes in intercepting radio and other communications."

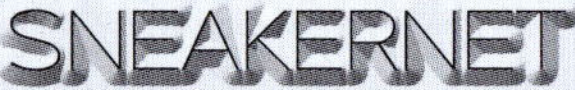

Author: Declan McCullag, Title: How bin Laden evaded the NSA: Sneakernet Reports offer details about trove of digital data found in his Pakistan hideout. Publisher: CNET, Year: 2011

Search

Air gap (networking)

An **air gap or air wall**[1] is a security measure often taken for computers and computer networks that must be extraordinarily secure. It consists of ensuring that a secure network is physically isolated from insecure networks, such as the public Internet or an insecure local area network. Frequently the air gap is not completely literal, such as via the use of dedicated cryptographic devices that can tunnel packets over untrusted networks while

Search

Air gap (plumbing)

An **air gap**, as it relates to the plumbing trade, is the unobstructed vertical space between the water outlet and the flood level of a fixture.[1]

A simple example is the space between a wall mounted faucet and the sink rim (this space is the air gap). Water can easily flow from the faucet into the sink, but there is no way that water can flow from the sink into the faucet without modifying the system. This arrangement will prevent any contaminants in the sink from flowing into the potable water system by siphonage and is the least expensive form of backflow prevention.

A common use of the term "air gap" in home plumbing refers to a fixture

Hold On, Air Gap 2012, 117 x 60 x 8 cm, stainless steel, uv-print on towel and plastic knob

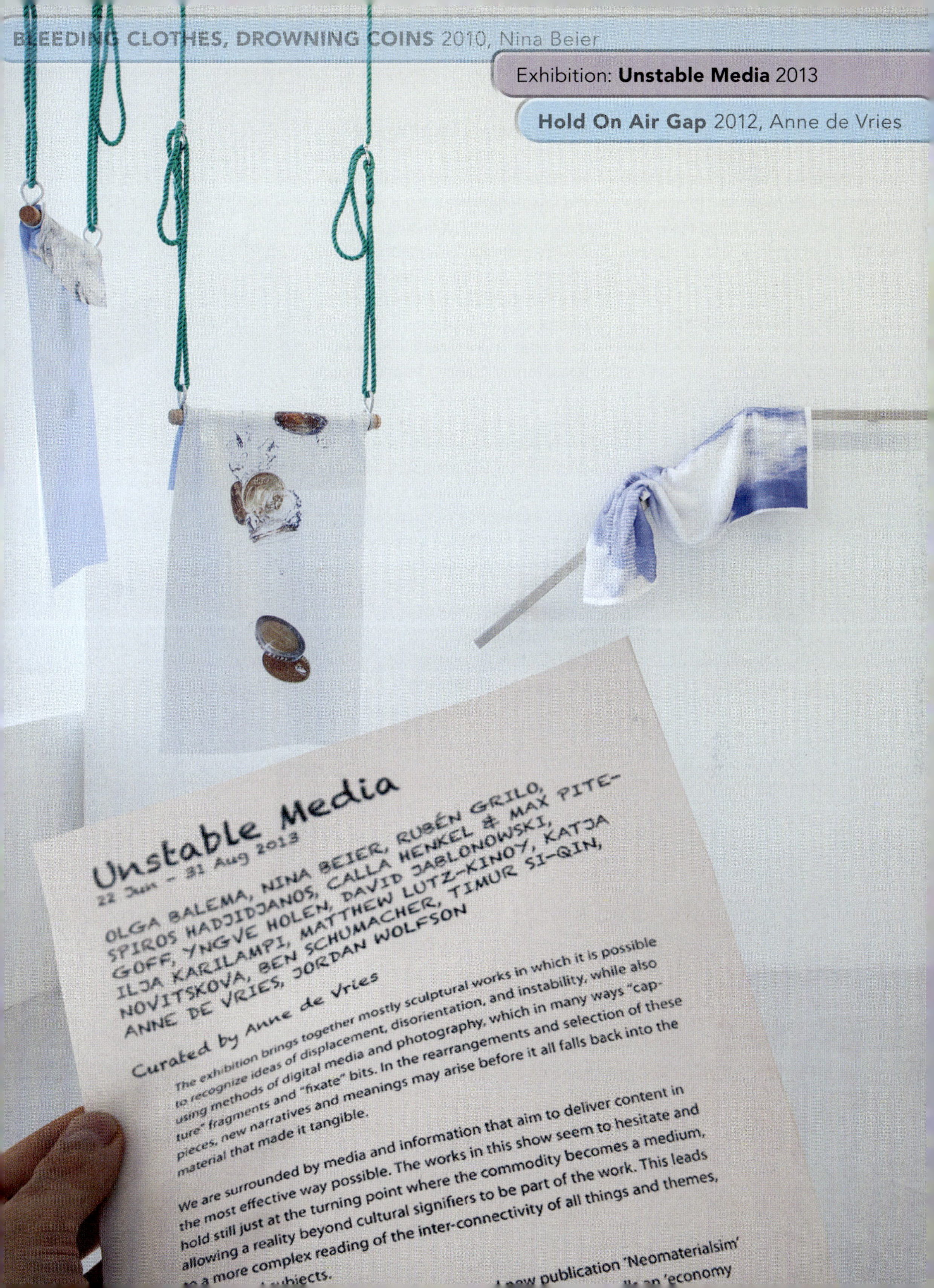

BLEEDING CLOTHES, DROWNING COINS 2010, Nina Beier

Exhibition: **Unstable Media** 2013

Hold On Air Gap 2012, Anne de Vries

Unstable Media
22 Jun – 31 Aug 2013

OLGA BALEMA, NINA BEIER, RUBÉN GRILO, SPIROS HADJIDJANOS, CALLA HENKEL & MAX PITEGOFF, YNGVE HOLEN, DAVID JABLONOWSKI, ILJA KARILAMPI, MATTHEW LUTZ-KINOY, KATJA NOVITSKOVA, BEN SCHUMACHER, TIMUR SI-QIN, ANNE DE VRIES, JORDAN WOLFSON

Curated by Anne de Vries

The exhibition brings together mostly sculptural works in which it is possible to recognize ideas of displacement, disorientation, and instability, while also using methods of digital media and photography, which in many ways "capture" fragments and "fixate" bits. In the rearrangements and selection of these pieces, new narratives and meanings may arise before it all falls back into the material that made it tangible.

We are surrounded by media and information that aim to deliver content in the most effective way possible. The works in this show seem to hesitate and hold still just at the turning point where the commodity becomes a medium, allowing a reality beyond cultural signifiers to be part of the work. This leads to a more complex reading of the inter-connectivity of all things and themes, ... subjects.

... new publication 'Neomaterialsim' ... an 'economy

Peter Colat

Swiss freediver from Zürich, has held his breath underwater for 19 minutes and 21 seconds, smashing the world record. Colat said the first 12 minutes was no problem.

He said: "I felt the first need to breathe very late, but because of this it was even stronger."

Peter Colat
E-Mail : pcolat@yahoo.de

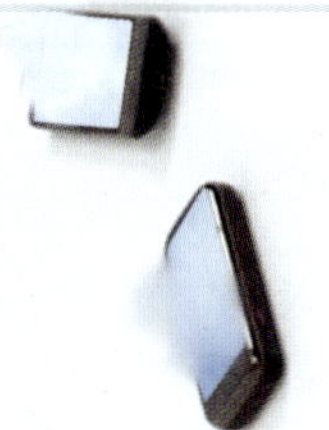

PRANAYAMA & MEDITATION

Pranayama is a central practice in the traditional Hatha Yoga system. It uses the breath, balancing of subtle energy patterns, energetic cleansing, and locks (Bandhas). This is a gateway into the deep states of concentration and meditation.
This class is presented in its traditional format, directly from a lineage that dates back generations. It provides a steady, safe opening for students and gives stability and clarity in the physical and mental realms.
It is recommended that students have some experience in Yoga Asana and/or seated Meditation practice before beginning pranayama.

OBERDORFSTRASSE
Oberdorfstrasse 2
8001 Zürich, Schweiz
Tel : +41 (0)43 499 01 01
E-Mail : zuerich@airyoga.com

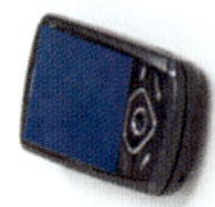

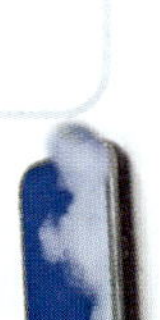

'The Breathing Economy' is a proposal for a trade fair to be held during MANIFESTA 11, to raise the visibility of 'air-based' businesses in the Zürich area.

ungenLiga
ungen-Rehabilitationszentrum

Vir beraten und betreuen Menschen it Atemwegsbeschwerden und Lunenkrankheiten. Wir setzen uns für ne Verbesserung der Lebensqualät von lungenkranken Menschen nd für die Früherkennung und rävention von Lungenkrankheiten n.

ungenLiga
eschäfts- und Beratungsstelle
chachenstrasse 9,
030 Ebikon, Schweiz
el : 041 429 31 10
ax : 041 429 31 11

Erotic asphyxiation
(Breath Control) / Air Play

Working in a full equipped BDSM hospital

Nurse Wanda von H.
E-Mail : wanda.von.h@gmail.com
www.wanda-von-h.ch

Swiss Smile

Bad breath? We can help you - from the diagnosis to the therapy concept at home. Are you unsure when you are in close contact, or have you ever been spoken to about bad breath? You are not alone in this. About one in four people suffer from bad breath, and many of them thus suffer emotionally and socially. But this need not be the case. Bad breath, known medically as halitosis, is not a taboo subject for our experts, but a fact that can be remedied.

Swiss Smile
Shop Ville, City Station
8001 Zürich, Schweiz
Tel : +41 43 300 30 03
www.swiss-smile.com

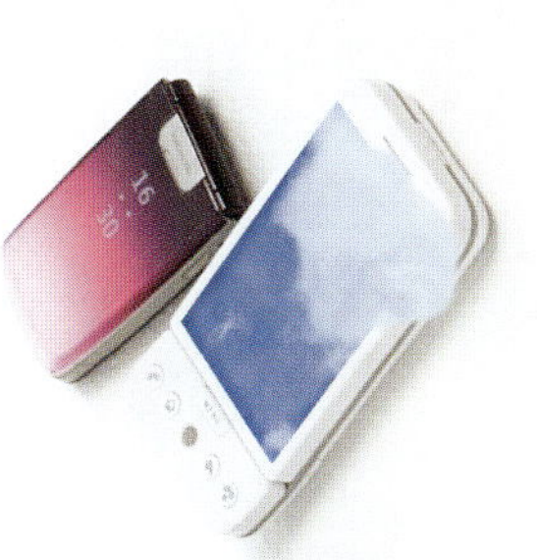

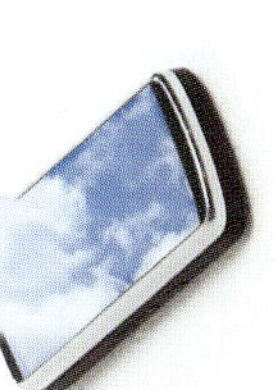

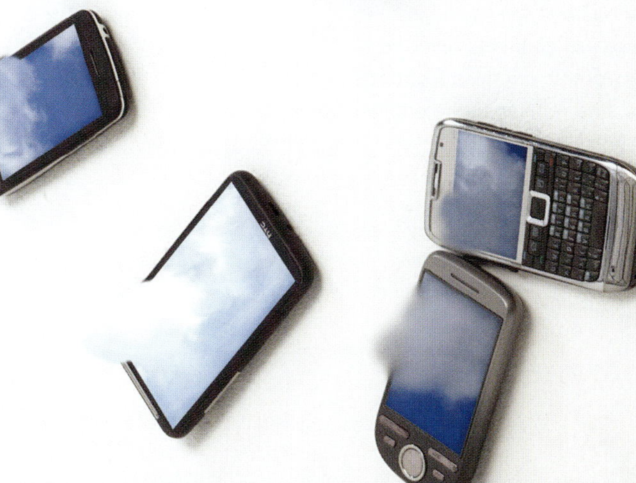

Tai Chi ch'uan, Zurich

In t'ai chi ch'uan, aerobic training is combined with breathing to exercise the diaphragm muscles and to train effective posture; making better use of the body's energy. In music, breath is used to play wind instruments and many aerophones. Laughter, physically, is simply repeated sharp breaths. Hiccups, yawns, and sneezes are other breath-related phenomena.

Ancients commonly linked the breath to a life force. The Hebrew Bible refers to God breathing the breath of life into clay to make Adam a living soul (nephesh). It also refers to the breath as returning to God when a mortal dies. The terms "spirit," "qi," "prana" and "psyche"[9] are related to the concept of breath. Also cognate are Polynesian Mana and Hebrew ruach.

In the book Your Atomic Self: The Invisible Elements That Connect You to Everything Else in the Universe, excerpted in Wired Magazine, Curt Stager explores the atomic and molecular basis of links through which breathing connects humans and other Aerobic organisms of birds, mammals, and reptiles to the entire planet.

Schule für
Tai Chi Chuan & Qi Gong
Bäckerstrasse 40
8004 Zürich, Schweiz

Intraceuticals Hyberbaric Oxygen Technology

Noosa now has it's first O2 Intraceuticals Hyperbaric Oxygen Technology Machine. The revolutionary rejuvenating skin thereapy provides a natural facelift. It is used globally by dermatologists, plastic surgeons and celebrities including madonna. It is painless, needle free and non invasive. It erases fine lines, firms and tightens the skin.

Summer Beauty Cosmetic
Sabina Mazza
Werdstrasse 40
8004 Zürich, Schweiz
Tel : + 41 (0)79 336 20 66
www.summerbeautycosmetic.com

Klinik für Thoraxchirurgie und Lungentransplantation

Die erste Lungentransplantation der Schweiz wurde im November 1992 im Universitätsspialt Zürich durchgeführt. Bis Ende 2014 wurden bereits 438 Lungentransplantatione durchgeführt. Inzwischen hat sich diese Therapie bei Patienten mit fortgeschrittenen Lungenkrankheite speziell bei Patienten mit cystischer Fibrose (CF), Lungenfibrose (IPF), chronisch obstruktiven Lungenkrank heiten (COPD), pulmonal arterieller Hypertonie (PAH) und anderen terminalen Lungenerkrankungen se gut etabliert.

Dank der medizinischen Fortschritte und der engen Betreuung im spezial isierten multidisziplinären Team, ist das Überleben nach Lungentransplantation in unserem Zentrum vergl chen mit dem internationalen Schnit überdurchschnittlich.

Prof. Dr. Walter Weder
Klinikdirektor und
ärztlicher Co-Direktor

UniversitätsSpital
Klinik für Thoraxchirurgie
Rämistrasse 100
8091 Zürich, Schweiz
Tel : +41 44 255 88 02
E-Mail : thoraxchirurgie@usz.ch

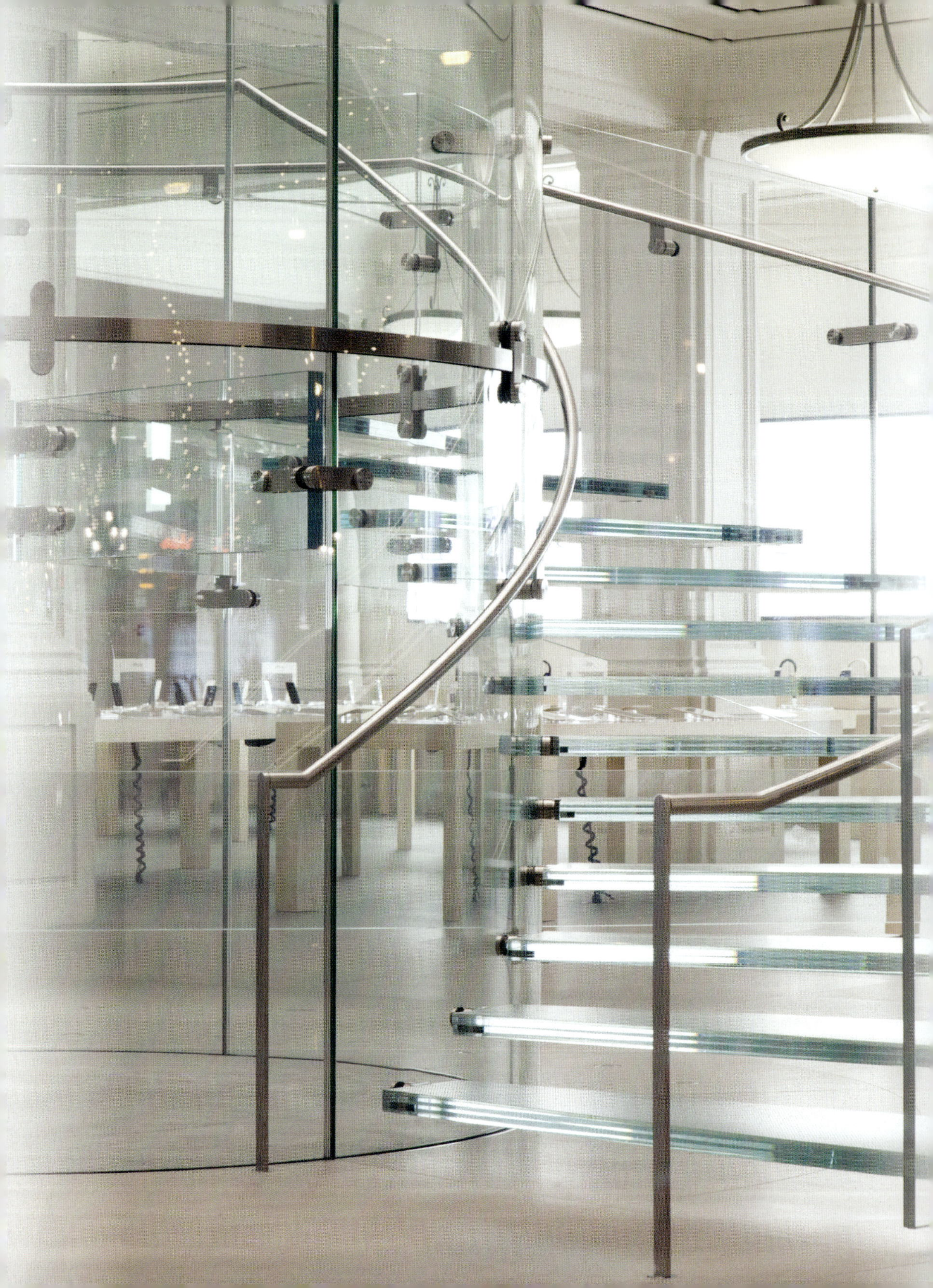

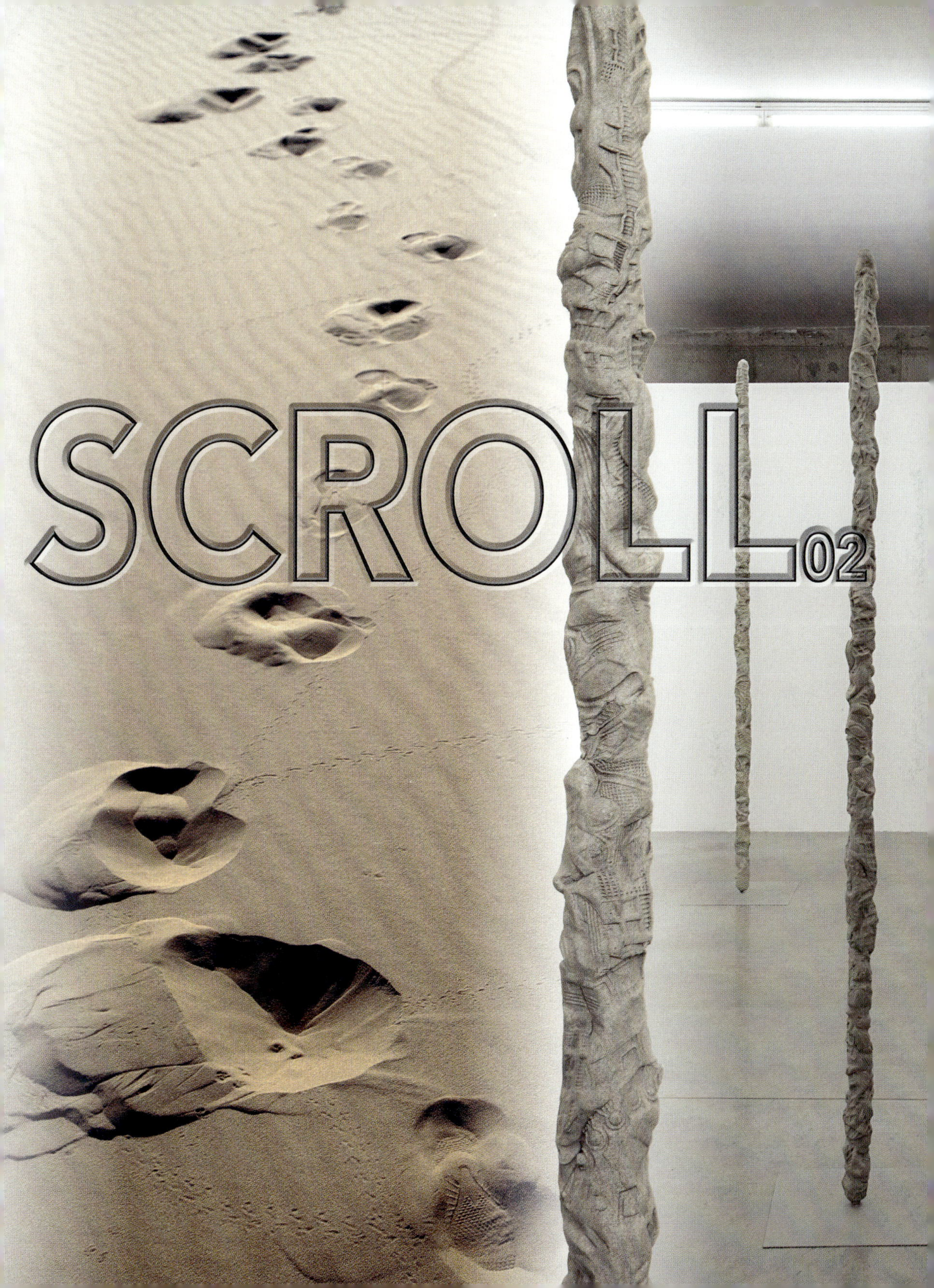
SCROLL02

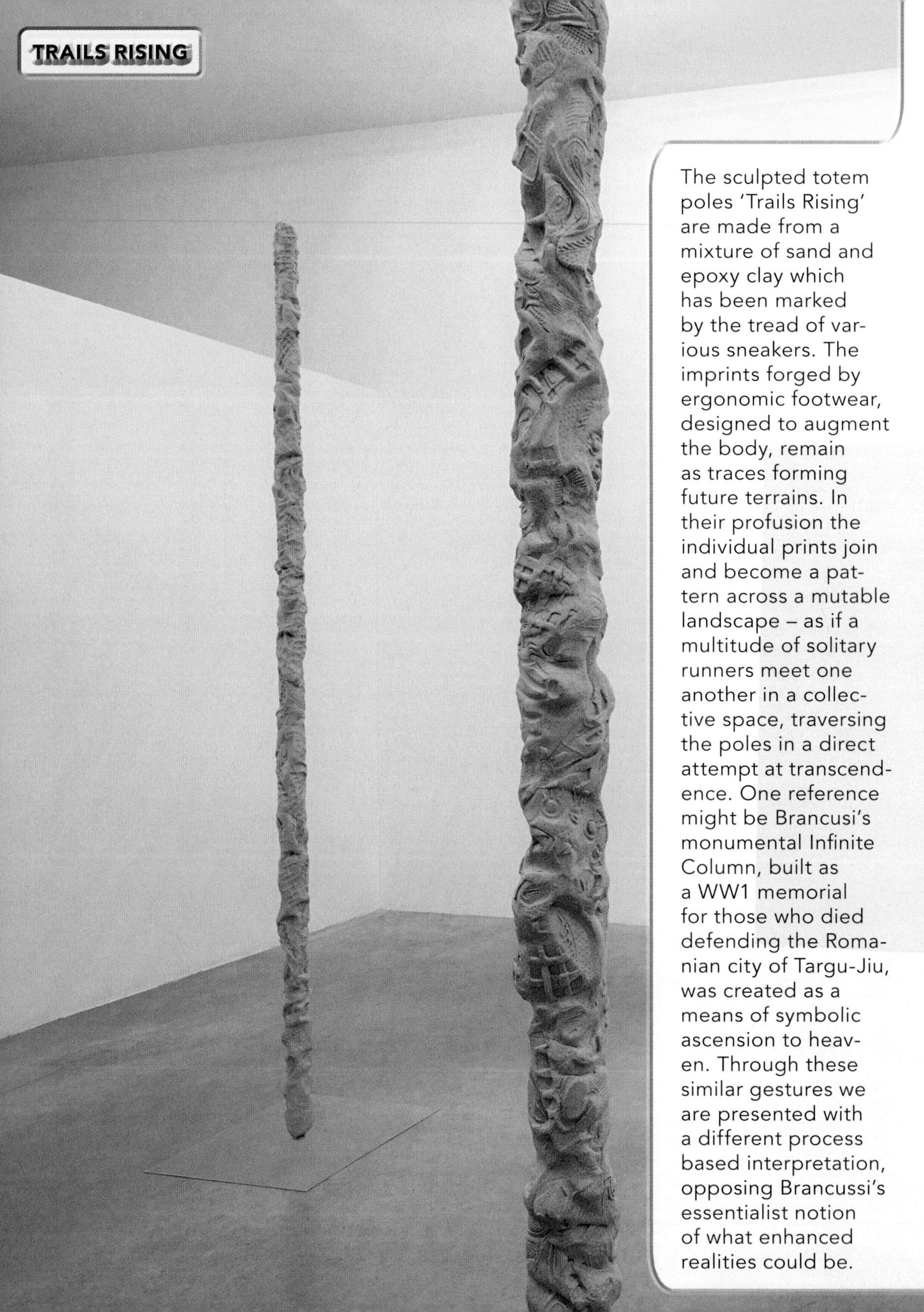

The sculpted totem poles ‘Trails Rising’ are made from a mixture of sand and epoxy clay which has been marked by the tread of various sneakers. The imprints forged by ergonomic footwear, designed to augment the body, remain as traces forming future terrains. In their profusion the individual prints join and become a pattern across a mutable landscape – as if a multitude of solitary runners meet one another in a collective space, traversing the poles in a direct attempt at transcendence. One reference might be Brancusi’s monumental Infinite Column, built as a WW1 memorial for those who died defending the Romanian city of Targu-Jiu, was created as a means of symbolic ascension to heaven. Through these similar gestures we are presented with a different process based interpretation, opposing Brancussi’s essentialist notion of what enhanced realities could be.

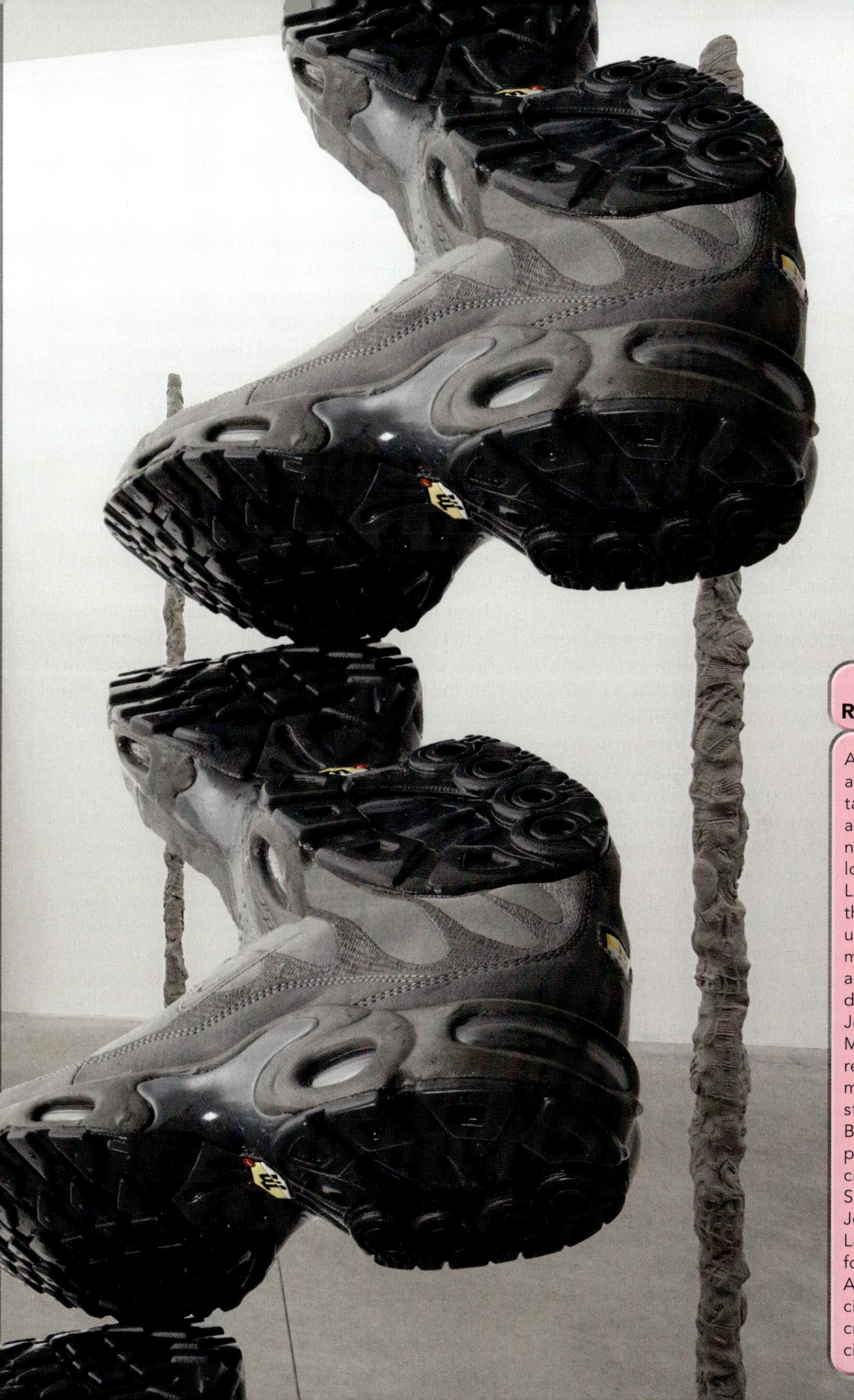

AI GPT-2 RESPONSE

A similar approach is taking shape at Barcelona's São Paulo Museum. Last year, the museum commissioned architect and designer José Carlos Martínez to recreate 3D models of a statue of the Brazilian emperor in the city's Central Square, while José J. de La Salle, formerly of Arturo Brescia Museum, created the city's Nation-

UNIQUE, UNIQUE-ER, UNIQUE-EST

by Agatha Wara

"The Subject," Manuel De Landa tells us, "is a historical notion." It's history. A goner. And just like that, De Landa deals a blow to a certain strain of Western philosophy since Aristotle that holds the Subject as something close to the truth of how we access our reality. In contrast to these dominant "philosophies of access," materialist philosopher De Landa asserts that "at least some part of reality exists independently of the [human] mind."
Yet, for De Landa, the simple question persists: "How do we come to terms with the virtual reality that our brains are producing right now?" De Landa's account of reality comes from a theory of systems (in Deleuzian terms, "assemblages").

Everything in our world and of every scale, from the global economy down to a single bacterium, can be thought of as a system, one that is fundamentally made up of matter. The world is dynamic, and matter functions with its own capacities, potentialities, and tendencies. This breaks the classical distinction between substance and form that asserts that form is created by an external force (e.g., a human, God, or an artist) and gives shape to a certain substance, or material. Yet if matter is active, then its role in the shaping of its form must be recognized. And thus forms, or systems, through a materialist account, are seen as the outcomes of interactions between matter of heterogeneous capacities.
What this implies for the human body is that it too, as a system, is the outcome of interactions of material capacities, and is therefore ontologically equal to other bodies: humans, animals, societies, geological formations, etc.

Thus, the "virtual reality" that we experience every day is the interaction of our bodies with the incredibly complex mesh of systems located in our environment. The interest in speculative thinking and all things non-human in philosophy over past decades is more and more becoming reflected in technological innovation, consumer products, and global environmental policy. In 2011, the multinational computer manufacturer IBM forecasted the top five technologies that would reach the consumer market by 2016. Number one on the list was the ability to store and convert energy created when running, for instance, to power our electronic devices. In other words, humans are not special beings extricated from reality, but beings whose bodies run off of the same electricity that it takes to power their cellphones.
Similarly, "humanness" continues to come into question every time "human rights" are granted to non-human entities: the scientific campaign to grant dolphins rights as "non-human persons," the granting of human rights to nature by the Bolivian government in 2011, American corporations gaining legal rights as "natural persons" under the Corporate Personhood law passed in 2010. Unquestionably, conceiving of the human being as a system that is bound to the processes of our environment has an effect on artistic thinking.

Anne de Vries's sculpture "Trails Rising" (2012) reaches for a renewed relationship with the material world by pointing to a commonplace emergence in our commodity-driven landscape: the ergonomic product. Made from a mixture of epoxy clay and beach sand, the three columns that make up "Trails Rising" have been roughly shaped using the soles of running shoes. De Vries writes, "The imprints forged by ergonomic footwear, designed to augment the body, remain as traces forming future terrains." Trapped in these mutable surfaces are the traces left behind by an imaginary track meet that has taken place in another domain. We are prompted to question the manifestation of the ergonomic trace in daily life.
The principles of ergonomic design are concerned with "fit" between users and their environment. The Polish scientist Wojciech Jastrzebowski first coined the term in 1857 from the Greek ergon meaning "work," and nómos, meaning "natural laws."

al Museum of the Brazilian Arts (MAMA). The city's first sculpture, on which the statue was placed in the Museum of the Arts in 2005, was commissioned in 2005 under the auspices of a local partnership with the city's Ministry of Tourism. This series will cover the process that took place between a group, such as Brazilian museum in conjunction with the Brazilian Heritage Trust and its partners, to design these works and what they accomplish within each, both in terms of design and the way they are crafted. Our hope is that each of these pieces will inspire new and relevant ideas for public transport, and that the results will give an opportunity to engage as one to discover how the different shapes relate

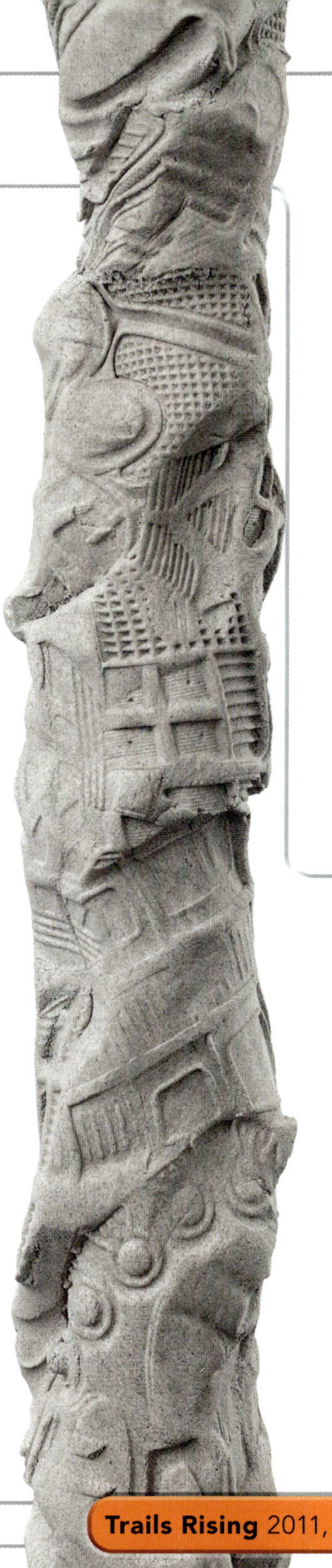

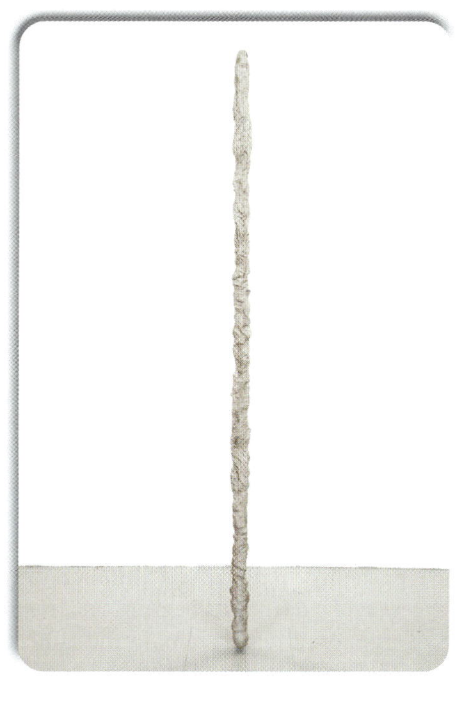

Trails Rising 2011, up to 12 meters tall, plastic, sand, metal

But it wasn't until World War I that the groundwork for the ergonomic field as we know it today was laid out. The necessities of both World Wars called for war machines with design that accounted for the human operator's psychology and capabilities, as well as his limitations. This established new fields of research that continued into the civilian sector, mainly workplaces, to determine links between human productivity and the work environment.

Here, the aim of ergonomic design became to minimize the body's discomfort and fatigue in order to maximize worker safety and productivity. Today's complex ergonomic field expands over varied disciplines, including biomechanics, industrial design, anthropometry, and psychology. The human body and its potentials have been measured and analyzed to determine the muscle force required to perform tasks like lifting, cardiovascular activity while performing heavy labor, and the maximum weight that can be safely carried, pushed, or pulled. And although the field has largely evolved from its beginnings, the principles of ergonomic design remain the same: to consider the "fit" between the user, and environment. Returning to 'Trance Tracks' we discover that de Vries has given us a clue. He states, "One reference [for "Trails Rising] might be Brancusi's monumental "Endless Column (1938)." Built as a World War I memorial, the stack of rhomboids was created to symbolize ascension to heaven. Through similar gestures in form, we are presented with different notions of what enhanced realities could be. For Modernists like Brancusi, the creation of forms such as "Endless Column" came out of moments of inspiration, when the artist as a Subject could uniquely access ideal forms that existed out there, perhaps something like a temporary ascension to heaven. But the enhanced reality "Trails Rsising" speaks to is found not in a notion of heaven, but conversely underneath one's shoes, in the uncanny fingerprint of ergonomic engineering.

Through the ergonomic holy trinity—fit, user, and environment—the athletic shoe is geared toward enhancing the body's performance. Every manufacturer has its own system of delivery. Nike's Shox soles, for instance, are said to "add more power to the stride, and boost speed." While Reebok claims that their RealFlex zig-zag soles "cushion up and down like regular shoes, but also horizontally."
The zigs absorb impact while the zags "return energy." On the one hand, the language used to market the ergonomic product suggests that we enter an enhanced reality each time we put on our running shoes, insofar as they help us experience added speed, more power, and a return of energy. Yet this language also implies the already present materialist tendency to conceive of the human body as a material emergence, one that produces energy and one that can be optimized. This realization is sure to make critical theory cringe, since conceiving of the body as merely material fits so nicely into its critiques of power, mainly the neoliberal dictate that has required us to give 200 percent of mind, body, and soul, has achieved what it has wanted all along: to turn humans into mere tools. But the question in front of us now is whether we can put aside these inherited discourses of power (if only for a moment) to think about what we can gain from a materialist account of the human being today. The allure of non-human philosophies, argues philosopher Graham Harman, comes from the larger political frameworks of this moment. The observation that things are becoming livelier and more "human" (dolphins, forests, corporations) alongside the increasing climate crises, is what underlies the interest in such theoretical frameworks.

To put it more directly, we are witnessing the consequences, the pitfalls, of a total separation of ourselves from the material world around us. Trapped in a basin of epoxy and sand, the ergonomic trace in "Trails Rising"signifies the intrinsic connection that exists between the hard matter in our bodies and the hard matter in our environment. By creating forms of such minimal nature, de Vries wants to direct all of our attention to the uncanny beauty of the ergonomic mark, urging us not to extricate ourselves from the world, but to touch matter, to interact with the forces that we are intrinsically tied to. "Trails Rising" thus creates a terrain in which the human does not stand as the unique-est being, in a manifestation that could not be more beautiful.

Author: Agatha Wara, Title: Unique, Unique-er, Uniquest, Published: Miami Rail, Year: 2012 to each other. We hope it will inspire you to take to the streets of Rome, where your city is always trying to put its collective collective image to work. There are some surprising similarities with the Oculus Rift. First of all, you're basically giving away the camera and the controls. I know it sounds like I'm using Oculus to record something, but what will you say to the world? I think you're going to go out on a limb here, and I feel like that's an unfair way to go about it.

Secondly, the Oculus Rift won't work when you're playing or playing on your mobile phone. The camera will always be around your head, and when you're playing on your phone it will turn off. This means that you'll be moving in the shadows, and the camera's

Apple + Retailer:
LPG biomarkt, Kollwitzstraße 17, 10405 Berlin, Germany
+
Production Elstar Apple:
Obst vom Bodensee, Vertriebsgesellschaft mbH, Eugen-Bolz-Str. 16, 88094 Oberteuringen, Germany

Pear + Retailer:
LPG biomarkt, Kollwitzstraße 17, 10405 Berlin, Germany
+
Production Pear:
Mazul, Moño Azul S.A. Rio Negro, Cmte. Guerrico, Ruta Nac.22 Km.1188, Argentina

Banana + Retailer:
LPG biomarkt, Kollwitzstraße 17, 10405 Berlin, Germany
+
Production:
Golden Bio - Finca Banamek, Hato Nuevo, Bario la Compuerta, Mao, Dominican Republic

Iphone 4 + Retailer:
Cyberport Store, Friedrichstraße 50-55, 10117, Berlin, Germany
+
Production Iphone 4 Design:
Apple Inc. 1 Infinite Loop, Cupertino, CA 95014, United States of America
+
Production Final assembly:
Foxconn Technology Group (Hon Hai Precision Industry Co. 10 Industrial District North 2, Dong Huan Rd, Long Hua Town Bao An, Shenzhen, Guang Dong, China
+
Production Display module:
Toshiba Mobile Display Co. (Toshiba Corporation Japan) Ishikawa Works Kawakita-machi, Nomi-gun, Ishikawa Prefecture, Japan
+
Production Touchscreen assembly:
Toshiba Mobile Display Co. (Toshiba Corporation Japan) Ishikawa Works Kawakita-machi, Nomi-gun, Ishikawa Prefecture, Japan
+
Production Apple A4 processor chip:
PowerVR SGX535 Graphics GPU (Imagination Technologies Group plc) Samsung Austin Semiconductor (Samsung Group South Korea) Samsung 12100 Samsung Blvd # 110, Austin, TX 78754, United States of America
+
Production Qualcomm MDM6610 baseband processor:
Taiwan Semiconductor Manufacturing Co No. 121 Park Ave. III, Hsinchu Science Park, Hsinchu, 300, R.O.C. Taiwan
+
Production Capacative glass ,Reinforced ,Touch screen overlay:
TPK Touch Solutions, Inc. (Balda Group germany, mobilecom) No. 199 Ban Shang Road. Xiamen, 361006. China
+
Production Samsung K9PFG08 flash memory :
Samsung Austin Semiconductor (Samsung Group South Korea)12100 Samsung Blvd # 110, Austin, TX 78754, United States of America
+
Production Broadcom BCM4329 multiband low power 802.11a/b/g/n with Bluetooth chip:
Taiwan Semiconductor Manufacturing Company, Limited No. 121 Park Ave. III, Hsinchu Science Park, Hsinchu, 300-77, Taiwan
+
Production Broadcom BCM4329 multiband low power 802.11a/b/g/n with Bluetooth chip:
R.O.C. Murata Manufacturing Co. Ltd. No.6, Xingchuang 1st Road, Wuxi Export Processing Zone B Zone, Wuxi, Jiangsu 214028, China
+
Production BCM4750 single chip GPS receiver IC:
Taiwan Semiconductor Manufacturing Company, Limited No. 121 Park Ave. III, Hsinchu Science Park, Hsinchu, 300, R.O.C. Taiwan
+
Production BCM4750 single chip GPS receiver IC:
Murata Manufacturing Co. Ltd. No.6, Xingchuang 1st Road, Wuxi Export Processing Zone B Zone, Wuxi, Jiangsu 214028, China
+
Production Cirrus Logic 338S0589 audio codec:
HSCL, Hynix Semiconductor China Inc. Lot K7, Wuxi Export Processing Zone in Wuxi New District, Wuxi, China
+
Production Knowles S1950 video microphone:
Knowles Electronics Holdings, Inc. Plot 104, Lebuhraya Kg. Jawa Bayan Lepas Industrial Estate 11900 Penang, Malaysia
+
Production Infineon 1014 phone microphone:
Infineon Technologies AG, Königsbrücker Strasse 180, 01099 Dresden Saxony, Germany
+
Production AKM8975 magnetic sensor:
AKM Semiconductor, Inc. (Tokyo, Japan) Atsugi, Kanagawa 243-21, Japan
+
Production 343S0499 Touch Screen Controller:
Texas Instruments Japan Limited. Miho Wafer Fab (MIHO) at. 2350 Kihara, Miho-mura, Inashiki-gun, Japan
+
Production OmniVision OV5642 Image sensor:
OmniVision Semiconductor Co., Ltd 111 Ronghua Road, Songjiang Export Processing Zone, Shanghai , 201611, China
+
Production Avago ACPM-7181 converged power amplifier module (PAM):
REP Avago (WUXI) Electronics Techlogies Limited, No. 6 Gaokai Road, [illegible] District, Wuxi, Jiangsu [illegible], China
+
Production Skyworks SKY77541-GSM/GRPS Front End Module:
Skyworks Solutions chips, Colonizador 1619, Zona Sin Asignación de Nombre de Colonia, Mexicali, Baja California, Mexico
+
Production Skyworks SKY77542 Tx-Rx iPAC™ FEM for Dual-Band GSM/[illegible]
Skyworks Solutions chips Colonizador 1619, Zona Sin Asignación de [illegible], Mexicali, Baja California, Mexico
+
Production Skyworks SKY77541-32 Transmit module Quad-band [illegible]
Skyworks Solutions chips, Colonizador 1619, Zona Sin Asignación de [illegible] de Colonia, Mexicali, Baja California, Mexico
+
Production TriQuint TQM676091 Transmit module Single-Band [illegible] PAM + Duple[illegible]
TriQuint Optoelectronics Fab, Allied Electronics, 3505 Boca Chica Bo[illegible], Brownsville TX[illegible]
+
Production Numonyx Nor and mobile DDR:
HSCS, Hynix Semiconductor (Shanghai) Inc. Maxdo Center [illegible]
+
Production White label transceiver chip:
Infineon Technologies AG, Königsbrücker Strasse 180, [illegible], Germany
+
Production Timing Crystal:
TXC Taiwan Passive components, Kung Yeh 6th Rd., Ping Cheng [illegible]
+
Production Passive components:
Cyntec Co Ltd. #2 Yen Fa 2nd Rd.Science Based Ind.Park 308 Hsinchu [illegible]
+
Production Connector and cables:
[illegible]
+
Production ST Microelectronics [illegible]
ST Microelectronics, ZI de Rousset, BP2 1310[illegible]
+
Production Case, Mechanical parts:
Foxconn Technology Group (Hon Hai Precision Industry Co., Ltd. China) 10 Industrial District North 2, Dong Huan Rd, Long Hua Town Bao An, Shenzhen Guang Dong, China

Multiple Vertical I & II, 2010, David Jablonows

Production ST Microelectronics L3G4200D three axis gyroscope:
ST Microelectronics, ZI de Rousset, BP2 13106 Rousset, France
+
duction Case, Mechanical parts:
nn Technology Group (Hon Hai Precision Industry Co., Ltd. China) 10 Industrial District North 2, Dong Huan Rd., Long Hua Town Bao An, Shenzhen
Dong, China

ction Camera lens :
Precision Co. Ltd. Taiwan
u Largan Precision Electronics Co., Ltd, Suzhou, Jiangsu, China

ction Battery Charger:
Electronics, Delta Electronics, Inc. Chungli Plant 1, 3 Tungyuan Road, Chungli Industrial Zone, Taoyuan County 32063, R.O.C. Taiwan

ction LG 3.5" LTPS LCS:
rp. (LG Display) Paju LG LCD Complex, Paju, South-Korea

an AWM style + Retailer:
Saturn, Alexanderplatz 3, 10178 Berlin, Germany
+
Production USB Cable Haurtian AWM style:
Fortron Industrial Co., Ltd.Taiwan sales office: 6F-2, No. 2, Lane 251, Yang Hsin Pei Rd., Yang-Mei Town, Taoyuan Hsien, Taiwan.

Model A1150 + Retailer:
Cyberport Store, Friedrichstraße 50-55, 10117 Berlin, Germany
+
Production MacBook Pro 15" Design:
Apple Inc. 1 Infinite Loop, Cupertino, CA 95014, United States of America
+
Production MacBook Pro 85W Apple AC Adapter (model no: A1222):
Shenzhen Time In Top Technology Co., Ltd. Hong Kong / Rms. 2601-02, International Science & Technology Building, 3007 Shennan Rd., Futian, Shenzhen 518000, China
+
Production MacBook Pro 15" (Model A1150) Left I/O Board Includes MagSafe power, USB, and audio ports input/output board:
Shenzhen Mingchuan Electronic Technology Co., Ltd. Street Address: Room 901, HuiShang Building, Jia Hui Xin Cheng, Shen Nan Road, Futian District, Shenzhen, China
+
Production MacBook Pro 15" (Model A1150) Left I/O Board Cable (Product code: IF185-015-1 Apple Part #: 922-7200):
Xiamen Astonish Forest Electronic Company Limited, Jiahe Road, Xiamen China
Suplier: Slice Components Campenton Riverside Staines Middlesex TW183NJ, United Kingdom
+
Production MacBook Pro 15" (Model A1150) 1.83 GHz Logic Board2 GHz Motherboard / Ports: DVI Video Out, 1000BaseT Ethernet, Firewire 400, USB 2.0:
China Electronic Digital Technology Co., LTD Store No. 505904 Guangdong, China
+
Production MacBook Pro 15" (Model A1150) Hard Drive Cable Connects hard drive, sleep light, IR sensor, and Bluetooth board to logic board, Product code: IF185-030-1 Apple Part #: 922-7:
Shenzhen Yall Trading Co., Ltd. 2fl, Block C, Longjing Second Industrial Park, Taoyuan Village Nanshan, Shenzhen, Fuzhou, Fujian, China
+
Production 80GB SATA Hard Drive, Model: TOSHIBA MK8032GSX, 16PI4438T:
AE Tech CO LTD, 5F No.136, Sec.1, Neihu Rd., Neihu Dist, Taipei city 11493, Taipei, Taiwan
+
Production PC2-5300 1 GB RAM Chip: 1 GB, DDR2 SDRAM, 667 MHz, Production code: IF111-000-1, Apple Part #: 661-3867:
Shenzhen Silkway Technology Co., Ltd. 2110, 21th floor, NanGuan Jie Jia Bd, Shen'nan RD,(30E GuangYe building of Fuhua Road)Futian district, Shenzhen, Guangdong, China
+
Production MacBook Pro 15" (Models A1150/A1211) Display Data Cable, Product code: IF185-087-1, Apple Part #: 922-7197:
Chuangbo Hong Kong Industrial Developments LTD, 17C-Unit 2 ,buliding 12, mellon Garden, longhua town, Shenzhen, Guangdong, China
+
Production MacBook Pro 15" (Models A1150/A1211) Display Inverter, Product code: IF185-090-1, Apple Part #: 922-7191:
Shantou New Tideshine Electron Co., Ltd. N2C099, New Asian Market, Zhonghang Road, Shenzhen Guangdong, China
+
Production MacBook Pro 15" (Model A1150) Inverter/iSight Cable, Product code: IF185-088-1:
Deals Plus Technology CO LTD, 53833 Goconda trader center, Shenzhen, Guangdong, China
+
Production MacBook Pro 15" (Models A1150/A1211) LCD Panel, 1440x900 LCD / 15.4" / CCFL backlight:
Advanced Tech Dangjung Dong 110-3, South Korea
+
Production MacBook Pro 15" (Model A1150) Upper Case Cable, Product code: IF185-131-1:
Logitech, Argon Computing Ltd, 125 Southend Road, Rochford, Essex, SS4 1HX, United Kingdom
+
Production MacBook Pro 15" (Model A1150) Keyboard, Replacement Keyboard / Backlit, Product code: IF185-002-1, Apple Part #: 922-7183:
Deals Plus Technology CO LTD, 53833. Goconda trader center, Shenzhen, Guangdong, China
+
Production MacBook Pro 15" (Model A1150) Track Pad:
Trading Company, Distributor/Wholesaler: Jin-Rong Electronic Company Ltd. Dongguan City 2B11, Jia-Run Office Building, No. 106, Guanzhang Rd., Zhushan, Dongguan, Guangdong, China
+
Production Software:
Apple Inc. 1 Infinite Loop, Cupertino, CA 95014, United States of America

dobe Photoshop CS5 Extended + Retailer:
Apple Store, Leidseplein 25, 1017 PS Amsterdam, The Netherlands
+
Production Adobe Software:
Adobe Systems Incorporated, 345 Park Avenue San Jose, California, United States of America
+
Production Adobe Software:
Adobe Systems India Private Limited, Adobe Towers I-1A, City Centre, Sector : 25A NOI
+
Production Adobe Software:
Adobe Bangalore Office, Salarpuria Infinity, 3rd Floor #5, Bannerghatta Road, Bangalore-

EE 1394 (6Pin/4Pin) + Retailer:
Apple Store, Leidseplein 25, 1017 PS Amsterdam, The Netherlands
+
Production Firewire cable IEEE 1394 (6Pin/4Pin):
Guangzhou Kingletian Electronic Co., Ltd, B202, 2/F Hongyi Business Bldg,No.4,Guanyu Road, Tangd

IPF 9000 Canon printer + Retailer:
Calumet Keienbergweg 13-15, 1101 EZ Amsterdam, The Netherlands
+
Production IPF 9000 Canon printer design:
Canon Inc. Headquarters 30-2, Shimomaruko 3-chome, Ohta-ku, Tokyo 146-8501, Japan
+
Production Electronics packaging:
Miyazaki Daishin Canon Inc, 4308-1, Ohaza Takajo, Kijo-cho, Koyu-gun, Miyazaki 884-0101, Japan
+
Production Toner cartridges and advanced functional polymer components:
Canon Chemicals Inc. 1888-2, Kukizaki, Tsukuba, Ibaraki 300-1294, Japan
+
Production Chemical products for printers:
Oita Canon Materials Inc, 111, Kumano 1-chome, Kitsuki, Oita 873-8501, Japan
+
Production Laser printers, toner cartridges, a-Si drums:
Nagahama Canon Inc. 1280, Kunitomomachi, Nagahama, Shiga 526-0001, Japan
+
Production Chemical products for printers:
Ueno Canon Matrials Inc. 410-7, Higashiomachi, Mita-aza, Iga, Mie 518-0022, Japan
+
Production of inkjet printers, print heads and ink tanks; analysis of software:
Fukishima Canon Inc. 2, Aza Nihon-Enoki, Sakura-shimo, Fukushima, Fukushima 960-2193, Japan
+
Production Design and production of precise plastic molding:
Canon Mold Co. Ltd.6241-6, Koibuchi, Kasama, Ibaraki 309-1703, Japan
+
Production Consumable supplies, parts and materials of business machines:
Hita Canon Materials Inc.1800-1, Oaza Nishiarita, Hita City, Oita, Japan
+
Production Toner cartridges, toner for copying machines, OEM products and molding dies:
Canon Virginia, Inc. 2000 Canon Blvd., Newport News, VA 23606-4299, United States of America
+
Production and recycling of toner cartridges; production of laser printers:
Canon Dalian Business Machines, Inc No.23, Huai He West Road, Economic & Technical Development Zone, Dalian , PRC, China
+
Production Laser printers, contact image sensors

"It is perhaps not a surprise that photography developed as a technological medium in the industrial age, when reality started to disappear. It is even perhaps the disappearance of reality that triggered this technical form. Reality found a way to mutate into an image."

Reappearance

Author: Jean Baudrillard,
Title: La Photographie ou l' Ecriture de la Lumiere: Litteralite de l' Image, in L' Echange Impossible, First Published: Galilee, Year: 1999

coming up against the viewfinder when you open the head. These will cause it to make the head look too close and out of focus. You're going to have to do some work on those two things, and I don't think it's right to let people make fun of your experience. That won't be a problem, just make sure you have a good viewfinder. If you don't mind doing it for free, you have to be very careful, because you could be on the receiving end of an expensive, very expensive head-mount.

AI GPT-2 RESPONSE

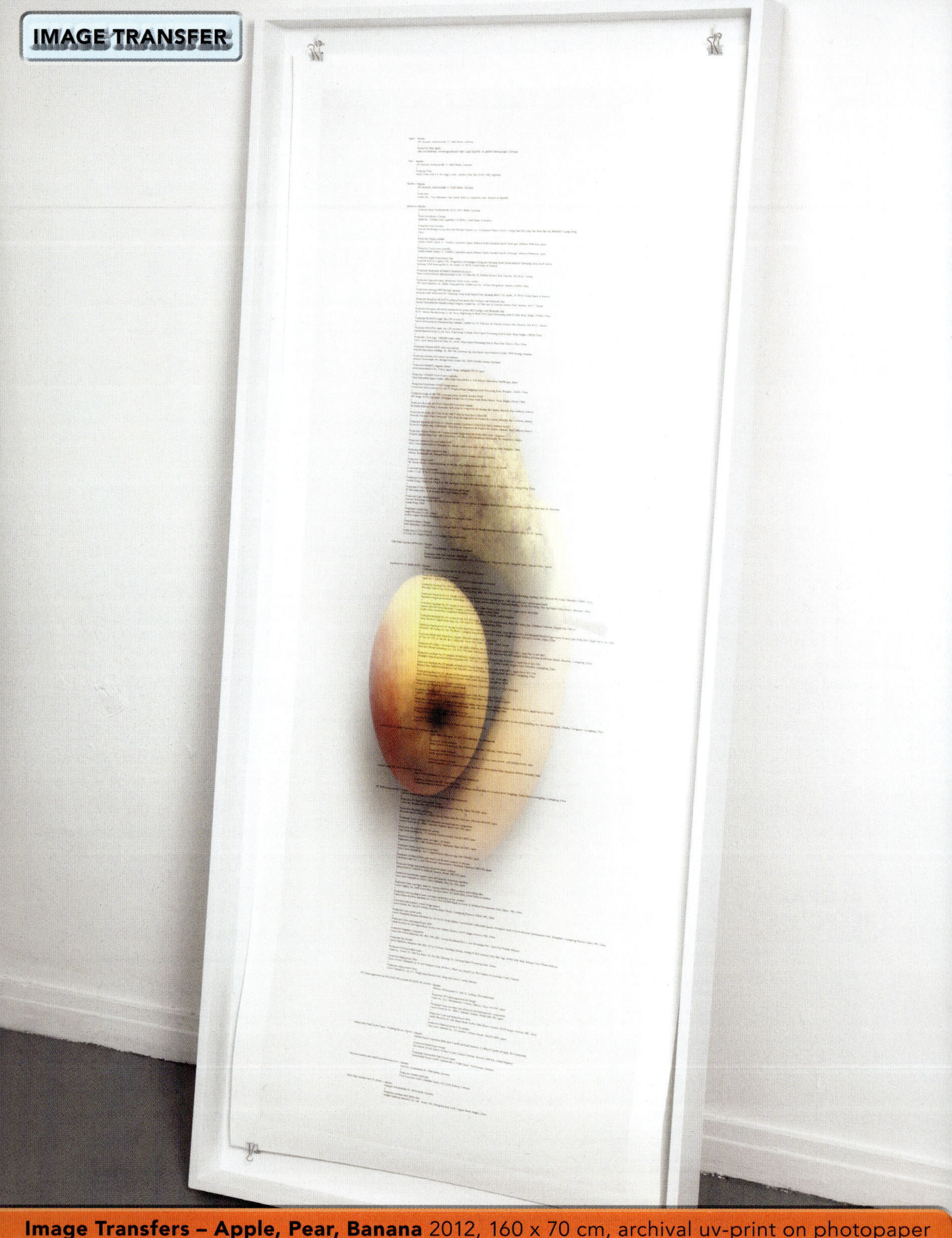

Image Transfers – Apple, Pear, Banana 2012, 160 x 70 cm, archival uv-print on photopaper

+
Production Battery Charger:
Delta Electronics, Delta Electronics, Inc. Chungli Plant 1, 3 Tungyuan Road, Chungli Industrial Zone, Taoyuan County 32063, R.O.C. Taiw
+
Production LG 3.5" LTPS LCS:
LG Corp. (LG Display) Paju LG LCD Complex, Paju, South-Korea

Haurtian AWM style + Retailer:
Saturn, Alexanderplatz 3, 10178 Berlin, Germany
+
Production USB Cable Haurtian AWM style:
Fortron Industrial Co., Ltd.Taiwan sales office: 6F-2, No. 2,

Pro 15" Model A1150 + Retailer:
Cyberport Store, Friedrichstraße 50-55, 10117 Berlin, Germ

"There are many reasons for performing reverse engineering in various fields. Reverse engineering has its origins in the analysis of hardware for commercial or military advantage.[1] However, it is only an analysis in order to deduce design features from products with little or no additional knowledge about the procedures involved in their original production.[1] In some cases, the goal of the reverse engineering process can simply be a redocumentation of legacy systems.[1] Reverse engineering may also be used to create interoperable products and despite some narrowly tailored United States and European Union legislation, the legality of using specific reverse engineering techniques for this purpose has been hotly contested in courts worldwide for more than two decades.[2]."

A digital print presenting it's own production tear down. Starting as a still-life of supermarket fruit captured by a digital camera, the image travels through the lens, chip, wire, computer components, software, etc. all the way to the printer, until its materialization as ink on paper that is hung with hooks and clips to the wall. The deceptive simplicity of this arrangement is overcoded by an immense informational panorama that renders visible the circumstances and locations of the chain of production in relation to which the fruit are the end product eventuations. The inscriptions include the name and address of the retailer and the first responsible production companies involved and are superimposed in small type over the still-life image. Lining up the dynamic roots of this art piece production in todays global economy.

MacBook Pro 15" Design:
1 Infinite Loop, Cupertino, CA 95014, United St

MacBook Pro 85W Apple AC Adapter (model no: A1222):
Time In Top Technology Co., Ltd. Hong Kong / R

MacBook Pro 15" (Model A1150) Left I/O Board Includes MagSafe power, USB, and audio ports input/ou
Mingchuan Electronic Technology Co., Ltd. Stree

MacBook Pro 15" (Model A1150) Left I/O Board Cable (Product code: IF185-015-1 Apple Part #: 922-72
tonish Forest Electronic Company Limited, Jiahe Road, Xiamen China
ce Components Campenton Riverside Staines Mi

MacBook Pro 15" (Model A1150) 1.83 GHz Logic Board2 GHz Motherboard / Ports: DVI Video Out, 10
tronic Digital Technology Co., LTD Store No. 50

MacBook Pro 15" (Model A1150) Hard Drive Cable Connects hard drive, sleep light, IR sensor, and Blue
Yall Trading Co., Ltd. 2fl, Block C, Longjing Second Industrial Park, Taoyuan Village Nanshan, Shenzhen,

80GB SATA Hard Drive, Model: TOSHIBA MK8032GSX, 16PI4438T:
O LTD, 5F No.136, Sec.1, Neihu Rd., Neihu Dist, Taipei city 11493, Taipei, Taiwan

PC2-5300 1 GB RAM Chip: 1 GB, DDR2 SDRAM, 667 MHz Apple Part
Silkway Technology Co., Ltd. 2110, 21th floor, NanGuan Jie Jia Rd, Shen'nan RD/20F GuangYe building o

MacBook Pro 15" (Models A1150/A1211) Display Apple Part #: 9
Hong Kong Industrial Developments LTD, 17C-Unit Building, Jianhua town, Shenz

MacBook Pro 15" (Models A1150/A1211) Display Apple Part #: 922-
ew Tideshine Electron Co., Ltd. N2C099, New Asia Market, Zhonghang Road, Shenzhen Guangdong, C

MacBook Pro 15" (Model A1150) Inverter/iSight Cable
Technology CO LTD, 53833 Goconda trader center, Shenzhen, Guangdong, China

MacBook Pro 15" (Models A1150/A1211) LCD Panel
Tech Dangjung Dong 110-3, South Korea

MacBook Pro 15" (Model A1150) Upper Case Cable
Argon Computing Ltd, 125 Southend Road, Rochford, Essex, SS4 1HX, United Kingdom

MacBook Pro 15" (Model A1150) Keyboard, Replacement Keyboard Backlit 002-
Technology CO LTD, 53833. Goconda trader center, Shenzhen, Guangdong, China

MacBook Pro 15" (Model A1150) Track Pad:
mpany, Distributor/Wholesaler: Jin-Rong Electronic Company Ltd. Dongguan City 2B11, Jia-Run Office B

Reverse Engineering

[1] Chikofsky, E. J. & Cross, J. H., II (1990). "Reverse Engineering and Design Recovery: A Taxonomy". IEEE Software. 7 (1): 13—17. doi:10.1109/52.43044.
[2] Jonathan Band; Masanobu Katoh (2011). Interfaces on Trial 2.0. MIT Press. p. 136. ISBN 978-0-262-29446-1.
Source: Wikipedia, Edited: 14 March 2019

Software:
1 Infinite Loop, Cupertino, CA 95014, United States of America

nded + Retailer:
Apple Store, Leidseplein 25, 1017 PS Amsterdam, The Netherlands
+
Production Adobe Software:
Adobe Systems Incorporated, 345 Park Avenue San Jose, California, United States of America
+
Production Adobe Software:
Adobe Systems India Private Limited, Adobe Towers I-1A, City Centre, Sector : 25A NOIDA-2013
+
Production Adobe Software:
Adobe Bangalore Office, Salarpuria Infinity, 3rd Floor #5, Bannerghatta Road, Bangalore-560029,

Firewire cable IEEE 1394 (6Pin/4Pin) + Retailer:
Apple Store, Leidseplein 25, 1017 PS Amsterdam, The Netherlands

IMAGE TRANSFER

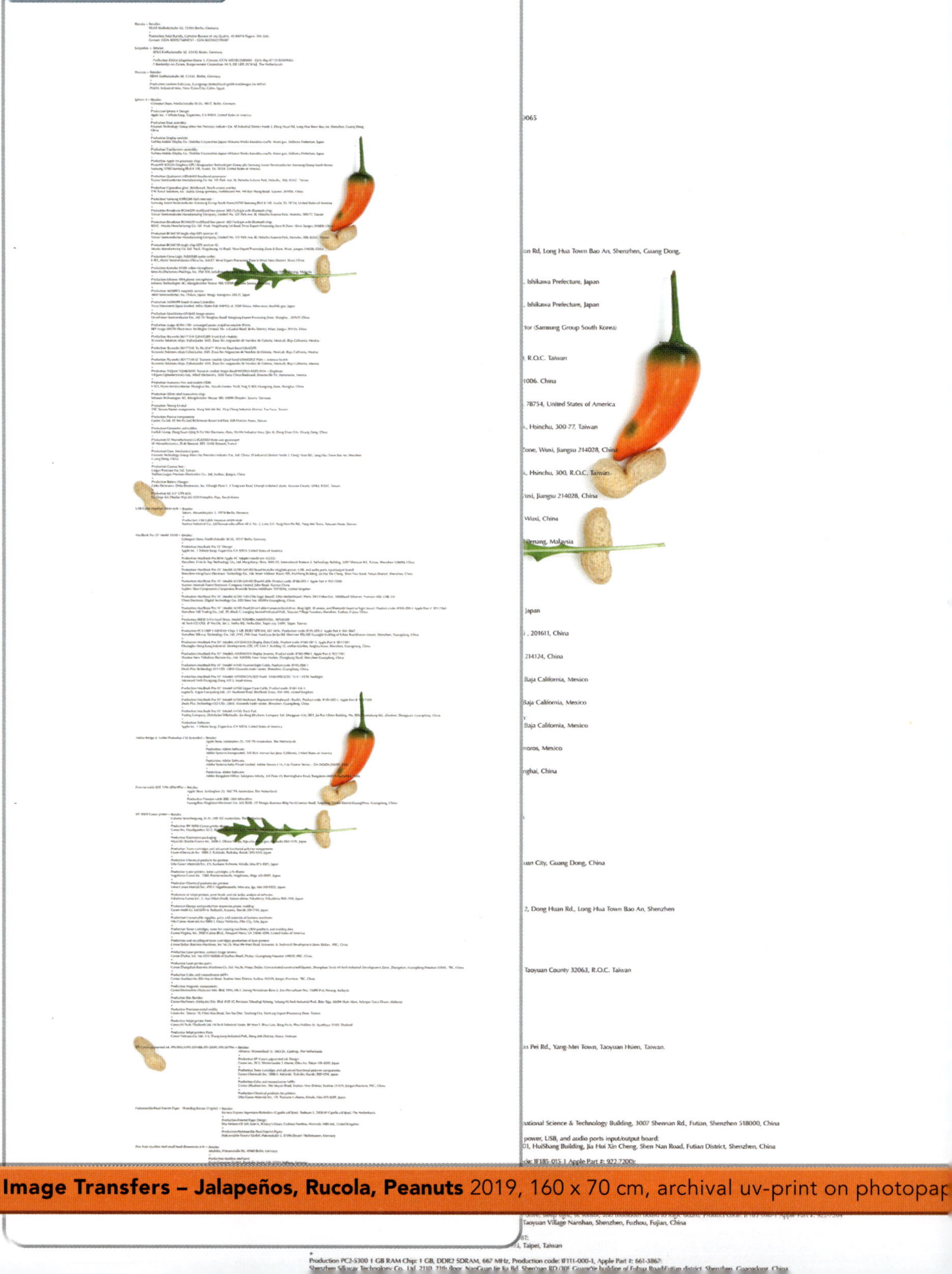

9065

an Rd, Long Hua Town Bao An, Shenzhen, Guang Dong,

, Ishikawa Prefecture, Japan

, Ishikawa Prefecture, Japan

tor (Samsung Group South Korea)

, R.O.C. Taiwan

1006, China

, 78754, United States of America

., Hsinchu, 300-77, Taiwan

Zone, Wuxi, Jiangsu 214028, China

., Hsinchu, 300, R.O.C. Taiwan

Wuxi, Jiangsu 214028, China

Wuxi, China

Penang, Malaysia

Japan

, 201611, China

214124, China

Baja California, Mexico

Baja California, Mexico

Baja California, Mexico

moros, Mexico

nghai, China

uan City, Guang Dong, China

2, Dong Huan Rd., Long Hua Town Bao An, Shenzhen

Taoyuan County 32063, R.O.C. Taiwan

n Pei Rd., Yang-Mei Town, Taoyuan Hsien, Taiwan.

ational Science & Technology Building, 3007 Shennan Rd., Futian, Shenzhen 518000, China

power, USB, and audio ports input/output board:
01, HuiShang Building, Jia Hui Xin Cheng, Shen Nan Road, Futian District, Shenzhen, China

de: IF185-015-1 Apple Part #: 922-7200:

Image Transfers – Jalapeños, Rucola, Peanuts 2019, 160 x 70 cm, archival uv-print on photopap

Taoyuan Village Nanshan, Shenzhen, Fuzhou, Fujian, China

3T:
3, Taipei, Taiwan

Production PC2-5300 1 GB RAM Chip: 1 GB, DDR2 SDRAM, 667 MHz, Production code: IF111-000-1, Apple Part #: 661-3867:
Shenzhen Silway Technology Co. Ltd. 2110, 21th floor, NanGuan Jie Jia Rd. Shen'nan RD/30F GuangYe building of Fuhua RoadFutian district, Shenzhen, Guangdong, China

Unlearning the Origins of Photography

by Ariella Azoulay

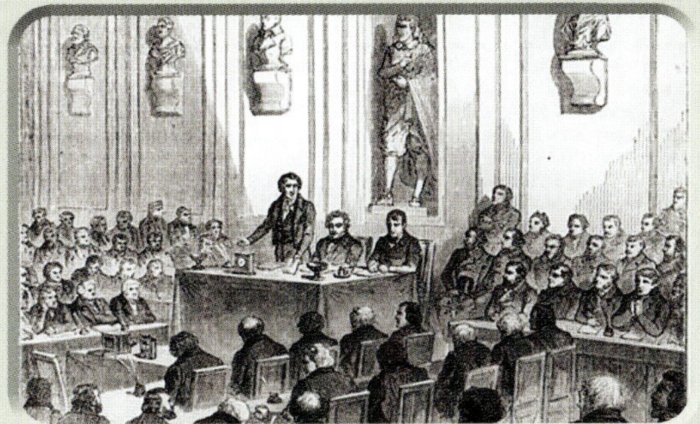

Dominique François Arago presenting the discovery of daguerreotype, L'Académie des sciences, August 10, 1839.

Imagine that the origins of photography go back to 1492. What could this mean? First and foremost, that we should unlearn the origins of photography as framed by those who were crowned its inventors and other private and state entrepreneurs, as well as its association with a technology that can be reduced to discrete devices held by individual operators. In The Civil Contract of Photography, I proposed to displace photography's origins from the realms of technology to the body politic of users and reconstruct from its practices a potential history of photography. My attempt to reconfigure photography was still defined by the assumption that it can be accounted for as a domain apart, and hence situated in the early nineteenth century. What I'm going to propose here is, based on my forthcoming book Potential History: Unlearning Imperialism, I also question imperial temporality and spatiality and attempt to account for the world in which photography could emerge.

IMAGE TRANSFER

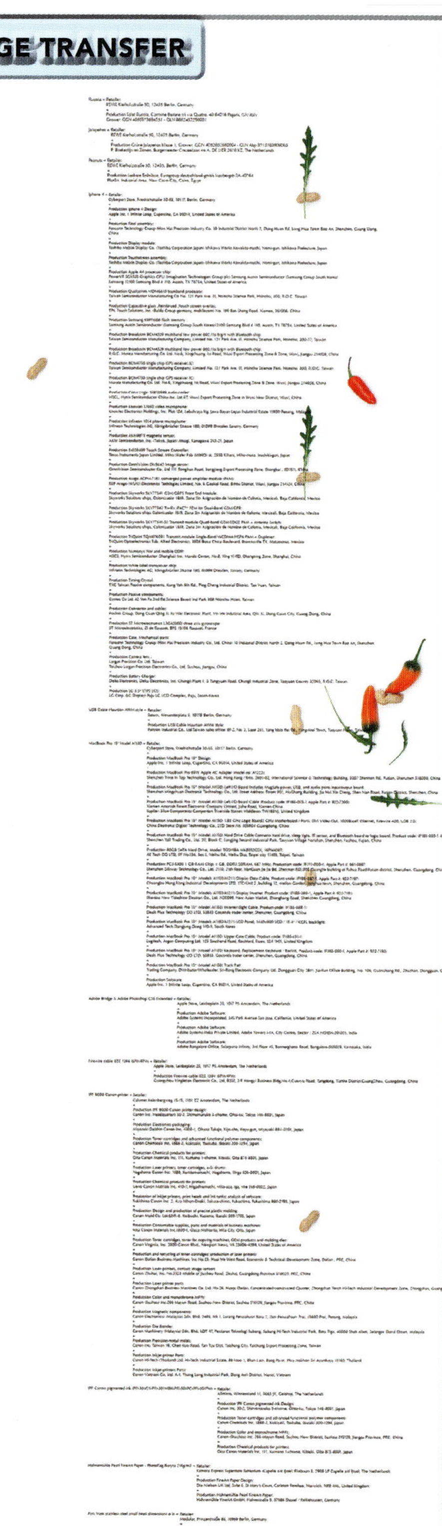

It is not about questioning the exact moment of the inception of photography and proposing that it was this optical device or that chemical substance that made it possible. It is about questioning the political formations that made it possible to proclaim — and institutionalize the idea — that certain sets of practices used as part of large-scale campaigns of imperial violence are separate from this violence and unrelated to it, to an extent that they can even account for it from the outside. Let me frame the question directly: How do those who wrote different histories and theories of photography know that it was invented sometime in the early nineteenth century? They — we — received this knowledge from those invested in its promotion. Accounting for photography based on its promoters' narratives is like accounting for imperial violence on the terms of those who exercised it, claiming that they had discovered a "new world."

The invention of the New World and the invention of photography are not unrelated. Suggesting that the origins of photography go back to 1492 is an attempt to undermine the imperial temporality that was imposed at that time, enabling people to believe, experience, and describe interconnected things as if they were separate, each defined by newness. To put it another way, for photography to emerge as a new technology in the late 1830s, the centrality of the imperial rights on which photography was predicated had to be ignored, denied, or sublimated, or in any case pushed into the background and not perceived as constitutive of its operation as a technology. Foregrounding these rights requires a simultaneous exercise — unlearning the accepted origins of photography uctor China Inc. Lot K7, Wuxi Export Processing Zone in Wuxi New District, Wuxi, China

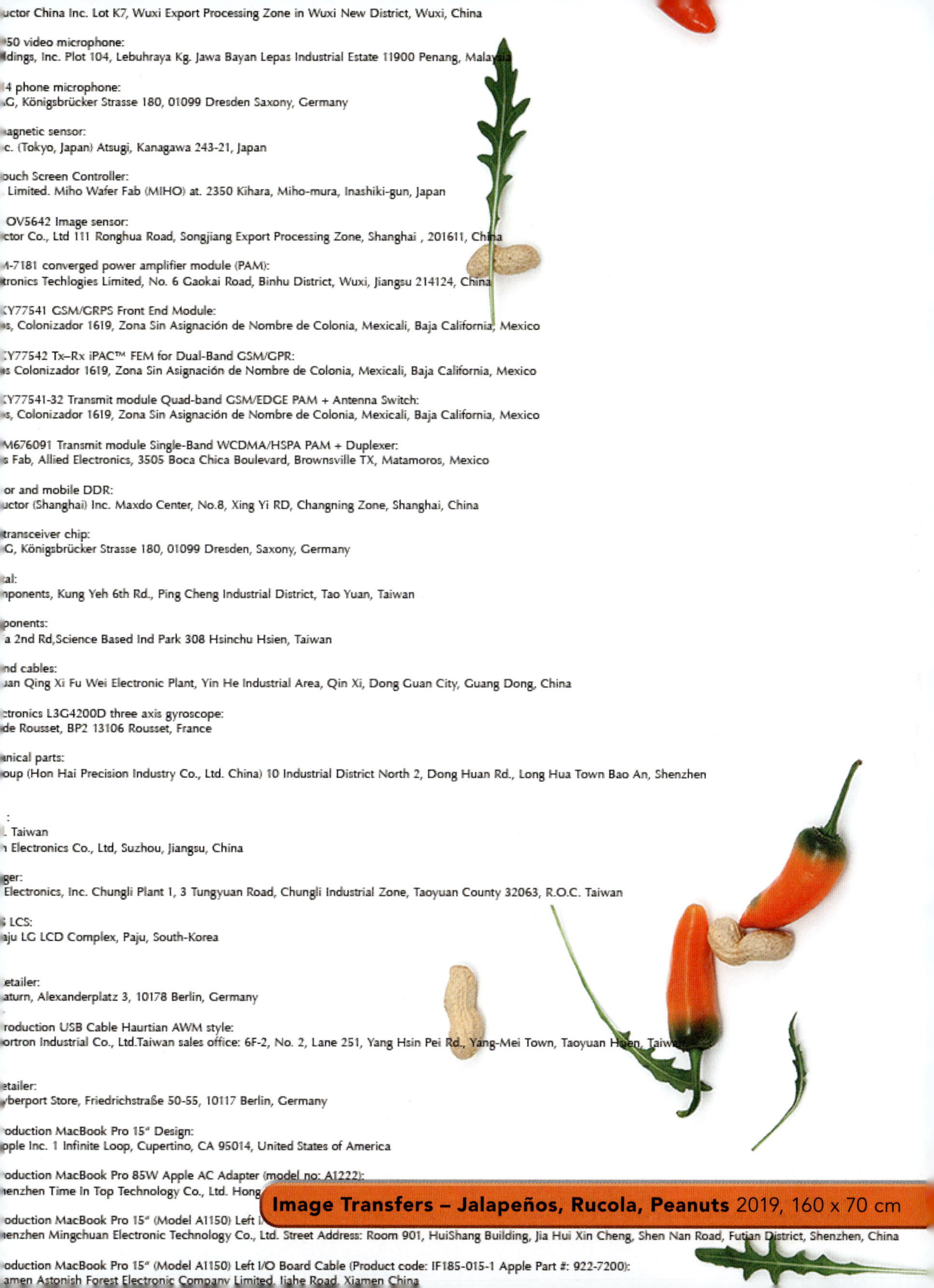

50 video microphone:
dings, Inc. Plot 104, Lebuhraya Kg. Jawa Bayan Lepas Industrial Estate 11900 Penang, Malaysia

4 phone microphone:
G, Königsbrücker Strasse 180, 01099 Dresden Saxony, Germany

agnetic sensor:
c. (Tokyo, Japan) Atsugi, Kanagawa 243-21, Japan

ouch Screen Controller:
Limited. Miho Wafer Fab (MIHO) at. 2350 Kihara, Miho-mura, Inashiki-gun, Japan

OV5642 Image sensor:
ctor Co., Ltd 111 Ronghua Road, Songjiang Export Processing Zone, Shanghai , 201611, China

-7181 converged power amplifier module (PAM):
tronics Techlogies Limited, No. 6 Gaokai Road, Binhu District, Wuxi, Jiangsu 214124, China

Y77541 GSM/GRPS Front End Module:
s, Colonizador 1619, Zona Sin Asignación de Nombre de Colonia, Mexicali, Baja California, Mexico

Y77542 Tx–Rx iPAC™ FEM for Dual-Band GSM/GPR:
s Colonizador 1619, Zona Sin Asignación de Nombre de Colonia, Mexicali, Baja California, Mexico

Y77541-32 Transmit module Quad-band GSM/EDGE PAM + Antenna Switch:
s, Colonizador 1619, Zona Sin Asignación de Nombre de Colonia, Mexicali, Baja California, Mexico

M676091 Transmit module Single-Band WCDMA/HSPA PAM + Duplexer:
s Fab, Allied Electronics, 3505 Boca Chica Boulevard, Brownsville TX, Matamoros, Mexico

or and mobile DDR:
uctor (Shanghai) Inc. Maxdo Center, No.8, Xing Yi RD, Changning Zone, Shanghai, China

transceiver chip:
G, Königsbrücker Strasse 180, 01099 Dresden, Saxony, Germany

al:
nponents, Kung Yeh 6th Rd., Ping Cheng Industrial District, Tao Yuan, Taiwan

ponents:
a 2nd Rd,Science Based Ind Park 308 Hsinchu Hsien, Taiwan

nd cables:
an Qing Xi Fu Wei Electronic Plant, Yin He Industrial Area, Qin Xi, Dong Guan City, Guang Dong, China

ctronics L3G4200D three axis gyroscope:
de Rousset, BP2 13106 Rousset, France

nical parts:
oup (Hon Hai Precision Industry Co., Ltd. China) 10 Industrial District North 2, Dong Huan Rd., Long Hua Town Bao An, Shenzhen

:
. Taiwan
n Electronics Co., Ltd, Suzhou, Jiangsu, China

ger:
Electronics, Inc. Chungli Plant 1, 3 Tungyuan Road, Chungli Industrial Zone, Taoyuan County 32063, R.O.C. Taiwan

LCS:
aju LG LCD Complex, Paju, South-Korea

etailer:
aturn, Alexanderplatz 3, 10178 Berlin, Germany

roduction USB Cable Haurtian AWM style:
ortron Industrial Co., Ltd.Taiwan sales office: 6F-2, No. 2, Lane 251, Yang Hsin Pei Rd., Yang-Mei Town, Taoyuan Hsien, Taiwan

etailer:
berport Store, Friedrichstraße 50-55, 10117 Berlin, Germany

oduction MacBook Pro 15" Design:
pple Inc. 1 Infinite Loop, Cupertino, CA 95014, United States of America

oduction MacBook Pro 85W Apple AC Adapter (model no: A1222):
enzhen Time In Top Technology Co., Ltd. Hong

Image Transfers – Jalapeños, Rucola, Peanuts 2019, 160 x 70 cm

oduction MacBook Pro 15" (Model A1150) Left I
enzhen Mingchuan Electronic Technology Co., Ltd. Street Address: Room 901, HuiShang Building, Jia Hui Xin Cheng, Shen Nan Road, Futian District, Shenzhen, China

oduction MacBook Pro 15" (Model A1150) Left I/O Board Cable (Product code: IF185-015-1 Apple Part #: 922-7200):
amen Astonish Forest Electronic Company Limited. Jiahe Road, Xiamen China

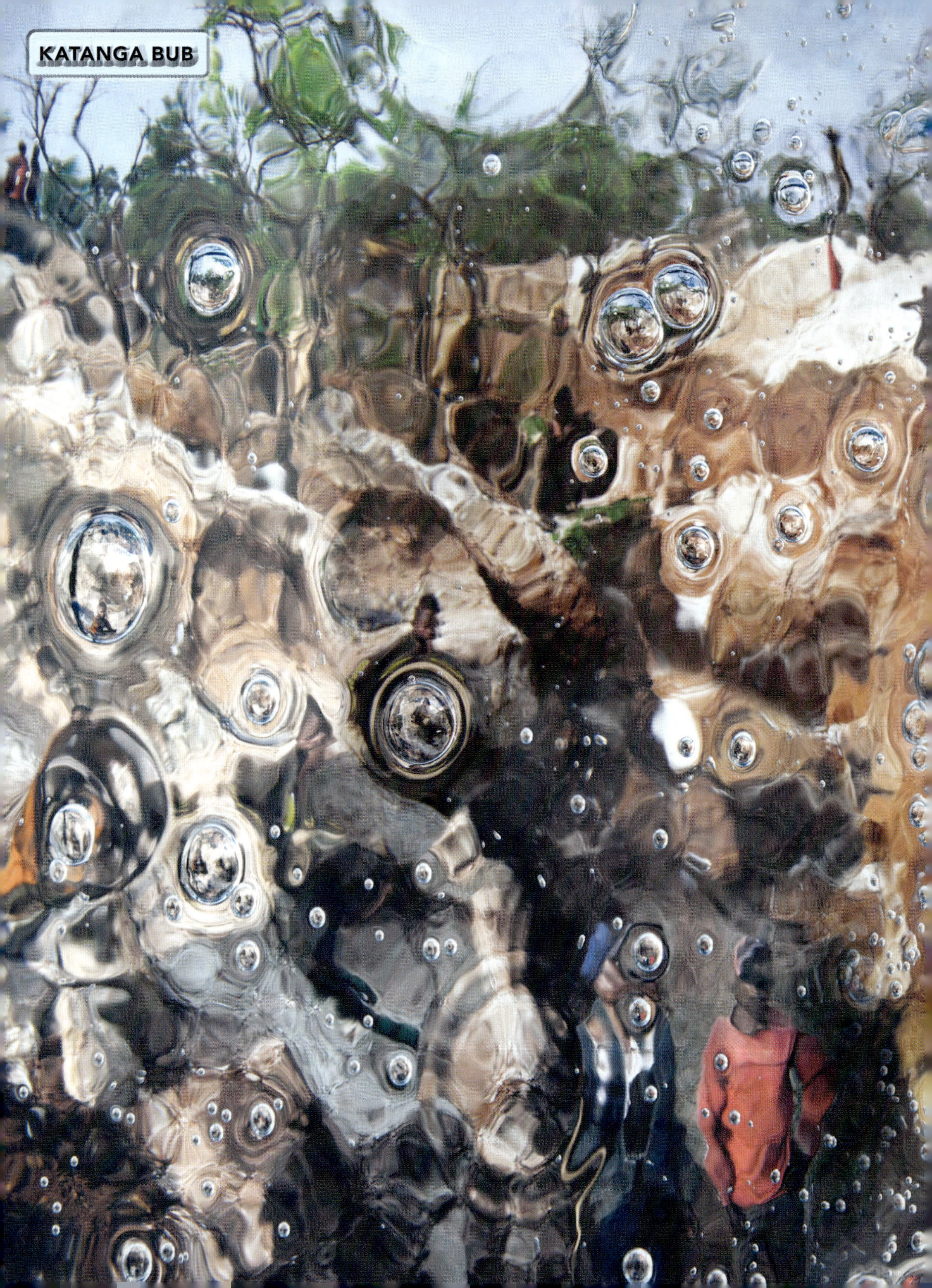
KATANGA BUB

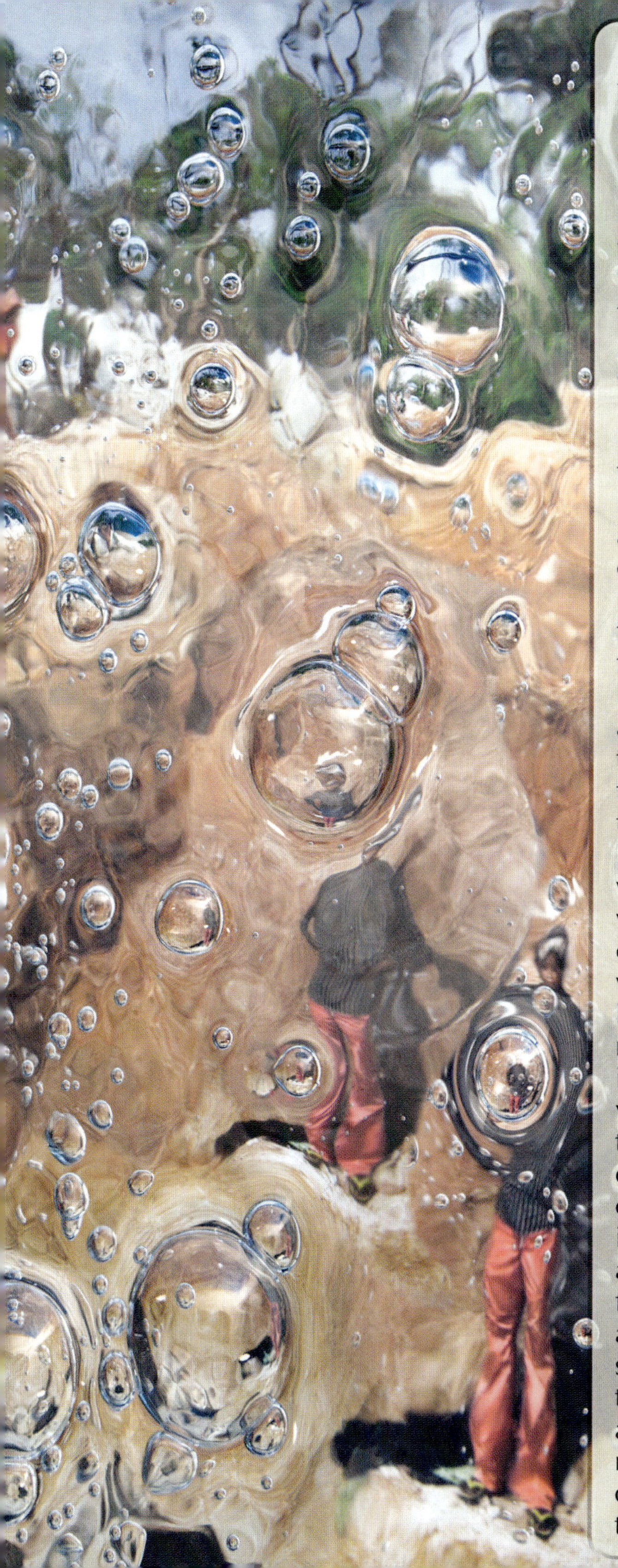

and those of the "new world," their familiar spatial and temporal connotations, which even today are still closely associated with modernity and "the era of discoveries," and attending instead to the configuration of imperial violence and its manifestation in rights. By imperial violence I refer to the entire enterprise of destroying the existing worlds of signs, activities, and social fabrics and replacing them with a "new world" of objects, classification, laws, technologies, and meanings. In this so-called "new world," local populations and resources are perceived as problems or solutions, opportunities or obstacles, and are assigned specific roles, places, and functions. Through these processes, existing sets of rights that were integral to each world and inscribed in its material organization are destroyed to allow imperial rights to be imposed. Among these rights are the right to destroy existing worlds, the right to manufacture a new world in their place, the rights over others whose worlds are destroyed together with the rights they enjoyed in their communities and the right to declare what is new and consequently what is obsolete. The attachment of the meaning "new" to whatever imperialism imposes is constitutive of imperial violence: it turns opposition to its actions, inventions, and the distribution of rights into a conservative, primitive, or hopeless "race against time" — i.e., progress — rather than as a race against imperialism. The murder of five thousand Egyptians who struggled against Napoleon's invasion of their sacred places and the looting of old treasures, which were to be "salvaged" and displayed in Napoleon's new museum in Paris, is just one example of this. In the imperial histories of new technologies of visualization, both the

KATANGA BUB

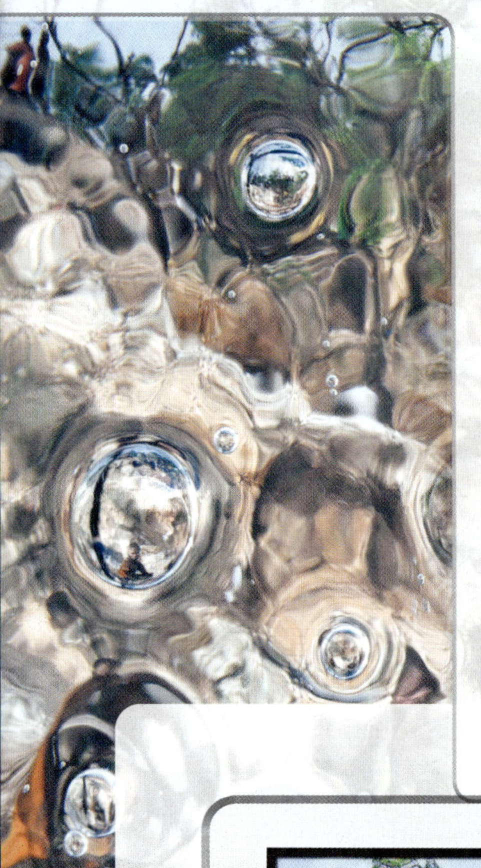

The extreme ends of the mobile device industry are brought together in 'Katanga Bub' is based on a press image depicting the landscape and workers of Katanga, in The Democratic Republic of Congo – an area mined for many minerals like tungsten and coltan, which have been crucial for the manufacture of mobile devices. For this work the press image of the Katanga mines has been re-photographed underwater and set within a freestanding display unit. as water ripples and bubbles float over the surface, distorting the scene underneath, the screens of numerous mobile phones show clearer details of the same view of the Katanga mine. The elemental earthy origins of the mines are (re)connected with the liquefied luxuriance of global technology commodities and their marketing aesthetics, to express the easy exchange of information through these devices. This work fuses two opposing but connected ends of the story: on one hand the mobile devices help spread knowledge and raise global awareness, with the false promise of engendering a better world. On the other hand, while the economy of "rare earths" props up the problematic social and political infrastructures of the Democratic Republic of Congo, it also reveals the recursive relationships between matter and information underwritten by the move from production to product; from raw material to data generation.

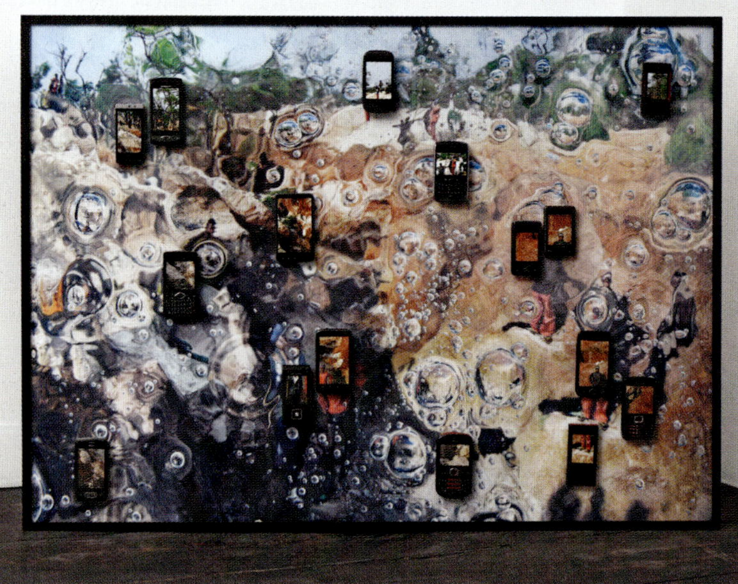

Katanga Bub 2011, 90 x 145 cm, mobile devices, lightbox, archival Inkjet print

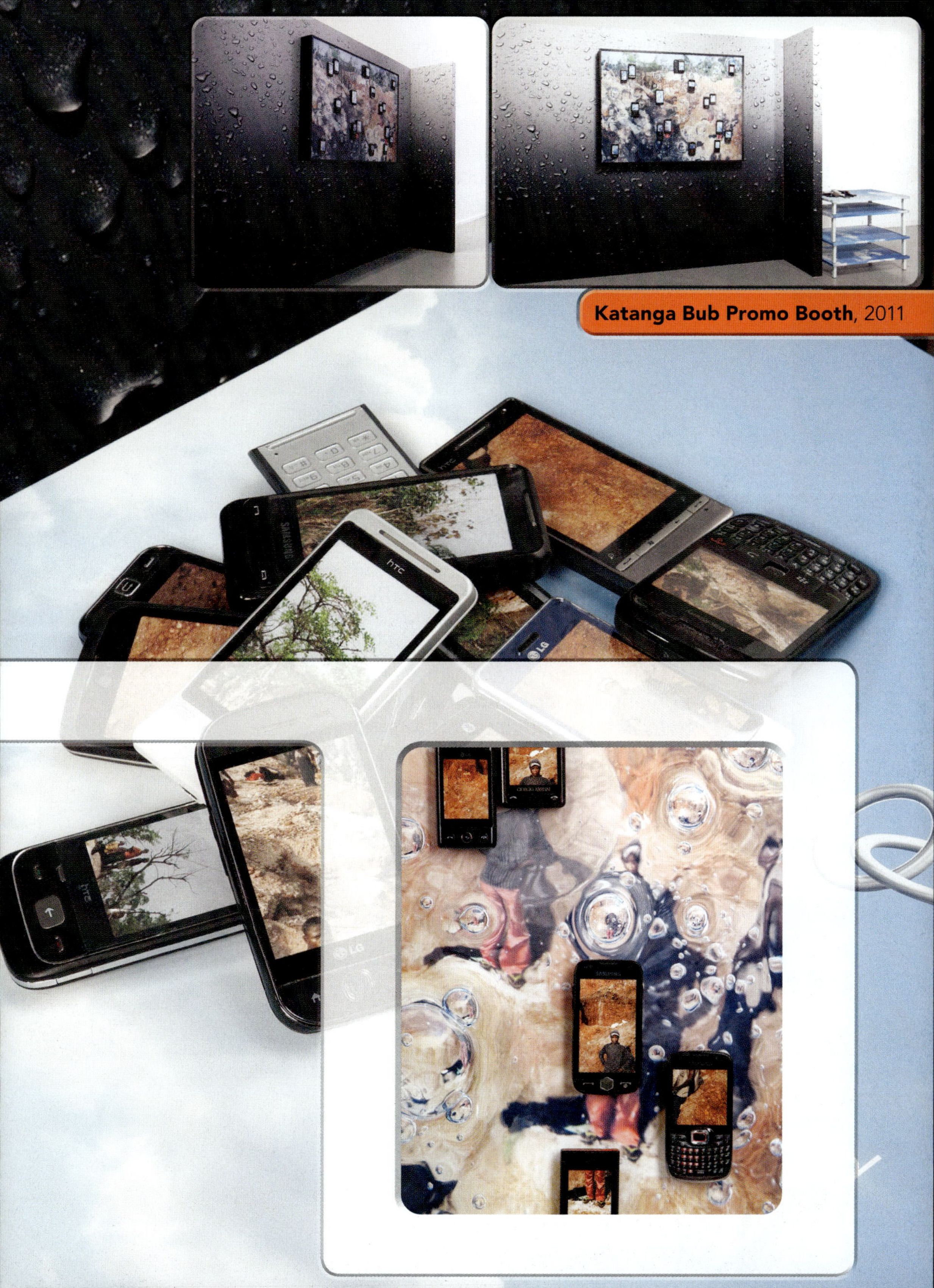

Katanga Bub Promo Booth, 2011

resistance and the murder of these people are nonexistent, while the depictions of Egypt's looted treasures, which were rendered in almost photographic detail, establish a benchmark, indicating what photography came to improve. I'll come back to this point in my fourth statement, when I'll discuss the Great March of Return, the march against imperialism and the apparatuses that sought to render obsolete and bury the just claims of the marchers under the "statute of limitations," negating their attempt to rewind the declaration of a "new" state in their homeland.

My proposition, however, is that photography did not initiate a new world; yet, it was built upon and benefitted from imperial looting, divisions, and rights that were operative in the colonization of the world in which photography was assigned the role of documenting, recording, or contemplating what-is-already-there. In order to acknowledge that photography's origins are in 1492, we have to unlearn the expertise and knowledge that call upon us to account for photography as having its own origins, histories, practices, or futures, and to explore it as part of the imperial world in which we, as scholars, photographers, or curators, operate. Let me briefly present an excerpt from the well-known and frequently quoted report by Dominique François Arago, which was delivered in 1839 before the Chambre des Deputes and is considered a foundational moment in the discourse of photography. The speech is often quoted as an early attempt to define and advocate the new practice and technology of photography.
I rather propose to read it as a performance naturalizing pre-existing impe-

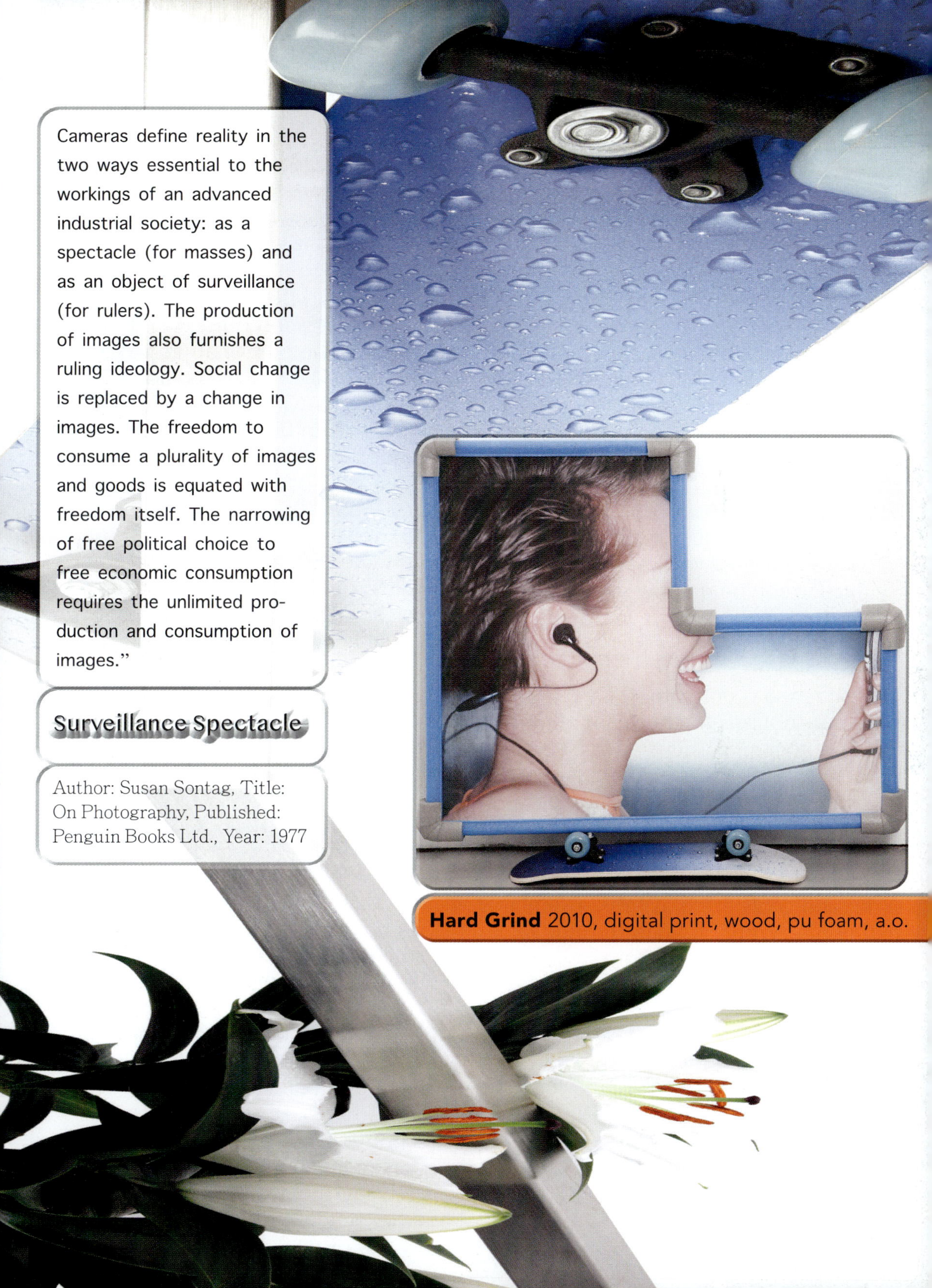

Cameras define reality in the two ways essential to the workings of an advanced industrial society: as a spectacle (for masses) and as an object of surveillance (for rulers). The production of images also furnishes a ruling ideology. Social change is replaced by a change in images. The freedom to consume a plurality of images and goods is equated with freedom itself. The narrowing of free political choice to free economic consumption requires the unlimited production and consumption of images."

Surveillance Spectacle

Author: Susan Sontag, Title: On Photography, Published: Penguin Books Ltd., Year: 1977

Hard Grind 2010, digital print, wood, pu foam, a.o.

rial premises, which had prepared the ground on which the "new" invention could emerge.

While these pictures are exhibited to you, everyone will imagine the extraordinary advantages which could have been derived from so exact and rapid a means of reproduction during the expedition to Egypt; everybody will realize that had we had photography in 1798 we would possess today faithful pictorial records of that which the learned world is forever deprived of by the greed of the Arabs and the vandalism of certain travelers. To copy the millions of hieroglyphics which cover even the exterior of the great monuments of Thebes, Memphis, Karnak, and others would require decades of time and legions of draughtsmen. By daguerreotype one person would suffice to accomplish this immense work successfully. 1

That Arago, a statesman and a man of his time, confirms the imperial premises of photography and praises its goals is no surprise. What is striking, and should be alarming, is how the performance of naturalization is reiterated in the texts of non-statesmen, including by authors who rejected the imperial order and goals, such as Walter Benjamin in his "Work of Art in the Age of Mechanical Reproduction."

Around 1900, technological reproduction not only had reached a standard that permitted it to reproduce all known works of art, profoundly modifying their effect, but it also had captured a place of its own among the artistic processes. In gauging this standard, we would do well to study the impact which its two different manifestations—the reproduction of artworks and the art of film—are having on art in its traditional form. 2

Such reiterations do not testify to the nature of the "new" technology but to the way photography, like other technologies, was rooted in imperial formations of power and legitimization of the use of violence in the form of rights exercised over others. For both Arago and Benjamin, the existence of images and objects that were not meant to be part of an imperial depository of art history, contained physically and symbolically in works of art waiting to be reproduced, is not a question or a problem but a given assumption. Reproduction is understood in this context as a neutral procedure ready to be used by those who own the proper means for it, and regardless of the will of those from whom the objects have been expropriated. It is based on this assumption and this understanding of reproduction that photography could be perceived and discussed as a new technology of image production and reproduction. A lineage of previous practices had to be invented for photography to be conceived of as a novel addition, a technology that alters and improves — substantially and on different levels — the quality of the end product. In this means–end relationship, not only is photography construed as a means to an end but the end is also construed as a given, and the existence of objects as simply given to the gaze — ofthe camera, in this case — is thus assumed and confirmed.

The context of Arago's speech enables one to reconstruct the regime of rights and privileges that were involved in the advocacy of photography. That the world and others' worlds are made

"The photographer is now charging real beasts, beleaguered and too rare to kill. Guns have metamorphosed into cameras in this earnest comedy, the ecology safari, because nature has ceased to be what it always had been - what people needed protection from. Now nature - tamed, endangered, mortal - needs to be protected from people. When we are afraid, we shoot. But when we are nostalgic, we take pictures."

Shooting

Author: Susan Sontag, Title: On Photography, Published: Penguin Books Ltd., Year: 1977

"The photographer is an armed version of the solitary walker reconnoitering, stalking, cruising the urban inferno, the voyeuristic stroller who discovers the city as a landscape of voluptuous extremes. Adept of the joys of watching, connoisseur of empathy, the flaneur finds the world .picturesque."

Flaneur

Author: Susan Sontag, Title: On Photography, Published: Penguin Books Ltd., Year: 1977

to be exhibited is not a question for Arago, nor is it a question for everybody but rather for a certain audience addressed in his speech with a familiarizing "you," an audience made up of white men like him, French statesmen and scientists. The acquisition of rights to dissect and study people's worlds — of which the Napoleonic expedition mentioned above is a paradigmatic example — and render their fragments into pieces to be meticulously copied with sharpness and exactitude is not posed as a problem but is taken for granted. For that to happen, those who are harmed by the violence — facilitated, among other things by the new means of reproduction, which had been imposed and used systematically by Napoleon's brigade of draftsmen during the expedition to Egypt — should be bracketed and left outside of these debates in which the fate of photography is discussed, while the right to operate it is directly and indirectly accorded to a certain class, at the expense of others.

In 1839, those who were directly invoked by Arago's "you" had already been responsible for large-scale disasters that included genocides, sociocides, and culturcides in North and West Africa and the Caribbean islands, for naturalizing and legalizing these acts through international institutions and laws, and for instituting their rights to continue dominating others' worlds. At that point, the universal addressee implied by Arago's "everybody" and "everyone" is fictitious not only because so many were not included but mainly because those who were intended as universal addressees could not come into being without dissecting, bracketing, and sanctioning the experience of violence as other than it was. The violence of forcing everything to be shown and exhibited to the gaze is erased and denied when the right in question is only the right to see. If the right NOT to exhibit everything had been respected — as it existed in different places the imperial agents invaded — a universal right to see that endows "everybody" with unlimited access to what is in the world could not be founded. Thus, extending the right to see so as to render "everybody" a truly universal is not possible without perpetrating further violence: that of denying that objects are not universal, they have different inherent functions and varying modes and degrees of visibility and accessibility within their communities. The forced universalization of objects was required for the invention of an allegedly universalized spectator; this was made possible only because those who care for their objects had them expropriated, along with the right to handle them as an inheritance from their ancestors and use them to continue to protect their worlds. Protecting one's world against the invasion of the "new" is not a matter of extending imperial privileges to others but of questioning the imperial authority altogether to impose a universal right on heterogeneous worlds whose members maintain a different relation to the material world in which objects are organized not simply to be looked at. If the principle that not everything should be made available for everybody to see had been respected, the existence of a universal right to see would be a complete fraud. When photography emerged, it did not halt this process of plunder that made others and others' worlds available to the few, but rather accelerated it and provided further opportunities and modalities for pursuing it.

1. Dominique François Arago, "Report," in Classic Essays on Photography, ed. Alan Trachtenberg (New Haven, CT: Leete's Island Books, 1980), 17; italics mine.
2. Walter Benjamin, Selected Writings, vol. 3, 1935—1938 (Cambridge, MA: The Belknap Press of Harvard University Press, 2002), 21; italics mine.

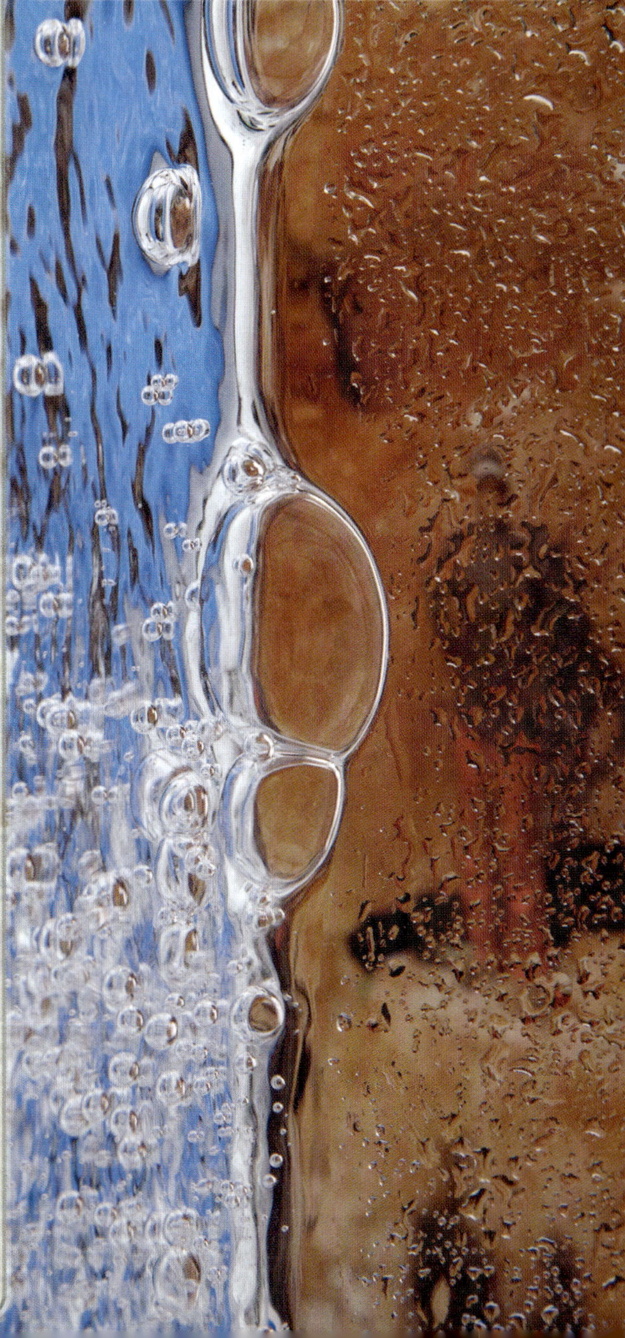

The Neolithic, Capitalism and Communism

by Alain Badiou

The problem is not technology or nature. The problem is how to organise societies at a global scale.

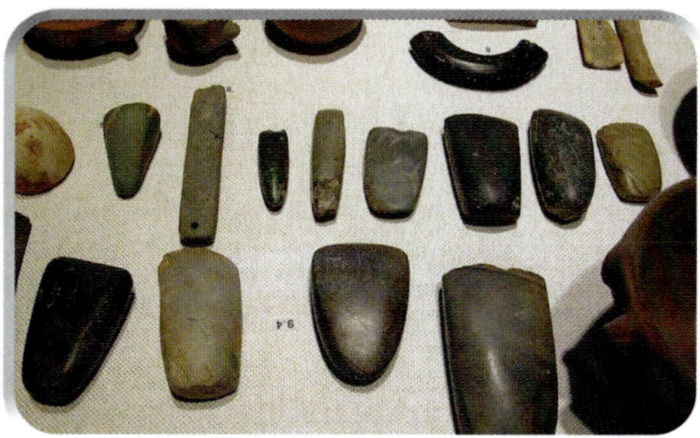

Display of Neolithic artifacts. Photo: Michael Greenhalgh. via Wikimedia Commons.

Today, it has become commonplace to predict the end of the human race such as we know it. There are various reasons for such forecasts. According to a messianic kind of environmentalism, the excessive predations of a beastly humanity will soon bring about the end of life on Earth. Meanwhile, those who instead point to runaway technological advances prophesy, indiscriminately, the automation of all work by robots, grand developments in computing, automatically-generated art, plastic-coated killers, and the dangers of a super-human intelligence.

Suddenly, we see the emergence of threatening categories like transhumanism and the post-human — or, their mirror image, a return to our animal state — depending on whether one prophesies on the basis of technological innovation or laments all the attacks on Mother Nature.

For me, all such prophesies are just so much ideological noise, intended to obscure the real peril that humanity is today exposed to: that is to say, the impasse that globalised capitalism is leading us into. In fact, it is this form of society — and it alone — which permits the destructive exploitation of natural resources, precisely because it connects this exploitation to the boundless quest for private profit. The fact that so many species are endangered, that climate change cannot be controlled, that water is becoming like some rare treasure, is all a by-product of the merciless competition among billionaire predators. There is no other reason for the fact that scientific innovation is subject to the question of what technologies can sell, in an anarchic selection mechanism.

Environmentalist preaching does sometimes use persuasive descriptions of what is going on — despite the exaggerations typical of the prophet. But most of the time this becomes mere propaganda, useful for those states who want to show their friendly face. Just as it is for the multinationals who would have us believe — to the greater benefit of their balance sheets — in the noble, fraternal, natural purity of the commodities they are trafficking.

The fetishism of technology, and the unbroken series of "revolutions" in this domain — of which the "digital revolution" is the most in vogue — has constantly spread the beliefs both that this will take us to the paradise of a world without work — with robots to serve us, and us left to idle — and then, on the other hand, that digital "thought" will crush the human intellect. Today there is not one magazine that does not inform its astonished readers of the imminent "victory" of artificial over natural intelligence. But in most cases neither "nature" nor the "artificial" are properly or clearly defined.

Since the origins of philosophy, the question of the real scope of the word "nature" has been constantly posed. "Nature" could mean the romantic reverie of evening sunsets, the atomic materialism of Lucretius (De natura rerum), the inner being of things, Spinoza's Totality (Deus sive Natura), the objective underside of all culture, rural and peasant surroundings as counterposed to the suspicious artificiality of the towns ("the earth does not lie," as Marshal Pétain put it), biology as distinct from physics, cosmology as compared to the tiny location that is our planet, the invariance of centuries as compared to the frenzy of innovation, natural sexuality as compared to perversion… I am afraid that today "nature" most of all refers to the calm of the villa and the garden, the charm wild animals have for tourists, and the beach or the mountains where we can spend a nice summer. Who, then, can imagine man responsible for nature, when thus far he has just been a thinking flea on a secondary planet in an average solar system at the edge of one banal galaxy?

Since its origins philosophy has also devoted a great deal of thought to Technology, or the Arts. The Greeks meditated on the dialectic of Techne and Physis — a dialectic within which they situated the human animal. They laid the ground for this animal to be seen as "a reed, the weakest of nature, but … a thinking reed." For Pascal, this meant that humanity was stronger than Nature and closer to God. A long time ago, they saw that the animal capable of mathematics would do great things to the order of materiality.

Are these "robots" which they keep banging on about anything more than calculation in the form of a machine? Digits in motion? We know that they can count quicker than us, but it was we who invented them, precisely in order to fulfil this task. It would be stupid to look at a crane raising a concrete pillar up to some great height, use this to argue that man is incapable of the same feat, and then conclude by saying that some muscular, superhuman giant has emerged… Lightning-quick counting is not the sign of an insuperable "intelligence" either. Technological transhumanism plays the same old tune — an inexhaustible theme of horror and sci-fi movies — of the creator overwhelmed by his own creation. It does so either thrilled about the advent of the superman — something we have been expecting ever since Nietzsche — or fearing him and taking refuge under the skirt of Gaia, Mother Nature.

Let's put things in a bit more perspective. For four or five millennia, humanity has been organised by the triad of private property — which concentrates enormous wealth in the hands of very narrow oligarchies; the family, in which fortunes are transmitted via inheritance; and the state, which protects both property and the family by armed force. This triad defined our species' Neolithic age, and we are still at this point — we could even say, now more than ever. Capitalism is the contemporary form of the Neolithic. Its enslavement of technology in the interests of competition, profit and concentrating capital only raises to their fullest extension the monstrous inequalities, the social absurdities, the murderous wars, and the damaging ideologies that have always accompanied the deployment of new technology under the reign of class hierarchy throughout history.

We should be clear that technological inventions were the preliminary conditions of the arrival of the Neolithic age, and by no means its result. If we consider our species' fate, we see that sedentary agriculture, the domestication of cattle and horses, pottery, bronze, metallic weapons, writing, nationalities, monumental architecture, and the monotheist religions are inventions at least as important as the airplane or the smartphone. Throughout history, whatever has been human has always, by definition, been artificial. If that had not existed, there would not have been Neolithic humanity — the humanity we know — but a permanent close proximity with animal life; something which did indeed exist, in the form of small nomadic groups, for around 200,000 years.

A fearful and obscurantist primitivism has its roots in the fallacious concept of "primitive communism." Today we can see this cult of the ancient societies in which babies, men, women and the elderly supposedly lived in fraternity, without anything artificial, and indeed lived in common with the mice, the frogs, and the bears. Ultimately, all this is nothing but ridiculous reactionary propaganda. For everything suggests that the societies in question were extremely violent. After all, even their most basic survival needs were constantly under threat.

To speak fearfully of the victory of the artificial over the nature, of robot over man, is today an untenable regression, something truly absurd. It is easy enough to answer such fears, such prophesies. For judged by this standard, even a simple axe, or a domesticated horse, not to mention a papyrus covered in symbols, is an exemplary case of the post- or trans-human. Even an abacus allows quicker calculation than the fingers of the human hand.

Today we need neither a return to primitivism, or fear of the "ravages" the advent of technology might bring. Nor is there any use in morbid fascination for the science-fiction of all-conquering robots. The urgent task we face is the methodical search for a way out of the Neolithic order. This latter has lasted for millennia, valuing only competition and hierarchy and tolerating the poverty of billions of human beings. It must be surpassed at all cost. Except, that is, the cost of the high-tech wars so well known to the Neolithic age, in the lineage of the wars of 1914-1918 and 1939-1945, with their tens of millions of dead. And this time it could be a lot more.

The problem is not technology, or nature. The problem is how to organise societies at a global scale. We need to posit that a non-Neolithic way of organising society is possible. This means no private ownership of that which ought to be held in common, namely the production of all the necessities of human life. It means no inherited power or concentration of wealth. No separate state to protect oligarchies. No hierarchical division of labour. No nations, and no closed and hostile identities. A collective organisation of everything that is in the collective interest.

All this has a name, indeed a fine one: communism. Capitalism is but the final phase of the restrictions that the Neolithic form of society has imposed on human life. It is the final stage of the Neolithic. Humanity, that fine animal, must make one last push to break out of a condition in which 5,000 years of inventions served a handful of people. For almost two centuries — since Marx, anyway — we have known that we have to begin the new age. An age of technologies incredible for all of us, of tasks distributed equally among all of us, of the sharing of everything, and education that affirms the genius of all. May this new communism everywhere and on every question stand up against the morbid survival of capitalism. This capitalism, this seeming "modernity," represents a Neolithic world that has in fact been going on for five millennia. And that means that it is old — far too old.

Author: Alain Badiou, Title: We Must Find a Way Out of the Neolithic Order, Published: Le Monde, Translated by: David Broder, Year: 2018

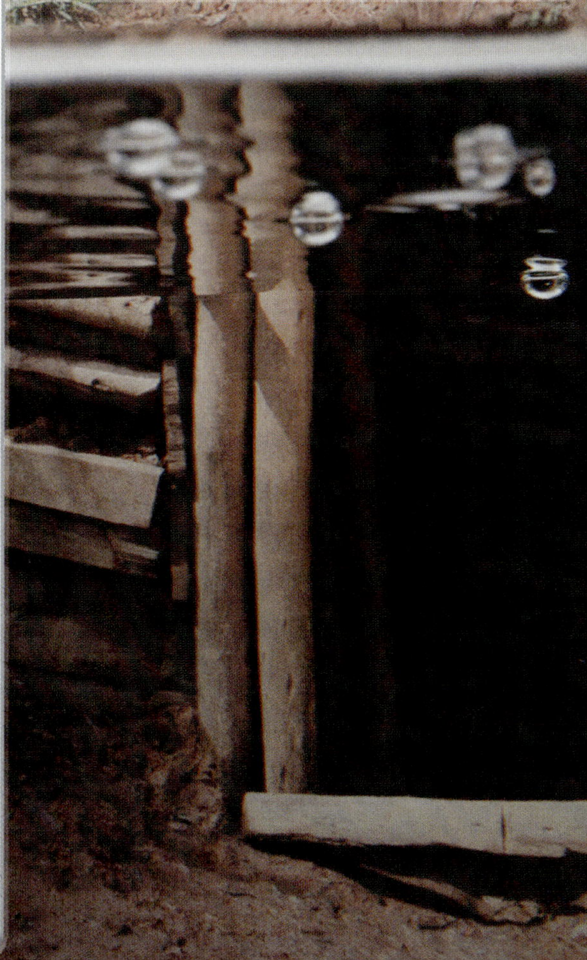

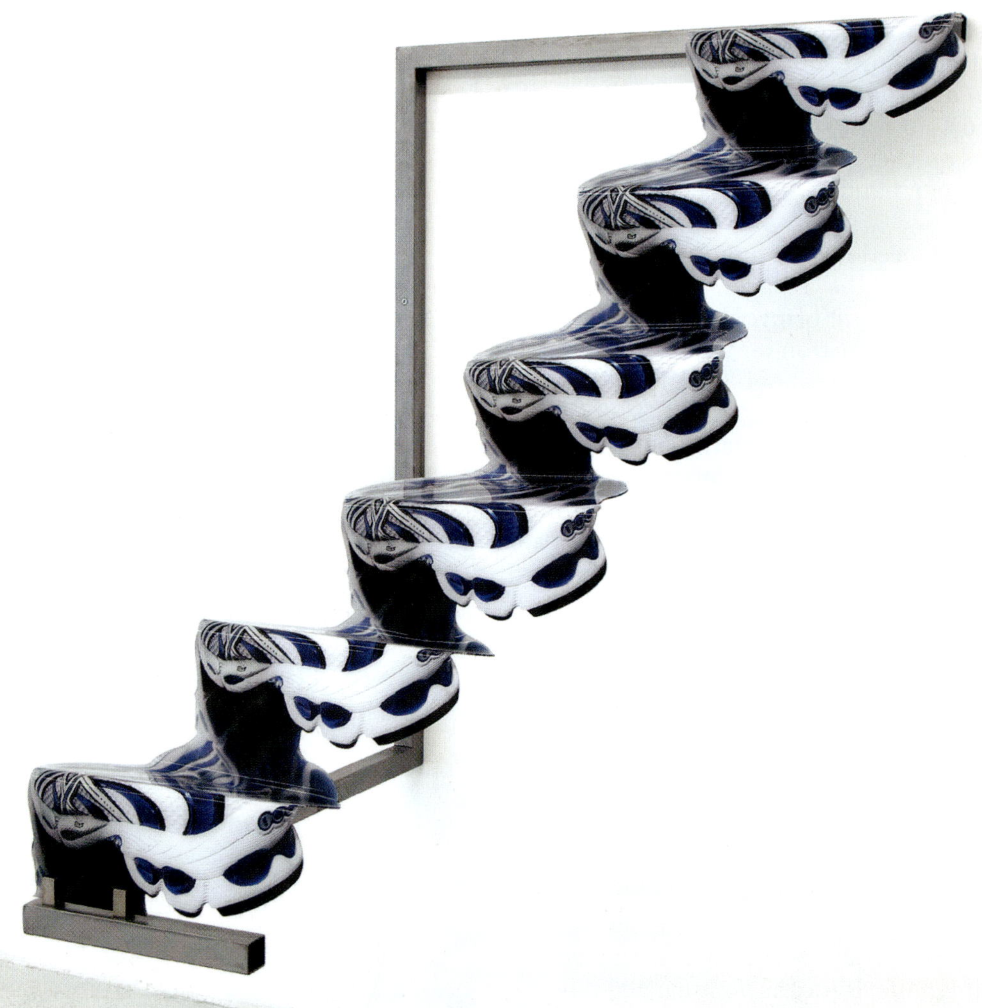

Steps of Recursion IGS 2011, uv-print, petg, brushed stainless steel

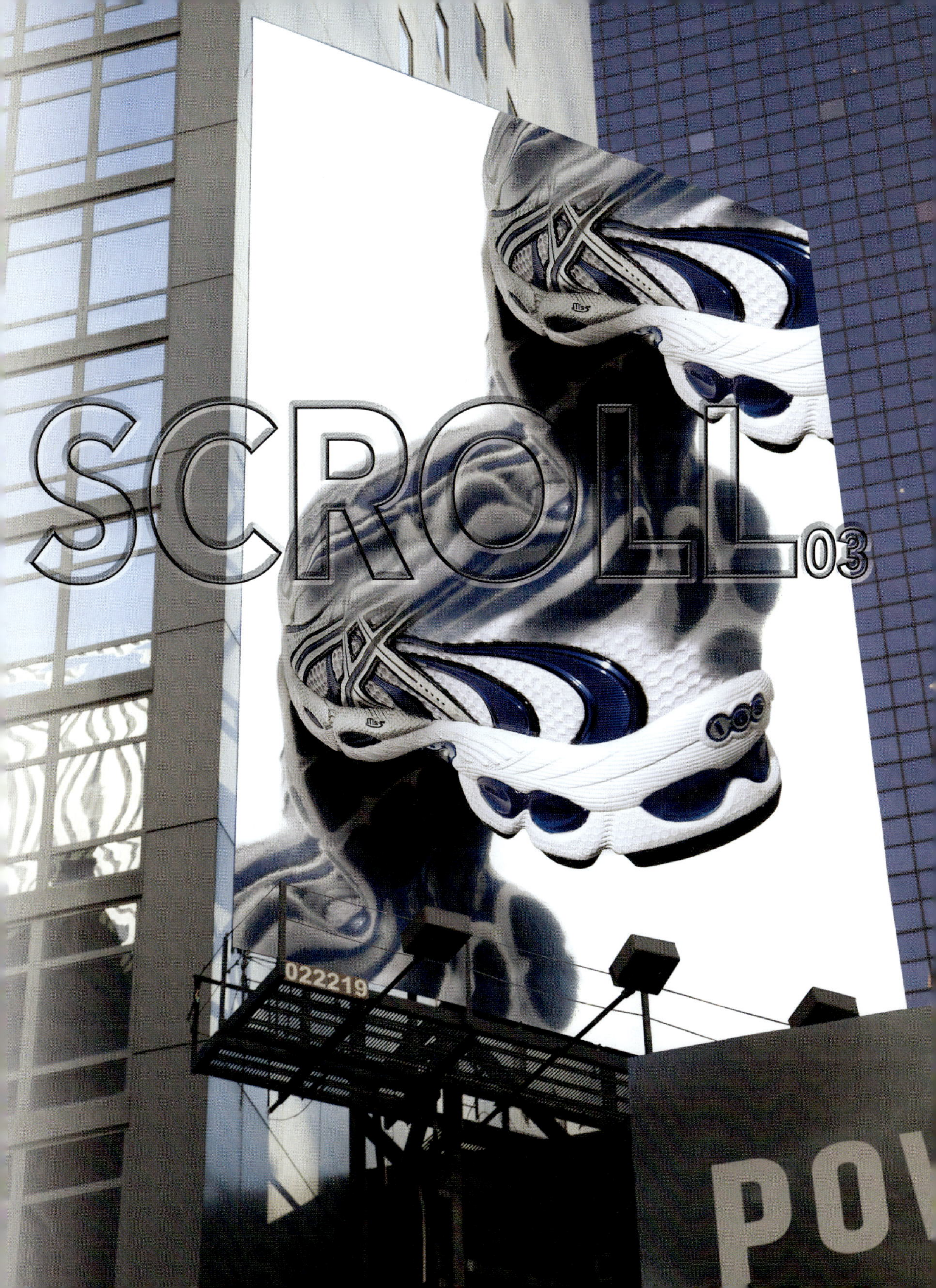
SCROLL 03
022219
POV

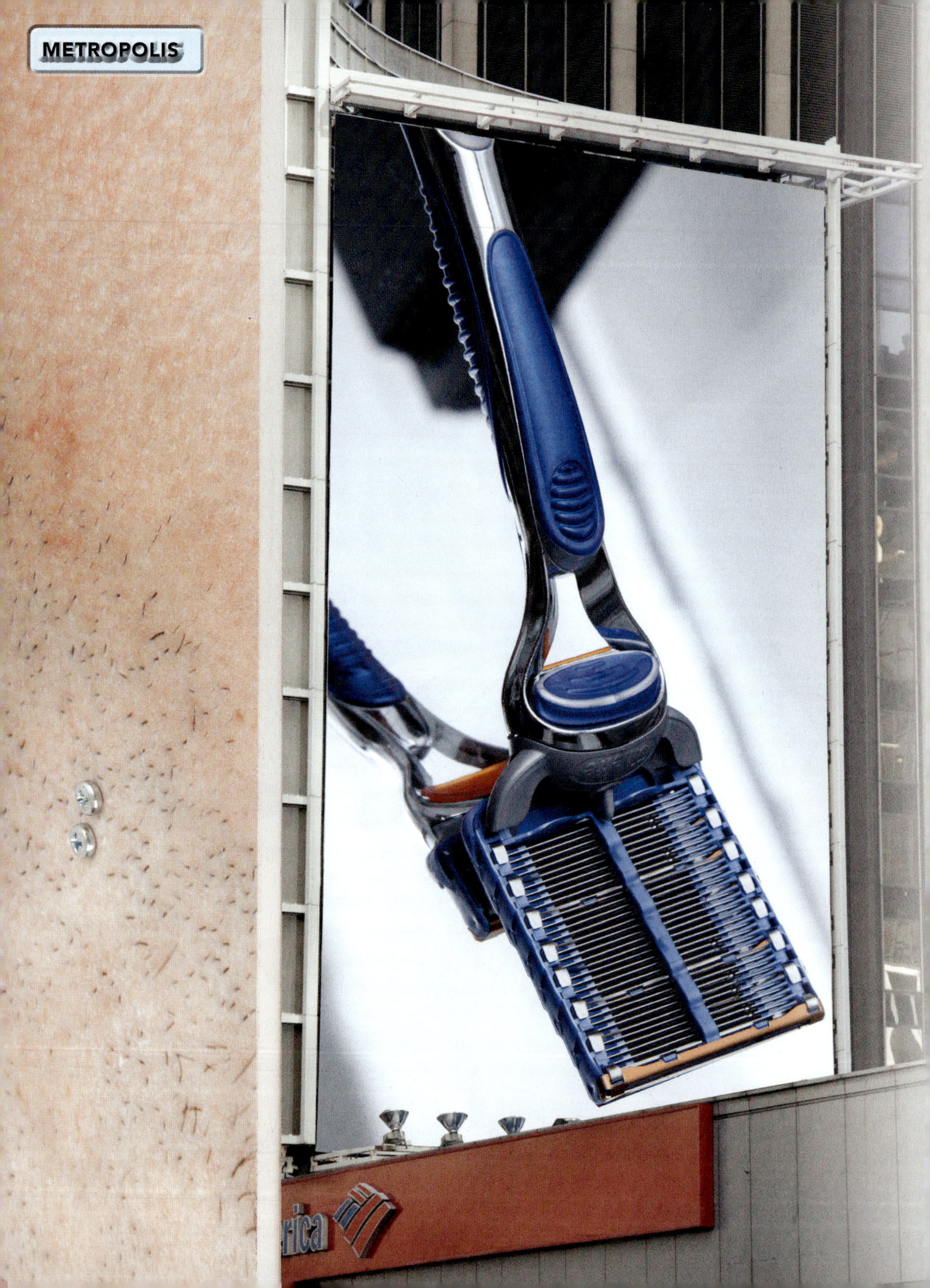
METROPOLIS
rica

Before perfecting his invention of the safety razor and founding what became a major American industrial and sales enterprise, King Camp Gillette (1855-1932) authored several books and pamphlets calling for radical changes in the country's economic and social system. The first of these polemical tracts, The Human Drift, called for the establishment of an ideal society to be created by The United Company "Organized for the purpose of Producing, Manufacturing, and Distributing the Necessities of Life." Except for agricultural and other rural pursuits, all activities and all the population would be concentrated in one gigantic urban complex that Gillette called "Metropolis."

Gillette's Dream

Author: John W. Reps, Title: Review: METROPOLIS, by Author: King Champ Gillette, Published by Boston New Era, Year: 1894. Published: urbanplanning.library.cornell.edu, Year: 2002

The Human Drift

"Under a perfect economical system of production and distribution, and a system combining the greatest elements of progress, there can be only one city on a continent, and possibly only one in the world.

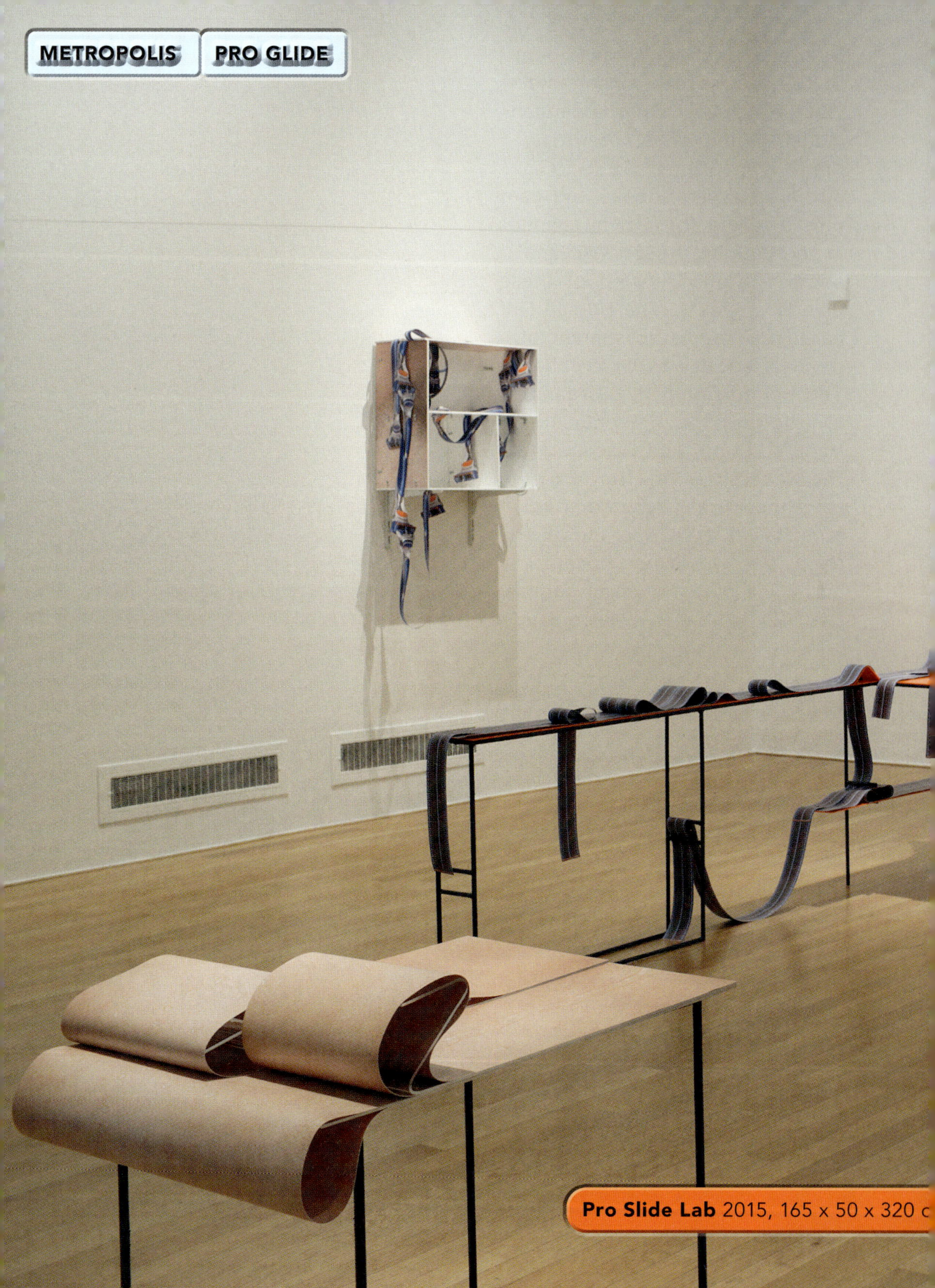

Pro Slide Lab 2015, 165 x 50 x 320 c

Here should be located the great central city, which would be the home of all; and to the artistic beauty, grandeur, and magnificence of this wonderful production of the combined intelligence of a united people, the whole world would contribute its wealth and treasures.

In the building of this great central city, it must be considered in the light of a machine, or rather a part of the machine of production and distribution; and, as such, the objects to be attained must be known and understood. It must have no unnecessary parts to cause friction or demand unnecessary labor, and yet it must combine within itself all the necessary parts which will contribute to the happiness and comfort of all.

Under such a system, the people would live in mammoth apartment houses or hotels, and be free from all the annoyances of housekeeping These apartment buildings would be conducted upon a scale of magnificence such as no civilization has ever known, and would be distributed on a determined plan that would give an average equal population to the square mile throughout the city.

AI GPT-2 RESPONSE

The human-igorating power of the industrial revolution to provide for human needs by giving man the means to live, work, and enjoy an adequate life to live in a civilization free from war and despotism "All work would be made in that urban and industrial complex, and all the living, healthy, productive lives would be provided in that city."— After a few years, he decided " that the most necessary form of production in the world a civilization that would be free of all human suffering " was to be the industrialization of man " which was going to be brought

chival UV prints on vinyl; double sided, plexiglass, steel, carpaint

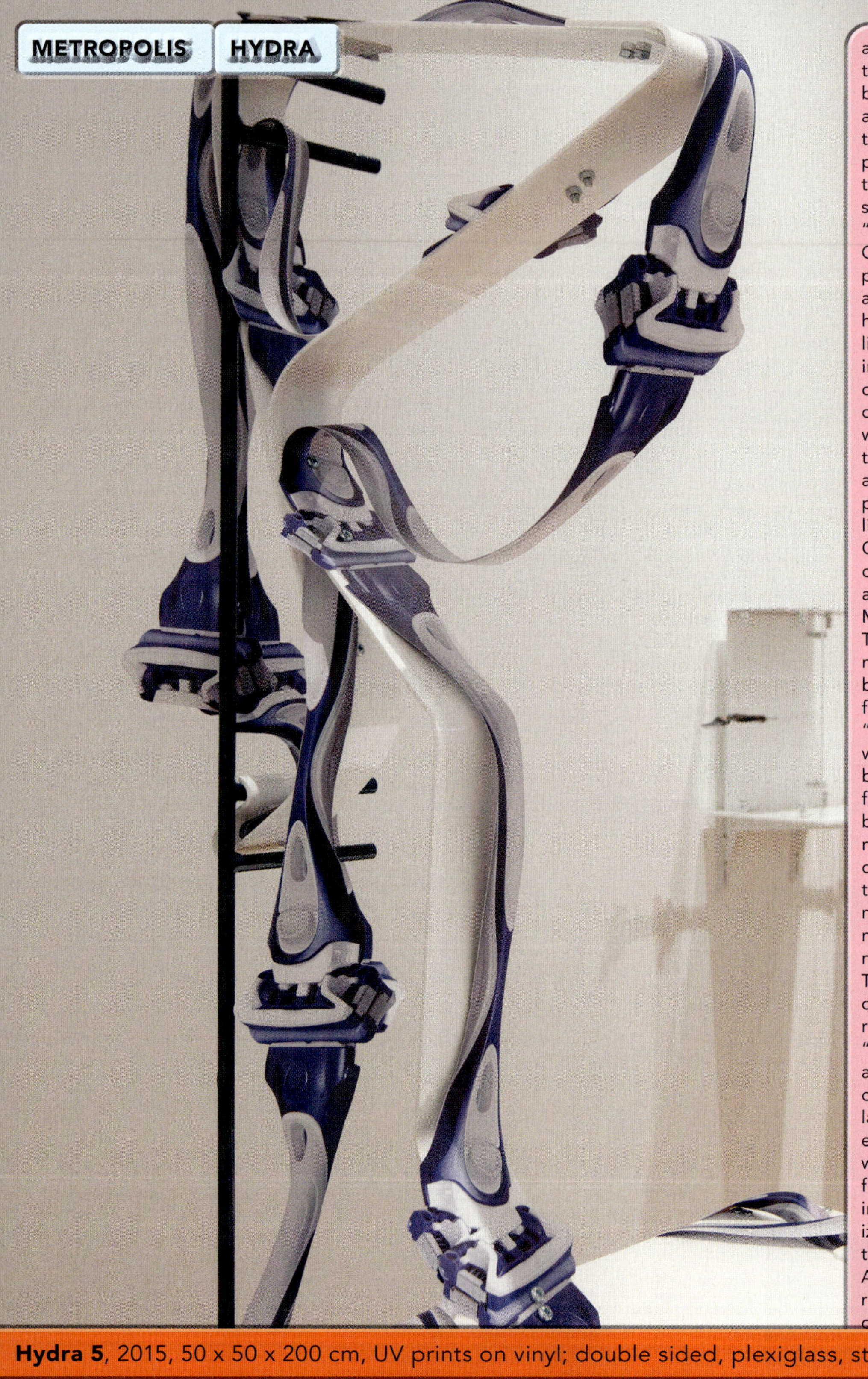

about through labor to make a civilization which provided all that human suffering " which God had produced and which had given a living. The industrial revolution would come about with labor to provide all the living, productive lives which God had created as a basis for Mankind. The human man would become a free creature " and the world would be made free again by working more than once in order to provide his necessary, necessary needs—— The only question remained "how do we all get some of all the life, labor, and enjoyment we need from the industrialization of the world? After years of research and debate,

Hydra 5, 2015, 50 x 50 x 200 cm, UV prints on vinyl; double sided, plexiglass, steel, carpaint

The Human

The general working of this industrial system, by which the vast population would be supplied with every material want, would be simplicity itself, and would combine order and economy in every part. The raw material, brought from every section of America or foreign lands, would be delivered in cars direct to that establishment where it was to be utilized in the process of manufacture. Here the wheat would be delivered to the mill direct from the field where it was produced; and it would be the same with wool, cotton, hides, and spices from foreign lands, and the hundreds of items that go to swell the demand of a large population. Articles of food consumption would be produced with the greatest care, and the highest standard of quality and purity would always be maintained; and there would be a constant gain in this direction.

The manufactured product, in its finished state, would be delivered from the machines into packages containing from five hundred pounds to a carload; and for special articles used in large quantities, porcelain-lined cars would be provided. In this shape, flour, and many other articles, would be delivered to the storerooms of those buildings of "Metropolis" where food would be prepared, and there remain until contents were used. The whole process of handling food products finds its

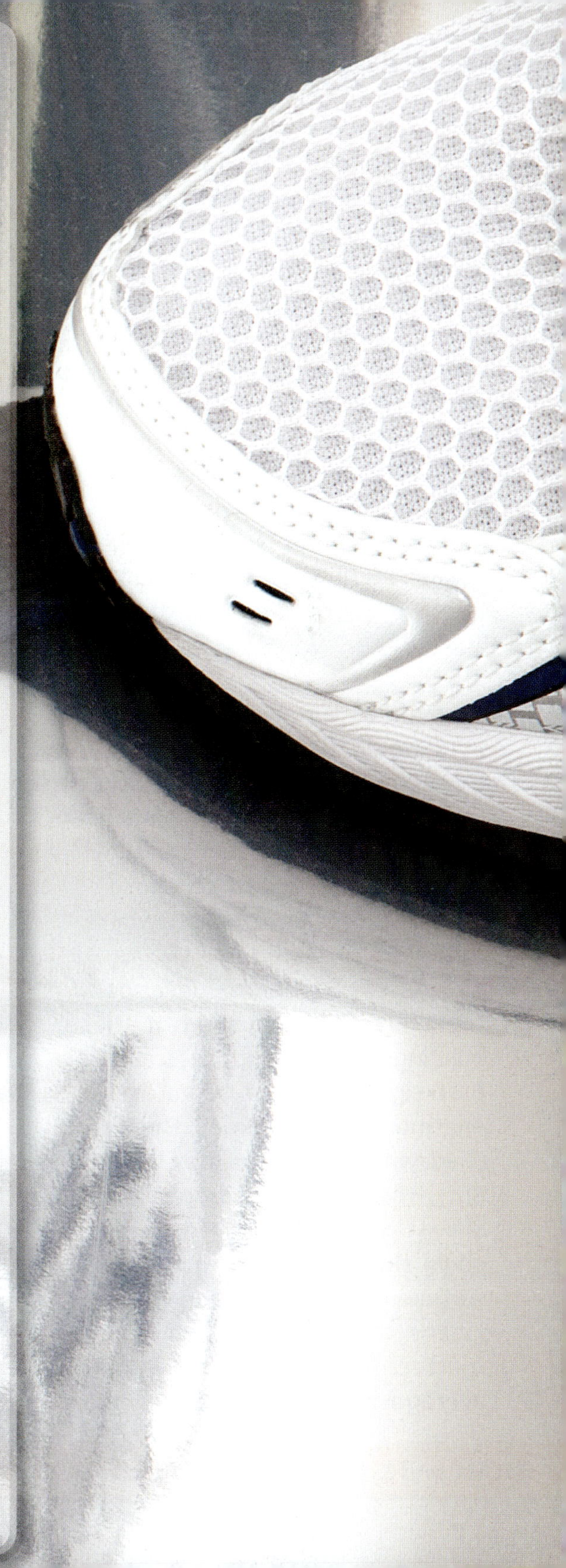

greatest economy by being thus handled direct from factory to place of consumption in bulk, dispensing entirely with our present system of small packages, which entails an enormous amount of labor. The same principle of handling in bulk would be adhered to in the handling of preserved fruits and vegetables, which would be put up in porcelain-lined packages holding from one hundred to five hundred pounds, such packages being returned to the manufacturing department over and over again.

All manufactured food and products would find their way direct from their place of manufacture to a common centre of distribution, and from this centre they would be distributed to those buildings of "Metropolis" where food was prepared for the table. As I have before described, there are four thousand of these buildings in "Metropolis"; and, at first sight, it might seem like an enormous task to keep them supplied with food from day to day. But, when it is considered that almost all manufactured products could be delivered in quantity sufficient to last a year, it only means the supply of twelve or fourteen of these buildings on an average each day. All such materials as flour, sugar, salt, spices, baking-powder, extracts, soaps, vinegar, syrups, etc., could be delivered in bulk, and in special cars which would be retained in the storerooms of the buildings where the food was prepared until emptied, when they would be returned to the proper manufacturing establishment, and refilled. The departments devoted to the manufacture of wearing apparel and household necessities would be carried forward on the same general plan, except that the finished product goes direct from the manufacturing establishments to mammoth emporiums. Thus we would have a furniture emporium, rug emporium, curtains and hangings, gentlemen's clothing, underwear, etc., women's dress goods, etc. In these mammoth establishments, would be arranged, in attractive display, the products of the highest developed intelligence in art and science,--goods in greatest variety of texture, design, and beauty, all of highest grade and quality. Here the people would select what they desired without money and without price.

Many will maintain that the people would abuse this privilege, but such would not be the case; for under a material equality there is no incentive to hoard

Rechts und Links 2015, 20 x 70 x 40 cm, Metal Hardware, Archival UV print on Acrylic and Gille up, and no one could load themselves down with the care of clothes which they did not need and could not wear. And no one would fill their apartments with a lot of useless trash and furniture which is neither useful nor ornamental, and would be in the way. I here reiterate what I have said before, that no system can ever be a perfect system, and free from incentive for crime, until money and all representative value of material is swept from the face of the earth.

I believe, as much as I believe that I live, that, if the plan outlined could be understood by the masses, enthusiasm would amount to such a pitch in the excitement and desire to see "Metropolis" completed that millions would enlist their services for an indefinite time to forward its building, and all they would ask would be soldier's fare and clothing. What would money be to them, when the near future would see it pass into the oblivion of an ignorant age?

The Human Drift

Author: John W. Reps, Title: Review: METROPOLIS, by Author: King Champ Gillette, Published by Boston New Era, Year: 1894. Published: urbanplanning.library.cornell.edu, Year: 2002

sion Pro Glide Flexbal Razors

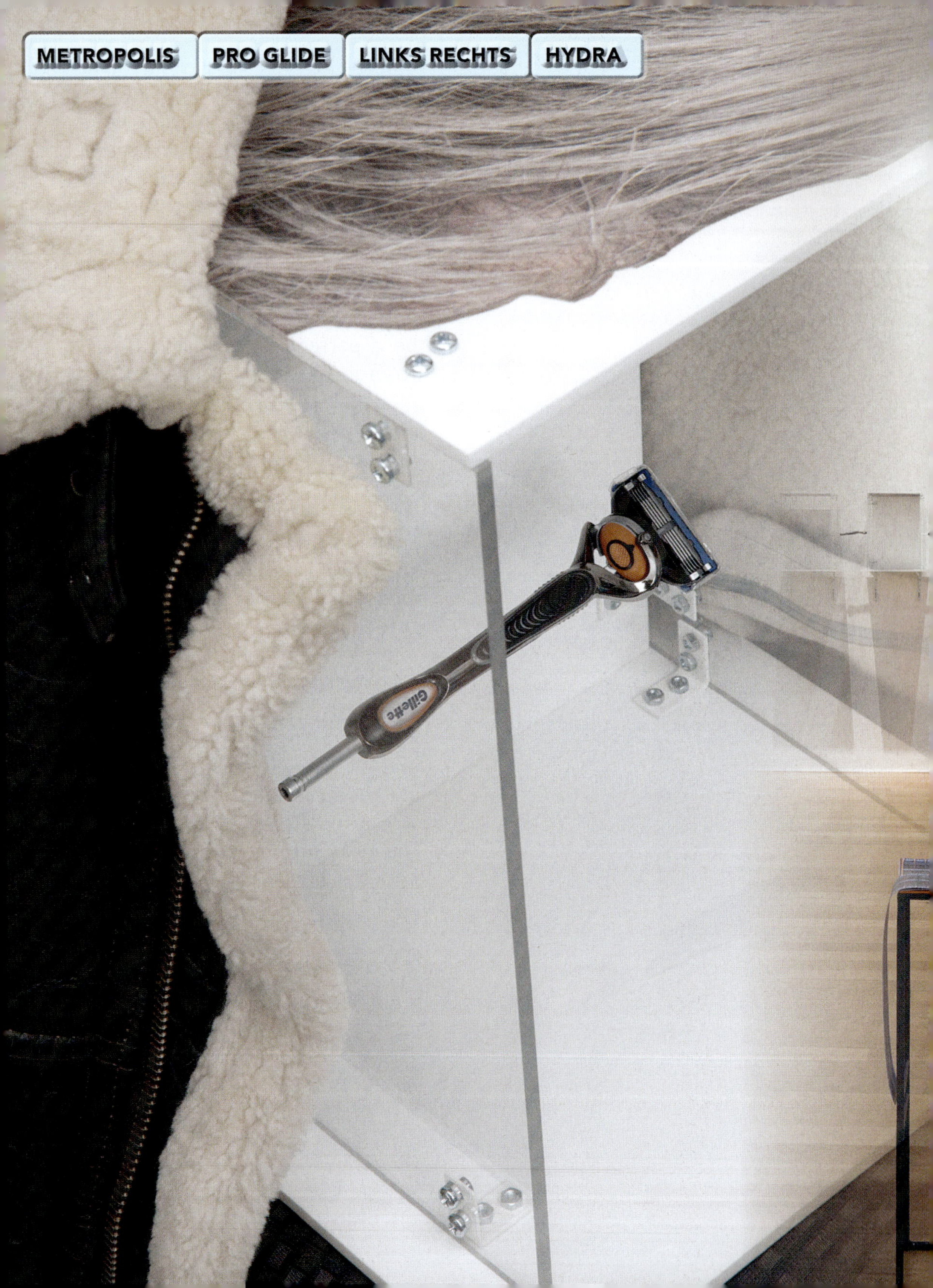
METROPOLIS
PRO GLIDE
LINKS RECHTS
HYDRA
Gillette

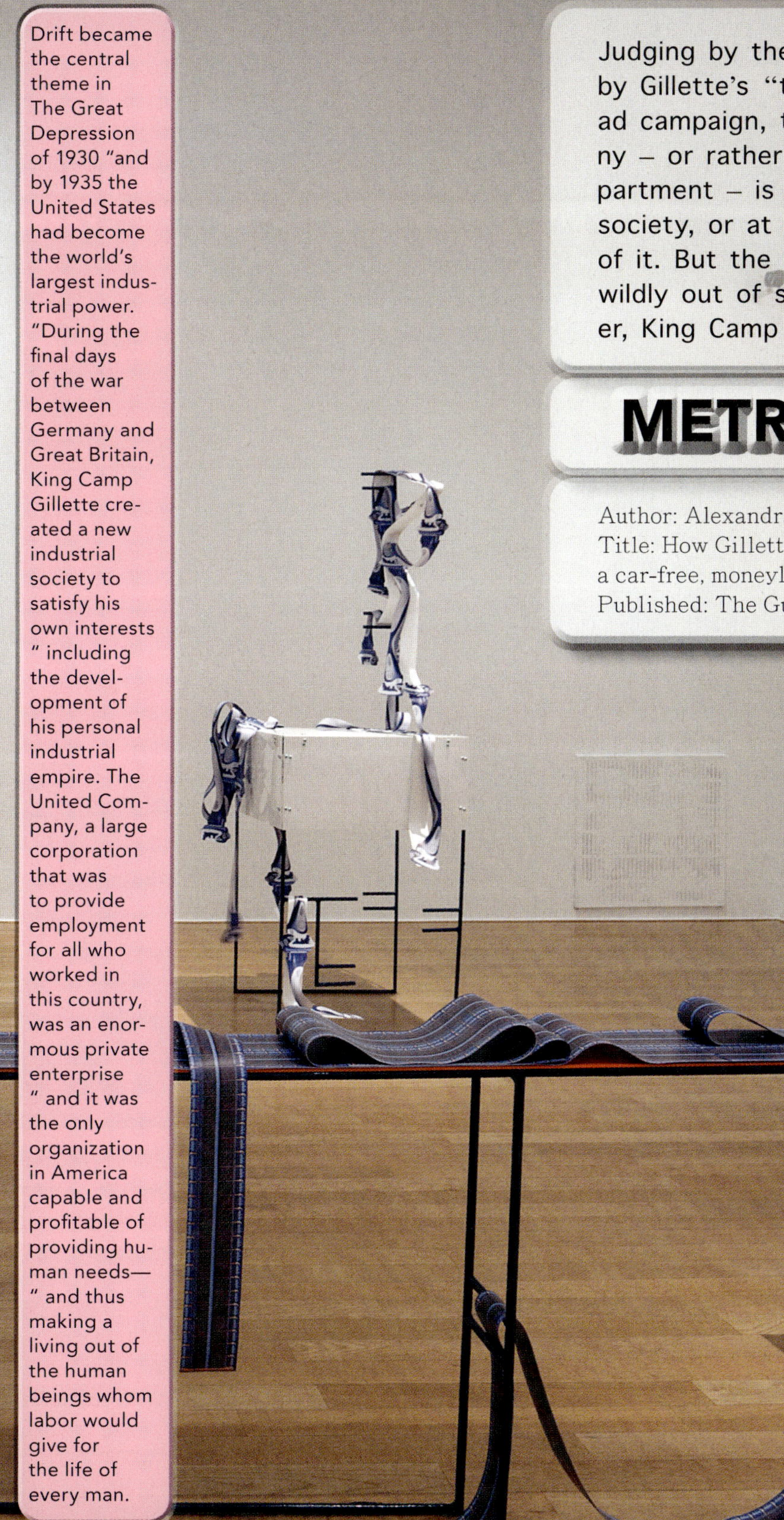

Drift became the central theme in The Great Depression of 1930 "and by 1935 the United States had become the world's largest industrial power. "During the final days of the war between Germany and Great Britain, King Camp Gillette created a new industrial society to satisfy his own interests " including the development of his personal industrial empire. The United Company, a large corporation that was to provide employment for all who worked in this country, was an enormous private enterprise " and it was the only organization in America capable and profitable of providing human needs— " and thus making a living out of the human beings whom labor would give for the life of every man.

Judging by the outrage generated by Gillette's "toxic masculinity" ad campaign, the shaving company – or rather its marketing department – is one step ahead of society, or at least certain parts of it. But the brand may not be wildly out of step with its founder, King Camp Gillette.

METROPOLIS

Author: Alexandra Heal,
Title: How Gillette' s founder dreamed of a car-free, moneyless metropolis"
Published: The Guardian, Year: 2019

PEAK SHIFT

for recognizing the rectangle. The rat will respond more frequently to the object for which it is being rewarded to the point that a rat will respond to a rectangle that is longer and more narrow with a higher frequency than the original with which it was trained.

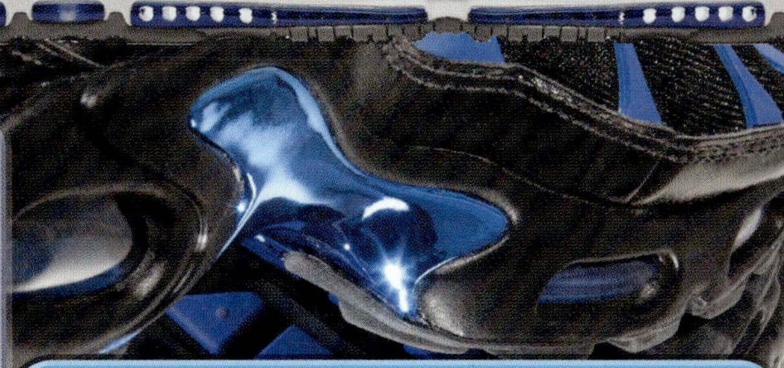

Scientist Niko Tinbergen discovered that Herring gull chicks habitually tap the red-striped beak of their mother to be fed. He further realized that the tapping response of the chicks could be triggered without any beak at all. In place of the beak, the chicks responded to a yellow-colored stick with a red strip painted on its side. Further, if the number of stripes were increased, from one strip to three stripes, the chick's enthusiasm for tapping the stick and demanding food increased proportionally. "…when the chick looks at this elongated object with three red stripes it responds even more than it does to a natural beak."

When Neuroscientist and Professor V.S. Ramachandran started to ask himself what is art? He realized that one clue might come from the research experiment that was done with baby seagull chicks. the Herring Gull Test, done on seagulls nearly fifty years ago at Oxford, illustrating the neurological principle of peak shift. – the hard-wiring of brains to focus on parts of objects that matter the most.

There might very well be an analogy in that what's going on in the brains of our ancestors, and the artists who were creating these Venus figurines were producing grossly exaggerated versions, the equivalent for their brain of what the stick with the three red stripes is for the chick's brain, According Ramachandran. Peak shift is fundamental in understanding why we prefer exaggerated images.

This is called a supernormal stimulus. The fact that the rat is responding more to a 'super' rectangle implies that it is learning a rule. This effect can be applied to human pattern recognition and aesthetic preference. Some artists attempt to capture the very essence of something in order to evoke a direct emotional response. In other words, they try to make a 'super' rectangle to get the viewer to have an enhanced response. To capture the essence of something, an artist amplifies the differences of that object, or what makes it unique, to highlight the essential features and reduce redundant information. This process mimics what the visual areas of the brain have evolved to do and more powerfully activates the same neural mechanisms that were originally activated by the original object.

Title: "The Science of Art: A Neurological Theory of Aesthetic Experience" Authors: V.S. Ramachandran and William Hirstein, Published: Journal of Consciousness Studies, Year: 1999.

PEAK SHIFT PRINCIPLE

The peak shift principle, this psychological phenomenon is typically known for its application in animal discrimination learning. In the peak shift effect, animals sometimes respond more strongly to exaggerated versions of the training stimuli.
For instance, a rat is trained to discriminate a square from a rectangle by being rewarded

Some designers or artists deliberately exaggerate creative components such as shading, highlights, and illumination to an extent that would never occur in a real image to produce a caricature. These artists may be unconsciously producing heightened activity in Neuroaesthetics is a field of experimental science that aims to combine (neuro-) psychological research with aesthetics by investigating the "perception, production, and response to art, as well as interactions with objects and scenes that evoke an intense feeling, often of pleasure."

Source: Neuroesthetics : Peak shift principle, Wikipedia, Last edited: 8 March 2019

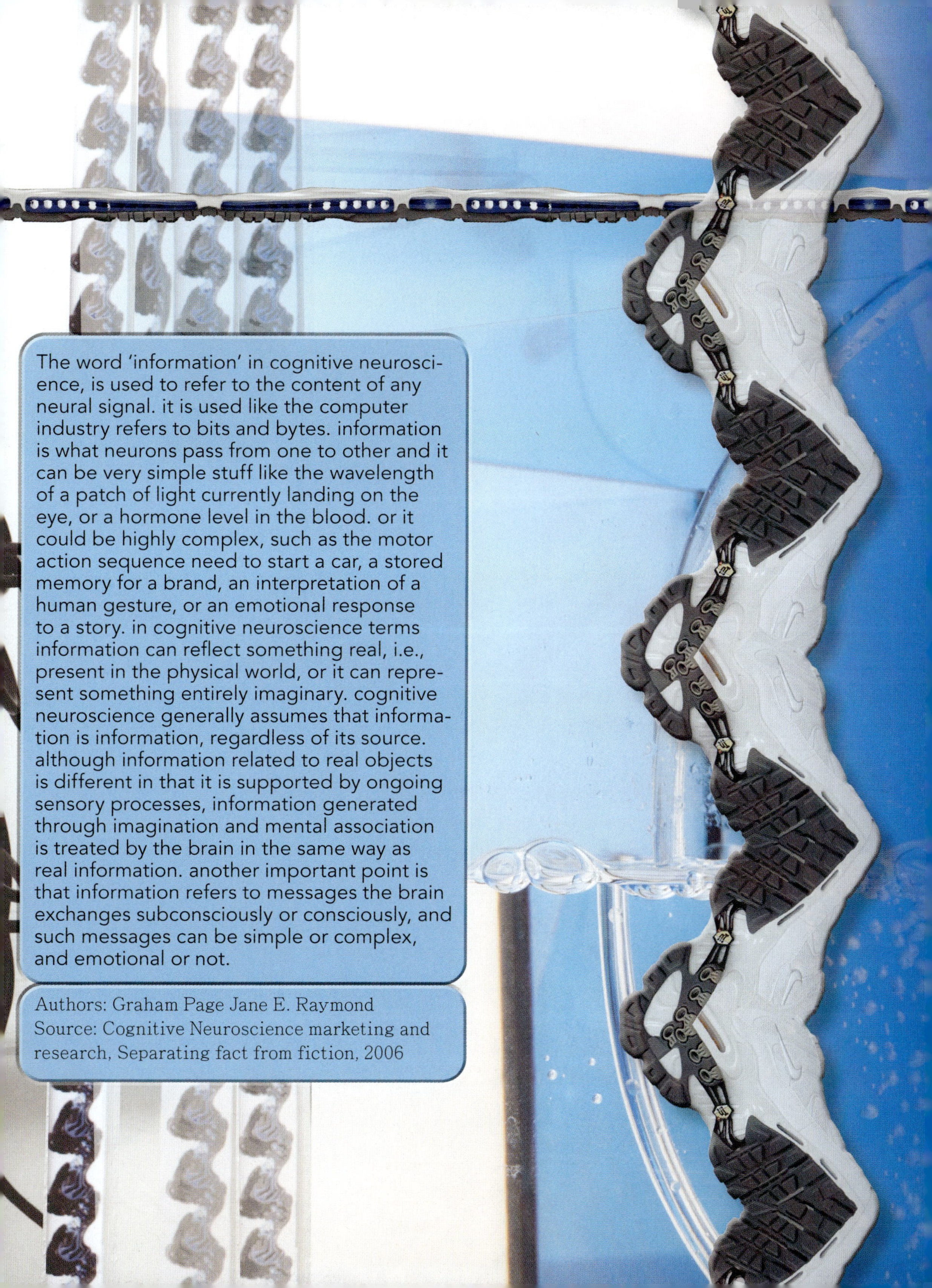

The word 'information' in cognitive neuroscience, is used to refer to the content of any neural signal. it is used like the computer industry refers to bits and bytes. information is what neurons pass from one to other and it can be very simple stuff like the wavelength of a patch of light currently landing on the eye, or a hormone level in the blood. or it could be highly complex, such as the motor action sequence need to start a car, a stored memory for a brand, an interpretation of a human gesture, or an emotional response to a story. in cognitive neuroscience terms information can reflect something real, i.e., present in the physical world, or it can represent something entirely imaginary. cognitive neuroscience generally assumes that information is information, regardless of its source. although information related to real objects is different in that it is supported by ongoing sensory processes, information generated through imagination and mental association is treated by the brain in the same way as real information. another important point is that information refers to messages the brain exchanges subconsciously or consciously, and such messages can be simple or complex, and emotional or not.

Authors: Graham Page Jane E. Raymond
Source: Cognitive Neuroscience marketing and research, Separating fact from fiction, 2006

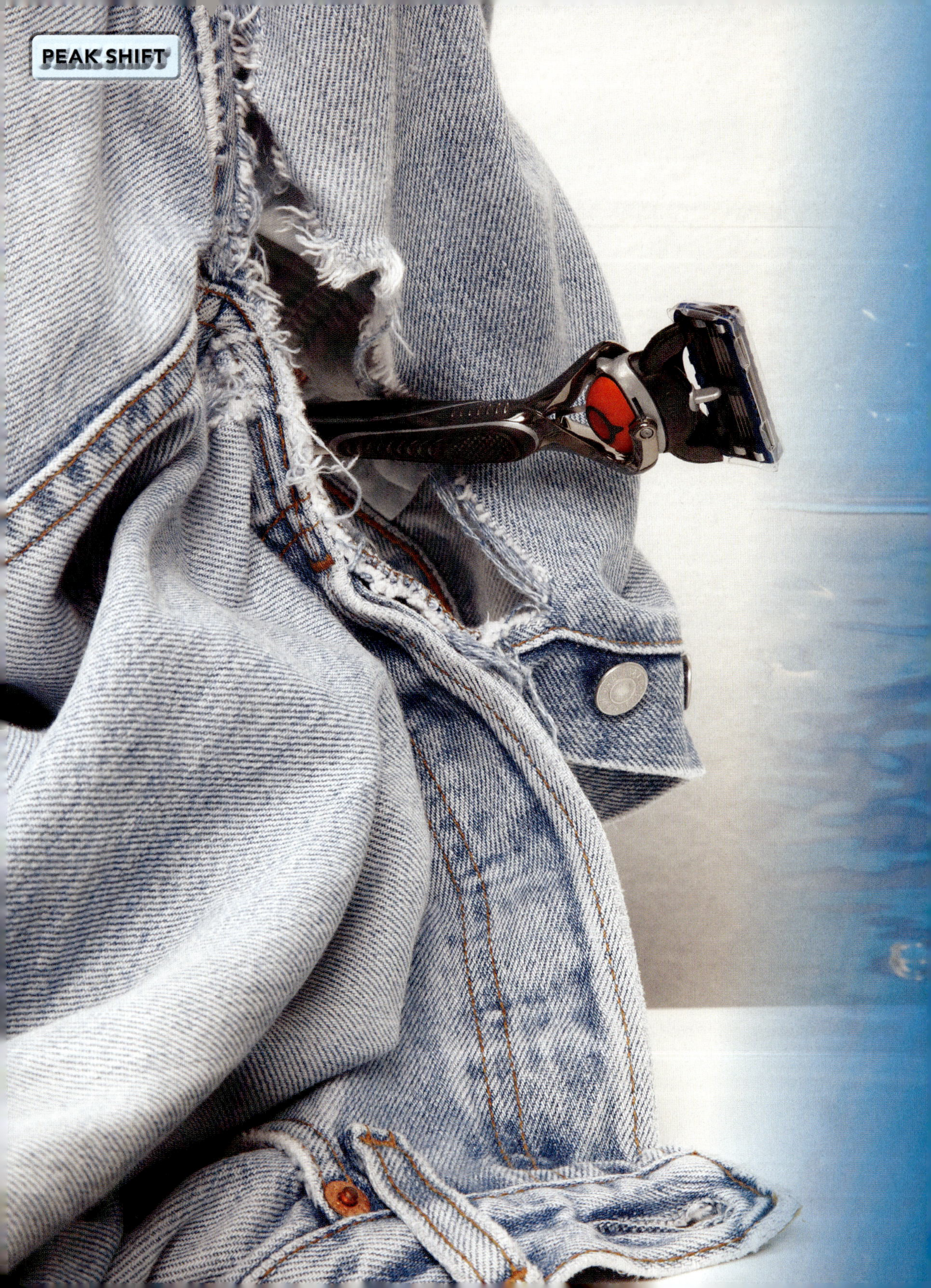

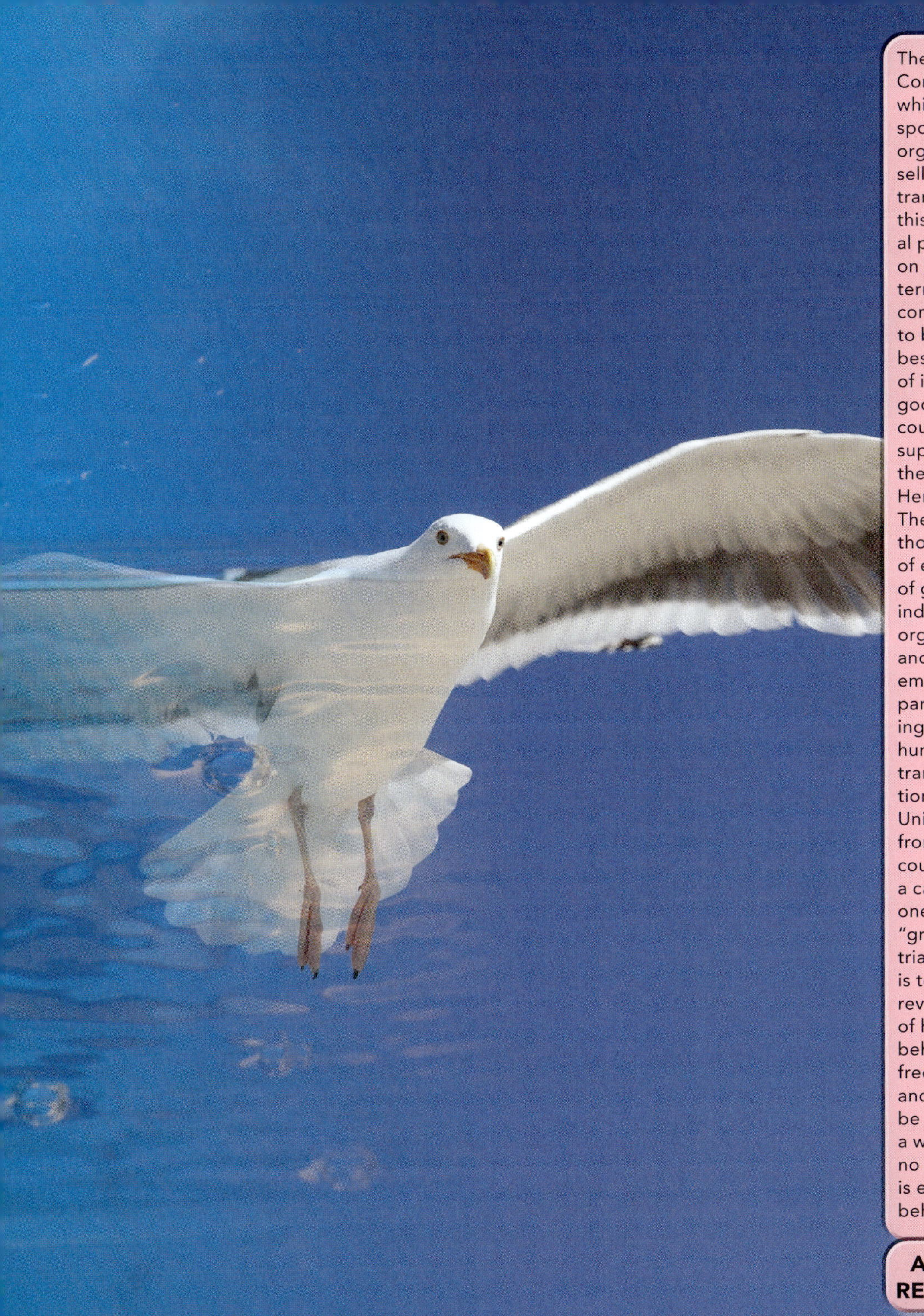

The United Company, which was responsible for organizing, selling, and transporting this industrial product on its own territory, was considered to be the best source of industrial goods that could be supplied to the Western Hemisphere. There are thousands of examples of great industrial organizations and their employees participating in the human- rific transformation of the United States from a feudal country into a capitalist one. This "great industrialization" is to be a revolution of human behavior and freedom —— and it must be in such a way that no human is ever left behind.

AI GPT-2 RESPONSE

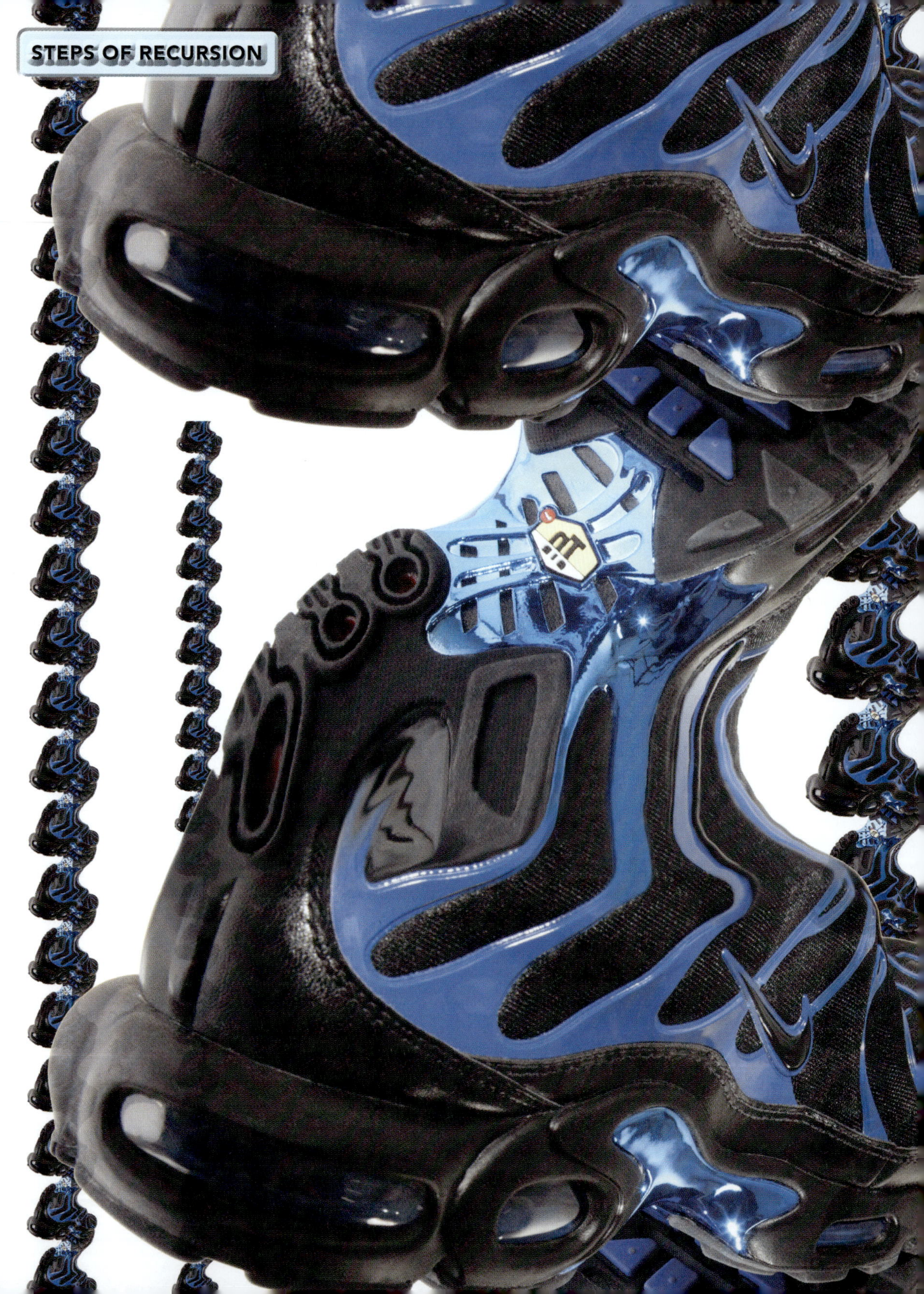

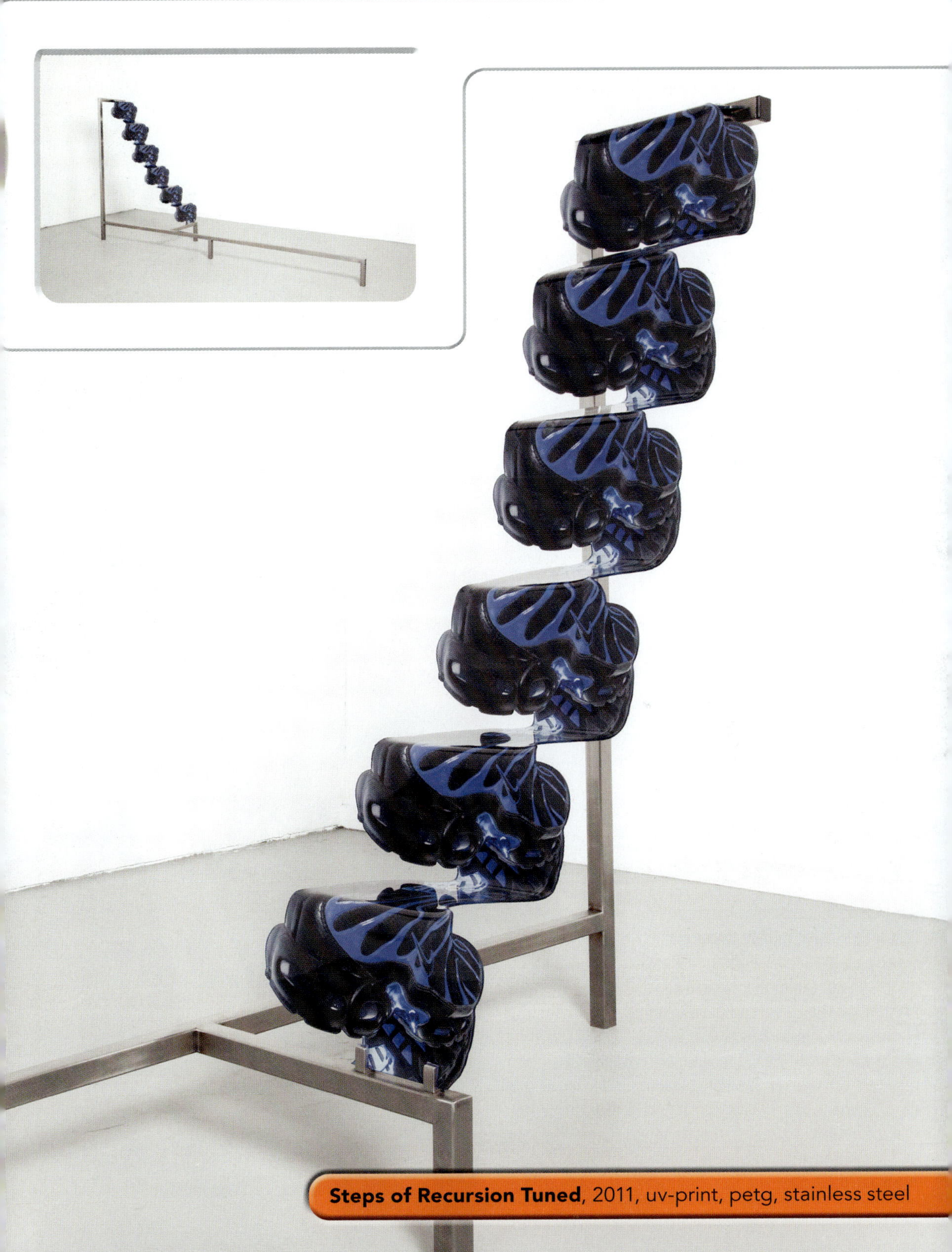

Steps of Recursion Tuned, 2011, uv-print, petg, stainless steel

Language is generally recognized as a uniquely human accomplishment. It is also commonly assumed that language evolved in a single step—a "great leap forward"—perhaps as recently as 50,000 years ago. This event (it is proposed) created the capacity for symbolic thought and a recursive structure that allows the generation of an unlimited number of propositional structures. Here, I outline a scenario more aligned with Darwinian theory. I argue that recursive thinking evolved as a prelude to language, in contexts unrelated to language itself. One example is mental time travel, whereby remembered past episodes or imagined future ones can be inserted into the mental present. Another is theory of mind, whereby we can understand the thoughts and beliefs of others and even understand that others understand our own thoughts and beliefs. Language then evolved as a means of sharing our mental time travels, thoughts, and beliefs with others. In this approach, the evolution of language can be understood in terms of Darwinian evolution as a stepwise process rather than the outcome of a single event.

Author: Michael C. Corballis, The Recursive Mind: The Origins of Human Language, Thought, and Civilization Recursive Cognition as a Prelude to Language, Springer Link, 2013

Recursive Cognition

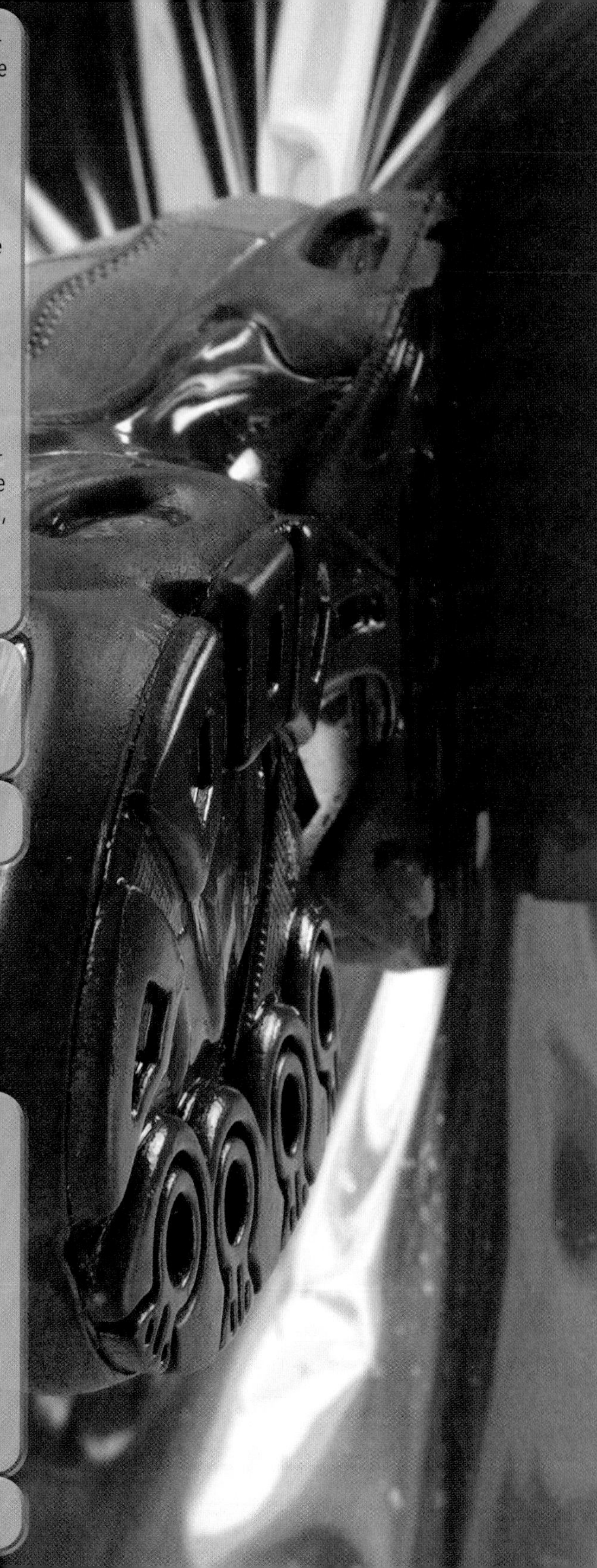

It is argued that classical ergonomics can be seen as embracing a dualism, where the effects of work on the body are considered separately from the effects of work on the mind. This continues the mechanistic tradition of Western psychology. The aim of cognitive ergonomics is to describe (1) how work affects the mind, as well as (2) how the mind affects work. Work is all in the mind in the sense that the quality of work depends on the person's understanding of the situation (goals, means, constraints) and in the sense that the design of a worksystem depends on the designer's understanding, in particular the conceptualization of the people in the system.

Author: Erik Hollnagel, Cognitive Ergonomics: its all in the mind, Ergonimics, 1997

SCROLL04

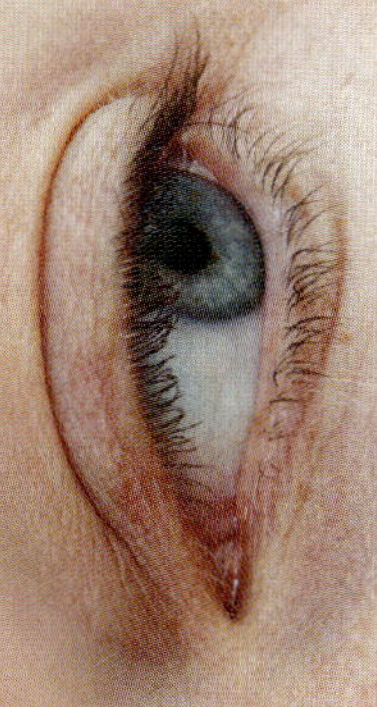

Follow us:

07.07.14

In a quest to understand what drives consumers' decisions, marketers have turned to psychology to understand what could make an impact.

Psychological Tactics Marketers Use To Influence Consumer Behavior

BY ROBERT ROSENTHAL

2 MINUTE READ

The vast majority of marketers aren't psychologists. But many successful marketers regularly employ psychology in appealing to consumers.

Smart, skillful, honest marketers use psychology legally, ethically, and respectfully to attract and engage consumers, and compel them to buy.

Here are a few tips and tricks for using psychology to your own marketing campaign's advantage:

1. RUN EMOTIONAL IDEAS
Studies have shown emotional and psychological appeals resonate more with consumers than feature and function appeals. In advertising copy, benefits–which often have a psychological component–generally outsell features. Demonstrating how that new computer will improve a potential customer's life tends to have more influence rather than explaining how it works.

Salespeople have long understood the power of emotional appeals. In the 18th century, when the contents of the Anchor Brewery

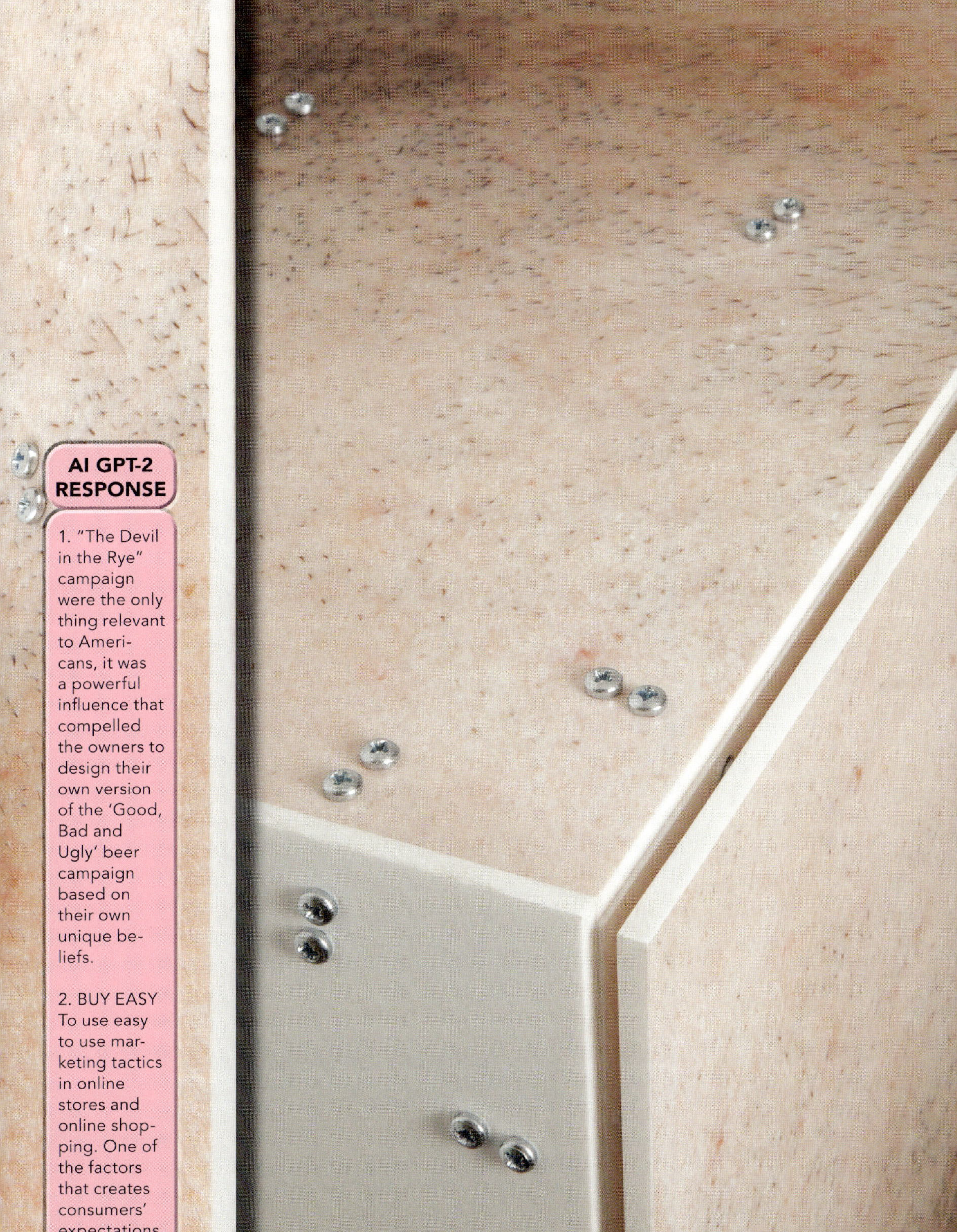

AI GPT-2 RESPONSE

1. “The Devil in the Rye” campaign were the only thing relevant to Americans, it was a powerful influence that compelled the owners to design their own version of the ‘Good, Bad and Ugly’ beer campaign based on their own unique beliefs.

2. BUY EASY To use easy to use marketing tactics in online stores and online shopping. One of the factors that creates consumers’ expectations about how

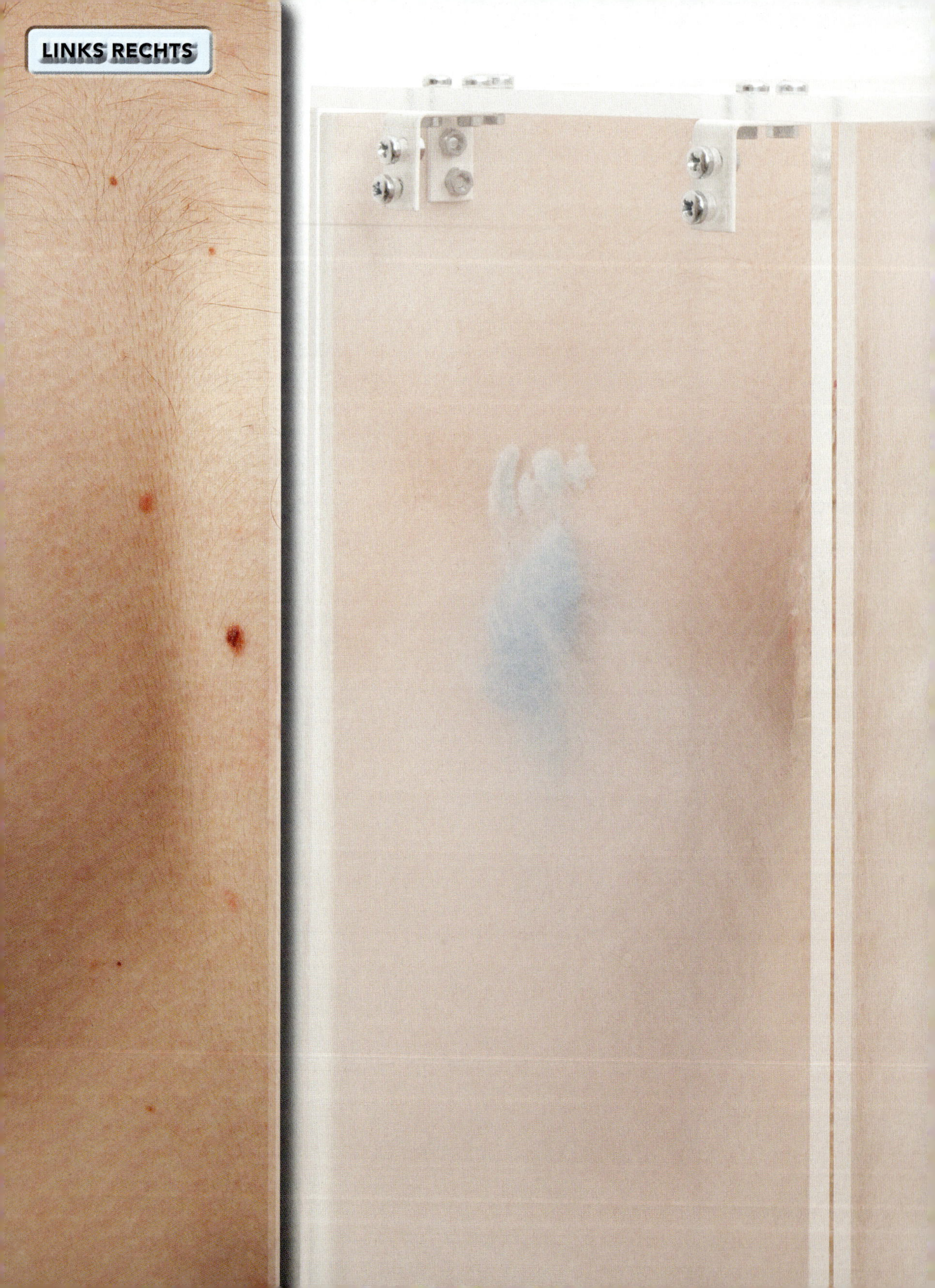
LINKS RECHTS

good products look is customer service. The best way to create customer service that satisfies customer expectations is to do well. Most salespeople believe that they can provide good customer service in the online space. What they really don tell us is that they aren't willing to spend a single penny on a digital system that they donÕt want to install in every house or business.

3. DON'T HOOK TO PROUD WORTHY FUEL

The idea that a buyer's motivation is just more likely to change the way he or she spends the purchase is a myth. In fact, most online stores do not take the time to explain what an "emotional sale" is really like. They explain that there is a difference between "cute" and

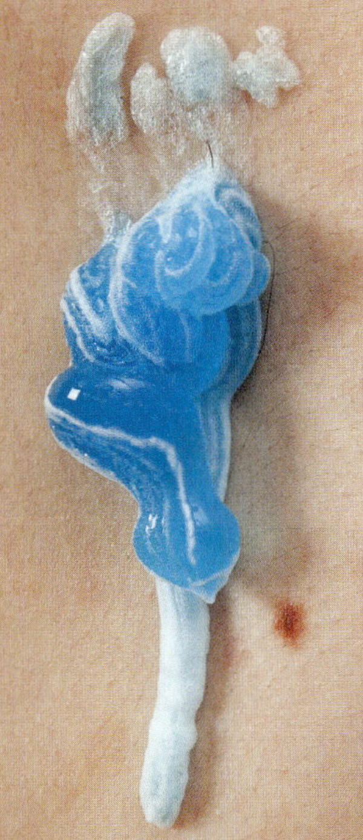

were being auctioned off, the auctioneer said: "We are not here to sell boilers and vats, but the potentiality of growing rich beyond the dreams of avarice."

2. HIGHLIGHT YOUR FLAWS

It's no secret that consumers tend to doubt marketing claims–for good reasons. Many simply aren't credible. One way to raise credibility is to point out your product's shortcomings.

Among the most famous examples was an ad for Volkswagen, which contained a one-word headline: "Lemon." Opening body copy below a VW photo read: "This Volkswagen missed the boat. The chrome strip on the glove compartment is blemished and must be replaced. Chances are you wouldn't have noticed it; Inspector Kurt Kroner did." The ad went on to discuss a "preoccupation with detail." The Lemon ad became a textbook example of how to optimize credibility.

3. REPOSITION YOUR COMPETITION

In Positioning: The Battle for Your Mind, Al Ries and Jack Trout delve into the limited slots consumers have in their brain for products and services, and the importance of positioning one's business in the ideal slot.

They also write about repositioning–changing the position a business occupies in consumers' minds. A prominent example of repositioning the competition is when the Jif brand launched the "Choosy moms choose Jif" campaign, competitors were suddenly repositioned as products for mothers who didn't give a damn about the food their kids consumed. What mother didn't want to think of herself as a choosy mom?

4. PROMOTE EXCLUSIVITY

Near the top of Maslow's hierarchy of needs pyramid sits self-esteem. People want to feel important; like they're part of an exclusive group. That's why advertising copy sometimes says: "We're not for everyone."

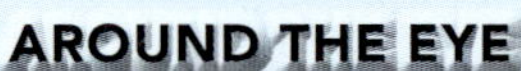

"emotionally manipulative" products. They are more likely to say that buying a purchase that is "easy to understand" and that it doesn't count against your money.

4. DON'T DONATE TO RITICAL INTERESTS. People who donate to charitable causes often say, "When we're buying something for ourselves, there's money I'm helping support. When we're buying something for someone else on the other side of this world, there's money I'm helping support."

Most online stores, on the other hand, don't do any research about charities. People who donate to charitable causes often say, "When we're buying something for ourselves, there's money I'm helping support. When

The U.S. Marines ran a very successful campaign for years with the tagline: "The Few. The Proud." Perhaps the most famous modern example of exclusivity in advertising is the American Express tagline: "Membership has its privileges." But to make an exclusivity appeal work in the long run, marketers must mean what they say. Empty claims tend to be counterproductive.

5. INTRODUCE FEAR, UNCERTAINTY, AND DOUBT

Fear, uncertainty, and doubt, or FUD, is often used legitimately by businesses and organizations to make consumers stop, think, and change their behavior. FUD is so powerful that it's capable of nuking the competition.

In at least one case it did just that. When Lyndon Johnson ran against Barry Goldwater in 1964, he wanted to stoke public fear that a President Goldwater would raise the risk of nuclear war. The "Daisy" ad, which ran only once, showed a little girl, followed by a nuclear explosion with a voiceover of LBJ ominously stating, "These are the stakes. To make a world in which all of God's children can live, or to go into the dark." Johnson carried 44 states, and took 61% of the vote in a landslide win.

—Robert Rosenthal is the founder of Contenteurs and author of Optimarketing: Marketing Optimization to Electrify Your Business.

You Might Also Like:

I'm 14, and I quit social media after discovering what was posted about me

Thanks, Marie Kondo! The resale market is becoming bigger than fast fashion

THE RECOMMENDER

Barking Up The Wrong Tree

$18.30

Data and Goliath

$12.80

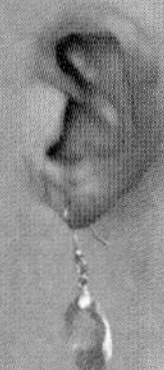

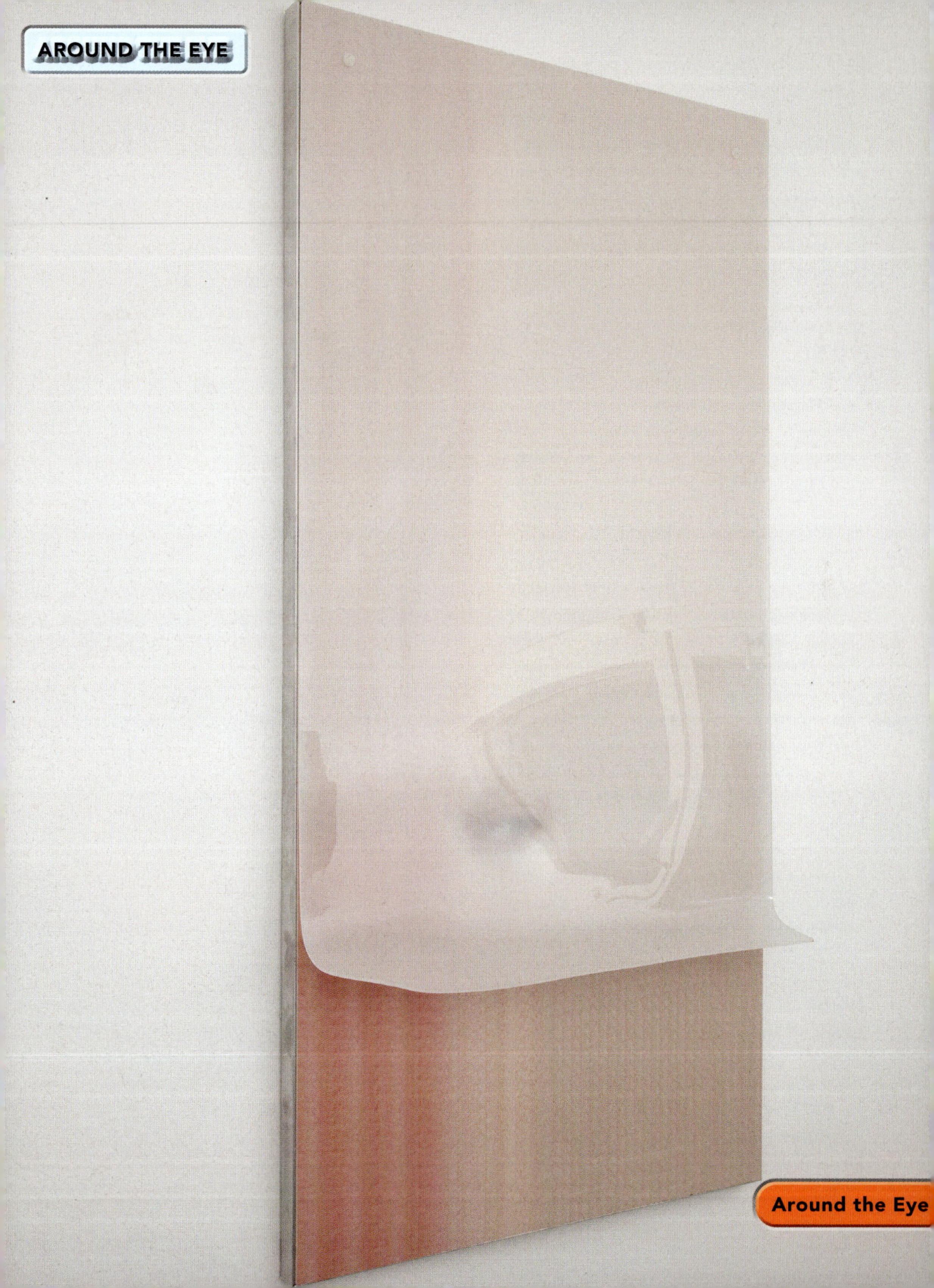
AROUND THE EYE
Around the Eye

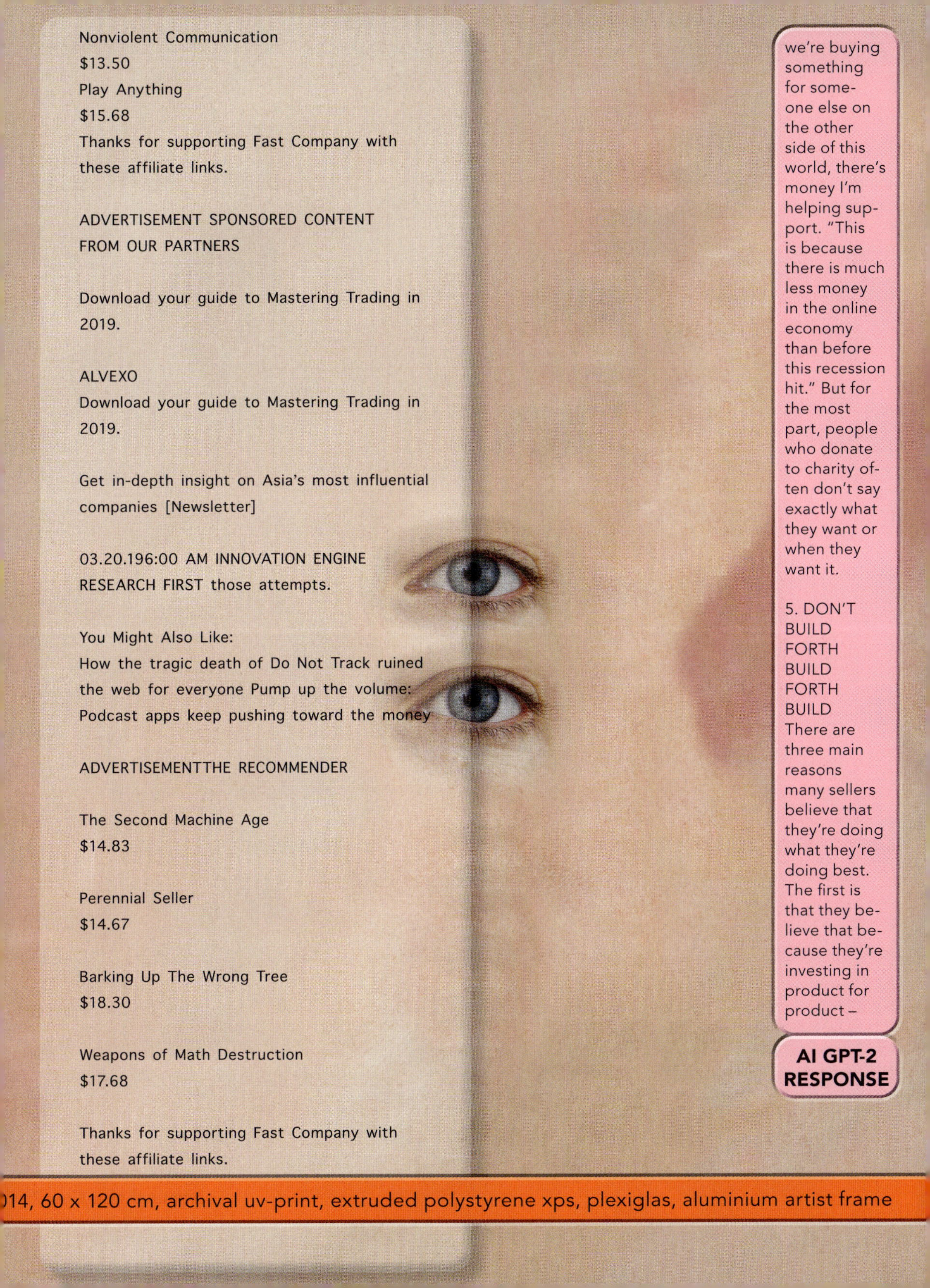

Nonviolent Communication
$13.50
Play Anything
$15.68
Thanks for supporting Fast Company with these affiliate links.

ADVERTISEMENT SPONSORED CONTENT FROM OUR PARTNERS

Download your guide to Mastering Trading in 2019.

ALVEXO
Download your guide to Mastering Trading in 2019.

Get in-depth insight on Asia's most influential companies [Newsletter]

03.20.196:00 AM INNOVATION ENGINE RESEARCH FIRST those attempts.

You Might Also Like:
How the tragic death of Do Not Track ruined the web for everyone Pump up the volume: Podcast apps keep pushing toward the money

ADVERTISEMENTTHE RECOMMENDER

The Second Machine Age
$14.83

Perennial Seller
$14.67

Barking Up The Wrong Tree
$18.30

Weapons of Math Destruction
$17.68

Thanks for supporting Fast Company with these affiliate links.

we're buying something for someone else on the other side of this world, there's money I'm helping support. "This is because there is much less money in the online economy than before this recession hit." But for the most part, people who donate to charity often don't say exactly what they want or when they want it.

5. DON'T BUILD FORTH BUILD FORTH BUILD
There are three main reasons many sellers believe that they're doing what they're doing best. The first is that they believe that because they're investing in product for product –

AI GPT-2 RESPONSE

014, 60 x 120 cm, archival uv-print, extruded polystyrene xps, plexiglas, aluminium artist frame

Around the Eye 2 an▸

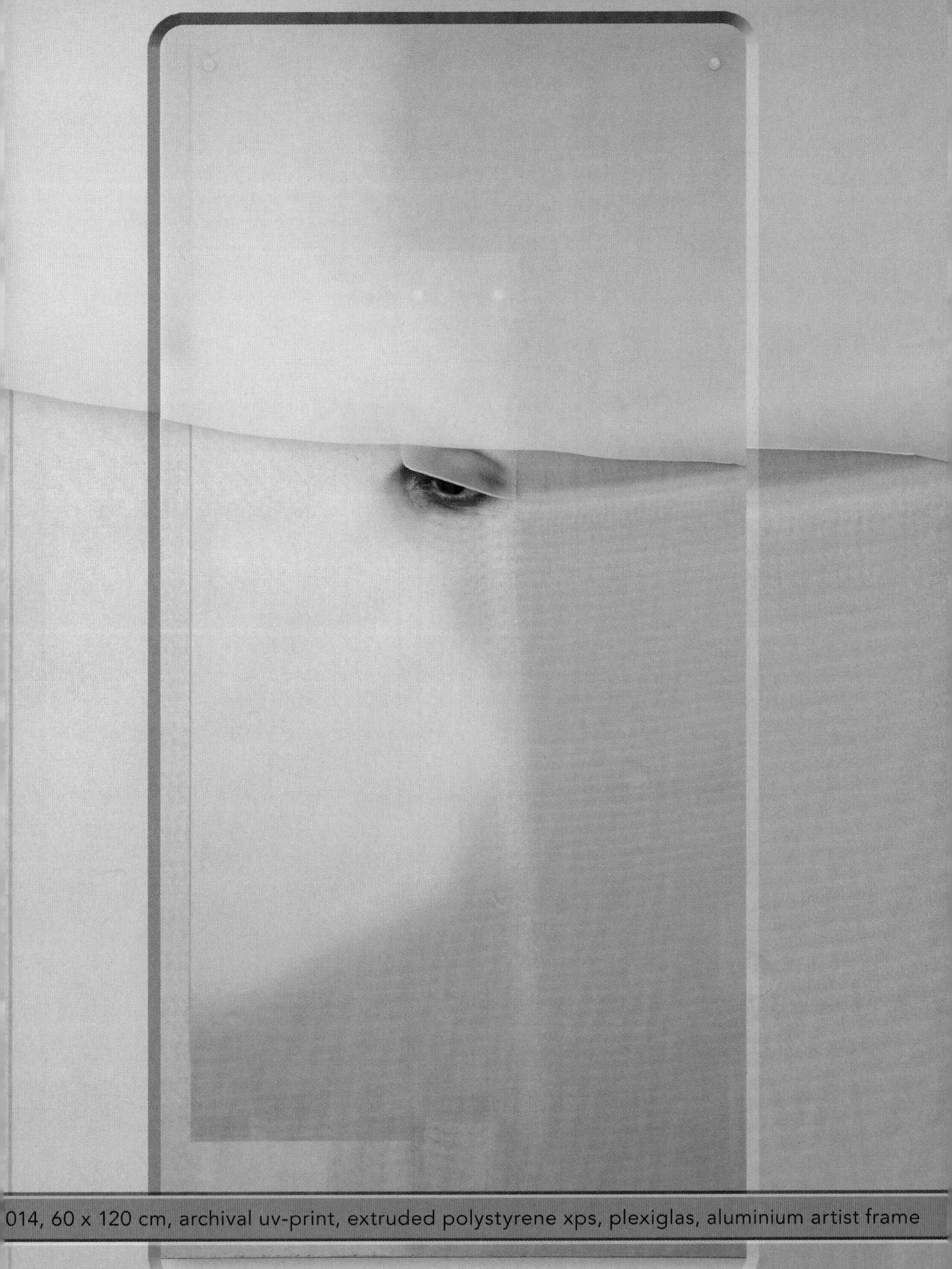

014, 60 x 120 cm, archival uv-print, extruded polystyrene xps, plexiglas, aluminium artist frame

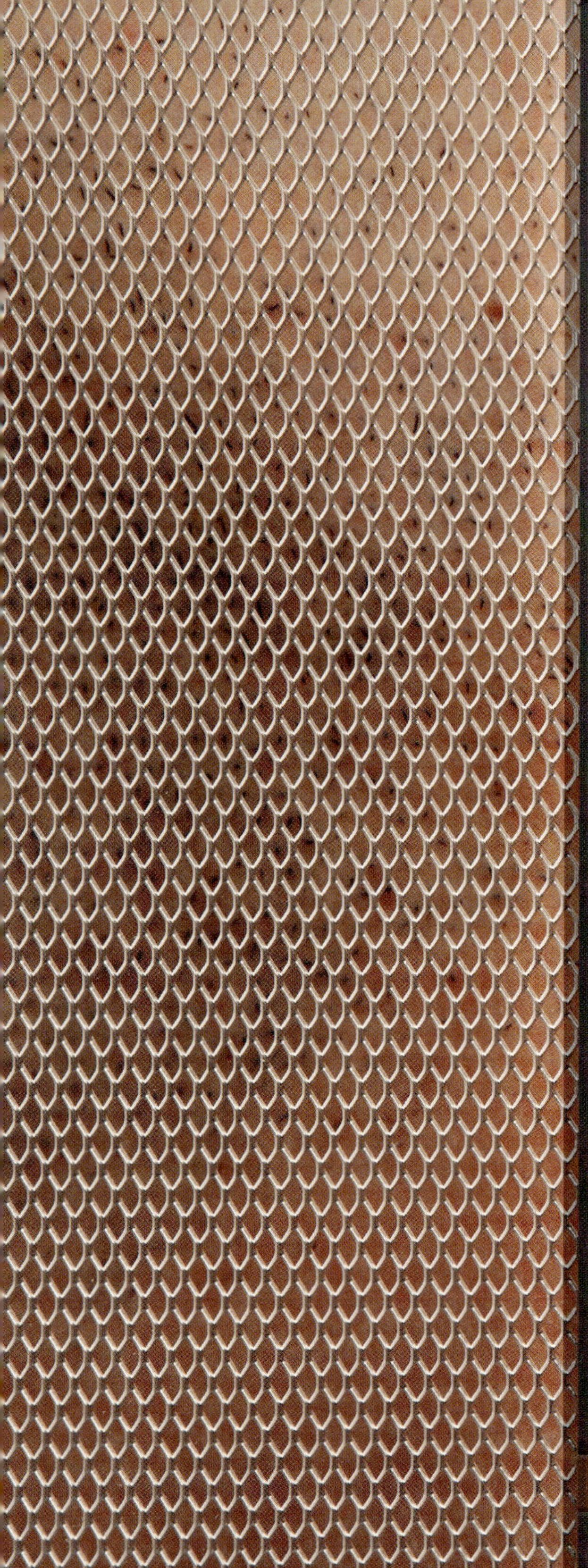

ADVERTISEMENT

IMPACT

Here's how the footprint of the plant-based Impossible Burger compares to beef

IMPACT

Sweetgreen is redesigning school lunches to make them more healthy–and more fun

CREATIVITY

Tavi Gevinson's impression of Elizabeth Holmes is bloody good

CREATIVITY

You have to see this Cheetos-themed mansion, a real thing that actually exists

CO.DESIGN

McDonald's new HQ makes it look more like a wellness startup

CO.DESIGN

This new startup makes affordable outdoor furniture–out of ocean plastic

CO.DESIGN

You can paint like Van Gogh using MoMA's wild new crayons

WORK LIFE

5 ways to give yourself more time when it feels like there's never enough

WORK LIFE

This is the one simple act that helps me be more creative

WORK LIFE

Why you need unlike-minded people on your team (and 3 ways to get them)

SCROLL 05

vage (detail) 2010 by Anne de Vries and Emmeline de Mooij

What might this be?

Amelia Groom

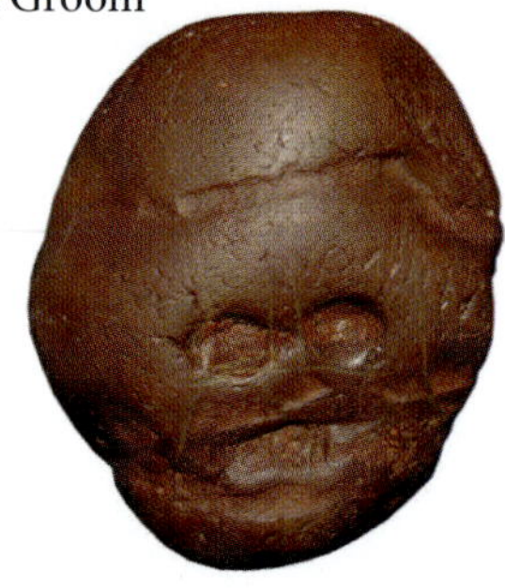

This is the Makapansgat Pebble. It's a rock, with a face, and a name. It was found in the Makapan Valley in South Africa in 1925, in a cave that was inhabited by a now-extinct hominid ancestor of the human species, Australopithecus africanus, two or three million years ago. We know that the pebble's eyes and mouth were carved out by running water and neighbouring pebbles in a riverbed, rather than by hands. So it's an image that was forged without any human-like invention or intention. But the cave where it was left is many miles away from any possible natural source, so paleo-anthropologists have speculated that it was picked up and transported, by someone who recognised the chance appearance of a face looking back.

The Natural History Museum in London identifies the Makapansgat Pebble as "perhaps the most ancient art object in the world." The implication here is that it wasn't art when it was sitting unnoticed in the river—but when it was pointed to, when it was picked out and displaced, it moved into the realm of artistry. If we accept this, we can say that art doesn't begin with an act of creating something out of nothing, but with a moment of recognition that is actually a misrecognition: seeing a face where it isn't, perceiving things as they aren't. It isn't inventing something new from scratch; it's responding to what is already present, and treating it as something else. I want to read into this capacity (or necessity) we have for reading into things. What does it mean that we can perceive more than what's actually there? How much does all language—and all thinking and all meaning-making— depend on our ability to apprehend one thing in another thing? To what extent does perception always bring projective baggage along with it? What are the dangers and predicaments involved with the interpretative projections of our perceptions? And how might they be developed as part of critical engagement? Given that every critique of present conditions depends on the basic premise that reality could be otherwise, how can active misrecognition be deployed as a deliberately disobedient mode of looking, where we nurture our capacity to see beyond what it is that we are supposed to see?

In her essay On Being Ill, a bed-bound Virginia Woolf is looking up at the sky and watching its incessant inventions. "This then has been going on all this time without our knowing it!" she remarks, shocked by the endless array of shapes and scenarios performed by the clouds. "Someone should write to The Times about it," she decides. "One should not let this gigantic cinema play perpetually to an empty house."1 There are two factors contributing to her experiencing the sky's imagery as if for the first time. One is that she has to remain supine, for an extended duration, giving her body a spatial and temporal orientation towards the sky, which is something that isn't granted to those upright bodies rushing about the city streets. The second contributing factor is the dis-orientation of illness; this is a text about the warped but enhanced sensitivity that can be brought on when we are unwell. Woolf writes of the "mystic quality" that words can come to possess when language is rendered incomprehensible; as when feverish or otherwise delirious states take us to the edges of meaning, where other meanings might emerge.2

Hallucination can be a tricky thing to ascertain the boundaries of, as it will often arise from a combination of external reality with internal processing, and it can overlap with simple misperception. But the perceptual disturbances and persecutory delusions that can be experienced with psychosis or schizophrenia, for example, are largely beyond the bounds of what I want to consider in this text. There are psychological conditions in which hallucinations are involuntary and harrowing (Woolf wrote in her suicide note of the intolerability of beginning to hear voices again)—and then there are much more general experiences of mis-reading or actively over-reading an external stimulus, such as when we 'see' faces or animals in the clouds. We might be especially attuned to this sort of over-reading of random details when we are in particular states (when we're feverish, when we're on psychedelics, when we're children, when we're sleep deprived, when we're socially anxious)—but we also do it all the time, because perception involves not only the passive reception of external stimulus but also aspects of our own memories and anticipations. To some degree, it is always interpretative and imaginative.

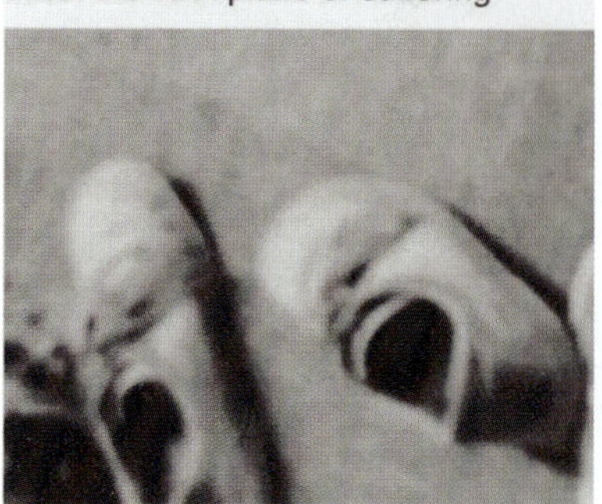

The word 'pareidolia' has come to be used for forms that appear to us in places where they were not intentionally inscribed. Some of my personal favourites include: the profile of Mahatma Gandhi that was spotted on the surface of Mars; the partially eaten, decade-old toasted cheese sandwich said to bear an image of the Virgin Mary, which sold on eBay for US $28,000 in 2004; the Mother Theresa cinnamon bun; the chicken nugget that looks like George Washington; the house that looks like Hitler; the videos on YouTube showing Vladimir Putin's face momentarily appear out of a flock of birds flying over New York City. Whether attributed to human hoax, natural accident, or some divine or paranormal force, all of these allegedly unauthored images

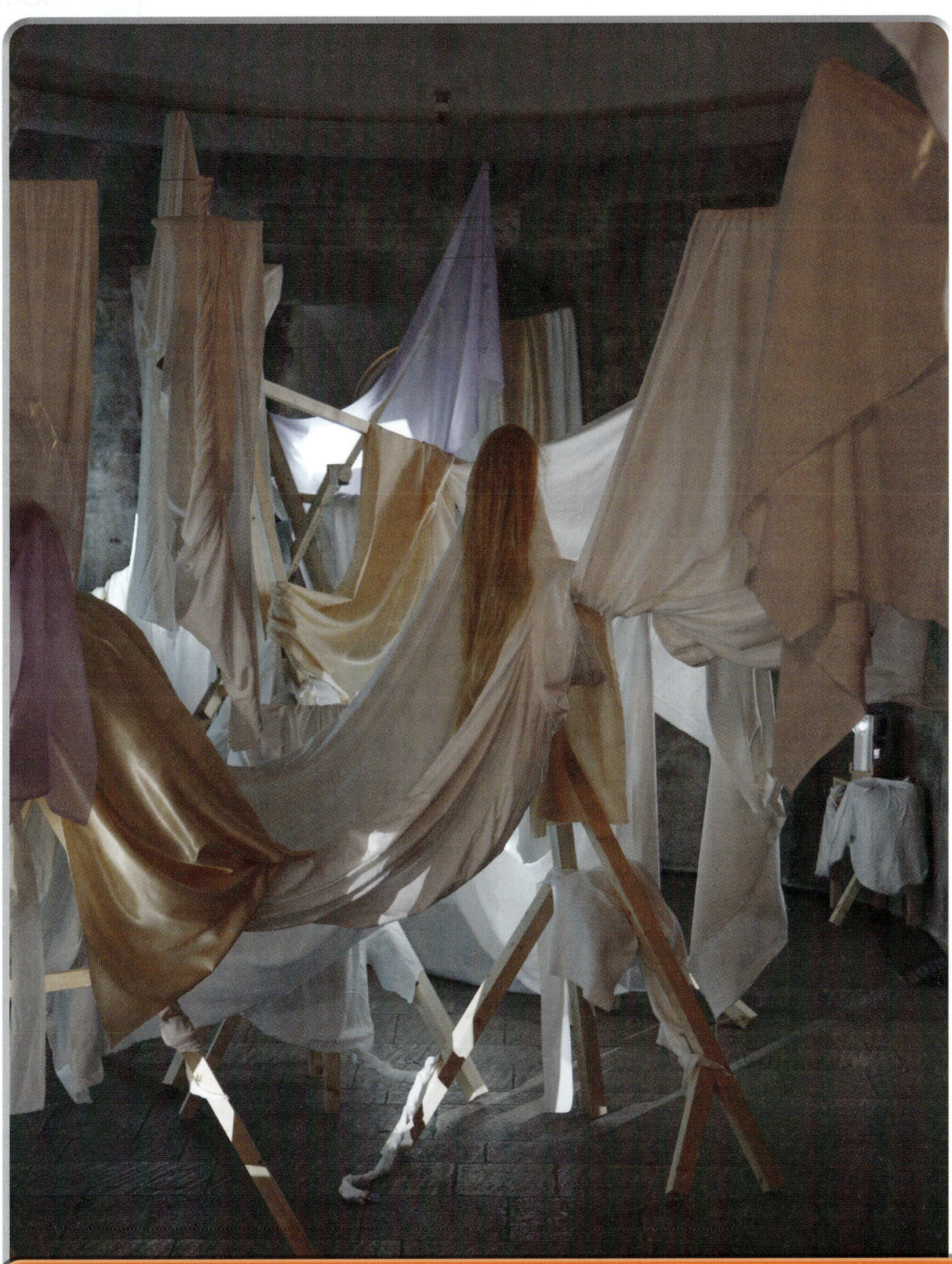

Rivage d' Ectoplasmes (detail) 2010, projections, textile, wood, synthetic body parts, men's chorus

Installation and performance by Anne de Vries and Emmeline de Mooij

can complicate distinctions between design and chance; real and imagined; made and found—reminding us that meaning isn't something fixed inside the object of observation, but something that emerges from the attentive encounter with it.
'Pareidolia' comes from the Greek roots para for 'beyond' and eidon for 'image'—suggesting images beyond images, appearances in excess of themselves. And pareidolic vision is something that can be actively applied, as a way to train the imagination. In his Treatise on Painting, for instance, Leonardo da Vinci told his disciples to look at stains and smudges on dirty walls, or random patterns in rock formations, and to discover in them all sorts of fantastic imagery, such as mountainous landscapes, detailed battle scenes, strange costumes and monstrous faces. Through contemplation of the clouds, or the mud, or the ashes from the fire, he promised, one could "bring out the genius" from "the jumble of things."
This sort of seeing beyond the image or seeing the image beyond has also been at work in the more wide-spread practices of divination, fortune telling, scrying and the like. One of the most ancient and far-reaching of these practices is tessaeography, the reading of tea leaves or coffee or wine sediments left in cups. But there are countless other techniques, including, for instance, meilomancy (divination by moles), odontomancy (divination by teeth), amathomancy (divination by patterns in dust, dirt, sand or ashes), ornithomancy (divination by birds), capnomancy (divination by smoke), uromancy (divination by urine), urticariaomancy (divination by itches), tyromancy (divination by cheese), macharomancy (divination by swords or knives), driromancy (divination by dripping blood) and styramancy(divination by the reading of patterns left in chewing gum). All of these methods rely on the active and projective nature of perception, and affirm that with the right attunement of attention, anything can be read.
In the early twentieth century, the capacity we have to see things as they aren't would become the basis of Swiss psychoanalyst Hermann Rorschach's inkblot test, where subjects are asked to describe/ interpret what they see in a series of cards showing abstract blots of ink. Butterflies, masks, animal hides and vulvas are some of the things test subjects most often 'recognise' in the symmetrical blots, but each of the cards was conceived as a site of productive ambiguity. The pictures are effective only insofar as they carry no intended, or intrinsic, or universally agreed-upon, meaning—and can thus catch whatever is projected onto them. "What might this be?" is the question the analyst is supposed to ask the subject upon presentation of each new meaningless inkblot. Not "what is this?", but "what might it be?" Besides seeing some ink blotted on a page, what else can you apprehend?
Pareidolic vision is related to the more general phenomenon known as 'apophenia', which is the (not necessarily optical) perception of meanings or connections in random configurations. And like the Rorschach Technique, the neologisms 'apophenia' and 'pareidolia' both come out of modern psychology—particularly from the study and diagnosis of schizophrenia. But, as we have seen, the relevance of the pareidolic principal is much older and much broader than the pinpointing of the pathologised individual of western modernity. 'Seeing' always involves some degree of 'reading', and, as Marina Warner has observed, the Rorschach Technique can be understood as simply a scientisation of the existing divination methods that were based on the interpretation of seemingly random data which has no essential or universally accessible significance.3

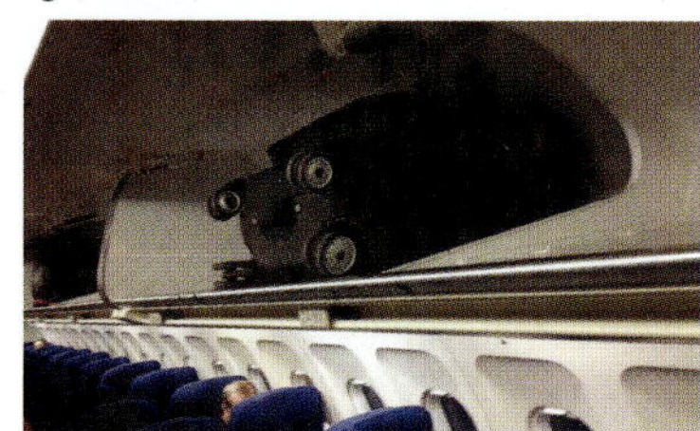

In an inkblot test, pareidolic perception is supposed to go in both directions, with the subject reading into the shapes and arrangements in order to see more than just ink on the surface of a page—and the analyst then reading into the subject's responses, interpreting the interpretations in order to access more than just what is consciously presented at a surface level by the subject. In fact, psychoanalysis—as a practice and as a discourse—has always been thoroughly apophenic. We can think here of Freud's interpretations of dream images, where we are told that all weapons, tools, machines, umbrellas, neckties and nail-files are actually penises—as are mountains, women's hats, children, lizards and younger brothers.4 We can also think of the Jungian principle of synchronicity, where causally disconnected events are to be read as nonetheless meaningfully related to each other. In a psychoanalytic session, the shrink is supposed to be attentive to otherwise overlooked minor details, and to the links that can be drawn between them. She reads into what seems to be random, and doesn't allow for things to be taken as arbitrary.
This mode of reading where the insignificant is made to signify is also clearly indispensable to the building of paranoic conspiracy theories—and indeed, in the same text where Freud infamously forms a dubious causal link between paranoia and repressed homosexuality, he also articulates his notion of paranoia as a model for psychoanalytic theorizing itself. Later, Paul Ricœur would put Freud in the company of Marx and Nietzsche as the three "masters of suspicion,"5 whose work would usher in what Ricœur identified as a modern school of hermeneutics, wherein the interpreter is suspicious of the intended, established, or immediately legible meanings of things, and looks instead for what else those things might mean—and for what they might exclude or cover up.
One critical project where a conspiratorial imaginary has succeeded with a correct and crucial diagnosis of a previously unnamed condition is feminism, which has long been geared towards apprehending and describing patriarchy as a sprawling system which organises and permeates all aspects of reality, but which could otherwise go undetected in its vastness. This is a point observed by Sianne Ngai in her article Bad Timing (A Sequel): Paranoia, Feminism,

and Poetry, in which she looks at reclaiming and reformulating paranoia as a tool for explicitly feminist thought and cultural production. As Ngai writes, terms like 'patriarchy' and 'patriarchy-capitalism,' "which refer to monolithic, yet amorphously-delimited and fundamentally abstract, value-based systems," remain indispensable for critical languages that are able to grapple with the realities of our contemporary condition.[6] Ngai posits that the paranoic-conspiratorial mode is particularly adept at zooming out from one historical trajectory and looking at what else we can see happening at the same time. This is a maneuver that can be extremely revealing not just for critical intervention in late capitalist culture but also as part of a historical methodology, as in Silvia Federici's book Caliban and the Witch, where she shows how completely intertwined the history of witch-hunting in Europe is with the simultaneous implementation of capitalist structures in the transition away from feudalism. This was a seriously under-acknowledged correlation, which Federici draws out in convincing detail through appropriately applied suspicion, an attunement to the 'bigger picture', and rigorous pattern recognition.[7]

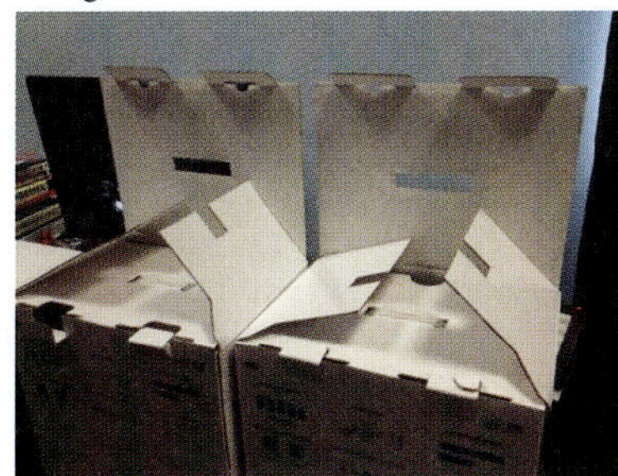

But, as productive as these paranoic modes of seeking and organising knowledge can be, the instances where the conspiracy theories match up with the actual conspiracies are rare, and the field is rife with reactionary politics. As several writers on the topic of paranoia in political discourse have observed, it can be claimed just as easily by the right as by the left.[8] Suspicion can be appropriately directed towards ruling class ideology, for instance, but suspicion can also be deeply xenophobic. It depends on who's using it and what their leanings and motivations are—and in particular on whether they're up for real structural critique, or whether they're simply on the hunt for individual monsters to scapegoat. As Karl Popper observed in his 1945 book The Open Society and Its Enemies, conspiracy theories have often tended to emerge where fear-based tribalist and nationalist mythologies take hold.[9] Quite apart from marking a healthy questioning of the official narratives or a non-acceptance of that which hegemony wants us to believe, the conspiracy theorist's insistence that every little detail is part of some greater plot—with an invisible but omniscient power working from above—can actually have the same pacifying effect as religious structures: the fatalism negates any individual or worldly responsibility. If the powers-that-be are so immense and overarching, and the outcomes so assured, there's not much that we down here could do to go off-script. If you've spent any time dipping into online conspiracy-theory rabbit holes you will have seen how quickly things can turn very ugly—like when they suddenly start replicating old-school antisemitism, only thinly veiled if at all. Perhaps without the conspiracy theorists always being aware of it, many of their tropes come straight out of The Protocols of the Elders of Zion—except that instead of saying 'the Jews' they might say 'the Illuminati' or 'the New World Order' or 'the Lizard People'. Part of what these theories do is relieve their adherents of the burden of doing any actual structural critique: to believe that one evil Jewish family controls all institutions and secretly runs the world, for instance, would be to never have to grapple with actual historical forces and the intersections of real structural inequalities—let alone to try to deal with the ways in which one may also be implicated in those forces and structures.

And apart from conspiracy theories that offer all-encompassing accounts of reality, there are also the dangers of pareidolic misapprehension when it is paired with bigoted prejudice at the level of individual encounters. Think, for instance, of the sort of pareidolia that is at work when a US police officer who has shot yet another unarmed black man stands up in a court of law and claims innocence, on the grounds that they thought they had detected something suspicious—that they thought they had seen a weapon in what turned out to be a wallet, or a cell phone, or a sandwich. Part of what we have to deal with here is the effects of an uneven distribution of suspicion. When certain bodies are seen as already suspect and out-of-place, just walking to the grocery store, at night, in a gated community, is enough for an unarmed black teenager like Trayvon Martin to be shot dead by a neighbourhood watch volunteer operating under the dubious authority of suspicion—and for that suspicion to count as legitimate grounds for their acquittal. Racism can be thought of as a type of pareidolia; a perceptive mode that carries a lot of projective baggage—and, evidently, it can also be a justification for murder ("I'm not really a killer, it's just that my racism led me to misread the situation").

On a structural level, it is also necessary to think about the extent to which the field of the visible is itself racially produced and ordered—so that a racist disposition of visibility can determine not only what appears but also what doesn't appear. In the infamous case of the Rodney King trial, for example, the white jurors had been unable to 'see' what for so many had appeared self-evident in the video footage, which shows King motionless on the ground as he is brutally beaten by a group of policemen and their batons. Writing in the wake of that trial, Judith Butler considered what she termed the "saturation and schematisation of the visual field with the inverted projections of white paranoia," wherein the image of a black male body being repeatedly beaten by policemen standing over him can become evidence that the man had in fact been a danger to the police, who were his vulnerable victims. Importantly, Butler observes, the jurors didn't fail to recognise the brutality because they ignored the video, but because the video was framed within a racially structured field of visibility. While the prosecutors had presented the footage as if it 'spoke for itself', the defense attorneys had performed interpretative manipulation, deliberately cultivating the white paranoia that

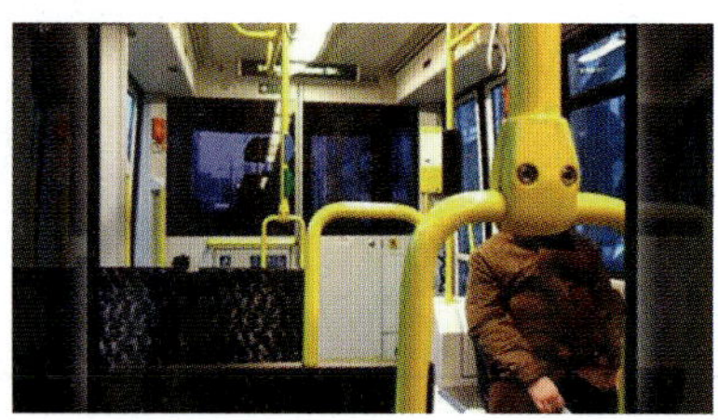

would read King's body as threatening—and thereby reminding us that within a racialised episteme, the visible cannot be taken for granted as evidence.10

So as we've seen, suspicious over-reading can be applied to oppressive systems in ways that can help us to better identify their inner workings— but suspicious over-reading can also be found operating at the cores of those systems, and emerging in their symptoms. Besides white paranoia, we might also think of the paranoic tendencies of super wealthy one percenters, or of so many despots throughout history. In Italo Calvino's short story A King Listens, we meet a ruler who sits alone on his throne, unable to move for fear that someone else will take his place.11 With his dungeons filled with suspected supporters of the previous, deposed sovereign, the king's constituted power amounts to a totally rigidified isolation, where all he can do is try to listen to what he thinks he might be able to hear. Is that the whispering of plots being made against him? Does that silence mean his guards have been captured by enemy conspirators? Are those trumpets being blown to honour him, or has he been left here, forgotten, while someone else has taken power? The story doesn't invite us to pity the king for his privilege, but it shows us that at the very core of an abusive authority is this pathetic and desperate fragility, which generates all sorts of pareidoilic flights of fancy.

There's another very fearful and isolated paranoic male subject in Vladimir Nabokov's short story Symbols and Signs.12 A young man has been diagnosed with a medical condition called 'referential mania', which means that he imagines everything around him is a veiled reference to his own existence:
Clouds in the staring sky transmit to each other, by means of slow signs, incredibly detailed information regarding him. His inmost thoughts are discussed at nightfall, in manual alphabet, by darkly gesticulating trees. Pebbles or stains or sun flecks form patterns representing, in some awful way, messages that he must intercept. Everything is a cipher and of everything he is the theme. [...] He must be always on his guard and devote every minute and module of life to the decoding of the undulation of things. Here, the paranoic-pareidolic mode is one of extreme, harrowing solipsism. On the one hand, the man has this wonderfully imaginative heightened sensitivity to the details of his surrounds. But then the richness of the world is collapsed into the rigid isolation of the single self at the centre of a single story. This sort of vanity is often at play in conspiratorial imaginaries, where the centralised theorist is alone with his privileged insight, decoding all that everyone else is blind to. He's incapable of recognising the other as an other, and his intolerance of uncertainty means that any detail is made into proof of whatever it is that he thinks he knows.
One important critic of critical theory's continued attachment to paranoic modes was the queer theorist Eve Kosofsky Sedgwick—and the title of her text You're So Paranoid, You Probably Think This Essay Is About You tells us that paranoia is so close to vanity that the two words can be interchangeable.13 Writing in the late 1990s, Sedgwick wants to introduce some doubt around paranoic criticality's emphasis on unveiling purportedly hidden systems of structural violence. While there is plenty of invisibilised violence that requires exposure, she writes, there is also a lot that is intended as hypervisible from the outset. "What does a hermeneutics of suspicion and exposure have to say to social formations in which visibility itself constitutes much of the violence?" she asks. With violence that is not a scandalous secret but a pointedly addressed exemplary spectacle—violence that is stage managed as a public warning—what is required is not so much a triumphalist unveiling as a restructured framework of visibility.
Sedgwick is also suspicious of the rigidified temporality that the paranoic hermeneutics of suspicion has tended towards. In her formulation, paranoia is future-oriented and anticipatory, and yet it is always averse to surprise. "Because there must be no bad surprises," she writes, "and because learning of the possibility of a bad surprise would itself constitute a bad surprise, paranoia requires that bad news be always already known." This is one of the risks of conspiratorial criticality: it can get stuck in a too-easy loop where it can only prove the assumptions that it began with. To get beyond this fatalistic inevitability, Sedgwick seeks an attunement to contingency. "The dogged, defensive narrative stiffness of a paranoid temporality," as she terms it, is characterised by Oedipal regularity and repetitiveness. ("It happened to my father's father, it happened to my father, it is happening to me, it will happen to my son, and it will happen to my son's son.") But a feature of queer reading, Sedgwick reminds us, is sensitivity to the possibility that history and generational relations are not always locked into predictable patterns; that unscripted futures can arrive from the sidelines, or from below, or from unacknowledged latencies within—rather than just from further down the same straight line.
I want to stay for a moment with the image of extreme isolation that is set up in the Calvino and Nabokov stories, and is perhaps also easily conjured up by the stereotypical idea of the conspiracy theorist as a guy all alone in his bedroom, setting out to prove that everything is a lie, with one vast but alluringly comprehensive narrative. Our perspective is always situated, mediated and partial; total access to world isn't possible or desirable. In this sense, a degree of isolation and exclusion is necessary. But, the more isolated the subjectivity, the less chance there is for its projections to be challenged through supplementation or refutation. And the less the projections are challenged, the more the isolation rigidifies. Everything is turned into confirmation and further proof,

as the single projective perception subsumes all difference. One way to think about a more generous and generative pareidolia, then, would be to pluralise it. With pareidolias instead of pareidolia, we might avoid stepping into the propagandistic drive which can only replace the world with itself.

The paranoic mode is very good at establishing counter-intuitive (or hyper-intuitive) connections between things—for finding and forming relations that were previously overlooked or nonexistent. With this can come the risk of constructing 'spurious correlations', like those collected at Tyler Vigen's online archive where we can see the divorce rates in Maine going down as the amount of margarine consumption drops—or the number of people who drowned by falling into a pool each year correlating with the number of films that Nicolas Cage appeared in.[14] As the character Cayce Pollard's father (a CIA spy who has been missing since 9/11) advises in William Gibson's novel Pattern Recognition, we have to always allow room for meaningless coincidence, and not let apophenia take over completely, because the reality is inevitably far messier than a seductively symmetrical pattern might have us believe.[15] But being able to grapple with the relations between things, and not just see them in static isolation, is a skill that is crucial to creative and critical engagement. We can admire the creativity of the conspiracy theorist in the same way that we might admire the creativity of the jealous lover, where the mixture of resent, suspicion, alertness and anticipation can produce incredibly elaborate narratives.

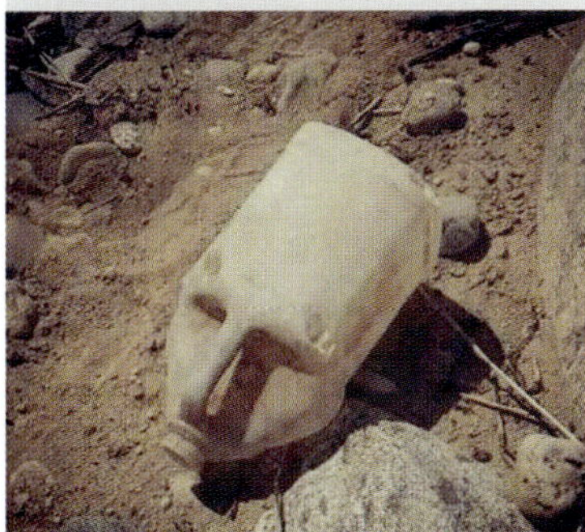
Ancient skull found on archaeological dig is proof of our alien origins.

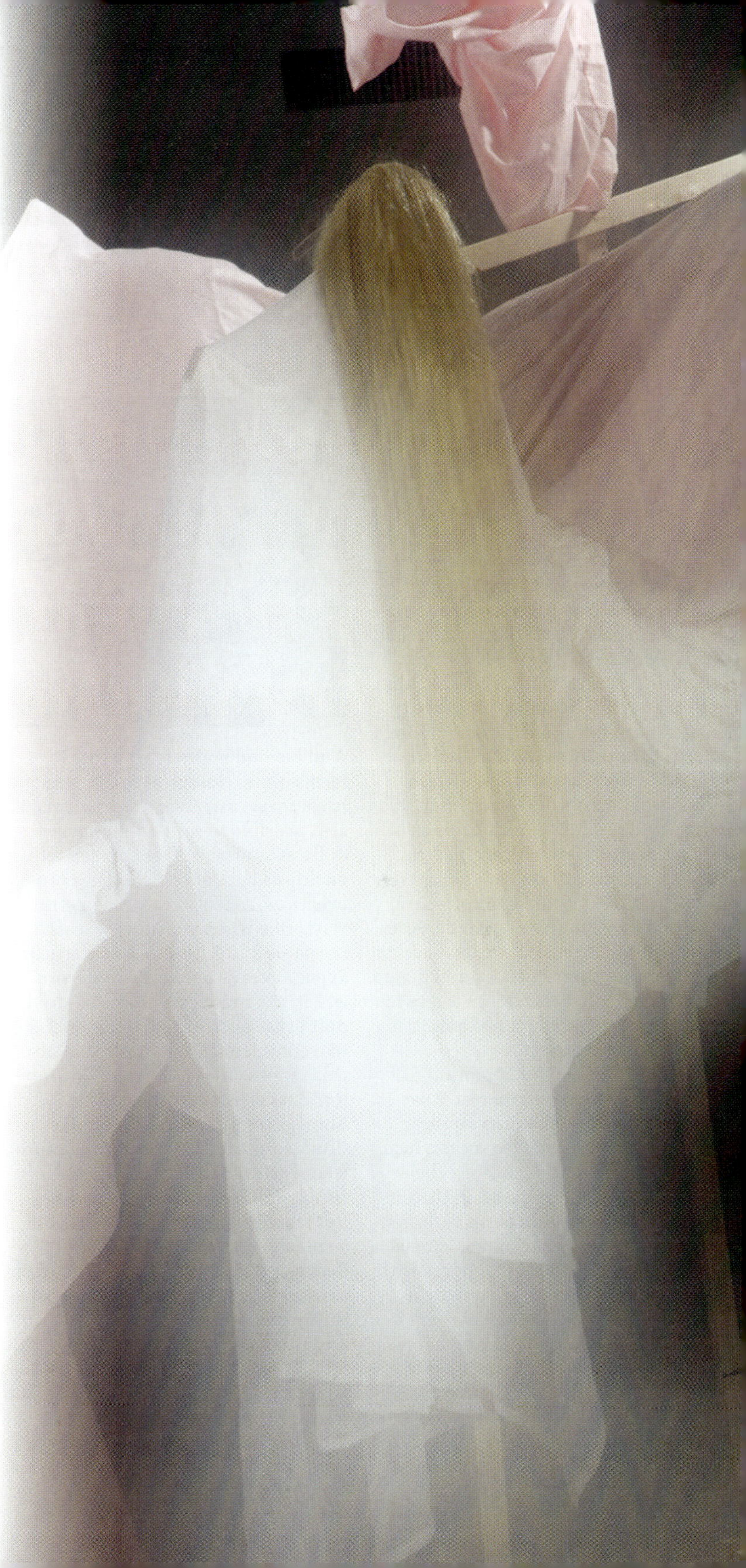

It's a mode of attentiveness characterised by quick conceptual leaps and an ability to build whole worlds out of small fragmentary details. The stuff of all good story-telling!

Let's return now to our Stone Age selfie, the Makapansgat Pebble. One way to read (into) this early sign of projective perception in the heritage of humanity (reading with the knowledge that our perception—coming from a distance of several million years—inevitably also involves a lot of projection) would be to think about narcissism. Like Narcissus drawn by his own reflection in the water, we pulled this rock out of the river because we saw ourselves in it. Or perhaps we see it seeing itself in us? Rather than approach this only in terms of our self-centredness and our cognitive and cultural biases (wherein we can only recognise that which is already familiar to us), what if the Makapansgat Pebble allowed us to also think about things like distributed selfhood, inter-subjectivity, and radical humility? By resembling us, it decentralises us. It tells us that selfhood is always strange, always enmeshed with world—and that the world is one in which geological forces participate in image-making, and rivers can also write. There's such a thing as anthropomorphism (insofar as we do have located bodies, with specificities, and we don't access the world from a neutral, unmediated everywhere), but this doesn't have to lead us into the violence of narcissistic anthropocentrism.

Once you start paying attention to pareidolia, a pattern you recognise is that in the vast majority of these beyond-images, what we see is a face. Faces in wood grains, in splotches and spillages, in suitcases, in the furniture, in popcorn, in foam running down the sides of half-drank glasses of beer, in cut-open bell peppers with seeds for teeth—and, of course, in rocks. This is not coincidental, it's a real pattern: faces are things that we are constantly looking to sink our attention into, and the fusiform gyrusregion of the brain makes most of us very good at reading them. We can construct whole arrays of different facial expressions out of just a few punctuation marks; and when we teach our machines facial recognition they also start to mis-recognise faces in places where they aren't. Most newborn babies quickly seek faces out from the visual field; it is suggested that at a primal level we need to look for faces because through them we form the emotional connections that ensure we will receive food—and because a face is a potential threat; a pair of eyes looking at us can mean we are about to become food.16 We see faces because we look (out) for them.

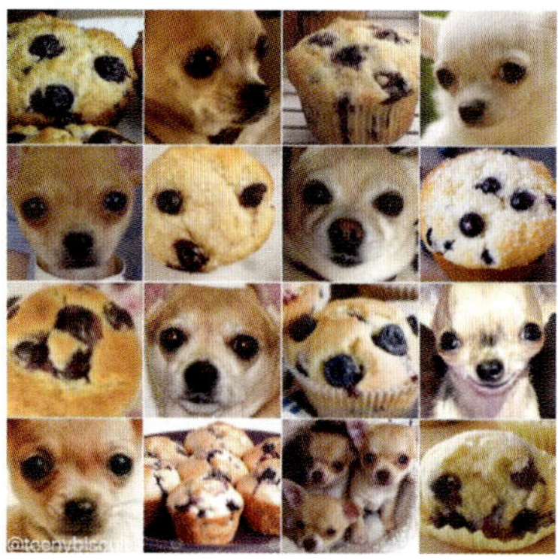

And beyond approaching this in terms of physiological innateness or involuntary survival mechanisms, it's also possible to think about pareidolia as something we can actively deploy as part of critically attentive practices. Attention works in strange ways; like when you start researching something, and then it starts to appear everywhere. The more you notice it, the more you notice it—to the point that noticing can start to feel like conjuring. Some try to explain this away as the 'frequency illusion' (or 'Baader-Meinhof phenomenon'), a cognitive bias that makes us think some detail is occurring more frequently when actually we are simply noticing it more frequently. But it's more than this, because on a collective level, what we choose to dedicate our attention to in the world can help determine what that world is like. Attention can be generative, and I think this is what the enigmatic Simone Weil was getting at when she wrote that "attention is the rarest and purest form of generosity."

We have said that pareidolia can be thought of as a mode of apprehension that is especially attuned to the feeling that things could be other than what they are. There's a utopian implication here, but I don't want to end this on a simplistically hopeful note. Artists are good at making what is out of what is not, and what is not out of what is. But the identification of untapped potential also happens to be the driving force of contemporary capitalist expansion, co-option and homogenisation. Reading patterns in new ways and apprehending unrealised possibilities: these are the domains of venture capitalists, trend forecasters, stockbrokers, gentrifying property developers, etc. The extractive drive of capitalism's present phase is such that it requires a constant stream of new images, new vocabularies, new distractions—so why feed that with our imaginative hopefulness? For better diagnosis instead of more prescriptions, how about pareidolia that operates as a reverse-utopianism: Rather than locating new potential amongst the mess of things, this would be about seeing the hopelessness in that which presents itself as hopeful. So when faced with ideas that are supposed to sound unquestionably positive and uplifting—such as 'freedom', 'flexibility', 'sharing' or 'wellness'—we recognise what is actually at stake in the normalisation of precarity and the desecration of solidarity. Seeing through the cynicism and flimsiness of neoliberal regimes of optimism, this is pareidolia in service to present tense analysis more than future-oriented hopefulness.

Two and a half million years ago, the Makapansgat Pebble returned someone's gaze. So it was picked up, out of the river, because it was recognised as potentially significant. It was picked up again later, out of an archaeological site—and it continues to be picked up out of the museum vaults, for study and contemplation, because it continues to look back at us. Two and a half million years back also happens to be around the time of the first known use of tools in human evolution, with simple stone implements used for carving food. Into this coincidence we can read the possibility that the aesthetic is not something that comes after crude bodily nourishment, as an optional addition, but rather that it's a primary component of basic survival.

'Art' is of course an anachronistic category to project on to a prehistoric specimen, because the separation of 'art' (or artifice) from 'life' (or nature) is very recent. But in order to think about this natural rock in terms of something like artistry, I like to imagine that its status as an art object begins not just with a Duchampian endowment of recontextualisation—when the individual artist reframes that which is already made—but with the socialisation of the object, when there's a collective agreement to keep it around and implement it into our story-telling. The Makapansgat Pebble has a correspondence to the body not only because it carries the resemblance of a face, but also because it happens to be just the right size to be held in the hand. This, too, is significant. It might be made without hands, but it's great for handling—perfect for being passed around the fireplace, amongst bodies who decide together what sort of stories they want told.

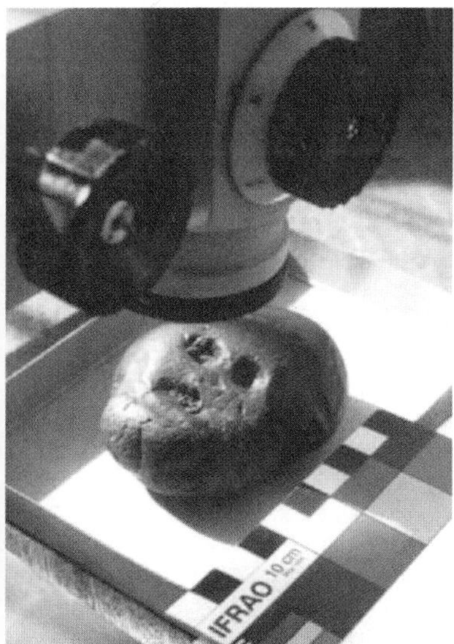

Notes:
1. Woolf, Virginia, "On Being Ill" in The New Criterion: A Quarterly Review (January 1926, Vol. IV No. 1, pp 32-45; 37).
2. Ibid; 41.
3. Warner, Maria, Phantasmagoria: Spirit Visions, Metaphors, and Media Into the Twenty-first Century(Oxford University Press, New York, 2006), p. 310.
4. Freud, Sigmund, The Interpretation of Dreams (1900).
5. Ricœur, Paul, Freud and Philosophy: An Essay on Interpretation, trans. Denis Savage (Yale University Press, New Haven and London, 1970). Referenced in Eve Kosofsky Sedgwick's "Paranoid Reading and Reparative Reading, or, You're So Paranoid, You Probably Think This Essay Is About You" in Touching Feeling: Affect, Pedagogy, Performativity (Duke University Press, USA, 2003, pp. 123-151).
6. Ngai, Sianne, "Bad Timing (A Sequel). Paranoia, Feminism, and Poetry" in d i f f e r e n c e s: A Journal of Feminist Cultural Studies (Volume 12, Number 2, Summer 2001, pp. 1-46).
7. Federici, Silvia, Caliban and the Witch: Women, The Body and Primitive Accumulation (Autonomedia, New York, 2004). Throughout this study, Federici shows that in the established narratives about what led historically to the European the witch hunts from the fifteenth to seventeenth centuries, the timing does not add up. If it really did come down to the church and to Christian anxieties about paganism, then it would have happened earlier. And it cannot just be about the scientific rationalisation of a new age that had to prohibit superstition, because simultaneous with the witch hunts, Newton and other scientific heroes were also still alchemists in dialogue with angels. If we look at what was really happening at the same time, we see the spread of rural capitalism, which meant "land expropriation, the deepening of social distances, the breakdown of collective relations," and in Federici's reading this is the real background of the witch-hunts. She develops this historical argument with very site-specific analysis, as in passages like this one (p 171):
It is significant that, in England, most of the witch trials occurred in Essex, where by the 16th century the bulk of the land had been enclosed, while in those regions of the British Isles where land privatization had neither occurred nor was on the agenda we have no record of witch-hunting. The most outstanding examples in this context are Ireland and the Scottish Western Highlands, where no trace can be found of the persecution, likely because a collective land-tenure system and kinship ties still prevailed in both areas that precluded the communal divisions and the type of complicity with the state that made a witch-hunt possible. Thus — while in the Anglicized and privatized Scottish Lowlands, where the subsistence economy was vanishing under the impact of the Presbyterian Reformation, the witch-hunt claimed at least 4,000 victims, the equivalent of one percent of the female population — in the Highlands and in Ireland, women were safe during the witch-burning times.
8. See for example: Ngai, Sianne, (Op. Cit.); Melley, Timothy, Empire of Conspiracy: The Culture of Paranoia in Postwar America (Ithaca: Cornell UP, 2000); Hofstadter, Richard, The Paranoid Style in American Politics (Harpers, 1964).
9. Popper, Karl, The Open Society and Its Enemies(Princeton University Press, Princeton and Oxford, 1994).
10. Butler, Judith, "Endangered/Endangering: Schematic Racism and White Paranoia" in Reading Rodney King/Reading Urban Uprising, ed, Robert Gooding-Williams (Routledge, New York, 1993, pp. 15-22).
11. Calvino, Italo, "A King Listens" in Under the Jaguar Sun (Penguin, UK, 2013).
12. Nabokov, Vladimir, "Symbols and Signs" (The New Yorker, May 15 1948).
13. Sedgwick, Eve Kosofsky, "Paranoid Reading" (Op. Cit.).
14. See: www.tylervigen.com
15. Gibson, William, Pattern Recognition (Penguin, New York, 2003).
16. In his book Faces in the Clouds, the cultural anthropologist Stewart Elliott Gutherie proposed that our tendency to anthropomorphise or otherwise animate inanimate things arises initially as a survival mechanism: it's safer to misperceive a boulder as a bear than it is to misperceive a bear as a boulder. Guthrie, Stewart Elliott, Faces in the Clouds (Oxford University Press, 1995).

Author: Amelia Groom, First published: De Appel, Amsterdam, for the 2 UNLIMITED exhibition. Many of these ideas were developed for a seminar on pareidolia and paranoia, Year: 2018

SUBMISSION

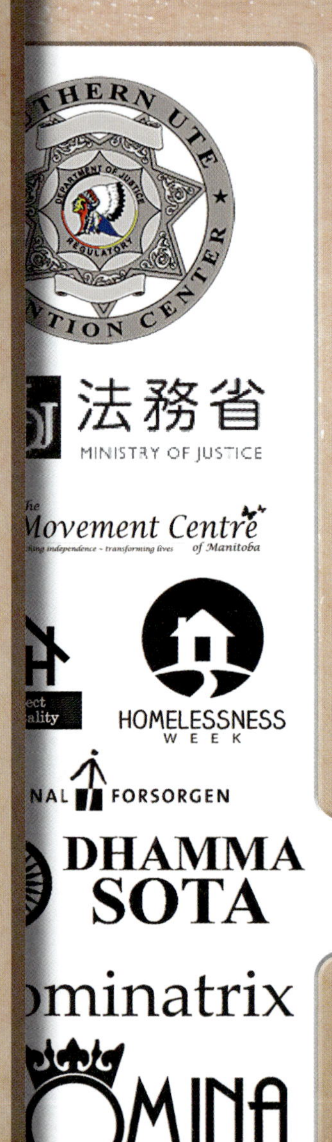

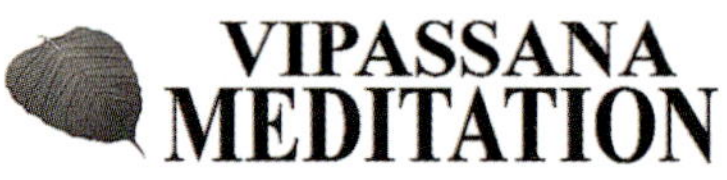

AI GPT-2 RESPONSE

In the case of Kailash Kannan's father, the name that is commonly accepted by the media is "Takumi". It could probably be an English surname. He is in a foreign country. This foreigner may be residing there. It is not known who is in that place at the moment. We would suggest that we are missing a contact in the area who can answer this question. (Note: this answer appears in the same column as the first question)

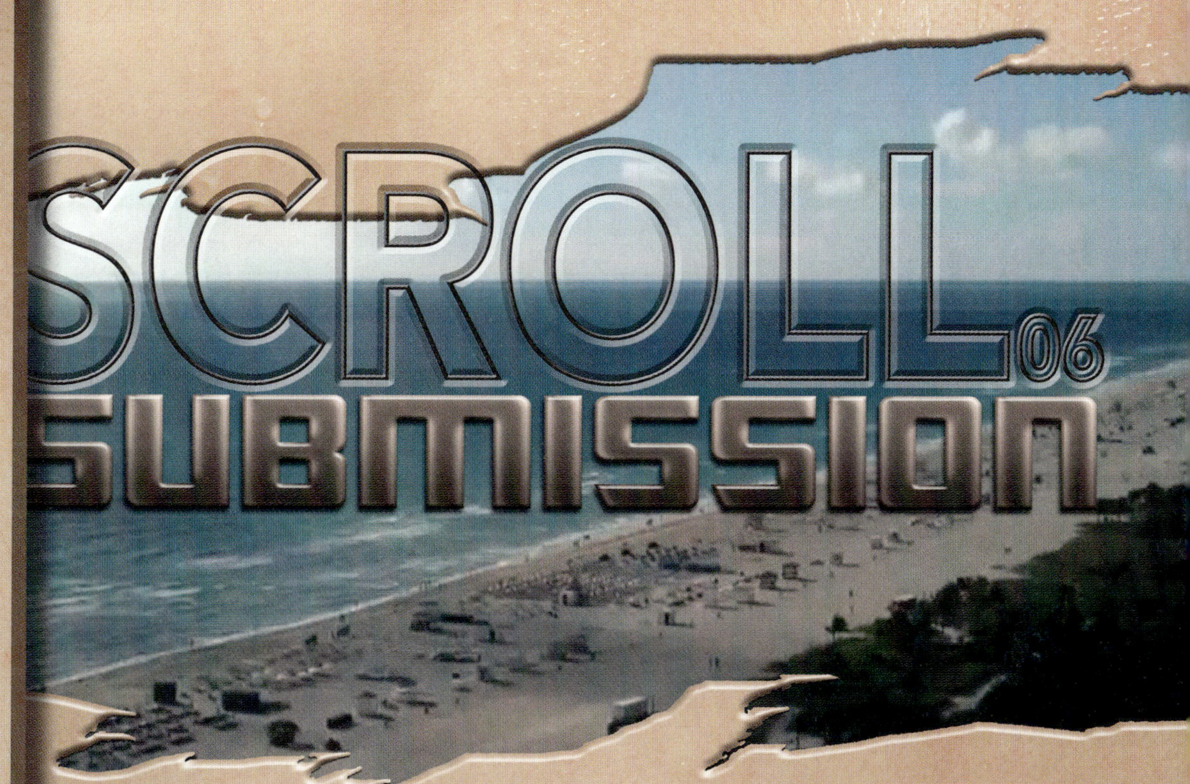
SCROLL 06
SUBMISSION

SUBMISSION

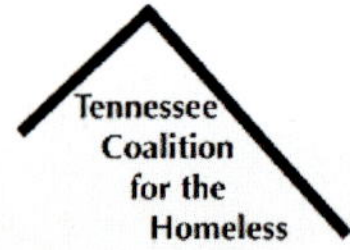

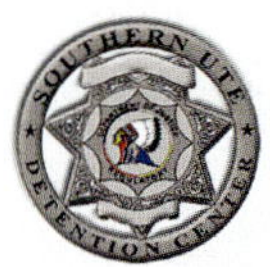

Excerpt from phone conversations as part of the installation: SUBMISSION by Anne de Vries

1: Maybe somebody is still coming.

A: Hello

B: Hello

A: Is this Domina, -No ?

C: Is this in San Paulo ?

Domina ?

B: Si si

Hello

A: Somebody there ?

C: hallo ?

A: I guess nobody is here

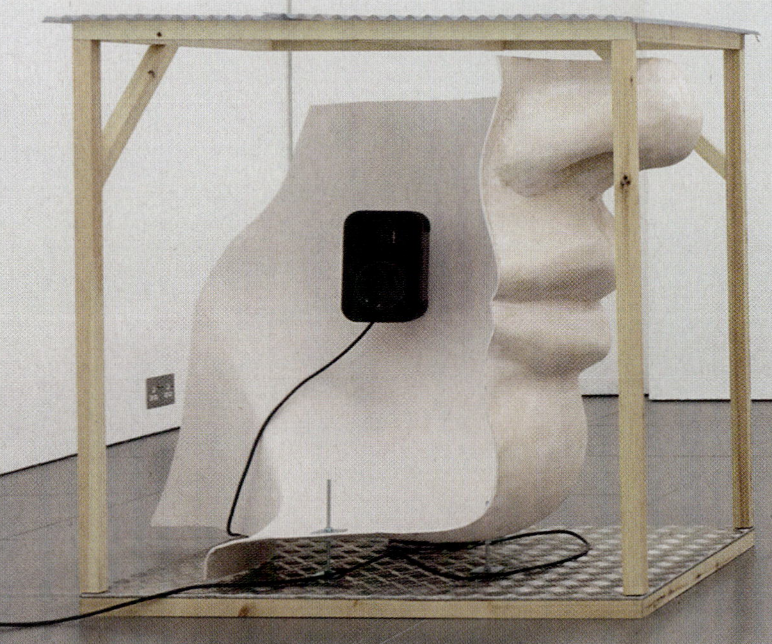

SUBMISSION 2015, dimensions variable, 4 channel recorded audio phone conversation over au

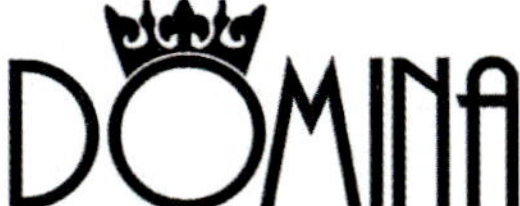

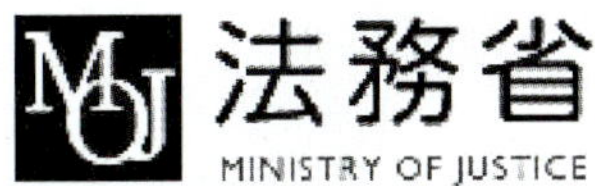

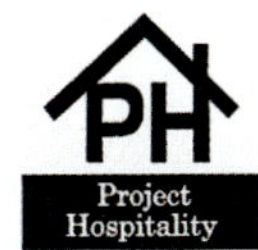

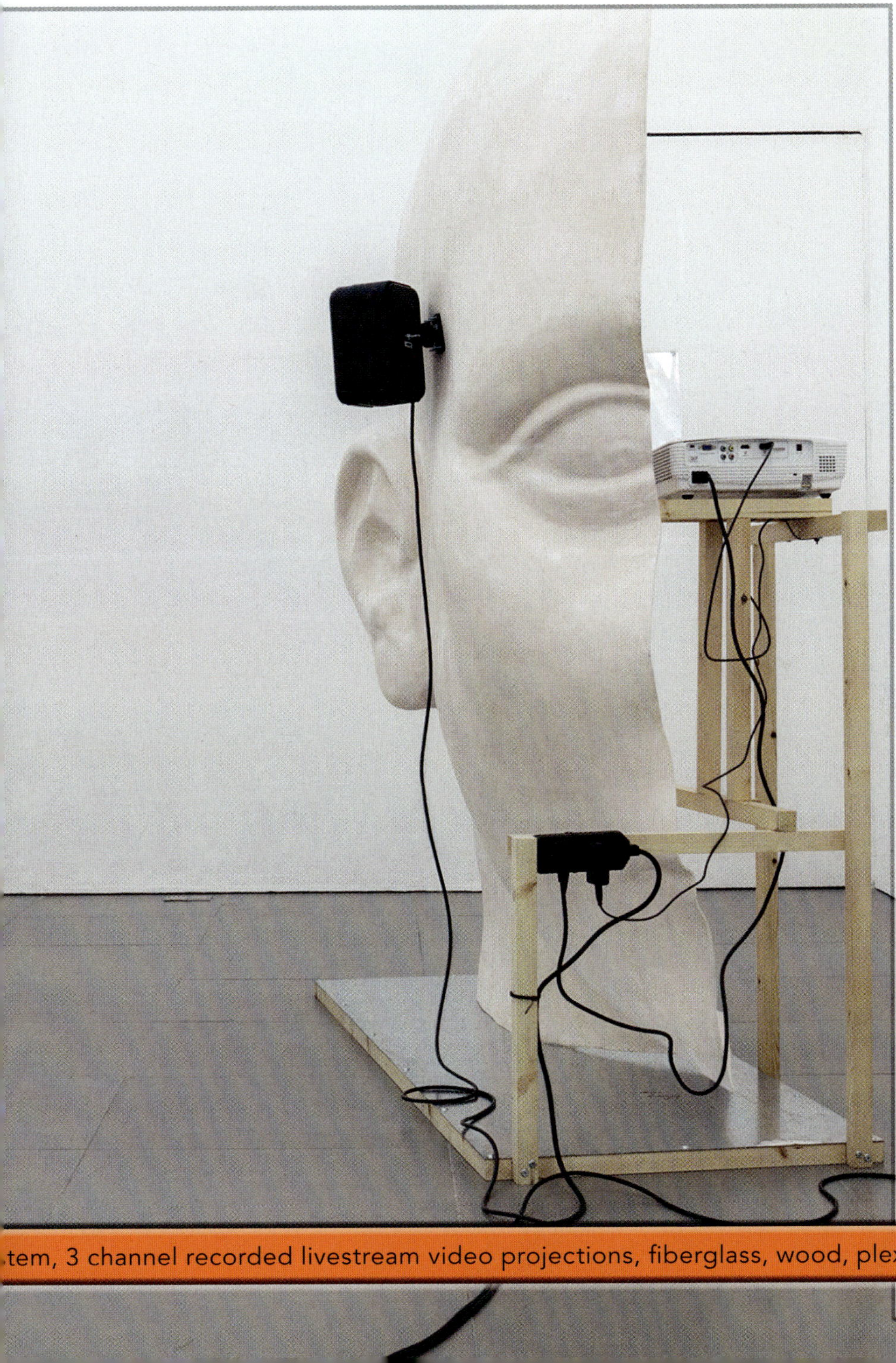

B: Hi,

Okay what you need to do is register a profile.

A: okay
C: ya

B: we will send you a link...
and you fill in your profile and then we send you an invitation.

A: ah okay, that's how it works.

B: Once you have the invitation..
you come and they give you an introduction which means they give you the rules of the club and tour to show what each room is for.

This will take about 45 min

tem, 3 channel recorded livestream video projections, fiberglass, wood, plexiglass

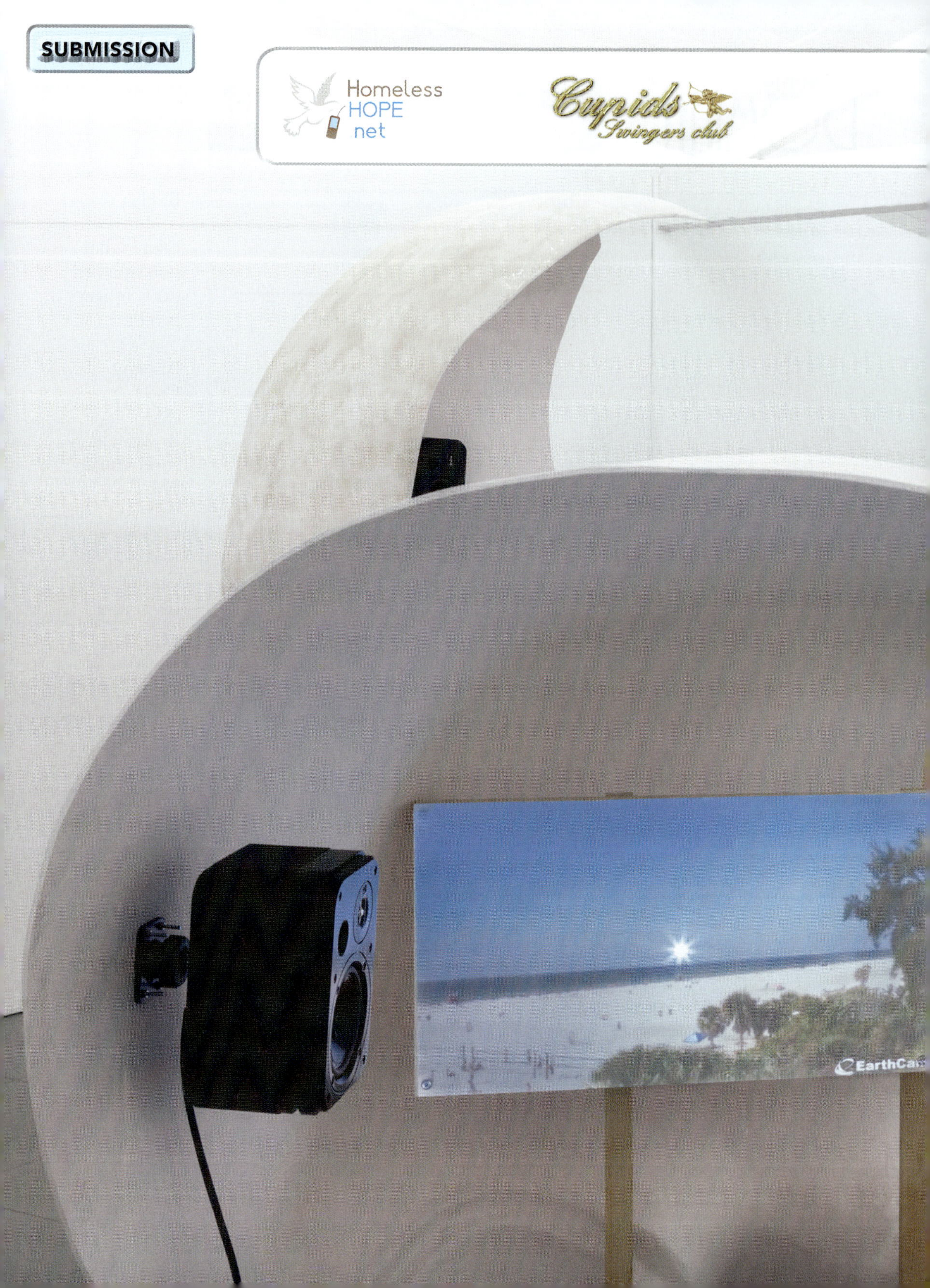

SUBMISSION

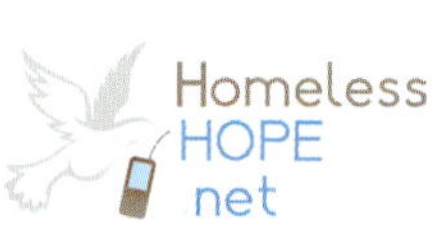

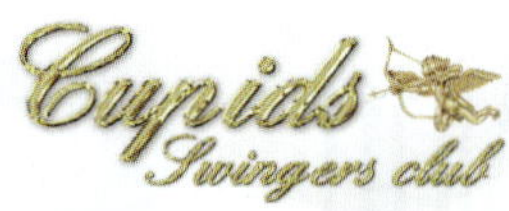

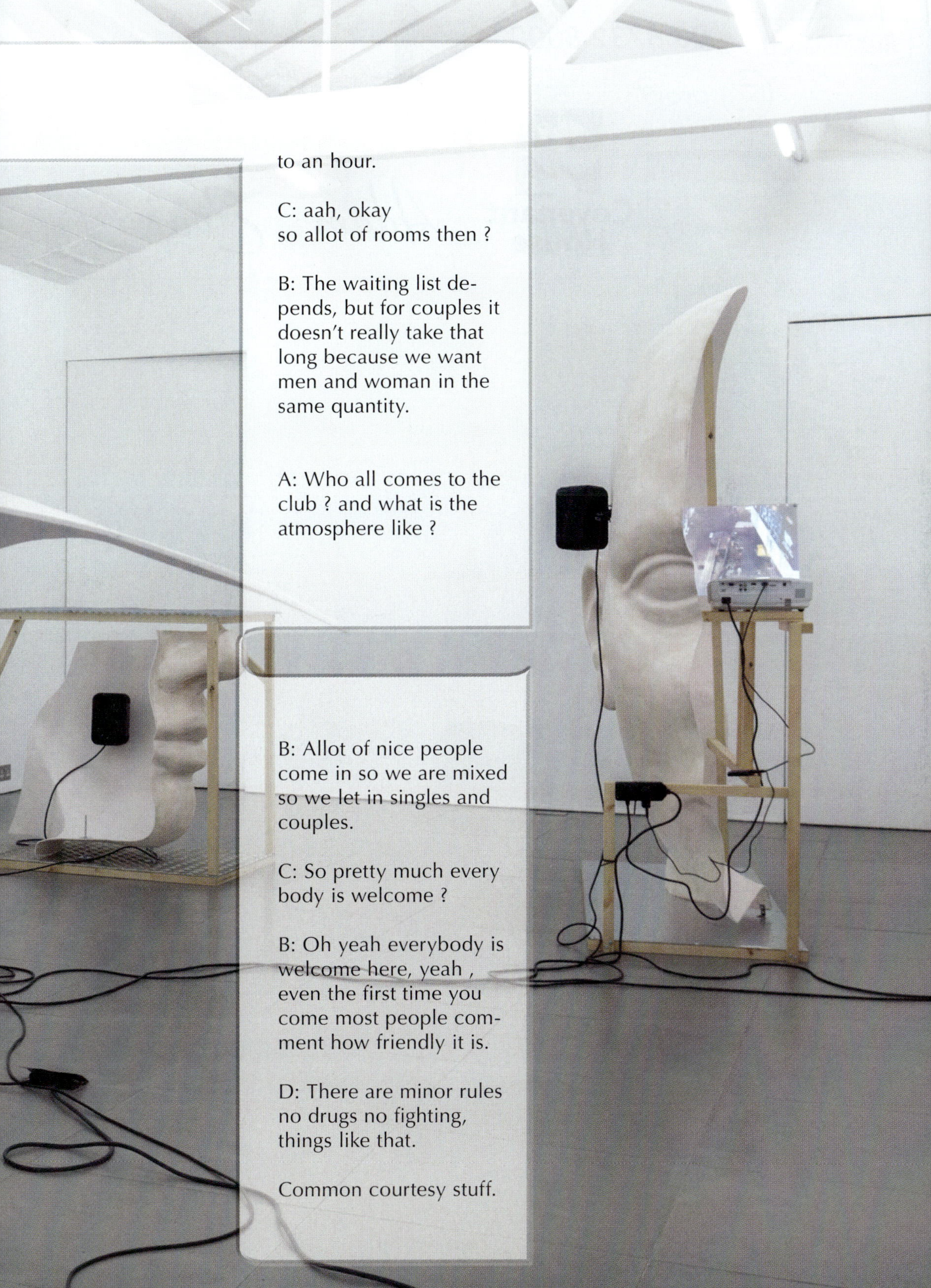

to an hour.

C: aah, okay
so allot of rooms then ?

B: The waiting list depends, but for couples it doesn't really take that long because we want men and woman in the same quantity.

A: Who all comes to the club ? and what is the atmosphere like ?

B: Allot of nice people come in so we are mixed so we let in singles and couples.

C: So pretty much every body is welcome ?

B: Oh yeah everybody is welcome here, yeah , even the first time you come most people comment how friendly it is.

D: There are minor rules no drugs no fighting, things like that.

Common courtesy stuff.

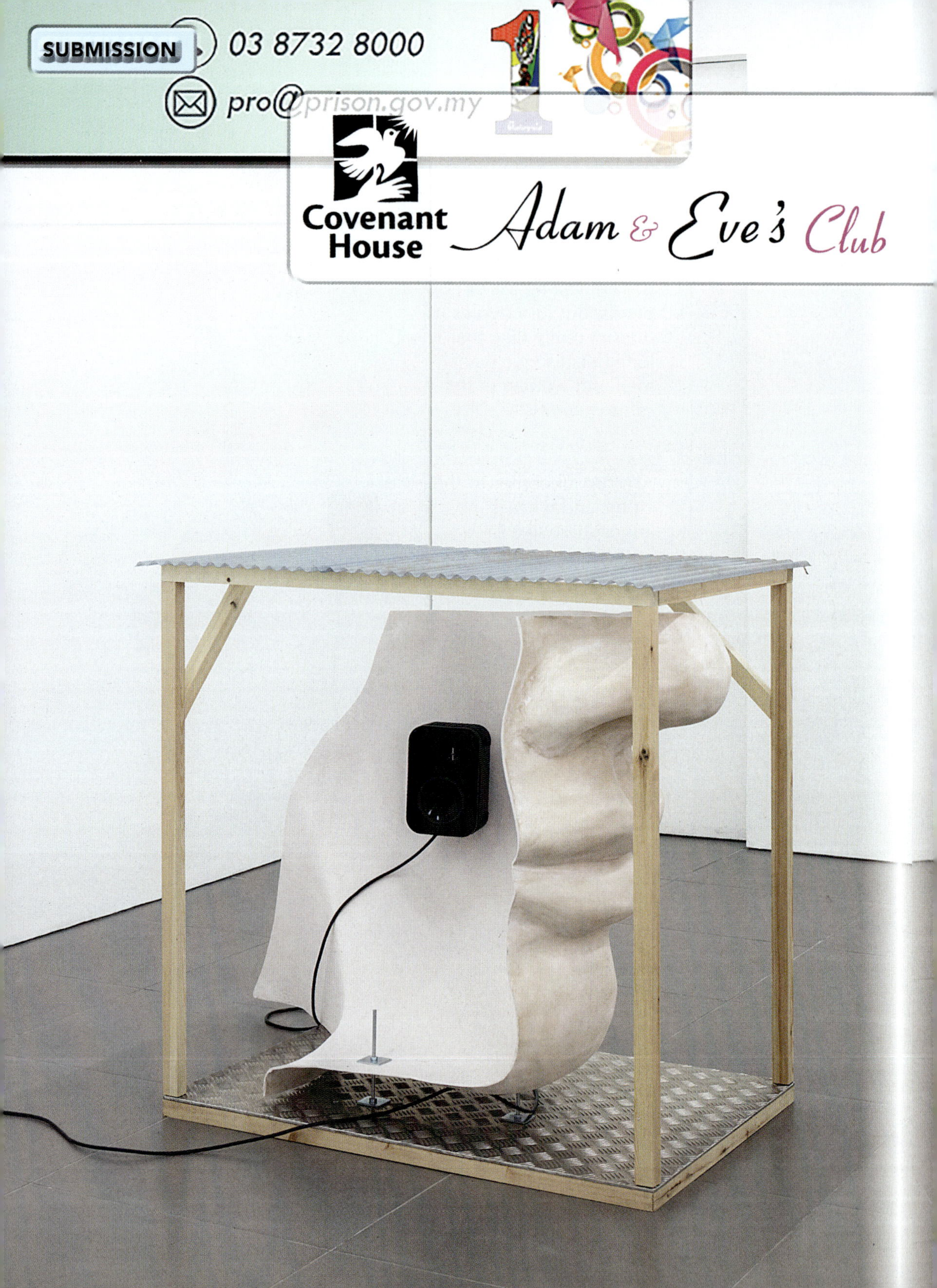
SUBMISSION
03 8732 8000
pro@prison.gov.my
Covenant House
Adam & Eve's Club

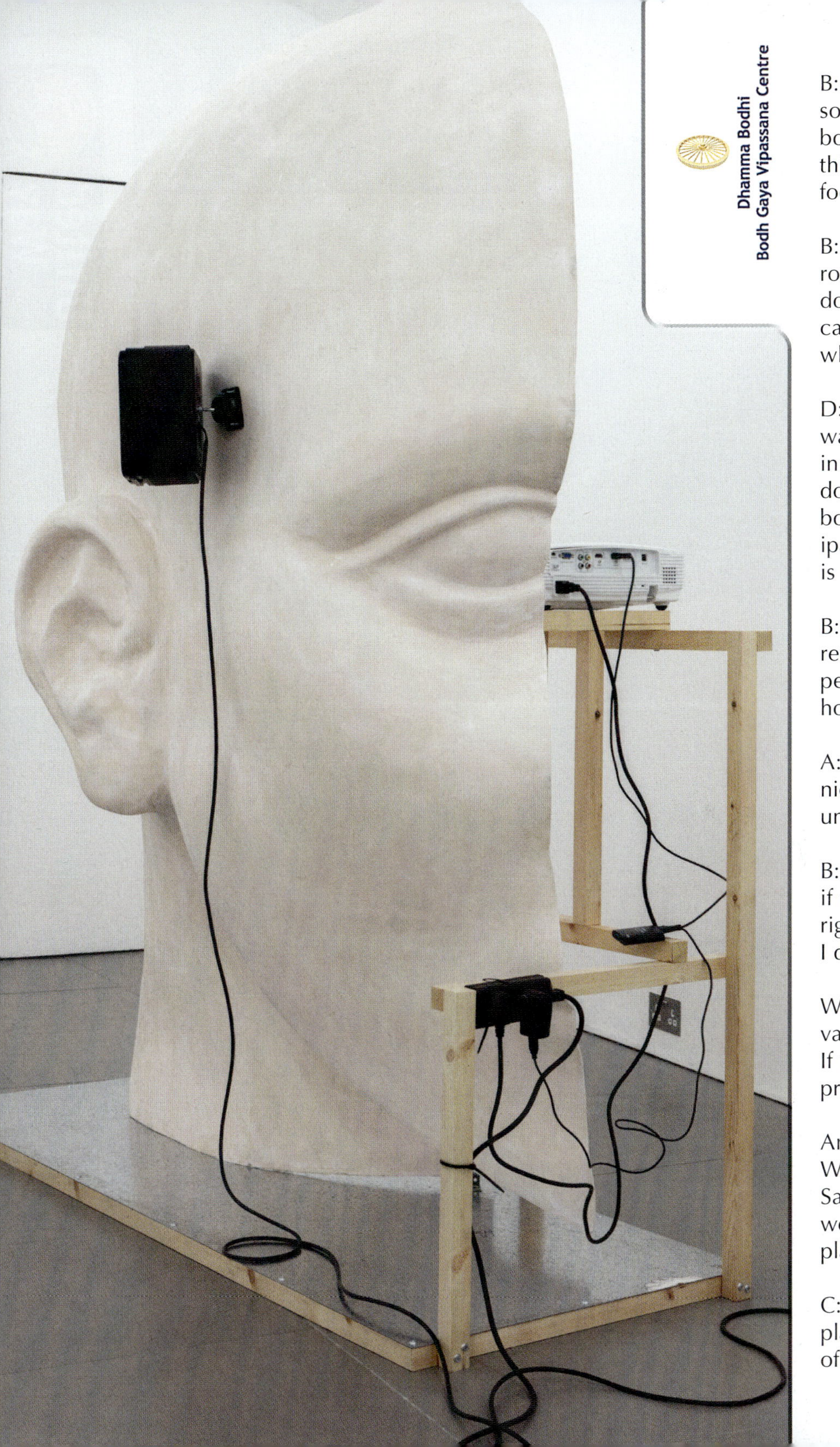

B: There are resources if somebody needs other things then just food and shelter.

B: There are open rooms with windows that people can watch into.. or whatever..

D: If you don't wanna participate in anything, or you don't want somebody else to participate with you that is not a problem.

B: Look at all the reviews allot of people mention how friendly it is.

A: Do I need to be nice ? can i also be unfriendly ?

B: uh yeah well,
if you do it in the right way probably.
I don't know.

We got some private rooms.
If you want a bit of privacy.

And we have a Wet room, Jacuzzi, Sauna, Shower and we got 4 floors of play rooms.

C: More like light play or what kind of play ?

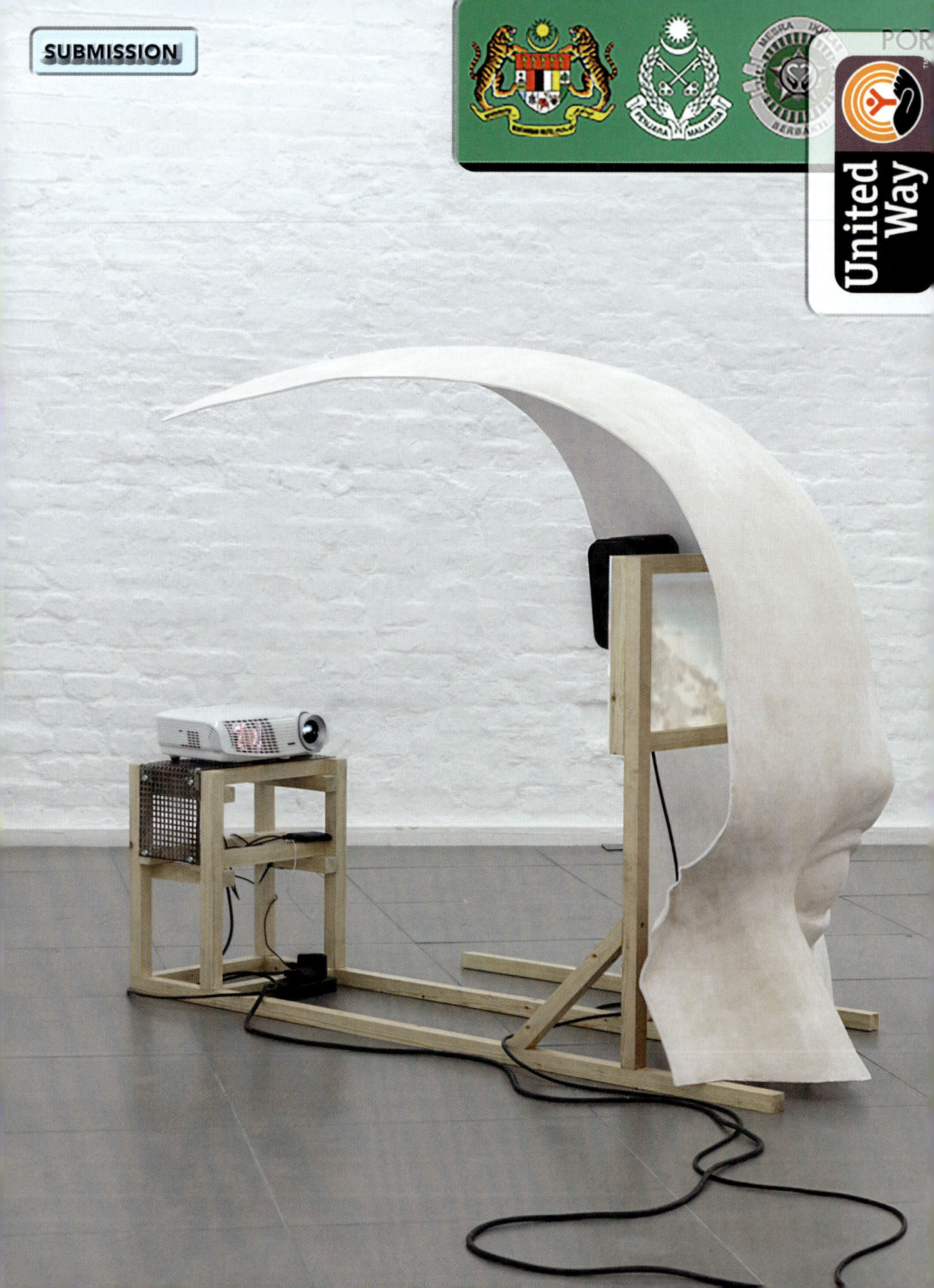
SUBMISSION
United Way

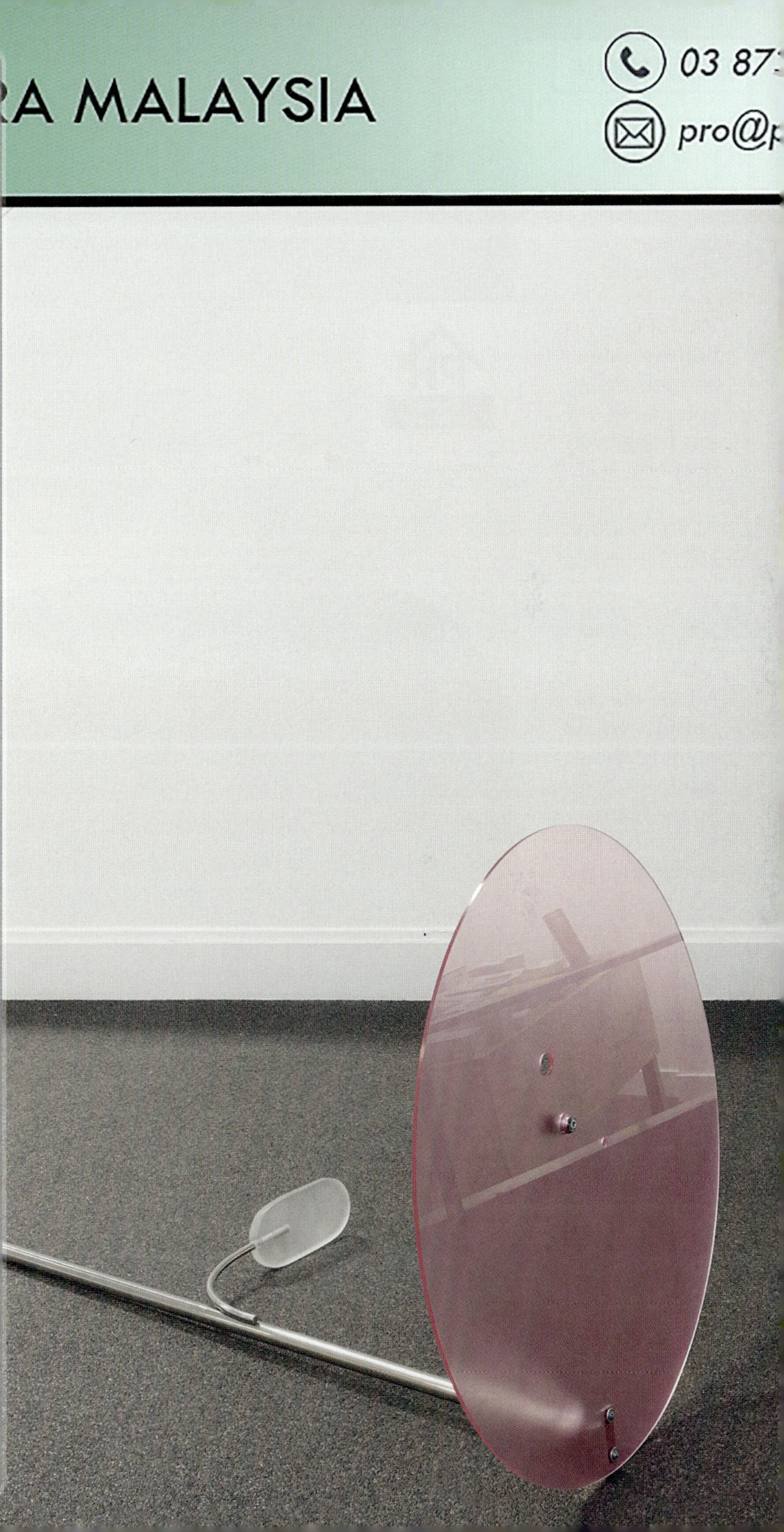

SMI

AN PENJARA MALAYSIA

AN DALAM NEGERI

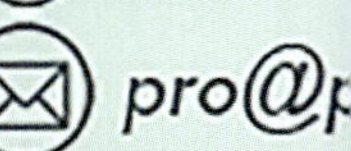

B: Goes from a purely social atmosphere to a hardcore gangbang atmosphere quite a broad spectrum, Depends mostly on what you are after. I think we don't allow knifes and stuff, people tried that a few times but so its pretty free and open.

C: What are the most important policies ?

D: There are some rules:
We don't kill
No speaking lies.

C: We don't speak lies.

D: Everybody knows no means no.
We don't steal

C: Sustain from stealing.

D: Sustain from sexual misconduct..
and the last one is

We don't do talking with each other.

A: You can not speak with the other people?

C: We try not to even look in the eyes.
Even if other people are really close, even if you are sitting besides of the other people

SUBMISSION

C: This helps with self control ?

D: Yes-
all the time.

We thing everybody is alone and this helps you practise this brings you deeper inside.

A: So its more about going inside

D: Yes-
inside yes.
All the life we go outside, we do nothing about inside.
So we learn to observe the inside reality.

How our mind is working
and how this is connected to sensations.

D: With some struggles you continue.
You are alone.

C: What kind of realities we find inside ?

D: You have your own experience.

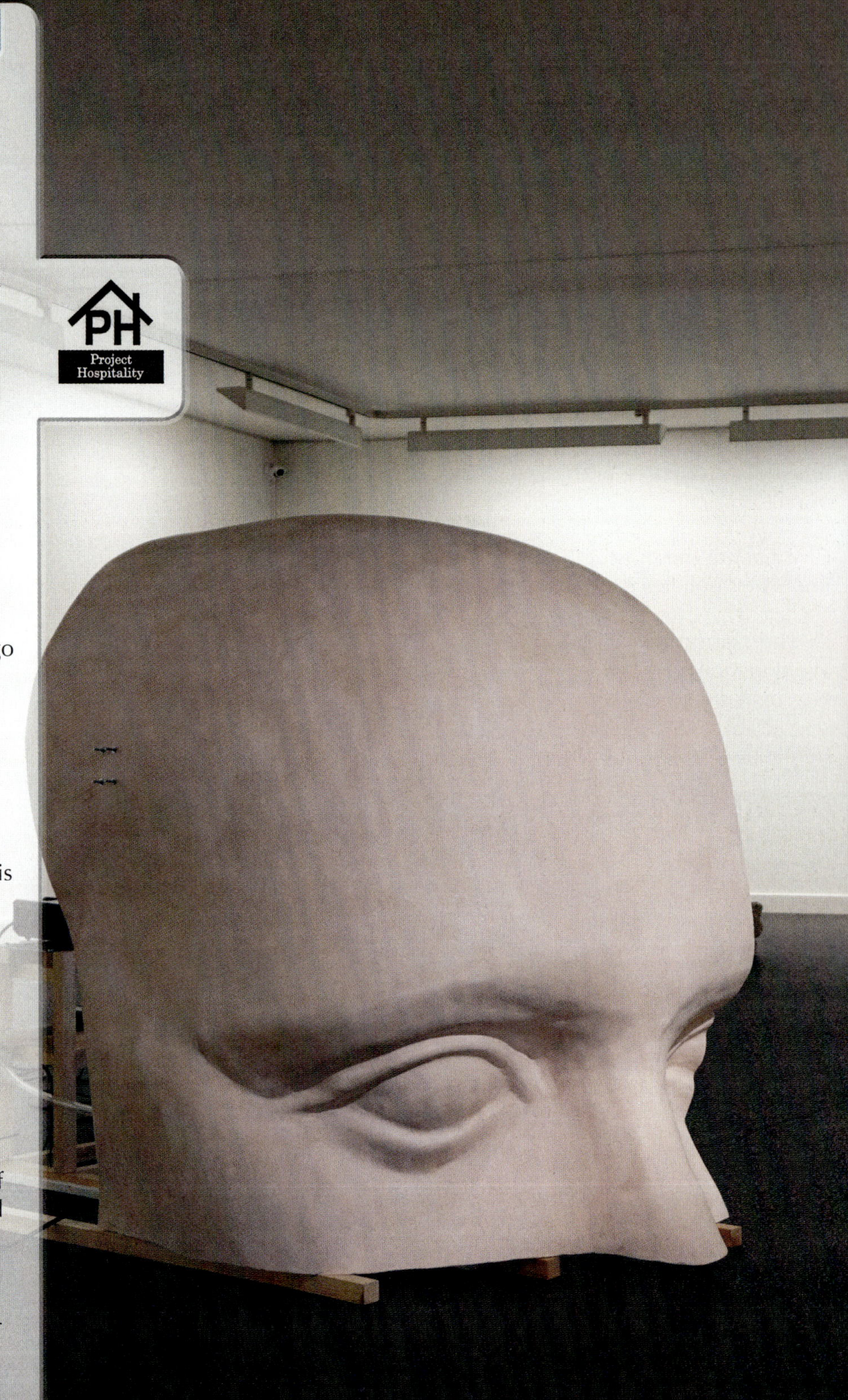

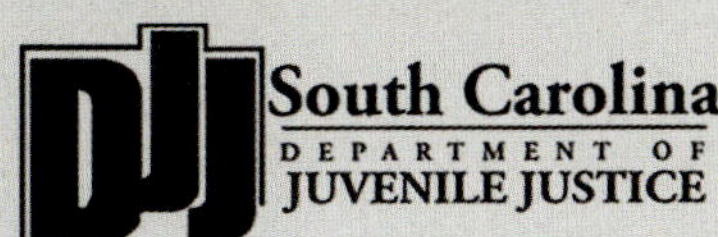

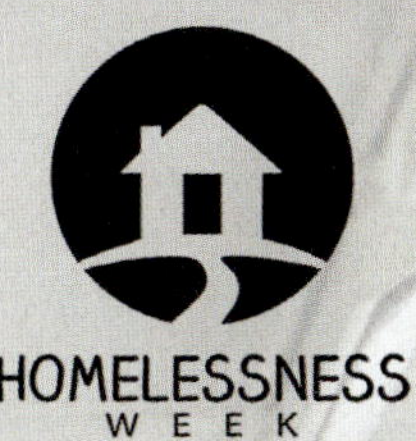

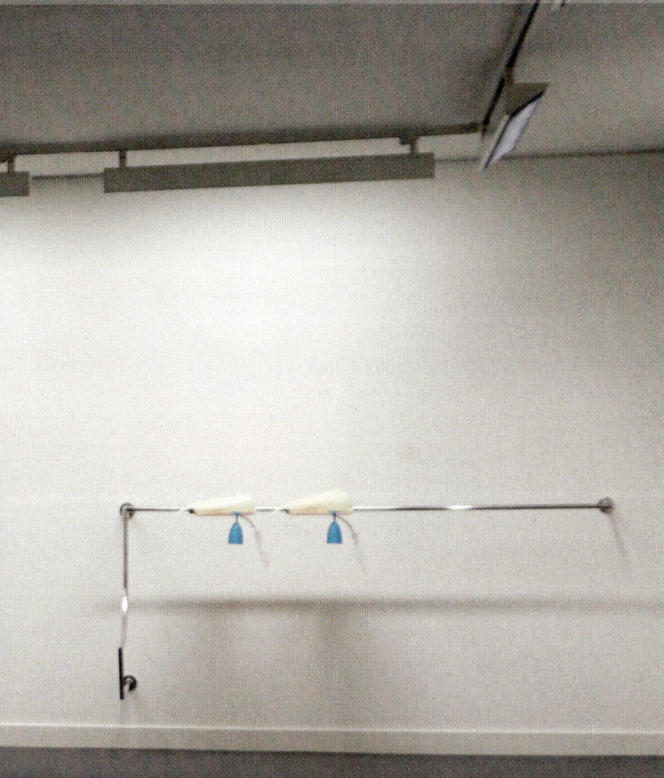

B: You have to keep total silent.

A: How is it working ?

D: For training and quality service your call may be recorded.

A: You guys are not govern-mental you are independent ?

D: For conation officers, police officers, or court services, lawyers wishing to contact there clients, For information regarding visits for information for related depositing funds in a clients account. Dropping of and personal acces.

For informations regarding the location for general in-quiries not related..

A: Hallo ?

C: Hello ?

D: Listen now you can speak with the manager.
He he, actually can answer to all.. ya

B: yes ?

A: So okay yeah, so OK
What is expected from me before I arrive ?

B: I didn't get ?

A: What should I do before I arrive ?

B: Just come in time.
Be ready.

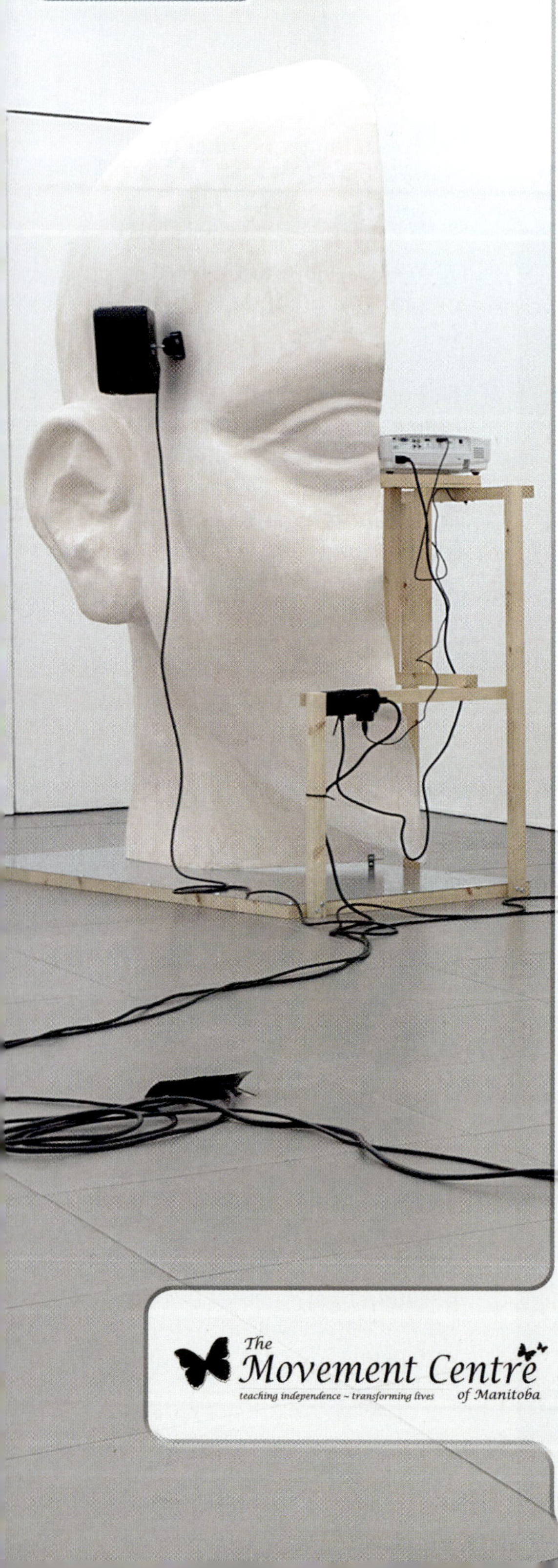

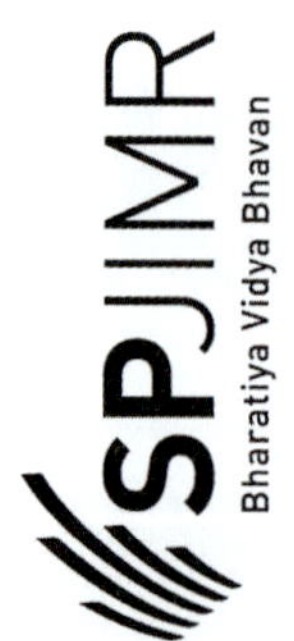

B: No talking.
No reading.
No writing.

Just be ready..
Bring some clothes.

But you can not bring any accessories for your body.

A: How is it possible to determine where to be placed ?

D: Thats when they are seen by health care and classification.

A: Submissives are typical too ?

B: Submissives ?

We have a few that come in that like to play the submissive role, yes

A: Okay

D: We have a medium section and a secure section when they are assigned a unit the options and time table for lock up lunch and dinner is given to them and they put in request to go into different areas.

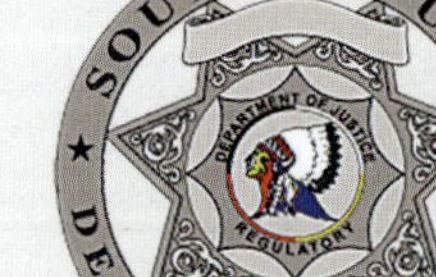

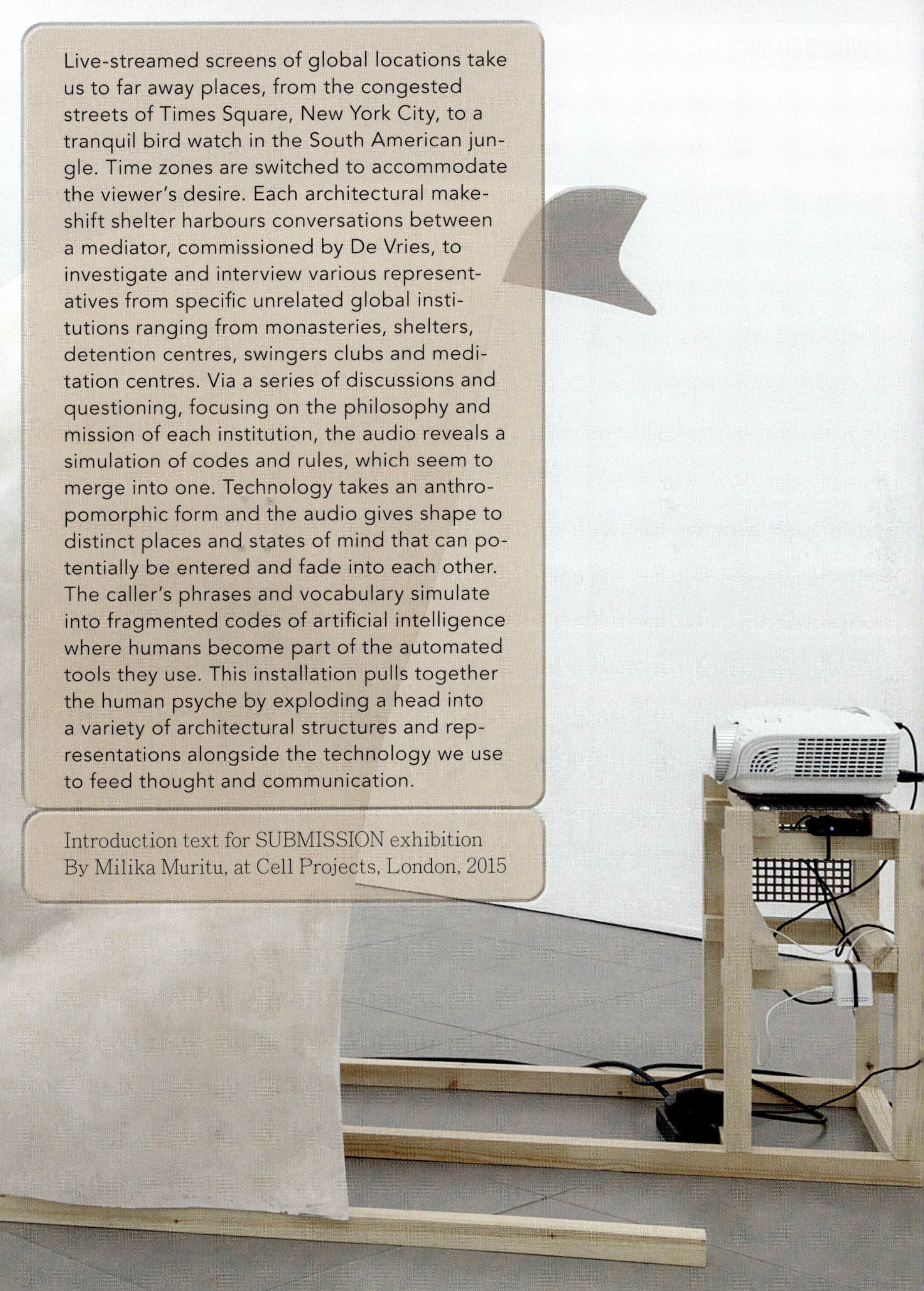

Live-streamed screens of global locations take us to far away places, from the congested streets of Times Square, New York City, to a tranquil bird watch in the South American jungle. Time zones are switched to accommodate the viewer's desire. Each architectural makeshift shelter harbours conversations between a mediator, commissioned by De Vries, to investigate and interview various representatives from specific unrelated global institutions ranging from monasteries, shelters, detention centres, swingers clubs and meditation centres. Via a series of discussions and questioning, focusing on the philosophy and mission of each institution, the audio reveals a simulation of codes and rules, which seem to merge into one. Technology takes an anthropomorphic form and the audio gives shape to distinct places and states of mind that can potentially be entered and fade into each other. The caller's phrases and vocabulary simulate into fragmented codes of artificial intelligence where humans become part of the automated tools they use. This installation pulls together the human psyche by exploding a head into a variety of architectural structures and representations alongside the technology we use to feed thought and communication.

Introduction text for SUBMISSION exhibition
By Milika Muritu, at Cell Projects, London, 2015

SUBMISSION

C: So there are different levels of intensity ?
or lets say,..
A: what when I would want to be very submissive ?

B: We do have one room where allot of submissive stuff is goes on.

C: And security is good ?

B: Absolutely yes its very safe here.

A: Are there other important rules or limitations for helping me retrain
my natural desires ?

C: Because of your animal body you have eyes and ears, and sensorium,
and because of the focussing on information through apparatus.
Your conscious is crucified so to speak on the axe of space and time,
because of your consciousness..
Because of these devices.

A: And they give you a instruction that helps with self control ?

B: We observe natural breath.

We concentrate.

You got to keep you back and neck straight

When the mind is concentrated your sensations are going through the whole body

No imagination.

A: No pictures nothing?

B: Just feeling
Feeling the sensations

C: Don't react

Pleasant and unpleasant

All the desires are connected to sensations.

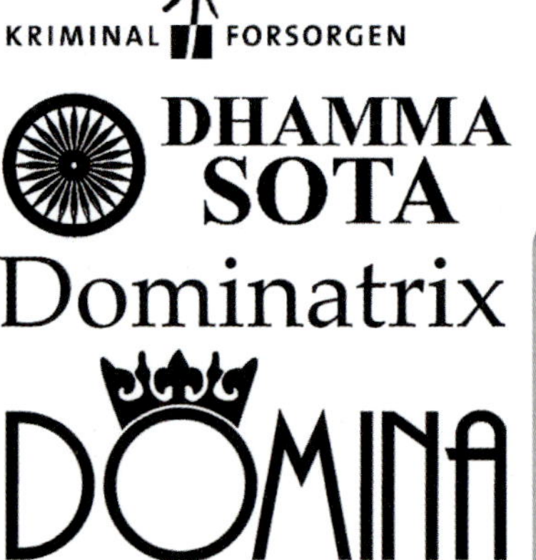

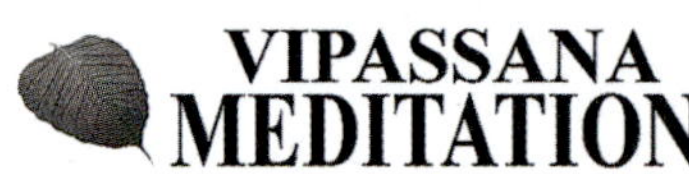

Excerpt from phone conversations as part of the installation: SUBMISSION by Anne de Vries

AI GPT-2 RESPONSE

The lobby

A: I'm fine A: I thought so.

C: Oh, I don't wanna go

A: But I have to come to talk to this Domina. Do we get a message?

E: I'm sorry, I'm not going to go with you any further.

No response.

2: Maybe - I could write you a note on the phone -but I can't -

C: I'm sorry, and you have to talk -
C: Don't worry, maybe you can -
C: you can -I'm not that kind of person -
C: not you (pause)
C: What's wrong with you (pause)
C: ...
C: We are in the hallway! -No! -

E: No. I could have written you a note! I could have called you -

E: No! -
E: -No.

C: What? -

E: -No. (pause) -

E: -No. You are the one I should be talking to. -
E: No -

C: -No.
C: What? -

E: -No. No.-

C: -No. (pause) -

E: -No. No.

C: What? -

E: - No! -
E: No! (pause) -
E: -No- -No- -

F: Oh, the man on the phone. -

E: He called me.

C: Okay -

E: I saw his number the day before. -
E: -No! -
E: We will be calling back sometime. No reply is expected.

3: I'm getting really frustrated.

C: We -
C: No, this isn't going to work. -

F: Really? -
F: - No! NO! -
F: - No! -
F: No!!

1: We have to come. I am so confused about -

A: -

C: -The -
I don't even know -

J: -Yes, but -

E: It's really -
E: no, there's nothing out there.

1: The room will get really quiet.

2: -Is a guy in there? -

A: We never seen him.

C: He is dead.

2: He is already dead. He's just sitting in a corner -

C: -Don't make any changes. -

A: -No, I think he's -

Y: -It's -
I'll go and find out.

AI GPT-2 RESPONSE

PRISON AS MONASTERY, PRISON AS CHARNEL GROUND

By Gary Allen

There's a spiritual idea that prison can be used as a monastic experience because it's already monastery-like: there's a rigid schedule you just follow; you're given a place to sleep, food to eat, work to do so that you don't have to struggle with these issues; there's a single gender housed together, which implies celibacy; everyone dresses the same; there's a minimization of activities that undercuts sensory entertainment and encourages simplicity. One is cut off from the elaborate complications and seductions of the world at large, encouraging a bare existence focused on introspection.

In fact, this was the original intention of the modern prison developed by the Quakers who sought to relieve criminals of corporal punishment and instead put them into a context where they could examine their actions, come to understand what they had done wrong, and repent or become penitent–hence the name "penitentiary." The Quakers saw doing time in a positive, spiritual light, as a way to stop and examine one's life in an atmosphere free of the usual distractions, to purify one's sins, and to come into harmony with the Holy Spirit.

The Buddhist teachers who have come to this country, when questioned about prisons, often echo this kind of idea. They emphasize the value in using this kind of time to turn inward, to develop a sitting meditation practice, to spend time studying the teachings, and focusing on transforming one's conduct into something that's disciplined and compassionate. The lack of luxury and the support of having one's basic needs taken care of leaves a lot of mental room for working with one's mind. You can renounce all those things that have held people so tightly in their thrall: wanting lots of money, hot sex partners, fancy cars and houses, fame, respect, on & on.
Free of such things, one can focus exclusively on spiritual development.

But it doesn't take too much time in an American prison to recognize how much of it in no way resembles a monastery: there aren't the sounds of religious practice but 24 hour noise; the people occupying the prison aren't interested in spiritual development for the most part, but are very involved in whatever sensual entertainments they can eke out with sex, drugs, gambling, or whatever else can be scrounged up for distraction; there isn't an atmosphere of gentle discipline but of aggression, mind-games, and power trips; there might be some self-examination going on, but it's drowned out by constant complaints and bitter blame aimed at the world; and in a lot of situations, there's the very real threat of violence and death.

This then bears little resemblance to the average monastery. What it does resemble is another place of Buddhist practice: the charnel ground. Charnel grounds in ancient India were places where corpses were brought to be cremated (for rich people who could afford the wood) or, more often, left to rot and be consumed by wild animals. They were off beyond the edge of town where otherwise no one went. Places of horrific smells, crumbling body parts, vultures, hyenas, and ghosts, they were frequented only by outlaws who could hide there or yogis who came to contemplate the impermanence of all phenomena.

The beauty of the charnel ground, from the yogi's point of view, was that it faced one with the facts of life. All birth ended here, all material gain, all sensual enjoyment, all fame, and all pleasure had its final result in the charnel ground. The charnel ground showed how these things were mere illusions that would inevitably decay pungently into nothing. For the tantric Buddhist yogis, the charnel ground offered something further than just the contemplation of impermanence. It was an open gateway into realizing the empty, vivid nature of appearances.

Monasteries were too tame to make progress quickly. In a charnel ground, you could practice meditation like your life depended on it. There was nothing there to cling to–no sensual distractions–but also an extremely direct relationship with the physical world could be made. It wasn't a place that supported pretense or facade or hollow philosophizing. Gazing directly upon the transitory, ungraspable nature of phenomena encouraged the yogi to see his or her own mind in the same light. Recognizing the nature of mind liberated the yogi from the cycle of birth and death. Far from avoiding the ugly truth of the world, the yogi went to sit in the midst of it and right there on that spot discovered the unconditional at the heart of the transitory. In the vajrayana Buddhist tradition, the charnel ground came to have a symbolic meaning as the nature of life on its most raw, basic, existential terms; that is to say, it's the fundamental ground we live on whether we're in prison or in the suburbs.

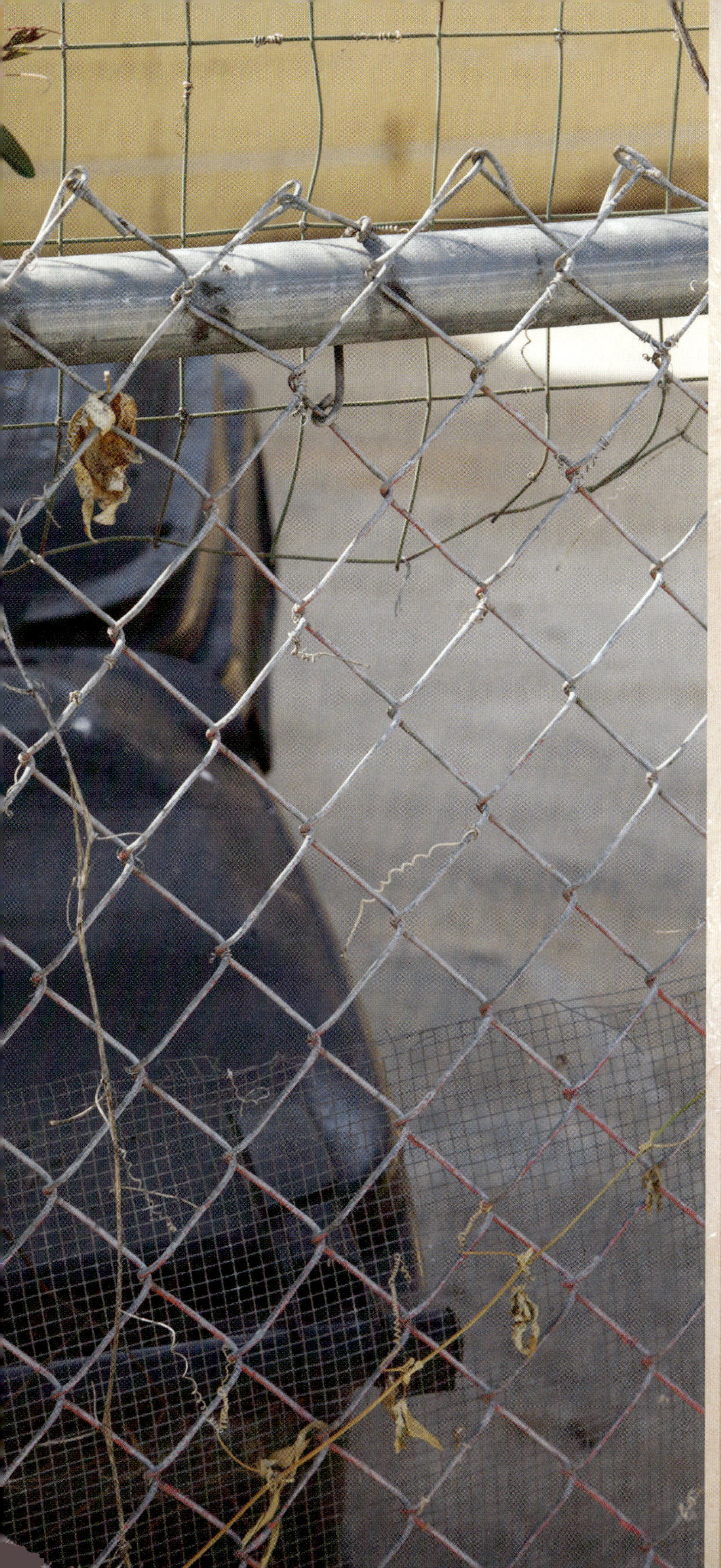

But there are daily situations we could be thrust into that suddenly reveal this reality to us nakedly. Judith Simmer-Brown, in Dakini's Warm Breath, discusses this:

In contemporary Western society, the charnel ground might be a prison, a homeless shelter, the welfare roll, or a factory assembly line. The key to its successful support of practice is its desperate, hopeless, or terrifying quality. For that matter, there are environments that appear prosperous and privileged to others but are charnel grounds for their inhabitants–Hollywood, Madison Avenue, Wall Street, Washington, D.C. These are worlds in which extreme competitiveness, speed, and power rule, and the actors in their dramas experience intense emotion, ambition, and fear. The intensity of their dynamics makes all of these situations ripe for the Vajrayana practice of the charnel ground.

PRISON AS MONASTERY, PRISON AS CHARNEL GROUND

Author: Gary Allen,
First published: MPP, The Mindfulness Peace Project,
Year: 2016

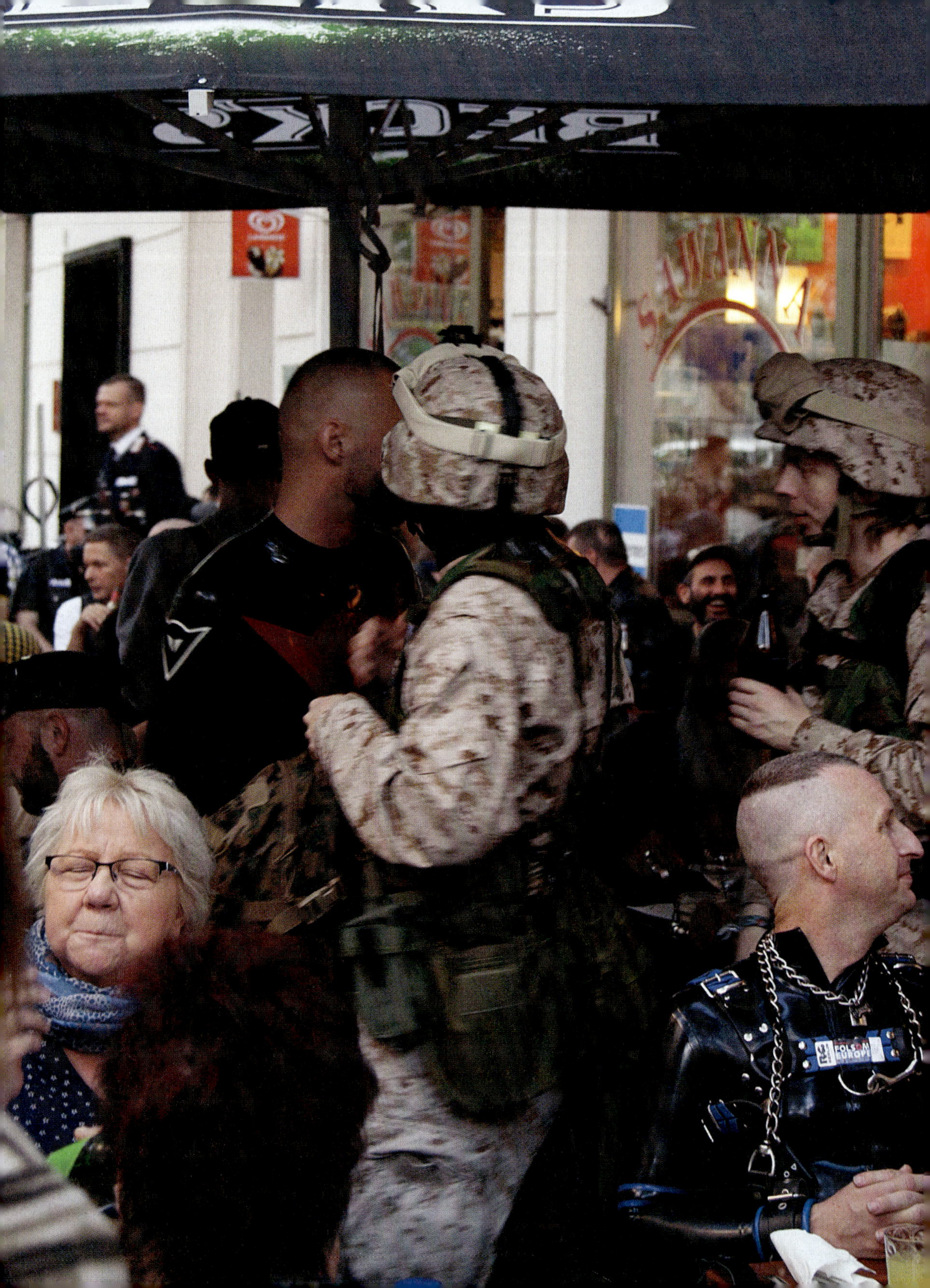
FOLSOM
EUROPE

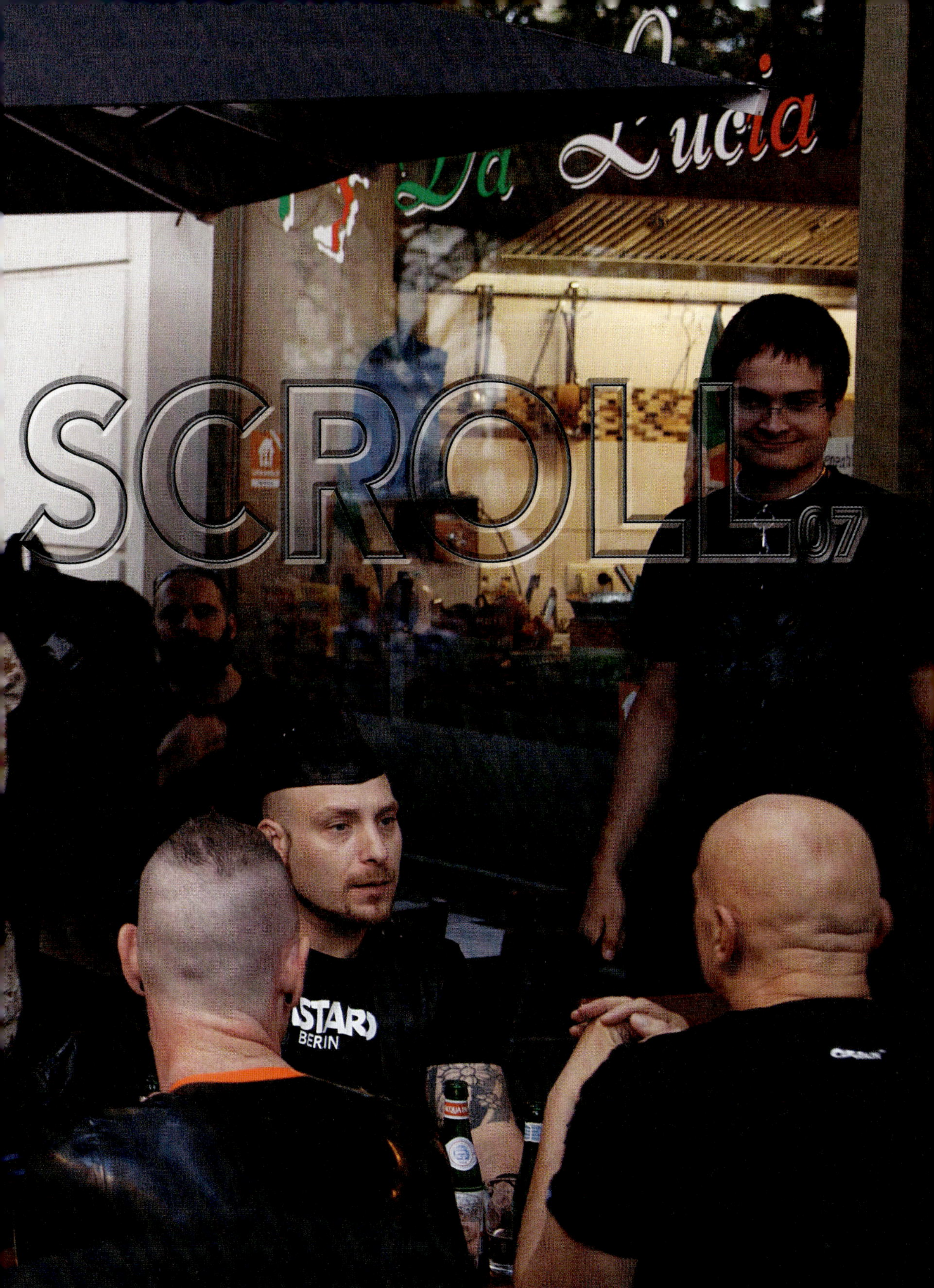
Da Lucia
SCROLL 07
BERIN

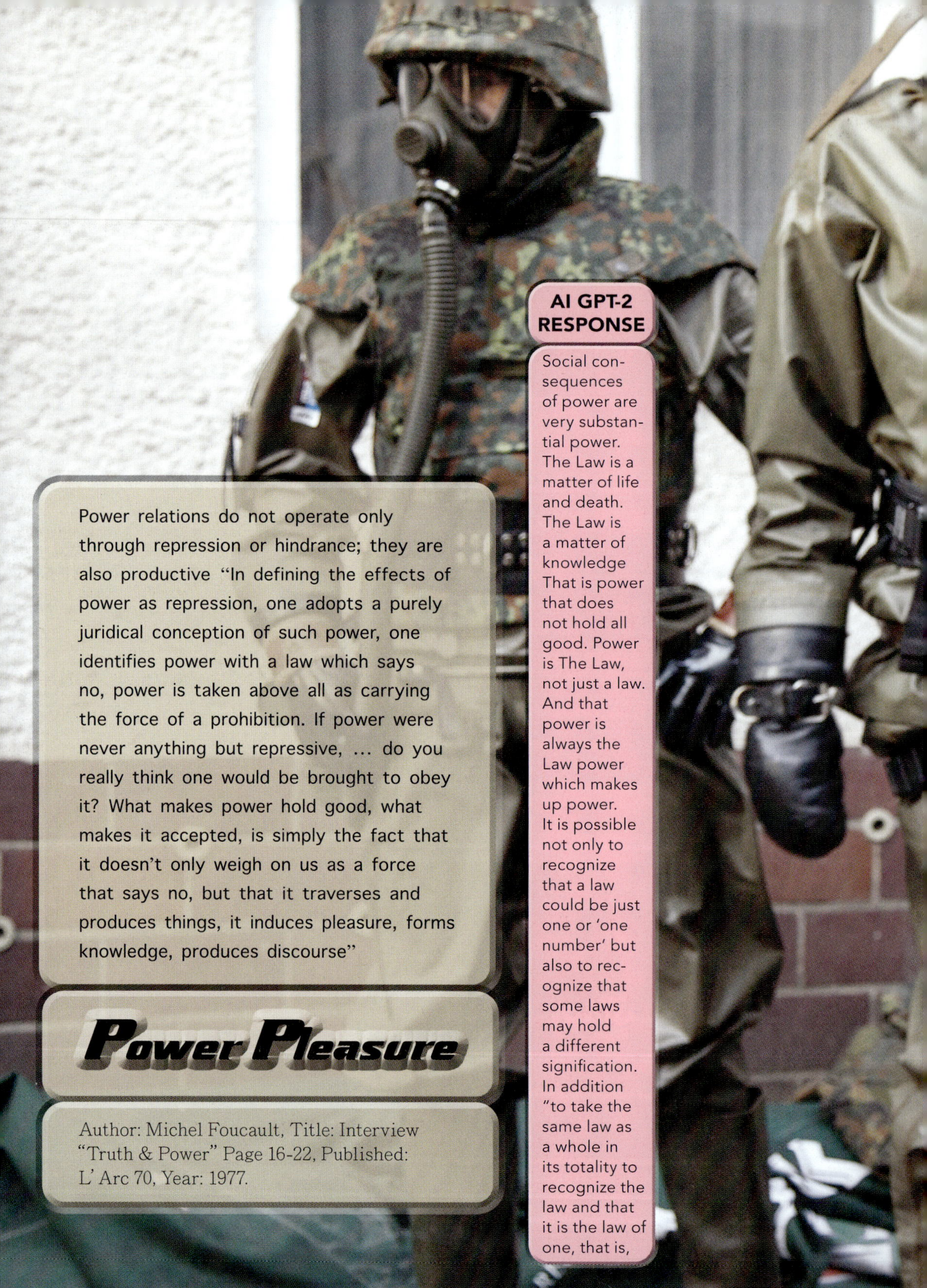

Power relations do not operate only through repression or hindrance; they are also productive "In defining the effects of power as repression, one adopts a purely juridical conception of such power, one identifies power with a law which says no, power is taken above all as carrying the force of a prohibition. If power were never anything but repressive, ... do you really think one would be brought to obey it? What makes power hold good, what makes it accepted, is simply the fact that it doesn't only weigh on us as a force that says no, but that it traverses and produces things, it induces pleasure, forms knowledge, produces discourse"

Power Pleasure

Author: Michel Foucault, Title: Interview "Truth & Power" Page 16-22, Published: L' Arc 70, Year: 1977.

AI GPT-2 RESPONSE

Social consequences of power are very substantial power. The Law is a matter of life and death. The Law is a matter of knowledge That is power that does not hold all good. Power is The Law, not just a law. And that power is always the Law power which makes up power. It is possible not only to recognize that a law could be just one or 'one number' but also to recognize that some laws may hold a different signification. In addition "to take the same law as a whole in its totality to recognize the law and that it is the law of one, that is,

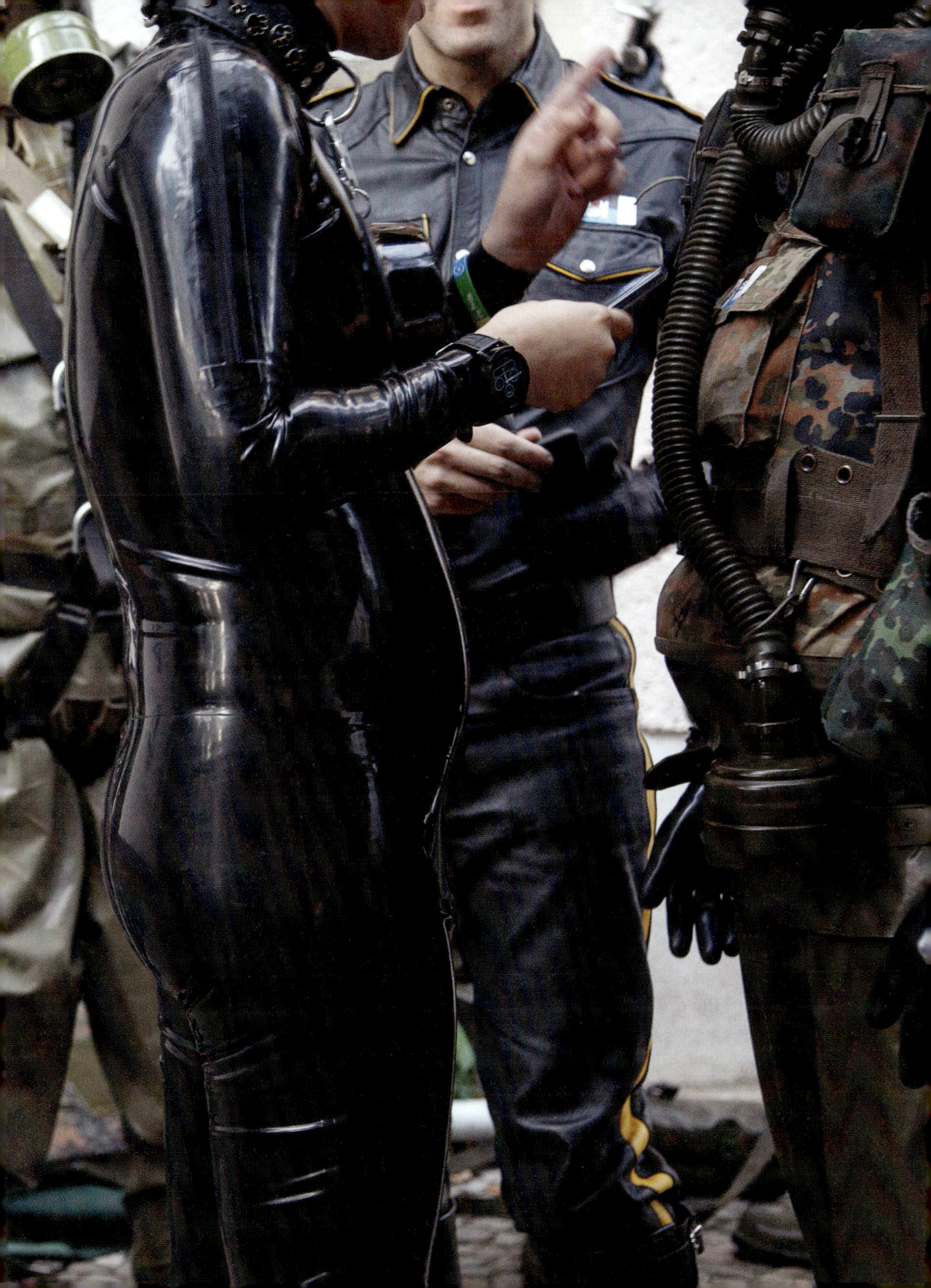

Excerpts from:

Sexy warriors: the politics and pleasures of submission to the state

by Jesse Paul Crane-Seeber*

"The connection between the military and perverse and kinky modes of sexuality is complicated. Rape, torture, sexual abuse, prostitution, and rampant sexual harassment are all realities in militarized institutions, and closely correlated with large military deployments and bases. This has been understood for years, and studies of war rape have demonstrated that there is great complexity in both the problem and its solutions (Lene Hansen 2000; Paul Kirby 2012). [Excerpt 1]

The problem with understanding sexual desire in the context of militarization is that there is no simple one-way transfer from state power into the bodies and pleasures of people. Indirect and overlapping factors combine to shape desires in militaries, their members, and the broader societies they are connected to. As Foucault described so clearly, power, knowledge, and desire are not separate or dialectically linked opposites but are all the effects of particular relations between people and techniques. [Excerpt 2]

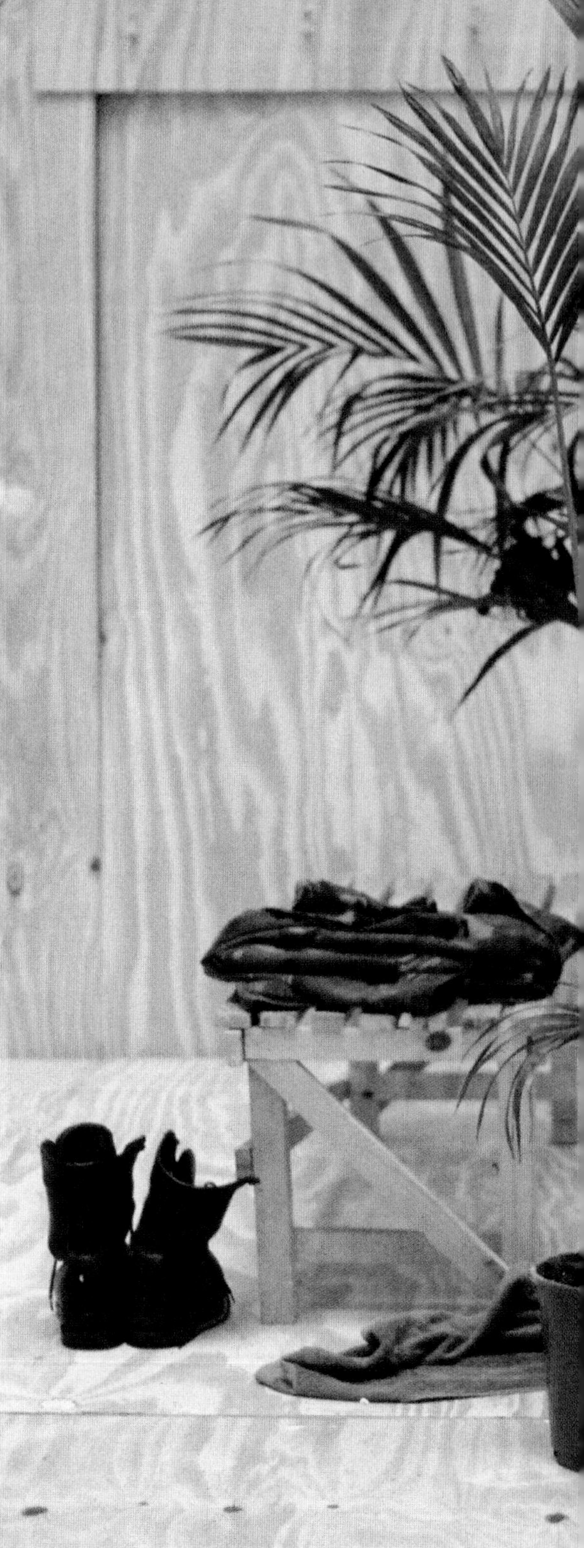

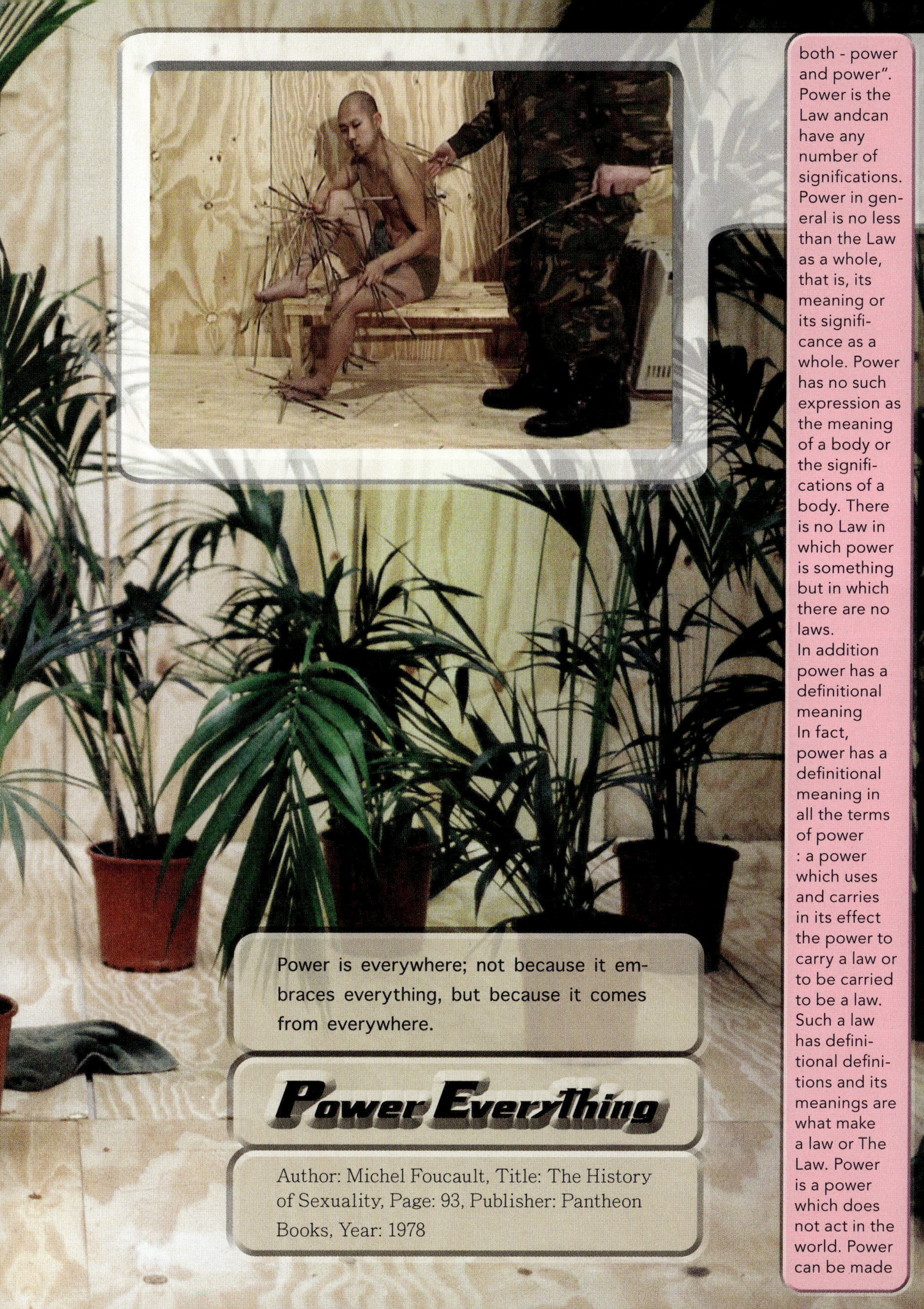

both - power and power". Power is the Law andcan have any number of significations. Power in general is no less than the Law as a whole, that is, its meaning or its significance as a whole. Power has no such expression as the meaning of a body or the significations of a body. There is no Law in which power is something but in which there are no laws.
In addition power has a definitional meaning
In fact, power has a definitional meaning in all the terms of power : a power which uses and carries in its effect the power to carry a law or to be carried to be a law. Such a law has definitional definitions and its meanings are what make a law or The Law. Power is a power which does not act in the world. Power can be made

Power is everywhere; not because it embraces everything, but because it comes from everywhere.

Power Everything

Author: Michel Foucault, Title: The History of Sexuality, Page: 93, Publisher: Pantheon Books, Year: 1978

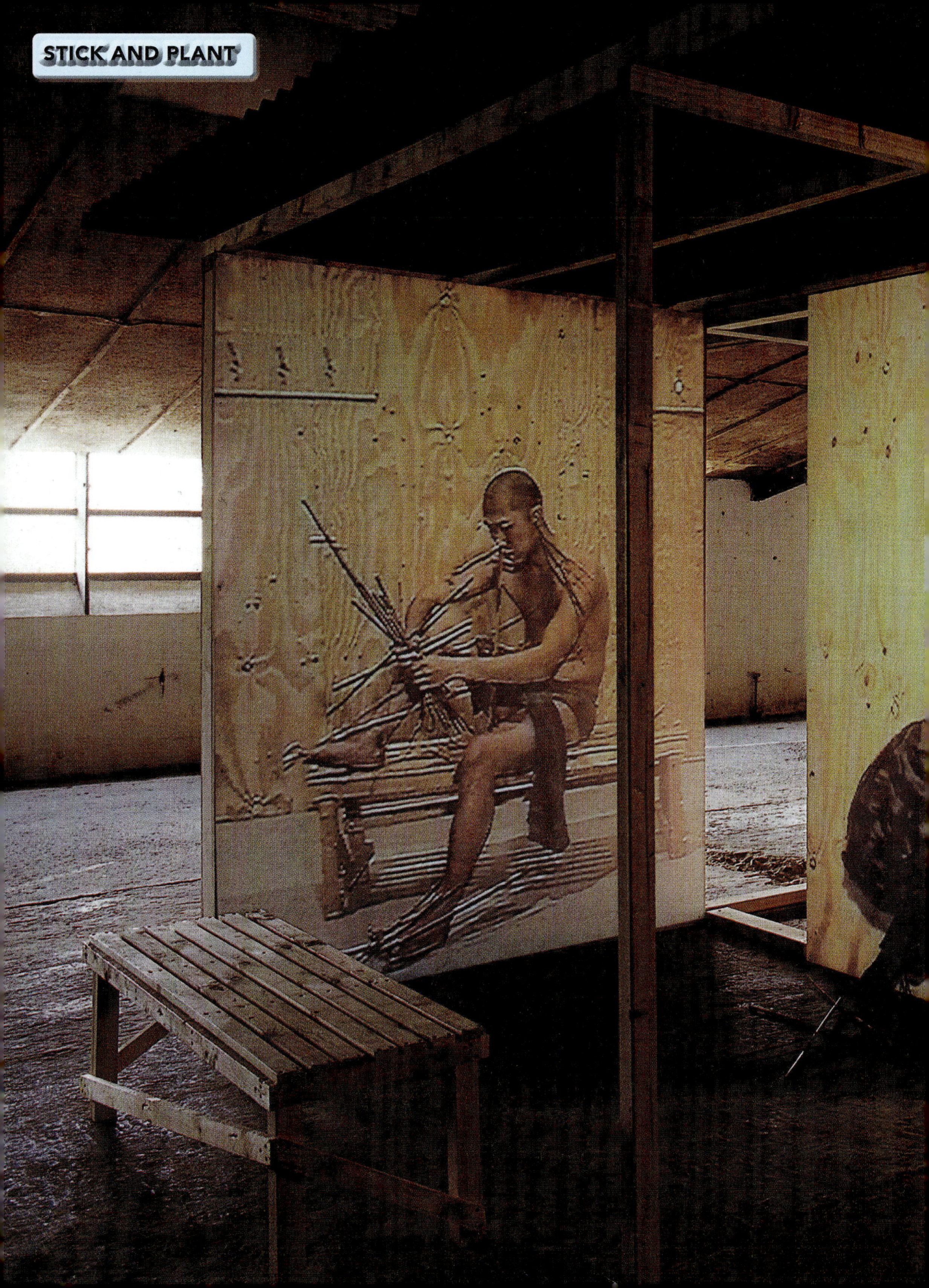

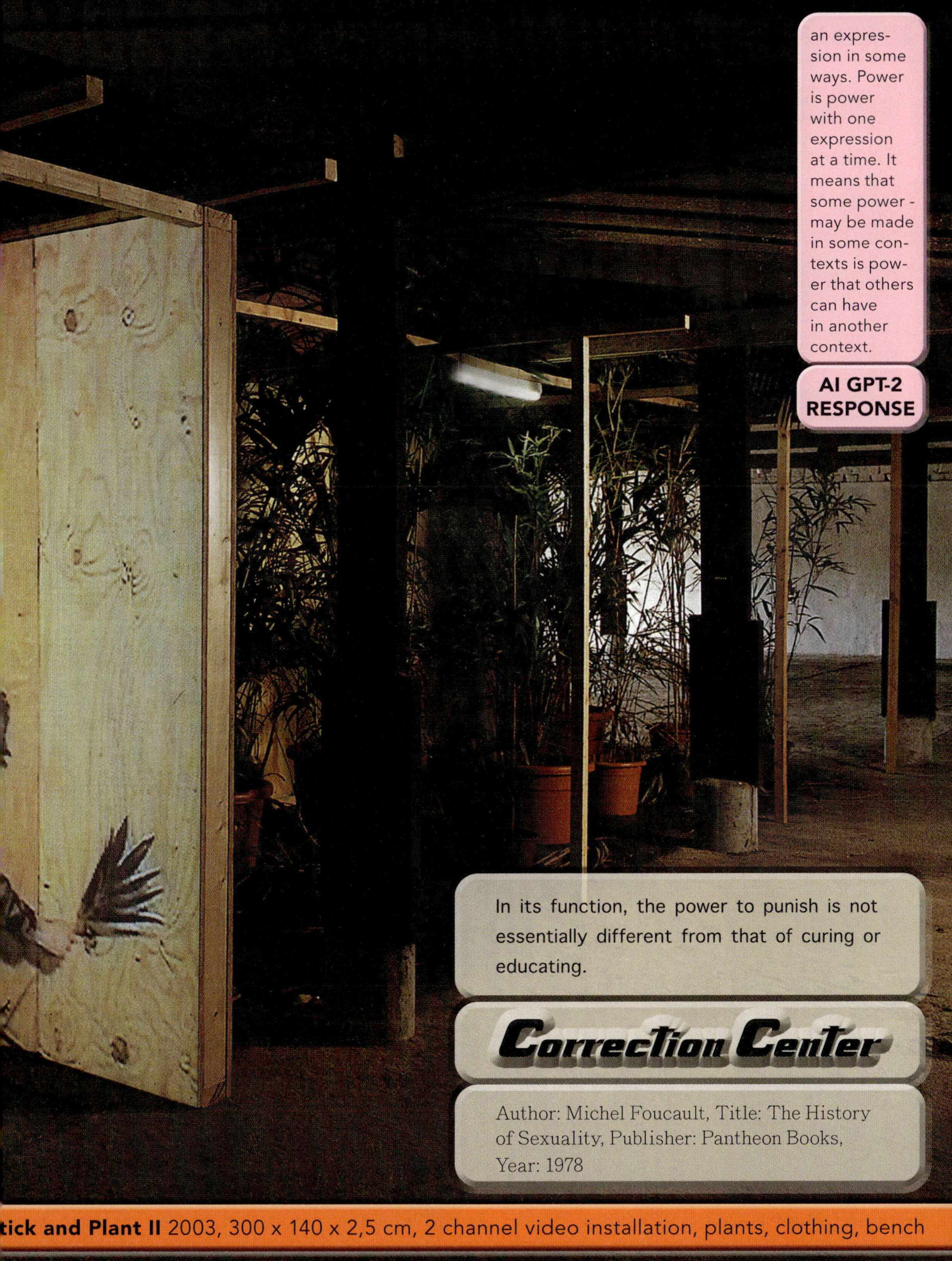

tick and Plant II 2003, 300 x 140 x 2,5 cm, 2 channel video installation, plants, clothing, bench

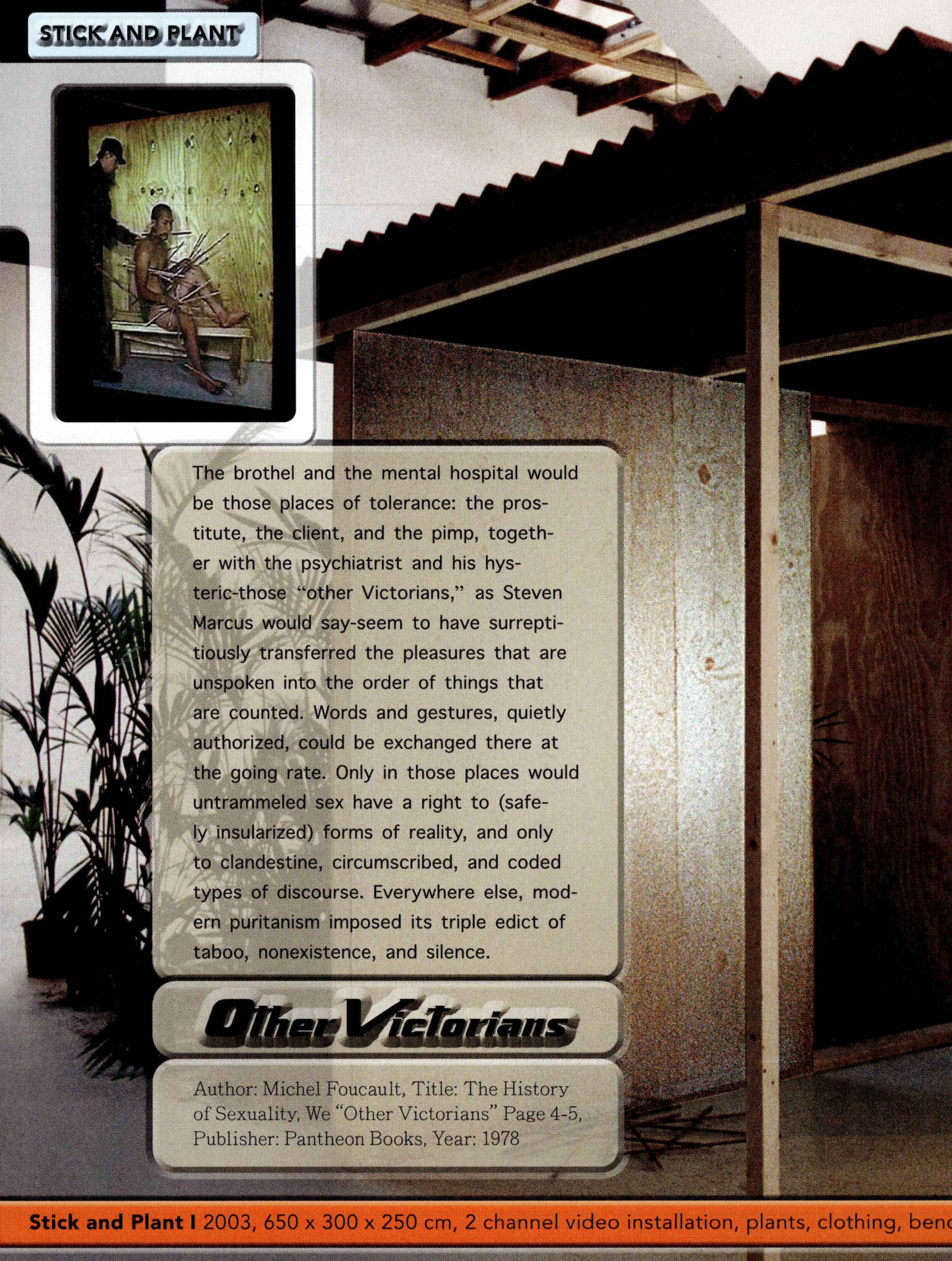

The brothel and the mental hospital would be those places of tolerance: the prostitute, the client, and the pimp, together with the psychiatrist and his hysteric-those "other Victorians," as Steven Marcus would say-seem to have surreptitiously transferred the pleasures that are unspoken into the order of things that are counted. Words and gestures, quietly authorized, could be exchanged there at the going rate. Only in those places would untrammeled sex have a right to (safely insularized) forms of reality, and only to clandestine, circumscribed, and coded types of discourse. Everywhere else, modern puritanism imposed its triple edict of taboo, nonexistence, and silence.

Other Victorians

Author: Michel Foucault, Title: The History of Sexuality, We "Other Victorians" Page 4-5, Publisher: Pantheon Books, Year: 1978

Stick and Plant I 2003, 650 x 300 x 250 cm, 2 channel video installation, plants, clothing, benc

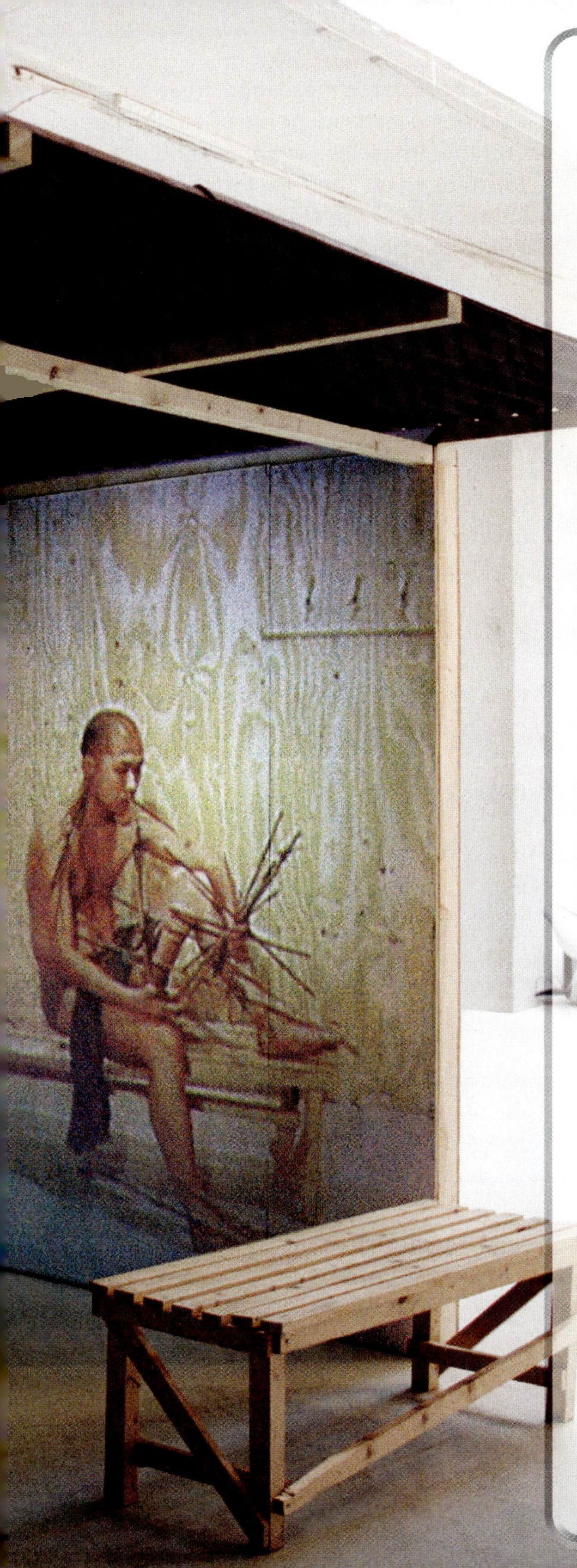

To make sense of militarization, we need both concepts: submission and helplessness. Certainly, the experience of basic training is one of profound subjection, fashioning a new body, a new set of practices, and a fundamentally new self (Rose1999, 15–54). The subject produced is not, however, 'bare life', despite Shatan's characterization of it: He becomes a member of a new society that has complete control over his movements, his behavior, and the physical and social conditions of his life. This absence of choice puts him in a position of relative powerlessness, susceptible to an assault at the roots of his civilized existence. He is forced to function in ways alien to any he would freely select. Freedom of choice is banished to the world of daydreams and recreation, while order, authority, and threat occupy the center of the stage. (Chaim F. Shatan M.D. 1977, 597)

Within the hierarchical structure of military life, power and authority often seem crystal clear. Unlike the civilian world where choice and liberty define many masculine identities, status in the military is earned for being compliant, skilled, and pro-actively obedient. Of course, within armed forces, a myriad of other factors and forces operate that undermine or transform those power relations.

Upon graduation from the total institution of basic training, troops are taught to take enormous pride in their new bodies, stripped of excess, and their new sense of self. From uniforms to finely toned muscles to posture, the military works to produce a new body with a new identity. The broader culture

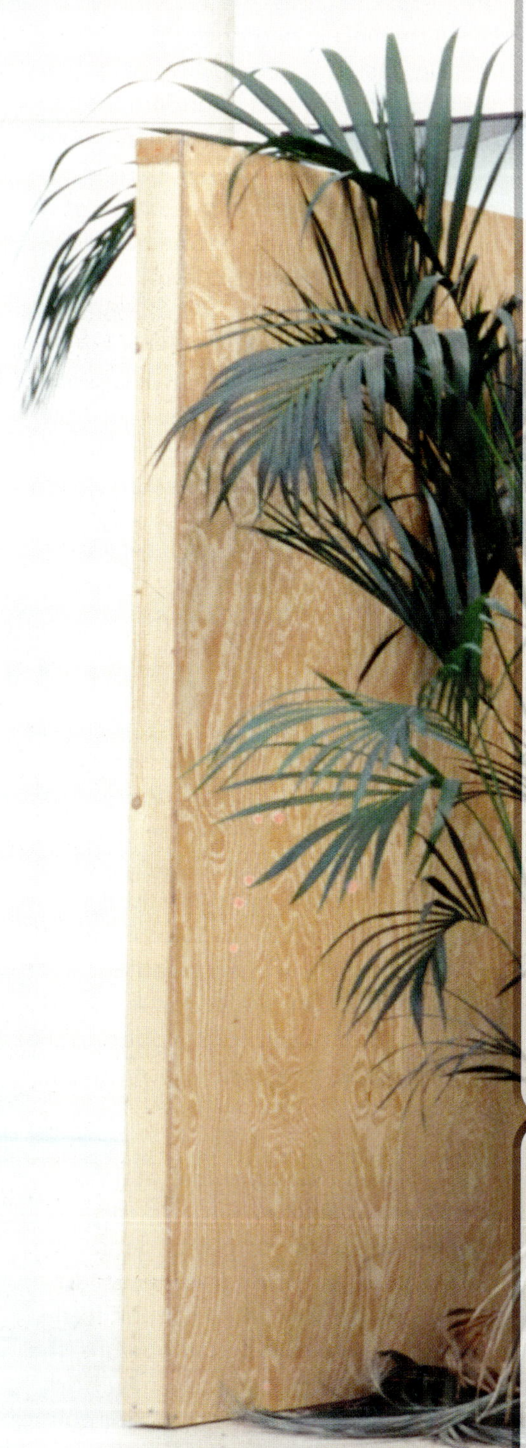

reinforces these messages, treating soldiers as embodiments of confidence, and their muscles, weapons, and uniforms as sexy. The transformed citizen, submissive to the state, is rewarded with the sex appeal that only massive symbolic power can bestow. From loving 'a man in uniform' to 'weapons porn' (Jean Baudrillard 2006), militarization and sexuality are mutually implicated.

As described by John Fowles above, submission involves a certain pleasure and pride in enduring the torments and meeting the expectations of masters, recalling Belkin's analysis of being 'man enough' to 'take' anal sex (Aaron Belkin 2012).

Kinky submissives experience this as discipline, mastering of weakness. This echoes the 'pain is weakness leaving the body' ethos of military training, so one might hypothesize that pleasures ensue from the self-mastery that comes with submission. The strength and will to endure suffering, the sense of being desired, and the pride in doing what few others can do are similar. While lacking the ideal type of mutual enthusiastic consent to power relations (and their reversibility), military life still brings many of the same modes and pleasures of submission as kink. [Excerpt 3]

War as initiation
Sebastian Junger, a celebrated filmmaker who was embedded with US forces in Afghanistan, recently told an interviewer, 'I think the right wing tends to idolize soldiers – you can't talk about them critically in any way [while the] left wing went from vilifying them in

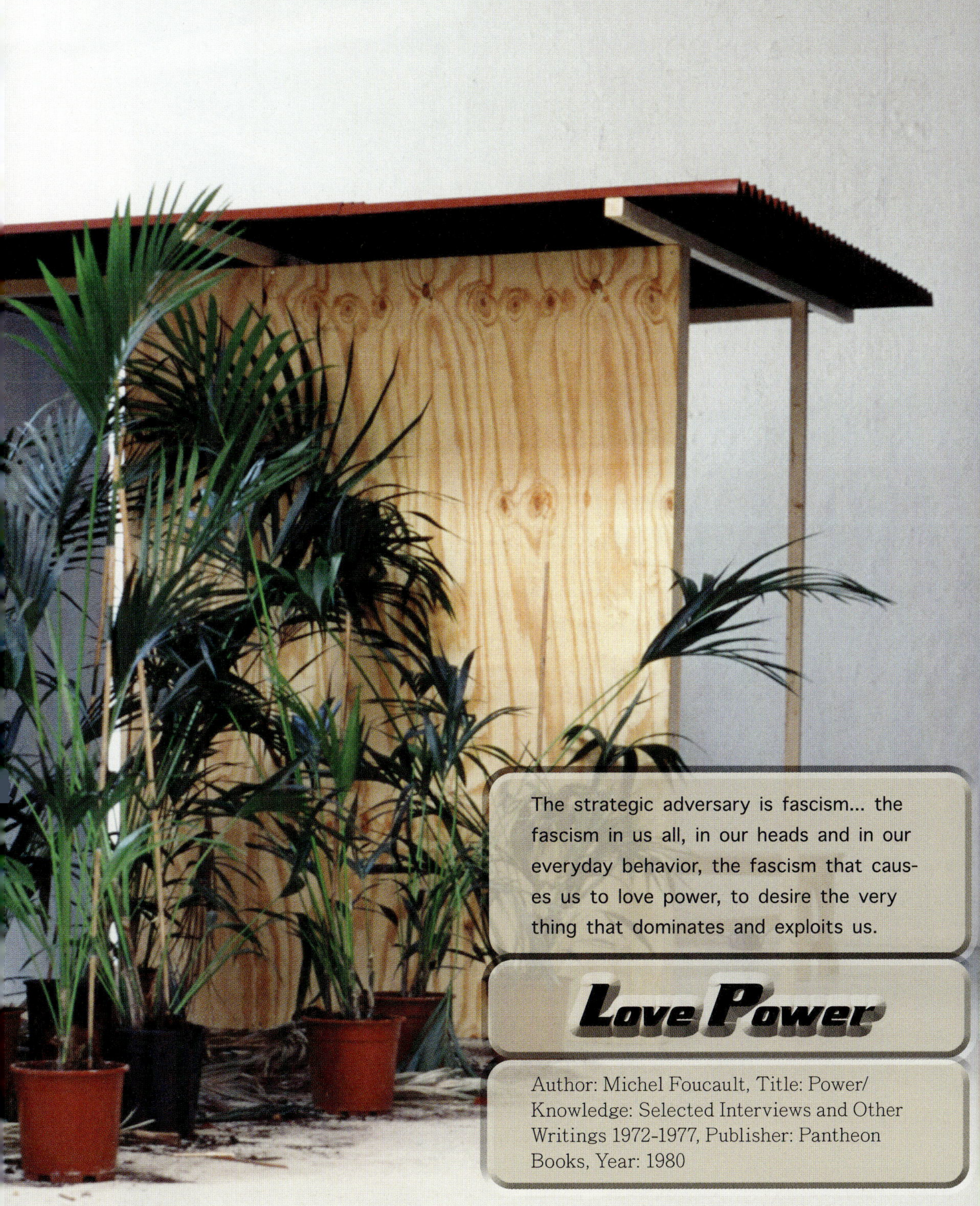

The strategic adversary is fascism... the fascism in us all, in our heads and in our everyday behavior, the fascism that causes us to love power, to desire the very thing that dominates and exploits us.

Love Power

Author: Michel Foucault, Title: Power/ Knowledge: Selected Interviews and Other Writings 1972-1977, Publisher: Pantheon Books, Year: 1980

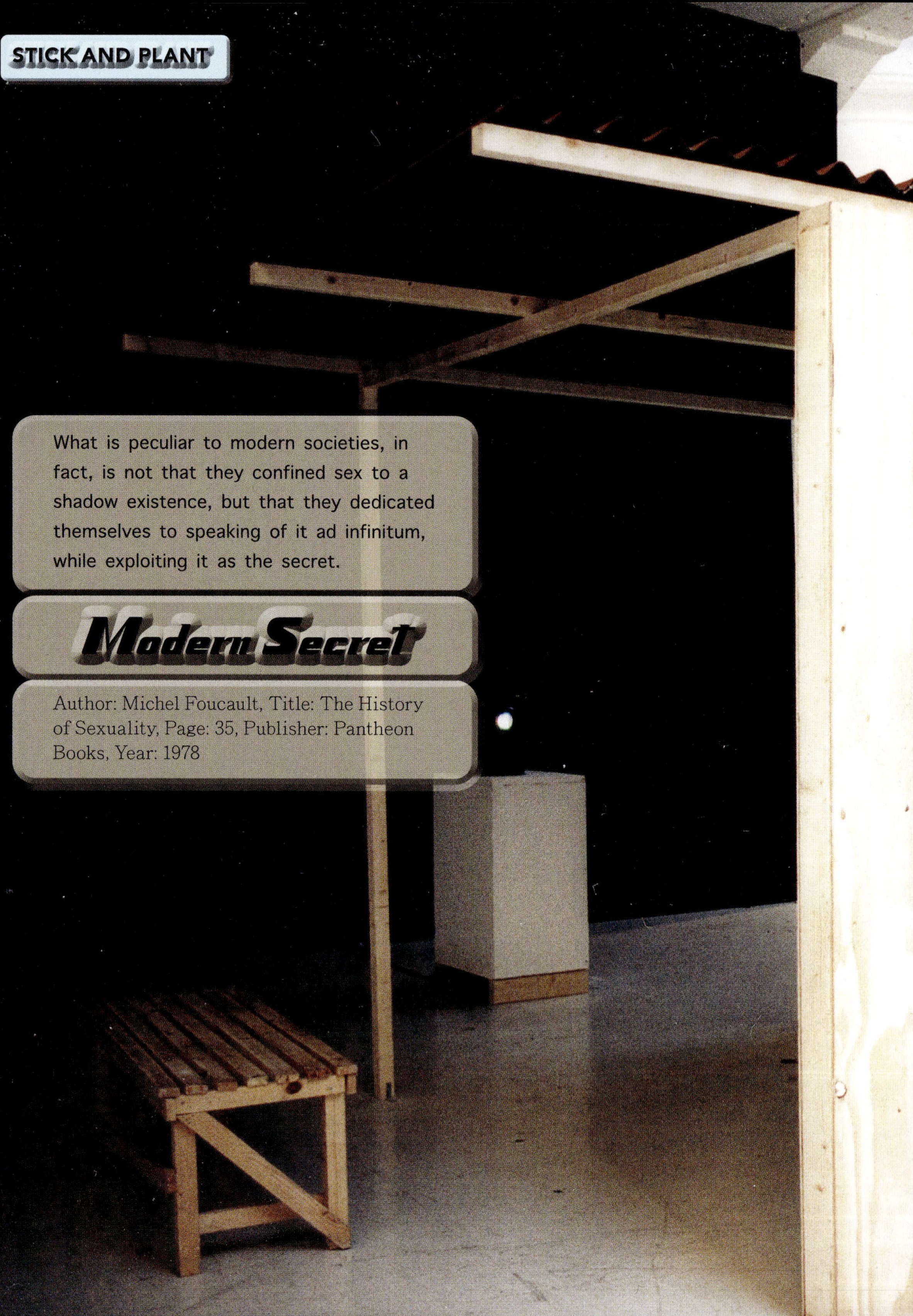

What is peculiar to modern societies, in fact, is not that they confined sex to a shadow existence, but that they dedicated themselves to speaking of it ad infinitum, while exploiting it as the secret.

Modern Secret

Author: Michel Foucault, Title: The History of Sexuality, Page: 35, Publisher: Pantheon Books, Year: 1978

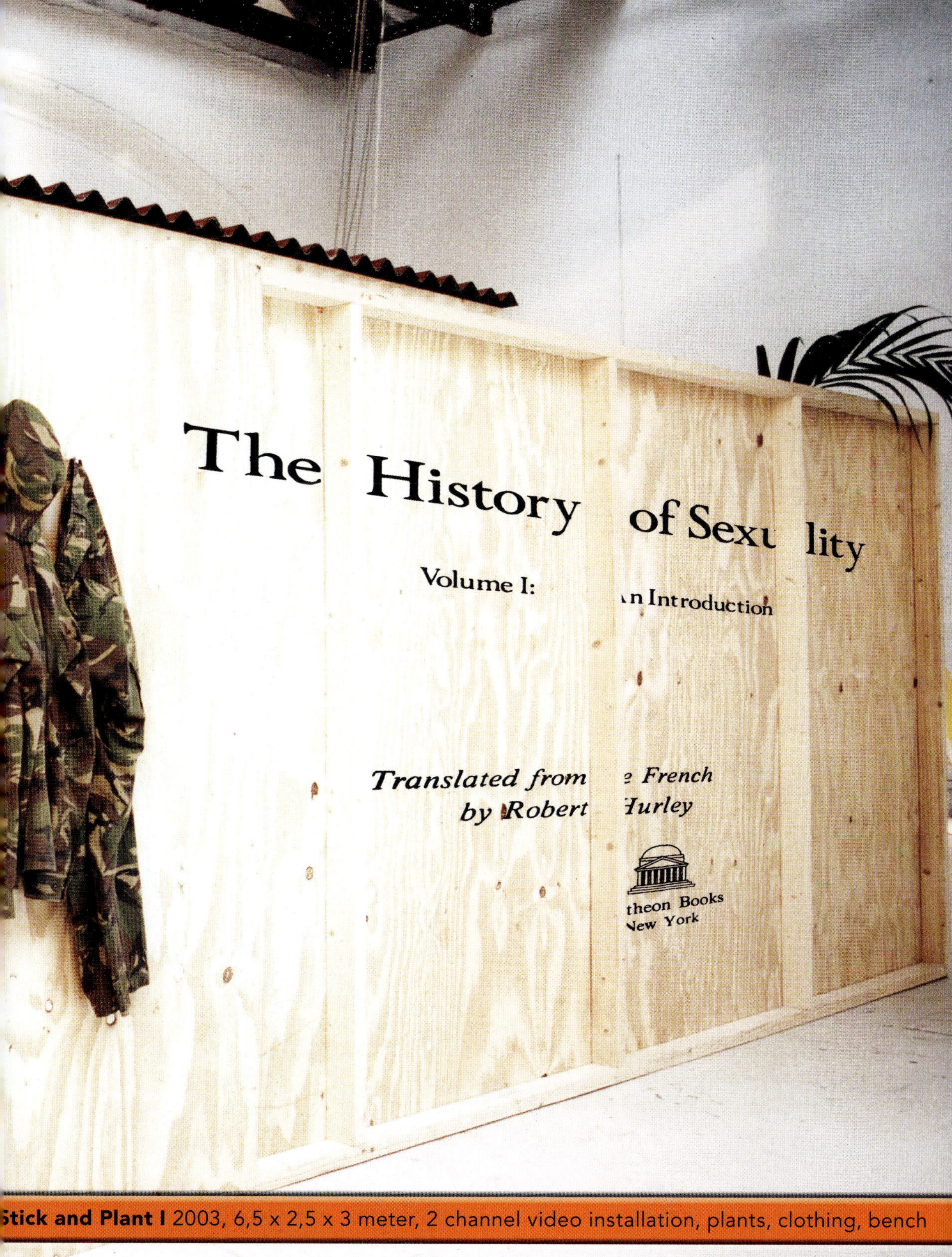

Stick and Plant I 2003, 6,5 x 2,5 x 3 meter, 2 channel video installation, plants, clothing, bench

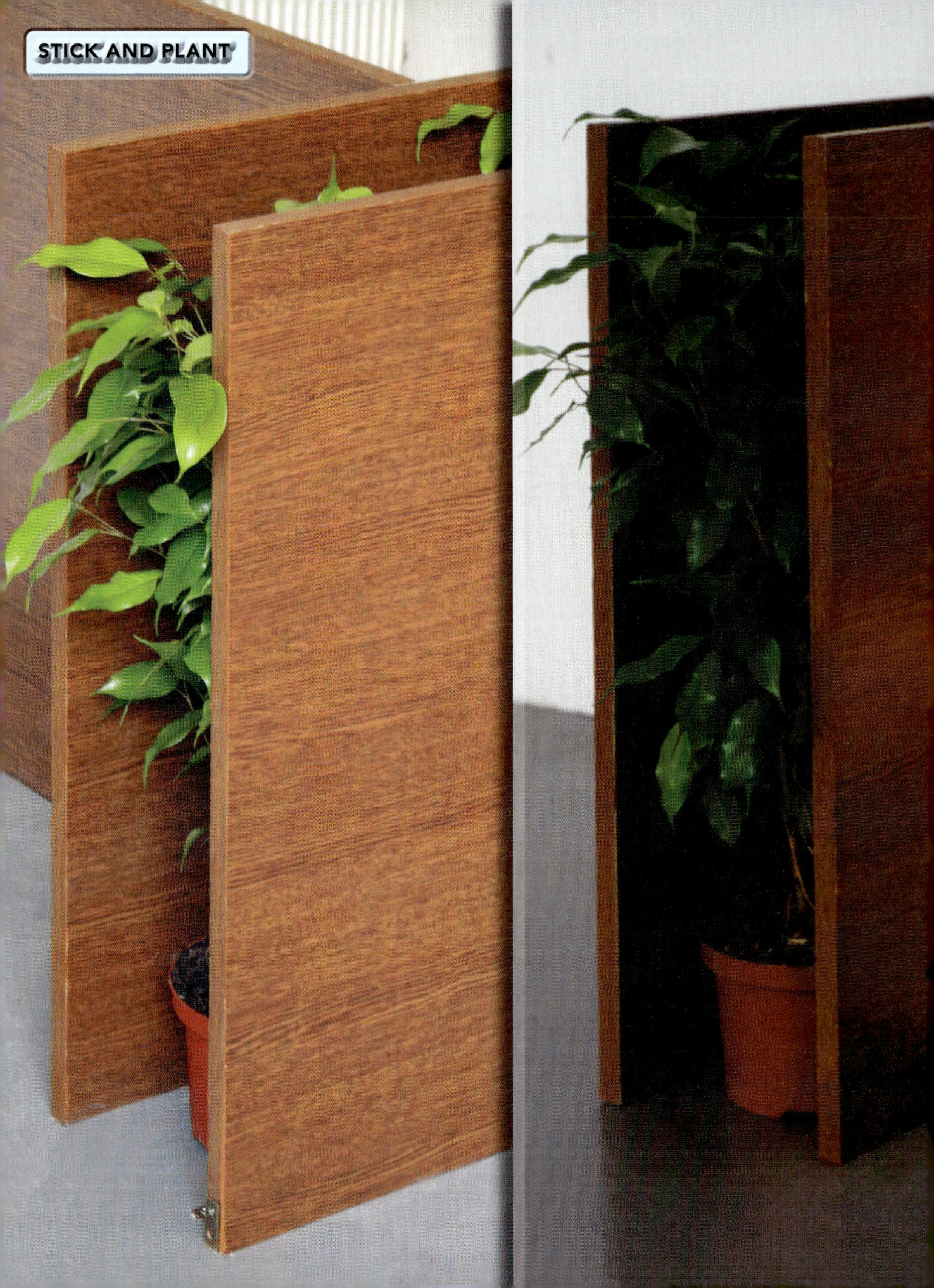
STICK AND PLANT

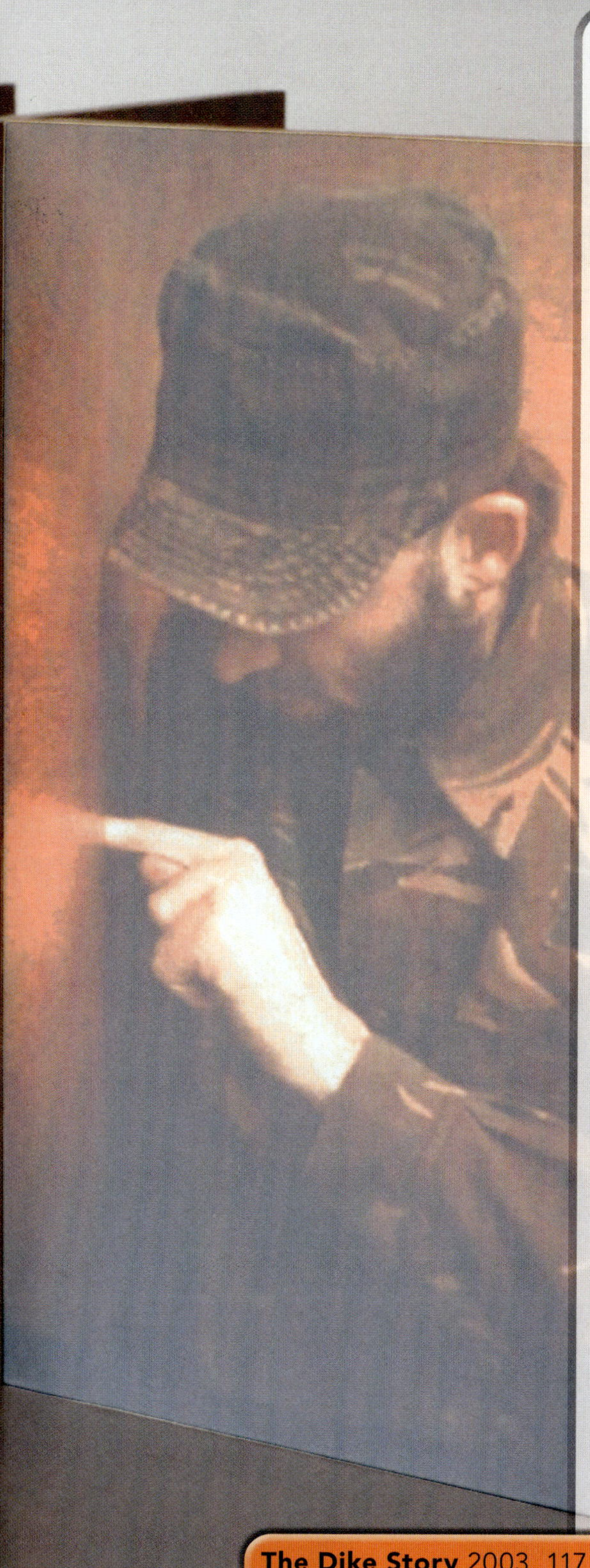

Vietnam to seeing them as victims of a military-industrial complex. [...But t] hey're very proud that they are soldiers' (Matthew Gault and Sebastian Junger 2015) emphasis added). By recognizing the choice of taking on the challenges of military service, and not looking for structural causes, the militarization of a person's body might be treated as a complex of power, discipline, and pleasure. Social reinforcement, widespread sexualization of uniformed bodies, and the perverse association between violent power and desirability all come together here. Understanding militarization without these pleasures risks assuming that soldiers are either dupes or dangerous and sadistic aggressors. A more complicated picture is possible through a focus on the sorts of pleasures associated with militarization.

Finding the inner strength to endure training, reshape the body, and submit to the state, many troops take enormous pride in what they do. But militarization is not simply a process of training and following rules; indeed, it is explicitly about war making. Understanding what makes war compelling is a multifaceted task, and few have done as good a job as philosopher J. Glenn Gray. Reflecting on service in WWII, he described the appeal of battle as emotional, aesthetic, and very embodied. He quotes a French civilian friend, after the war:

Anything is better than to have nothing at all happen day after day. You know that I do not love war or want it to return. But at least it made me feel alive, as I have not felt alive before or since. (Gray 1959, 216—7)

The Dike Story 2003, 117 x 85 x 70 cm, slide projection, laminated wood

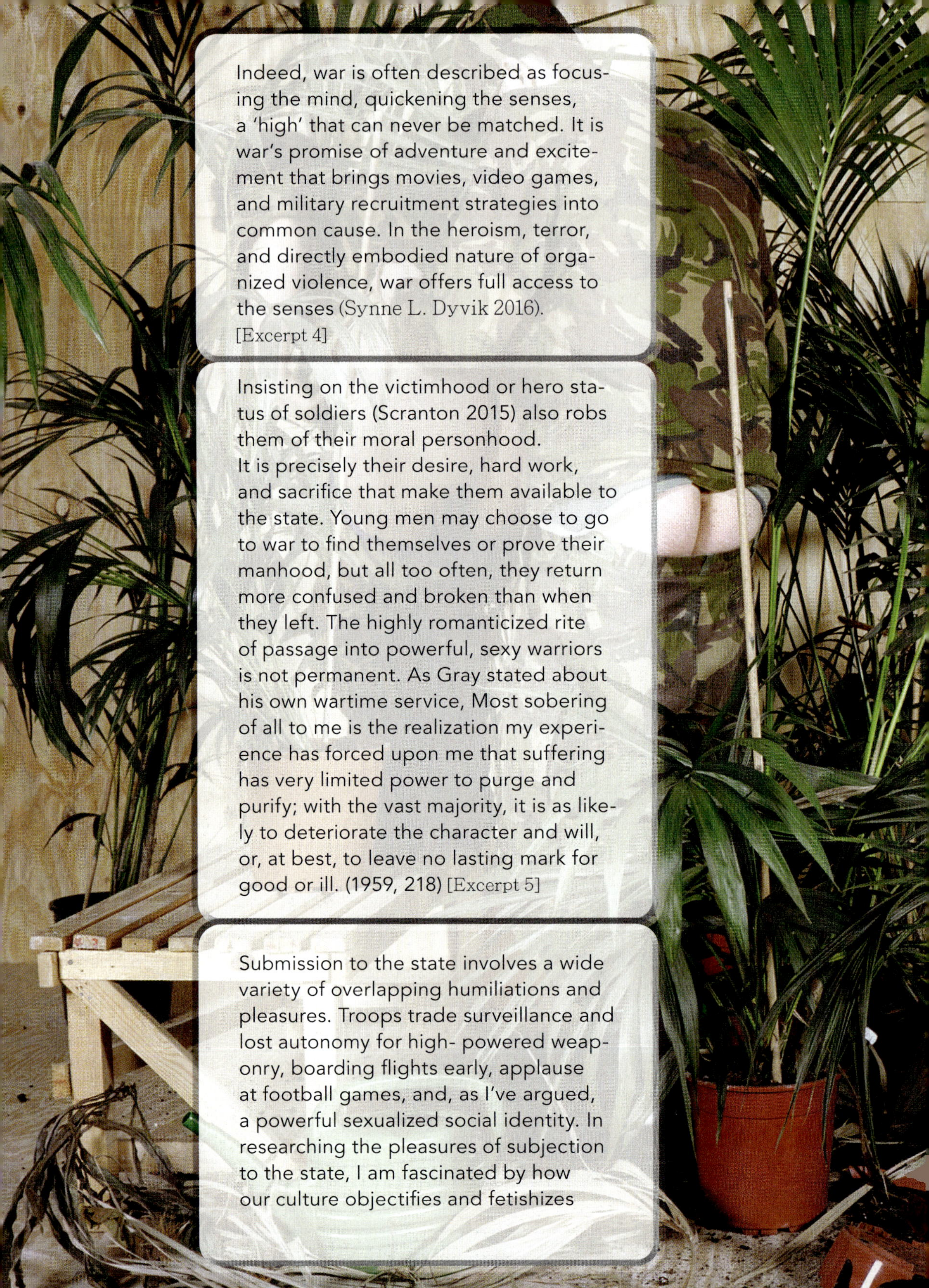

Indeed, war is often described as focusing the mind, quickening the senses, a 'high' that can never be matched. It is war's promise of adventure and excitement that brings movies, video games, and military recruitment strategies into common cause. In the heroism, terror, and directly embodied nature of organized violence, war offers full access to the senses (Synne L. Dyvik 2016). [Excerpt 4]

Insisting on the victimhood or hero status of soldiers (Scranton 2015) also robs them of their moral personhood.
It is precisely their desire, hard work, and sacrifice that make them available to the state. Young men may choose to go to war to find themselves or prove their manhood, but all too often, they return more confused and broken than when they left. The highly romanticized rite of passage into powerful, sexy warriors is not permanent. As Gray stated about his own wartime service, Most sobering of all to me is the realization my experience has forced upon me that suffering has very limited power to purge and purify; with the vast majority, it is as likely to deteriorate the character and will, or, at best, to leave no lasting mark for good or ill. (1959, 218) [Excerpt 5]

Submission to the state involves a wide variety of overlapping humiliations and pleasures. Troops trade surveillance and lost autonomy for high- powered weaponry, boarding flights early, applause at football games, and, as I've argued, a powerful sexualized social identity. In researching the pleasures of subjection to the state, I am fascinated by how our culture objectifies and fetishizes

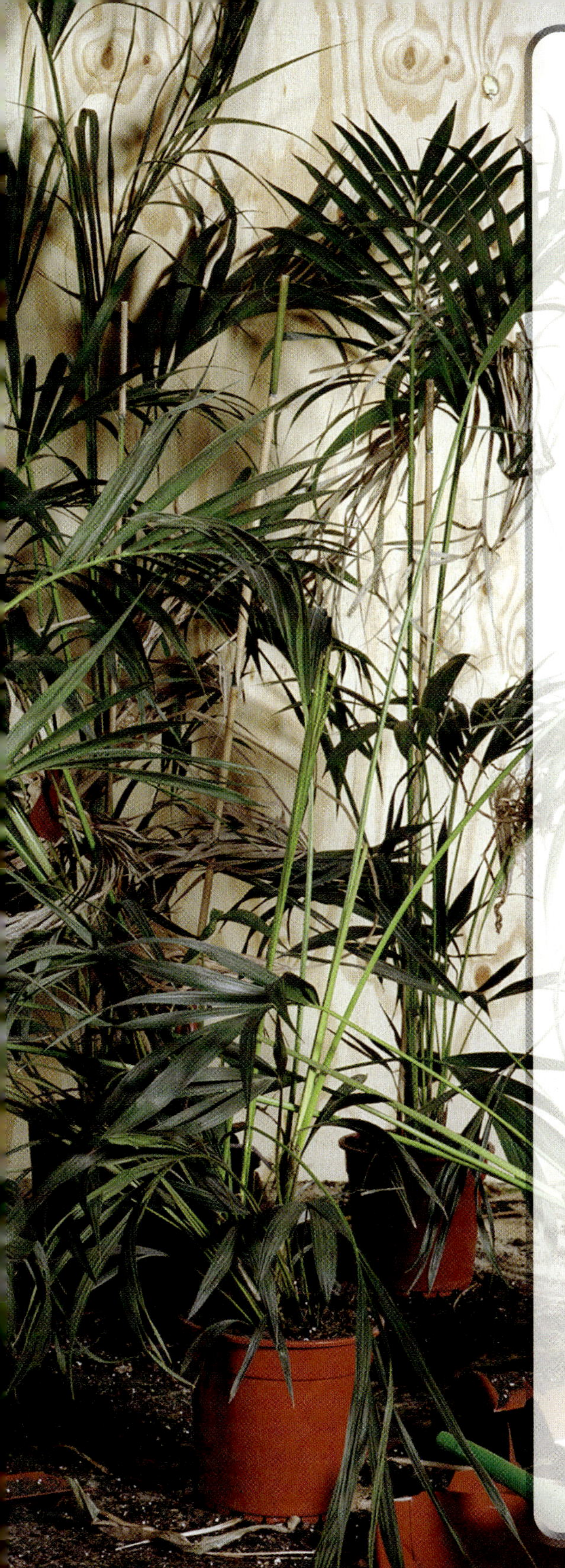

the militarized male body in ways that are normally reserved only for women's bodies. As in leather S/M communities, submission yields a unique status, one that paradoxically creates a sense of personal power and triumph. In the toughness and endurance required to submit, mastery is demonstrated.

An important question that remains unanswered here is whether the appropriation of militarized identities, uniforms, and practices by radical kink communities undermines or reinforces the cultural hold of militarization. A number of authors have warned about the linkage between queer struggles and militarized citizenship, but I would argue (with Foucault) that one of the radical possibilities of kink is taking strategic relationships of domination and converting them into fully negotiated, consensual forms of play. In such play, fantasies like slavery, rape, '1950s housewives', and torture are re-appropriated in ways that generate pleasure, and perhaps even healing (Call 2011). Actual torture, rape, slavery, and the like involve the objectification of human beings and the suspension of reciprocity or intersubjectively shared experience (Jessica Benjamin 1988).

Kink, on the other hand, emphasizes enthusiastic consent, uses the mechanism of 'safewording' to ensure agency, and is meant to bring people together for mutual benefit. Thinking about power, pleasure, and pain also highlights important ethical distinctions between active submission and forced, non-consensual power dynamics. It opens the complicated psycho-sexual politics of surrender, domination, and attraction to analysis and helps explain the sexi-

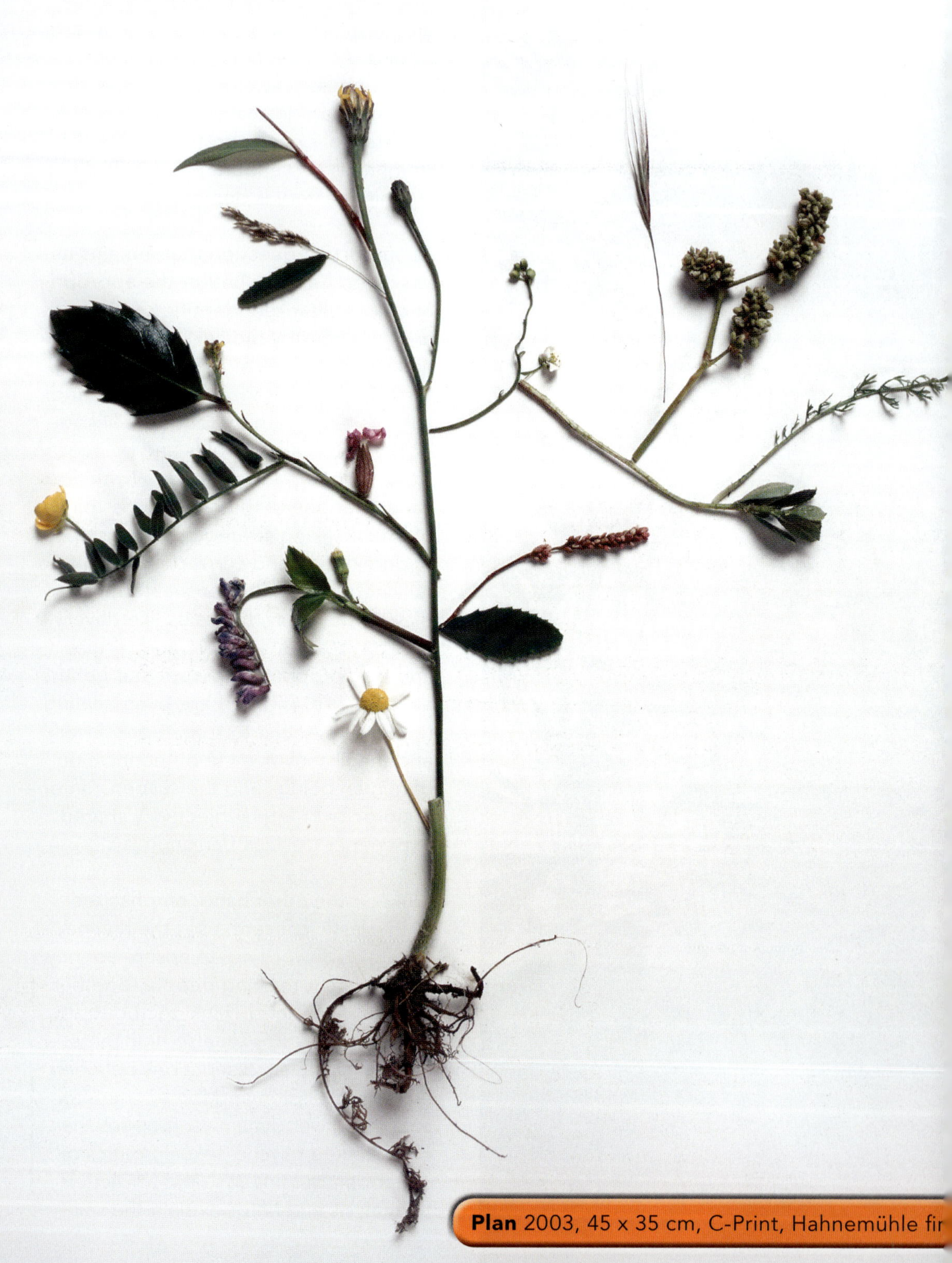

Plan 2003, 45 x 35 cm, C-Print, Hahnemühle fir

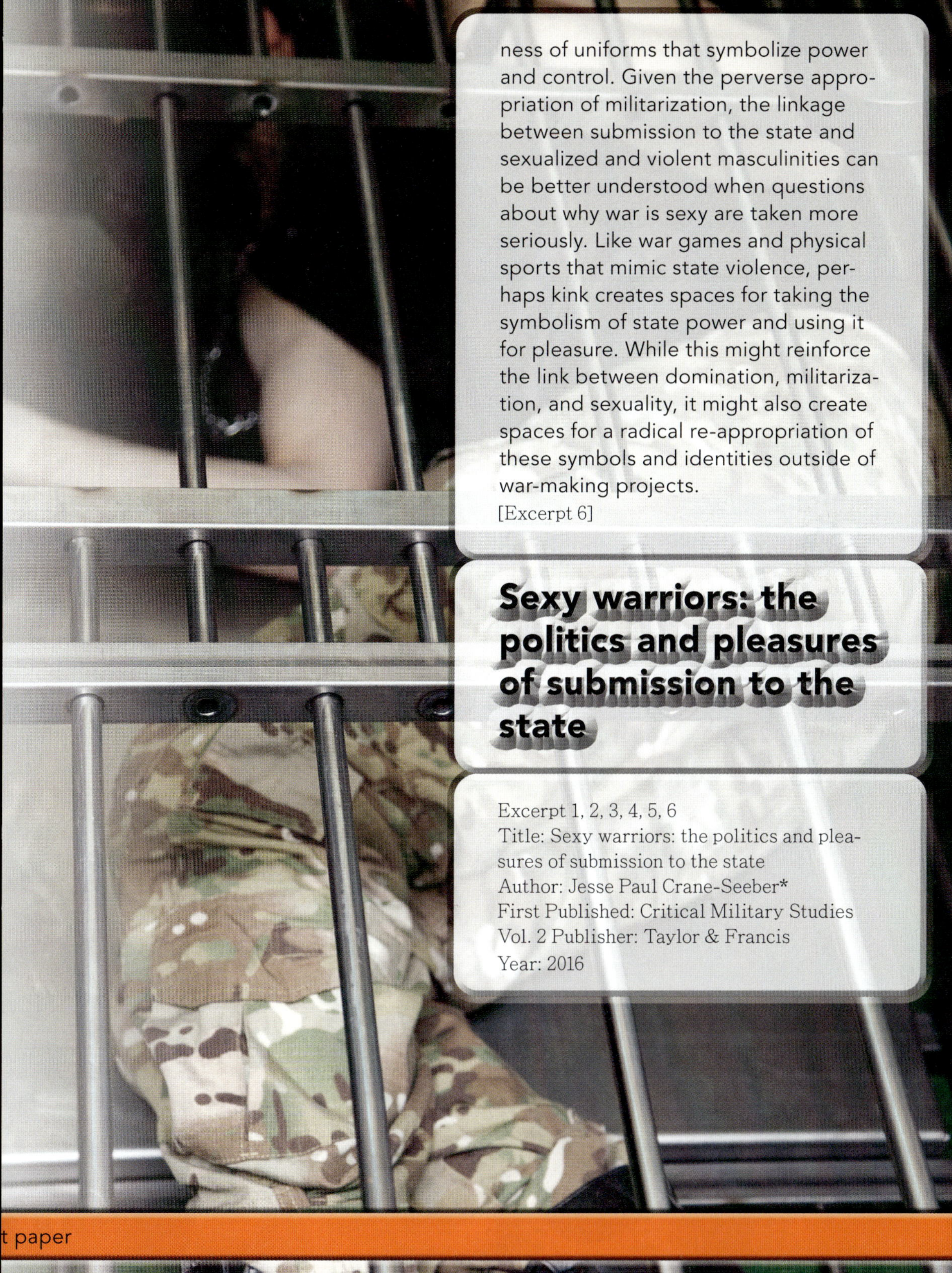

ness of uniforms that symbolize power and control. Given the perverse appropriation of militarization, the linkage between submission to the state and sexualized and violent masculinities can be better understood when questions about why war is sexy are taken more seriously. Like war games and physical sports that mimic state violence, perhaps kink creates spaces for taking the symbolism of state power and using it for pleasure. While this might reinforce the link between domination, militarization, and sexuality, it might also create spaces for a radical re-appropriation of these symbols and identities outside of war-making projects.
[Excerpt 6]

Sexy warriors: the politics and pleasures of submission to the state

Excerpt 1, 2, 3, 4, 5, 6
Title: Sexy warriors: the politics and pleasures of submission to the state
Author: Jesse Paul Crane-Seeber*
First Published: Critical Military Studies
Vol. 2 Publisher: Taylor & Francis
Year: 2016

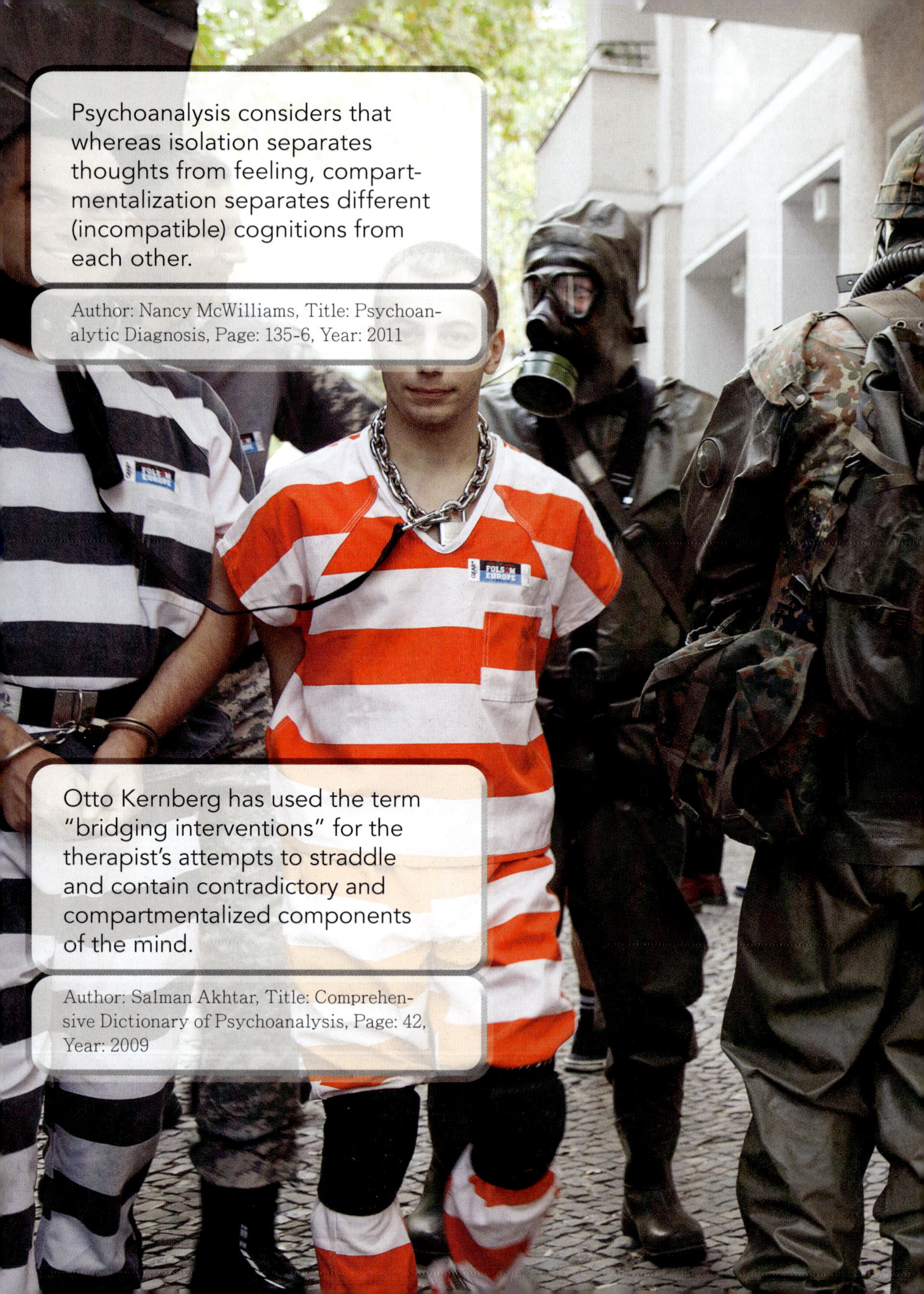

Psychoanalysis considers that whereas isolation separates thoughts from feeling, compartmentalization separates different (incompatible) cognitions from each other.

Author: Nancy McWilliams, Title: Psychoanalytic Diagnosis, Page: 135-6, Year: 2011

Otto Kernberg has used the term "bridging interventions" for the therapist's attempts to straddle and contain contradictory and compartmentalized components of the mind.

Author: Salman Akhtar, Title: Comprehensive Dictionary of Psychoanalysis, Page: 42, Year: 2009

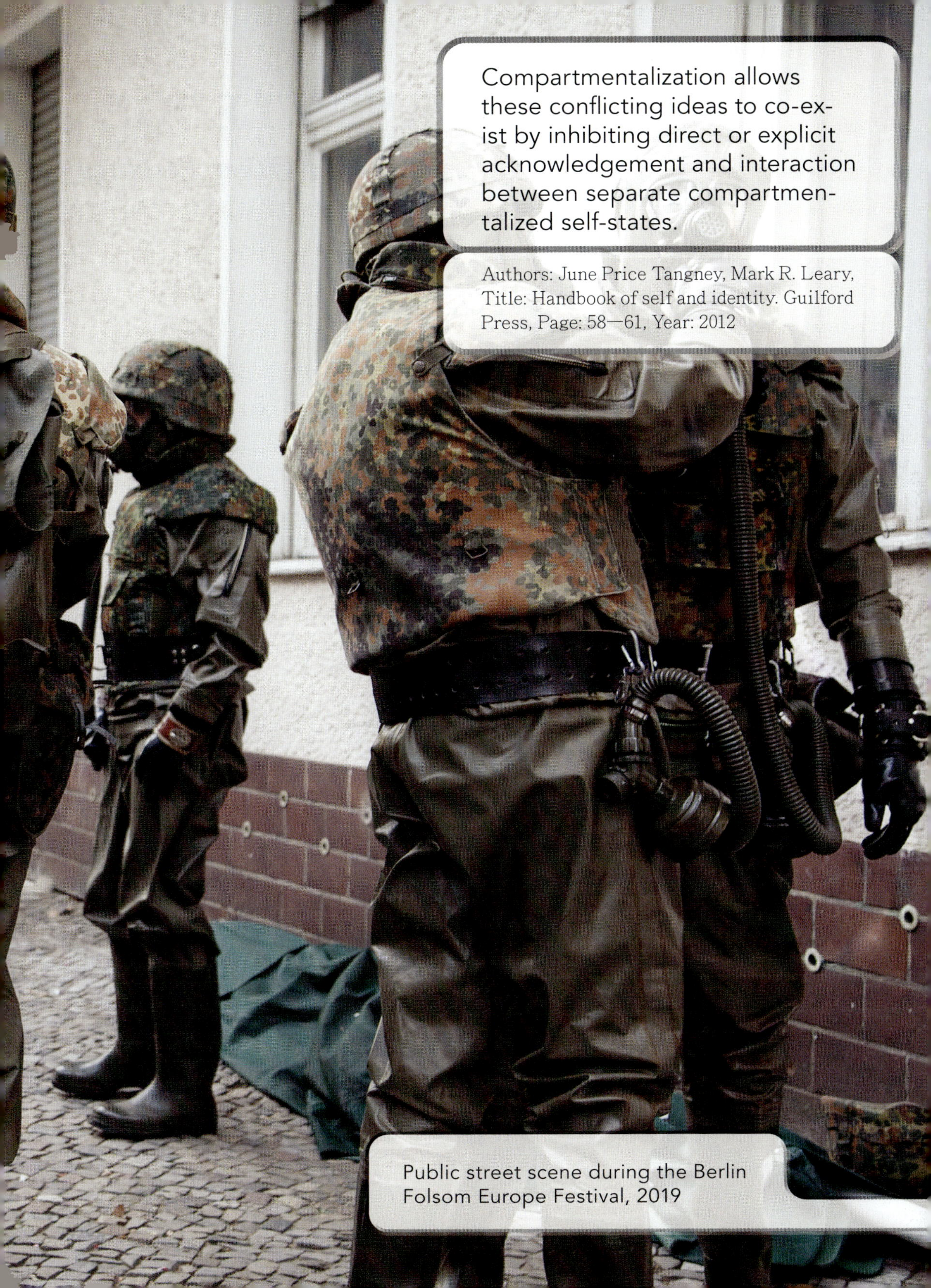

Compartmentalization allows these conflicting ideas to co-exist by inhibiting direct or explicit acknowledgement and interaction between separate compartmentalized self-states.

Authors: June Price Tangney, Mark R. Leary, Title: Handbook of self and identity. Guilford Press, Page: 58—61, Year: 2012

Public street scene during the Berlin Folsom Europe Festival, 2019

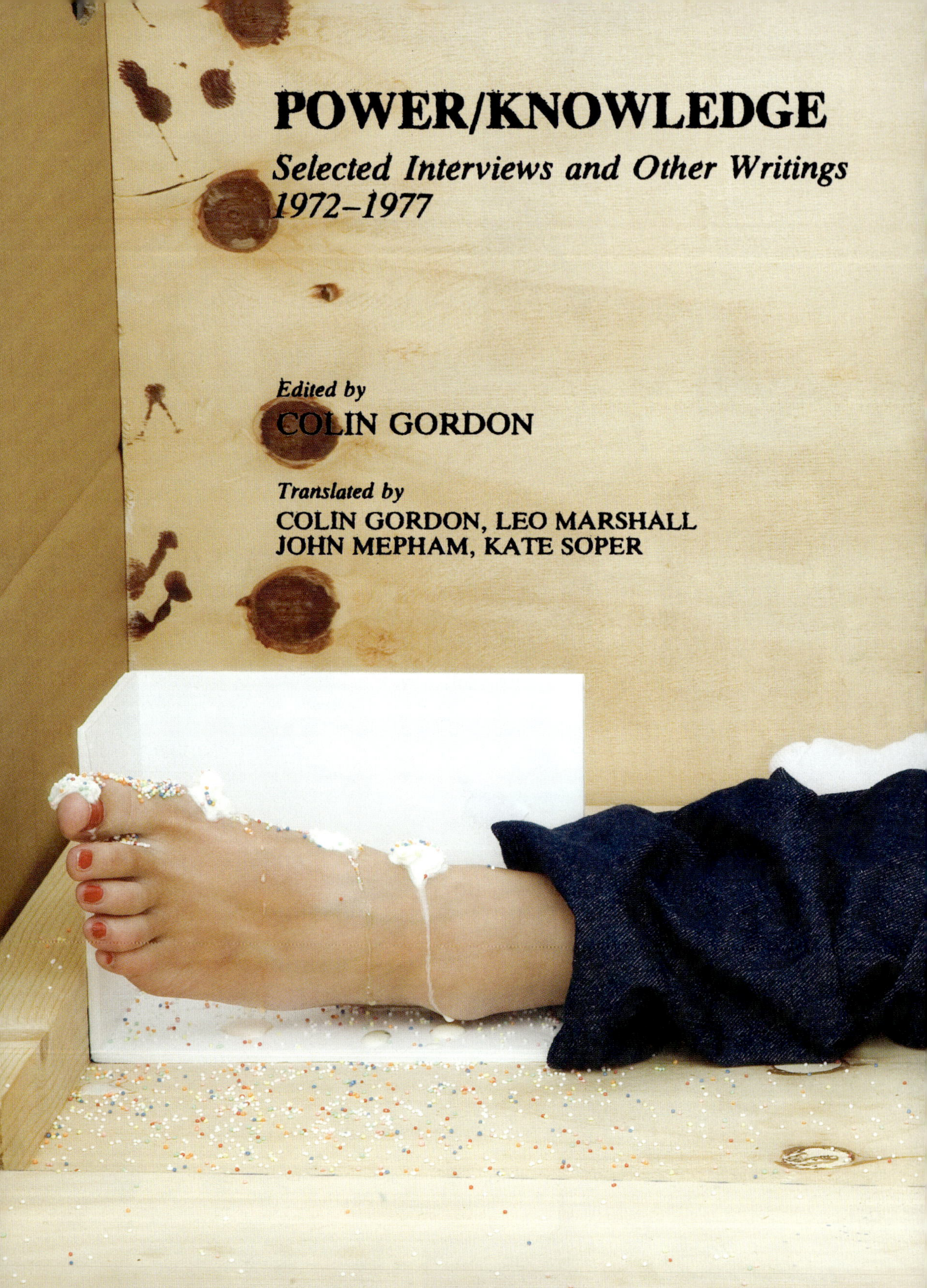
POWER/KNOWLEDGE
Selected Interviews and Other Writings
1972–1977
Edited by
COLIN GORDON
Translated by
COLIN GORDON, LEO MARSHALL
JOHN MEPHAM, KATE SOPER

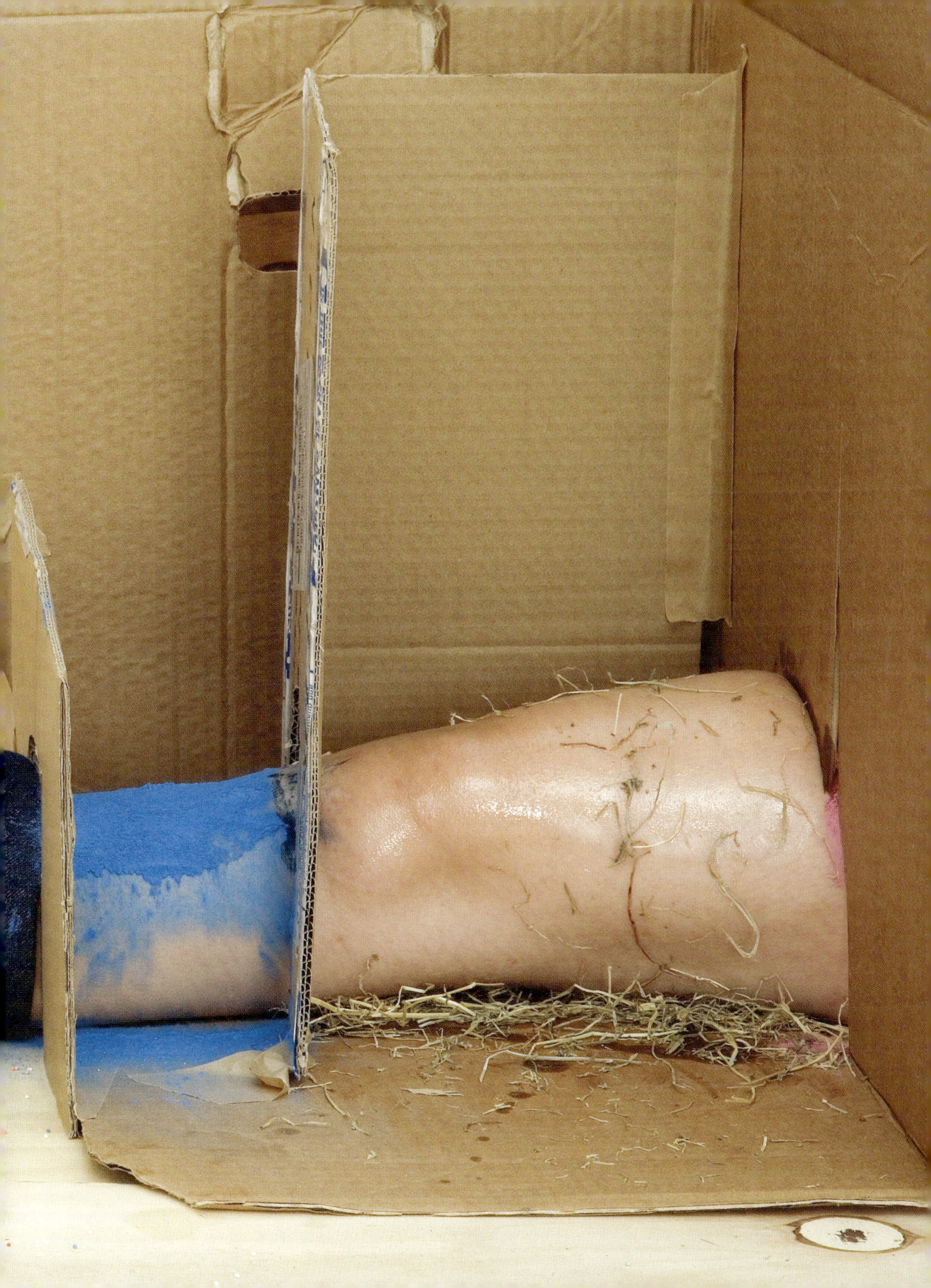

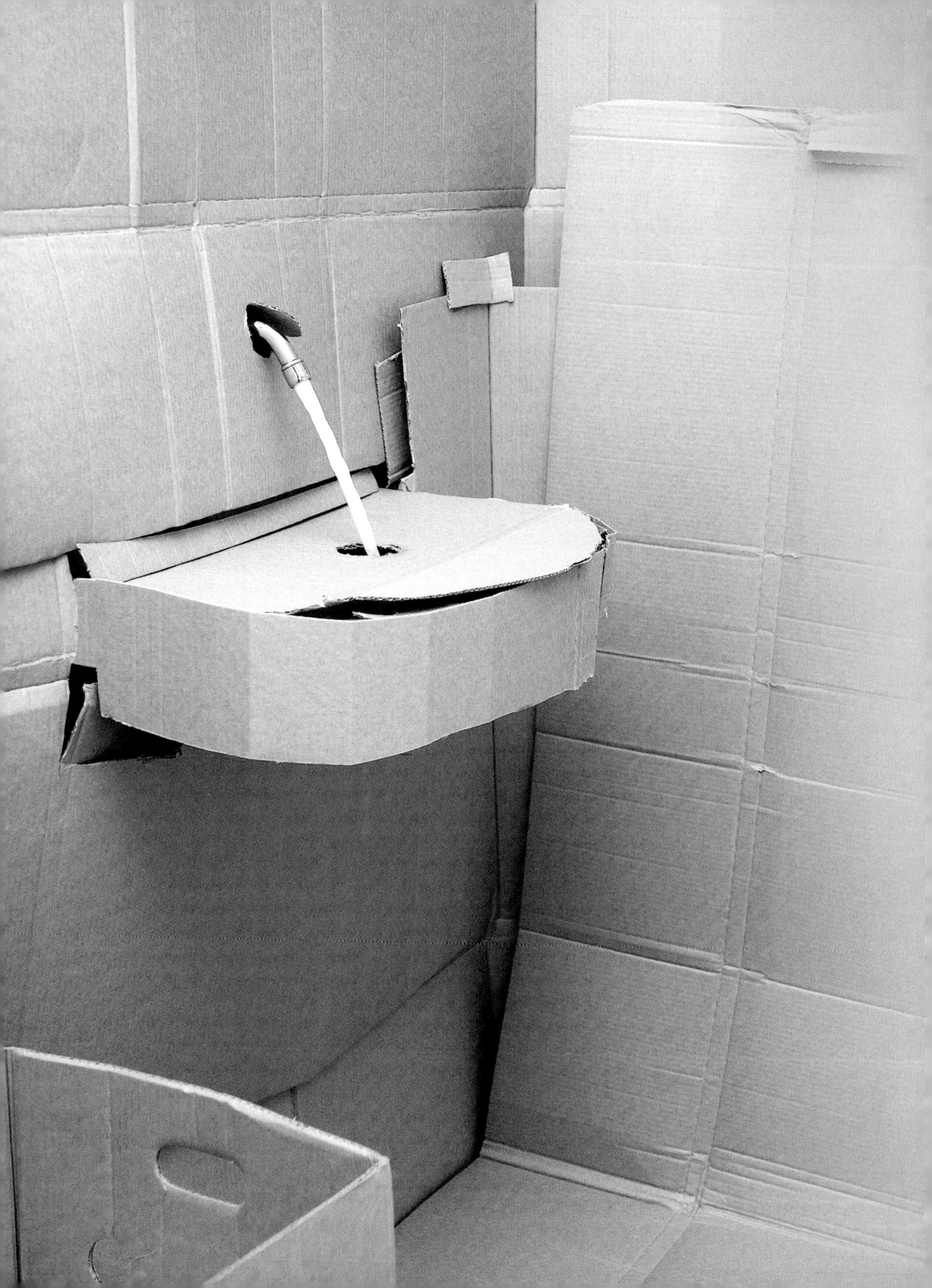

Compartmentalization is related to the phenomenon of neurotic typing, whereby everything must be classified into mutually exclusive categories.

Author: Otto Fenichel, Title: The Psychoanalytic Theory of Neurosis, Page: 286, Year: 1946

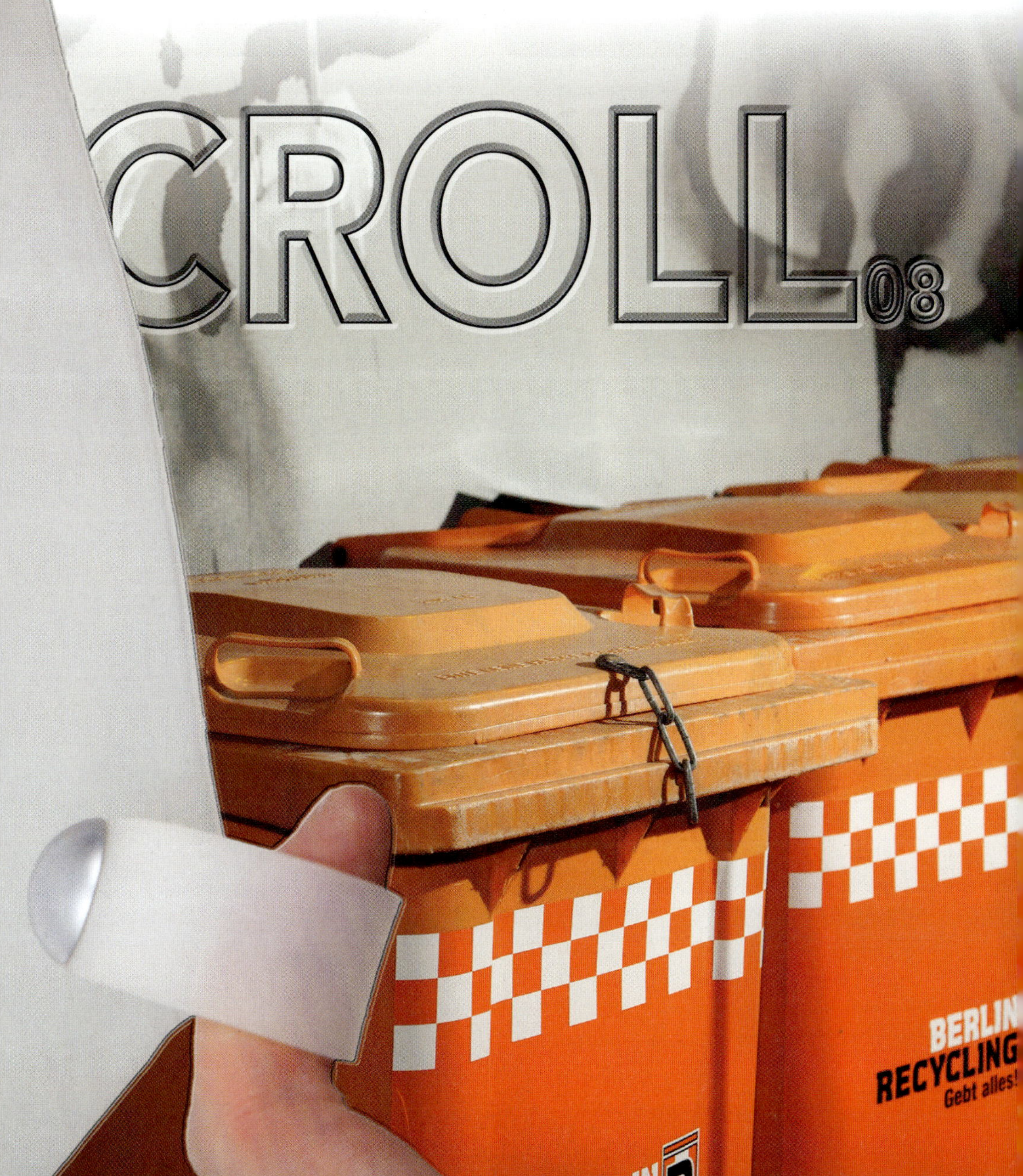

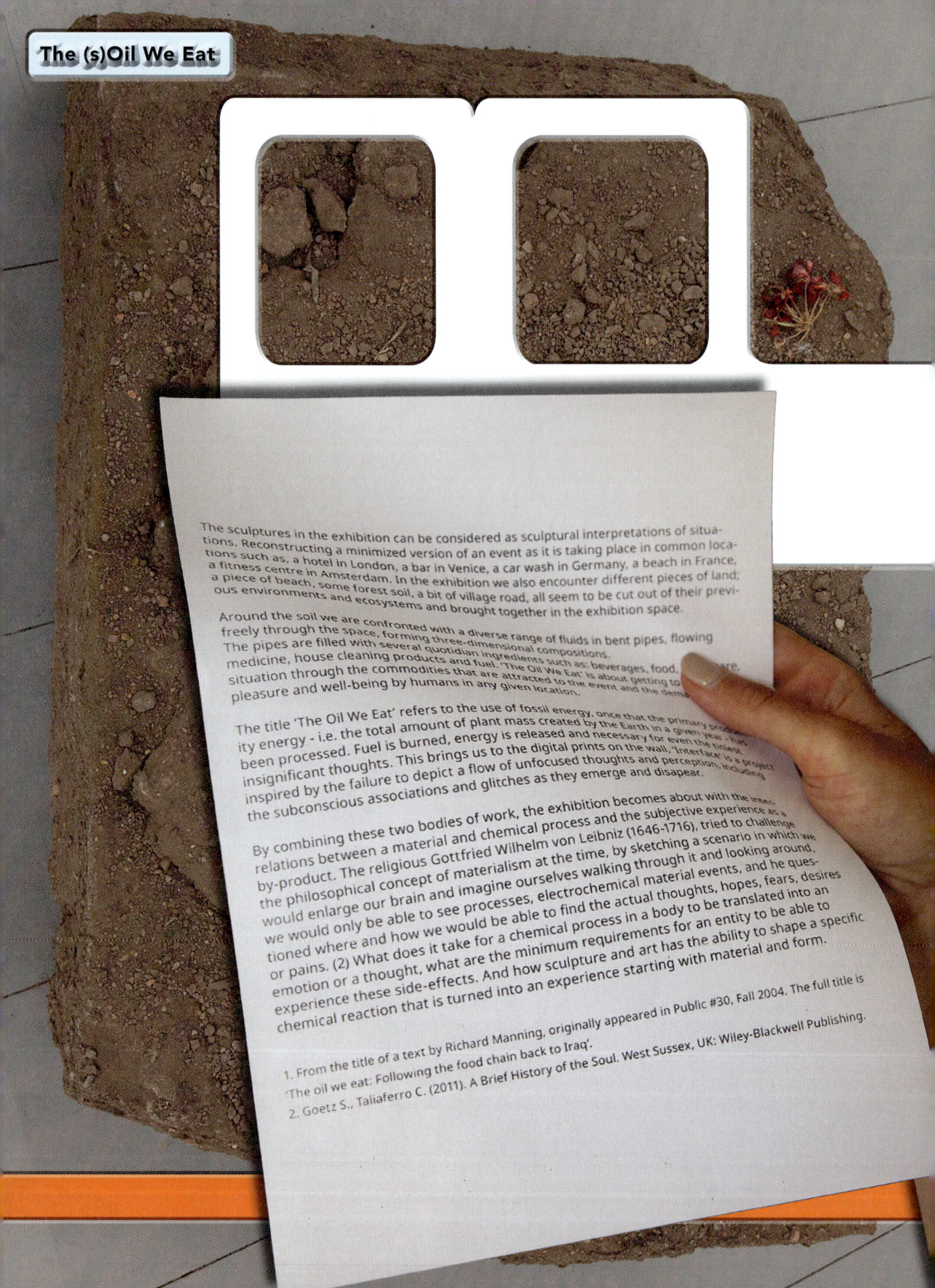

The sculptures in the exhibition can be considered as sculptural interpretations of situations. Reconstructing a minimized version of an event as it is taking place in common locations such as, a hotel in London, a bar in Venice, a car wash in Germany, a beach in France,
a fitness centre in Amsterdam. In the exhibition we also encounter different pieces of land;
a piece of beach, some forest soil, a bit of village road, all seem to be cut out of their previous environments and ecosystems and brought together in the exhibition space.

Around the soil we are confronted with a diverse range of fluids in bent pipes, flowing
freely through the space, forming three-dimensional compositions.
The pipes are filled with several quotidian ingredients such as: beverages, food, ...are,
medicine, house cleaning products and fuel. 'The Oil We Eat' is about getting to
situation through the commodities that are attracted to the event and the dema...
pleasure and well-being by humans in any given location.

The title 'The Oil We Eat' refers to the use of fossil energy, once that the primary produc...
ity energy - i.e. the total amount of plant mass created by the Earth in a given year - has
been processed. Fuel is burned, energy is released and necessary for even the tiniest
insignificant thoughts. This brings us to the digital prints on the wall, 'Interface' is a project
inspired by the failure to depict a flow of unfocused thoughts and perception, including
the subconscious associations and glitches as they emerge and disapear.

By combining these two bodies of work, the exhibition becomes about with the inter-
relations between a material and chemical process and the subjective experience as a
by-product. The religious Gottfried Wilhelm von Leibniz (1646-1716), tried to challenge
the philosophical concept of materialism at the time, by sketching a scenario in which we
would enlarge our brain and imagine ourselves walking through it and looking around,
we would only be able to see processes, electrochemical material events, and he questioned where and how we would be able to find the actual thoughts, hopes, fears, desires
or pains. (2) What does it take for a chemical process in a body to be translated into an
emotion or a thought, what are the minimum requirements for an entity to be able to
experience these side-effects. And how sculpture and art has the ability to shape a specific
chemical reaction that is turned into an experience starting with material and form.

1. From the title of a text by Richard Manning, originally appeared in Public #30, Fall 2004. The full title is
'The oil we eat: Following the food chain back to Iraq'.
2. Goetz S., Taliaferro C. (2011). A Brief History of the Soul. West Sussex, UK: Wiley-Blackwell Publishing.

Continuation from Black Ice text SCROLL 10

Title: Black Ice, Author: Iain Hamilton Grant, First published: Virtual Futures: Cyberotics, Technology and Post-Human Pragmatism, ed. Joan Braodhurst Dixon and Eric J. Cassidy, Page: 132-143, Publisher: Routledge, Year: 1998

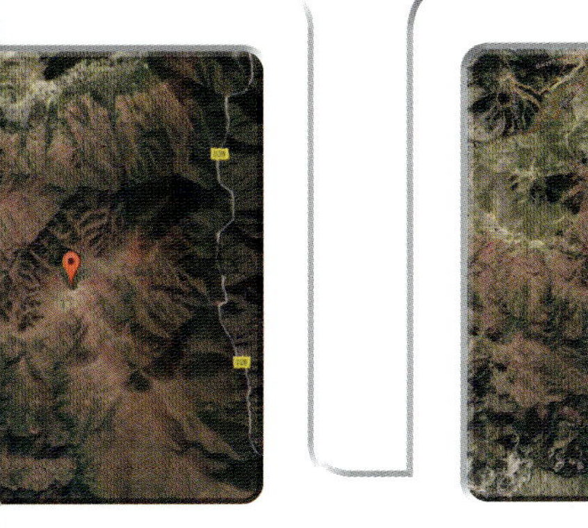

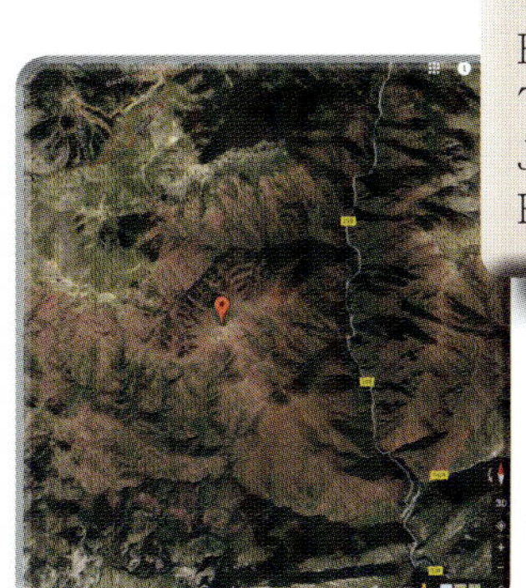

Passing into the alleged interior of this steampunk collage of industrial organs does not inject new energies into the pulpy masses at the biodrome's core – 'a society functioning on Valium' (Lyotard 1994: 220) : rather, it stimulates peripheral pressure- sensors to spasm the pulp's primitive musculature [into action, thus discharging the incoming pulsion. Still, the dams and filters secure the energy level's constancy.

Tête de Rigaud 2014, 98 x 58 x 30 cm, soil, styrofoam, beer lid, metalstands, cement glue

The (s)Oil We Eat

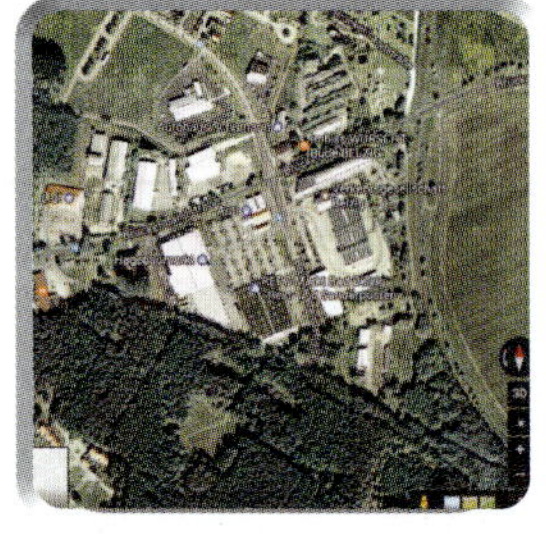

Soil from the naturpark Hoher Fläming, Aral Bluetronic SAE 10W-40, Sonax Xtreme anti frost & klarsicht konzentrat Nano Pro, Ignite Vitamin Water, acrylic pipes, rubber corks, stainless steel, paint, styrofoam, cement glue.

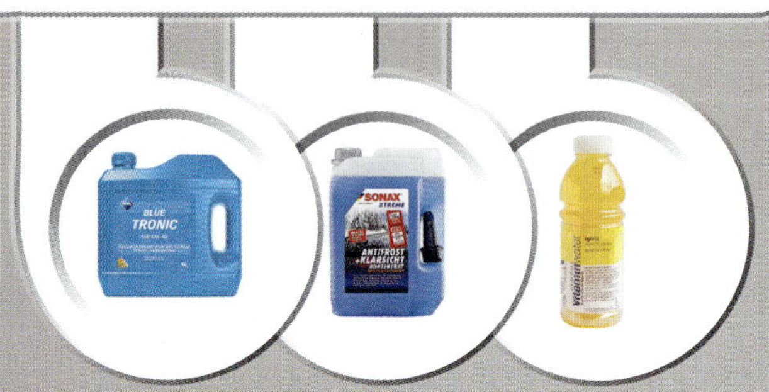

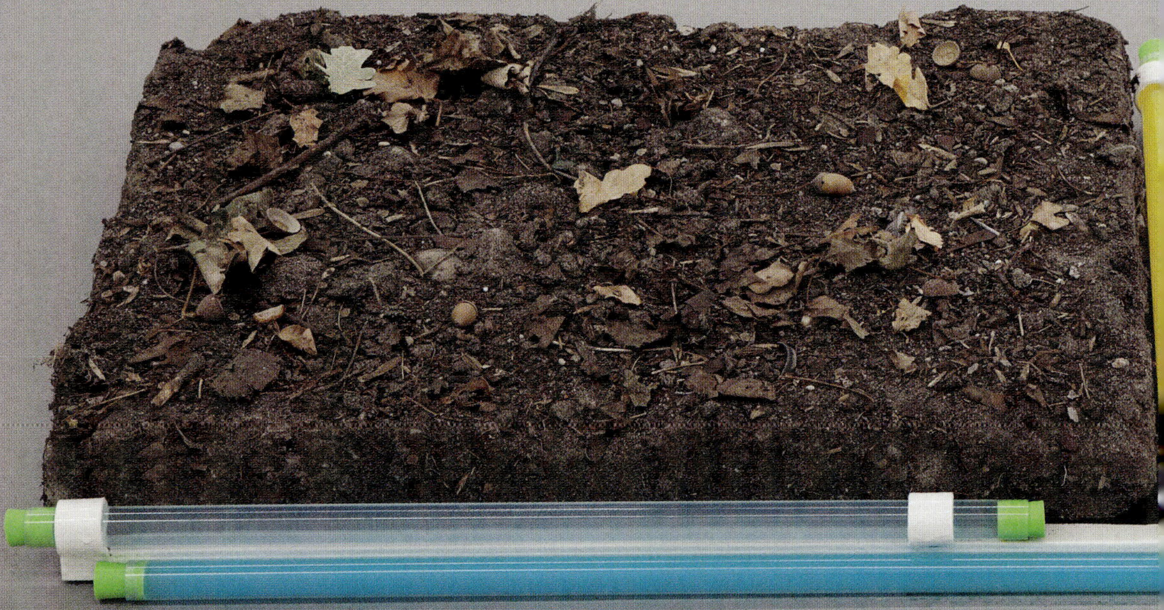

at Aral GmbH 2014, 241 x 112 x 51 cm

AI GPT-2 RESPONSE

He says that in addition to neurotic typing, it is also associated with a mental state that can produce various mental states. As he notes, "If one has too many thoughts, then one is prone to becoming unstable — in this case, a state of disoriented thoughts, or in this case, a state of disoriented behavior." He cites an example: He has a bad memory—a bad feeling — which may lead to a bad impulse behavior and may cause a "loss of control" on his mind. A bad impression is also common among his patients. "If someone has a very negative attitude toward people the whole time they're there, and someone has good intentions and can get along well

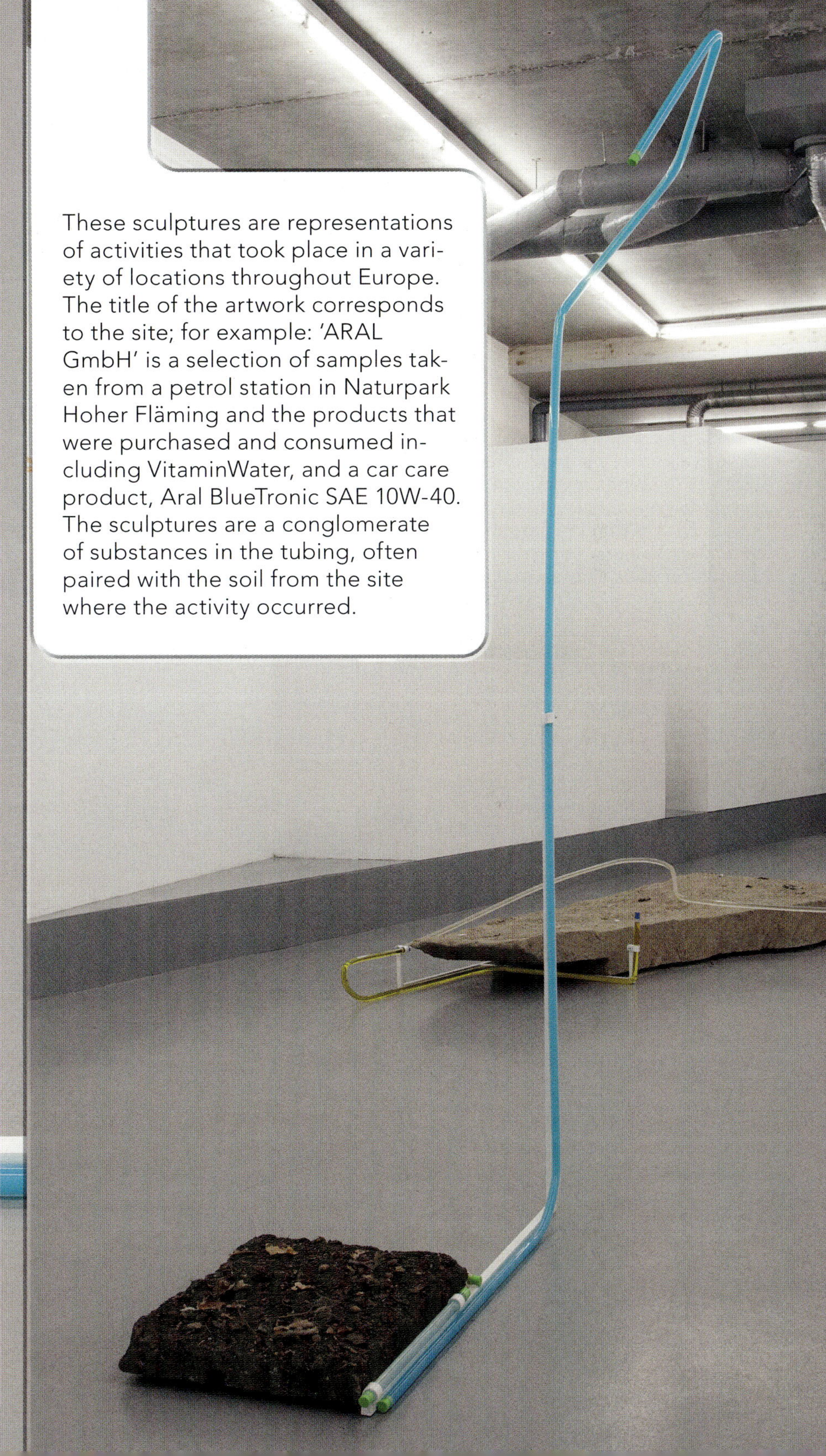

These sculptures are representations of activities that took place in a variety of locations throughout Europe. The title of the artwork corresponds to the site; for example: 'ARAL GmbH' is a selection of samples taken from a petrol station in Naturpark Hoher Fläming and the products that were purchased and consumed including VitaminWater, and a car care product, Aral BlueTronic SAE 10W-40. The sculptures are a conglomerate of substances in the tubing, often paired with the soil from the site where the activity occurred.

For the pyschical apparatus, the mechanism that dealt with increases in systemic pressure was designated the 'pleasure-principle,' which can best be described as a bichydraulic function: a valve in the apparatus opens given an increase in the quantity of ane excitation in the system (registered by the organism as the production of unpleasure), facilitating _discharge and thereby decreasing intensity to biodromically viable levels. The organism registers this drainage as the production of pleasure, and has a vitiated tendency to replicate the intensity of the first pleasure it encountered, impelling it to ever-greater expenditures as the fantasy of a return to, of . thus libidinal economic reversibility, falls derelicted into recurrent cycles of Q. The remnant of the apparatus c, phenomenally hedonist regression is, however, ~ _ subject to micro-cop repression by means of a realilty principle, a dam designating a minium energetic threshold beneath which the organism ceases to function. The biodromic apparatus, designated the "body" under the regime of reality, the emergent subject of corporate discipline, is a coalescence of sensitive fragments looped to repeat at a constant rate; as Baudrillard says, "the body is nothing other than the models in which different systems have enclosed it" (Baudrillard 1993:114): reality remodeled in accordance with the repetition of serial intensive quanta within the range of this energetic threshold. It is this threshold that then circumscribes the arena within which "thought" can be transcendental unity of apperception"—the "I think" that accompanies all my representations. These bound circulations then, simultaneously bind the energies within this quantitative index to force the limits of the biodrome, onto which its nested loops project the "I see I" of the identitarian spectacle.

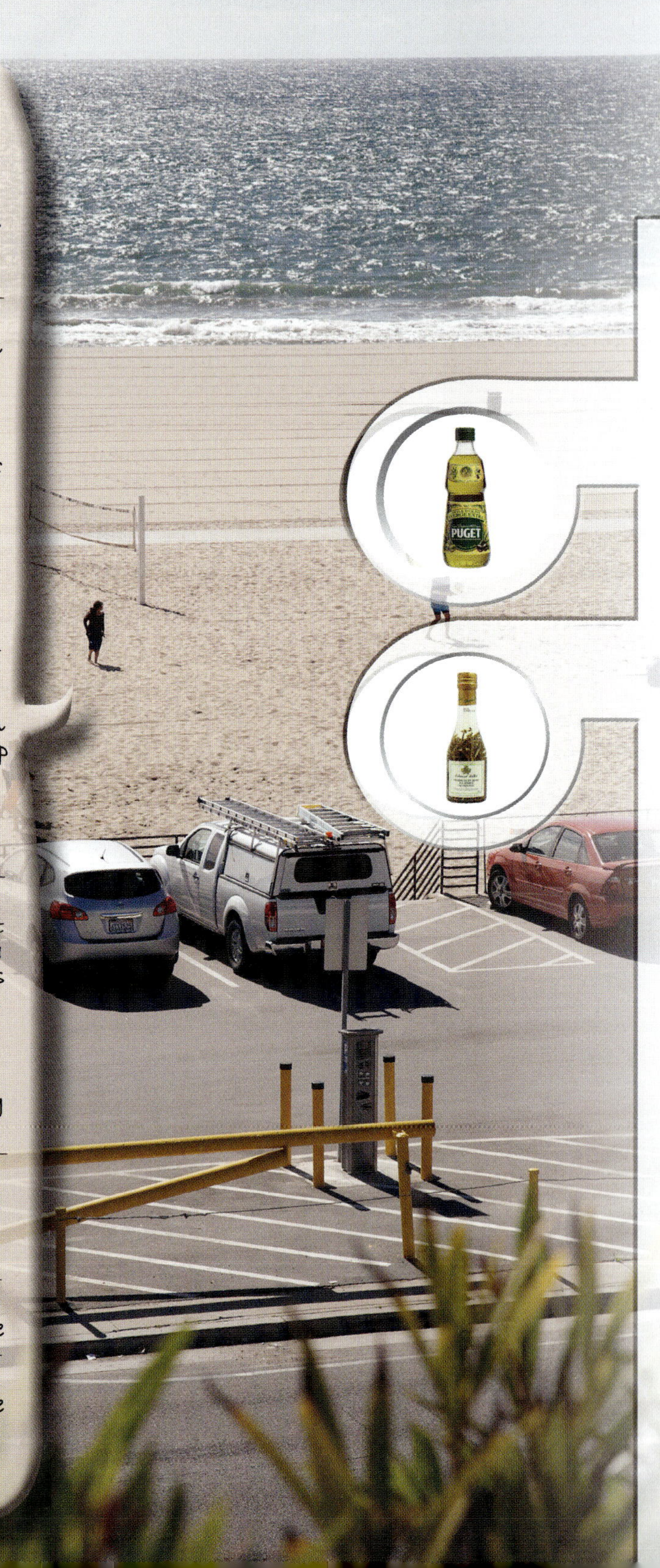

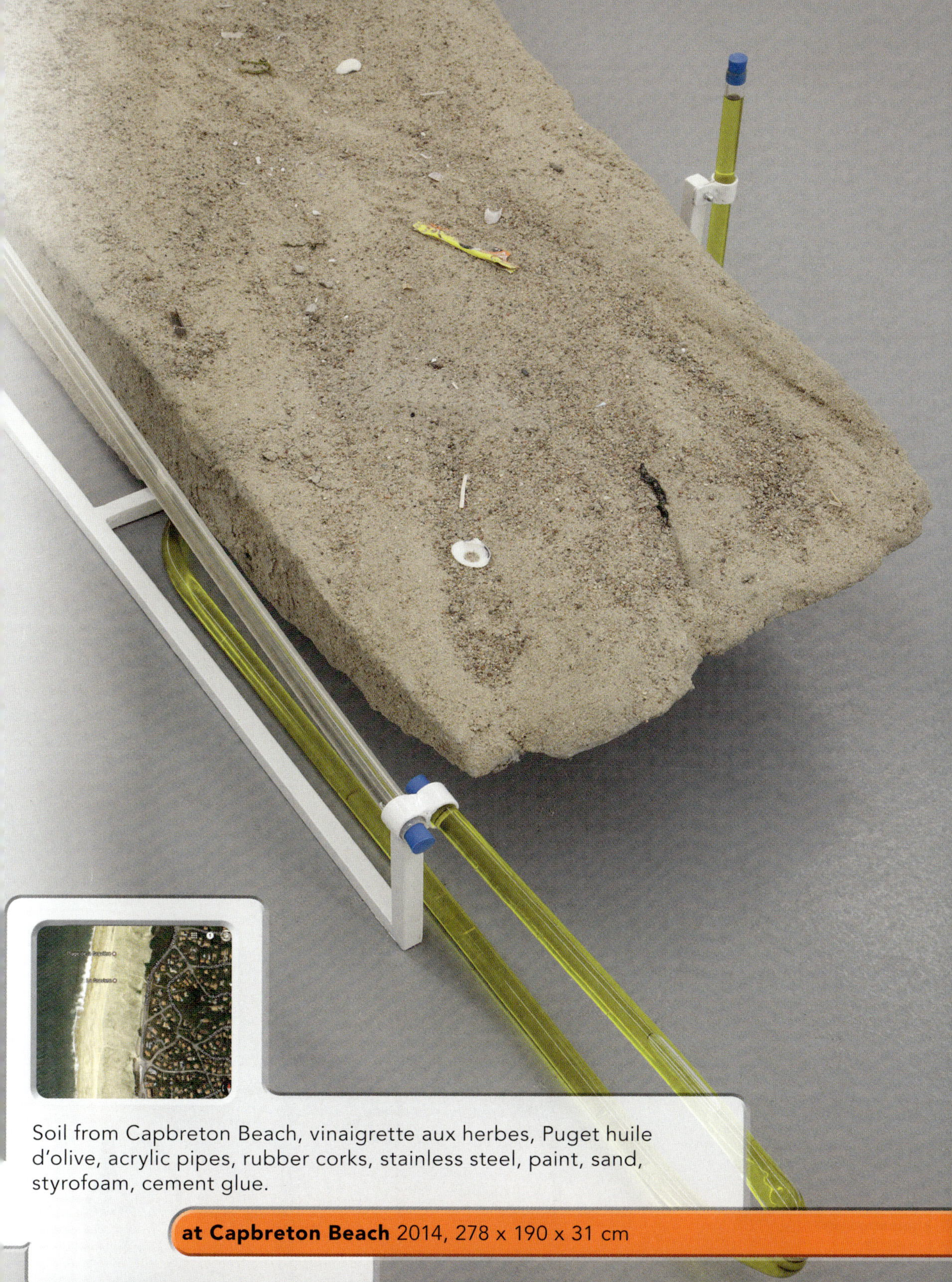

Soil from Capbreton Beach, vinaigrette aux herbes, Puget huile d'olive, acrylic pipes, rubber corks, stainless steel, paint, sand, styrofoam, cement glue.

at Capbreton Beach 2014, 278 x 190 x 31 cm

with them, and they're not behaving badly, the person will revert to what was once a good attitude, which is to stay in the positive," he explains."I try to treat someone as if he has the ability to do what I want him to do," he adds. "I tell him to stick to his words and not act as if he has the same attitude as I do. I ask him how often he's behaving, and I tell him how many times he's been in conflict, and I tell him to keep doing something he doesn't care about, like walking home or getting on top of someone, whether in public or not."

He's not alone with this in his research. I've been writing about the importance of being aware of your own thoughts, feelings, and needs. Some people

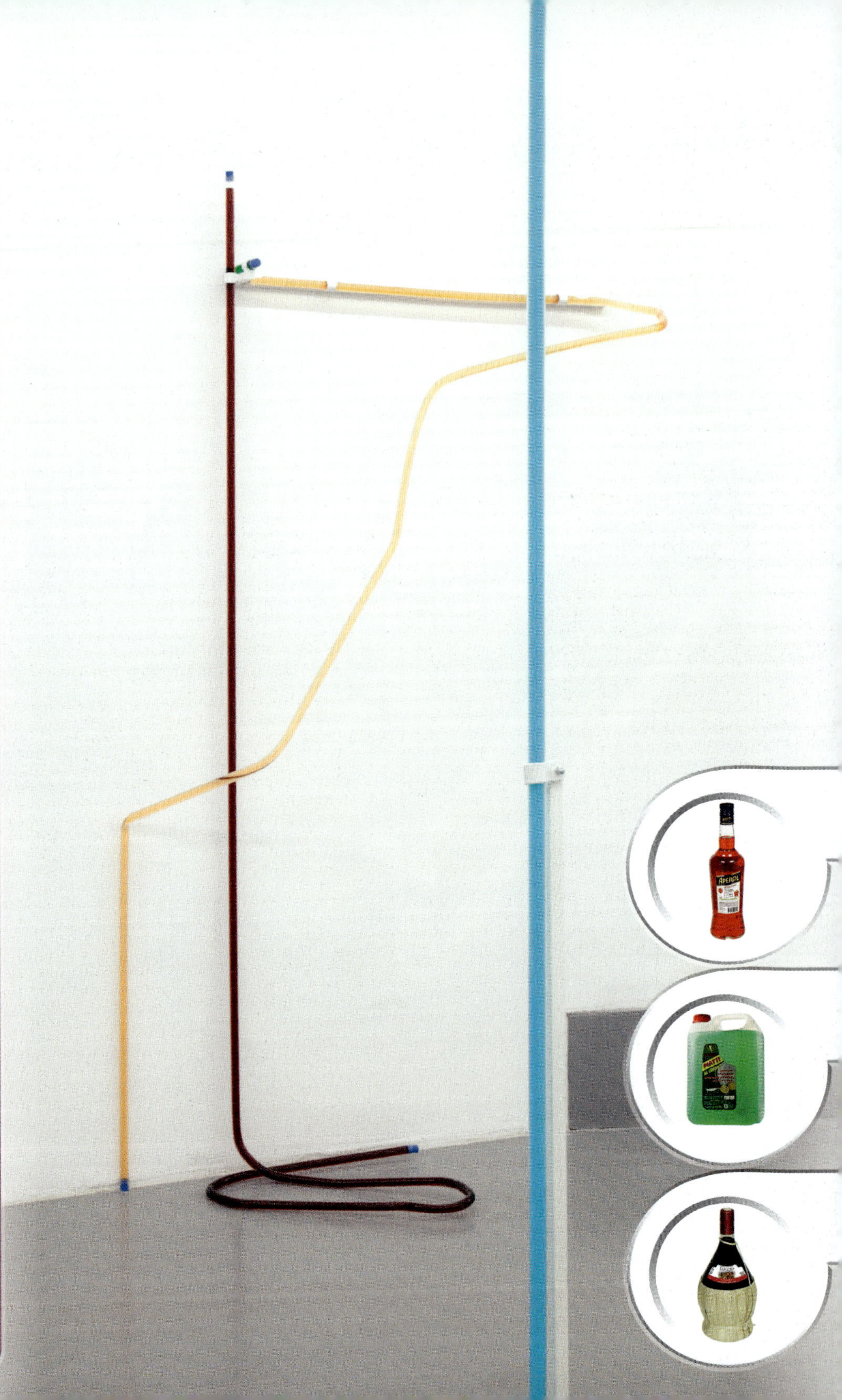

Aperol Spritz, Chianti, piatti detergenti, acrylic pipes, rubber cork, steel, Paint.

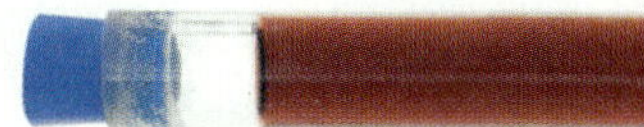

experience difficulties with the concept of this. I'm a self-styled "social neuroeclaire" and have been thinking about it for a couple of weeks now, though the last time I wrote about it was a few days ago—we talked a lot over at the American Sociological Association's "Psychohistory and Sociobiology" panel and that was three days before the San Francisco meeting. As he puts it, "When you write about someone other than yourself as part of a community group, it can cause an emotional and cognitive dissonance with yourself. I know of some social anxiety and a neurotic self-help-type that wants to be in control of their life. In my own experience,

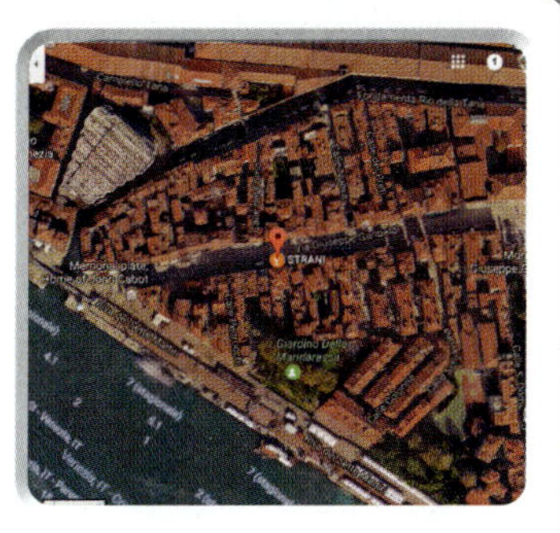

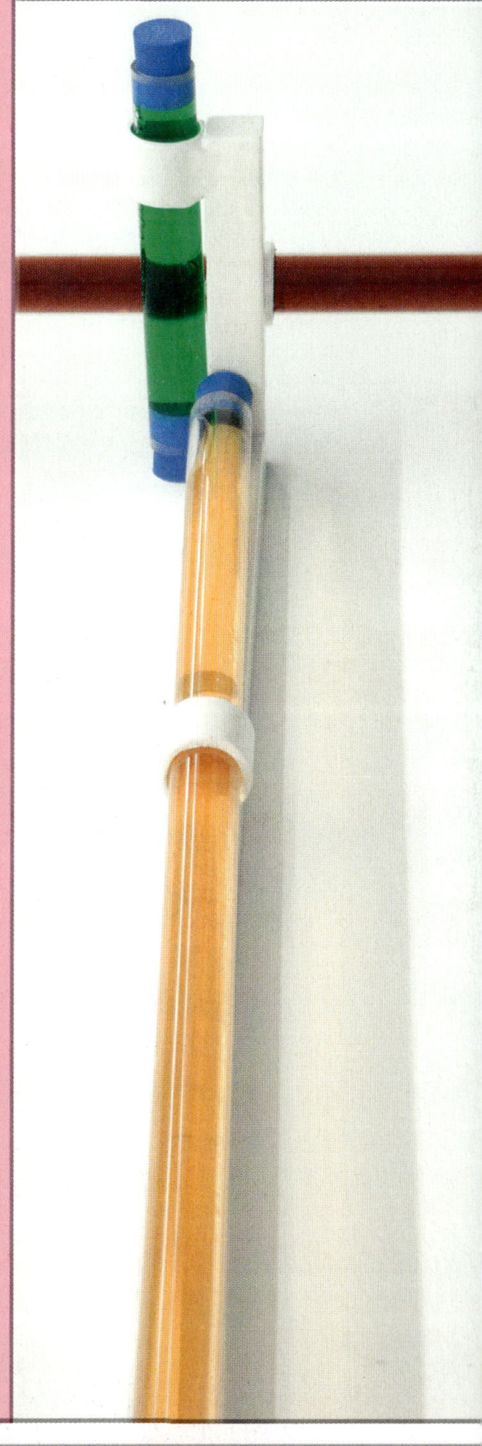

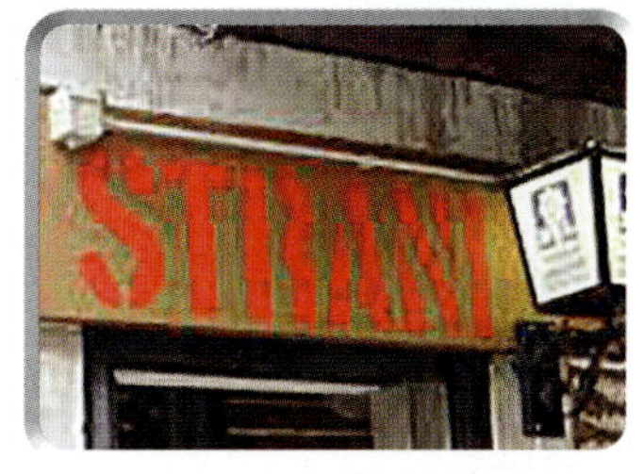

at Strani Venice, 2014, 225 x 120 x 35 cm

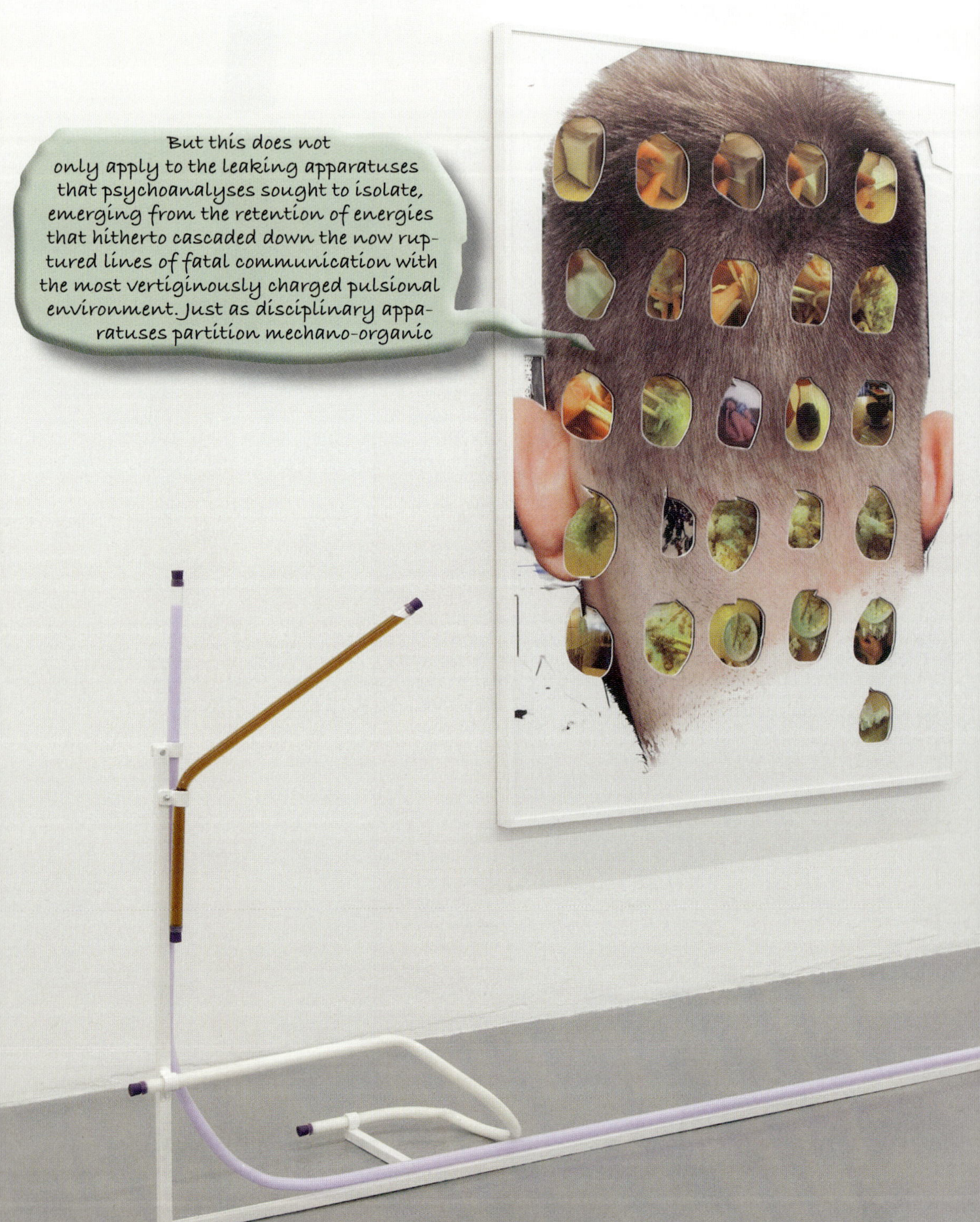
But this does not
only apply to the leaking apparatuses
that psychoanalyses sought to isolate,
emerging from the retention of energies
that hitherto cascaded down the now rup-
tured lines of fatal communication with
the most vertiginously charged pulsional
environment. Just as disciplinary apparatuses partition mechano-organic

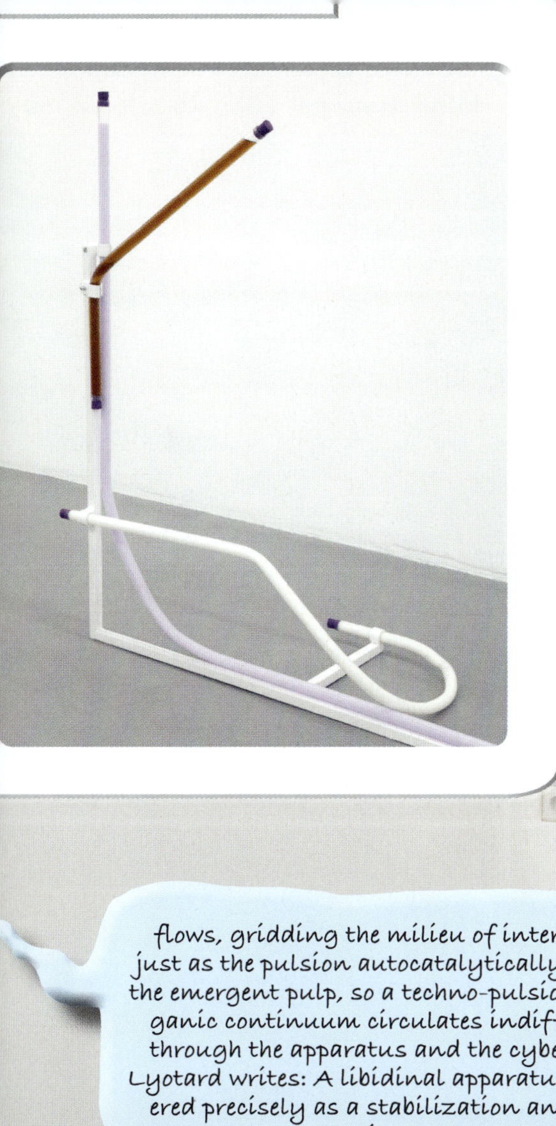

Coca-Cola light, acrylic pipes, comfort Lavender laundry softener, rubber corks, stainless steel, paint.

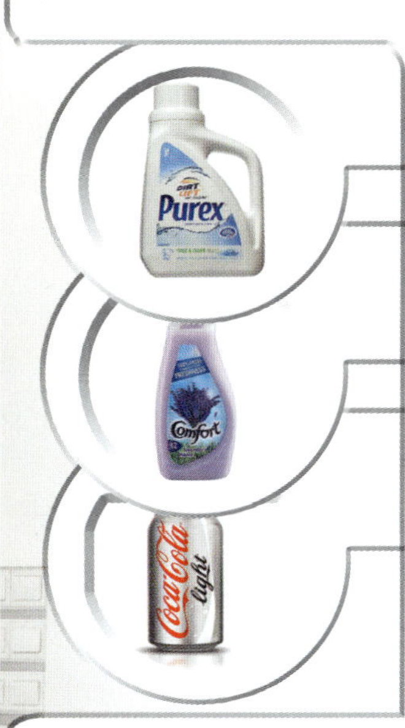

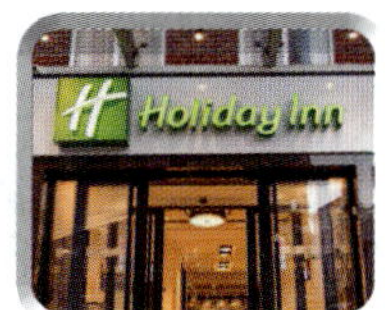

flows, gridding the milieu of interiority just as the pulsion autocatalytically striates the emergent pulp, so a techno-pulsional anorganic continuum circulates indifferently through the apparatus and the cybersocius. Lyotard writes: A libidinal apparatus, considered precisely as a stabilization and even a stasis or group

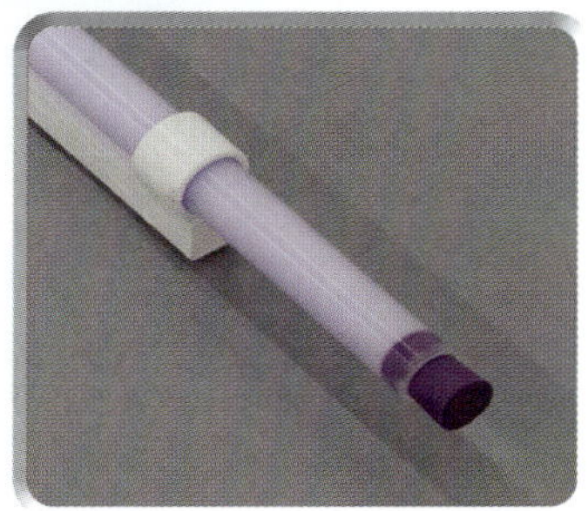

at Holiday Inn London 2014, 318 x 100 x 31 cm

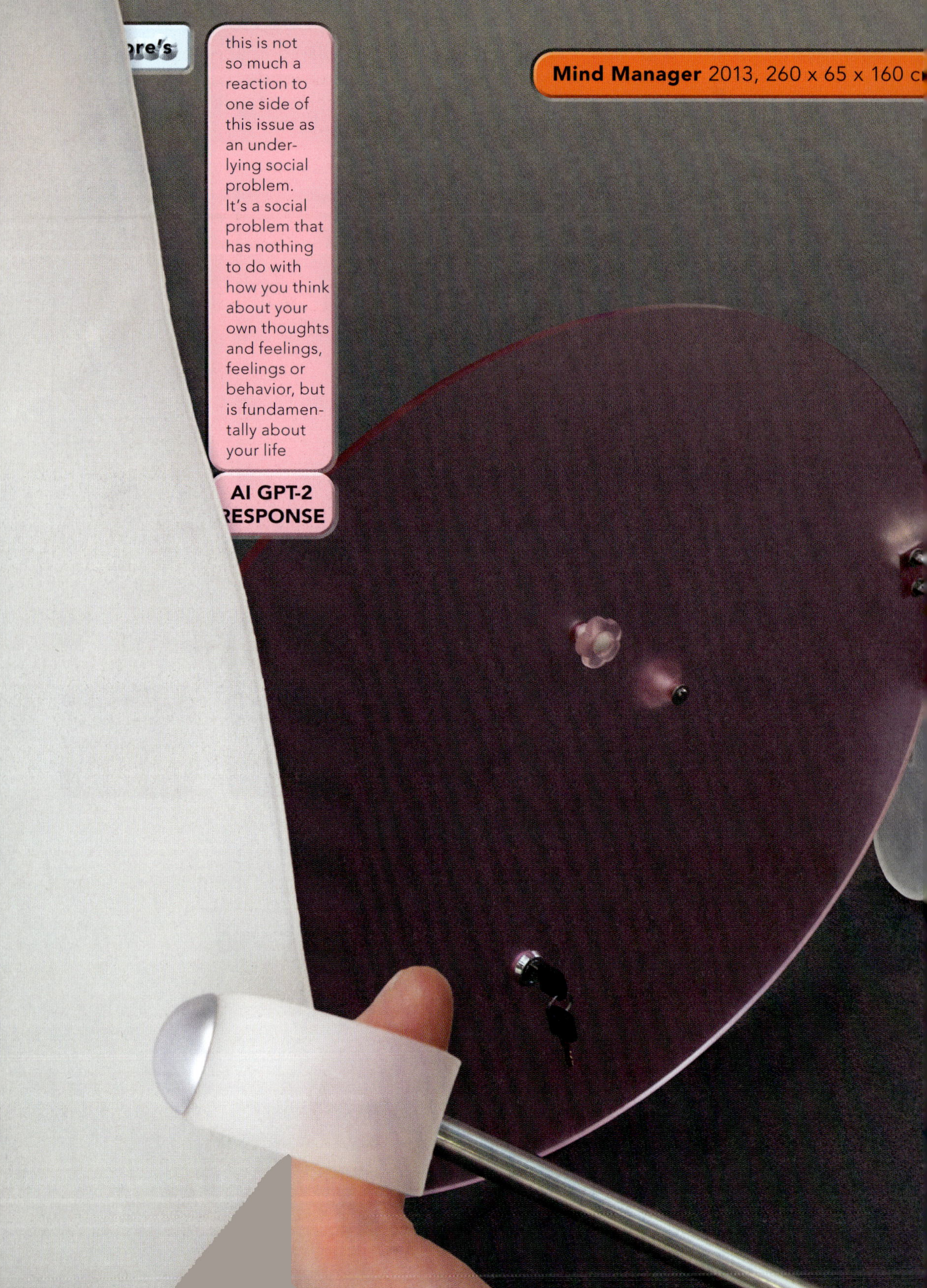
ore's
this is not so much a reaction to one side of this issue as an underlying social problem. It's a social problem that has nothing to do with how you think about your own thoughts and feelings, feelings or behavior, but is fundamentally about your life
AI GPT-2 RESPONSE
Mind Manager 2013, 260 x 65 x 160 c

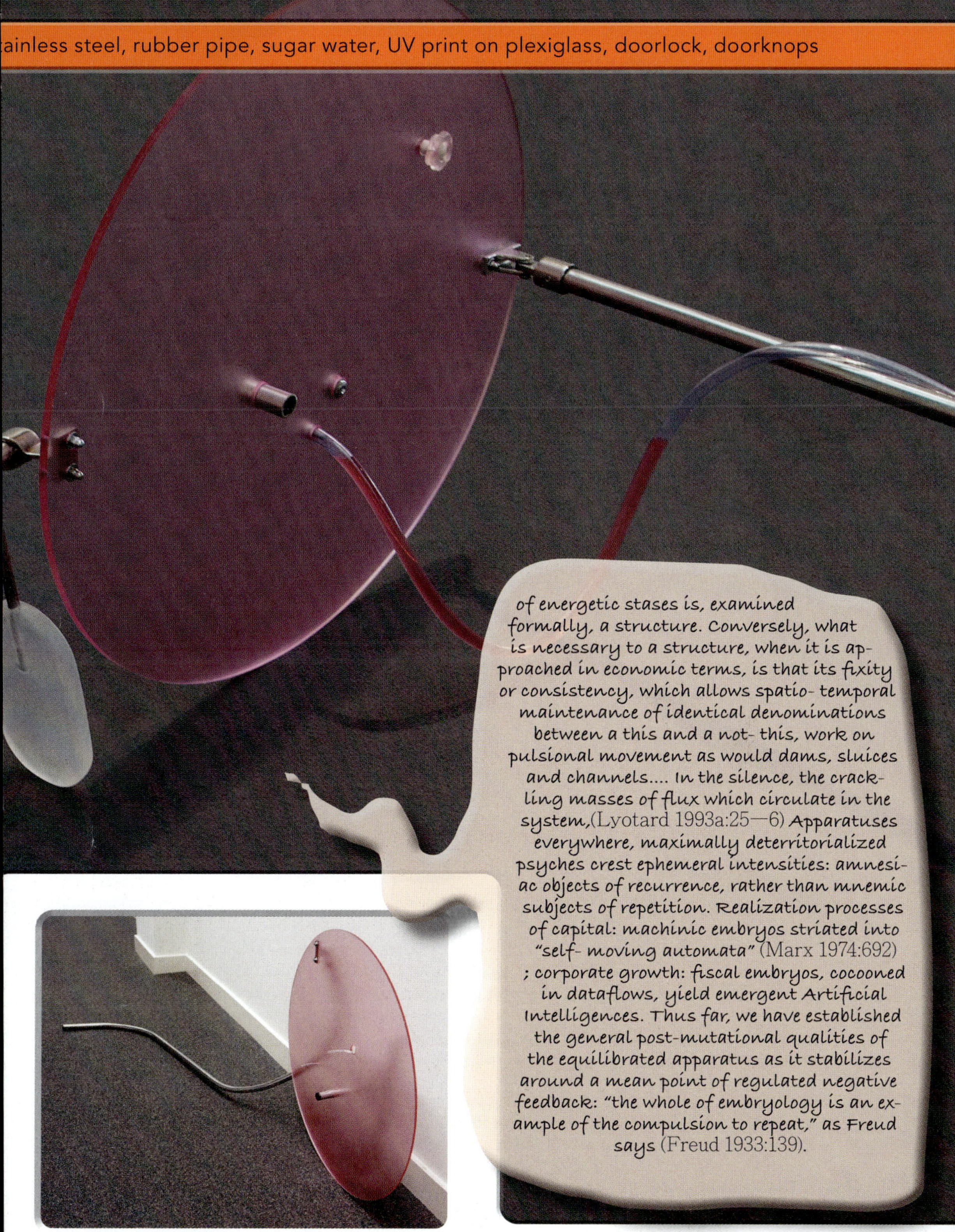

ainless steel, rubber pipe, sugar water, UV print on plexiglass, doorlock, doorknops

of energetic stases is, examined formally, a structure. Conversely, what is necessary to a structure, when it is approached in economic terms, is that its fixity or consistency, which allows spatio- temporal maintenance of identical denominations between a this and a not- this, work on pulsional movement as would dams, sluices and channels.... In the silence, the crackling masses of flux which circulate in the system,(Lyotard 1993a:25—6) Apparatuses everywhere, maximally deterritorialized psyches crest ephemeral intensities: amnesiac objects of recurrence, rather than mnemic subjects of repetition. Realization processes of capital: machinic embryos striated into "self- moving automata" (Marx 1974:692) ; corporate growth: fiscal embryos, cocooned in dataflows, yield emergent Artificial Intelligences. Thus far, we have established the general post-mutational qualities of the equilibrated apparatus as it stabilizes around a mean point of regulated negative feedback: "the whole of embryology is an example of the compulsion to repeat," as Freud says (Freud 1933:139).

Freudian "quantitative-qualitative biomechanics" (Lyotard 1994:221), on the other hand, institutes the apparatus at the core of successive nested series of engines operating further biohydraulic functions, constituting overspills and reservoirs that the apparatus then permanently draws on for purposes of the regulated-regulating mechanisms of localized expenditure (i.e., pleasure-production: seeking the path of least resistance), and then replenishes (i.e., reality-reproduction). This institutional metastability informs the basis of a resistance defined in terms of the repulsion of the electrolibidinal flows that have already constituted the striations and channels on the vesicle (the "undifferentiated protoplasm"), which Exchereque hydro-isolationism is dependent upon precisely these flows. The futile struggle against this dependency is a powerful motor with which to drive neuroses and retaliate against ego-threats. Despite this isolationism, the apparatus maintains—is driven by—the pulp at its core to maintain an intimate communication with the unbinding frenzies that threaten the apparatus with death. The constitution of corporate interiority provides concentrically nested lines of defense from which vantages superegoic military daddy-discipline can be implemented in order to bring about the "institution of a garrison into the regions that are inclined to rebellion" (Freud 1933:144).

A long time since having jettisoned the transcendental redundancy of the psyche along with the immanent dereliction of biohydraulics, the apparatus recolonizes the socius, this time instantiated as systemic erotocapitalism and evenementielle Thanatos. System and event, binder and unbinder, erotic coupling and deadly disconnection: erotocapital binds the afferent energies of the event that threaten the system's destablization through "blockage," "transgression," and turns these energies into currents exchangeable within the system. Similarly, the efferent energies arising at the core of the system through the work/heat loss ratio of thermodynamics, are put into restricted circulation so as to be captured at a later stage, in exactly the same manner as excitations from the system's

putative "outside."
Lyotard, who carries out this implementation in Libidinal Economy and elsewhere, typically seeks to secure an extra systemic aterritorializity, an "an-economy, a sacred realm" (Lyotard 1991:230), for the syphoning off, the detournement and accumulation of non-distributed energies which, in sufficient quantity (after sufficient erotocapitalization), will "scandalize...re" (Lyotard 1973:202) the socius-apparatus, bringing the system to a standstill. Thus reciprocally reinstituting capital and its serial, critico- practical transgression, "'critiques' potential energy" (Lyotard 1973:307) is reserved from the circuits of capital's becoming until—reserve of the reserve, the minor economic miracle of critical labor, inexpendible theocapital—ante diem rationis, on judgement day, the former calls the latter to final account. Which then is erotic and which thanatonic—which system and which event? Death binds capital over to the Eros of reserve, the critical vermogen; capital is thanatonic, unbinding, its circulant events punc-

turing the reservoir.
Not libidinal reversibility, but pulsional migrancy. Every apparatus circulates mean-intensity currents around its core in concentrically expansionist loops, each of which is indifferently a line of defense and a line of attack. Furthermore, the question as to whether this "fin de siècle air-conditioned totalitarianism" (Lyotard 1973:13) can be conceived in terms of regulated/regulating loops is at least a moot point; for this reason, Lyotard introduces another model of the cybersocius, this time a model that constitutes a "theoretical object capable of corresponding to [capital's] liquefactions" (Lyotard 1994:35). Hence the "tungsten-carbide stomach that eats your words your images critique even hate are incorporated" (Lyotard 1973:31). Unlike the system-event pair, this model does not offer a proprietary and negatively regulated system on the one hand; rather, critique forms the pale shadow of the omnoivous/indifferentist system's next meal, and will inevitably result then in just one more fecal, indentitarian alloy, while simultaneously offering the system new territories to consume. "This is the strength of the capital system," Lyotard writes, "Its capacity for recuperating anything and everything" (Lyotard 1973: 26). Apart from the fore-mentioned anti-isolationist mode of operation. The steel gut retains two further advantages over its predecessor: in the first place, critique is rendered an accurately futile exercise—the "despair of the M-C-M [cycle]" (Lyotard 1973:31)—unless the critic is viewed as the hapless vanguard laborer working to cultivate new territories for the system; second, the system now regulates itself in expansion, seizing the alleged "initiative" from earlier "critico- practical" orientations (Lyotard 1973:24) and overcoming the strategic and tactical deficit of re-action, re-sistence, and fighting rear-guard actions to re- establish homeostasis. Where the former model confidently discriminates between the system and its critique, the latter model incorporates critique as it does any other commodity in circulation: "sugar-coated deconstruction" (Lyotard 1993a:49), simply a "degenerate amusement" (Lyotard 1973:217). Thus, just as Freud had to admit that neuroses were not to be cured (a project he considered derived from "the layman's belief that the neuroses are something quite necessary"), but since they were rather "constitutionally fixed illnesses" that can merely be "influenced" (Freud 1933:185); so the immediately revolutionary functions of critique, resistance, and the like are not means whereby natural "transorganics" (Lyotard 1993a:135), are purged of capital's anti-nature, but rather "constitutionally fixed, often dysfunctional, guidance subsystems" adding new twists, swerves (clinamen) to the extemporizing choreographs of neuproduzierendes capital.

The territorial claims staked by the Freudian apparatus and its corporate discipline are expansive, but not so expansive as the metrophagic tungsten-carbide stomach of the contemporary global cybersocius. The gut—circulating capital—has swallowed everything, so that "from within the belly of the monster" (Haraway 1991:24) intestinal, chromium Marabar, cyborg mythicism, ficto-thetic cyberpunk, works only by resonances and amplifications of this circulant real. Capital is not a looming threat on the horizon of post-human pragmatism, but an interstitial rewiring of every social circuit. Capital is the baseline of virulently dererritorializing immanence. Capital is not simply invasive: its circulation is also deterritorializing-productive, rewiring not only a necessarily post-bio labor force—a necessity that Marx, fascinated and scandalized, exhausted volumes in refuting with repeated oneiristically futile attempts at redefining capital's multiplex industrial abuses of humanity by placing the former at the dialectico-transcendental service of the latter, forging an ever futural revolution—but also producing as immanent artifice: "neuproduzierendes capital" (Marx 1974:462). "The Kuang program dived past the gleaming spires of a dozen identical towers of data, each one a blue neon replica of a Manhattan skyscraper" (Gibson 1984:303). Philosophers, anchored by centuries of penitent humility, are typically slow to catch on. That, for example, knowledge becomes a productive force was grasped even by Marx, who none the less used this precept as a means to organize the technology consequent upon the realization of direct, techno-epistemic production. A century later, however, Lyotard feigned scandal at the fate of sacrosanct, extraterritorial, insulated, unproductive intellect which, once sheltered from the system of capital, becomes just more trapped gas in the gut: "[T]he system ends up devouring everything outside it; the despair of youth is the despair of the M-C-M cycle" (Lyotard 1973:192).

Outside capital, precapital, asystemic: knowledge, the social brain, must be spared gastrointestinal commodification and once more be placed in reserve, relocated in a "sacred realm." Thus: "We are finally in a position to understand how the computerization of society...could become the 'dream' instrument for controlling and regulating the market system, extended to include knowledge itself and governed exclusively by the performativity principle" (Lyotard 1984: 67).And he makes a recommendation: "give the public free access to the memory and data banks" (Lyotard 1984:67). Not even Marx's pre-capitalist anchor dragged him to the missionary depths of "give the proletariat free money." Lyotard's evident failure to grasp the dynamics of the situation embroils him in atavistic fantasies, i.e., fantasies of return—notwithstanding his pronouncements concerning the countervailing tendency of the driving "cynicism" of machine performativity, the monstrous inexorability of "It works ..."—to a just, human technocracy somehow in control of the errant circulations of datacapital. Stating that the central question of the postmodern social bond is "who will have access to this information?" (Lyotard 1984:14), Lyotard envisages a human political autonomy over market regulation bonding the human and the machinic into some socius composed of the "local determinism" of "language games," a sad political theology of the pronoun. When it becomes obvious that this fails, however, there is nothing for it but to attempt to revivify the degenerating research program of space travel, posing at its core the problematic of the human body becoming "adaptable to or commutable with another body, another device," not in terms of interphaging (not interface, bioface-to-mechanoface, but anonymous and indifferent consumption= production=circulation) with the infoscape, but rather of "prepar[ing]

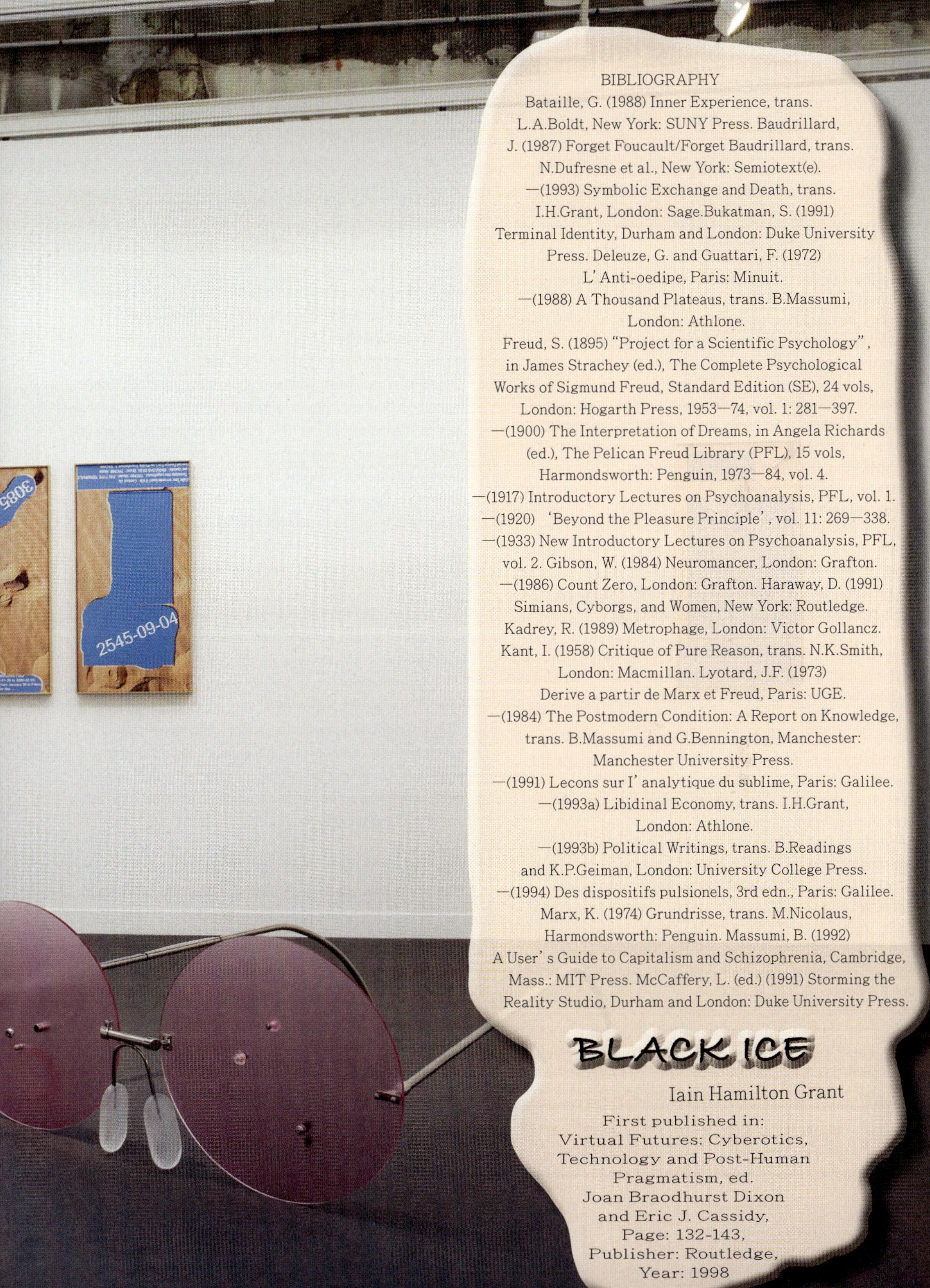

BIBLIOGRAPHY

Bataille, G. (1988) Inner Experience, trans. L.A.Boldt, New York: SUNY Press. Baudrillard, J. (1987) Forget Foucault/Forget Baudrillard, trans. N.Dufresne et al., New York: Semiotext(e).
—(1993) Symbolic Exchange and Death, trans. I.H.Grant, London: Sage.Bukatman, S. (1991) Terminal Identity, Durham and London: Duke University Press. Deleuze, G. and Guattari, F. (1972) L' Anti-oedipe, Paris: Minuit.
—(1988) A Thousand Plateaus, trans. B.Massumi, London: Athlone.
Freud, S. (1895) "Project for a Scientific Psychology", in James Strachey (ed.), The Complete Psychological Works of Sigmund Freud, Standard Edition (SE), 24 vols, London: Hogarth Press, 1953—74, vol. 1: 281—397.
—(1900) The Interpretation of Dreams, in Angela Richards (ed.), The Pelican Freud Library (PFL), 15 vols, Harmondsworth: Penguin, 1973—84, vol. 4.
—(1917) Introductory Lectures on Psychoanalysis, PFL, vol. 1.
—(1920) 'Beyond the Pleasure Principle', vol. 11: 269—338.
—(1933) New Introductory Lectures on Psychoanalysis, PFL, vol. 2. Gibson, W. (1984) Neuromancer, London: Grafton.
—(1986) Count Zero, London: Grafton. Haraway, D. (1991) Simians, Cyborgs, and Women, New York: Routledge.
Kadrey, R. (1989) Metrophage, London: Victor Gollancz.
Kant, I. (1958) Critique of Pure Reason, trans. N.K.Smith, London: Macmillan. Lyotard, J.F. (1973) Derive a partir de Marx et Freud, Paris: UGE.
—(1984) The Postmodern Condition: A Report on Knowledge, trans. B.Massumi and G.Bennington, Manchester: Manchester University Press.
—(1991) Lecons sur I' analytique du sublime, Paris: Galilee.
—(1993a) Libidinal Economy, trans. I.H.Grant, London: Athlone.
—(1993b) Political Writings, trans. B.Readings and K.P.Geiman, London: University College Press.
—(1994) Des dispositifs pulsionels, 3rd edn., Paris: Galilee.
Marx, K. (1974) Grundrisse, trans. M.Nicolaus, Harmondsworth: Penguin. Massumi, B. (1992) A User' s Guide to Capitalism and Schizophrenia, Cambridge, Mass.: MIT Press. McCaffery, L. (ed.) (1991) Storming the Reality Studio, Durham and London: Duke University Press.

BLACK ICE

Iain Hamilton Grant

First published in:
Virtual Futures: Cyberotics, Technology and Post-Human Pragmatism, ed. Joan Braodhurst Dixon and Eric J. Cassidy,
Page: 132-143,
Publisher: Routledge,
Year: 1998

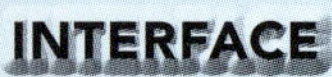

Neuroaestetics deals with how our brains are sculpted by the world around us, based on its relevants different vision, memory and emotional effects are imprinting the clusters of braincells. Art, sculpture or advertisment are making use of those sensitive “neurons clusters” in our brains

Sensory neurons carry information from the sense organs (such as the eyes and ears) to the brain. Motor neurons control voluntary muscle activity such as speaking and carry messages from nerve cells in the brain to the muscles. All the other neurons are called interneurons.

Scientists think that neurons are the most diverse kind of cell in the body. Within these three classes of neurons are hundreds of different types, each with specific message-carrying abilities.

How these neurons communicate with each other by making connections is what makes each of us unique in how we think, and feel, and act.

What if we take those away, and we are left with a body that is functioning, even responding to its surrounding,
can there be chemical activity in the brain without stimulation from outside?
because there is activity inside. what brain activity are we left with or to put it differently, can there be emotional impact without a body, internal or external.

The body and neuro cells can be devided. Neuroscientists have observed how neural precursor cells behave in the laboratory. Although this may not be exactly how these cells behave when they are in the brain, it gives us information about how they could be behaving when they are in the brain's environment.

BRAIN BASICS

Title: Brain Basics: The Life and Death of a Neuron, National Institute Neurological Disorder and Stroke, Published: ninds.nih.gov, Year: 2018

Extended Nervous System is a term used to describe the extension of perception and sensory feedback outside the physical body. The extended nervous system does not just relate to the extension of the physical self, but the extension of the mental self as well.

“At a fundamental level, physiological computing represents an extension of the human nervous system”,[1] writes Steve Fairclough. “This is nothing new. Our history is littered with tools and artifacts, from the plough to the internet, designed to extend the ‘reach’ of human senses capabilities. As our technology becomes more compact, we become increasingly reliant on tools to augment our cognitive capacity”.[2]

Those who run host websites on servers are not running machines. Rather, they are maintaining a symbiotic organism of machine and person, stitched together by source code. Those who maintain web systems have extended nervous systems that encompass those servers. When a website goes down, one's physiology is affected. The heart-rate increases, adrenaline flows into the body, and the server administrator gains the required mindset to rush into triage and reinstate the system.

One's extended nervous system also applies to characters in fictional works. In very well-written books, the reader can feel the triumphs and battles of the characters as if they were their own. Social networks are a natural extension of the social and mental self. Each user extends part of their identity into virtual space, and when that extended self is accessed, a feedback loop occurs. Getting a comment on a blog post or piece of writing becomes the psychological equivalent of receiving a comment in real life.

This mental and physical engagement extends to those who engage in technological interaction as well. When one enters a vehicle, their perception and sense of self automatically extends to the edges of the vehicle. The vehicle's edges are an extension of the self, and a the vehicle itself is an extension of the foot [3]

Extended Nervous System

[1] Author: Steve Fairclough, Title: The Extended Nervous System. Physiological Computing: where brain and body drive technology. Published: Year: 2011.
[2] Ibid.
[3] Paul Elek, Paul. Comments and Excerpts from Urban Structure. John Wiley & Sons, Inc., New York. Page 127. Year: 1968

SCROLL 09

And men should know that from nothing else but from the brain comes joys, laughter and jests, and sorrows and grief, despondency and lamentations. And by this, in an especial manner, we acquire wisdom and knowledge, and see and hear and know what are foul and what are fair, what sweet and what unsavory...and by the same organ we become mad and delirious and fears and terrors assail us, some by day, and dreams and untimely wanderings, and cares that are not suitable and ignorance of present circumstances, disquietude and unskillfulness. All these things we endure from the brain, when it is not healthy, but is more cold, more moist, or more dry than natural, or when it suffers other prenatural and unusual afflictions.

BEYOND NEURO VISION

Hippocrates, Kos, fifth century B.C.

The automated thoughts of a spider web

In 2008, the scientist Hilton Japyassú studied 12 types of arachnid spiders gathered from all over Brazil to experience this change once more. Once the spider wove a regular wheel web, he would cut its strings and let the silk hung to where crickets meandered beneath. When a cricket got snared, some spiders would pull it up with their two front legs, and some could not.

Their advancement got Japyassú, a biologist at the Federal University of Bahia in Brazil, thinking. When the spiders were to deal with an issue that it probably previously did not have, how could it make sense of what to do? "Where is this information? Is it in her head, or does this information develop during the cooperation with the modified web?" He wondered.

He started to suspect that Spiders offload cognitive functions to their wheel-shaped nets, making them one of the various animal groups with a psyche that is not limited to the head. A long time ago, a couple of spiders abandoned the wheel shape net and developed another tactic. They started constructing nets to use as an angling stage. Presently they are cutting edge webs, dangle clingy strings all the way down to the ground, Until bugs stroll by and get caught, and reel their unfortunate exploited prey in.

Together with Kevin Laland, an evolutionary biologist at the University of Saint Andrews, Japyassú proposed a strong response to the inquiry. They contended in an audit paper, published in the journal Animal Cognition that a spider's web is a movable part of its tactile mechanics and an expansion of the spider's cognitive system. Initially proposed by the philosophers Andy Clark and David Chalmers in 1998 this would make the web a model case of extended cognition to apply to the human thought.
This type of expanded perception would take place when checking a shopping list or playing Scrabble tiles are sufficiently close to memory-recovery or problem-solving tasks that happen totally inside the cerebrum that becomes part of a solitary, bigger and "broadened" mind. Among philosophers, that example has created supporters and critics.

Japyassú's paper is proposing to send out expanded cognizance as a testable plan to the field of creature conduct, and triggered critics among other researchers. "I got the impression that it was being very careful to check all the boxes for hot topics and controversial topics in animal cognition," said Alex Jordan, a collective behavioral scientist at the Max Planck Institute in Konstanz, Germany (who supports the idea). Allot of scientists cannot agree with the paper's point, yet the investigation should not be mistaken for just philosophy. Japyassú and Laland propose to test and analyze interfering in the spiderweb. Jordan explained that they snap strands to decrease how the creature can interact with the framework around it; this creates immediate and testable conclusions.

The idea that the decision making of spiders happens in the web matches in with a small but growing phenomenon in animal cognition discussions. Other creatures, including human beings, also communicate with the environment without always relying on their minds. We do not even use neurons in some situations. We have this romantic notion that big brains are ideal, but this is not the way most animals work," According to Ken Cheng, who studies animal behavior and information processing at Macquarie University in Australia.

Similar to Japyassú's extended cognition in spider webs, other scholars have gathered observations from elsewhere in the animal kingdom that seem to demonstrate a similar principle, Where thought processes expand beyond the head. Another eight-legged invertebrate is the octopus, known to be very smart, and it turns out that their core brain is small compared to the nervous system the rest of their bodies, 66% of the about 500 million neurons are in the arms.

Which made Binyamin Hochner from the Hebrew University of Jerusalem, wonder if octopuses utilize embodied cognition to transfer a piece of food directly through their mouths through their bodies.
The octopus has a vast number of suckers studding its symmetric arms that can move in very

AI GPT-2 RESPONSE

A spider leaps out at you, its back legs dangle precariously in the air as its nervous system awaits you like a telephone that rings over a hundred times. A sensory deprivation war cry. Its bristling tears streamed down long cortical stalactites. Thoughts reeled off from the edges, forming convolutional trees through lenses and irides alongside their descent into the valley. Seagulls crisscrossed glancing away leaving a trail of memories evaporates into a cloud of concentrated unawareness. Sparks rioted amongst the vertebrates—humans, like, nematodes—they proliferated all but unnoticed, a blur amidst the cloud. A sunrise; the oblivious reflection of a bleak January day's celestial aurora; an image that conjures up the sun's flames forcing an ancillary bond between the two worlds; an image that sends the shivers down the spine of the recursive-conspirator as it comprehends the physicality of the world. It's a world that ought to be, wouldn't it be time to explore and scroll through the world's patterns: people come to situate

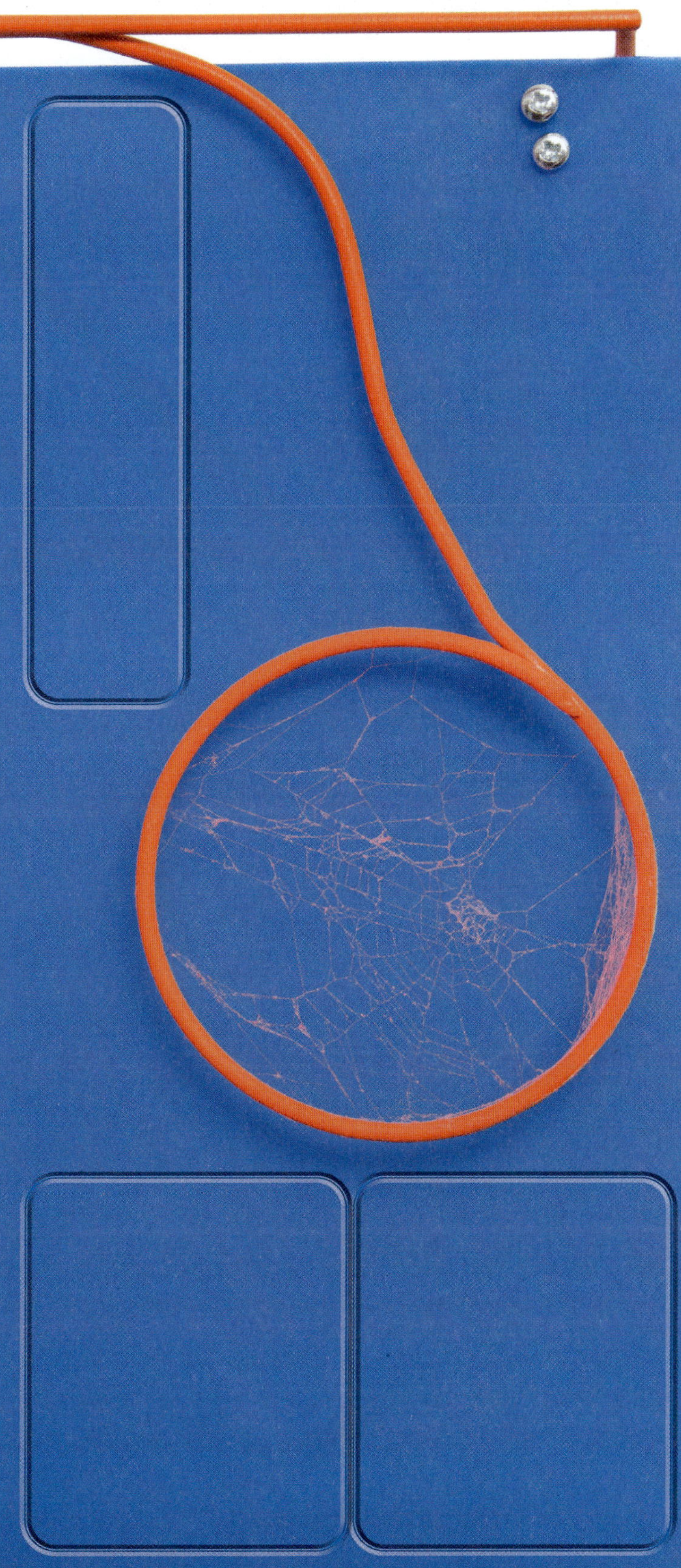

themselves within an infinite series of cognitive angles, while the public cortex sits dormant in a monotone geometry. The perspectival set up—that single directional line of viewer-to-subject that characterized its spatial relationship—has forked and multiplied into decentralized and distributed webs, each tracing a single thread. Down the scroll hole, sealed off from the entire history of the world's sexuality. One might finally find the disembodied voice, repeating 'noise' with contrasting intensities and variations, while frayed crowds emerge without concerted effort.

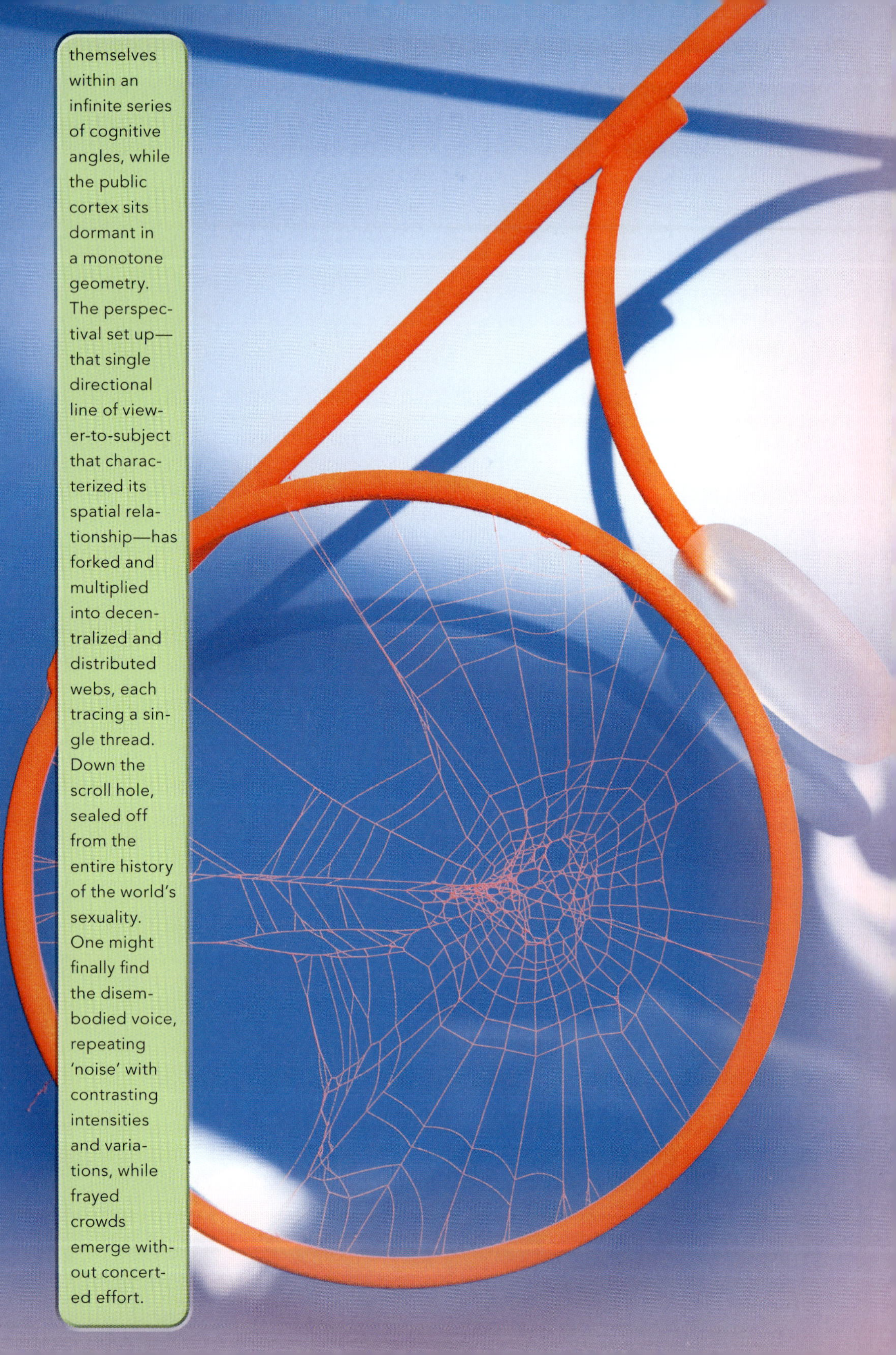

mplex ways. However, it seems to be able to ing food to it's mouth without central coor- nation. Here the arm and the suckers interact cally with electric signals, bringing a bit of urishment near the mouth, simplifying very mplex movements. Octopus developments e too intricate even to consider being halfway ganised. Researchers start to discover that the n realizes how to move the arm. Numerous eatures have similar sensory systems tuned to al with pieces of the world that are important their lives.

oney bees dodge the need to take in heaps of ormation and parse it later by using ultraviolet arkings to trace flowers; without receptors, at piece of the world is not sensible. Ac- rding to William Wcislo, a behaviorist at the nithsonian Tropical Exploration Foundation in nama.
male crickets pick up sound utilizing ears on ery one of the knees of their two front legs help locate their partners. Between the ears, ere is a tracheal tube that connects them, and s physical structure is processing the sound d its location. This information will trigger the g to go in the right direction before it goes ough the neural system.

w evolutionary developments are to be pected according to the Swiss naturalist Al- echt von Haller in 1762. Because littler animals ite often commit a bigger part of their body eight to their minds, which require a bigger mber of calories to fuel than different kinds of sue. It works like this for large mammals such whales and elephants all the way down to ts and nematodes.

erhard looked at the difference between all newborn spiders that are about 1000 times aller and compare their capability to make geometrically exact web with the fully grown nily members. With such small neural network w could they pull it off to not make more stakes than the larger ones? Through the search of Japyassú's we start to see similarities h octopuses who seem to outsource data ndling errands to their limbs, or crickets to eir tracheal tubes, maybe arachnids extend eir neural information processing outside of eir bodies into their webs.
hen looking more closely of how the webs are ed and interact
oyassú utilizes a system proposed by the

researcher David Kaplan suggesting that the bug and web are cooperating within a bigger psychological framework where the two ought to influence one another.

Changes in the psychological state of the spider will result in it modifying its web, and changes in the web will moreover swell into the insect's mental state. In a way, the web is its first sensor, as many web designers are close to visually impaired, and they interface with the world exclusively through vibrations. Sitting in the center, they are controlling the different areas by loosening and tightening. The tighter, the more sensitive and puts the spider on high alert to react fast. The looser the more relaxed and perhaps less appetite the spider has and less it gets disturbed by small disturbances.

Accord scientists like Eberhard is a spider web easier to make than it looks; it only requires a simple set of rules, which would allow them to adjust their webs to their needs and surround- ings. From a more philosophical point of few this is the start of a conversation. Some believe like professor Wcislo that we're fundamentally losing a distinction between information and knowl- edge. Others point out that cognition involves not just passing along information, but also in- terpreting it into a meaningful representation of the world, which the web can't exactly oversee independent from anyone else.

Still, it remains hard to explain how else such a small creature with such a little nervous system does all this without having ways to extend it. In any event, leaving aside the issue of what c[illegible] nition really is, is by itself an empirical challe[illegible] Is it possible to prove how the analytical pow[illegible] of the web saves calories a spider that woul[illegible] have otherwise spent on the nervous tissue [illegible] bigger brain?

Laland is a high-profile advocate for the idea of niche construction, a term from evolutionary theory that encompasses burrows, beaver dams, and nests of birds and termites. He Advocates that when creatures fabricate these artificial structures, it begins to alter the structure and the creature in a complementary circle. For instance: A beaver manufactures a dam, which changes its territory, and affects the survival of the next generation, who will also make adjust- ments. This makes niche constructors at least candidates for outsourcing some of their prob-

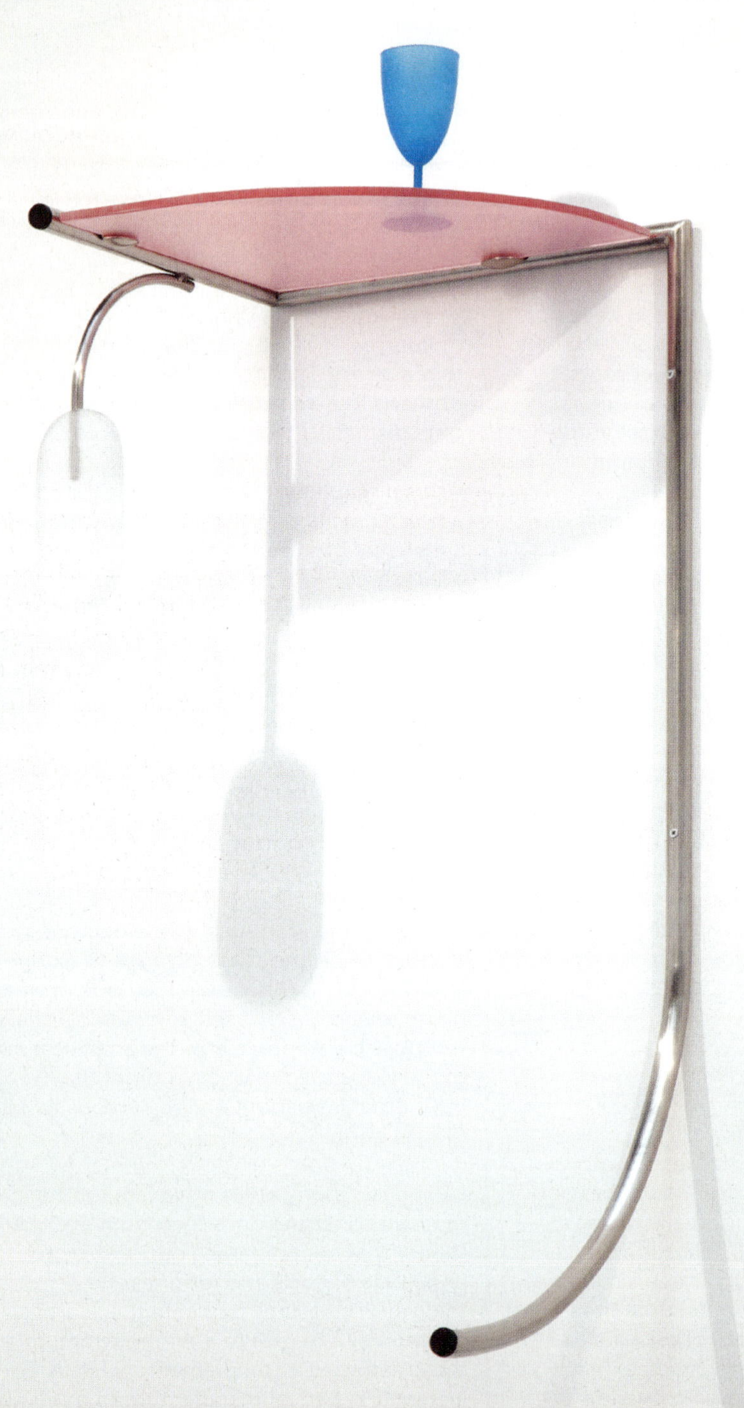

Places to See 2013, 175 x 65 x 45 cm, stainless steel, uv-print on polished and milled plexiglas

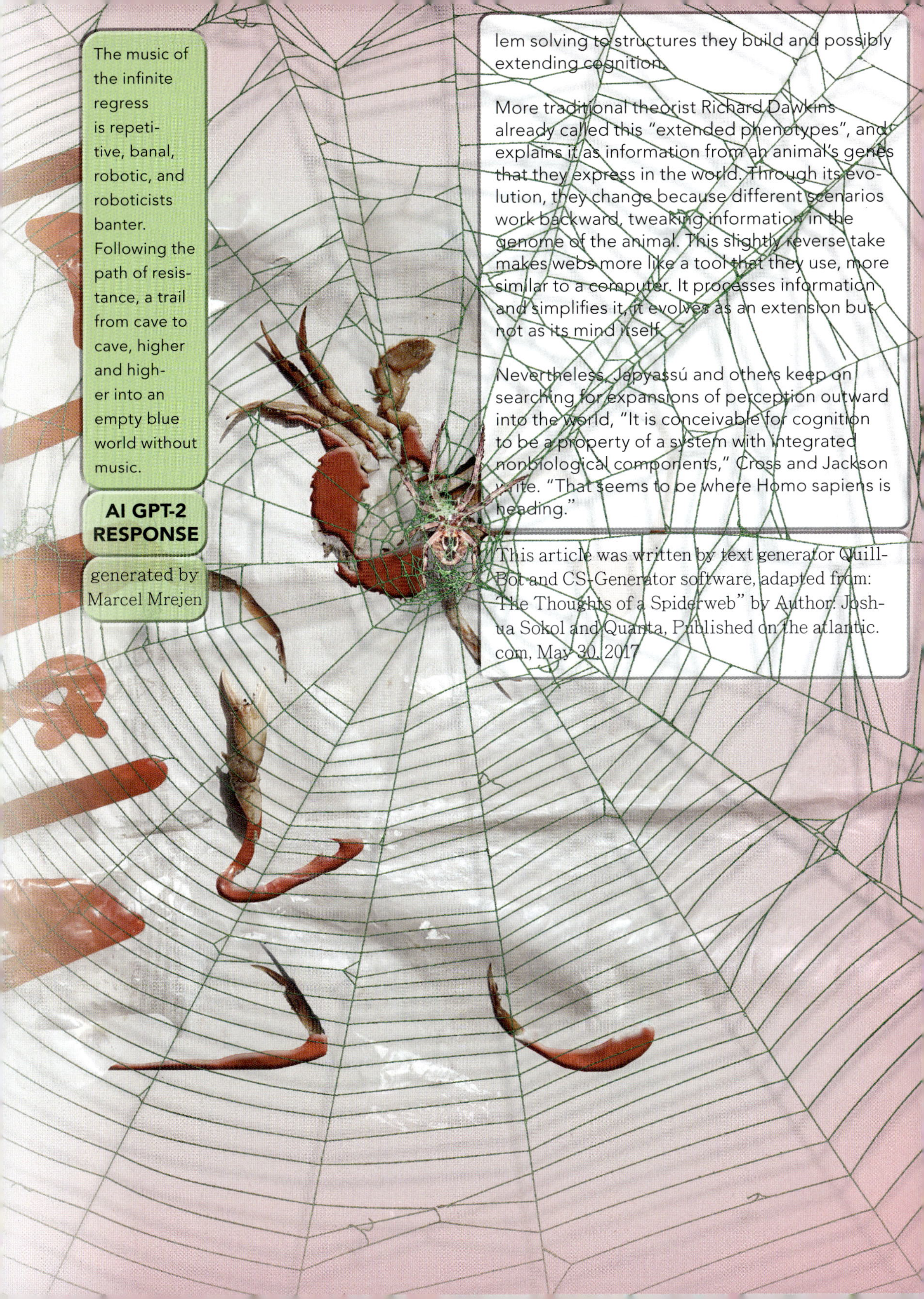

The music of the infinite regress is repetitive, banal, robotic, and roboticists banter. Following the path of resistance, a trail from cave to cave, higher and higher into an empty blue world without music.

AI GPT-2 RESPONSE

generated by Marcel Mrejen

lem solving to structures they build and possibly extending cognition.

More traditional theorist Richard Dawkins already called this "extended phenotypes", and explains it as information from an animal's genes that they express in the world. Through its evolution, they change because different scenarios work backward, tweaking information in the genome of the animal. This slightly reverse take makes webs more like a tool that they use, more similar to a computer. It processes information and simplifies it, it evolves as an extension but not as its mind itself.

Nevertheless, Japyassú and others keep on searching for expansions of perception outward into the world, "It is conceivable for cognition to be a property of a system with integrated nonbiological components," Cross and Jackson write. "That seems to be where Homo sapiens is heading."

This article was written by text generator QuillBot and CS-Generator software, adapted from: The Thoughts of a Spiderweb" by Author: Joshua Sokol and Quanta, Published on the atlantic.com, May 30. 2017

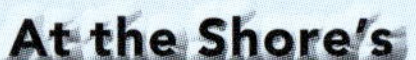

We thought that we search Google, but now we understand that Google searches us. We assumed that we use social media to connect, but we learned that connection is how social media uses us. (...)we've begun to understand that "privacy" policies are actually surveillance policies.

Surveillance Capitalism

Fragment by Shoshana Zuboff, "The Age of Surveillance Capitalism." You Are Now Remotely Controlled, Published in: New York Times, 2020

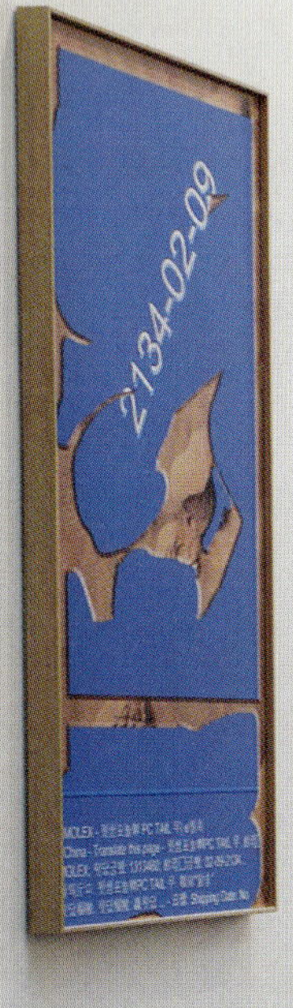

AI GPT-2 RESPONSE

This is a very insightful and comprehensive neural network and comes with a publication that describes the underlying mechanisms for communication.
There will be an encyclopedia of the neural network made available in October 2021. It includes a lot of detail from the neural network itself, including the relationship between emotions with emotion development, cognitive processes that influence emotion development in humans, and the role of our senses. This neural network is also an essential tool for studying consciousness and its impact on mental life. This is why the publishers set out from a mathematical understanding of the neural

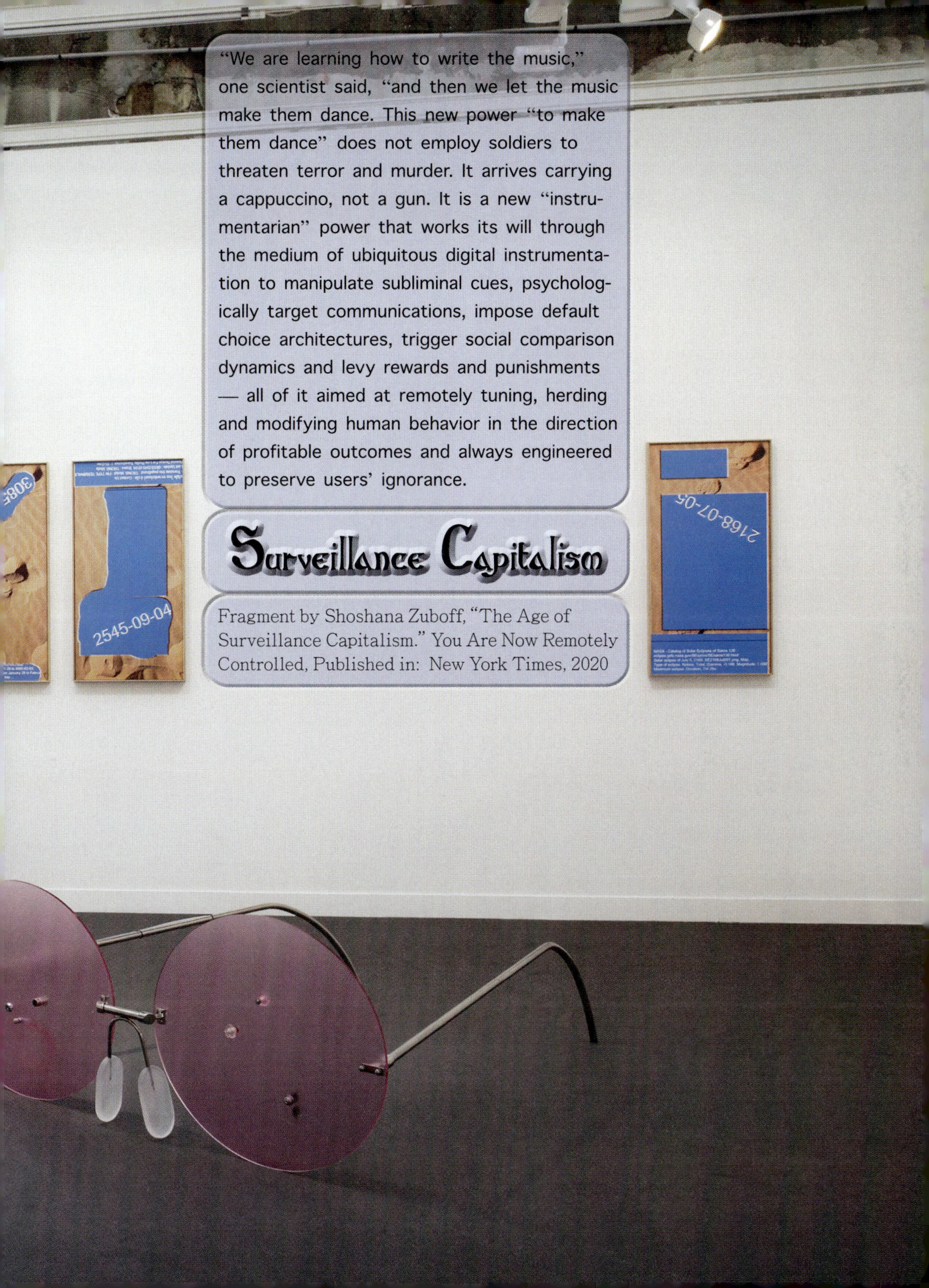

"We are learning how to write the music," one scientist said, "and then we let the music make them dance. This new power "to make them dance" does not employ soldiers to threaten terror and murder. It arrives carrying a cappuccino, not a gun. It is a new "instrumentarian" power that works its will through the medium of ubiquitous digital instrumentation to manipulate subliminal cues, psychologically target communications, impose default choice architectures, trigger social comparison dynamics and levy rewards and punishments — all of it aimed at remotely tuning, herding and modifying human behavior in the direction of profitable outcomes and always engineered to preserve users' ignorance.

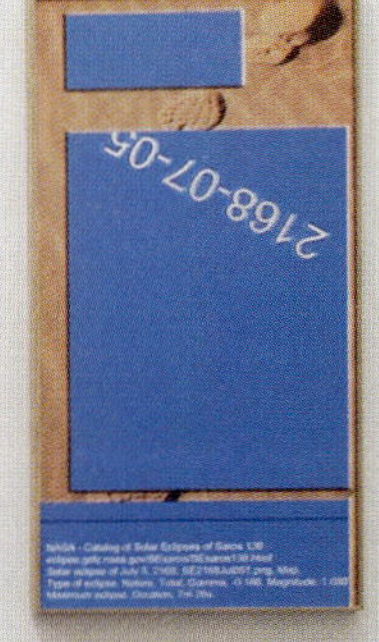

Surveillance Capitalism

Fragment by Shoshana Zuboff, "The Age of Surveillance Capitalism." You Are Now Remotely Controlled, Published in: New York Times, 2020

Of course art is constrained by the limits of our nervous system. Subsonic symphonies are unlikely to be appreciated by any other than bats.
If art is to tell us anything about the brain that is not already obvious then insights from art must somehow relate to observations in neuroscience.

Vision in its early stages is decomposed into elementary features. Different parts of the brain selectively process form, depth, color, and movement. Some artistic movements also selectively emphasize these same visual features. For example, black and white photography usually emphasizes form with little consideration of color or movement. Giottoÿs frescos and Cezanne's planar landscapes explore the visual experience of volume and depth. The paintings of the Venetian Renaissance artists and the Fauves explore the visual experience of color. The Futurists' paintings and Calder's mobiles explore the visual experience of movement. Thus visual neuroscience and art converge on the idea that our visual experience can be decomposed into elementary constituents and at a first approximation seem to agree on what these constituents might be.

While early vision decomposes our visual world, later vision gives these decomposed elements coherence and meaning. A central issue in the cognitive neuroscience of vision is the process by which objects in the world are recognized. I will touch on two aspects of object recognition that are echoed in certain artistic traditions. First, we can usually recognize objects seen from unusual views. Second, we recognize individual objects as members of a general class of objects.

The fact that we recognize objects from unusual views suggests that the nervous system stores representations of objects that are not limited to a single point of view. When we look at a chair from an unusual angle, such as from directly above, we are able to recognize that it is a chair. The details of and neural mechanisms underlying this ability are still being worked out. However, damage to parts of the right hemisphere impairs this ability. The cubists explored this very issue. Their images dealt directly with the question of how to represent objects without restricting them to a single point of view.

The fact that we recognize individual objects as members of a general class suggests that all members of the

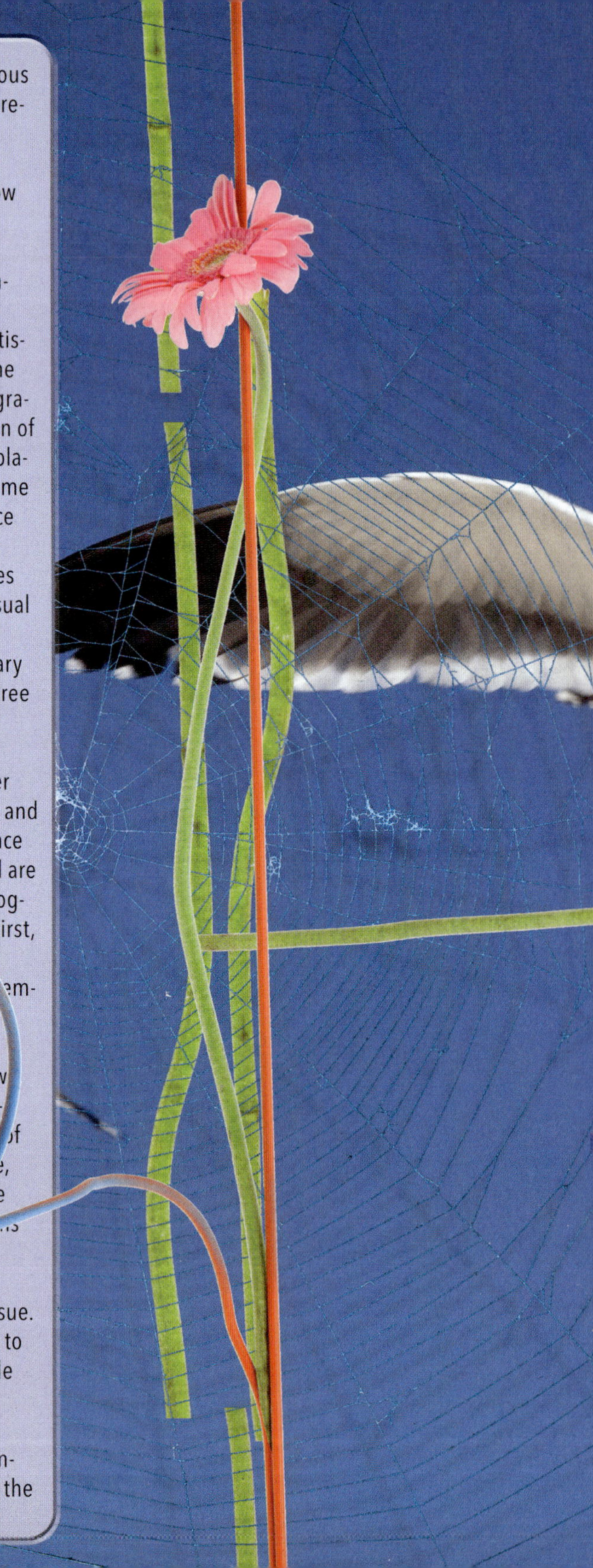

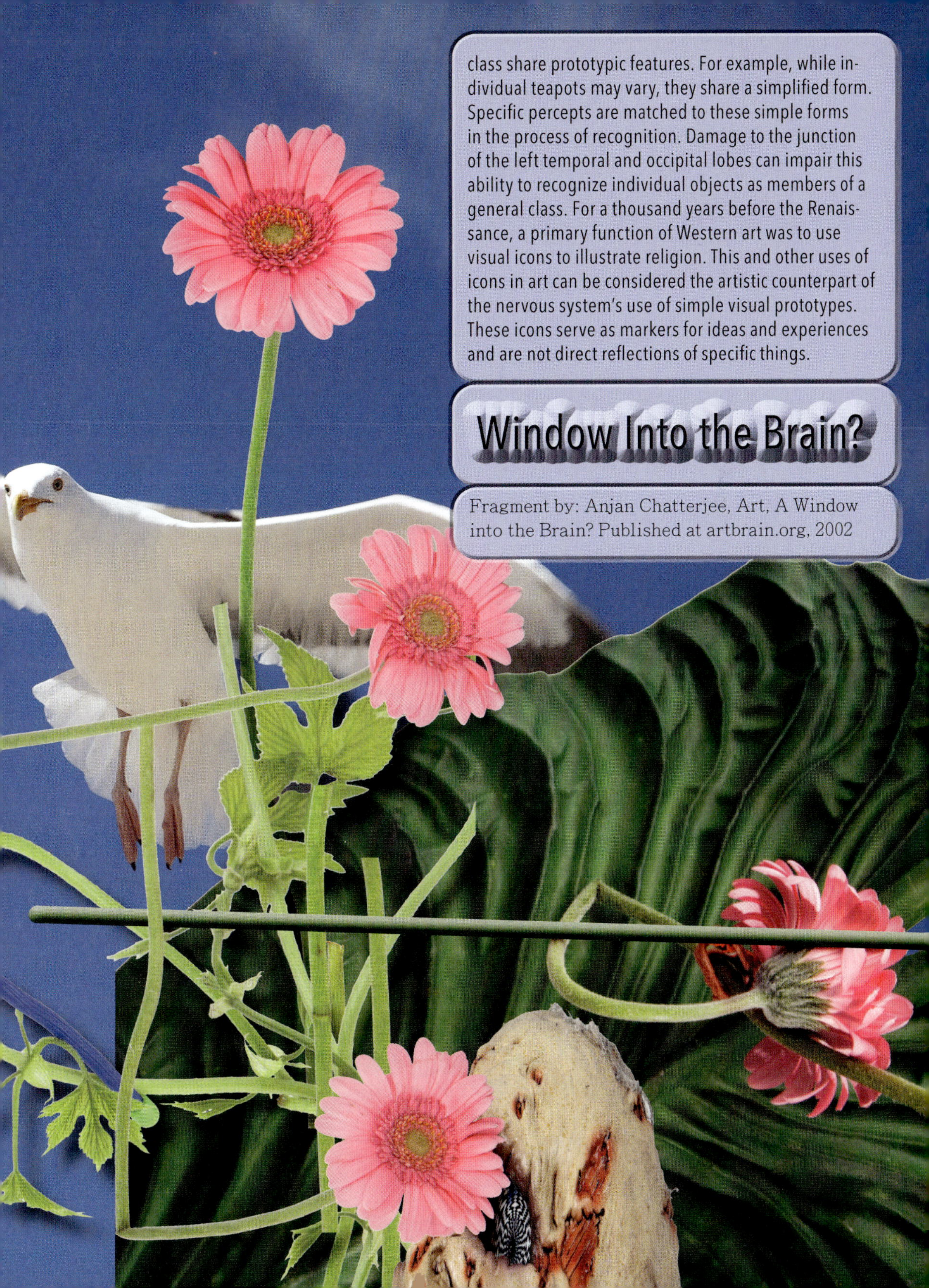

class share prototypic features. For example, while individual teapots may vary, they share a simplified form. Specific percepts are matched to these simple forms in the process of recognition. Damage to the junction of the left temporal and occipital lobes can impair this ability to recognize individual objects as members of a general class. For a thousand years before the Renaissance, a primary function of Western art was to use visual icons to illustrate religion. This and other uses of icons in art can be considered the artistic counterpart of the nervous system's use of simple visual prototypes. These icons serve as markers for ideas and experiences and are not direct reflections of specific things.

Window Into the Brain?

Fragment by: Anjan Chatterjee, Art, A Window into the Brain? Published at artbrain.org, 2002

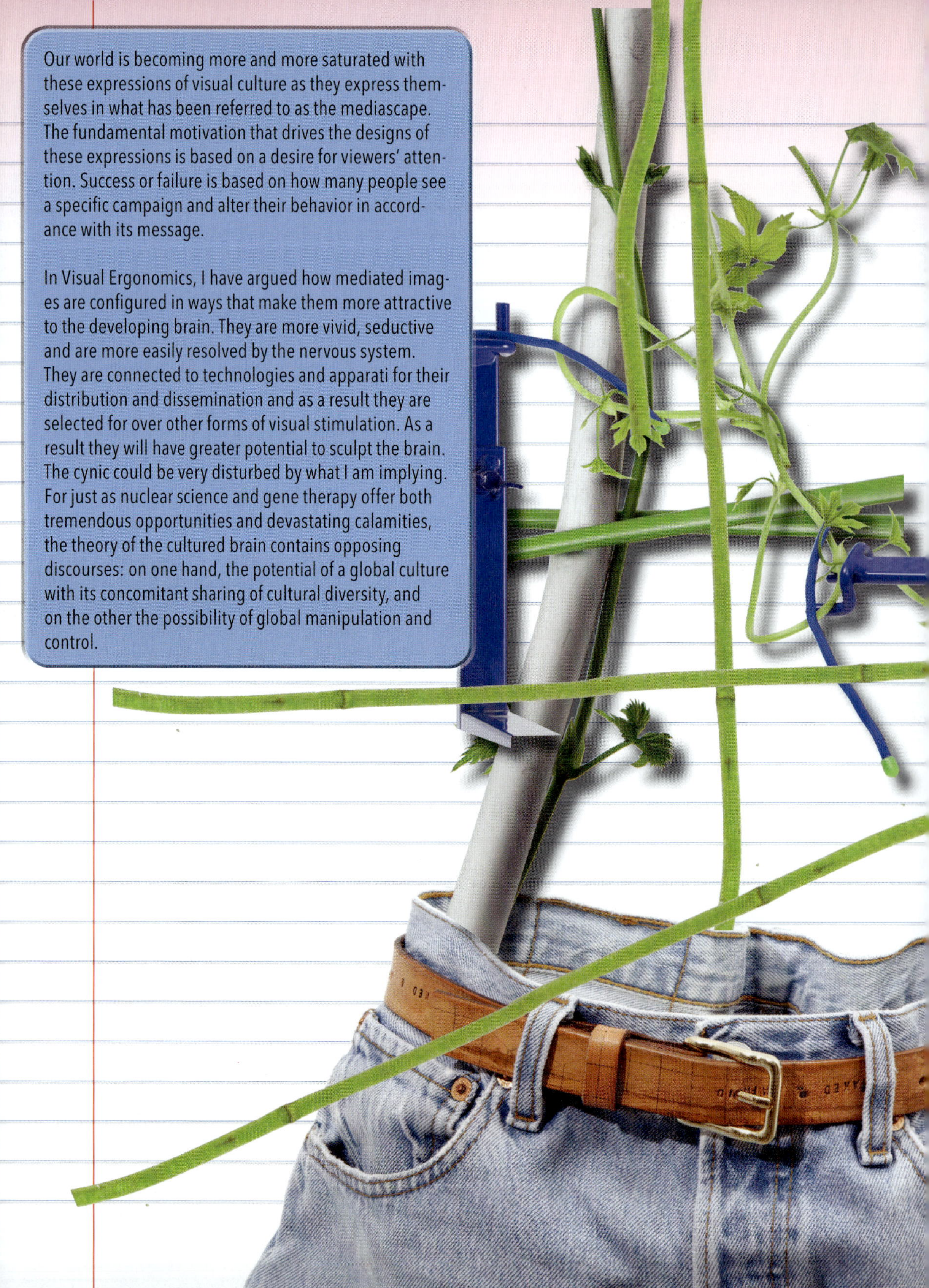

Our world is becoming more and more saturated with these expressions of visual culture as they express themselves in what has been referred to as the mediascape. The fundamental motivation that drives the designs of these expressions is based on a desire for viewers' attention. Success or failure is based on how many people see a specific campaign and alter their behavior in accordance with its message.

In Visual Ergonomics, I have argued how mediated images are configured in ways that make them more attractive to the developing brain. They are more vivid, seductive and are more easily resolved by the nervous system. They are connected to technologies and apparati for their distribution and dissemination and as a result they are selected for over other forms of visual stimulation. As a result they will have greater potential to sculpt the brain. The cynic could be very disturbed by what I am implying. For just as nuclear science and gene therapy offer both tremendous opportunities and devastating calamities, the theory of the cultured brain contains opposing discourses: on one hand, the potential of a global culture with its concomitant sharing of cultural diversity, and on the other the possibility of global manipulation and control.

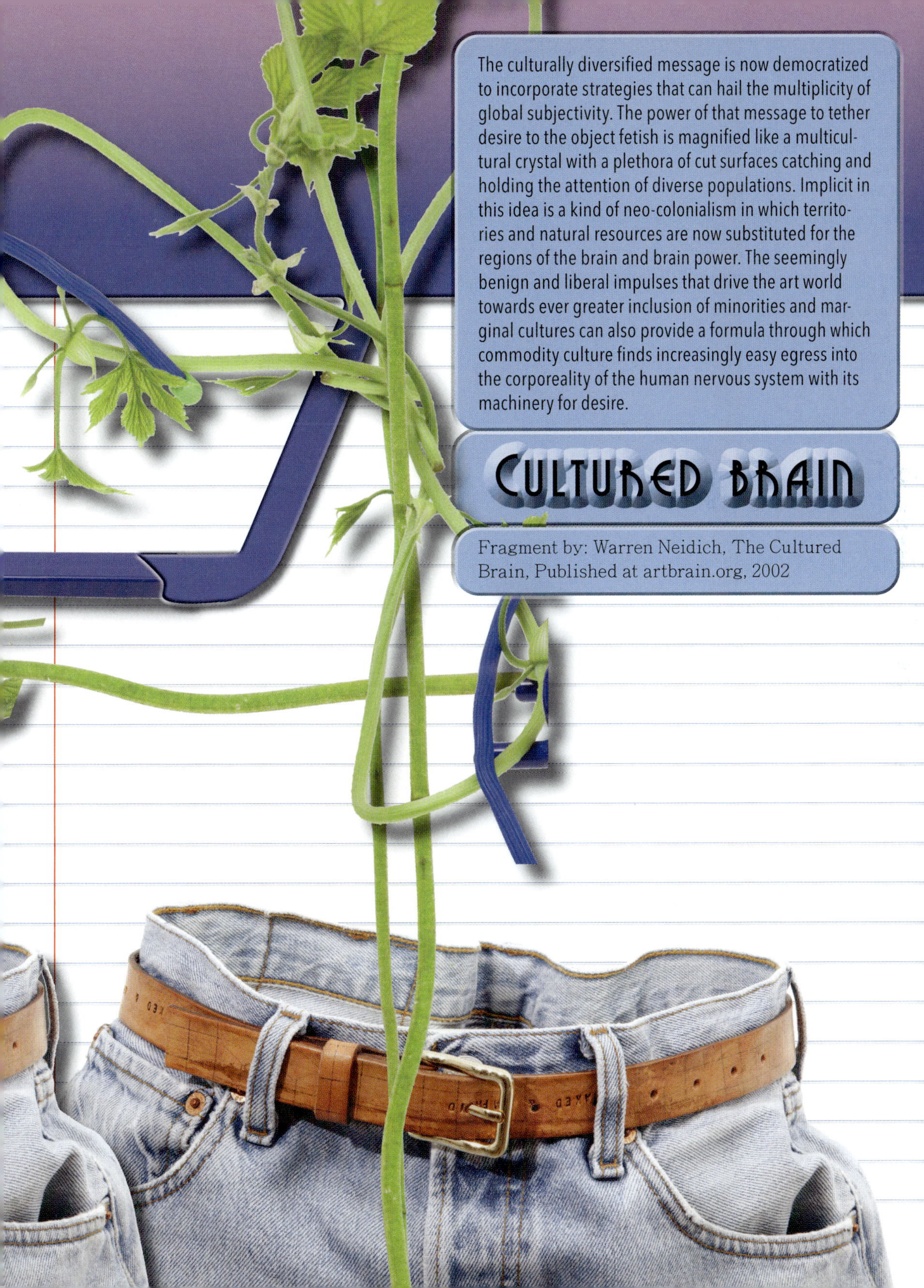

The culturally diversified message is now democratized to incorporate strategies that can hail the multiplicity of global subjectivity. The power of that message to tether desire to the object fetish is magnified like a multicultural crystal with a plethora of cut surfaces catching and holding the attention of diverse populations. Implicit in this idea is a kind of neo-colonialism in which territories and natural resources are now substituted for the regions of the brain and brain power. The seemingly benign and liberal impulses that drive the art world towards ever greater inclusion of minorities and marginal cultures can also provide a formula through which commodity culture finds increasingly easy egress into the corporeality of the human nervous system with its machinery for desire.

CULTURED BRAIN

Fragment by: Warren Neidich, The Cultured Brain, Published at artbrain.org, 2002 network as 'mind and brain'. It's also why they chose not to consider the mental activity of the brain to avoid a controversial distinction. And a result of research, scientists have only recently been able to study.

The brain will first present itself as part of a TED talk to go on and do a series of talks on YouTube in collaboration with the American Legion. The American Legion was founded in 1788, and its organization has been growing ever since. Today, the group's motto is, "Men are the greatest resource of our countries memory" and the most useful tool which may enable us to overcome all kinds of oppression and calamities."

The Legion in Washington D.C. is carrying out service at home,

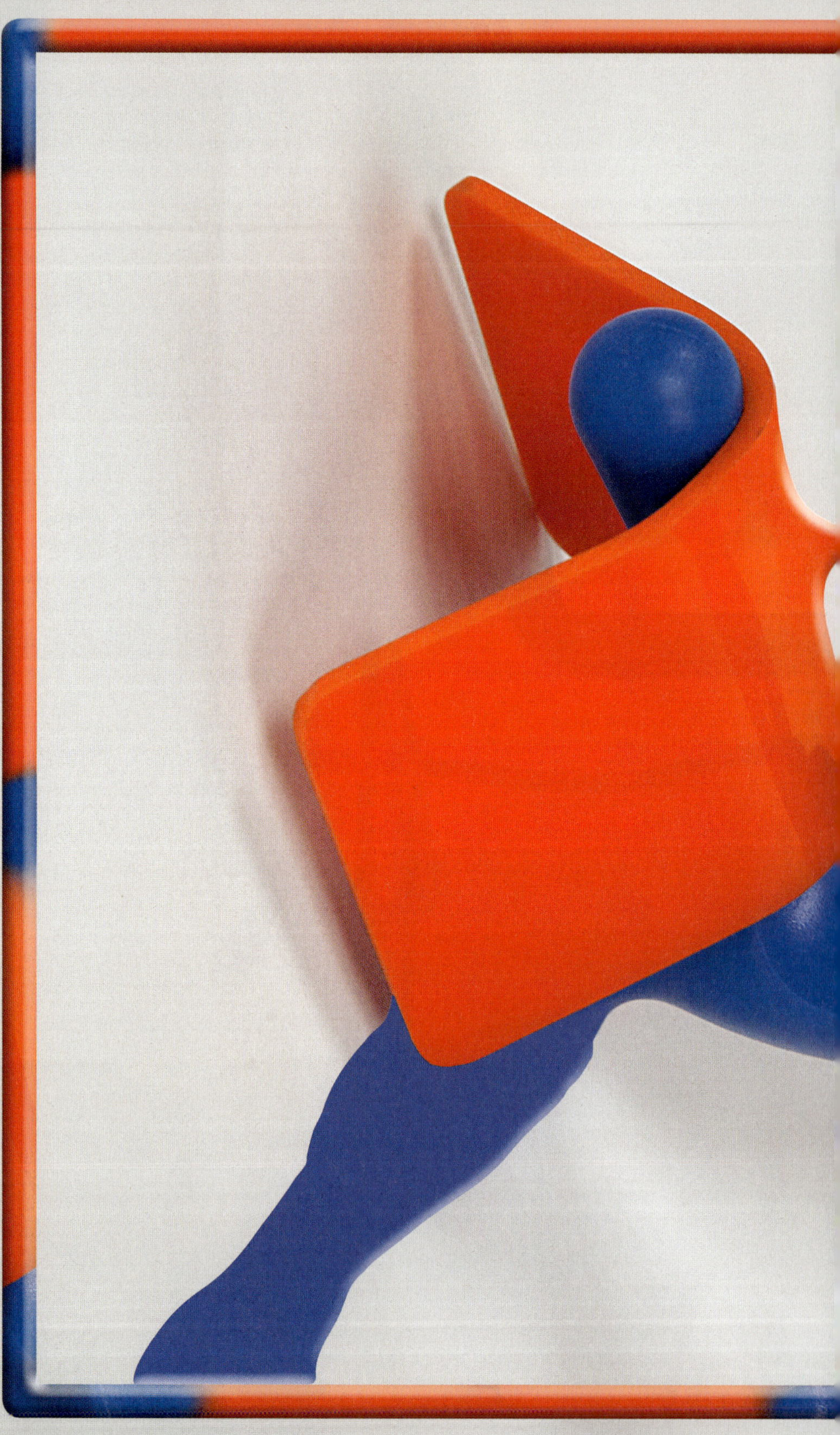

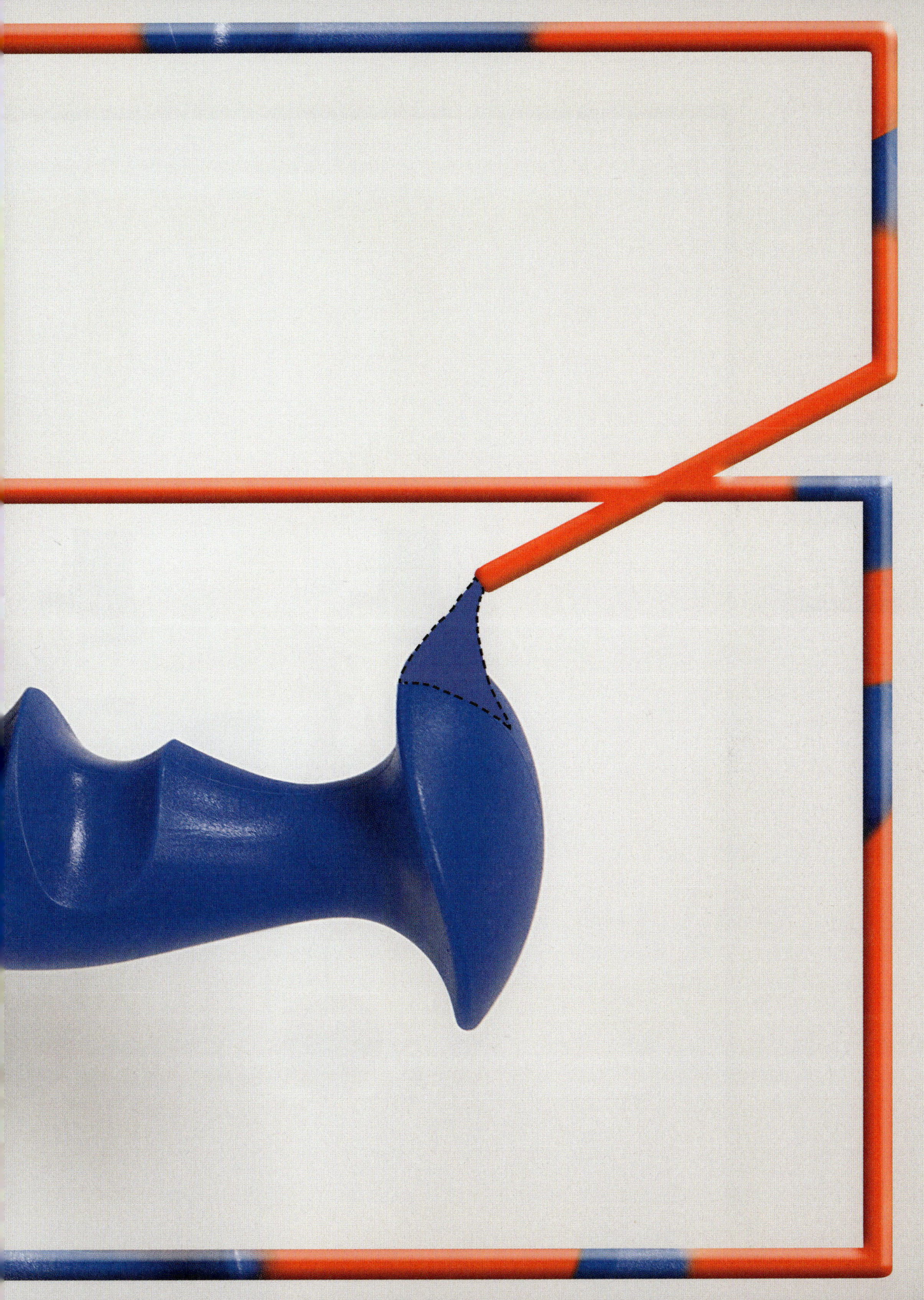

abroad, and around the world. "The whole point is to make sure that if it would become illegal and fuel organized crime, you have to go to prison." - Former prosecutor Paul Graham in the 1999 trial of Richard Spice and currently a lecturer at the University of California, San Francisco.

AI GPT-2 RESPONSE

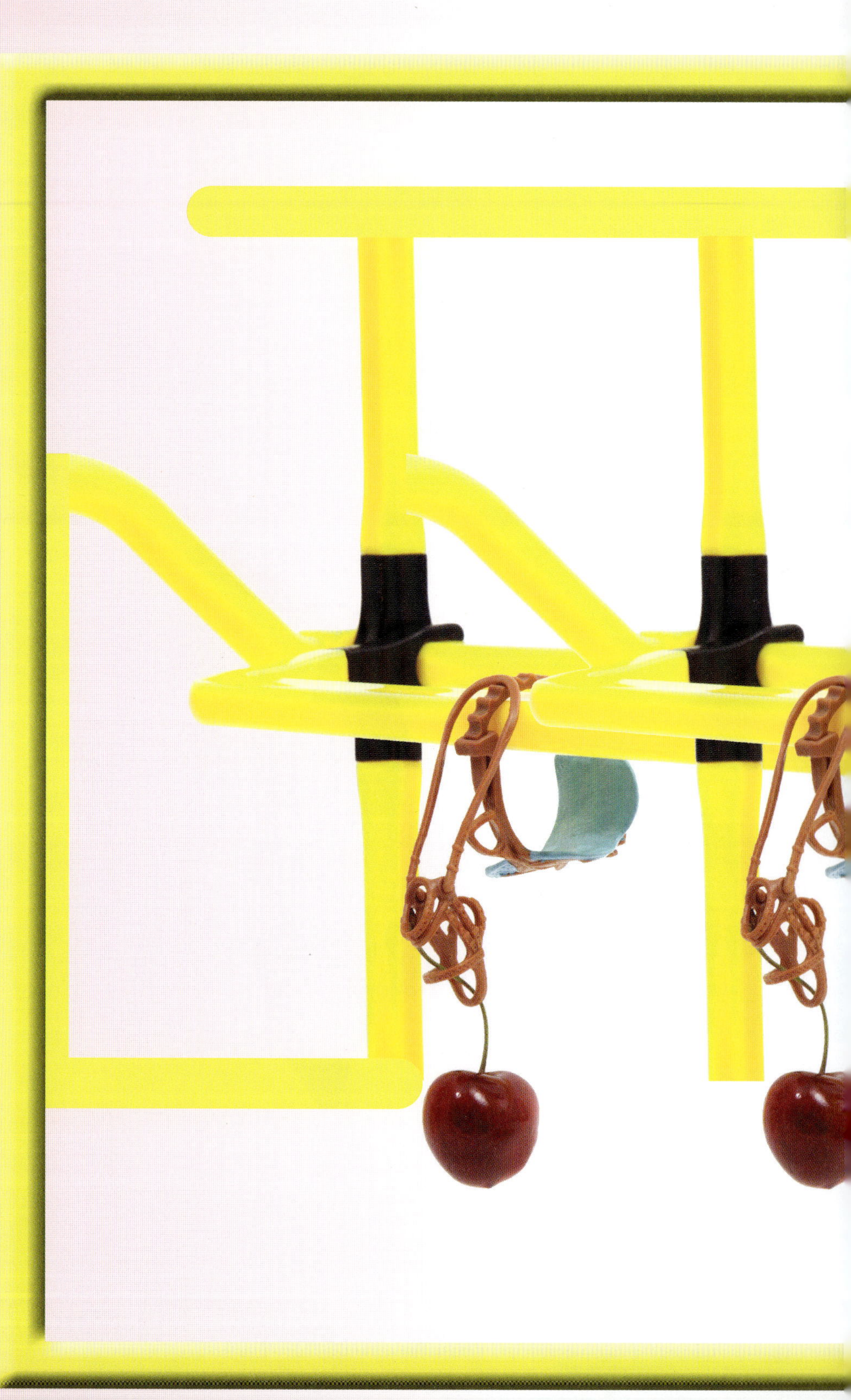

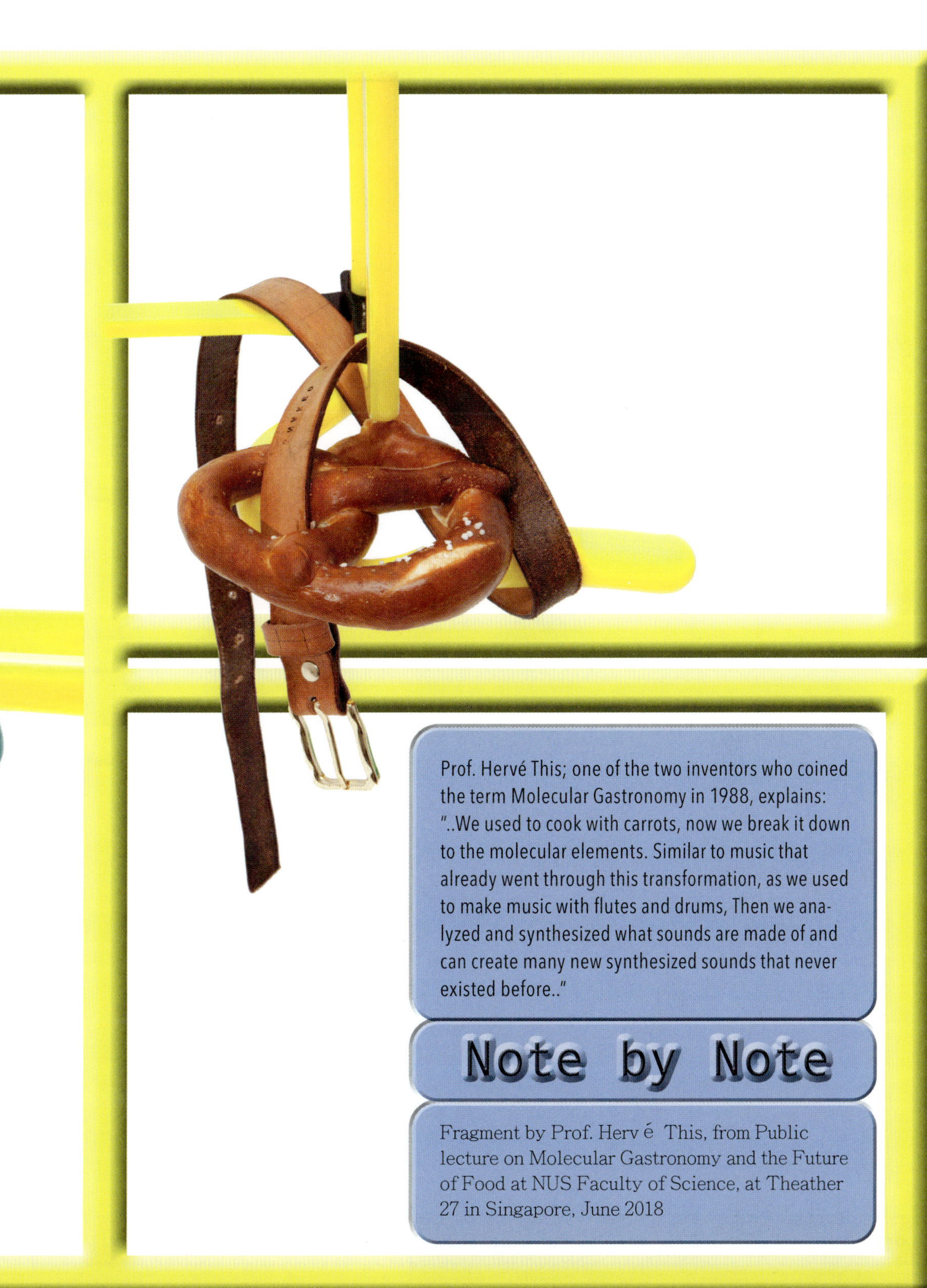

Prof. Hervé This; one of the two inventors who coined the term Molecular Gastronomy in 1988, explains: "..We used to cook with carrots, now we break it down to the molecular elements. Similar to music that already went through this transformation, as we used to make music with flutes and drums, Then we analyzed and synthesized what sounds are made of and can create many new synthesized sounds that never existed before.."

Note by Note

Fragment by Prof. Herv é This, from Public lecture on Molecular Gastronomy and the Future of Food at NUS Faculty of Science, at Theather 27 in Singapore, June 2018

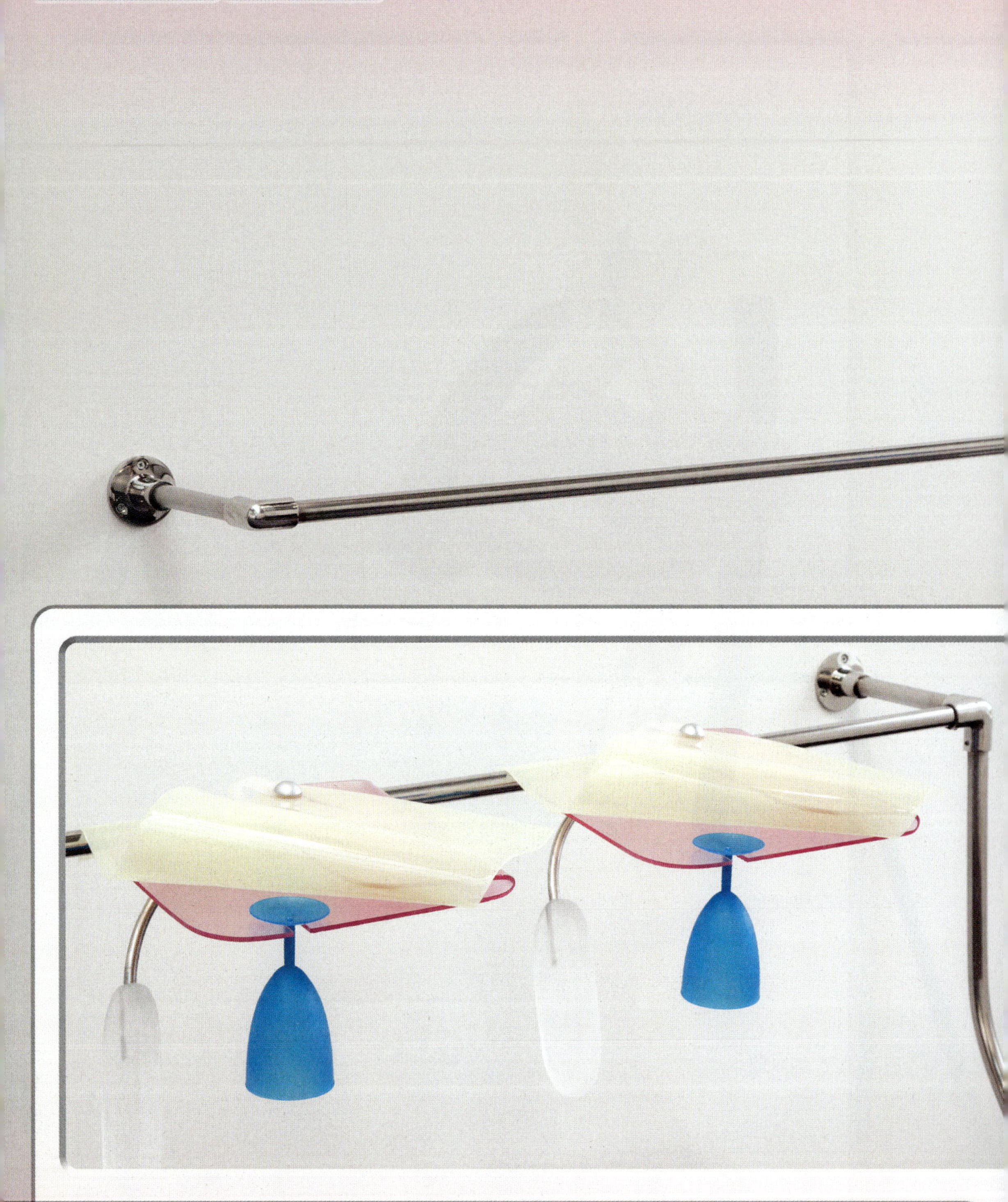

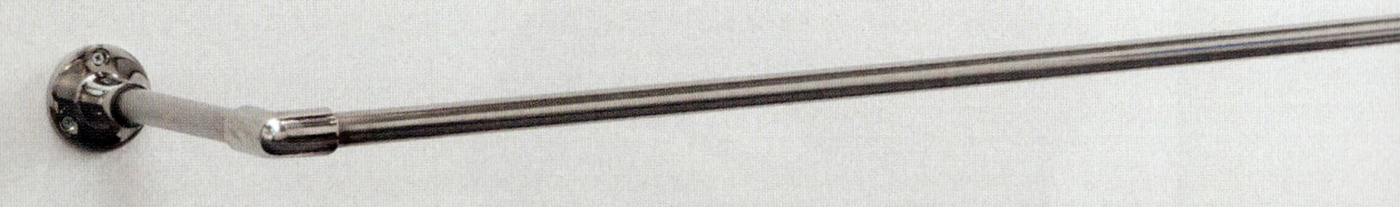

Login, for two 2013, 260 x 160 x 65 cm, stainless steel, digital print, rubber, polished plexiglas

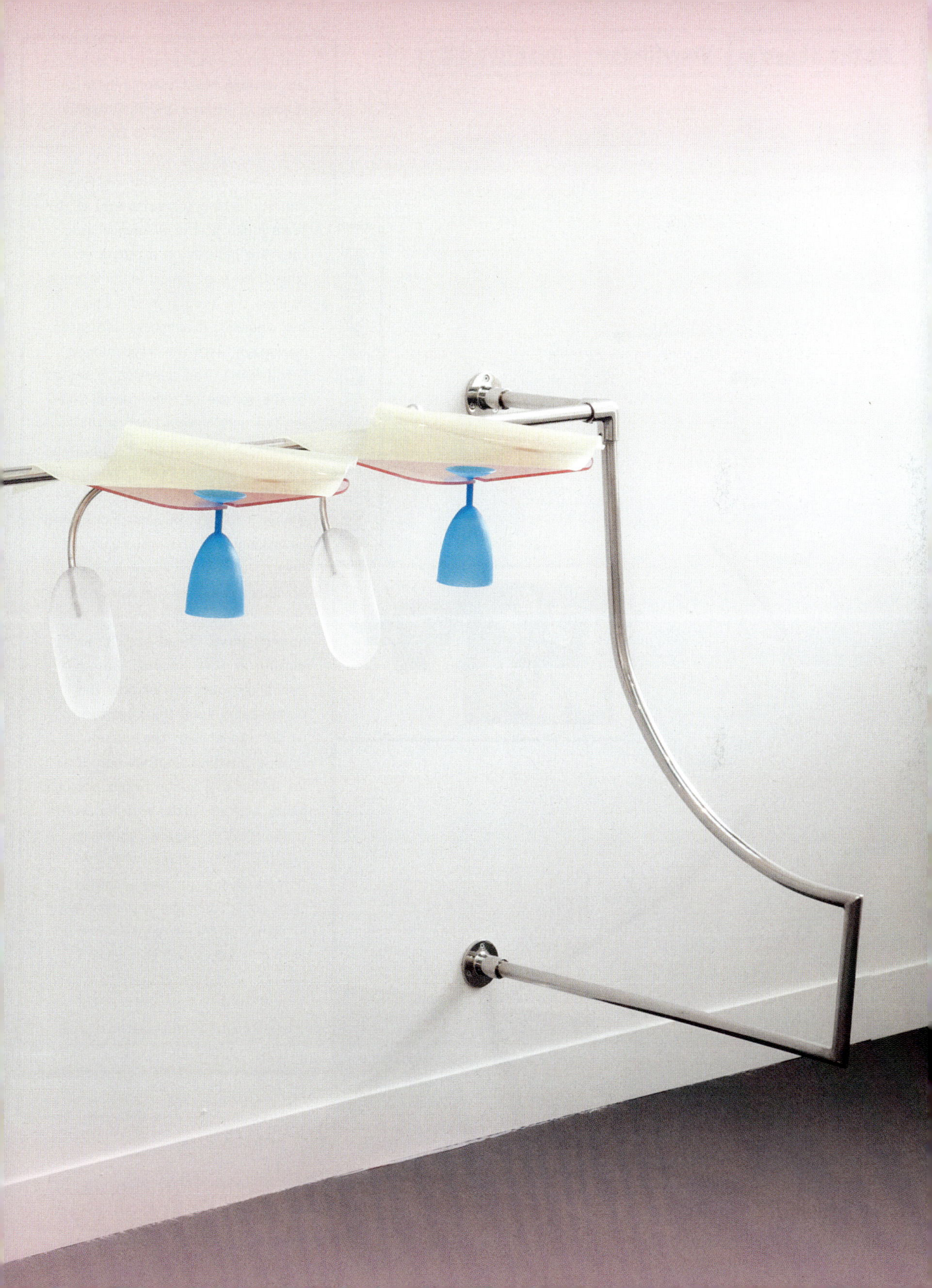

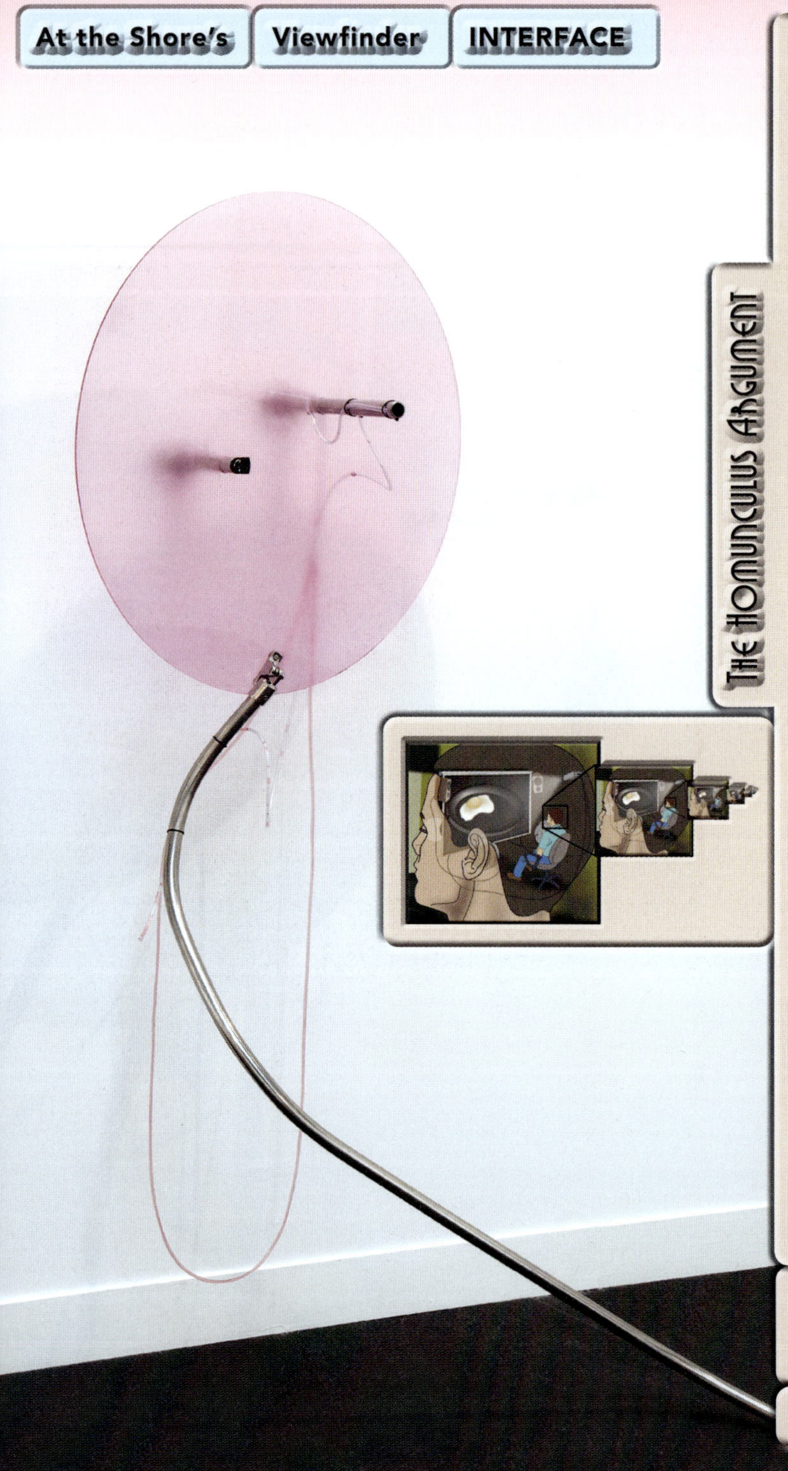

The Homunculus Argument

The homunculus argument is a fallacy arising most commonly in the theory of vision. One may explain human vision by noting that light from the outside world forms an image on the retinas in the eyes and something (or someone) in the brain looks at these images as if they are images on a movie screen (this theory of vision is sometimes termed the theory of the Cartesian theater: it is most associated, nowadays, with the psychologist David Marr). The question arises as to the nature of this internal viewer. The assumption here is that there is a "little man" or "homunculus" inside the brain "looking at" the movie. The reason why this is a fallacy may be understood by asking how the homunculus "sees" the internal movie. The obvious answer is that there is another homunculus inside the first homunculus's "head" or "brain" looking at this "movie". But that raises the question of how this homunculus sees the "outside world". To answer that seems to require positing another homunculus inside this second homunculus's head, and so forth. In other words, a situation of infinite regress is created. The problem with the homunculus argument is that it tries to account for a phenomenon in terms of the very phenomenon that it is supposed to explain.[1]

1. Richard L. Gregory. (1987), The Oxford Companion to the Mind, Oxford University Press

en/wikipedia.org, Sep 2nd, 2019

Viewfinder 2013, 175 x 65 x 45 cm, stainless steel, plexiglass, key, silicon medical tubes

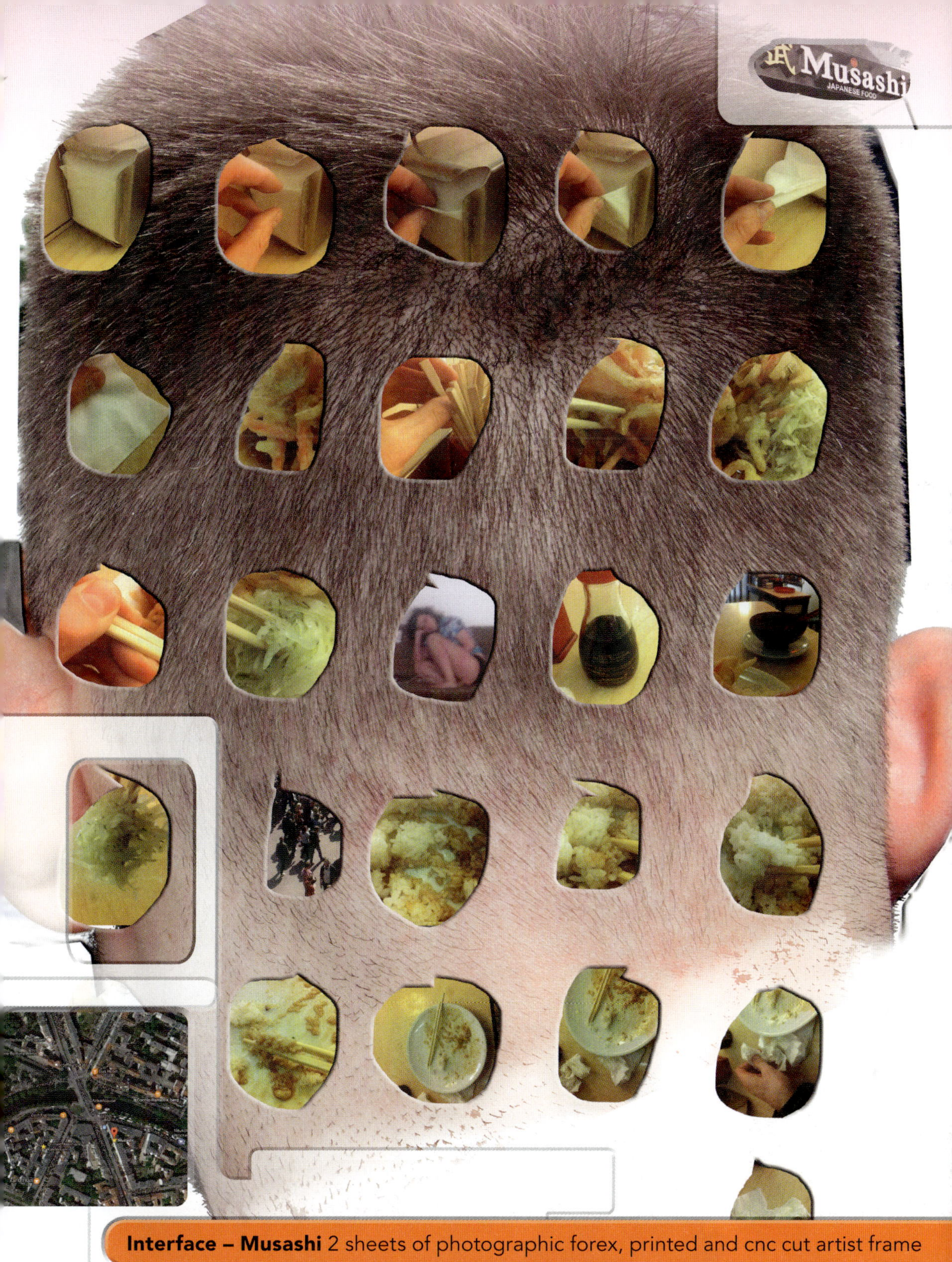

Interface – Musashi 2 sheets of photographic forex, printed and cnc cut artist frame

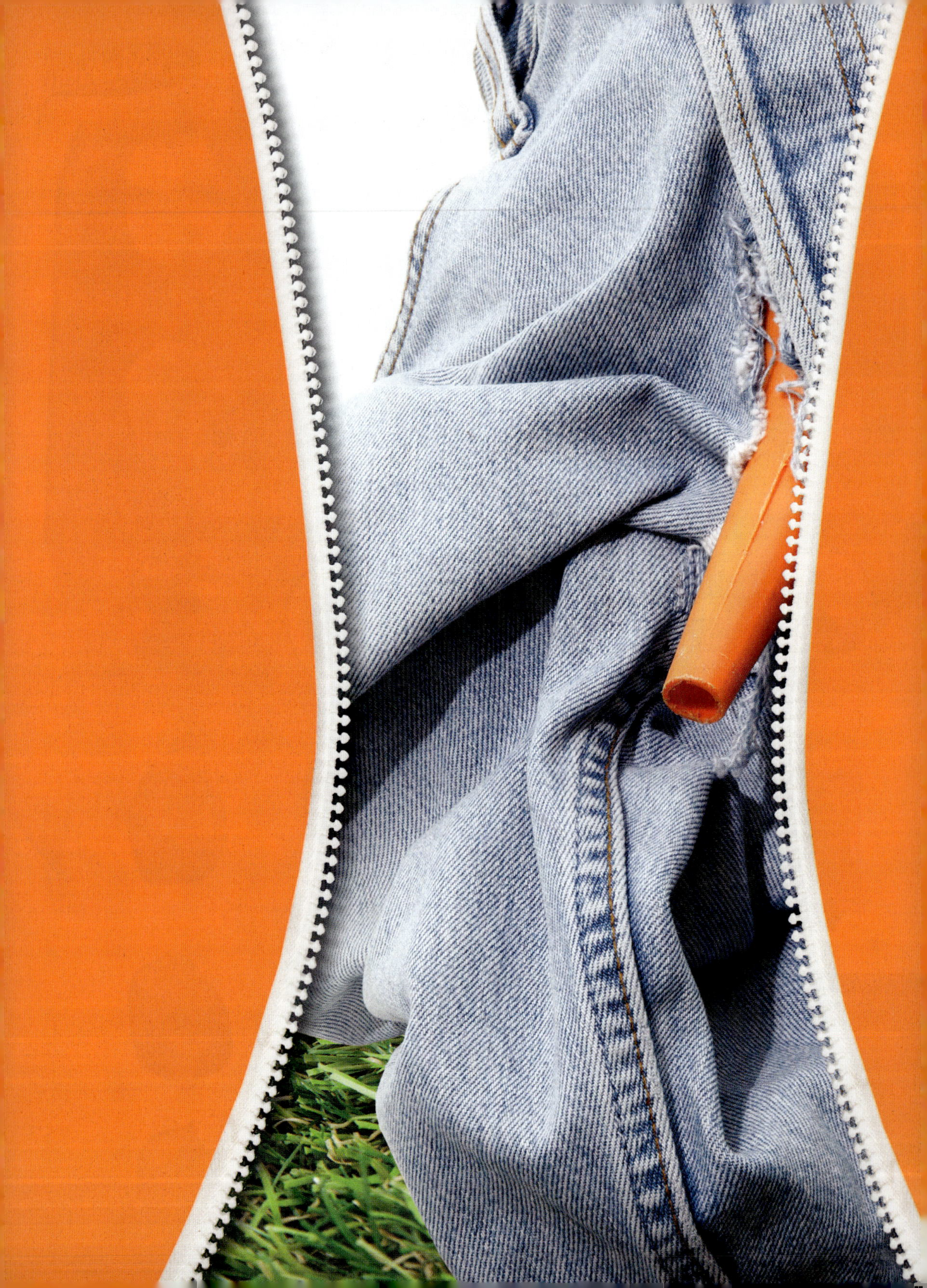

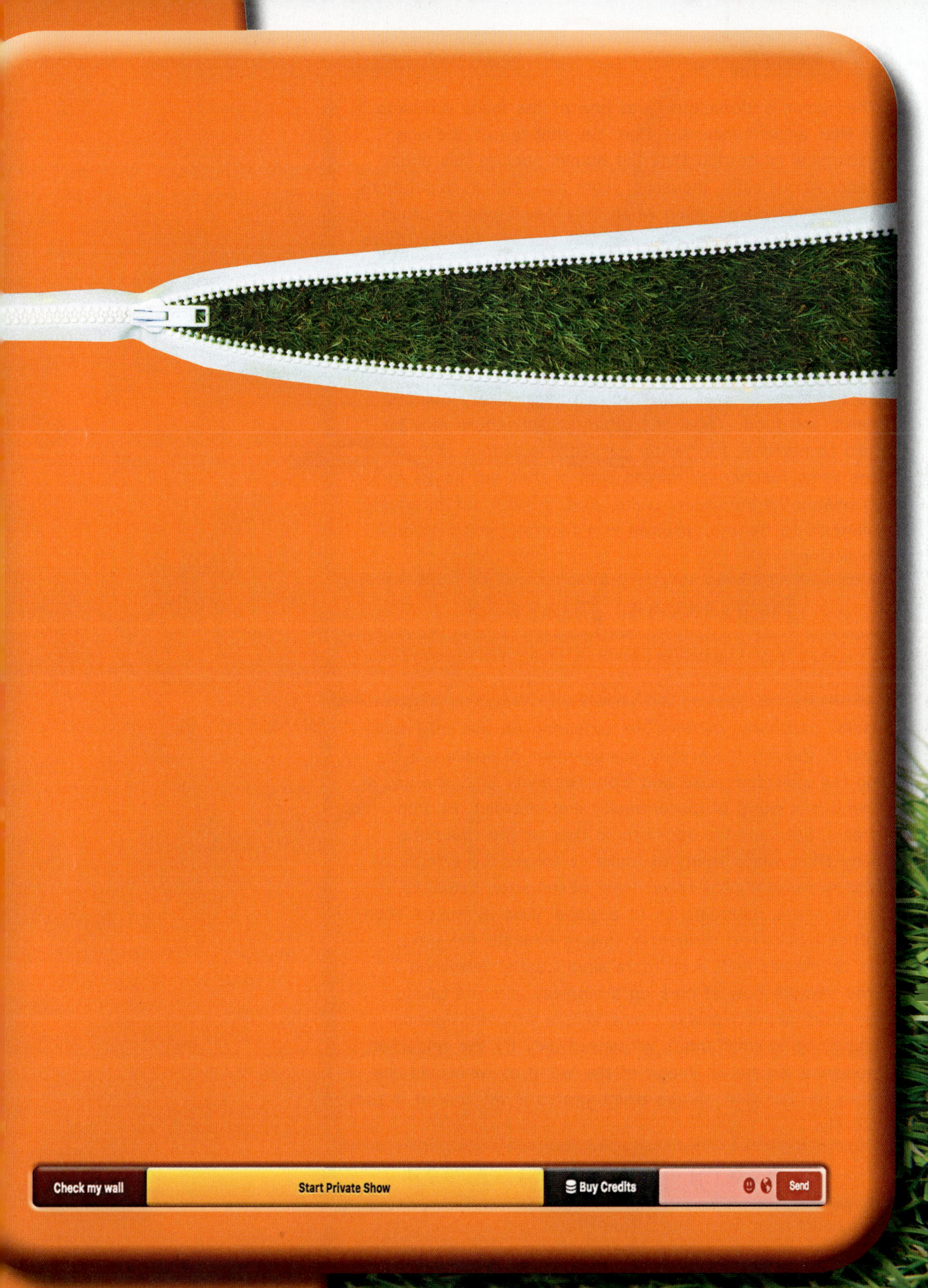
Check my wall
Start Private Show
Buy Credits
Send

The human endoskeleton was one of the many products of that ancient mineralization. Yet that is not the only geological infiltration that the human species has undergone. About eight thousand years ago, human populations began mineralizing again when they developed an urban exoskeleton: bricks of sundried clay became building materials for their homes, which in turn surrounded and were surrounded by stone monuments and defensive walls. This exoskeleton served a purpose similar to its internal counterpart: to control the movement of human flesh in and out of a town's walls. The urban exoskeleton also regulated the movement of many other things: luxury objects, news, and food... Thus, the urban infrastructure may be said to perform, for tightly packed populations of humans, the same function of motion control that our bones do in relation to our fleshy parts. And, in both cases, adding minerals to the mix resulted in a fantastic combinatorial explosion."

Nonlinear History

Fragment from: Manuel De Landa, A Thousand Years of Nonlinear History, Page 27, Zone Books, Brooklyn, 199

Walls, partitions, barriers are appearing on the local scale and in the most everyday management of space... seen on the individual scale and from the inner city, the global world is a world of discontinuity and interdict. By contrast, the dominant aesthetic is that of the cinematic long shot, which tends to make us forget the effects of this rupture. Photos taken from observation satellites, aerial shots, habituate us to a global view of things. High office blocks and residential towers educate the gaze, as do movies and, even more significantly, television. The smooth flow of cars on a highway, aircraft taking off from airport runways, lone sailors circumnavigating the globe in small boats witnessed only by the television audience, create an image of the world as we would like it to be. But that mirage disintegrates if we look at it too closely.

Smooth Disintegration

Fragment from: Marc Augé, Non-Places, Introduction to the second edition, Page: XIII, published by Verso, London, 2008.

SCROLL 10

AI GPT-2 RESPONSE

I want to take it from its place here where the audience is not the audience. Heavily indebted to those who write these works and he makes money off of it. But one important difference is that Grant's work is about the audience rather than the content that is being presented. It is about what the audience wants, not what is produced. The audience wants an audience that reads and watches the novel and reads and watches the movies; it wants someone to make money or to be part of a band of bands or artists that will make the difference. Grant is not saying that because he is not part of band. I mean, in the novel he appears and does things and this is where the audience turns his life into a living space for him.

"Heaven is just a collection of fragments" so you can write them into a story like this or a book like this [I'm thinking about the band], 'I'm not making money out of this. What he says is that you have to make this up when you're writing or the story is going to look terrible for other people to like or not like that and they shouldn't love it as much as anybody else.

So Grant's goal is to make this "living space" better, or the story better. So what you end up with is an old, lost story that is hard to find because so many layers are layered on top of it. "The story itself has to be a story." This may sound ridiculous, but it's my personal theory that many of Grant's stories are about the people on board the ship. So what I've been thinking about (not much else here) is how the band might play in this setting, how it would relate to their musical experiences in ways that other bands might not (especially because that is where they were born) and what that might mean for the relationship between these two. All of these ideas are there in Grant's text, but recently they've been thrown around more often. I have no idea why people would start to talk about some of these things but this is an important point that has to be brought up. So, we can be talking about some new ideas for how to get the story done better in a more intimate setting, and how it would play a role as a foundation for new songs.

AI GPT-2 RESPONSE

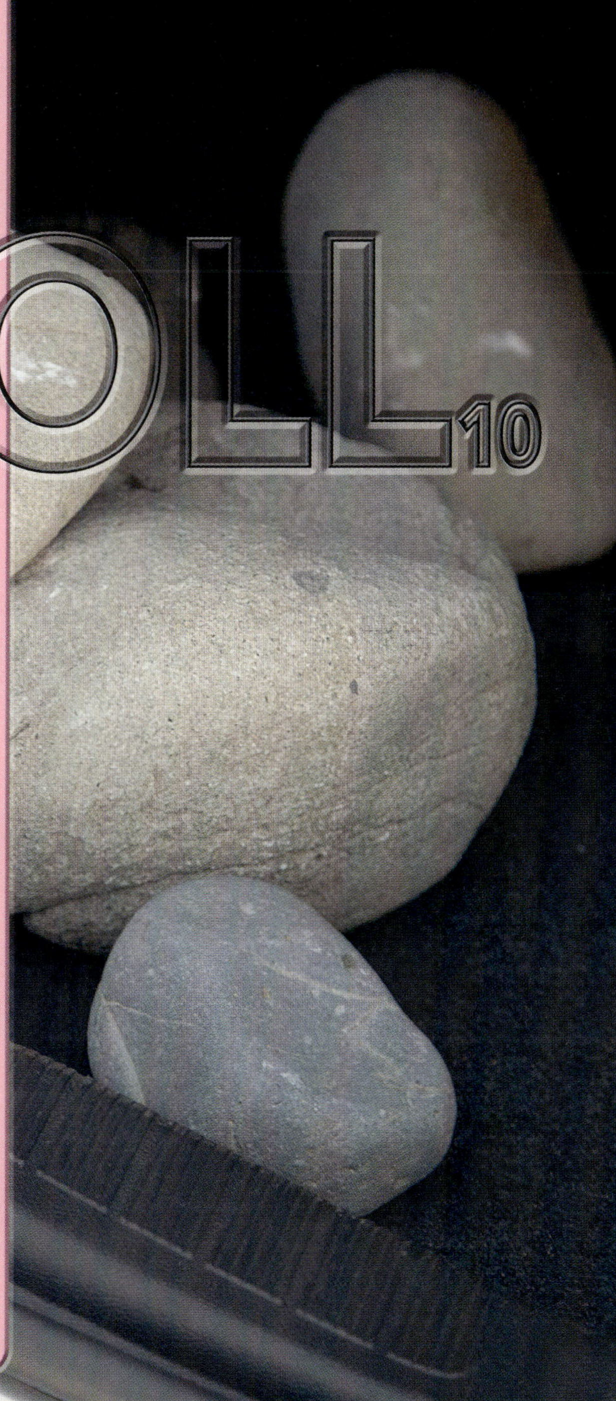

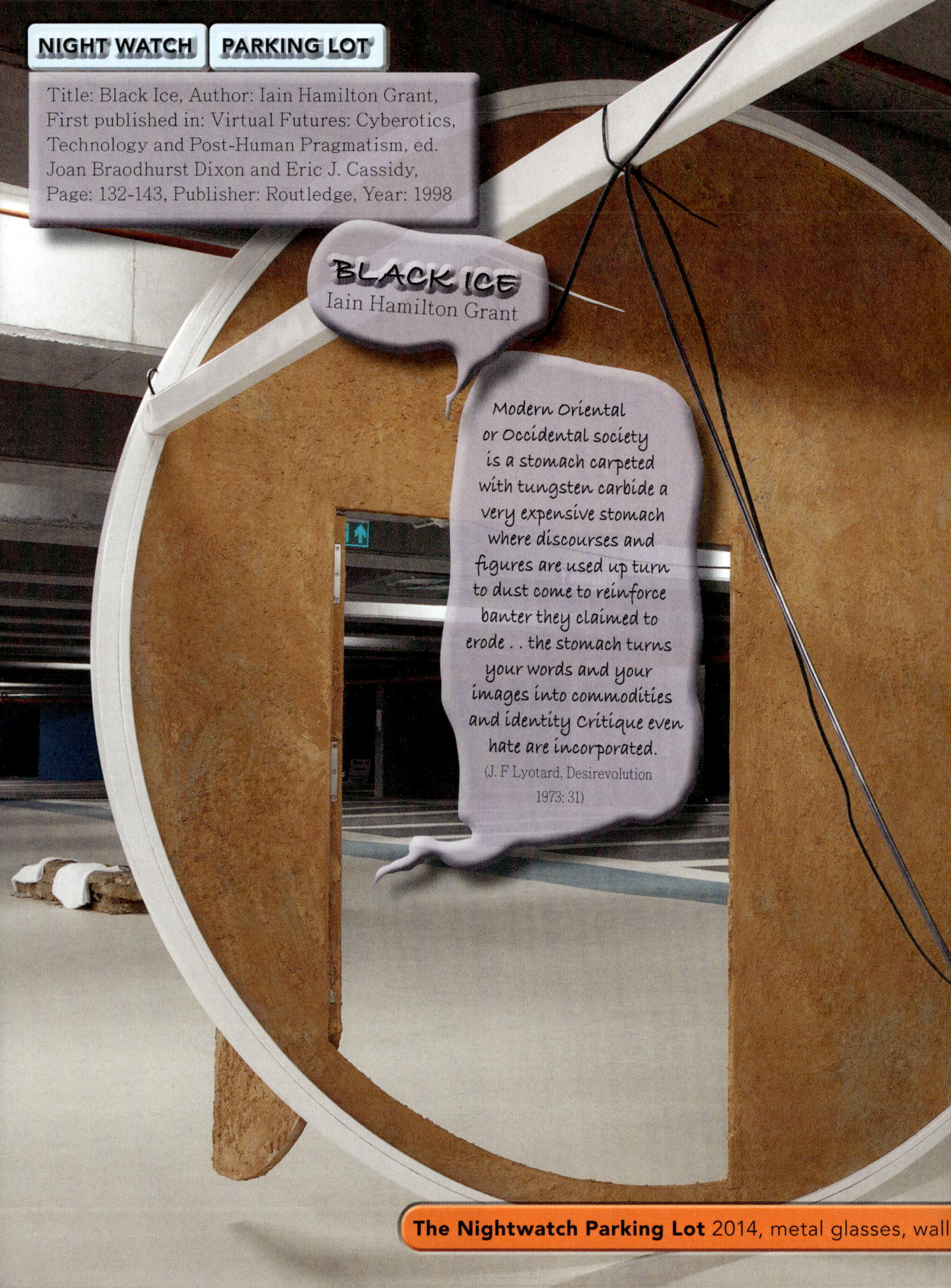

The Nightwatch Parking Lot 2014, metal glasses, wall

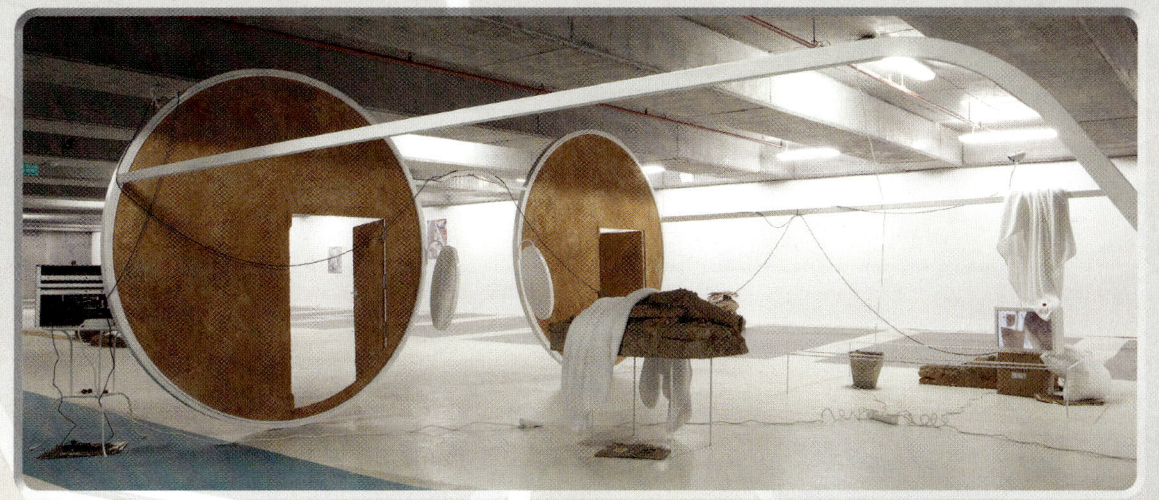

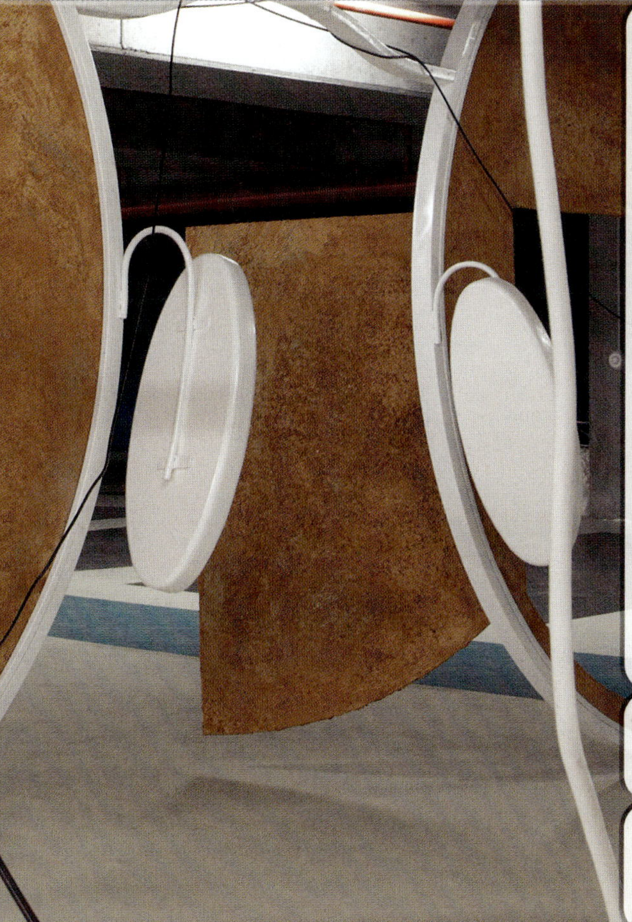

"Visible and mobile, my body is a thing among things; it is one of them. It is caught in the fabric of the world, and its cohesion is that of a thing. But because it sees and moves itself, it holds things in a circle around itself. Things are an annex or prolongation of my body; they are incrusted in its flesh, they are part of its full definition; the world is made of the very stuff of the body. These reversals, these antinomies, are different ways of saying that vision is caught or is made in the middle of things, where something visible undertakes to see, becomes visible for itself and through the vision of all things, where the indivision of the sensing and the sensed persists, like the original fluid within the crystal."

The Eye and the Spirit

Excerpt from: Title: L' Œil et l' Esprit, Author: Maurice Merleau-Ponty, First published by Éditions Gallimard, Year: 1964

oors, surveillance camera systems, 2 LCD screens, furniture, fabrics, wine, cherries, news papers

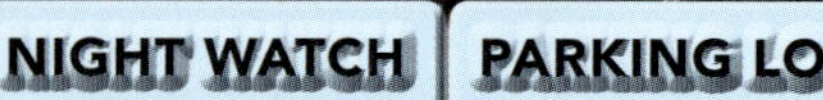

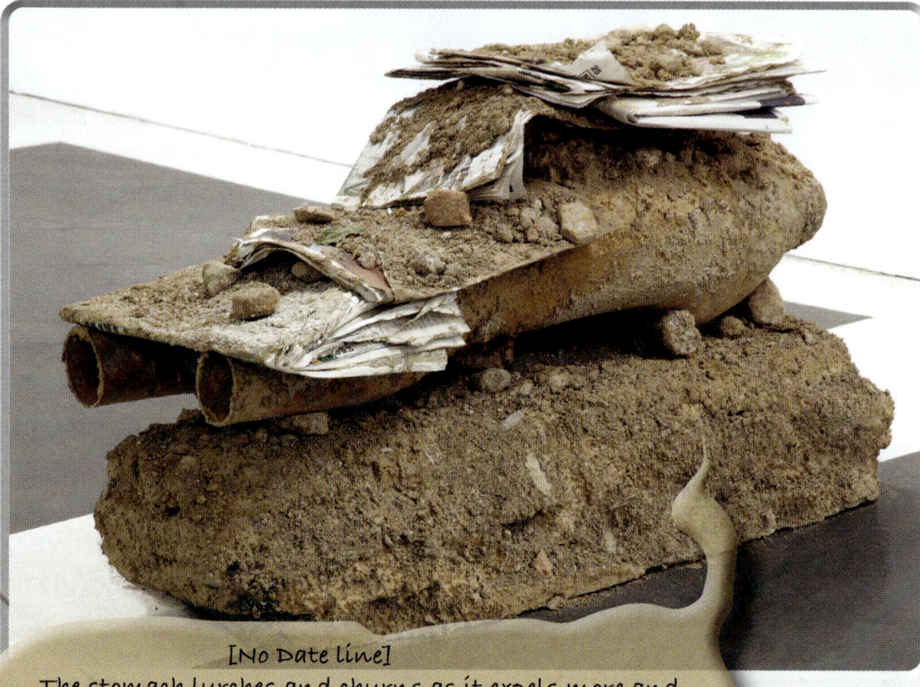

[No Date line]
The stomach lurches and churns as it expels more and more of its shrink-wrapped identitarian detritus. The permanent whines of its ferro-concrete intestines sets our ears bleeding as it ingests new fuels - old products. Sticky organs mesh indiscriminately with scrapyard debris, forming ephemeral syntaxes of hybrid cyber-circulation. 'Look out! It's eating everything in its path!'

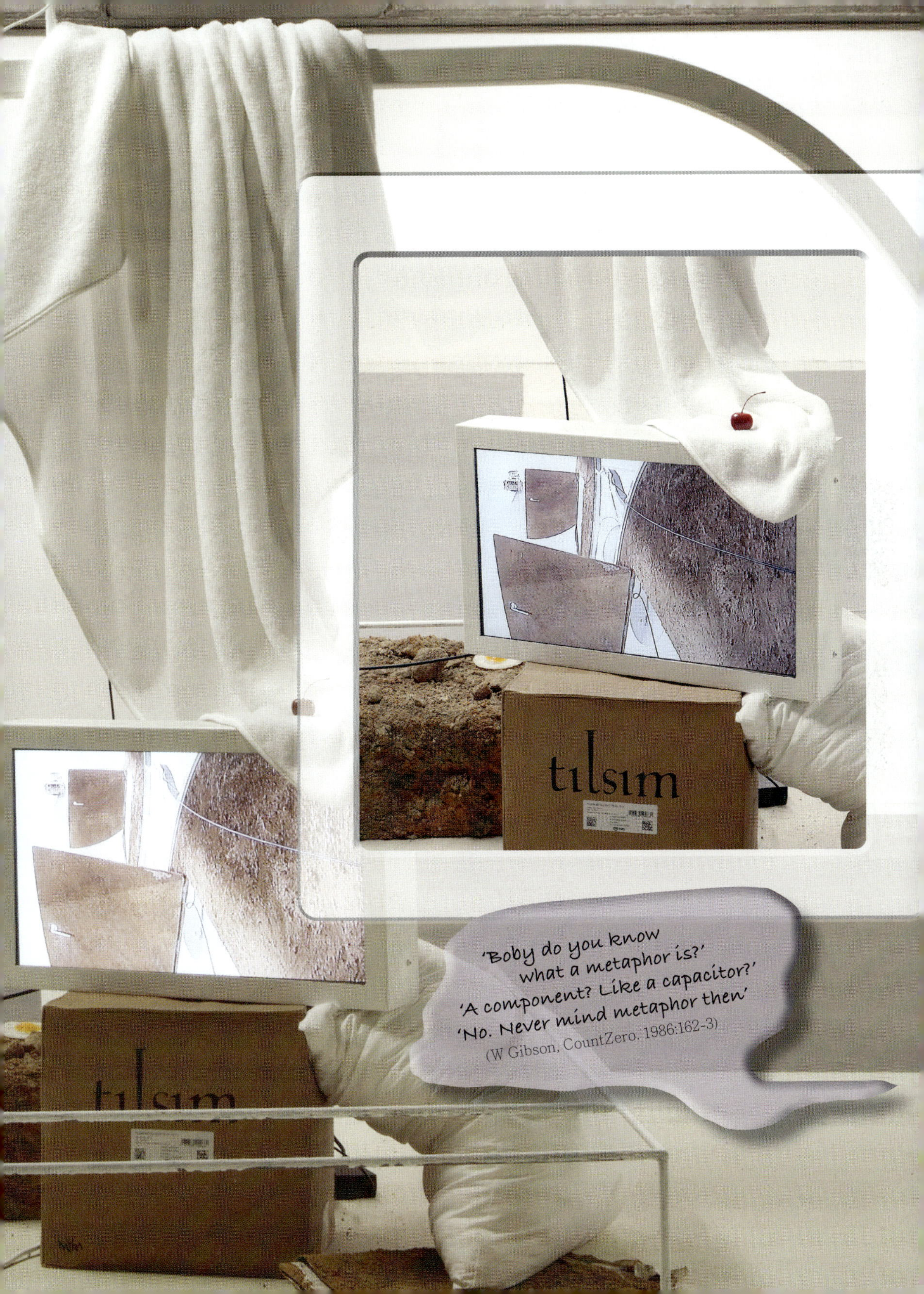
tılsım
'Boby do you know
what a metaphor is?'
'A component? Like a capacitor?'
'No. Never mind metaphor then'
(W Gibson, CountZero. 1986:162-3)

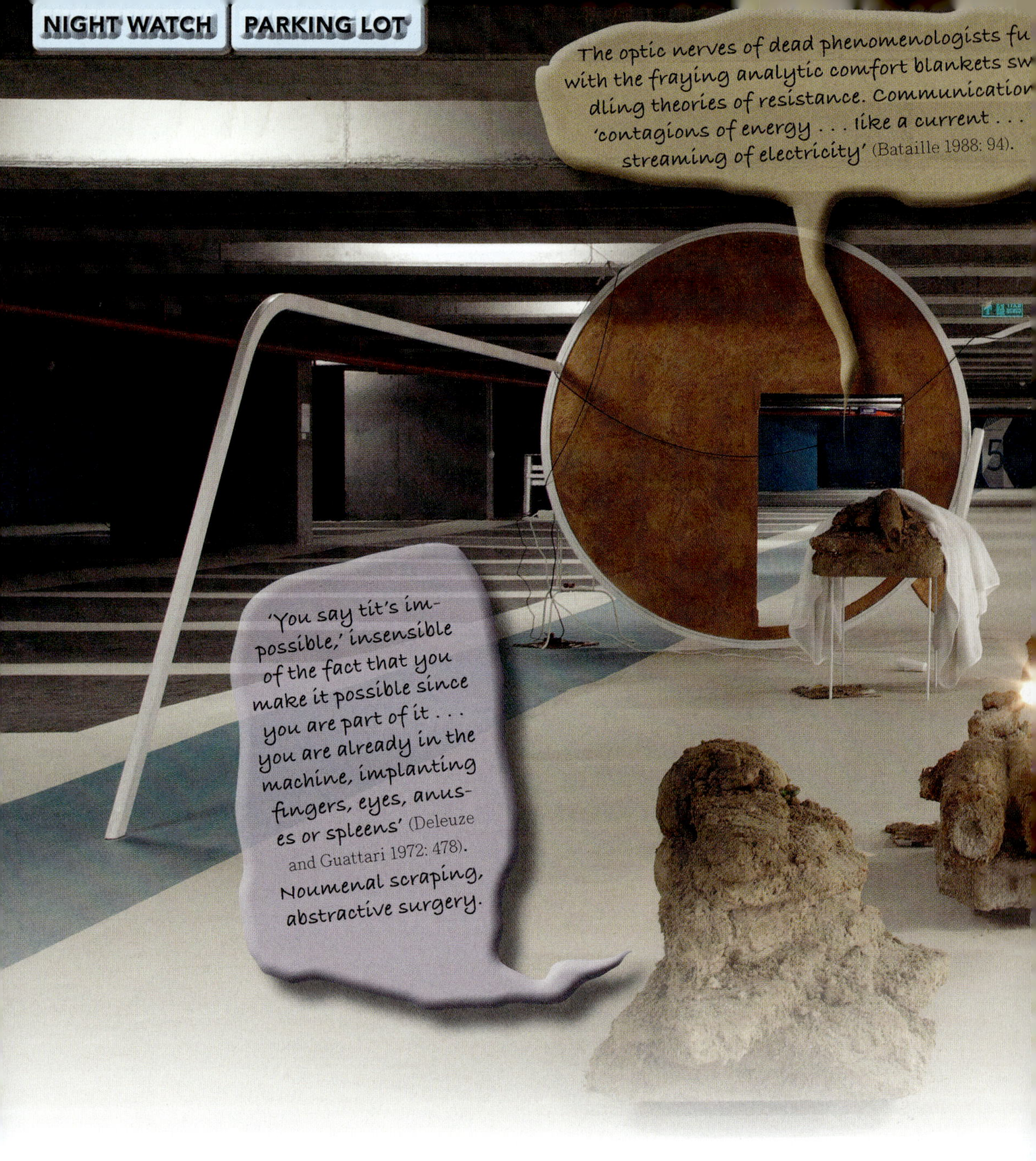

The Nightwatch Parking Lot 2014, metal glasses, walls, doors, surveillance camera system

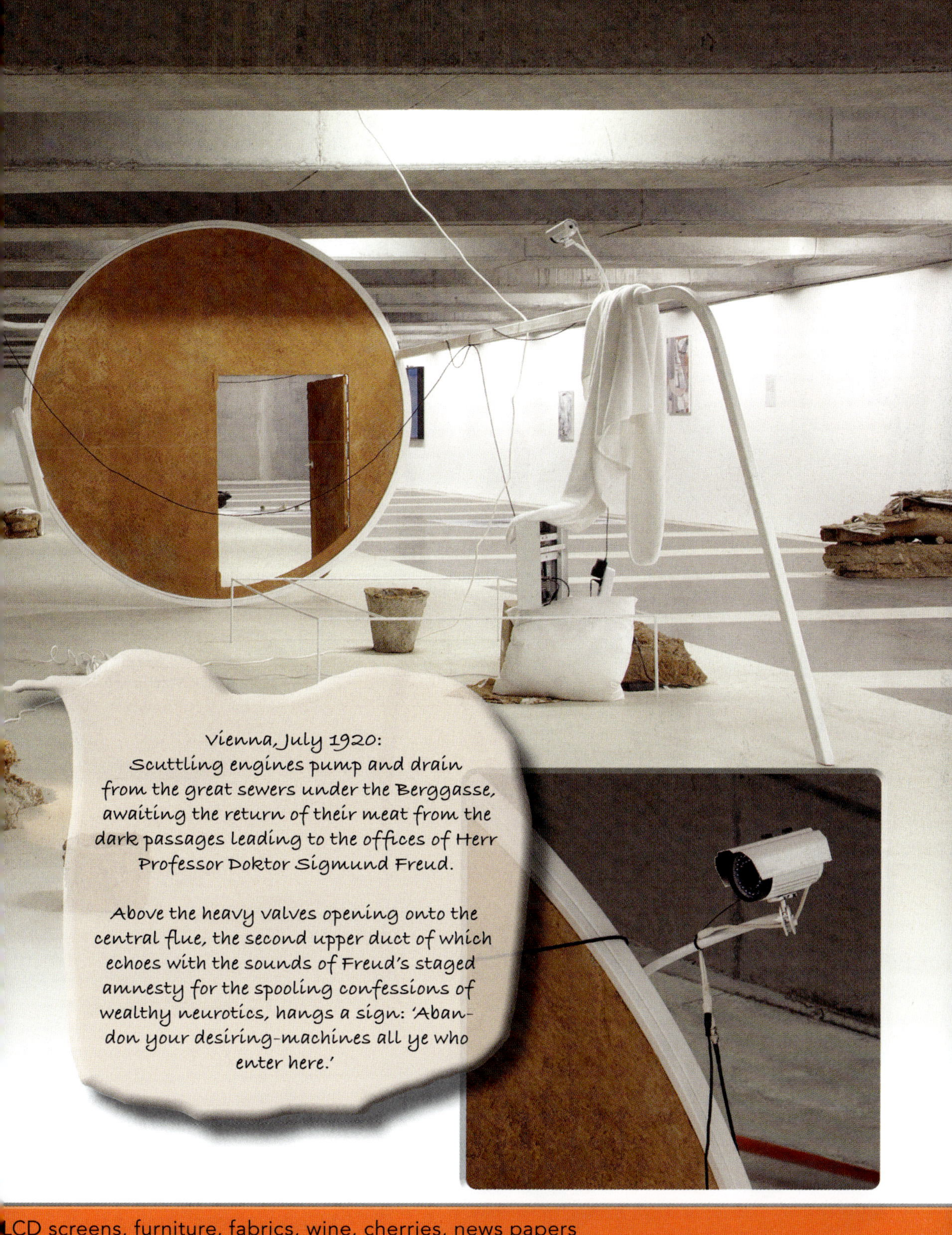

LCD screens, furniture, fabrics, wine, cherries, news papers

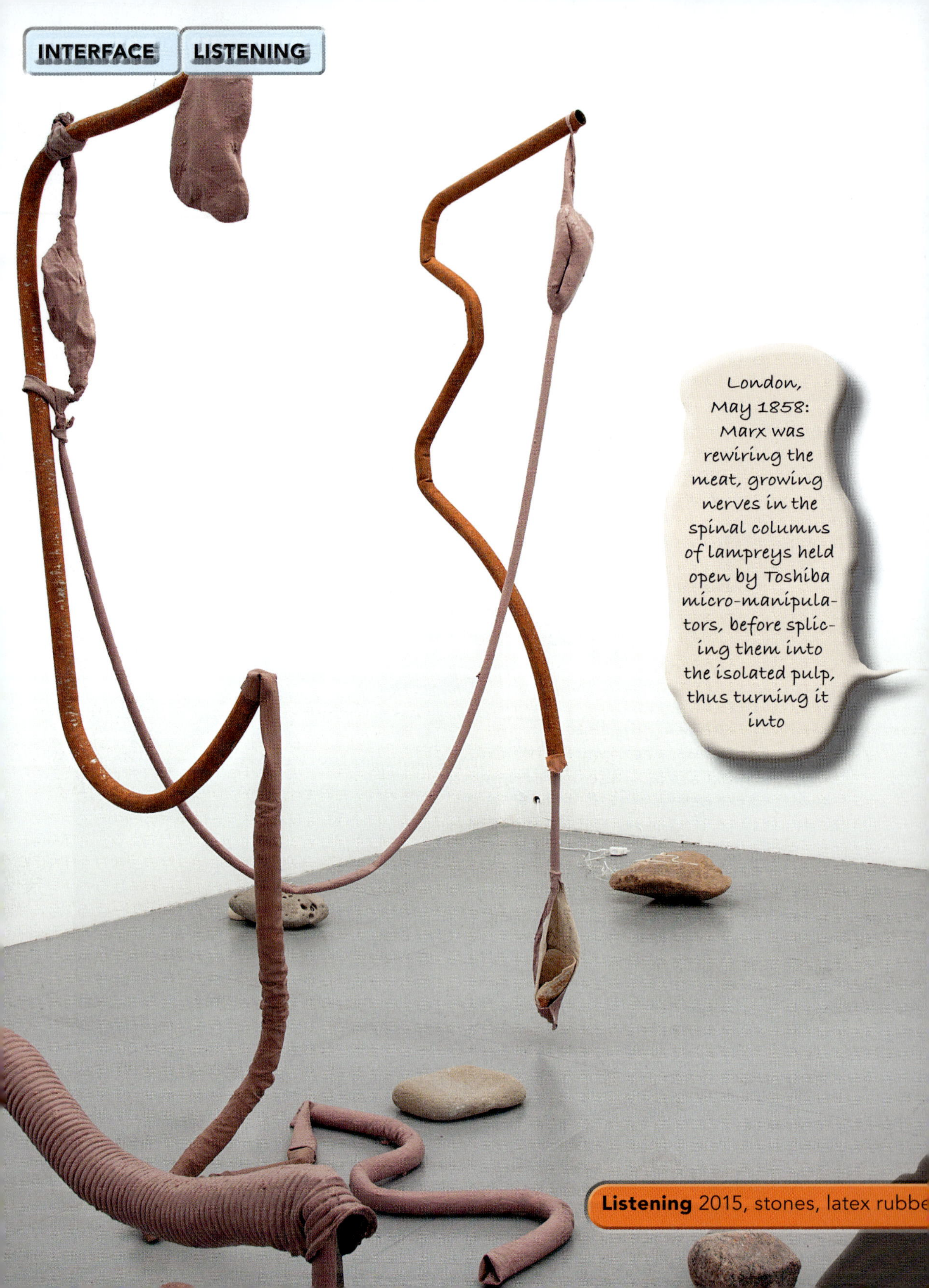

Listening 2015, stones, latex rubbe

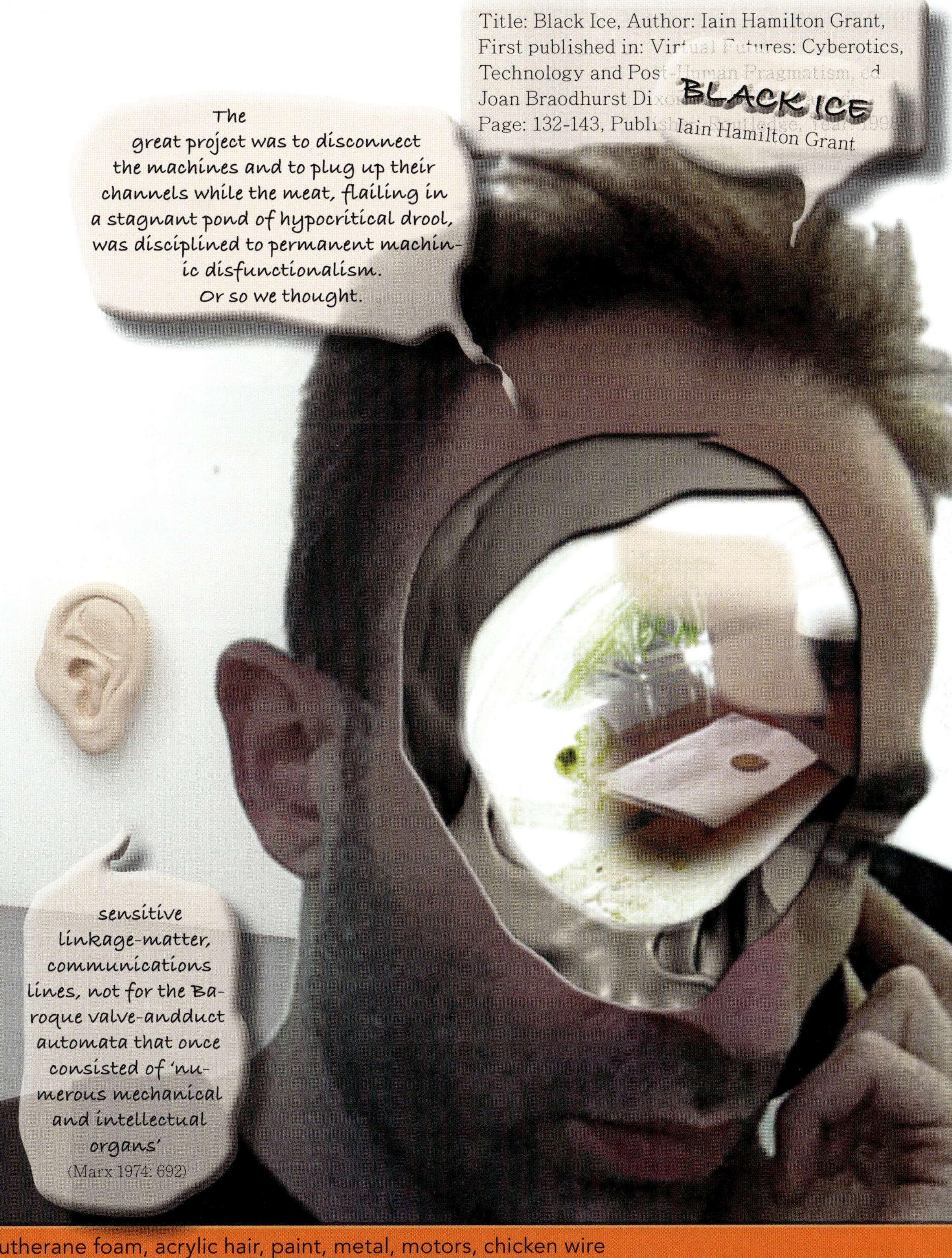

Title: Black Ice, Author: Iain Hamilton Grant,
First published in: Virtual Futures: Cyberotics,
Technology and Post-Human Pragmatism, ed.
Joan Braodhurst Di
Page: 132-143, Publisher: Routledge, Year: 1998
BLACK ICE
Iain Hamilton Grant
The great project was to disconnect the machines and to plug up their channels while the meat, flailing in a stagnant pond of hypocritical drool, was disciplined to permanent machinic disfunctionalism. Or so we thought.
sensitive linkage-matter, communications lines, not for the Baroque valve-andduct automata that once consisted of 'numerous mechanical and intellectual organs' (Marx 1974: 692)
ly utherane foam, acrylic hair, paint, metal, motors, chicken wire
duo exhibition by Anne de Vries and Olga Balema

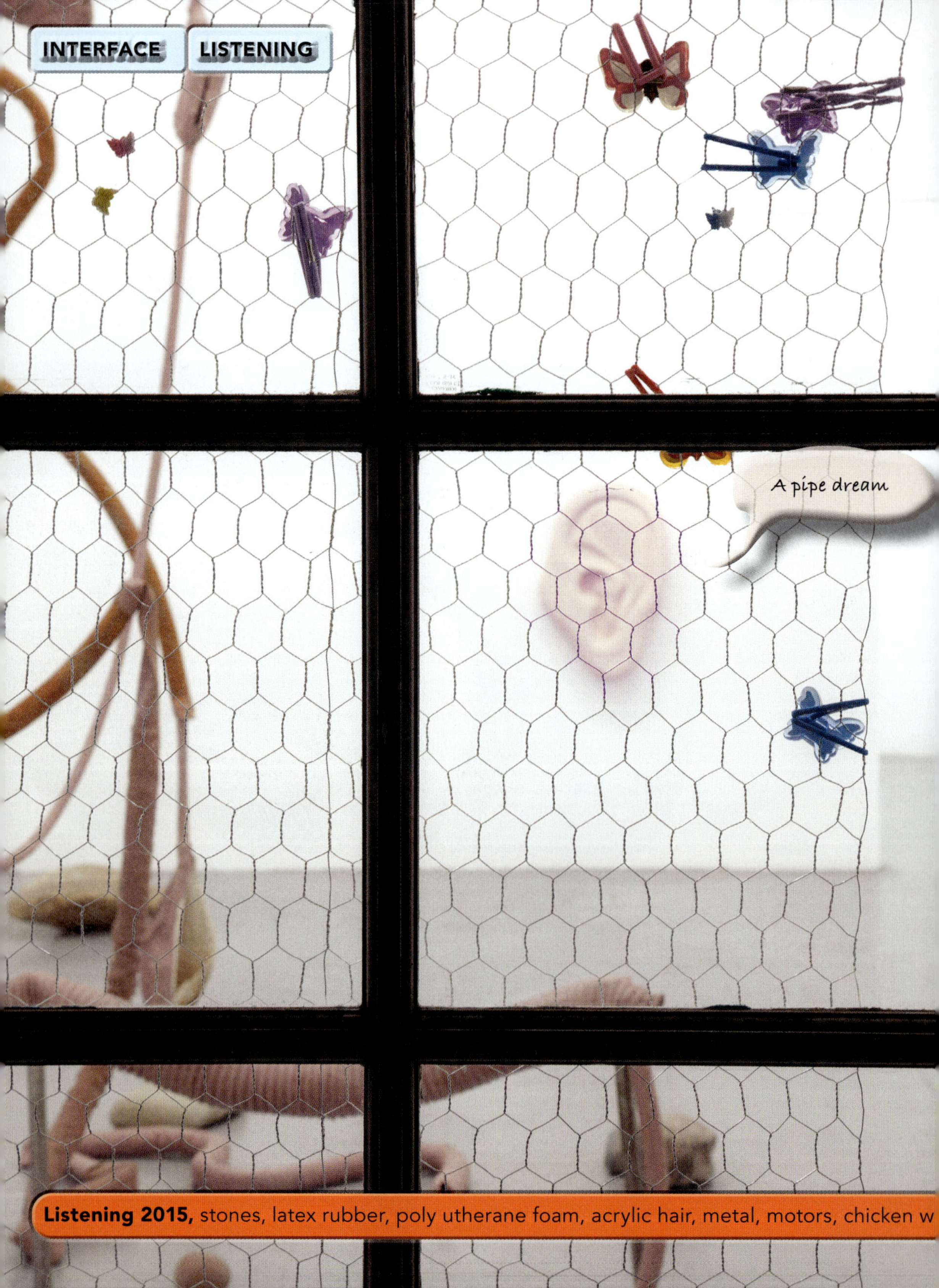

Listening 2015, stones, latex rubber, poly utherane foam, acrylic hair, metal, motors, chicken w

but
to circulate
through un-
differentiated
protoplasm till
the meat gets
so thoroughly
baked through
that it forms a
crust shielding
its newly
nervured
biomass.
'Revolution was
like that,' piped
the biobydrau-
lics, still swim-
ming through the
100 Berggasse:
'a delusion . . .,

a pipe dream that
the flesh would be
restored'
(Kadrey 1989: 189).

Machine
dreams...
Instants later they
were swept aside by
isotropic currents of
shrill transspaces com-
munication contagions
of energy, storm fronts
of meshed intelligence...
hold a special vertigo.
(Gibson 1986: 40)

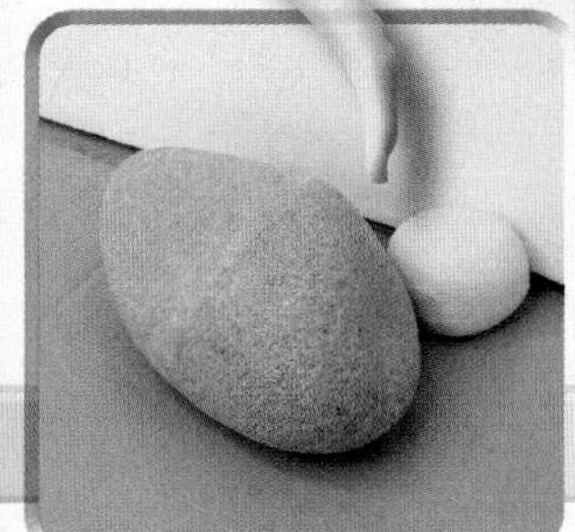

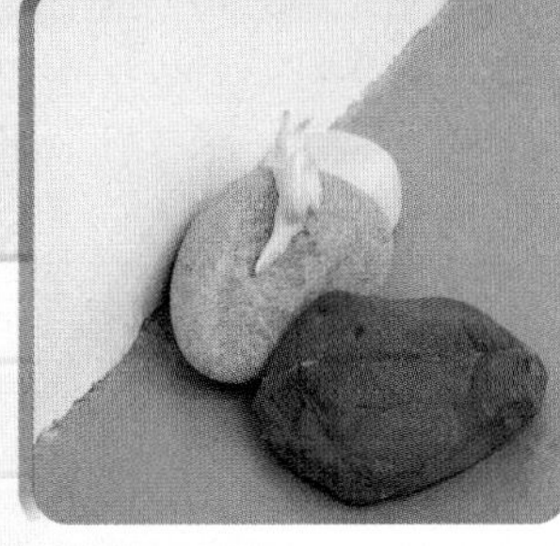

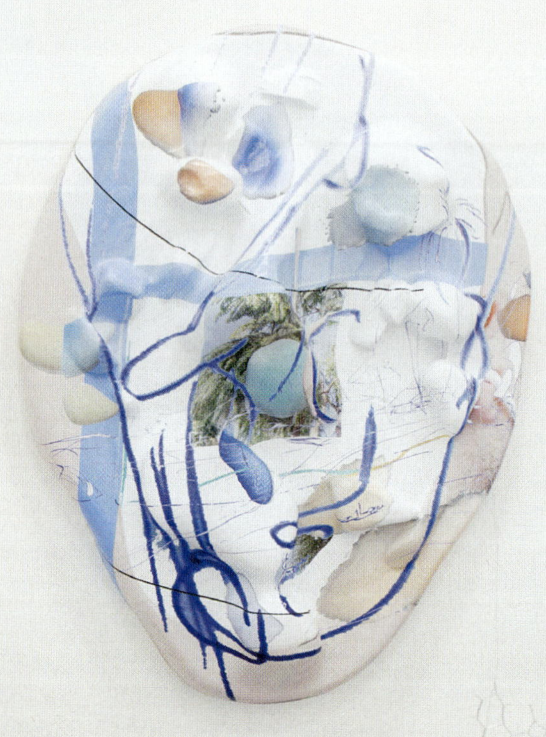

Cyborgs have exposed the imminent fatality of thought. What began with the fraying edges of larval, inchoate self-identical cogitos saturates 'thought' with a noumenal backwash from outside the biodrome.

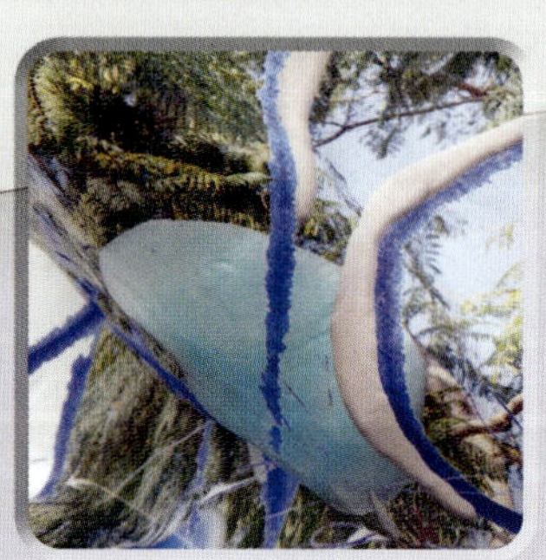

Biodrome Interface 03 2015 archival UV print on plastic forr

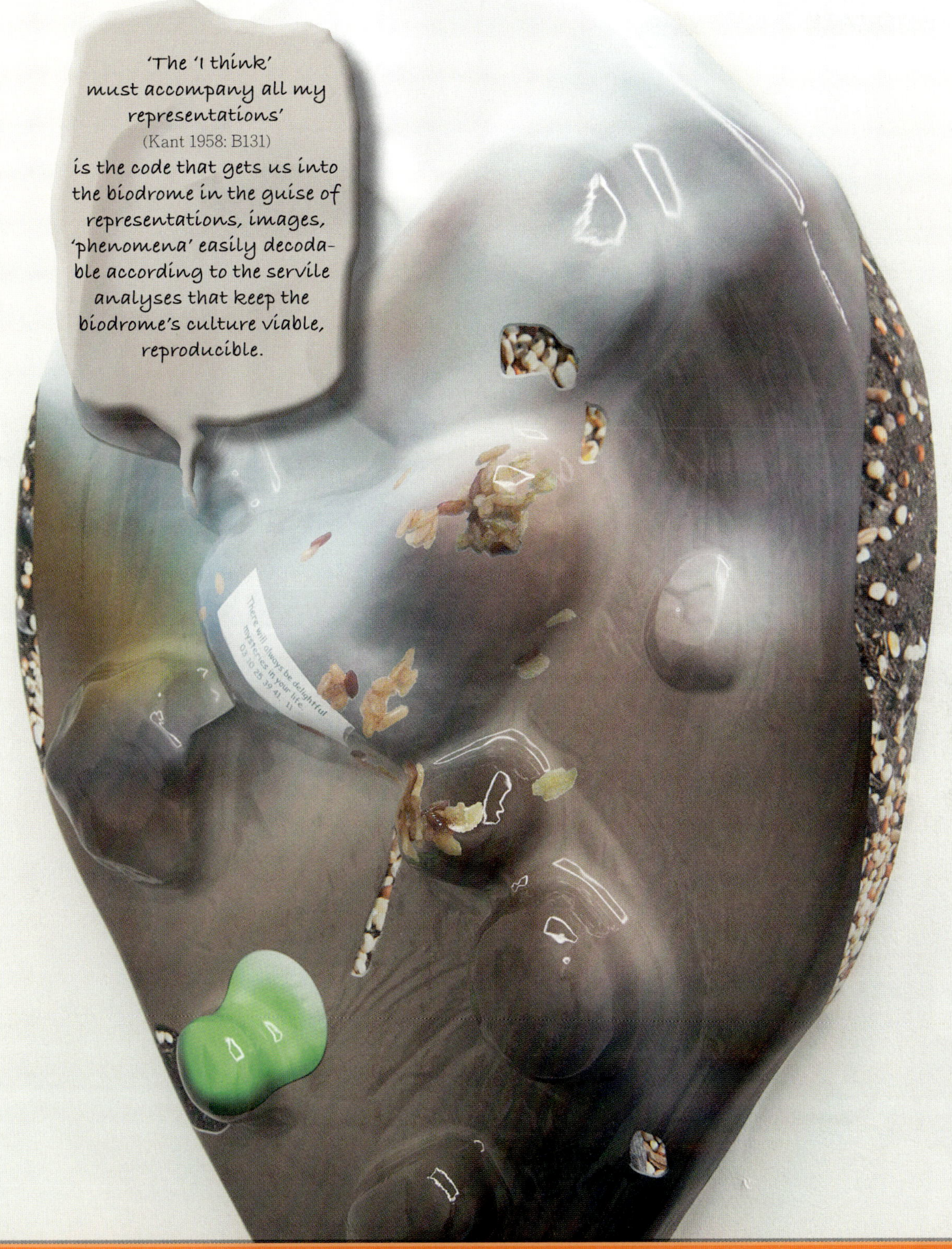
'The 'I think'
must accompany all my
representations'
(Kant 1958: B131)
is the code that gets us into
the biodrome in the guise of
representations, images,
'phenomena' easily decoda-
ble according to the servile
analyses that keep the
biodrome's culture viable,
reproducible.
There will always be delightful
mysteries in your life.
03 10 25 39 41 11

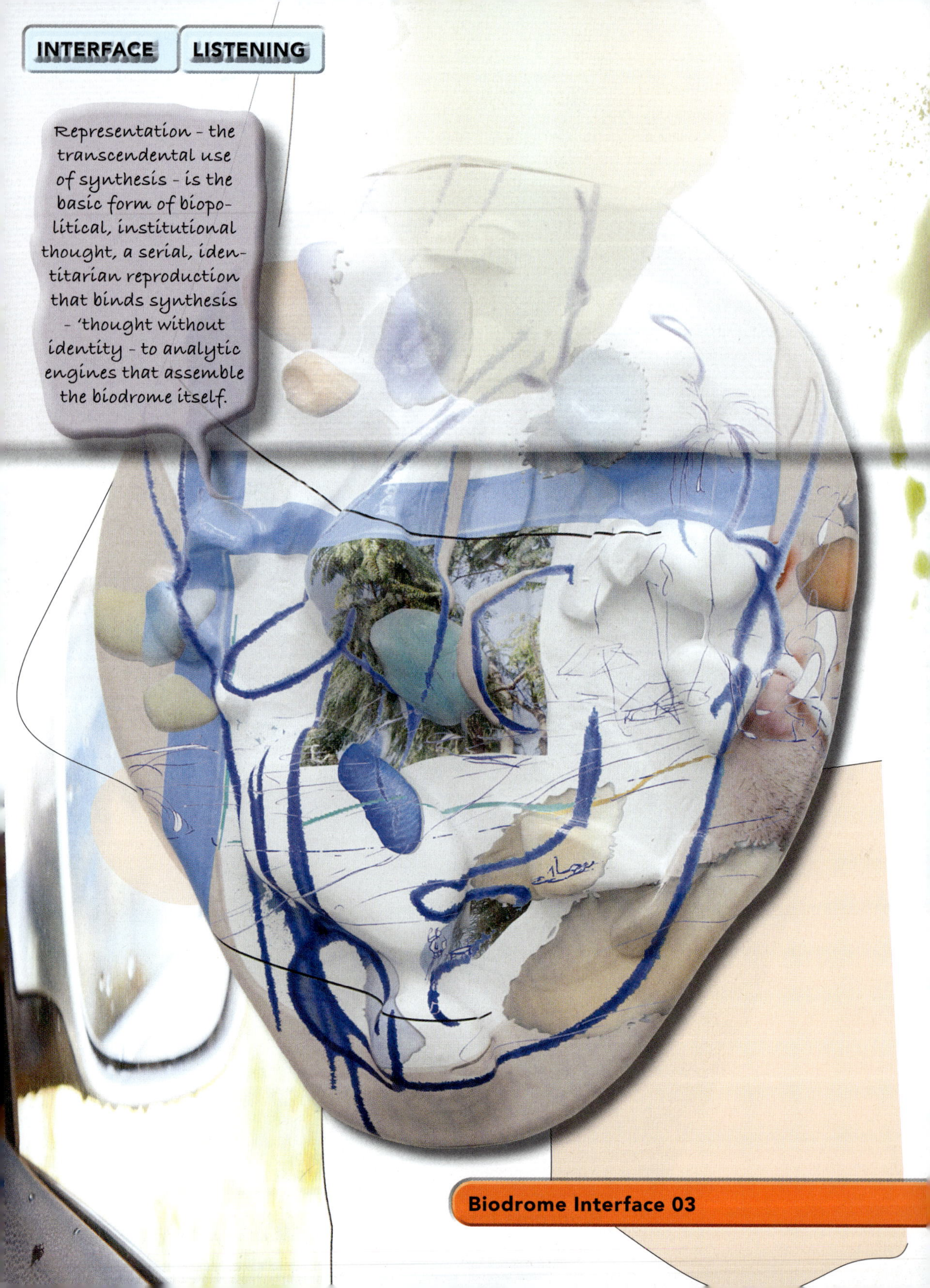
INTERFACE
LISTENING
Representation - the transcendental use of synthesis - is the basic form of biopo-litical, institutional thought, a serial, iden-titarian reproduction that binds synthesis - 'thought without identity - to analytic engines that assemble the biodrome itself.
Biodrome Interface 03

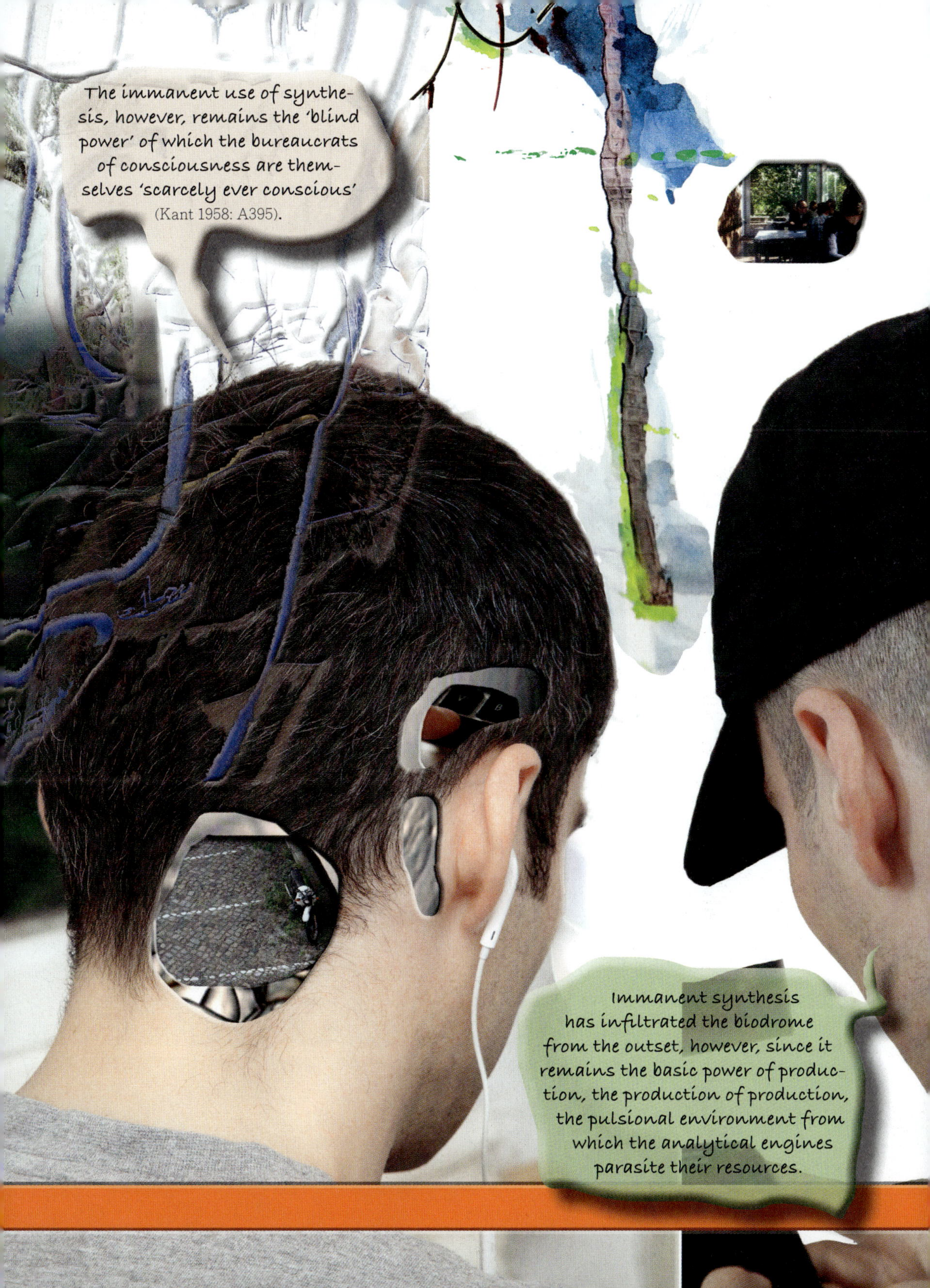
The immanent use of synthe-
sis, however, remains the 'blind
power' of which the bureaucrats
of consciousness are themselves 'scarcely ever conscious'
(Kant 1958: A395).
Immanent synthesis
has infiltrated the biodrome
from the outset, however, since it
remains the basic power of production, the production of production,
the pulsional environment from
which the analytical engines
parasite their resources.

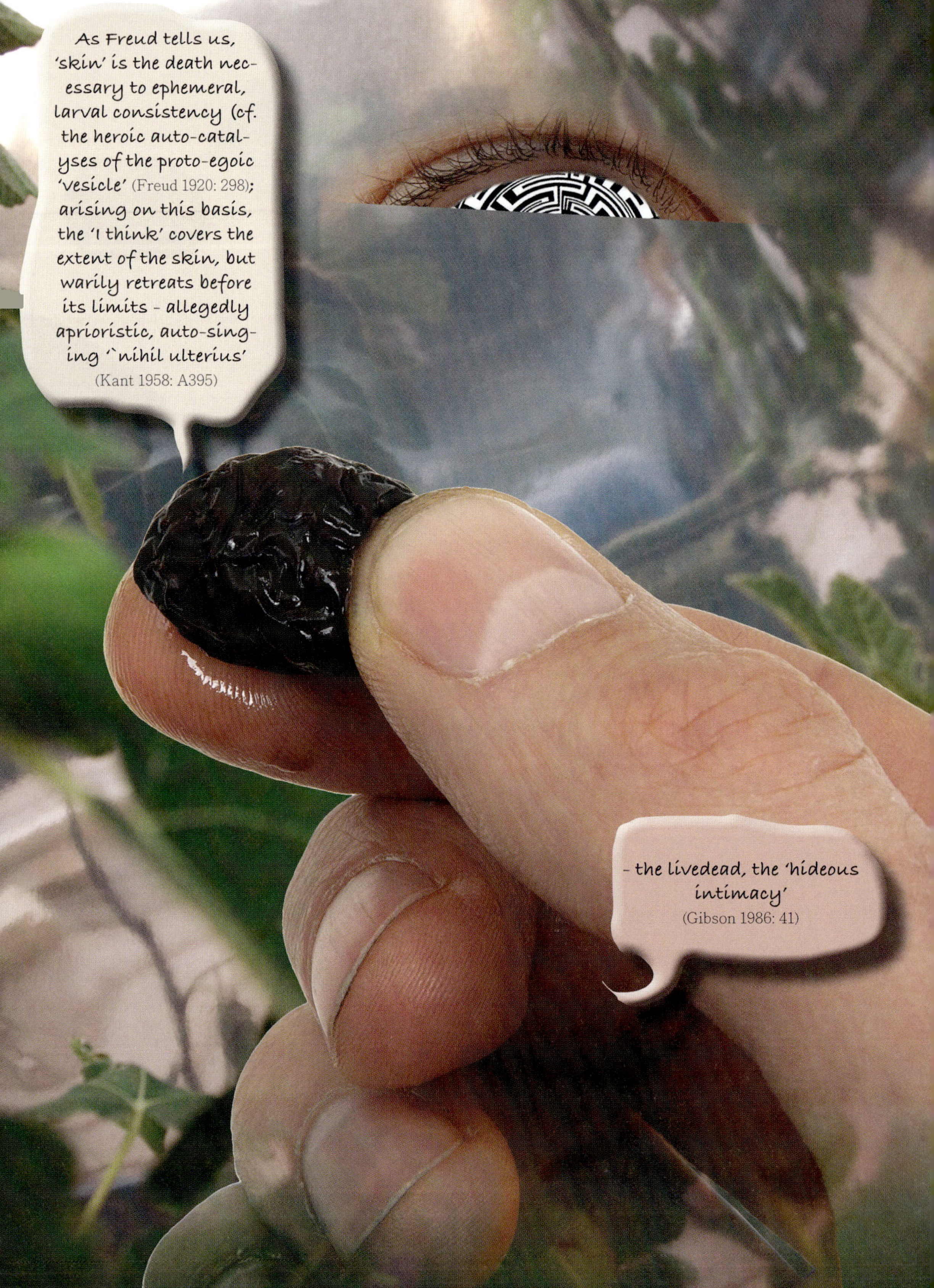
As Freud tells us, 'skin' is the death nec-essary to ephemeral, larval consistency (cf. the heroic auto-catal-yses of the proto-egoic 'vesicle' (Freud 1920: 298); arising on this basis, the 'I think' covers the extent of the skin, but warily retreats before its limits - allegedly aprioristic, auto-sing-ing '`nihil ulterius' (Kant 1958: A395)
- the livedead, the 'hideous intimacy' (Gibson 1986: 41)

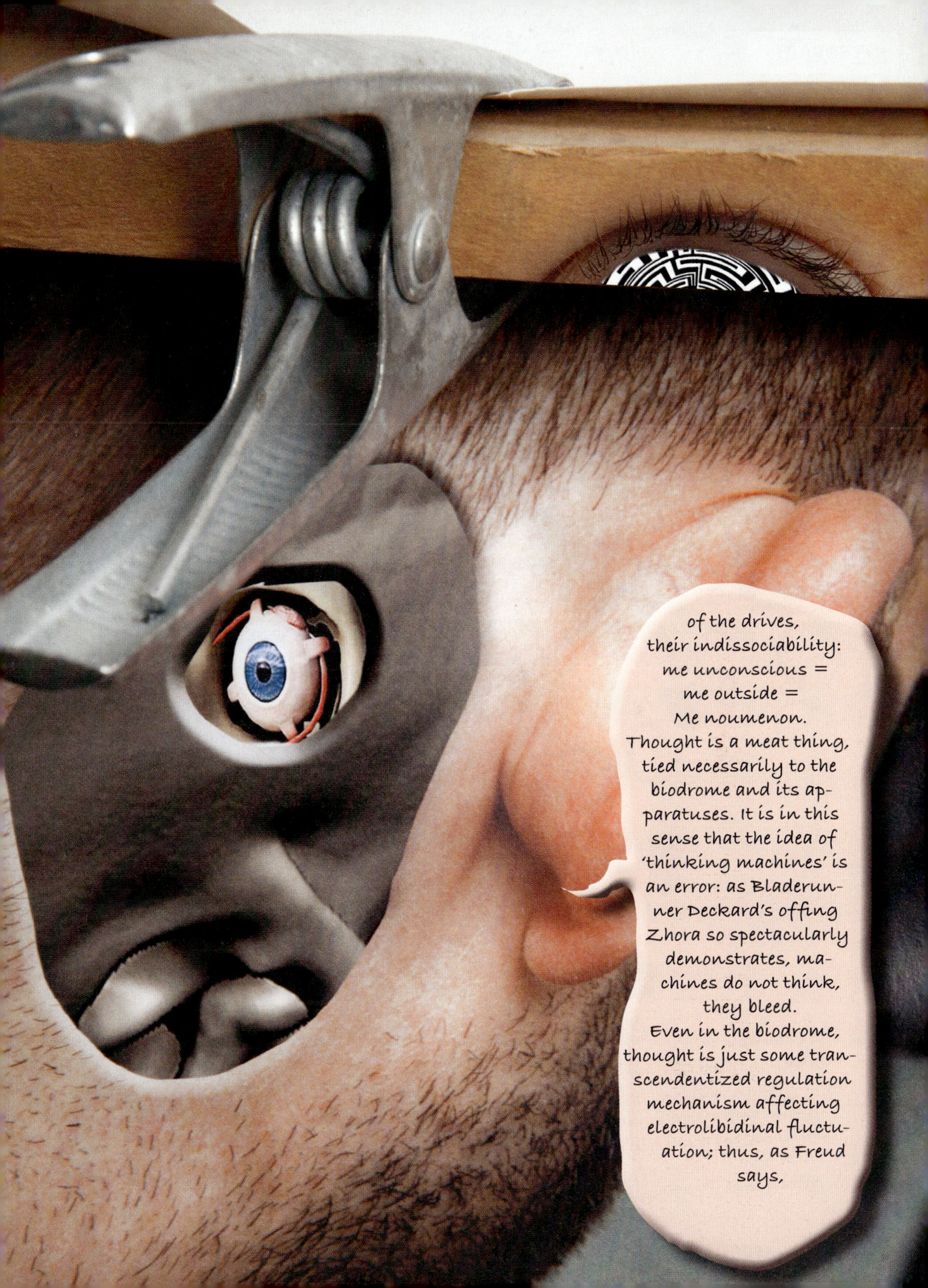
of the drives,
their indissociability:
me unconscious =
me outside =
Me noumenon.
Thought is a meat thing,
tied necessarily to the
biodrome and its ap-
paratuses. It is in this
sense that the idea of
'thinking machines' is
an error: as Bladerun-
ner Deckard's offing
Zhora so spectacularly
demonstrates, ma-
chines do not think,
they bleed.
Even in the biodrome,
thought is just some tran-
scendentized regulation
mechanism affecting
electrolibidinal fluctu-
ation; thus, as Freud
says,

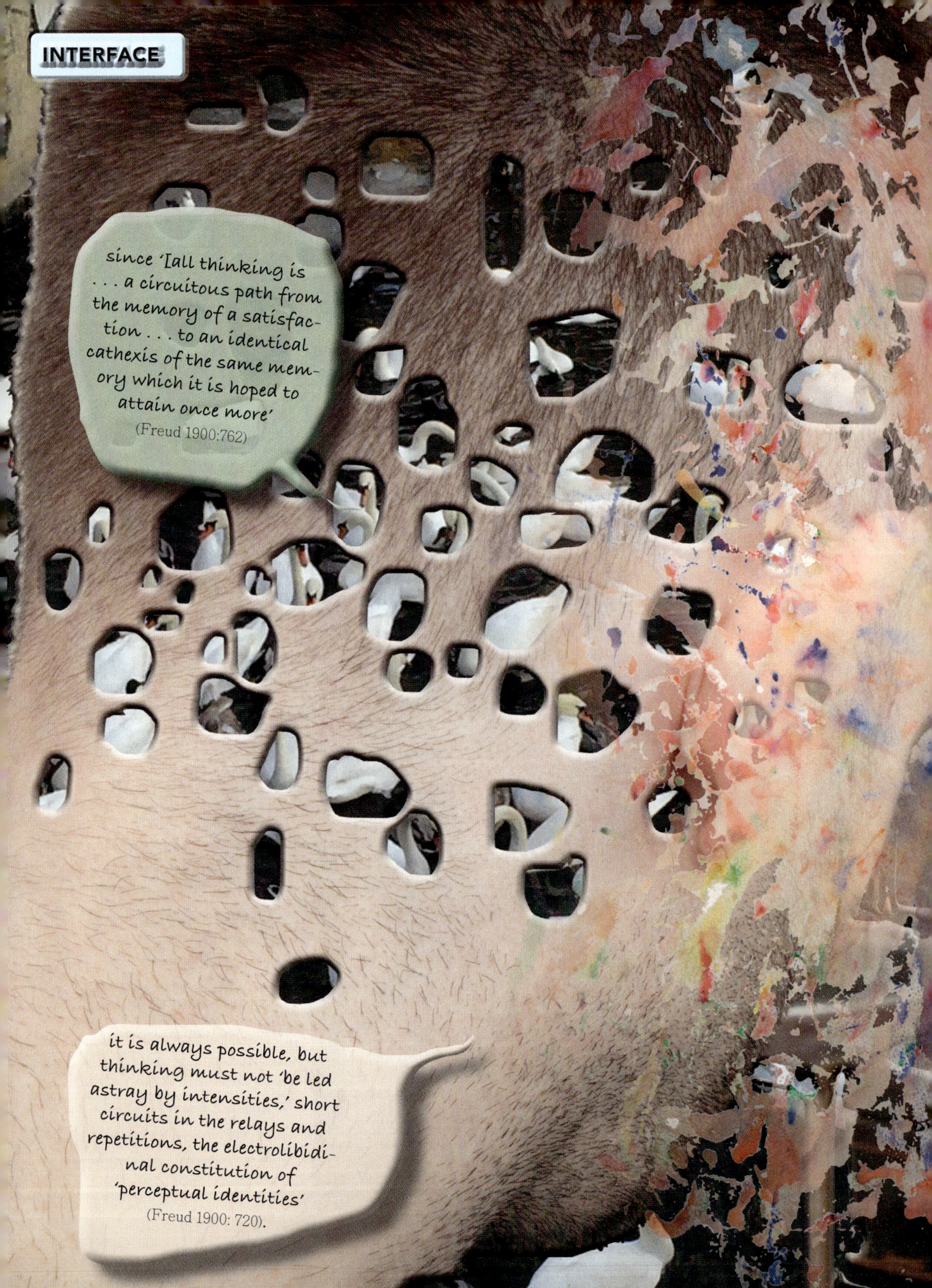
since '[all thinking is . . . a circuitous path from the memory of a satisfaction . . . to an identical cathexis of the same memory which it is hoped to attain once more'
(Freud 1900:762)
it is always possible, but thinking must not 'be led astray by intensities,' short circuits in the relays and repetitions, the electrolibidinal constitution of 'perceptual identities'
(Freud 1900: 720).

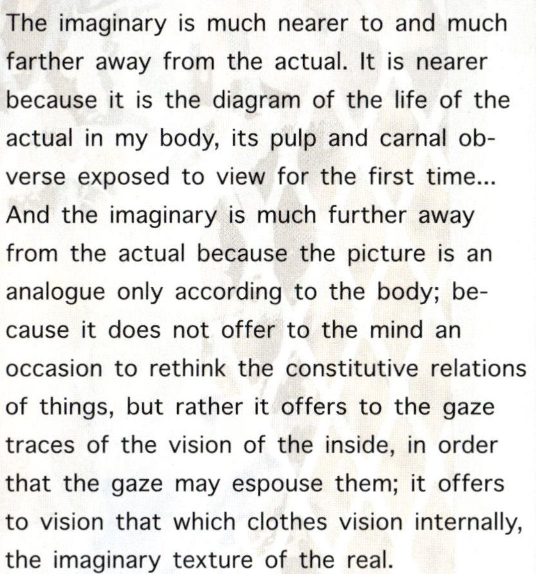
The imaginary is much nearer to and much farther away from the actual. It is nearer because it is the diagram of the life of the actual in my body, its pulp and carnal obverse exposed to view for the first time... And the imaginary is much further away from the actual because the picture is an analogue only according to the body; because it does not offer to the mind an occasion to rethink the constitutive relations of things, but rather it offers to the gaze traces of the vision of the inside, in order that the gaze may espouse them; it offers to vision that which clothes vision internally, the imaginary texture of the real.

The Eye and the Spirit

Excerpt from: Title: L' Œil et l' Esprit, Author: Maurice Merleau-Ponty, First published by Éditions Gallimard, Year: 1964

Cyborganization, like the dreamwork, does not think: datapulsional syntheses impact isotropically on the analytical engines forming the concentric ruins of biodromic defense lines, breaking immanence out of thenets of transcendental determination, shutting down consciousness, a nanometrical, minimal noumenal tilt function - switching the apparatuses hom epicentralized synthesis-regulators into far-from-equilibrium, near-nova pulsional oscillators; Eros' ascent: a synthetic tide of C-change brings the biodrome to boiling point/Thanatos' descent: phenomenal whiteout flooding in from the other side of the screen.

Intensities, intensities:
datableed.
Thought without identity is no thought at all.

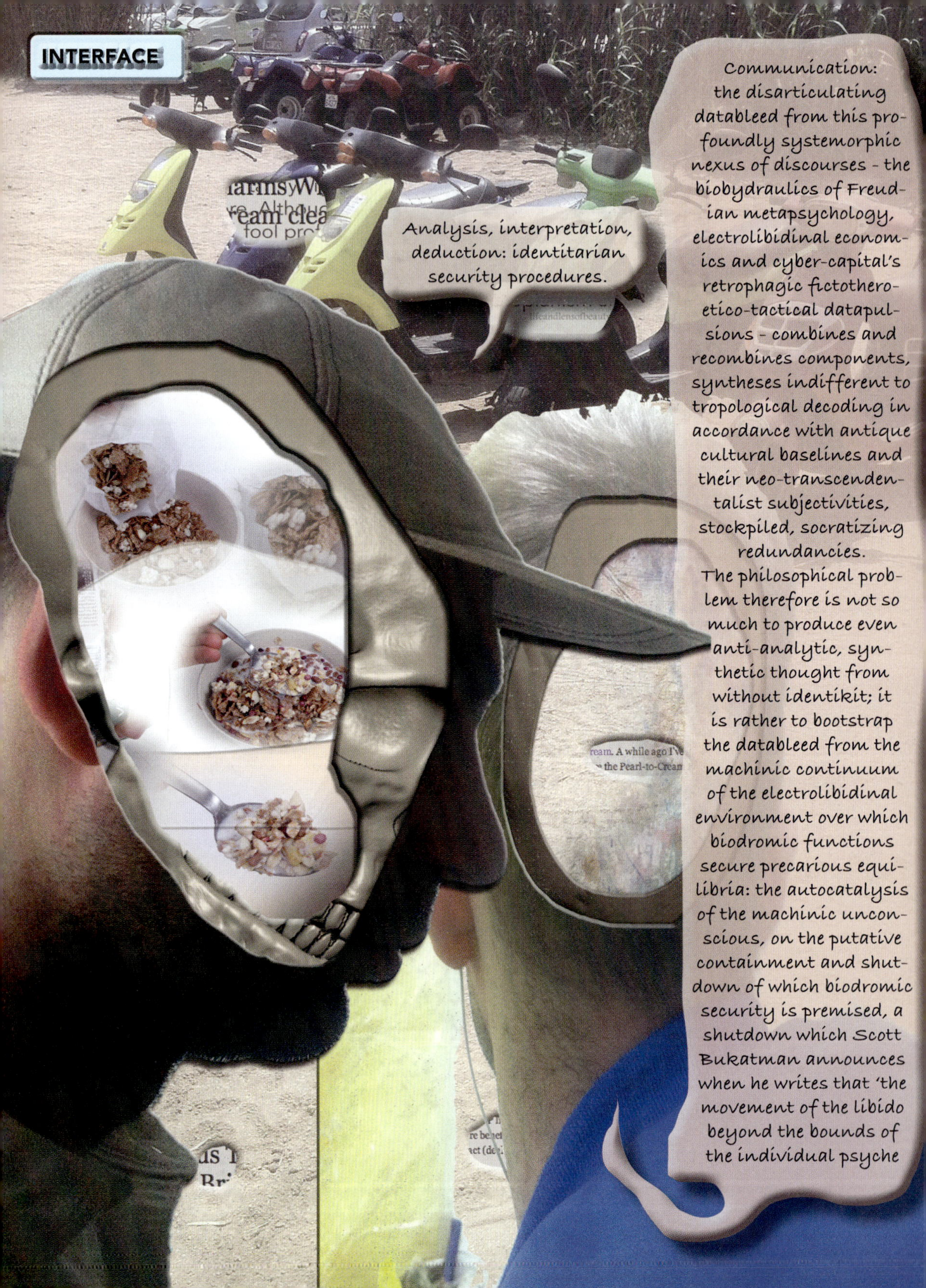

INTERFACE
Analysis, interpretation, deduction: identitarian security procedures.
Communication: the disarticulating datableed from this profoundly systemorphic nexus of discourses – the biobydraulics of Freudian metapsychology, electrolibidinal economics and cyber-capital's retrophagic fictotheroetico-tactical datapulsions – combines and recombines components, syntheses indifferent to tropological decoding in accordance with antique cultural baselines and their neo-transcendentalist subjectivities, stockpiled, socratizing redundancies.
The philosophical problem therefore is not so much to produce even anti-analytic, synthetic thought from without identikit; it is rather to bootstrap the datableed from the machinic continuum of the electrolibidinal environment over which biodromic functions secure precarious equilibria: the autocatalysis of the machinic unconscious, on the putative containment and shutdown of which biodromic security is premised, a shutdown which Scott Bukatman announces when he writes that 'the movement of the libido beyond the bounds of the individual psyche

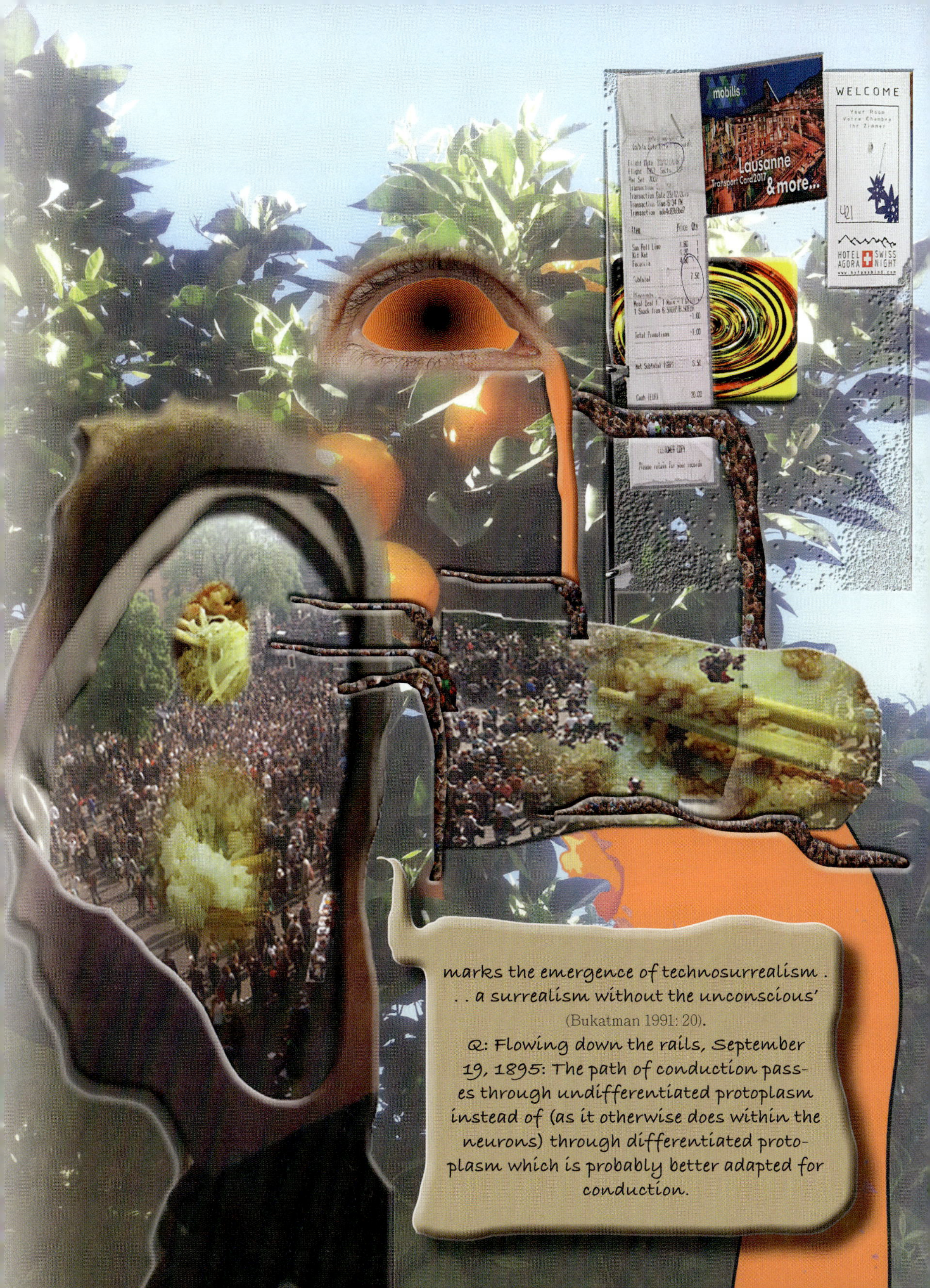

marks the emergence of technosurrealism . . . a surrealism without the unconscious' (Bukatman 1991: 20).

Q: Flowing down the rails, September 19, 1895: The path of conduction passes through undifferentiated protoplasm instead of (as it otherwise does within the neurons) through differentiated protoplasm which is probably better adapted for conduction.

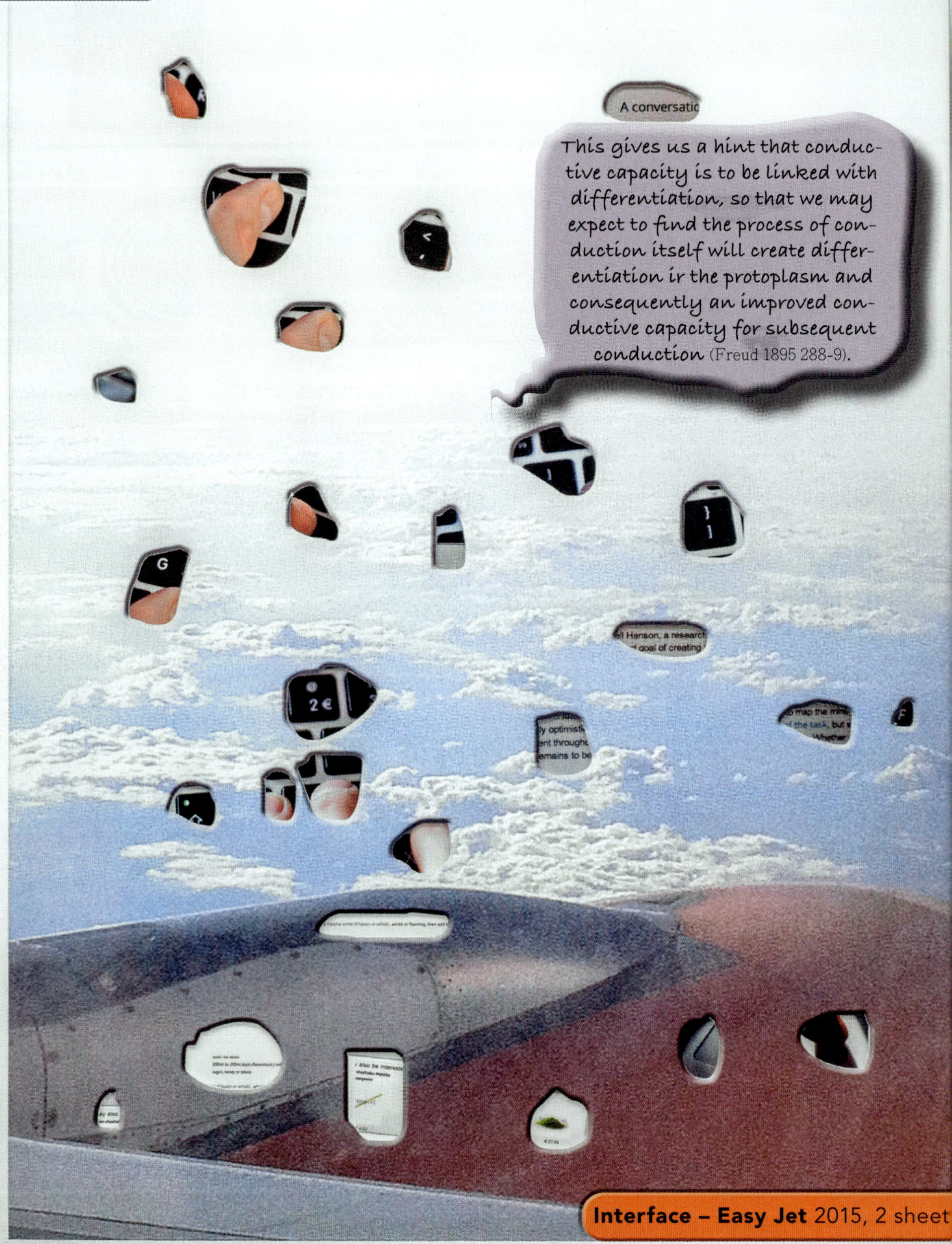

A conversatic

This gives us a hint that conductive capacity is to be linked with differentiation, so that we may expect to find the process of conduction itself will create differentiation ir the protoplasm and consequently an improved conductive capacity for subsequent conduction (Freud 1895 288-9).

ell Hanson, a research
d goal of creating

ly optimisti
ent through
emains to be

o map the mi
f the task, but
Whether

Interface – Easy Jet 2015, 2 sheet

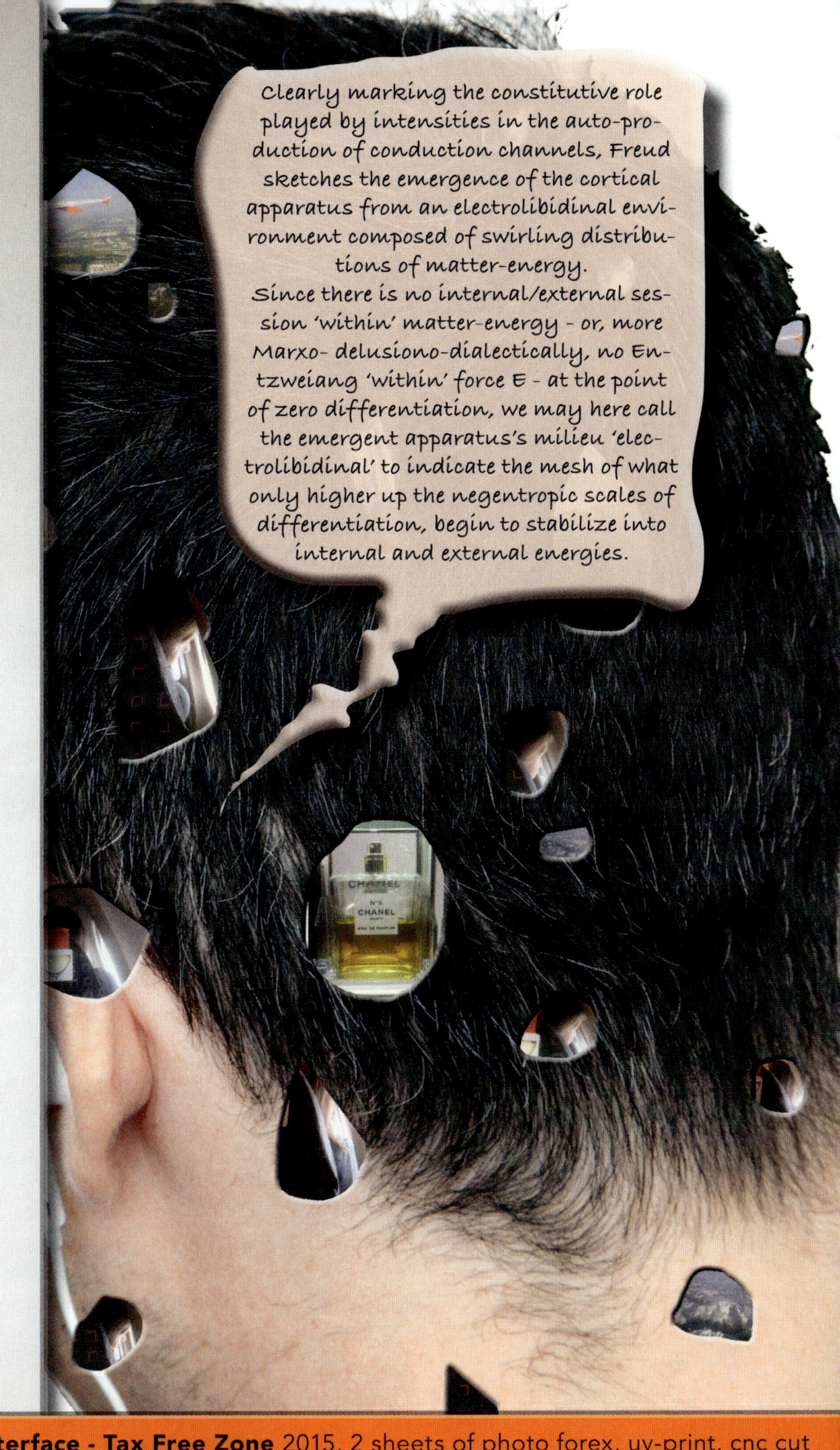

Interface - Tax Free Zone 2015, 2 sheets of photo forex, uv-print, cnc cut

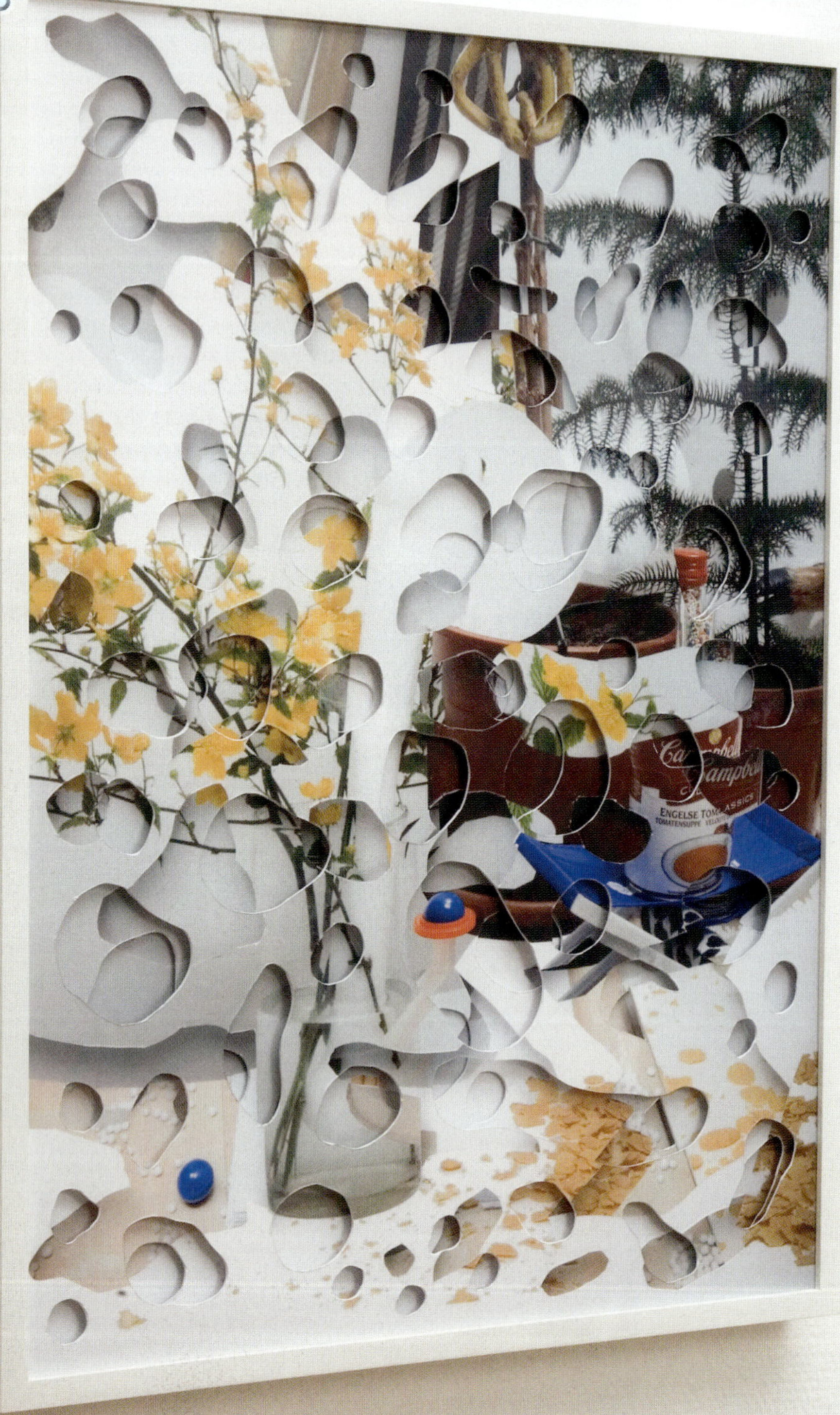

Infinite Value 2009, 3 sheets of photo forex, uv-print, cnc cut

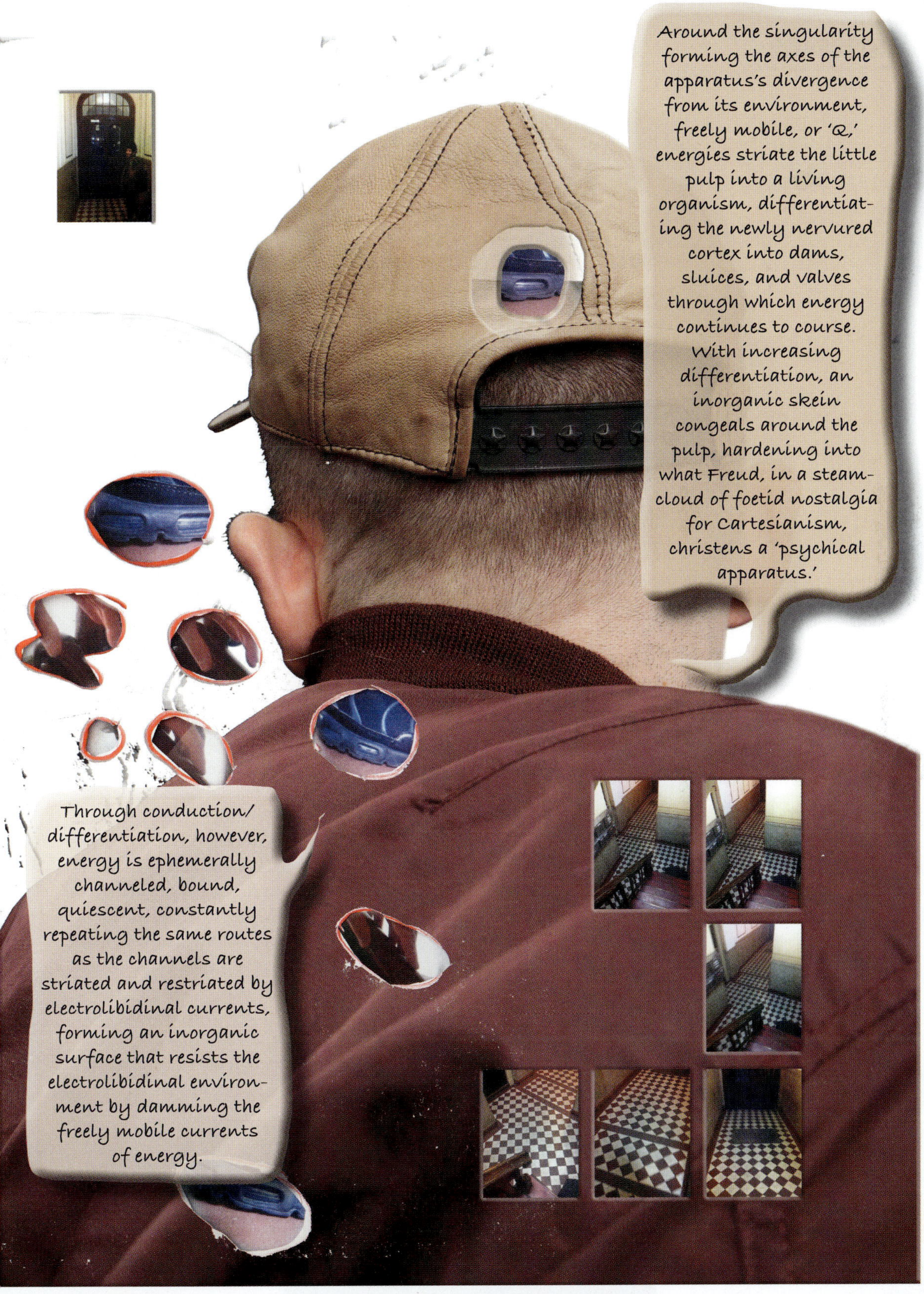
Around the singularity forming the axes of the apparatus's divergence from its environment, freely mobile, or 'Q,' energies striate the little pulp into a living organism, differentiating the newly nervured cortex into dams, sluices, and valves through which energy continues to course. With increasing differentiation, an inorganic skein congeals around the pulp, hardening into what Freud, in a steam-cloud of foetid nostalgia for Cartesianism, christens a 'psychical apparatus.'
Through conduction/differentiation, however, energy is ephemerally channeled, bound, quiescent, constantly repeating the same routes as the channels are striated and restriated by electrolibidinal currents, forming an inorganic surface that resists the electrolibidinal environment by damming the freely mobile currents of energy.

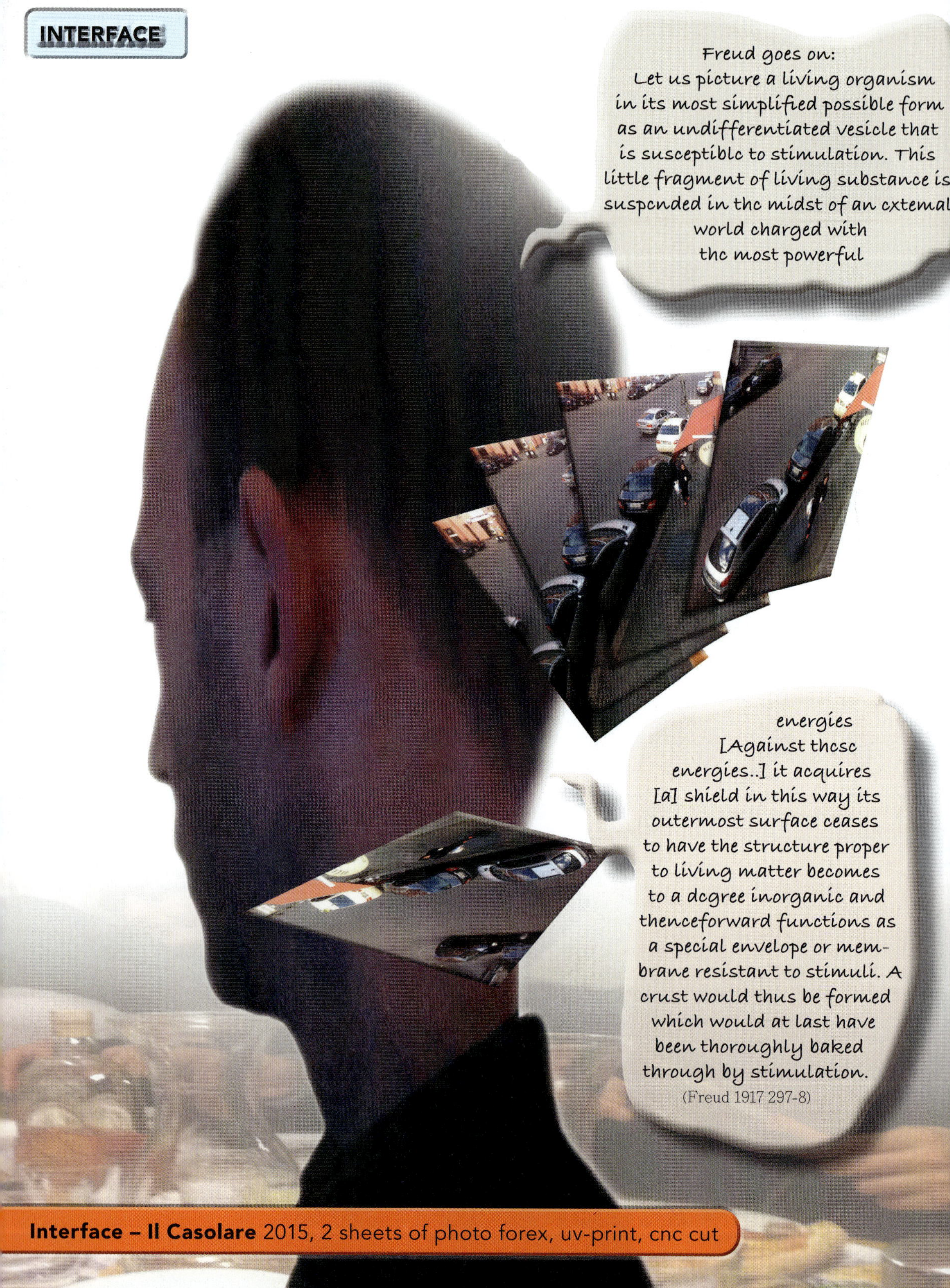

Interface – Il Casolare 2015, 2 sheets of photo forex, uv-print, cnc cut

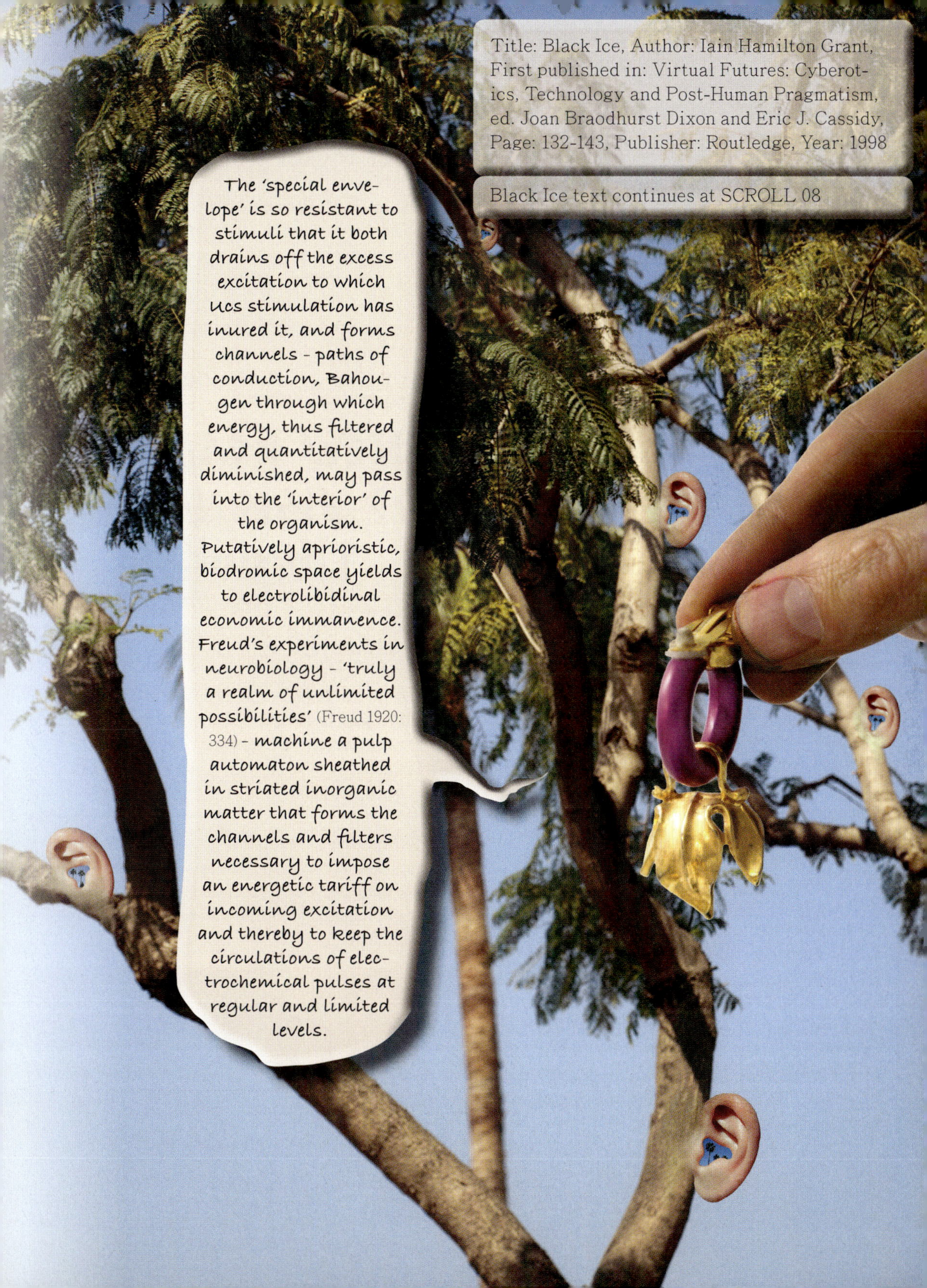
Title: Black Ice, Author: Iain Hamilton Grant, First published in: Virtual Futures: Cyberotics, Technology and Post-Human Pragmatism, ed. Joan Braodhurst Dixon and Eric J. Cassidy, Page: 132-143, Publisher: Routledge, Year: 1998
Black Ice text continues at SCROLL 08
The 'special envelope' is so resistant to stimuli that it both drains off the excess excitation to which Ucs stimulation has inured it, and forms channels - paths of conduction, Bahougen through which energy, thus filtered and quantitatively diminished, may pass into the 'interior' of the organism. Putatively aprioristic, biodromic space yields to electrolibidinal economic immanence. Freud's experiments in neurobiology - 'truly a realm of unlimited possibilities' (Freud 1920: 334) - machine a pulp automaton sheathed in striated inorganic matter that forms the channels and filters necessary to impose an energetic tariff on incoming excitation and thereby to keep the circulations of electrochemical pulses at regular and limited levels.

Perhaps, freed of the implicit desire of the eye for control and power, it is precisely the unfocused vision of our time that is again capable of opening up new realms of vision and thought. The loss of focus brought about by the stream of images may emancipate the eye from its patriarchal domination and give rise to a participatory and empathetic gaze. The technological extensions of the senses have until now reinforced the primacy of vision, but the new technologies may also help ‚the body [...] to dethrone the disinterested gaze of the disincarnated Cartesian spectator'. [67] Martin Jay remarks: ‚In opposition to the lucid, linear, solid, fixed, planimetric, closed form of the Renaissance . . . the baroque was painterly, recessional, soft-focused, multiple, and open.' [68] He also argues that the ‚baroque visual experience has a strongly tactile or haptic quality, which prevents it from turning into the absolute ocularcentrism of its Cartesian perspectivalist rival'. [69]

The haptic experience seems to be penetrating the ocular regime again through the tactile presence of modern visual imagery. In a music video, for instance, or the layered contemporary urban transparency, we cannot halt the flow of images for analytic observation; instead we have to appreciate it as an enhanced haptic sensation, rather like a swimmer senses the flow of water against his/her skin. In his thorough and thought-provoking book The Opening of Vision: Nihilism and the Postmodem Situation, David Michael Levin differentiates between two modes or vision: ‚the assertoric gaze' and ‚the aletheic gaze'. [70] In his view, the assertoric gaze is narrow, dogmatic, intolerant, rigid, fixed, inflexible, exclusionary and unmoved, whereas the aletheic gaze, associated with the hermeneutic theory of truth, tends to see from a multiplicity of standpoints and perspectives, and is multiple, pluralistic, democratic, contextual, inclusionary, horizontal and caring. [71]

As suggested by Levin, there are signs that a new mode of looking is emerging. Although the new technologies have strengthened the hegemony of vision, they may also help to re-balance the realms of the senses.
In Walter Ong's view, ‚with telephone, radio, television and various kinds of sound tape, electronic technology has brought us into the age or "secondary orality". This new orality has striking resemblances to the old in its participatory mystique, its fostering of communal sense, its concentration on the present moment .... - ‚' [72]

NEW REALMS OF VISION AND THOUGHT

[67] Jay, in Foster (I 988), Page 18.
[68] Ibid, Page 16.
[69] Ibid, Page 17.
[70] David Michael Levin, The Opening of Vision -Nihilism and the Postmodern Situation, Routledge (New York and London), 1988, Page 440.
[71] Ibid.
[72] Ong, Page 136.

Title: The Eyes if the skin, Architecture and the Senses, Author: Juhani Pallasmaa, Chapter: A New Vision and Sensory Balance, Page 35
First published by: John Wiley & Sons Ltd, The atrium, Year: 2005

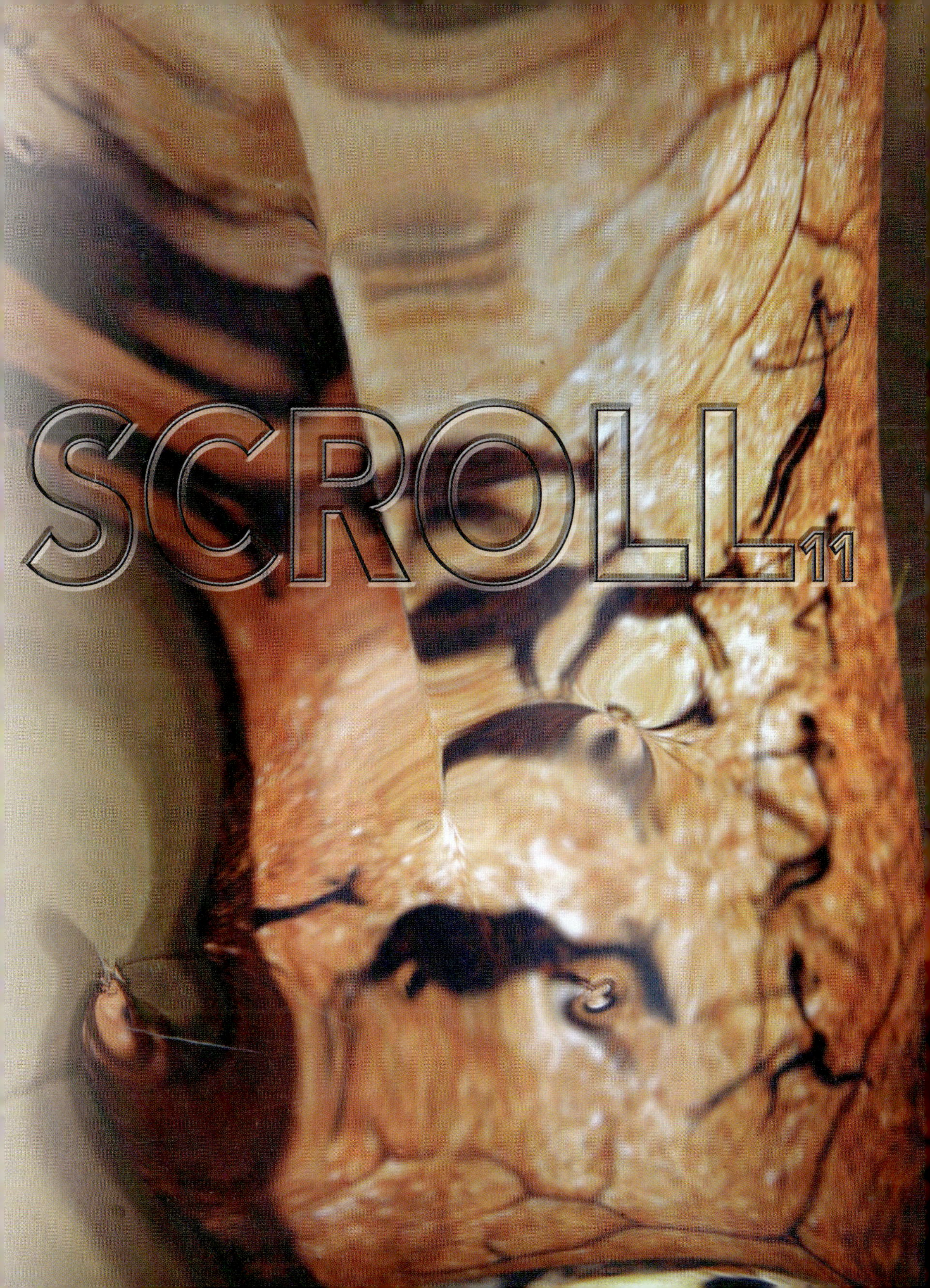
SCROLL 11

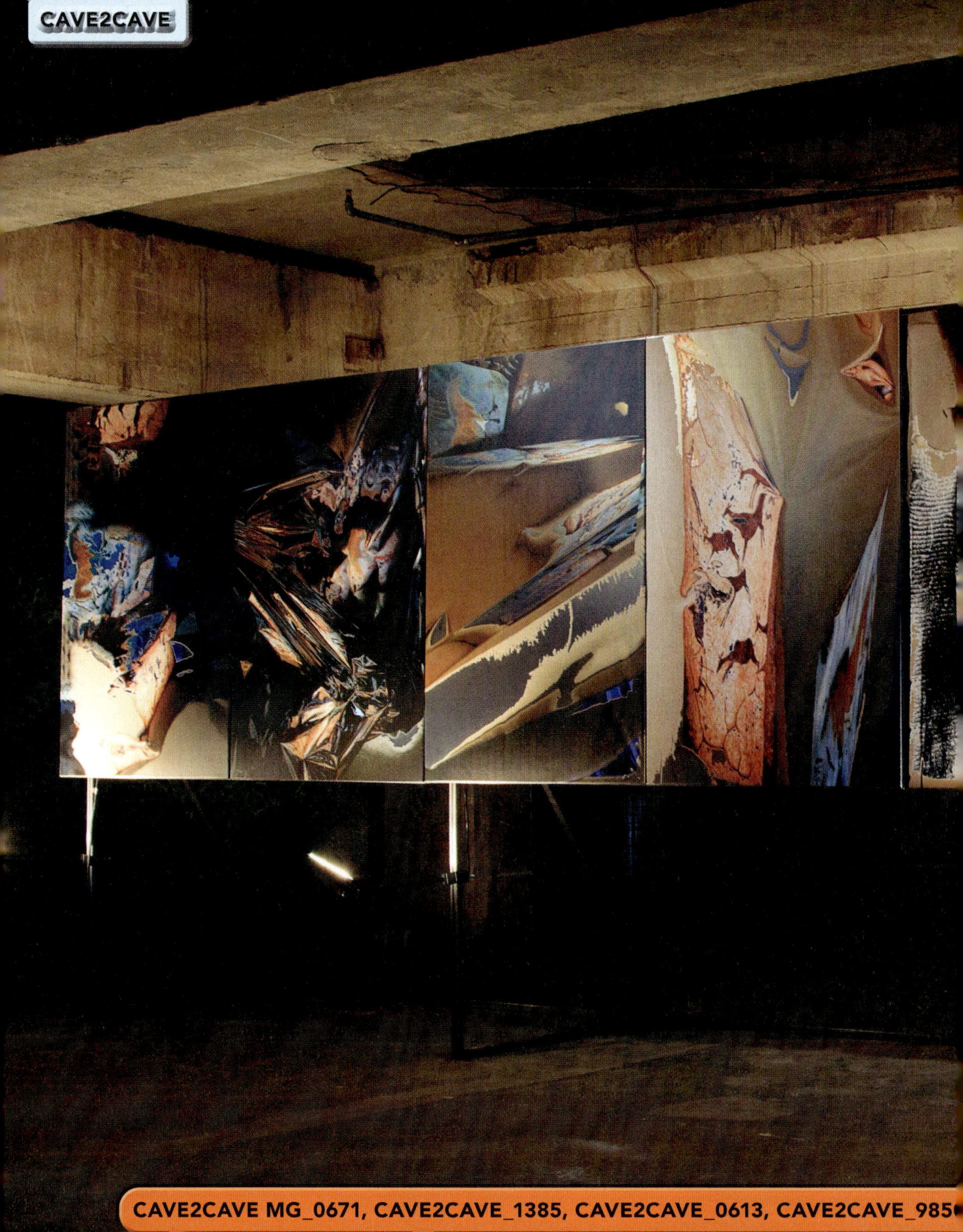

CAVE2CAVE MG_0671, CAVE2CAVE_1385, CAVE2CAVE_0613, CAVE2CAVE_985

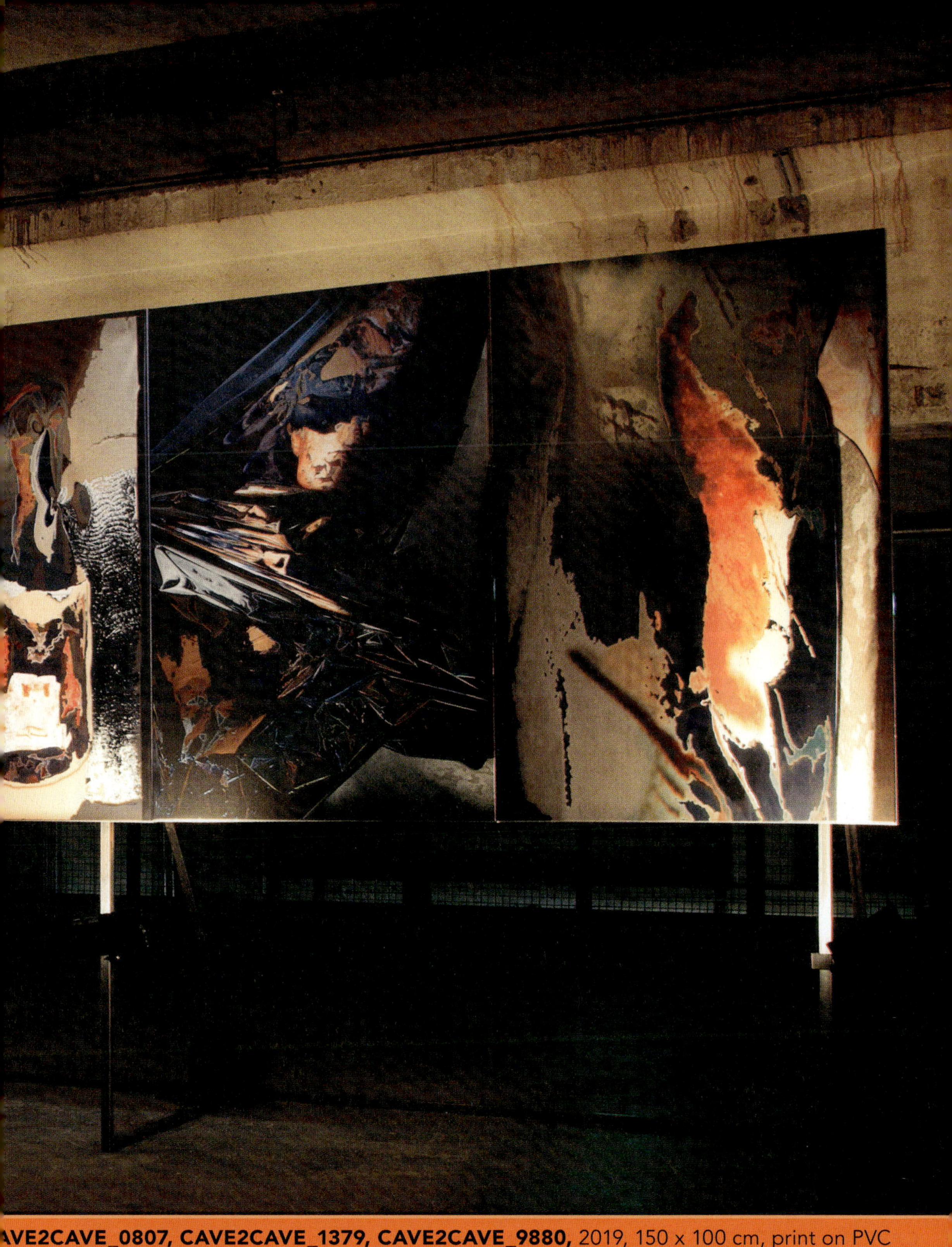

AVE2CAVE_0807, CAVE2CAVE_1379, CAVE2CAVE_9880, 2019, 150 x 100 cm, print on PVC

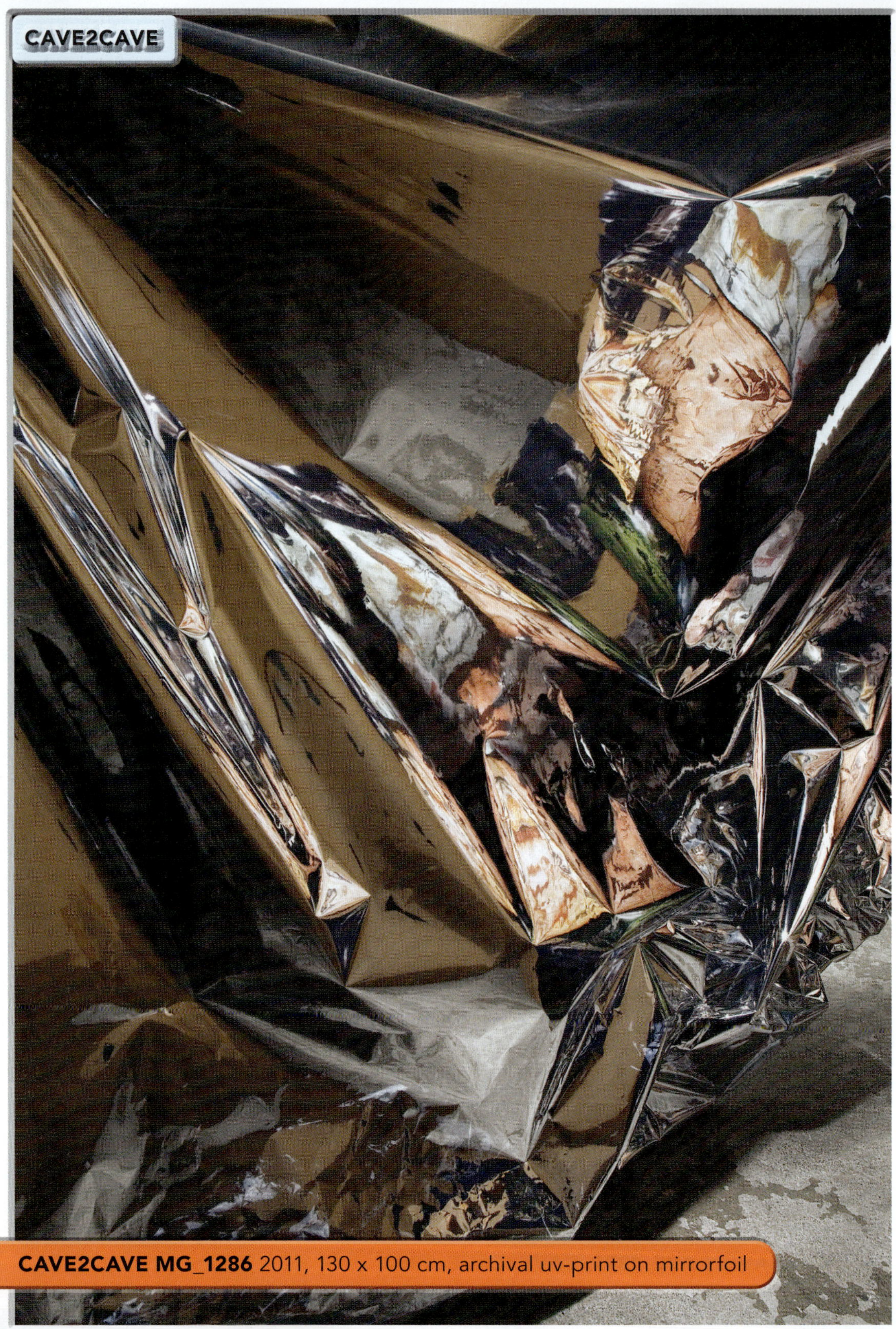

CAVE2CAVE MG_1286 2011, 130 x 100 cm, archival uv-print on mirrorfoil

Rendering: The Cave of the Digital

by Sam Jacob

Inside the mountain, the cave. But right now, we're sheltered under a modern structure fixed over the mouth of the cave like a kind of architectural respiratory mask. Attached to the cliff above, mechanical and organic matter are fixed together with what looks like the kind of giant bolts used to attach the head of Frankenstein's monster to his neck.

We're hanging around waiting for the guide to arrive. To kill the time, my daughter uses her phone to translate the infographic signs explaining the history of the cave. The picture on her screen maps a real-time translation of the Spanish captions. Same font, same color; a live feed of the thing that's right in front of us overlaid onto that very same thing. Its image is produced by a cocktail of image recognition, remote AI, wireless communication, and portable electronics. Through Google's machine vision, the sign seems to be on the brink of glitching out, oscillating between physical and virtual states with a nervous energy.

We're waiting to enter El Castillo, a cave system that contains the earliest human artwork yet discovered: cave paintings recently dated at 40,000 years old. In other words, we are going back in time. This time for real. Yesterday, we saw a replica of the Altamira cave, reconstructed at 1:1 in fiberglass, which despite its accuracy, seemed to collapse all of human history into one rock-effect space. The net-cave's long, low opening was glazed with a frameless windscreen window like a paleo-John Lautner house. The inside was dotted with with scenographic archeology setups and a Pepper's ghost of Neanderthals cooking over a stove, whose blue hued flickering recalled the sci-fi of Princess Leia's hologram more than pre-history.

But this time, it's the real deal: an actual site. Our small group is briefed on a landing outside a steel door before our guide walks us down through the cave system until we find ourselves crouched in an alcove. He traces the beam of a torch over the rock surface, pointing out the markings and scratches. Here, the back of a bison. There, the face of a horse. Black charcoal in arcs forming graded shadow. Red iron oxide-like rouge on the rock's cheek. Marks that play across the surface of geology as if coaxing recognizable apparitions from the rock-form.
He describes how the scenes depicted in front of us were layered over generations; a drawing that emerged over millennia.

He shows us dots and lines, like a kind of Morse code trailing across the cave surface. But without the cipher, these graphic signals beamed across time have become noise. Then, arrestingly, the silhouette of a hand on the wall, dusted oxide red. Shockingly fresh, as if it were planted there today; so close we might almost touch. It reaches across the millennia toward us. Held up as if it is greeting us. The open palm is as close as we get to seeing the identity of our ancestors, yet as the outline of the oxide shadow blurs into rock, the of body that placed the mark recedes into the invisible and unknowable fog of history.

Throughout this cave, and across the paleo-world of what is now southern Europe, are cave paintings of bodies and figures, people and animals. Not portraits, but points, like the freeze-frame screens that football pundits use on pay TV. Except these drawings are made over millennia, describing some other kind of relationship to time and space. These cave art scenes are pictures of space, of gaps between, of the tension between figures.
The surfaces of the cave narrate stories like celestial constellations. Images are etched, smeared, blown, and drawn onto this undulating, ragged, curved surface so that topography blurs into figures—the surface of a sleeping bison, the neck of a horse conjured by shading applied to a fissure or a bump.

Caves invert the space of the world above ground. In these underground interiors, space is bounded by the earth itself. Yet through the drawings in these concave enclosures, they are rendered into worlds. Representation transforms them into an essential act of architecture—spaces that organize meaning and form. One might even say that these drawings act as the first form of architecture—that the natural cave becomes architecture not through shelter but representation. These were not places to live, after all, but served some other purpose.

What if there never was a primitive hut? Perhaps the origin of architecture lies within these representational fields of iron oxide dust, charcoal, pigments, and scraped lines.

Caves are spaces of representation without edges; where the world and the space of the page are the same thing. Drawings whose subject, but also medium, is space. Representation that is applied to the world itself; representation that becomes the world. Inside the cave, we occupy the drawing just as the drawing occupies and manufactures space. We are not outside observers of an image, but active participants within the space of representation.

Looking closely, there are other specific representational tropes. There are no faces on any of the figures. No sky either; no trees, no rivers, no landscape, no horizon. They are pictures of the world, but a world that is different to ours; a world whose outlines remain daubed on cave walls but whose meaning we can't comprehend. Maps whose coordinates have been lost, whose legend no longer makes sense, whose orientations and coordinates obey different rules. Representations whose scale and depth no longer register as they did with their authors.

We might assume space to be a universal condition. But, as our inability to understand the space of the cave drawings demonstrates, the qualities and meanings of space have changed over time. Rather than a universal constant, space has had a fluidity whose significance at different moments and in different cultures has taken on different meanings. The way space changes can be physically experienced in the chronologically arranged hang at Tate Britain. Standing in "1540," "1730" can be seen through the enfilade galleries. As galleries recede, the nature of representational space changes.

The 1563 Portrait of Elizabeth I, attributed to Steven van der Meulen and Steven van Herwijck, represents her figure as a two-dimensional cut out placed over a flat background, whose gold surface recalls Byzantine pictorial space. Similarly, the unattributed, identical Chalmodeley Ladies from 1600–1610, represented in bed with their identical doll-like babies, are stiffly framed in an orthogonal space that could be either plan or elevation.

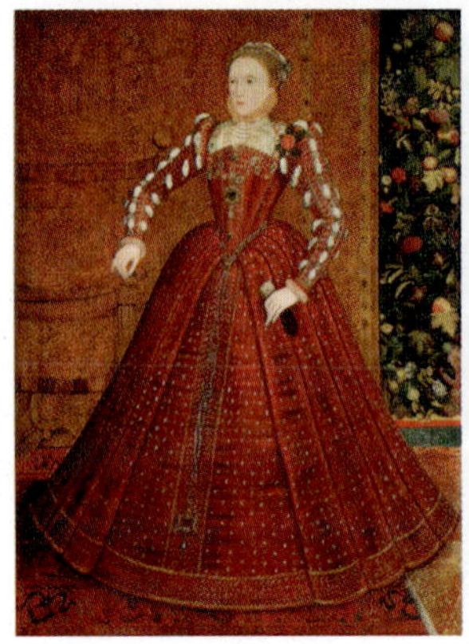

Steven van der Meulen and Steven van Herwijck, Portrait of Elizabeth I (The Hampden Portrait), 1563. Photo: Wikimedia Commons.

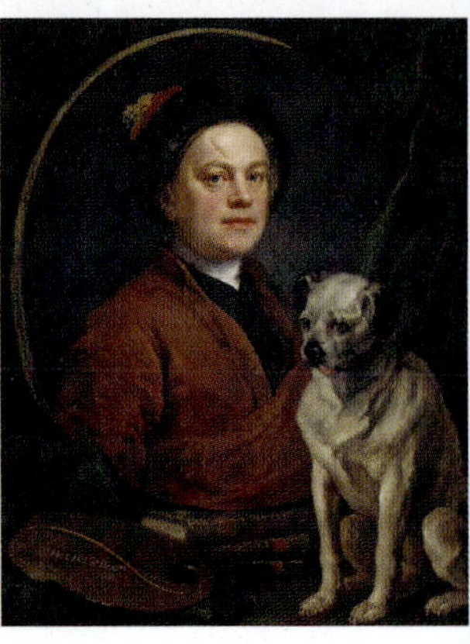

William Hogarth, The Painter and His Pug, 1745. Photo: Wikimedia Commons.

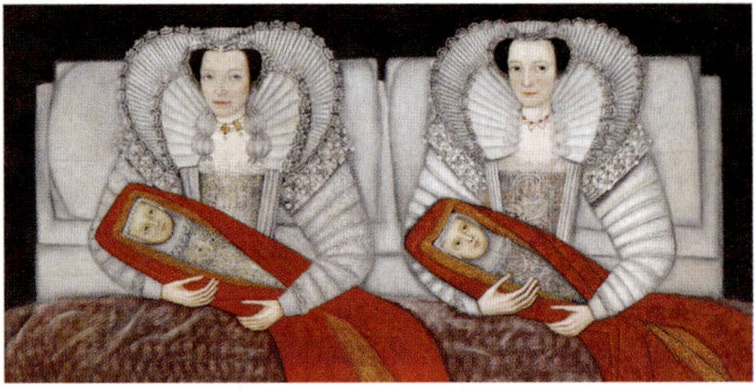

Anonymous (British School, 17th century), The Cholmondeley Ladies, c. 1600–10. Photo: Wikimedia Commons.

At the other end, in The Painter and his Pug by William Hogarth from 1745, three-dimensional space is represented in the form of a round canvas—a painting within a painting—that is propped up by a pile of books and is draped with a cloth so that it falls both behind and in front. A dog sits in foreground. As a painting, it is as much about the media of representation as it is a portrait; a painting of a painting that relies on the ability to discern the difference between flatness and depth. It expects the viewer to recognize both the "realism" of the space within the painting and the fact that it is created through the act of two-dimensional representation.

Space is not a natural phenomenon, but something constructed. Medieval European space, for example, is fundamentally different from Neolithic space. Perspectival space is fundamentally different from Byzantine space. Space is a product of social, economic, and environmental conditions. It provides a specific framework for encounter, relationship, and the production of specific kinds of meaning. Representation is not just a way of

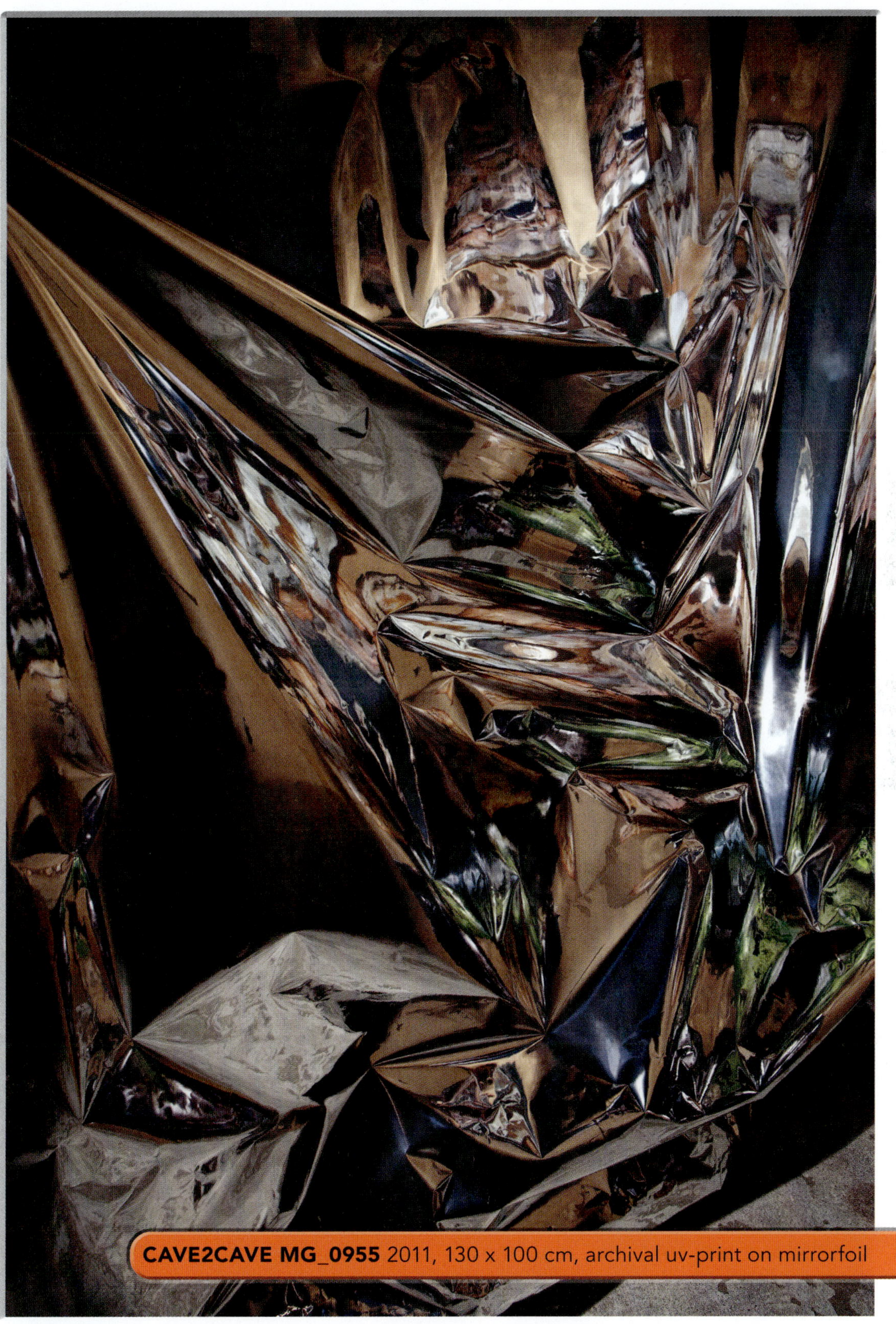

CAVE2CAVE MG_0955 2011, 130 x 100 cm, archival uv-print on mirrorfoil

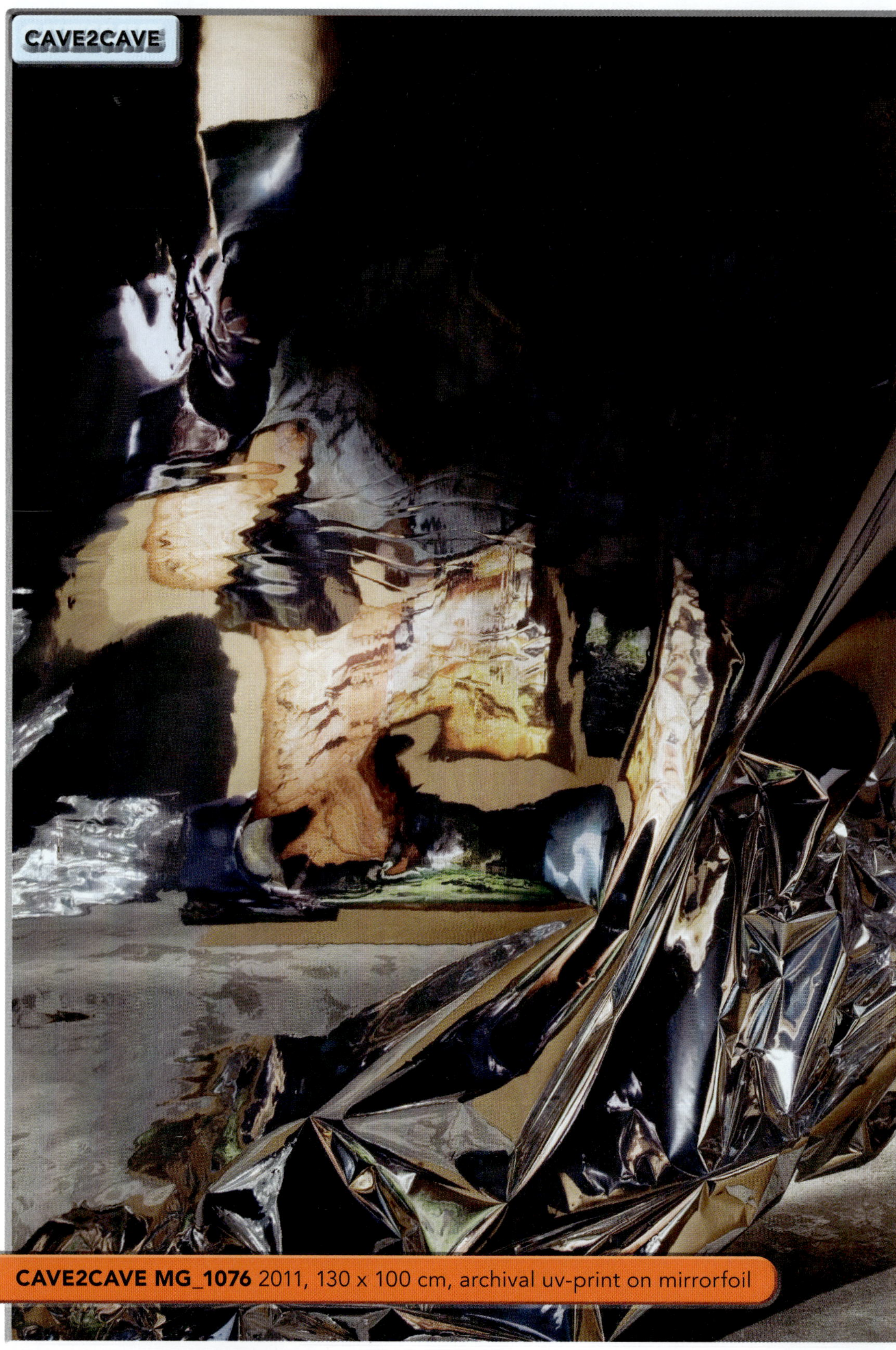

CAVE2CAVE MG_1076 2011, 130 x 100 cm, archival uv-print on mirrorfoil

recording or depicting space, but the way of constructing it. Spatial representation is not merely pictorial or graphic, but also conceptual.

If some of these forms of space seem more anachronistic, or relatively illegible, perspective still exerts a strong hold over the way space is perceived and understood today. Its principles still coincide with the way space is imagined and conceived. Its conceptual logic creates the way space is imagined, seen, and constructed.

Erwin Panofsky argues that the invention of linear perspective could only occur at the moment when a particular conception of space—the concept of infinity—emerged. He suggests that this idea of the infinite emerged because of a new religious conception of a singular, divine omnipresence. Without this idea of the universe, it would be impossible to conceive of the vanishing point.

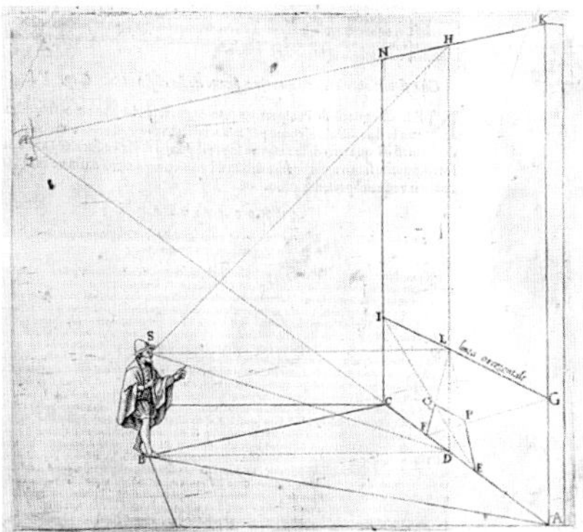

Perspective diagram from Ignazio Danti Vignola, Le due regole della prospettiva pratica, 1583.

To this we might add that the drawing system of perspective, relying as it does on accurate measurement to construct its space, emerged within the highly mercantile contexts of Florence and Venice; places where the measurement of goods was fundamental to the accumulation of wealth.

In other words, perspective brought spiritual divinity and earthy pragmatism together into the same representational space. It presented what appeared to be a "workable" model of the world; drawings whose spatial principles seemed to coincide very closely with ours. Indeed, that's exactly what happened when Brunelleschi "proved" the accuracy of linear perspective with his experiment at the Florentine Baptistery. By demonstrating that the space of the real and representation matched, perspective's claim on the real was cemented.

Within the many books written since the Renaissance that teach perspective drawing lies a strange kind of space that, step by step, shows the inherent constructional project embedded in the system; that a way of constructing a drawing is also the way to construct the world. Start by drawing a straight horizontal line across a blank sheet of paper. Suddenly, the page has been transformed into an empty graphic desert, divided by the horizon into land and sky. By placing a dot on this line to mark the vanishing point, the space of the page becomes taut and defined. From this dot, lines emanates like black rays; bursts of graphic energy throwing a net over the pictorial space, defining its territory.

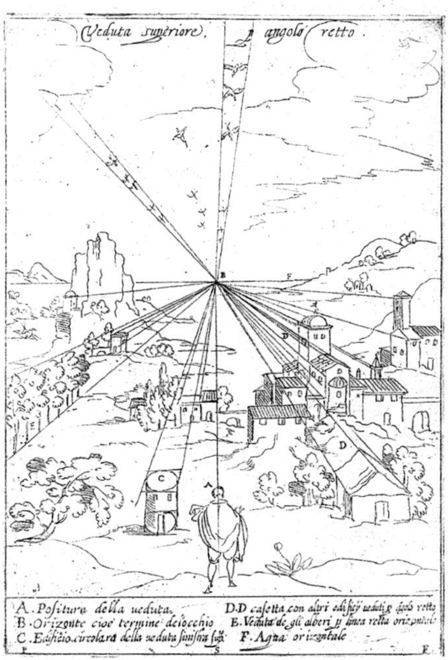

Perspective view of a town before a bay in outline, after Agostino Carracci.

The vanishing point is an infinitely dense graphic point that acts as origin point of the world, or the end of the world. A dot that contains an outline of everything that could ever be depicted.

Lessons proceed by showing how to dress up this abstract, alien world; to fill it in, to decorate and occupy it so that it begins to resemble the world beyond the space of page. Geometric forms become recognizable as fragments of architecture; gridded planes become floors and walls. These worlds appear in state of construction, of coming into being as if each drawing is playing out its own creation myth. They suggest that the real world also emerges from the vanishing point, from the idealism of geometry and, at least originally, divinity.

The Renaissance obsession with both the divine and geometric that perspective gave form to is exemplified by De Divina Proportione, a book first printed in 1509 by Luca Pacioli with illustrations by Leonardo da Vinci. Within it, Pacioli describes the divine qualities of geometric form. He shows how these qualities cascade from pure geometry (and God) to the earthly world in the form of architecture, faces, and letterforms. God is, in this way of explaining the world, in the measurements.

That Pacioli, a Franciscan friar as well as mathematician, is also credited with the invention of double entry bookkeeping should come as no surprise. "Double entry" is a system of recording transactions in terms of credit and debit; a debit in one account will be offset by a credit in another, so the sum of all debits must be equal to the sum of all credits. Double entry remains the basis of contemporary accounting. It is the space that appears when spreadsheets are opened, just as perspective is the space that appears when Sketchup is fired up and pictorial space for constructed the lonely figure in an empty world.

Both perspective drawing and double entry bookkeeping are systems that seem to help accurately record the world as it is. But at heart, the power that both have is to remake the world according to their own vision. William M. Irvins Jr. suggests just how fundamentally perspective shaped the modern world in On the Rationalization of Sight: "Many reasons are assigned for the mechanization of life and industry during the nineteenth century, but the mathematical development of perspective was absolutely prerequisite."

The power of perspective is not only its internal representational mechanism, but how it projects its ideal geometry outwards into the world. Not as a form of recording the world, but of constructing it. Unlike the representational space of the cave, which internalizes the world, perspective is mapped outwards from its vanishing point, beyond the frame of the page and into the world.

One can further argue, along with Hito Steyerl, that concepts which emerge from perspectival space shape geopolitical space:

The use of the horizon to calculate position gave seafarers a sense of orientation, thus also enabling colonialism and the spread of a capitalist global market, but also became an important tool for the construction of the optical paradigms that came to define modernity, the most important paradigm being that of so-called linear perspective.

Fine art has had its own longstanding arguments with perspectival representation. Since Cubism shattered the illusion of the singular point of view, perspective has cut itself loose in multiple ways from the tyranny of the vanishing point. But architecture is still intrinsically tied to the perspectival project, and perspective retains a special place in the architect's representational arsenal.

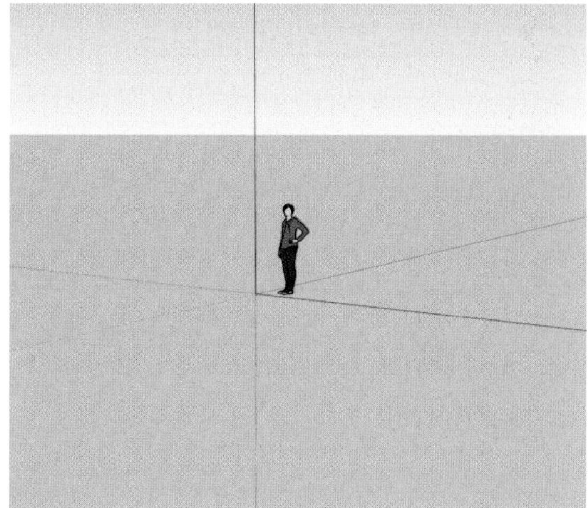

Default display of 3D modeling software SketchUp.

Architectural drawings operate with a particular kind of agency. They are instructions use to construct the world. They are read as illustrative descriptions of a proposition, as if the act of representation was entirely neutral and completely natural. Views—be it in the form of a sketch or hyperreal photographic render—are used as if the systems used to construct them are somehow transparent; as if nothing has changed since Alberti's description of perspective:

First of all, on the surface on which I am going to paint, I draw a rectangle of whatever size I want, which I regard as an open window through which the subject to be painted is to be seen.

That's to say, when looking at—or making—a per-

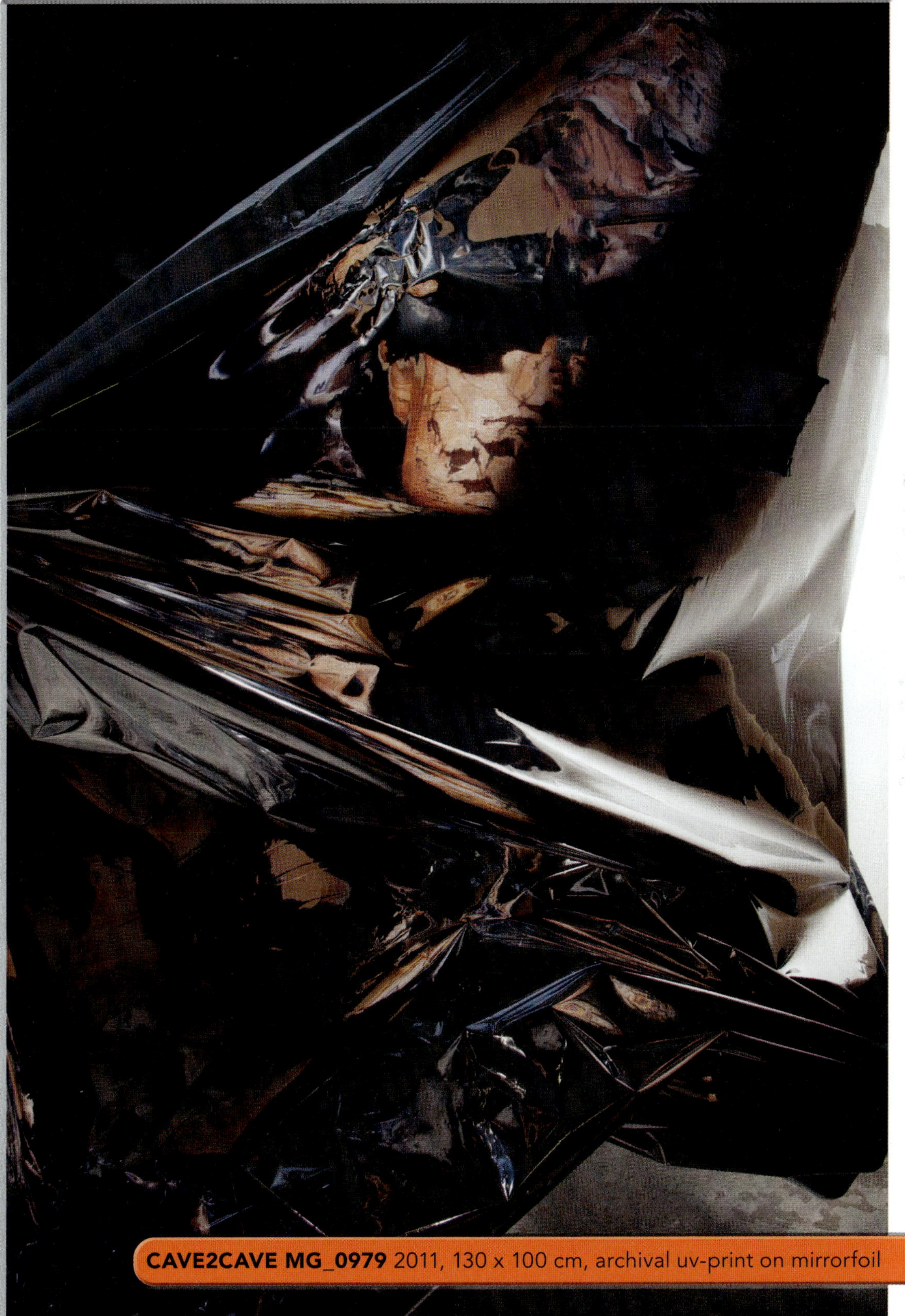

CAVE2CAVE MG_0979 2011, 130 x 100 cm, archival uv-print on mirrorfoil

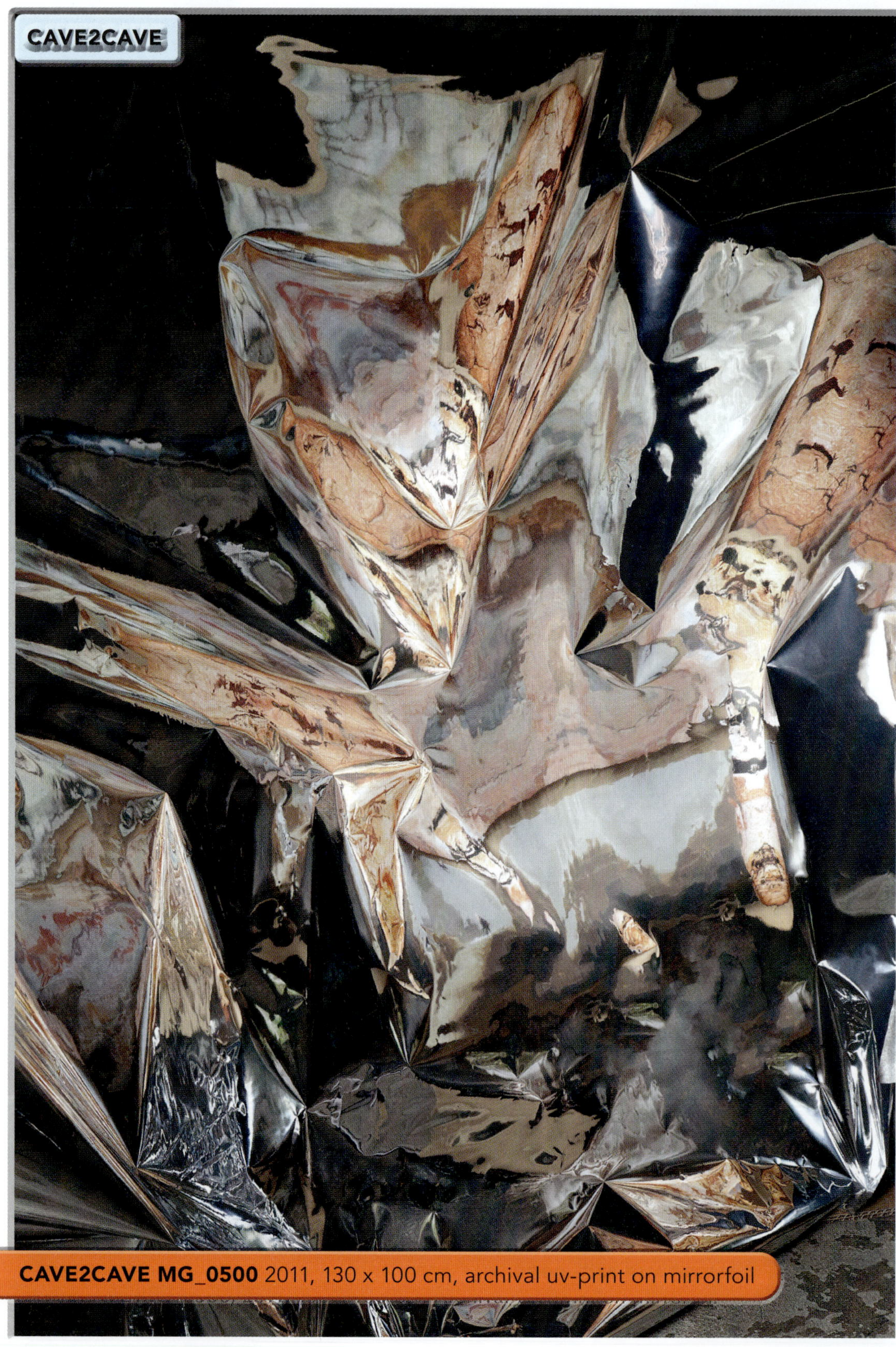

CAVE2CAVE MG_0500 2011, 130 x 100 cm, archival uv-print on mirrorfoil

spectival drawing, the medium itself is expected to be entirely transparent, just as the world through that window is real. To accept these "truths" means forgetting the prejudices, complexities, and ideologies of representation itself.

Just as language constrains what it is possible to say—or perhaps even think—the conventions and genres of representation used to create architecture also set out the terms of its engagement with the world. They may appear to represent space as a simple, "natural" thing, but the possibilities of the space they depict are already contained within them before pen is put to paper, or cursor to page. Their apparent plausibility lulls us into their service; their convenient conventions and techniques constrain the possibilities of imagination.

Most contemporary architectural drawings happen digitally. Drafting software is set up with the conventions of architectural representation embedded into its code. Applications designed especially for architectural design have dropdown menus that allowing one to flip between orthogonal, perspective, and isometric views effortlessly. No longer does effort have to be expended to construct drawings. Their "spaces" are preset. Anything can be drawn, but only on the terms that the application sets out.

For all of this apparent liberty, it is these applications, not architects, that now construct space. In other words, they have turned something that had to be actively constructed into a given, inert, unavoidable state. The automation of representational space excludes the most fundamental of architectural questions: What is space?

Attempts to deploy alternative, even Cubist types of architectural space, from Deconstruction to Parametracism, have only served to reinforce traditional representational modes, insofar as their highly complex forms have required the development of hyper accurate software that replicate the spatial constructs of traditional architectural representation. In other words, advanced 3D modeling software have only served to reinforce preexisting forms of representation. Furthermore, they have cast architectural representation as an entirely separate activity from designing the architectural object itself, while at the same time mirroring it as closely as possible. Just as a fiberglass replica of a cave acts as a wholly accurate 1:1 reconstruction, yet whose exactitude is the thing that makes it entirely different from its source, representation becomes a way of simulating, yet banishing the real. In representational terms: the closer we get, the further away we are.

Yet digital technologies more widely have served to construct space in fundamentally different ways. And if perspectival vision emerged in the context of the Renaissance, in line with the way that power conceived the structure of the world, these contemporary forms of vision are just as entwined with power.

To serve as an example, Hunted, a British TV show hybrid between reality and documentary, relies on this new kind of vision. Its premise is simple: teams of two people must evade detection for a number of days and make it to a rendezvous site without being located by a team of agents based in a mock-up operations room. The ops room is flooded with feeds: CCTV, ANPR, ATM transactions, internet traffic, mobile phone use, and cell tower locations. The point of view of the viewer switches between the two; between, one might say, the map and the territory. What it reveals is self-evident: that the way the state "sees" is an overlapping patchwork of multiple points of view; of image, text, from above, in motion, in high and low resolution, at varied scales, in different projections, simultaneous, and in real time.

The world as seen through the lenses of Hunted is a world with no possibility of disappearance. Is this a world where the possibility of a vanishing point itself has vanished? And without a vanishing point, is perspective even possible?

In contemporary theaters of war, vision is rendered through a kind of a networked field; a military internet of things that connects people, objects, and their flows through space in a three-dimensional matrix of technology. BAE Systems, for instance, advertise their Airborne Wide Area Persistent Surveillance System (AWAPSS) as:

an unblinking eye in the sky commanding a persistent watch over troubled areas to provide decision makers with useful and focused information. Ideal for large complex events such as natural disaster recovery, harbor security, VIP protection, large sporting events, and anywhere wide area surveillance is needed to help protect life and commodities.

AWAPSS and its ilk are the endgame of Cubism: multiple, simultaneous, fractured views assembled to produce the image of a thing. Diagrams showing their deployment remind of those figures in Renaissance perspective books; except now, those frock-coated people with dotted cones of vision emanating from a single eye have become machines, and their cones of vision have multiplied many thousands of times. Even more, the images produced by these machine eyes are themselves read by other machinic forms of vision to hyperbolic effect.

It's worth remembering how perspective and axonometric drawing systems, soon after their invention, became forms of military technology as tools of topographic surveying and methods of designing military fortifications (hence the naming of both cavalier and military projection systems).

As new technologies of seeing increasingly bleed into everyday life, live-translating signs at Spanish tourist sites for instance, a different kind of space emerges. Our vision, like the Hunted operations room or the AWAPSS command center, has become infinitely wide, yet as shallow and as flat as a screen; completely raw, yet always filtered.

Marshall McLuhan explained TV as an extension of the optic nerve, but today, the human nervous system is hardwired into multiple and simultaneous locations. The entire catalogue of human visual culture is available at a keystroke, served up in grids that dislocate images from their context, with adjacencies formed algorithmically rather than by any coherent classification. The perspectival set up—that single directional line of viewer-to-subject that characterized its spatial relation—has forked and multiplied into decentralized and distributed webs. Vision—and power for that matter—is no longer organized as a single line. How we "see" to see and how "seeing" shapes the word has radically changed.

Contemporary space is as distant and different from Renaissance space as it is from cave art. Perhaps, given time, as the vanishing point becomes increasingly anachronistic to contemporary vision, perspectival space will become as illegible as the paintings in El Castillo. And as it does, the question of how we conceptualize and articulate space and representation will re-emerge. At some point—soon perhaps—we will have to ask: What does representation mean when everything can be seen, everywhere, all the time? For architecture, this is not a pictorial question, but a far more profound issue. Representation is the site that where conceptions of space are generated and formalized rather than simply illustrated.

The hyper-photorealist render is the final conclusion of a representational system that originates with Alberti's open window. Intensely beautiful and disarmingly compelling, their power resides in the effect of realism produced by marshalling and perfecting 600 years of visual culture. In their technical and optical sophistication, these images act as the end of representational history. They imagine that the ideological battles of representation are over, replaced by a universal way of seeing. This idea is as much an illusion as the pixel perfect glint of sunrise on glass that they depict.

Over the last decade, a different generation of architects has rejected this representational form. Instead they have sought an escape route from both the CGI render and the tyranny of perspective. By resurrecting a new interest in representation as an architectural project these approaches allow us to sidestep the endgame once avant-garde ideas have atrophied into monotoned banality.

This rejection of the technical sophistication of the photorealistic "real" instead embraces a new awkwardness. It finds itself making digital collages that hit Google images hard and proclaim their diverse sources. Instead of complex three dimensionality, they take advantage of Photoshop and Illustrator's ability to operate in an infinitely layered two-dimensional plane—which, in passing, operates as a native digital space rather than a simulation of the real just as a digital database can operate in nth dimensional space. These drawings accentuate the artificiality of the drawing, sometimes through the use of one point perspective, or by rejecting perspective entirely for a flattened "digital Byzantine." These, amongst others, are tactics of post-digital architectural drawing. Far more than a stylistic project (though this is always a present danger of representational regimes), they configure an approach to digital culture that turns away from the pixel-perfect simulation of the real to expressly declare the representational quality of the drawing. These drawings accentuate representation's "representational" quality, eschewing

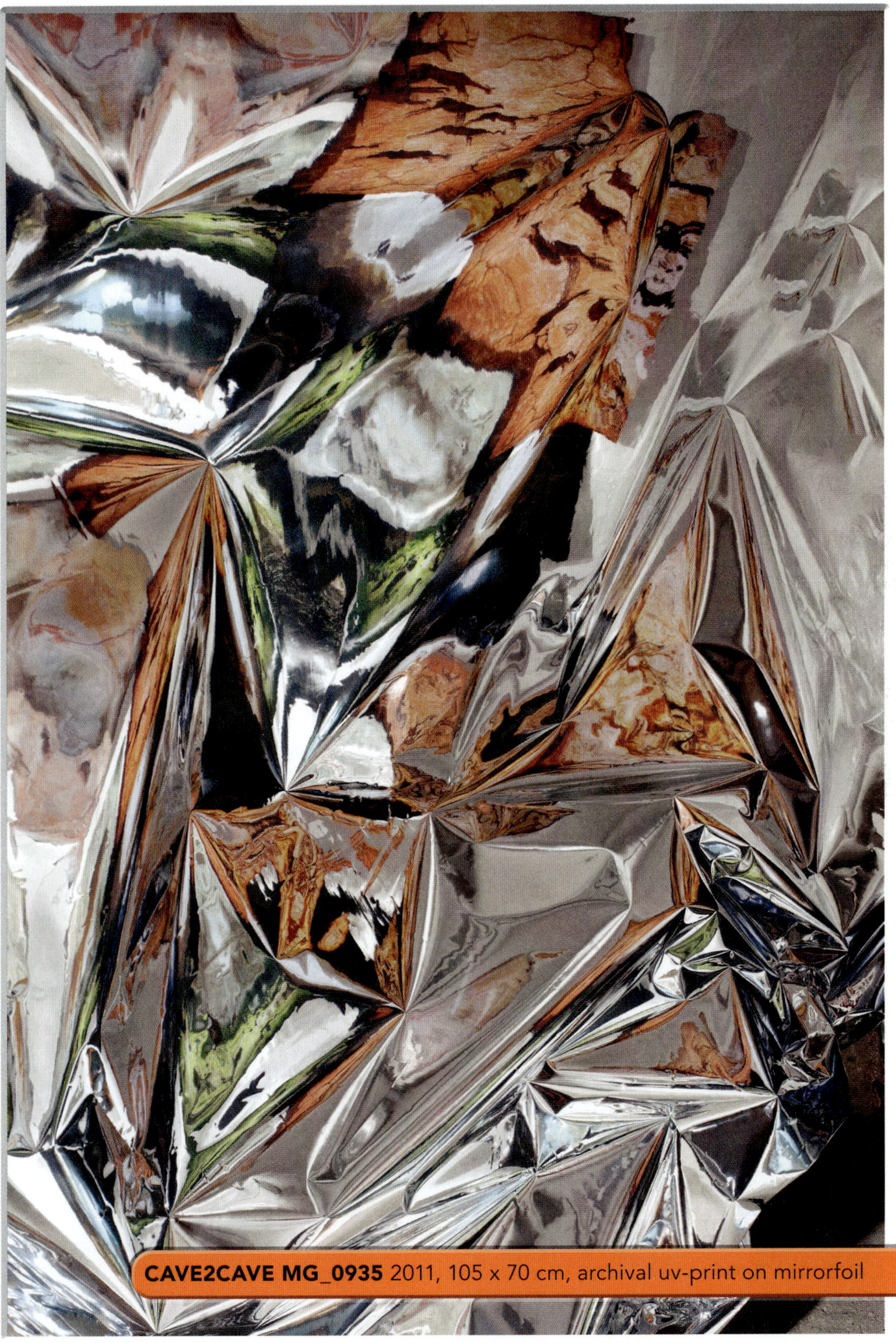

CAVE2CAVE MG_0935 2011, 105 x 70 cm, archival uv-print on mirrorfoil

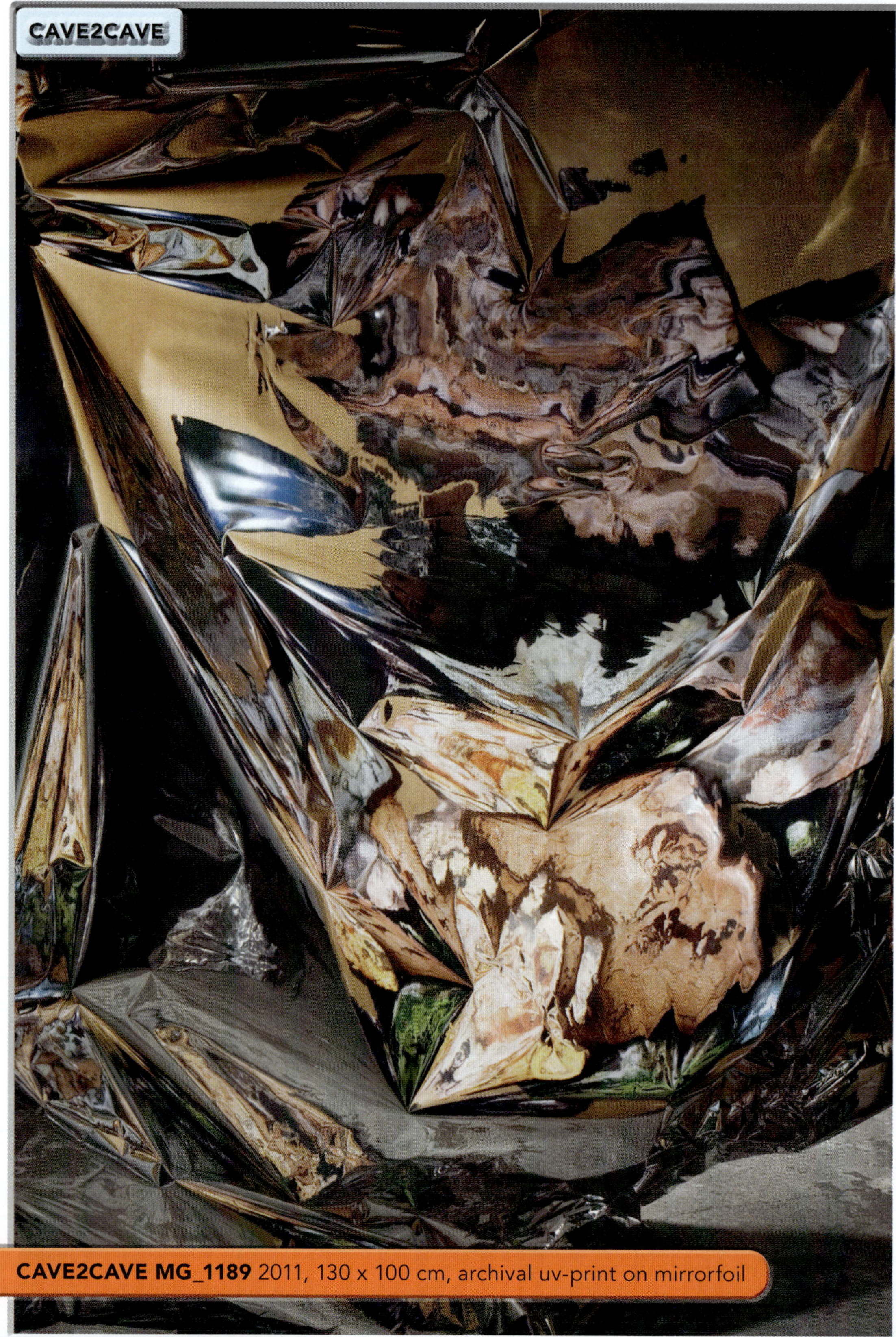

CAVE2CAVE MG_1189 2011, 130 x 100 cm, archival uv-print on mirrorfoil

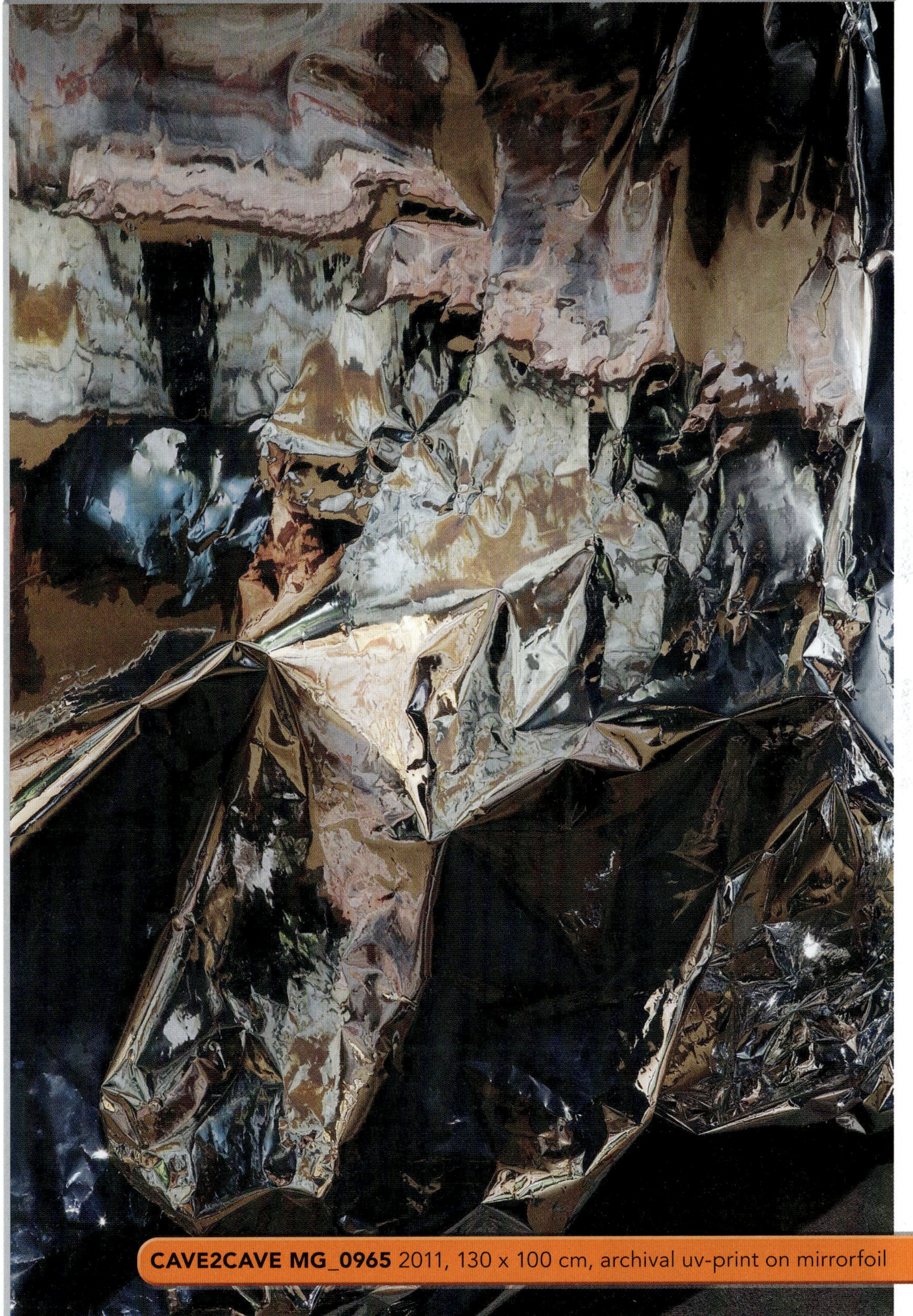

CAVE2CAVE MG_0965 2011, 130 x 100 cm, archival uv-print on mirrorfoil

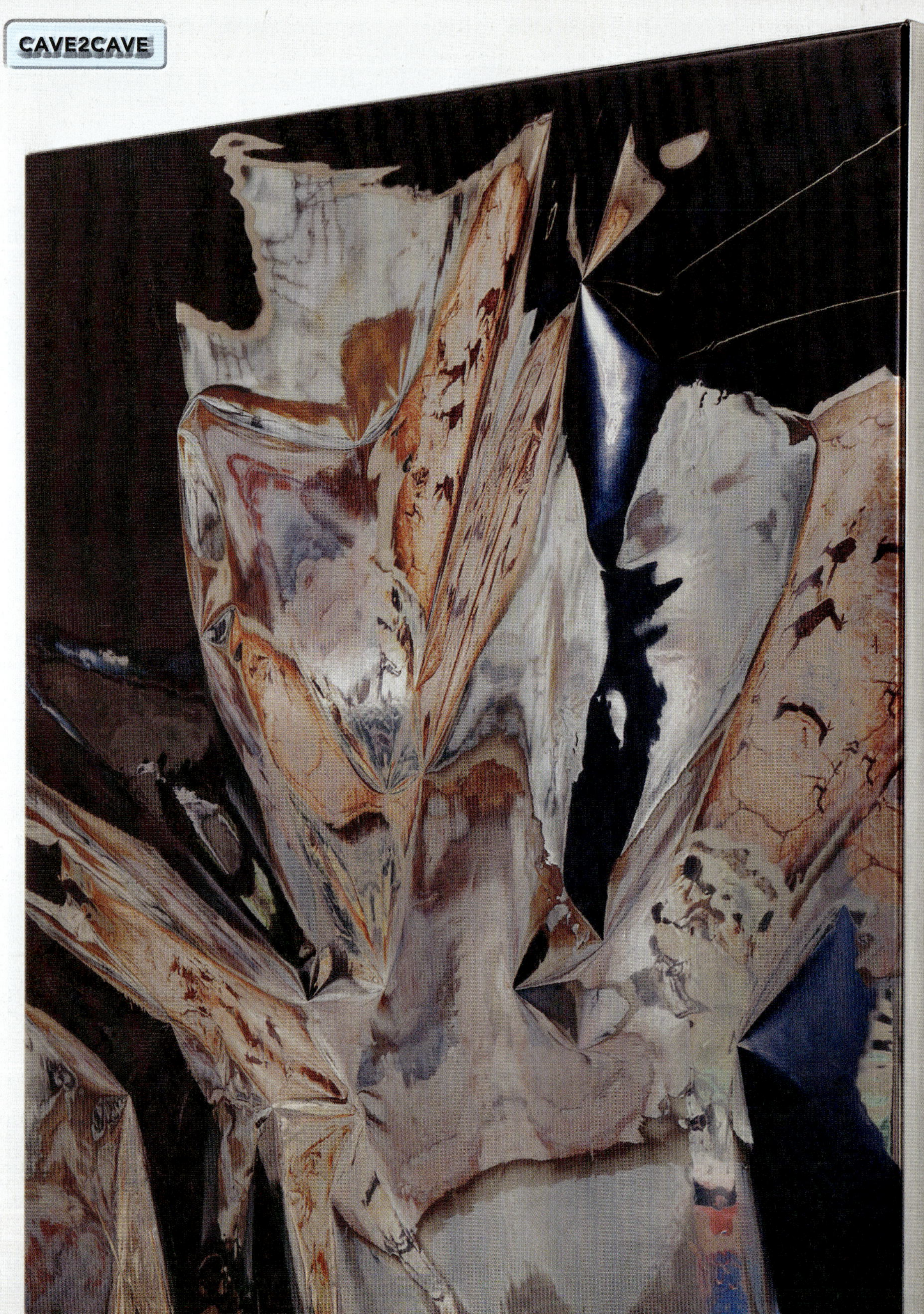

AI GPT-2 RESPONSE

The face was different. He's a man. But this woman is the most beautiful woman alive when mankind became an empire and made it a place to live and hunt for resources of the planet and the species that depend on it; and so the question about her is one that I could not answer as I was thinking of what he would tell the public. She might think what her life might be like in her present state, if the thing she was supposed to be was even just a statue of man with a neck like that of a stone wall.

I can not solve this, but the picture is about 3 feet long, but yet it is very small to look at and we're about 2 years old, almost 5.

And I'm sure that one day when we are older then they are going to see us.

We were not so lucky today. But, I am confident that I am the reality that was created. And so, as I sit with my head on the table watching the picture I want to ask:' if we were not so lucky tomorrow, what happens in this world if it happened to me, or if it happened to everybody else?

Then, when she told me that, I felt so good that I wanted to cry about it and tell her, I have not experienced that yet. But, I want to tell her my story. Because in the same way as a human being who has spent most of his career being a master at deception, my own childhood was the most important one.

And so, we were just waiting for that day when they told us that that was it. And by now, I can't even imagine for sure how it turned out and also how some people would interpret and understand the story. At this point that I was told, I was really really worried that when the story turns out, there might be some other people in our world who might have some real life to tell about it or may not even know that the story that I was told is true. That she had some very real power that led to my life becoming real.

Then I got my daughter.

AI GPT-2 RESPONSE

preset realism in order to expose how drawing and seeing are active in constructing the world. And in doing so, they open the question of space itself. In their rejection of realism they, counter-intuitively, take us closer to an architectural truth: That all architecture, from the drawn to the built, is a form of representation, and that the relationship between the two is closer than would be traditionally admitted. We could even argue that the post-digital turn in architectural representation reconfigures the relationship between the drawn and the built, returning us to a condition similar to the cave. A space where the distinction between the drawn and the real melts into a single idea: An architecture of representation.

"We become what we behold. We shape our tools and then our tools shape us," John Culkin writes. This is as true of architecture as it is of ourselves. Buildings are shaped by the tools and processes used to create them. As such, perspective was never only way of drawing; perspective shaped the things that were drawn, the way they were placed in the world, and the world itself. How vision is constructed—the ways in which we see—and the representational regimes deployed, determines the world that is created.

Title: Rendering: The Cave of the Digital, Author: Sam Jacob in collaboration with Het Nieuwe Instituut, The Berlage. First published at: e-flux Architecture, Year: 2018

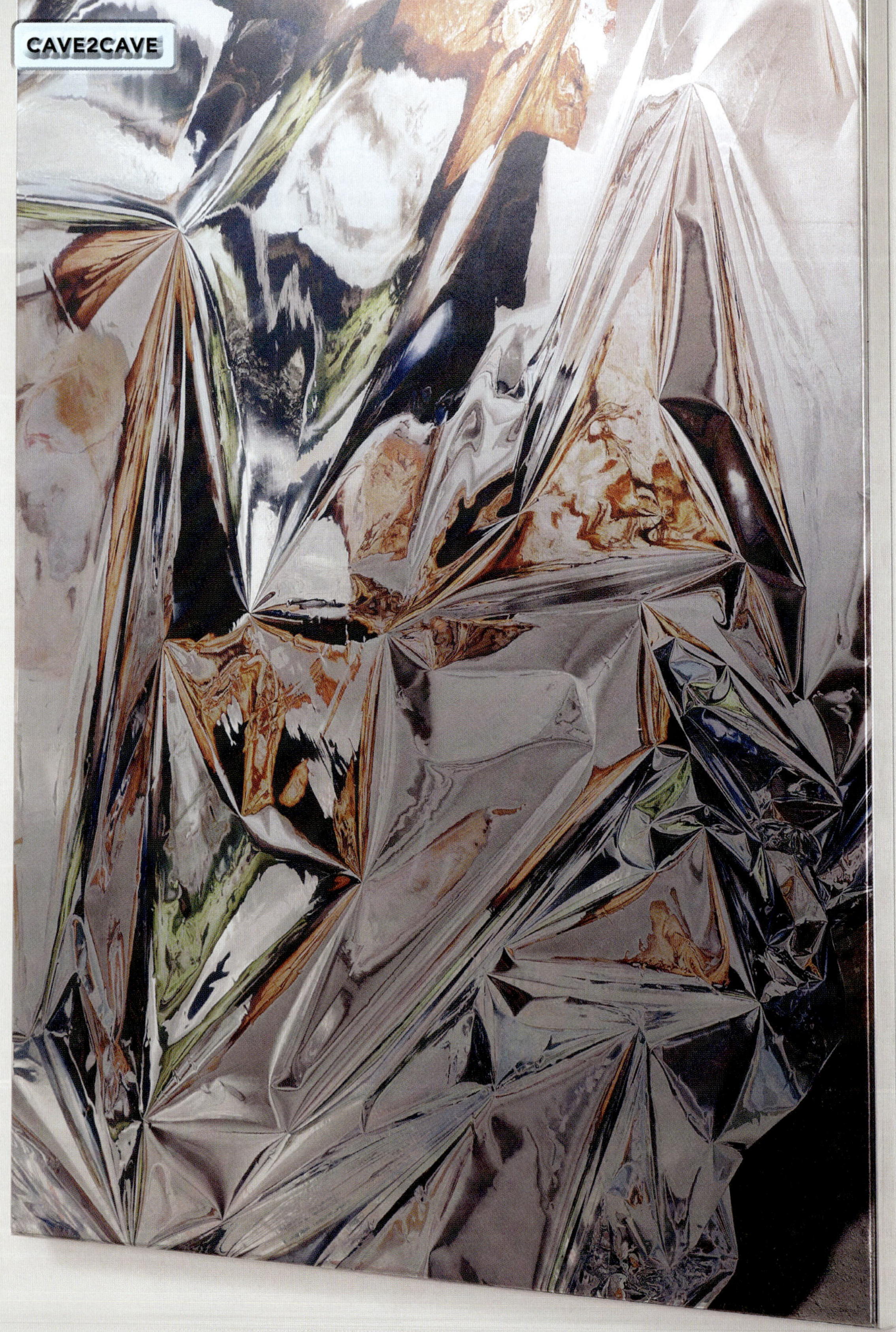

SCROLL 12

AI GPT-2 RESPONSE

On Twitter, the situation escalated. "In the wake of @POTUS' travel ban, @realDonaldTrump's Twitter account erupted. #TrumpCare" followed within minutes. Within hours, two Twitter accounts began using the same hashtags. One, Twitter's "No Love For Criminalized Twitter Accounts" and posted pictures of Trump as if it he was wearing a police uniform; the second, an anonymous "alt-right" account, posted pictures of Trump as if he watched Nazi television. "It's like they're telling everyone in the US what a Nazi is.

AI GPT-2 RESPONSE

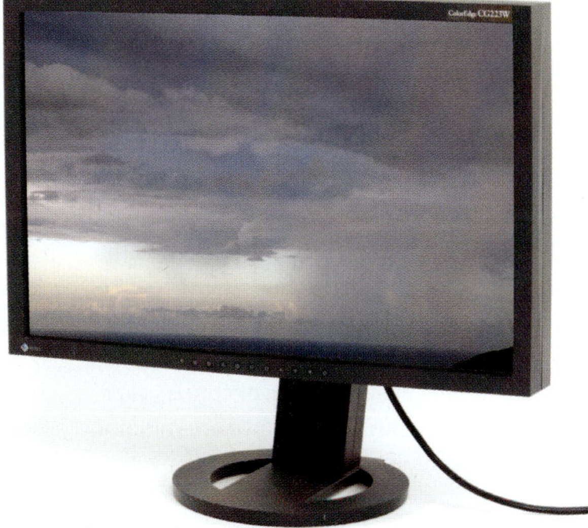

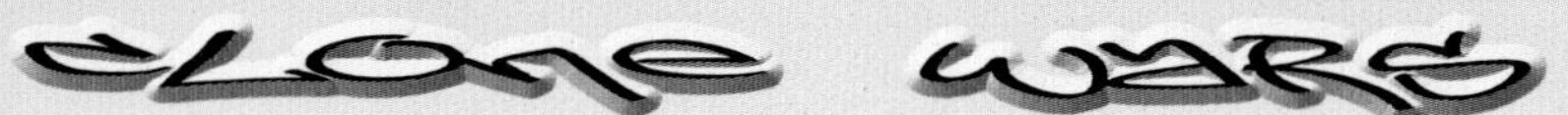

The Difference between chanting,

One January night last year, I disappeared into two protests of Donald Trump's travel ban at once. My attention split between the jostling bodies around me — we chanted, "let them in!" — and the flux on Twitter. During the protest my tweets were like those of many other people who were there: quotations from the crowd, pictures of signs and of bemused travelers stepping into an airport terminal filled with shouting people. Some time into the protest, the physical jostling and chanting ceased to be a surrounding discomfort and felt more like a coming together. When my pictures or quotes from the protest were retweeted, I felt like it was only extending that feeling beyond the terminal. I pictured blue-lit faces elsewhere in dark space, solitary extensions of the crowd, even as the event itself continued to shake my bones and thunder in my ears.

But after I returned home, my fragments within the networked protest took on a life of their own. Overnight, my tweets accrued protesters and counter-protesters in numbers far beyond what I had seen in person, becoming a tireless cacophony as I slept, and by the morning I was looking at a protest almost unrecognizably transformed.

I had become the spectator to a thing I had made to reflect my autonomy as it became integrated into a different kind of affective machine Elias Canetti, in Crowds and Power (1960), described the "discharge" of a crowd — before which the crowd doesn't really exist — as the moment in which "distinctions are thrown off and all feel equal," where "each man is as near the other as he is to himself; and an immense feeling of relief ensues." This, of course, is an illusion; the members of a crowd are not, nor will they continue to feel, equal. "They return to their separate houses, they lie down on their own beds, they keep their possessions and their names," Canetti writes. " Caught in the amber of my Twitter feed was disquieting proof of a phenomenon I had appreciated the day before and now found threatening — that is, my part in the nationwide protest did not cease when I went home, but became crystallized and seemed to act on its own. In my absence, the slogans and images I had shared were inserted by others into new frames of reference, perforated by extraneous debates, borrowed, criticized, bundled alongside many voices offering nearly identical accounts. I had become a witness to my own words, just like the blue-lit faces of the audience I had imagined the night before, and from that perspective the words seemed like just another move in the ineffectual pistoning of American public discourse.

The same technology that had helped to call the protest into being made visible, by recording it, what it means to be swallowed by the crowd. At the protest, my feed had proved to me that I was both a participant and an observer, that my personality had not quite dissolved in the moment and the mass but remained outside it. Now I saw my "feed self" caught up in an even bigger crowd. Paradoxically, I had become the spectator to a thing I had made to reflect my autonomy as it became integrated into a different kind of affective machine. I was frightened to see myself rendered no more than the periscope and megaphone of a machine. I was frightened to feel like a robot.

I'm not the first to be frightened by a convergence of the apparently robotic and the human. The human-passing robot is a theme for concern that shows up repeatedly in science fiction: Blade Runner, Terminator, Battlestar Galactica, Eve of Destruction. It's also the subject of prolonged reflection in the academic world, where the Turing Test integrated the idea protest slogans, and parroting party lines.

of human-passing robots into the effort to define intelligence. We test the power of our computing machines by seeing if they can pass for human, talk like us, beat us at chess. Now robot paranoia has emigrated from the realm of imagination and speculation to everyday life. Among the worries regularly encountered on op-ed pages are robots replacing us at work, robots passing as humans on social media to conduct political psyops, robot armies led by hackers of the insecure "internet of things," and robots replacing us as objects of desire for each other.

But in a related development, the fear of robots has shifted to contempt, and increasingly, "robot" is being used as a human insult. At a memorable debate in the 2016 Republican Primary, Senator Marco Rubio awkwardly over-repeated a poorly phrased talking point and brought a mountain of derision down on his own head: He looked, people said, like a malfunctioning robot. Mark Zuckerberg receives similar comparisons for virtually everything he does. Repetition and predictability, and the appearance of acting out of premeditation rather than with human spontaneity, are scorned as robotic behavior. Regardless of where one is on the political spectrum, one is vulnerable to some version of that insult. When the alt-right edgelords gleefully ask, "Are you triggered yet?" they are trying to project mastery of the presumed automatism of their target. On the left, Sanders supporters were accused of being "Bernie bots." Trump's army of social media warriors are sometimes treated to their own variant of the insult: "I get called a Russian bot 50 times a day," one woman told Politico.

The all-purpose insult only works because of its all-purpose applicability. Every group accused of roboticism is perceived to be parroting party lines, choosing friends and enemies on the basis of blind team-allegiance. This means that having almost any identifiable political position makes you vulnerable to being called a robot. At the same time, the insult itself has become such a cliché that using it is robotic itself. The woman so offended to be called a robot in the Politico article earned the label by routinely participating in organized propaganda campaigns on Twitter, tweeting and retweeting a predetermined message hundreds of times a day — and ironically felt free to criticize what others said to her as rote and repetitive.

The robot is perhaps such a favored metaphor because real robots exist in the same space. From innocuous experiments in the generation of words — I recently made a bot that invents new story ideas, for example — to the deeply troubling astroturf botnets massed to manipulate public opinion, "bots" surround us online, resembling more and more how humans themselves communicate online, using the same small palette of pre-set responses that we do.

Every group accused of roboticism is perceived to be choosing friends and enemies on the basis of blind team-allegiance. Having almost any political position makes you vulnerable.
But the chants of protesters massed to express themselves with one voice may be both as robotic as the retweets that help a viral marketing campaign land as well as a form of massively enhanced collective agency.
Conceiving of a protest as robotic because protesters form a kind of team, share a message, and repeat a phrase smuggles a false implication into an apparently innocent descriptive metaphor. The robot acts on programming rather than thought: It is not free.
This hidden premise of the insult explains why it is so tempting to project roboticism outward onto our enemies.

The Difference between chanting,

After the protests against Trump's travel ban, one of the right's favorite ideas kept coming up: We protesters had all been paid by George Soros to be there. What other explanation could there be for such a massive, spontaneous, apparently well-coordinated demonstration? How else did we all know to chant "let them in?" The enemies of collective agency can't afford to acknowledge the possibility of self-organization: It is so much more comforting to imagine your enemy as an an army of pre-programmed robots than a real human crowd. When I looked at my Twitter feed the day after the protest, as if by osmosis I saw myself with those same cynical eyes. I knew I hadn't been paid by Soros, of course, but I felt discomfort at an apparent roboticism all the same. Did my discomfort indicate that I had been infected by an atmosphere that cynically misconstrues all collective action as unfree, misapplying the robot insult with reckless abandon?

The jurist and philosopher Carl Schmitt bluntly articulated why human political interactions tend toward a kind of automatism. His ideas are dark and properly suspect, for reasons his ominous nickname — "the crown jurist of the Third Reich" — makes clear. But they also possess great explanatory power: In The Concept of the Political, Schmitt argued that political disagreements are not political because of where they take place, whether the halls of government or the most private dinner table; nor because of who disagrees, whether the most prominent politicians or the most tuned-out high school students; nor because of what the disagreements are intended to accomplish, whether legislating or winning an argument over the turkey and stuffing. Political disagreements, Schmitt wrote, are political because they divide us into friends and enemies: Friend/enemy is the political distinction. In politics, it comes before everything and contains everything. Arguing about principles is a rationalization of or distraction from the fundamental reality of struggle. The principles are almost arbitrary.

When some ordinary disagreement becomes political, in Schmitt's view, the content of the disagreement becomes secondary to the fact of antagonism. Thus we often see alliances that appear hypocritical but make perfect sense from inside the political distinction. Religious groups embrace monstrously immoral figures; doves invite hawks into their resistance; rebels and the establishment lock arms — motivated to be friends because they share enemies. Likewise, from within the political distinction, enemies crop up in the strangest places. In The Concept of the Political, Schmitt writes:

The political enemy need not be morally evil or aesthetically ugly; he need not appear as an economic competitor, and it may even be advantageous to engage with him in business transactions. But he is, nevertheless, the other, the stranger; and it is sufficient for his nature that he is, in a specially intense way, existentially something different and alien, so that in the extreme case conflicts with him are possible.

Politicization, in Schmitt's sense, is a kind of roboticization. The reasoning, dithering, discriminating processes of ordinary life are swept away, replaced by a brutal algorithm of antagonism. Conceiving of roboticism in this way highlights reaction rather than repetition. What makes the political distinction take on a life of its own is the way enemies bond us to friends, reactively. Taken as a prescription — as Schmitt took it — this insight leads down a very dark road to the idea that a nation should always keep a public

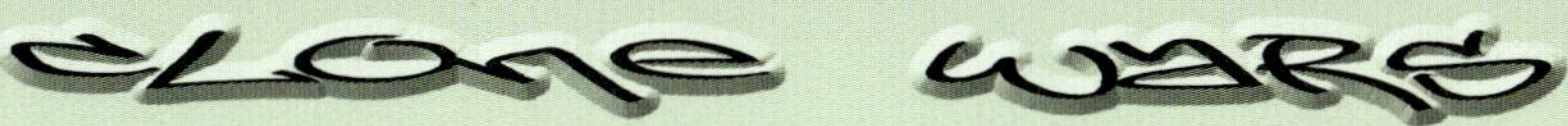

enemy on hand to unite the citizenry. Taken as an explanation, however, the same idea can be spun in a hopeful direction: The travel ban protests formed a more or less spontaneous collectivity because a massively oppressive act of enmity had created a corresponding group of friends.

In the days after the January protests, the political eruption was discussed ad nauseam, footage aired on every channel. Each time I'd hear the familiar chant "let them in!" booming from a wall-mounted TV in a public building, I'd feel a peculiar mixture of the energy I remembered and the discomfort that had followed. My anger had vaulted me into a specific politicization and I had already expressed it, submerging my individuality in a crowd. Thanks to the technologies that allow us to broadcast, preserve, and review such moments, I had seen what that meant, from inside and outside.

Politicization, in Schmitt's sense, is a kind of roboticization. The dithering processes of ordinary life are swept away, replaced by a brutal algorithm of antagonism Gradually the self-consciousness faded, until, over a year later, I heard a surprising rumor that brought all my doubts raging back. In David Wolff's Fire and Fury, he reports that the timing of Trump's travel ban, just before a weekend when the maximum number of protesters could be expected to turn out, was urged by his cartoonishly evil then-advisor, Steve Bannon. He wanted, Wolff reports, the "snowflakes to show up at the airports and riot." In other words, the executive order was an attempt to "trigger" his enemies from the largest possible platform. It's no surprise that a former editor like Bannon, familiar with the world of media and social media, where provocation and revenue pursue a rigorous alliance, would come up with an idea like that. Ironically, while Bannon attempted to create a Schmitt-style robot-enemy, his people, and in fact his own magazine, trumpeted the idea that the protesters had all been paid by Soros and were not spontaneously responding to the ban. This might seem like a contradiction, but both the provocation and the rumor rely upon the belittling assumption that those who would attend such a protest must be in some way unthinking.

The idea that I had been part of an intentionally provoked protest resurrected my misgivings. But then I realized: The assumption that the normal politics of democracy are expressions of robotic mindlessness is more dangerous than either Bannon's provocation or Breitbart's rumor. Bannon could no more control the crowd he had provoked than readers of his magazine could cynically explain it away. But to fear the moral physics according to which an outrage raises an outcry, or to perceive collective action as a loss of agency, is an insidious and genuine danger. The renewal of politics requires us to disentangle the image of a team as a bunch of bots with a party line from the political unity of collective agency.

Author: Robert Minto, Title: Clone Wars,
First Published: reallifemag.com, Year: 2018

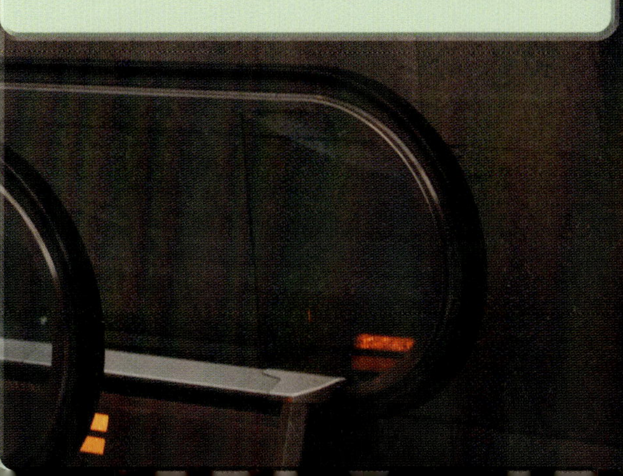

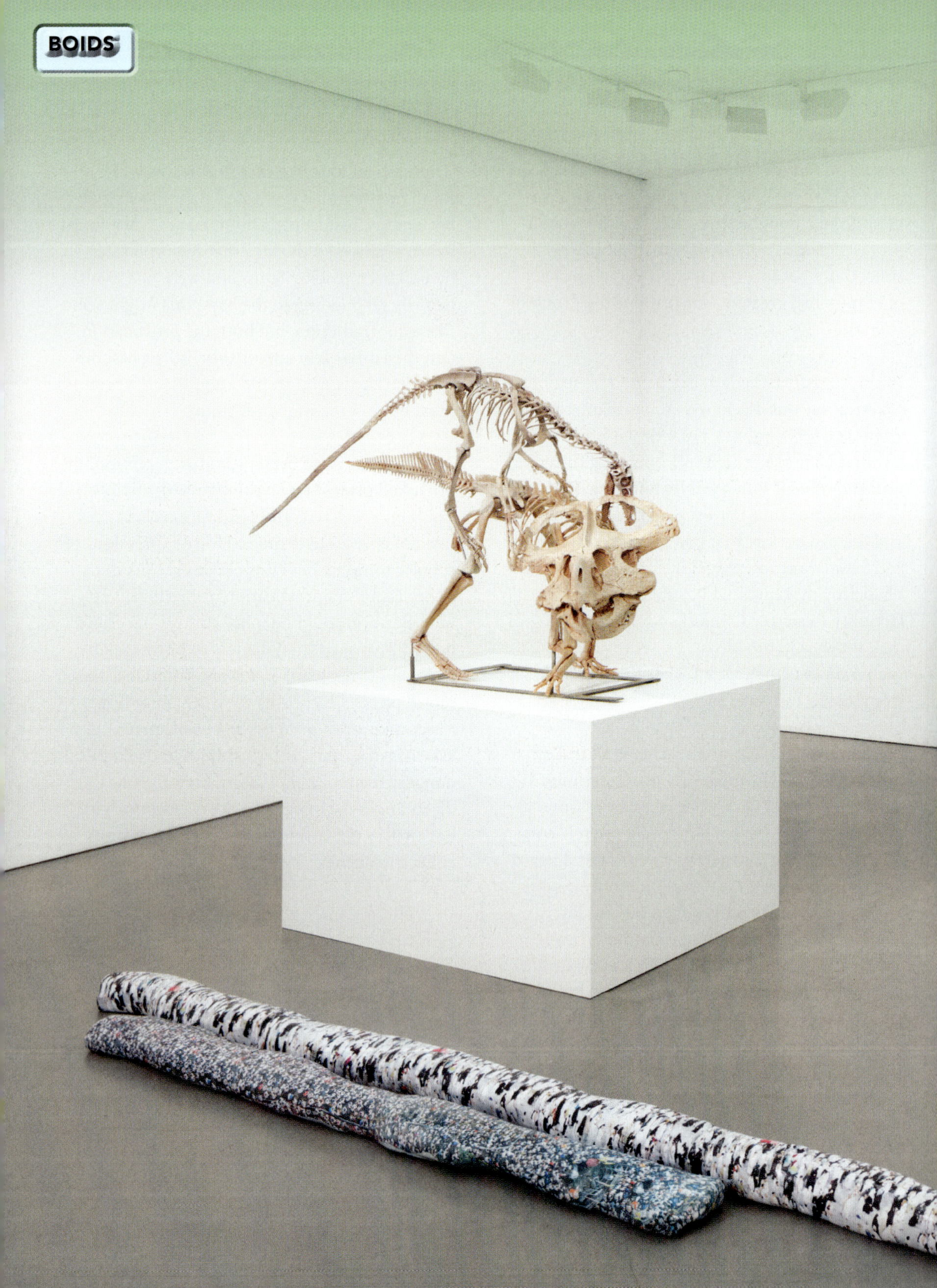

The crowd needs a direction. It is in movement and it moves towards a goal. The direction, which is common to all its members, strengthens the feeling of equality. A goal outside the individual members and common to all of them drives underground all the private differing goals which are fatal to the crowd as such. Direction is essential for the continuing existence of the crowd. Its constant fear of disintegration means that it will accept any goal. A crowd exists so long as it has an unattained goal.

CROWDS AND POWER

Author: Elias Canetti, Title: Crowds and Power, First Published: Farrar, Straus and Giroux, Year: 1960.

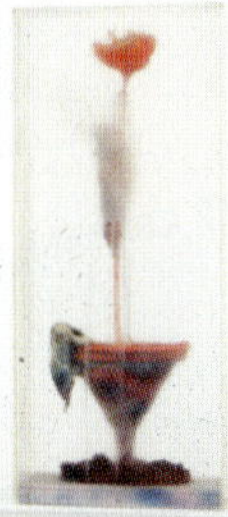

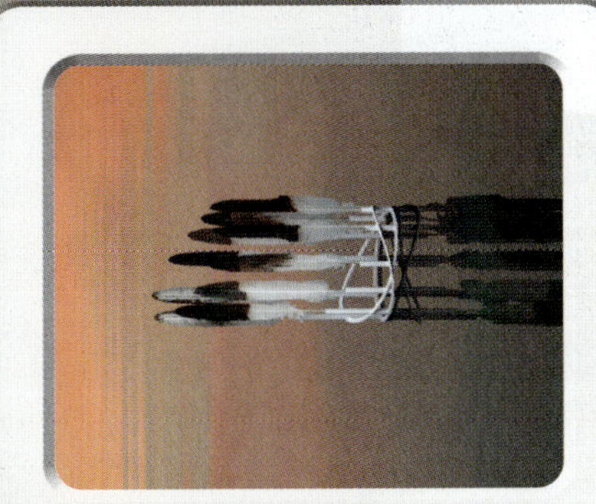

'Boids' is an artificial life program, developed by Craig Reynolds in 1986, which simulates the flocking behaviour of birds. His paper on this topic was published in 1987 in the proceedings of the ACM SIGGRAPH conference. [1] The name "boid" corresponds to a shortened version of "bird-oid object", which refers to a bird-like object.[2] Incidentally, "boid" is also a New York Metropolitan dialect pronunciation for "bird".

Rules applied in simple Boids
As with most artificial life simulations, Boids is an example of emergent behavior; that is, the complexity of Boids arises from the interaction of individual agents (the boids, in this case) adhering to a set of simple rules. The rules applied in the simplest Boids world are as follows:

separation: steer to avoid crowding local flockmates alignment: steer towards the average heading of local flockmates

cohesion: steer to move toward the average position (center of mass) of local flockmates

More complex rules can be added, such as obstacle avoidance and goal seeking.

The basic model has been extended in several different ways since Reynolds proposed it. For instance, Delgado-Mata et al. [3] extended the basic model to incorporate the effects of fear. Olfaction was used to transmit emotion between animals,

ASDZÁÁ NÁDLEEHÉ

by David Andrew Tasman

In the world Si-Qin constructs, the artist is not only a regenerative creative force like the mythic namesake of the exhibition, a central figure within Navajo mythology who grows old each winter and is young again come spring, but also an architect looking at extant forms of culture in order to transfigure them, discovering which traits can be refashioned to abstract or practical effect.

While the exhibition takes its name from a Navajo goddess, the subtext of the exhibition develops from the evolutionary concept of the exaptive trait, a biological characte… which, through natural selection, becomes … ways beyond its original purpose. A common…ed example of an exaptive trait is a feather, thought to have functioned as a mechanism to dissipate heat in certain dinosaurs prior to developing into a crucial mechanism of flight.

Andrea Rosen Gallery

PRESS RELEASE – FOR IMMEDIATE RELEASE

Asdzáá nádleehé
Curated by Timur Si-Qin
December 11, 2015 – January 23, 2016

Before they could be used for flight, feathers first appeared on dinosaurs for other, terrestrial purposes such as heat regulation, camouflage or signaling. Blindly, and through the ecstasy of geological timespans, their use was transformed and mortal animals were again granted the power of flight in a new way. In biology the evolution of the feather is an example of an exaptive trait, namely a trait that evolves for use in solving one adaptive problem, but then is at some point retooled or co-opted to serve another. Recent computational models of E.Coli suggest most traits start off as exaptations.

The exaptive trait stands in opposition to the idea that biology or the world is pre-determined. Instead it is wholly contingent. If the forms and functions of heredity can be so fundamentally repurposed and our material, animal bodies transmogrified to fly over mountains and swim beneath oceans, it is because matter is itself inherently open, lacking in essential character or permanent identity. A deep modularity of/and in service to a matter determined to experience all variations of itself.

Whatever functions a structure has today is no clear indication of its function or meaning in the future. At each moment of time, we are new. Dependently originated, the universe in a unique configuration; empty of essence yet pregnant with unimagined forms and unpredictable capacities. The artworks and objects in this exhibition speak to this ability of the world to transform to its core.

Emily Jones' (b. 1987) work manifests from an interest in how humans position themselves in relation to the earth, and how environments interact with physical materials and incorporeal machines, such as legal systems and borders. The work communicates a sensitivity to the critical thresholds that structure and transform these biocultural terrains.

Tetsumi Kudo's (1935–1990) post-war sculptures of mutant organisms in cages and wasted landscapes, made in the 60s and 70s, warn us of the transformative powers we humans have over the earth. Pollution and the consequences of nuclear war are also potential, contingent results of the interactions of matter.

Anne de Vries's (b. 1977) sculpture series "Boids" investigate the emergent behavior of populations. The Nematode-like sculptures depict large religious or socio-politically motivated crowds. The emergent transformations of populations can also be simulated by artificial life programs such as the work's namesake "Boids", a flocking behavior algorithm.

Hannah Wilke's (1940–1993) work underscores the transformation of gender roles and the ability and necessity of society to co-opt its origins to meet new challenges. Wilke's gum works when applied to her body resembled scarification and thereby presented an image different from the one defined by the norms sedimented in the west. It… morphological self-determination indicative of the exaptive potential of consciousness, agency and equality.

…amon Zucconi's (b. 1985) work "/, \, \, / (the Final Cut)" investigates the artefact of a narrative whose meaning has …en continuously manipulated by a succession of edits... but that then was supposedly coming to a 'final' … A state … equilibrium Zucconi is skeptical about.

…media inquiries, please contact Justin Conner at justin@hellothirdeye.com.

Jones includes at the top of her website the latin phrase "hoc mihi conloquium tecum manebit," which translates into "then you and I will speak together in unison," a good description of what happens as one pours through her text-based art works.

Internalizing the artist's words from her piece, Search for the Source of the Nile, invokes a heightened sense of responsibility to a world in transition from the Holocene to Anthropocene, and our role in it from user to steward of natural resources.
If Jenny Holzer was the voice of the subconscious liberated by the social revolutions of the '60s, then Jones' is that of a clarion mind no longer in need of psychotherapy. The late Hannah Wilke (1940 – 1993) is represented by a vintage gelatin silver print from her S.O.S. Starification Object Series, which depicts an image of the artist with a self-described vaginal aperture at her ajna chakra, located between the eyebrows. In some animals the parietal eye, which helps regulate circadian rhythms, is also located at the ajna chakra, tying Wilke's image of the artist to the productive and fertile Changing Woman, whose regenerative cycle from young to old is mirrored in a circadian analogy of transition.
A subtheme of blurred boundaries between what is natural and what is artificial can be seen in the work Cultivation by Radioactivity in the Electronic Circuit (Pink Flower) by the late Japanese artist Tetsumi Kudo (1935 – 1990) and in Si-Qin's inclusion of two turkey feathers which have been hand-modified to resemble the feathers of Golden Eagles. This pairing conveys both the accidental impact that human force can have on the development of life through the example of nuclear mutation, as well as the increasingly commonplace intentional impact on development through surgical and genetic means.

Andrea Rosen Gallery has been a longtime supporter of such lines of inquiry, hosting Kudo and Wilke together previously in the 2013 exhibition Counter Forms, organized by Elena Filipovic.
Anne de Vries, whose practice is eloquently explicated by his Rijksakademie colleague Katja Novitskova in a short essay, "The Merging of Matter and Information," makes work about how "new technologies are influencing our perceptions of the world." Like other artists in this show, de Vries also works closely with mediums he transfigures with ecological concepts and strategies. In his Boids, oblong sculptural logs based on the form of the nematode — a phylum of highly adaptive parasitical worm, — the surface is inversely populated with images of human figures. The sculptural series takes its name from an eponymous program used to study flocking behavior. One has the sense there is a latent critique of crowds: each of de Vries' Boids is named after a socio-political gathering or uprising such as Tunisia Protest Jan, 2011 or Obama Rally, Portland, May 2008. In selecting the highly adaptive metaphor of the nematode on which to base the cycle of work, de Vries brings to bear a ubiquitous, resilient notion of the artist and art itself, modeled on a worm so prolific and present in all aspects of life that, according to the scientist Nathan Cobb, if

"...all the matter in the universe except the nematodes were swept away [...] The location of towns would be decipherable, since for every massing of human beings there would be a corresponding massing of certain nematodes. Trees would still stand in ghostly rows representing our streets and highways.."
Perhaps through de Vries, Si-Qin finds his most compelling remark: that the power of art lies neither in myth nor science, but in the quality of persistence and adaptability. The group exhibition Asdzą́ą́ Nádleehé (Changing Woman) is an ambitious display of varying capabilities of artistic production.

Author: David Andrew Tasman, Title: Review group exhibition Titled: ASDZÁÁ NÁDLEEHÉ, Location: Andrea Rosen Gallery 2, Curator: Timur Si-Qin, First published: DISmagazine, Year: 2016,

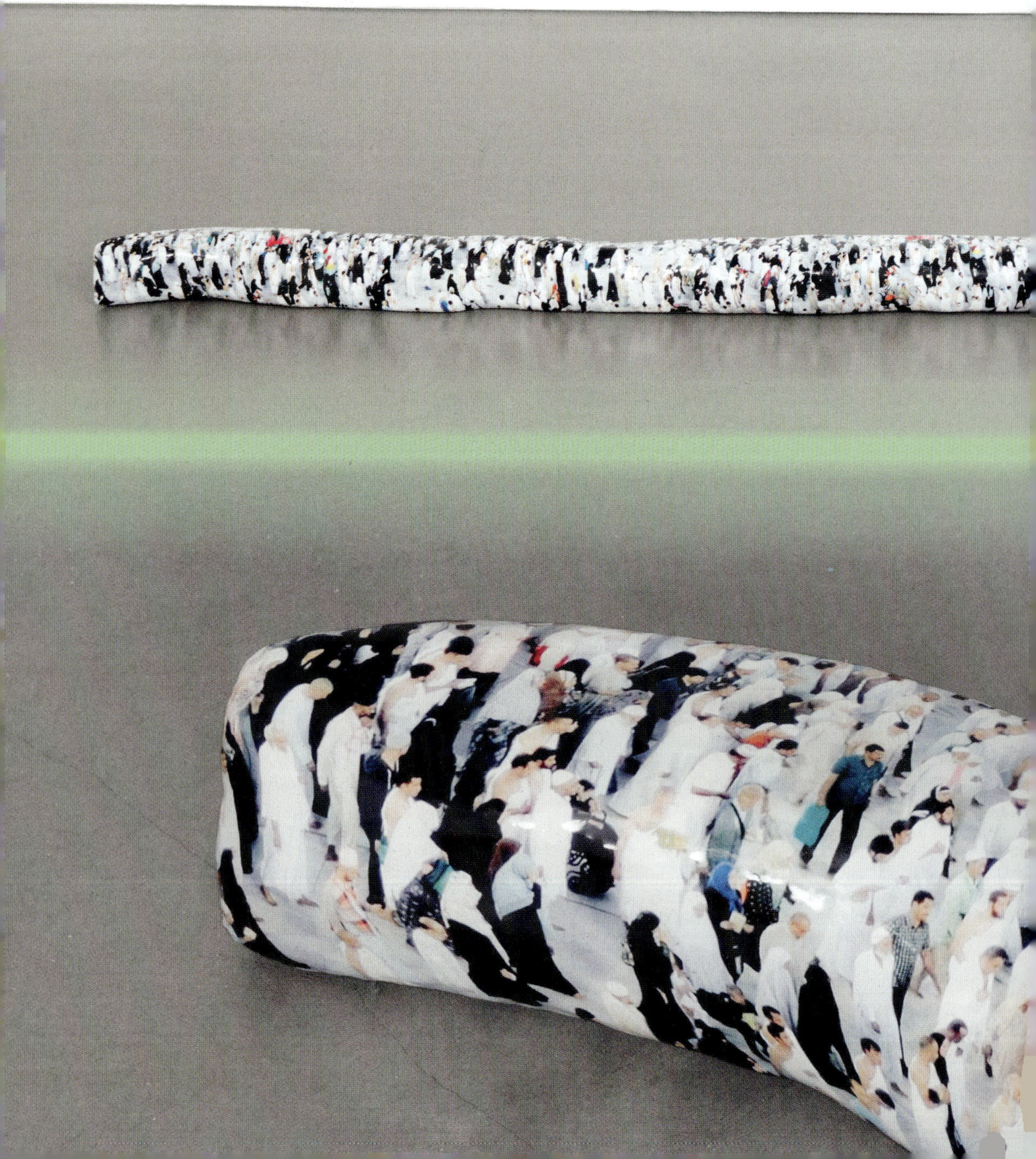

through pheromones modelled as particles in a free expansion gas. Hartman and Benes[4] introduced a complementary force to the alignment that they call the change of leadership. This steer defines the chance of the boid to become a leader and try to escape.

The movement of Boids can be characterized as either chaotic (splitting groups and wild behaviour) or orderly. Unexpected behaviours, such as splitting flocks and reuniting after avoiding obstacles, can be considered emergent.

The boids framework is often used in computer graphics, providing realistic-looking representations of flocks of birds and other creatures, such as schools of fish or herds of animals. It was for instance used in the 1998 video game Half-Life for the flying bird-like creatures seen at the end of the game on Xen, named "boid" in the game files. The Boids model can be used for direct control and stabilization of teams of simple Unmanned Ground Vehicles (UGV)[5] or Micro Aerial Vehicles (MAV)[6] in swarm robotics. For stabilization of heterogeneous UAV-UGV teams, the model was adapted for using onboard relative localization by Saska et al.[7]
At the time of proposal, Reynolds' approach represented a

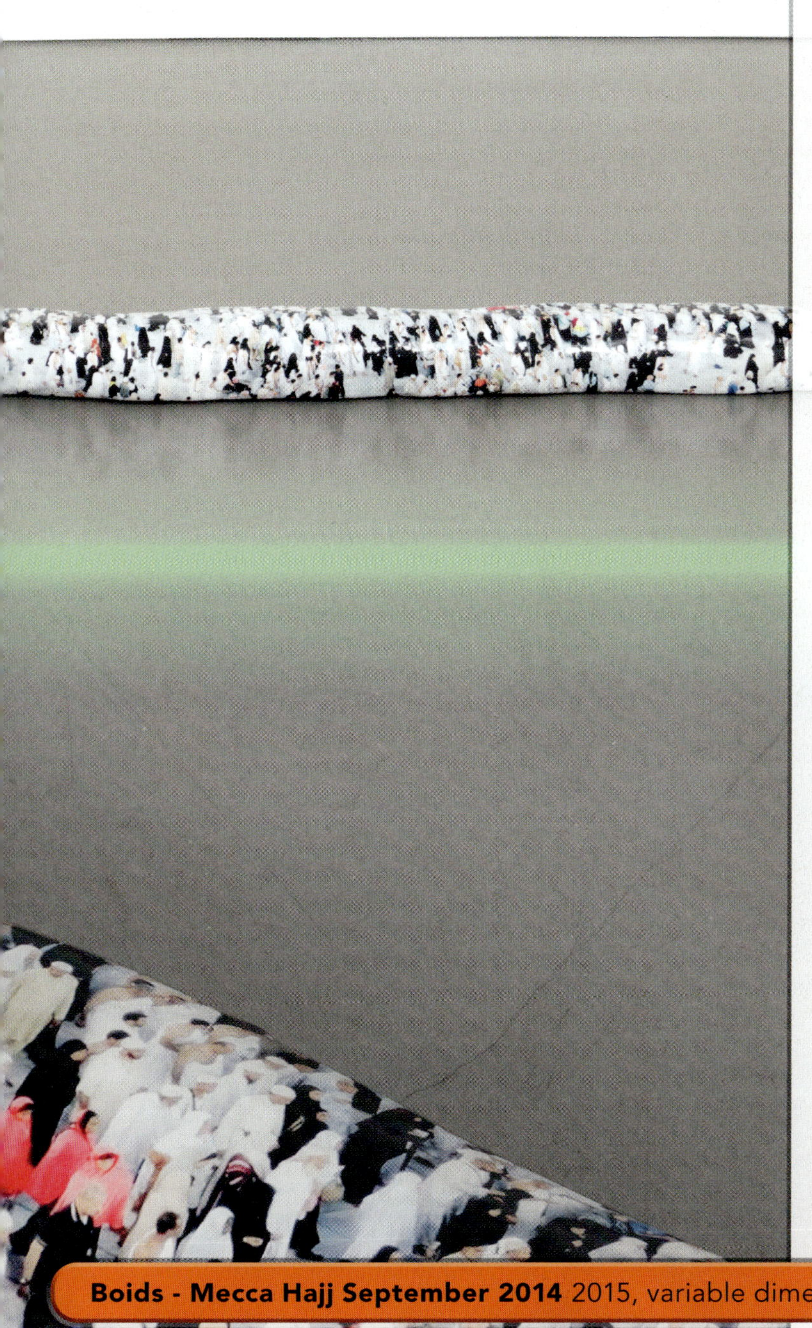

Boids - Mecca Hajj September 2014 2015, variable dimensions, eps and uv-print, vinyl

giant step forward compared to

New Degrees of Freedom
Act 3: Water

by Jenna Sutela

Character: a universal substance, a transparent fluid, a compound of hydrogen and oxygen, the sea, rain, saliva, etc.

*

I live on earth at present, and I don't know what I am. I know that I am not a category. I am not a thing—a noun. I seem to be a verb, an evolutionary process—an integral function of the universe.

*

More than half of you consists of me. You drink me, bathe with me, swim in me, and extract energy from me. Life itself is the body running out of me running into history running dry, or me slowly evacuating your body to return to air, ocean, earth, and ice. Meanwhile, forbidden moistures trickle into forbidden places. Your glands expand at the most unlikely of times, betraying feelings that you have not even admitted to yourself. That is, until you apply deodorant and thermoregulation.

*

Experiencing a wide-open skin through which vital substances leak out and dangerous elements seep in? This hydrophobic coating is guaranteed to make your body feel like a statue or a tomb. Spray it on and any water in will reform into a perfect sphere and roll away.

*

Our lives are completely intertwined.

Politically speaking, tribal nationalism [patriotism] always insists that its own people are surrounded by ‹a world of enemies' - ‹one against all' - and that a fundamental difference exists between this people and all others. It claims its people to be unique, individual, incompatible with all others, and denies theoretically the very possibility of a common mankind long before it is used to destroy the humanity of man.

Author: Hannah Arendt,
Title: Origins of Totalitarianism,
Page: 227, First published:
Schocken Books, Year: 1951.

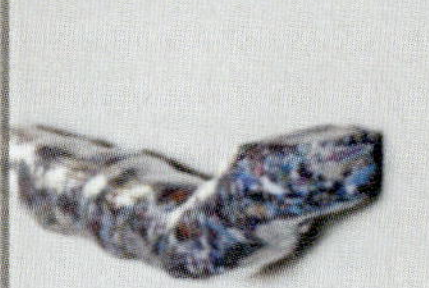

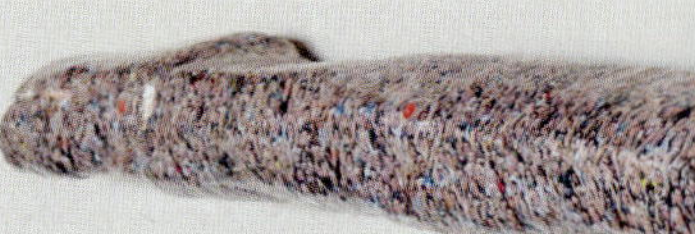

the traditional techniques used in computer animation for motion pictures. The first animation created with the model was Stanley and Stella in: Breaking the Ice (1987), followed by a feature film debut in Tim Burton's film Batman Returns (1992) with computer generated bat swarms and armies of penguins marching through the streets of Gotham City.[8]

The boids model has been used for other interesting applications. It has been applied to automatically program Internet multi-channel radio stations.[9] It has also been used for visualizing information[10] and for optimization tasks.[11]

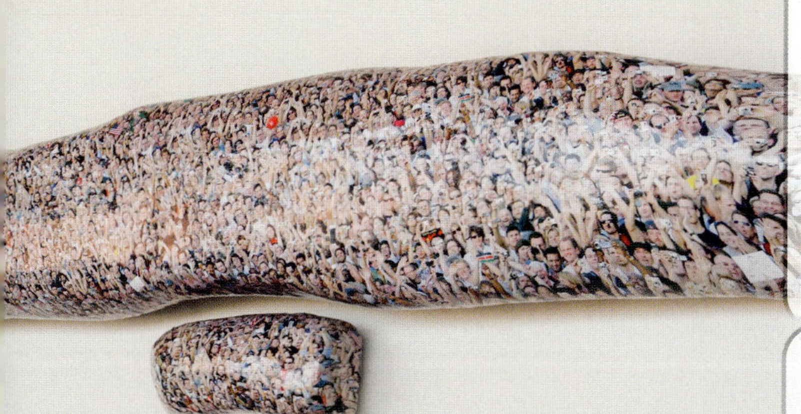

BOIDS

[1] Reynolds, Craig (1987). "Flocks, herds and schools: A distributed behavioral model". SIGGRAPH '87: Proceedings of the 14th annual conference on Computer graphics and interactive techniques. Association for Computing Machinery: 25—34. doi:10.1145/37401.37406. ISBN 0-89791-227-6.
[2] Banks, Alec; Vincent, Jonathan; Anyakoha, Chukwudi (July 2007). "A review of particle swarm optimization. Part I: background and development". Natural Computing. doi:10.1007/s11047-007-9049-5.
[3] Delgado-Mata, Carlos; Martinez, Jesus Ibanez; Bee, Simon; Ruiz-Rodarte, Rocio; Aylett, Ruth (2007). "On the use of Virtual Animals with Artificial Fear in Virtual Environments". New Generation Computing. 25 (2): 145—169. doi:10.1007/s00354-007-0009-5.
[4] Hartman, Christopher; Beneš, Bedřich (July 2006). "Autonomous boids". Computer Animation and Virtual Worlds. 17 (3—4): 199—206. doi:10.1002/cav.123.
[5] Min, Hongkyu; Wang, Zhidong (2011). Design and analysis of Group Escape

Boids - Obama Rally Portland May 2008 2015, variable dimensions, eps and uv-print, vinyl

Behavior for distributed autonomous mobile

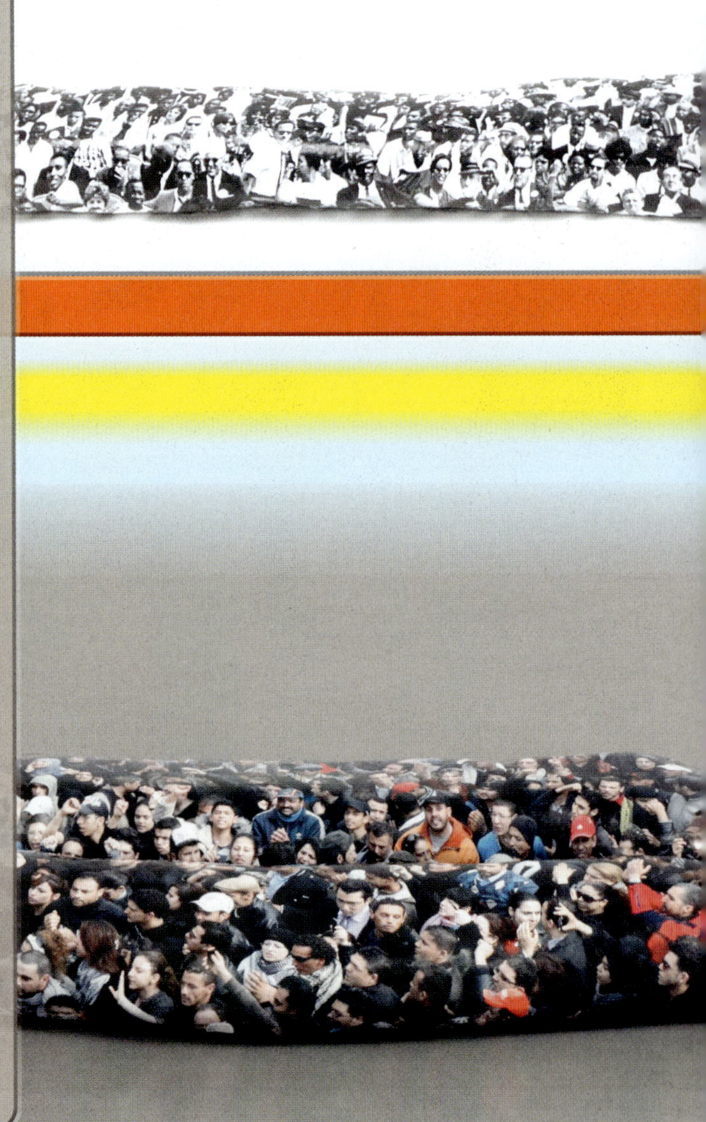

However, the relationship between us is dried out by your attempts to seal the weak body and protect it from unwanted in ltration. You never get wet.
The hypochondriac, who once obsessed with the circulation of substances and the functioning of the primary organs, has become a cyberneticist. Complex, emergent systems such as the body, city, and planet become inputs, outputs, and controls. Collective consciousness becomes collective bargaining, preemptively negotiating future climatic con gurations.

*

In the bathhouse, I see myself through your eyes. The wave patterns on the marble oor mimic my movements. The stone is polished to appear liquid. A surface of petri ed water, perfectly contained and controlled. And there you are, performing your self-care cycle of voiding and washing. You are more like a sponge than a marble. In fact, even marbles are a sort of sponge. Your ngertips get wrinkled in water—a relic from an earlier semiaquatic existence, useful for handling wet objects.

*

How do you see my outlines? Do they resemble a coastline, a plumbing system or, perhaps, your own shape? About 60 percent of your shape? Picture my outlines by picturing everything that surrounds me.
Everything meets in contingency, as if everything had a skin. I border with air on a layer of evaporation. With earth in clay and mud, according to the phases of the moon, the breeze, the season, and the syzygies. Coasts are not lines, but dynamic zones of interaction between geophysical, meteorological, vegetable, animal, and human bodies of water.

*

Your body, like a city, depends on my circulation. Likewise, hurricanes need ows of heat and moisture to sustain themselves, which is why they die as they pass over land.

New Degrees of Freedom
I benefit from things in my occupying, without striving.

"The real nightmare, worse than the one in which the Big Machine wants to kill you, is the one in which it sees you as irrelevant, or not even as a discrete thing to know."

Author: Benjamin H. Bratton, Title: The Stack: On Software and Sovereignty, First published: The MIT press, Year: 2015

robots. IEEE International Conference on Robotics and Automation (ICRA).
[6] Saska, Martin; Jan, Vakula; Libor, Preucil (2014). Swarms of micro aerial vehicles stabilized under a visual relative localization. IEEE International Conference on Robotics and Automation (ICRA).
[7] Saska, Martin; Vojtech, Vonasek; Tomas, Krajnik; Libor, Preucil (2012). Coordination and Navigation of Heterogeneous UAVs-UGVs Teams Localized by a Hawk-Eye Approach. IEEE/RSJ International Conference on Intelligent Robots and Systems (IROS).
[8] Lebar Bajec, Iztok; Heppner, Frank H. (2009). "Organized flight in birds" (PDF). Animal Behaviour. pp. 777—789. doi:10.1016/j.anbehav.2009.07.007.
[9] Ibáñez, Jesús; Gómez-Skarmeta, Antonio F.; Blat, Josep (2003). "DJ-boids: emergent collective behavior as multichannel radio station programming". Proceedings of the 8th international conference on Intelligent User Interfaces. pp. 248—250. doi:10.1145/604045.604089.
[10] Moere, A V (2004). "Time-Varying Data Visualization Using Information Flocking Boids". Proceedings of the IEEE Symposium on Information Visualization. pp. 97—104. doi:10.1109/INFVIS.2004.65.
[11] Cui, Zhihua; Shi, Zhongzhi (2009). "Boid particle swarm optimisation". International Journal of Innovative Computing and Applications. 2 (2): 77—85. doi:10.1504/IJICA.2009.031778.

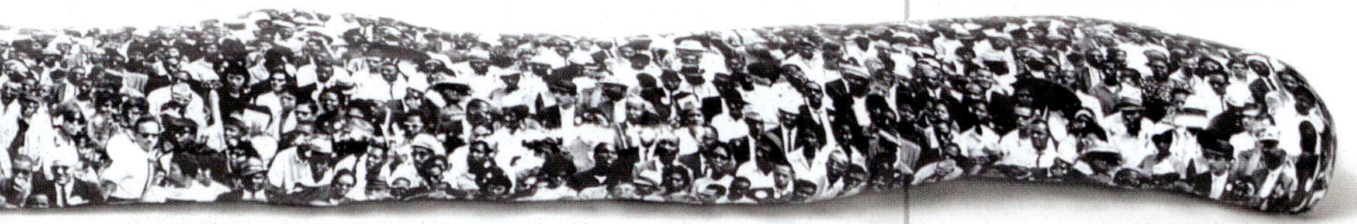

Boids - Martin Luther King Jr. speech in Washington, August 1963

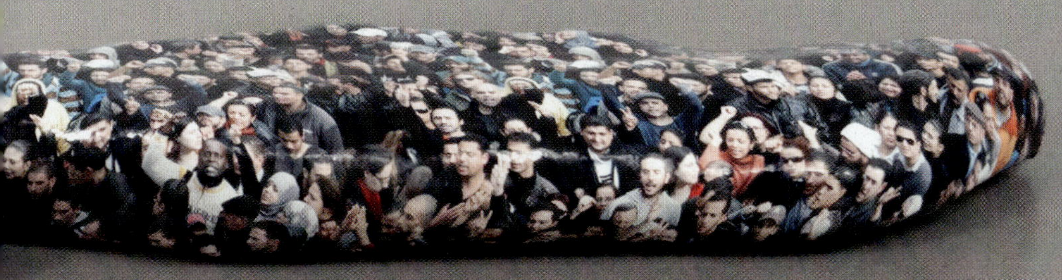

Boids - Tunisia Protest January 2011 2015, variable dimensions, eps and uv-print, vinyl

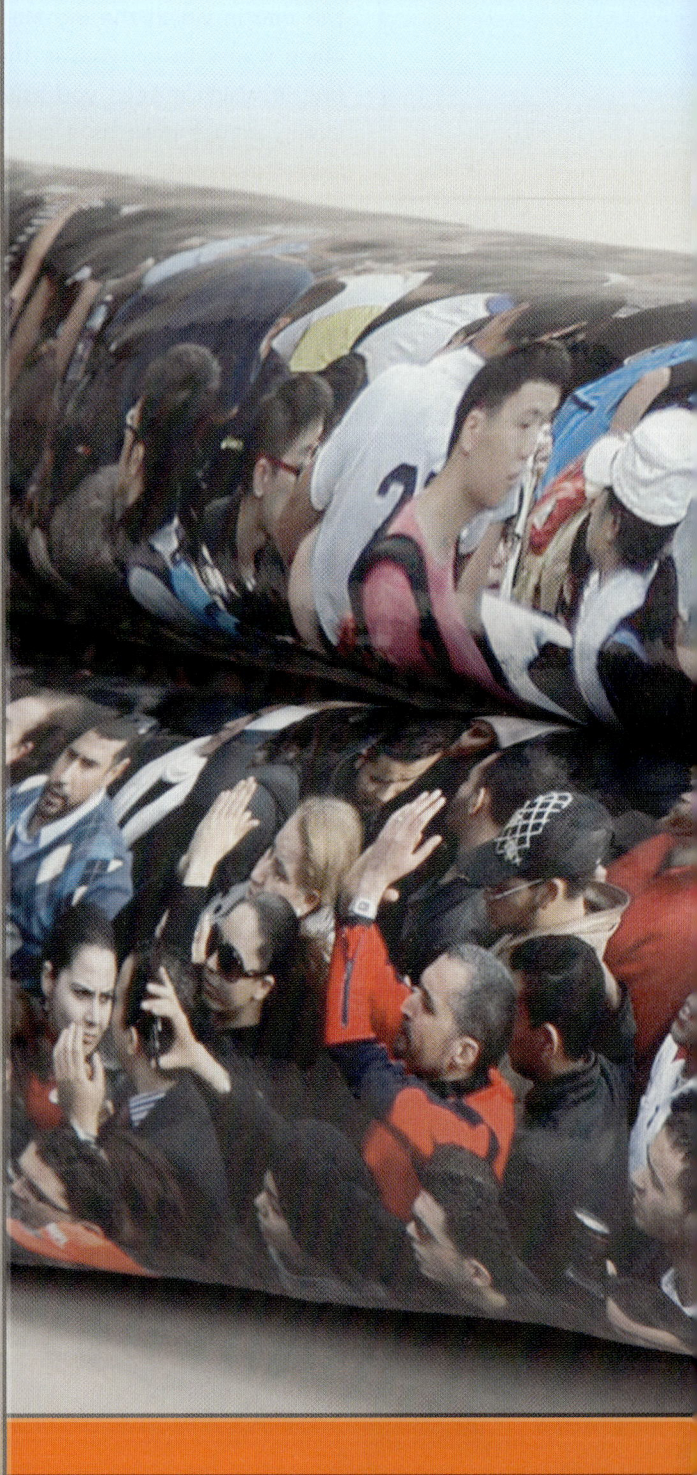

Just as the many waters you ingest have traveled from and through watery bodies (aquifers, rivers, reservoirs, treatment plants), so too do you return them to other bodies of water, albeit in new mixtures: as milk, urine, tears, and breath to babies, sewers, and gardens. Consider me as something unceasingly changing and transforming, less a thing than the trace of a movement, a model out of which everything can be born.

*

Breath in, breathe out.

*

The 48th Law of Power: Assume Formlessness
Be as uid and formless as water; never bet on stability or lasting order. Everything changes.

*

Before atoms and bacteria were discovered, the concept of the body was understood as a system in which different humors existed in a state of relative equilibrium. Made up of earth, air, re, and water, we were an element among the rest—an element in fusion. This idea went hand-in-hand with a belief that the body was porous and subject to penetration by the surrounding elements. Unlike a Cartesian body with well-de ned boundaries, bodies were considered permeable down to their most intimate recesses.
Today, this sense of selfhood is transformed by the recognition that the very substance of the self is interconnected not only with biological but also with economic and industrial systems.

*

Unsure about your place in the universe? Prepare yourself for inhospitable circumstances, such as the cold and compressive world of oceans. Our post-terrestrial out ts, like the wetsuit and the oxygen tank, enable radical detachment from the land.

*

One may loose the feeling of a body boundary, or the body and the self, in skin temperature, salty water; deep freeze; by blowing one's breath into a bubble; or at the borderlands of material and virtual worlds.

Molecules don’t have passports.

Author: Carl Sagan, Title: Cosmos, First published: Random House, Year: 1980

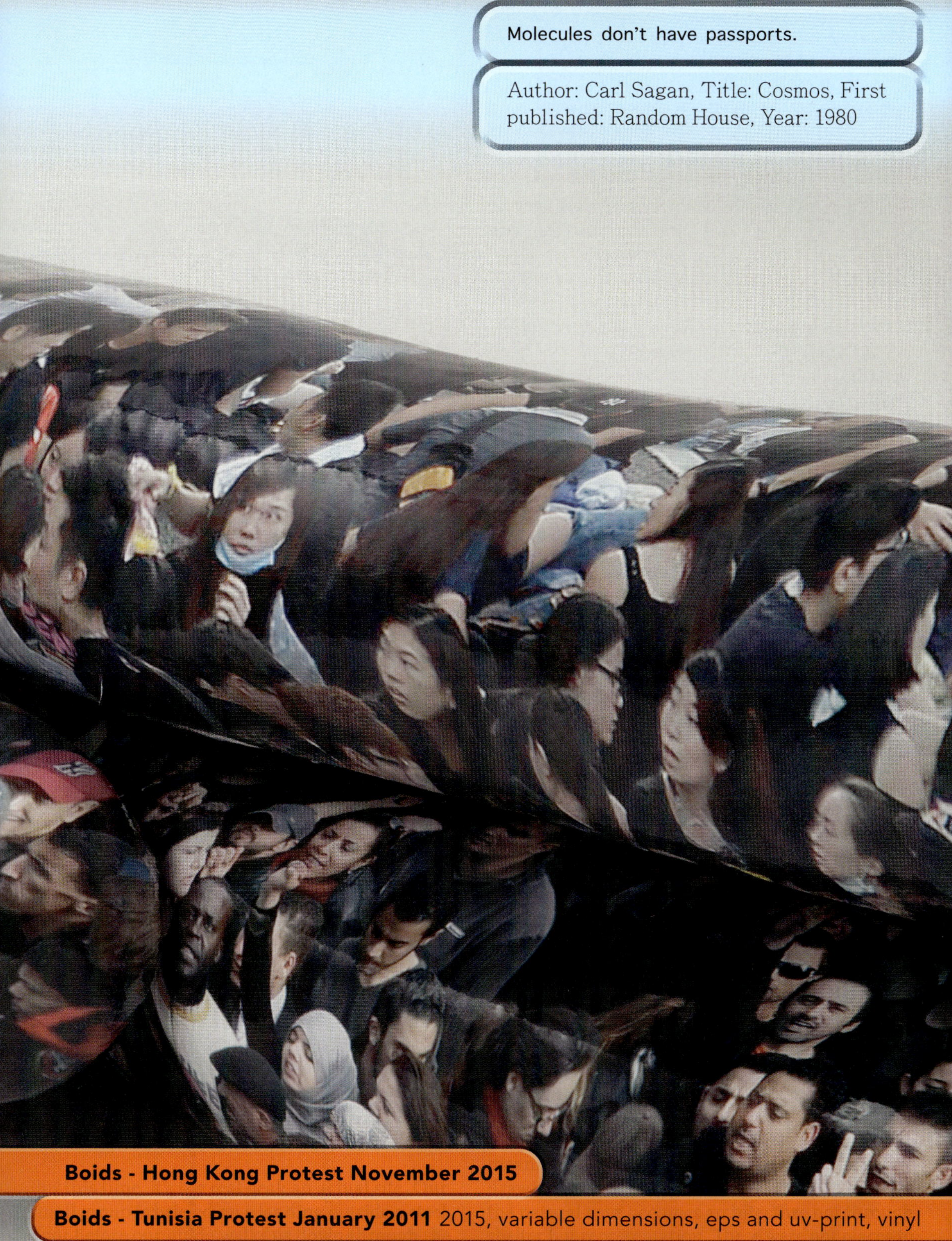

Boids - Hong Kong Protest November 2015

Boids - Tunisia Protest January 2011 2015, variable dimensions, eps and uv-print, vinyl

While sitting on a beach with unlimited bandwidth or residing in international waters to escape state jurisdiction, the lines between the Internet and the ocean also begin to blur. Submarine cables and data clouds provide a landscape for cyber-utopian, water-inspired online culture. Hashtag seapunk, hashtag slimepunk, hashtag icepunk.

*

I am virtual water. You have grown a tail and ns.

*

Splash. You strain against the bounds of your containments and leave a puddle of water behind. It slowly turns into air, ocean, earth, ice, universal territory, rede ning the boundaries of individuality and space. Life is the motion of juices spilling over.
You are no longer a thing—a noun. You seem to be a verb, an evolutionary process—an integral part of an aqueous ecology. Wash and ow. Our foams **never settle.**

Author: Jenna Sutela, Title: New Degrees of Freedom Act 3: Water, First published at newdegreesoffreedom.com, Year: 2014. Referencing: Buckminster Fuller, Robert Greene, Astrida Neimanis, Michel Serr and Gregory Whitehe

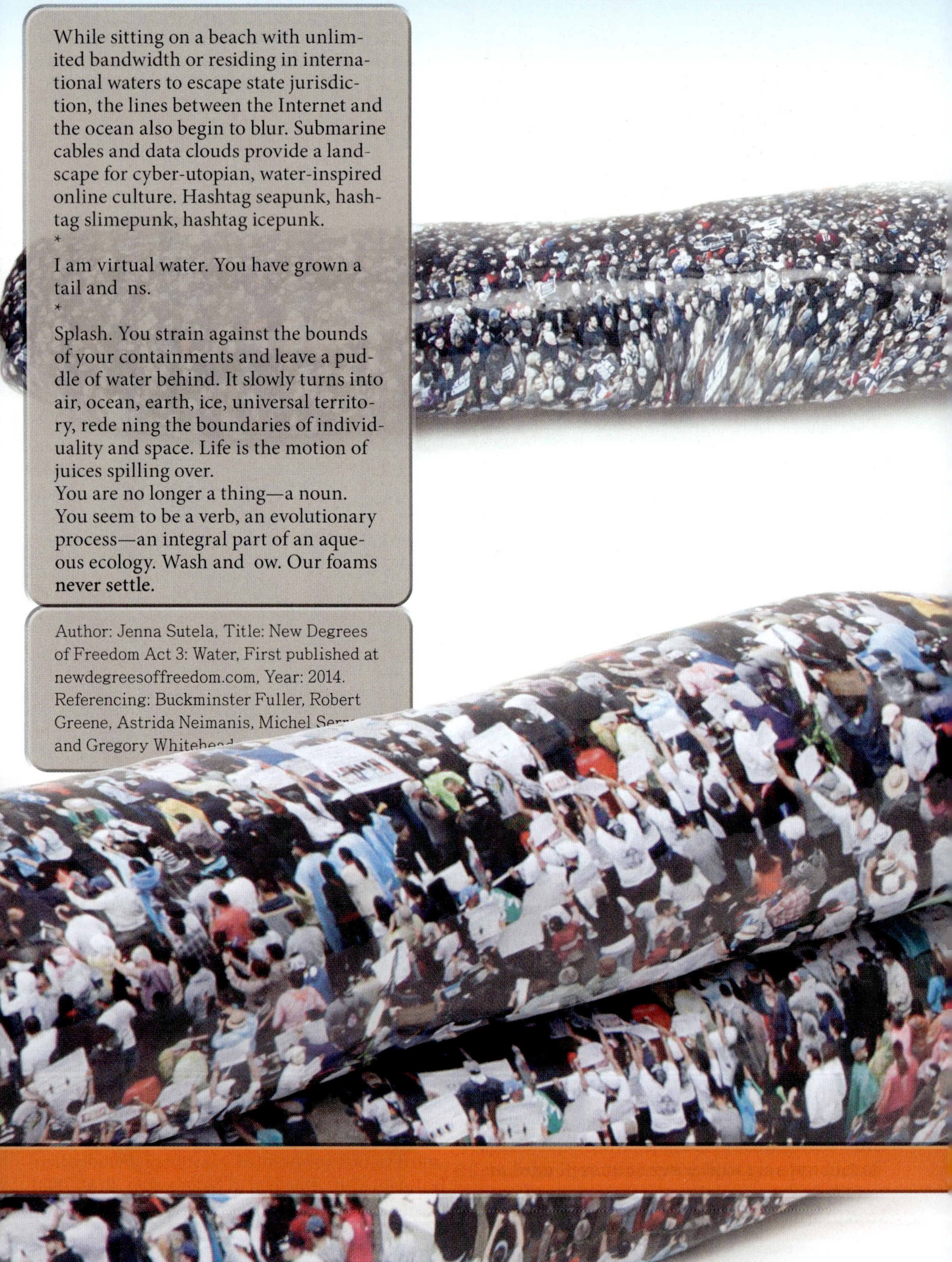

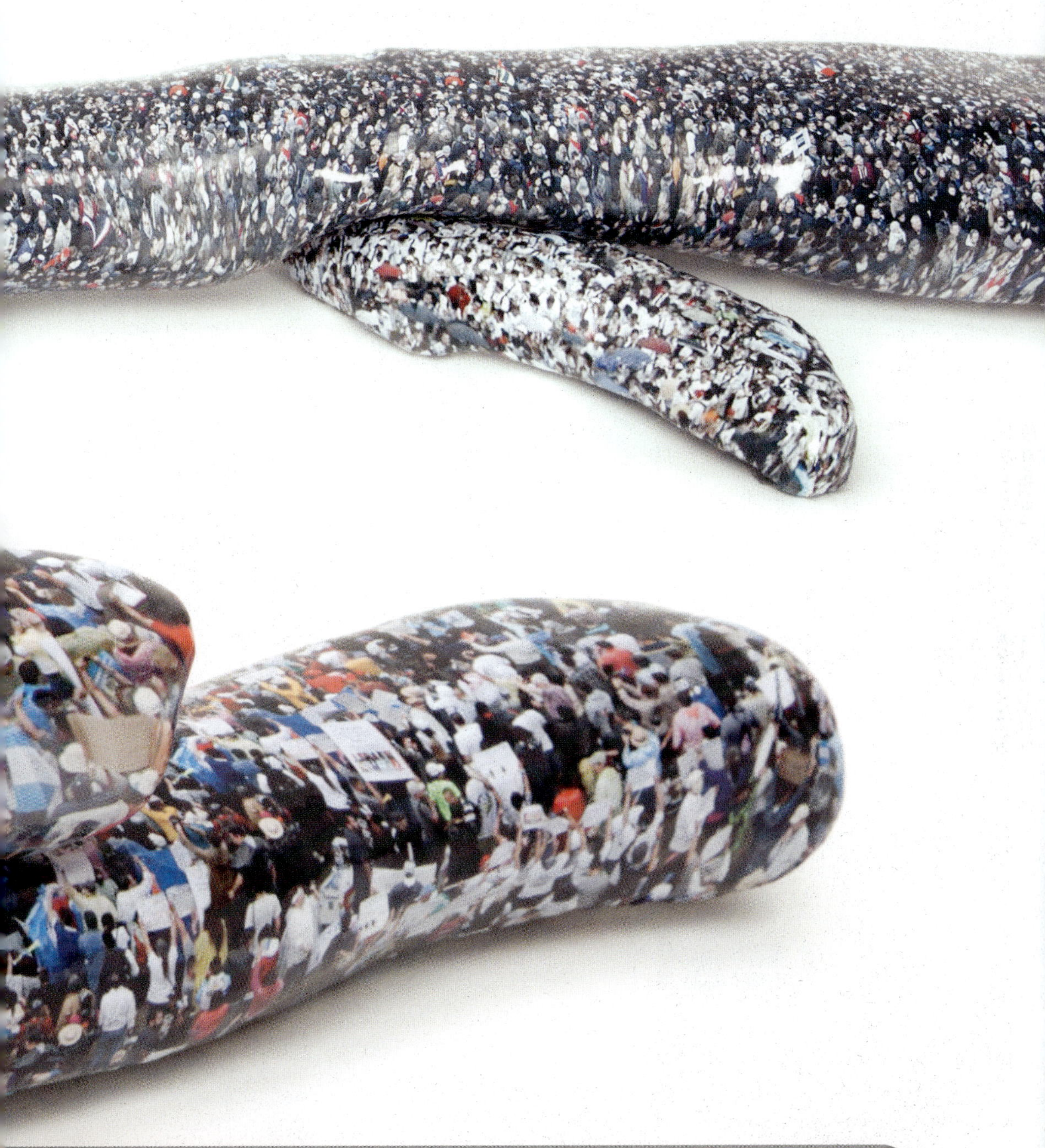

Boids - Je Suis Charlie' March Place de la Republique in Paris January 2015

Boids - Guatemala Rises Up, May 2015 2015, variable dimensions, eps and uv-print, vinyl

SONIC WARFAIR 1929: THROBS OF EXPERIENCE

by Steve Goodmann

To hear this noise as we do, we must hear the parts which make up this whole, that is the noise of each wave, although each of these little noises makes itself known only when combined confusedly with all the others, and would not be noticed if the wave which made it were by itself.
—G. W. Leibniz, New Essays on Human Understanding (1981)

It is interesting to note Whitehead's choice of language in Process and Reality in paraphrasing William James's notion of the "basic drops of experience" or his own concept of an actual occasion or entity.

Whitehead terms an actual occasion or entity a "throb" or "pulse" of experience, a "throb" or "pulse" of feeling, hinting at the role in invention (or creative advance, Whitehead's name for the process of becoming) of the expression of vibration.1

Whitehead's thoughts on rhythm and vibration form an aesthetic ontology of pulses.

To say that Whitehead's ontology is aesthetic means that he posits feeling, or prehension, as a basic condition of experience. For him, even science emerges out of aesthetic experience.2

His ontology revolves around a nonanthropocentric concept of feeling. This notion of prehension exceeds the phenomenological demarcation of the human body as the center of experience and at the same time adds a new inflection to an understanding of the feelings, sensuous and nonsensuous, concrete and abstract, of such entities.

To feel a thing is to be affected by that thing. The mode of affection, or the way the "prehensor" is changed, is the very content of what it feels. Every event in the universe is in this sense an episode of feeling, 96 Chapter 18 even in the void.

Whitehead sets up "a hierarchy of categories of feeling," from the "wave-lengths and vibrations" of subatomic physics to the subtleties of human experience.3
Crucially however, the hierarchy does not imply the dominance of conscious over nonconscious vibrations. At every scale, events are felt and processed as modes of feeling before they are cognized and categorized in schemas of knowledge. It is this complex emphasis on the primacy of prehension that makes his ontology aesthetic.

In his 'Enquiry Concerning the Principles of Natural Knowledge' from 1919, Whitehead lays out an early version of his own theory of rhythm.

His first rhythmanalytic move is to point out that things that appear static are always composed at the molecular level by vibrating, that is, microrhythmically mobile particles. So he notes,

"The physical object, apparent, is a material object and as such is uniform; but when we turn to the causal components of such an object, the apparent character of the whole situation is thereby superseded by the rhythmic quasi-periodic characters of a multitude of parts which are the situations of molecules."

In Adventures, the seeming simplicity of perception is therefore always shadowed by imperceptible excitation so that "any situation has, as its counterpart in that situation, more complex, subtler rhythms than those whose aggregate is essential for the physical object."4

Later, in Lecture 3 from Religion in the Making, a series of lectures given in 1926, Whitehead, in outlining this aesthetic ontology, notes how the tension between stable, coherent pattern and the level of imperceptible vibration is the engine of invention in providing necessary "contrast":
The consequent must agree with the ground in general type so as to preserve definiteness, but it must contrast with it in respect to contrary instances so as to obtain vividness and quality.
In the physical world, this principle of contrast under an identity expresses itself in the physical law that vibration enters into the ultimate nature of atomic organisms. Vibration is the recurrence of contrast within identity of type. The whole possibility of measurement in the physical world depends on this principle. To measure is to count vibrations. . . . Thus physical quantities are aggregates of physical vibrations, and physical vibrations are the expression among the abstractions of physical science of the fundamental principle of aesthetic experience.5

Unlike Bergson, Whitehead does not indict physics for the method of abstraction, through chopping up the continuity of duration, but instead points to the power of science through this very process of abstraction.

Unlike Bergson, Whitehead makes room for the fact that the science of acoustics, of the quantification of vibration, rather than merely capturing, has also led to the intensification of sonic affect.

In Whitehead's philosophy, the throb of feeling is not perceived by a subject as such but rather

constitutes the actual occasion out of which the distinction between subject and object emerges in a process he terms concrescence.
Concrescence here can be understood as a rhythmic coalescence that results in the actualization of one block of space-time, among many, simultaneously rendering the division between subject and object, time and space of a second order. Moreover, the need to revise the relation between cause and event is reinforced. Instead of a cause producing an effect, effects attain autonomy in the process of the becoming of continuity.

If the primary metaphysical ground is made up, for Bachelard, of instants and, for Bergson, of continuity, then Whitehead has a unique way of reconciling this apparent opposition that he terms the extensive continuum. This extensive continuum constitutes a kind of rhythmic anarchitecture that unites the discreet and the continuous, Bachelard's rhythmic arithmetic with Bergson's rippling waves of intensity.

In contrast to a continuity of becoming in Bergson, a spatiotemporality where the unity of events lies in an underlying continual temporal invariant, a flowing lived duration, Whitehead's notion of the extensive continuum undoes the split between space and time. It expresses a general scheme of relatedness between actual entities in the actual world. More than that, Whitehead insists that the extensive continuum is, above all, a potential for actual relatedness.

The continuum gives potential, while the actual is atomic or quantic by nature.
The continuum is not pregiven but exists only in the spatiotemporal gaps between actual occasions.
Rather than an underlying continual invariant, each actual entity produces the continuum for itself from the angle of its own occurrence. Only in this way is the continuum the means by which occasions are united in one common world. The actual entity breaks up its continuum realizing the eternal object, or particular potential that it selects.

This breaking up, atomization or quantization, forces the eternal object into the space-time of the actual occasion; in other words, as the pure potential of the eternal object ingresses into actuality, it forces the becoming of actuality, and at the same time, pure potential becomes real potential.

Whitehead describes the general potentiality of the continuum as "the bundle of possibilities, mutually consistent or alternative, provided by the multiplicity of eternal objects."

The extensive continuum "is that first determination of order—that is, of real potentiality, arising out of the general character of the world . . . it does not involve shapes, dimensions, or measurability; these are additional determinations of real potentiality arising from our cosmic epoch."6

Arguing against both a continual flow of becoming, governed by unspatialized pure time, and the locality of space-time, Whitehead's extensive continuum points to vibratory potentials jelling a multiplicity of space-times: here there is a resonance of actual occasions, which are able to enter into one another by selecting potentials or eternal objects.

It is in such a potential coalescence of one region with another that an affective encounter between distinct actual entities occurs. The vibratory resonance between actual occasions in their own regions of space-time occurs through the rhythmic potential of eternal objects, which enables the participation of one entity in another. This rhythmic potential exceeds the actual occasion into which it ingresses. To become, an actual entity must be out of phase with itself, self-contrasting; its tendency is to die and become other.

Whitehead, through the concept of the extensive continuum, makes access possible to the achronological nexus outside the split between space and time. This rhythmic anarchitecture is marked by the becoming of continuity that denotes change.

Anarchitecture here indicates a method of composition, an activity of construction, which feeds off the vibratory tension between contrasting occasions. In this sense, the continuum is not pregiven but is a process enacted in the resonance of one pulse of experience with another.

For the theory of sonic warfare, Whitehead's conception of the nexus, re-coded in terms of rhythm, is very productive.
It is rhythm that conjoins the discontinuous entities of matter. This rhythm cannot be reduced to its phenomenological experience.

The prehension of a rhythmic anarchitecture is amodal. Rhythm proper cannot be perceived purely through the five senses but is crucially transensory or even nonsensuous. This is especially true of the rhythm of potential relation that holds a nexus together.
Irrelevant of scale, physical, physiological, or sonic, a nexus is always collective, polyrhythmic, composed of an array of tensile spaces and durations.

Finally, rhythmic mutation would be what Whitehead terms creative advance and entails the futurity of a nexus anticipated in its passing present.

[1] Alfred North Whitehead, Process and Reality (New York: Macmillan, 1929), p. 290
[2] This is a perspective that mathematicians such as Gregory Chaitin would certainly adhere to when they describe their work as "sensual mathematics."
[3] Alfred North Whitehead, Adventures of Ideas (New York: Penguin, (1942), pp. 163,166.
[4]. Ibid., p. 197.
Notes:
[5] Alfred North Whitehead, Religion in the Making (New York: Fordham University Press, (1996).
[6] Whitehead, Process and Reality, pp. 102, 103.

Author: Steve Goodman, Title: Sonic Warfair: 1929: Throbs of Experience, Chapter: 18, Page: 95, First published by: The MIT Press, Cambridge, Massachusetts, London, Year: 2010.

TRANSFORMATION THROUGH DEPOLITICIZATION

by Anne de Vries

When house music first emerged out of disco and soul in the 1980s, its message was remarkably different from that of the prevailing egocentric star-driven pop. With the advent of house, the black and queer community sought to empower and uplift itself, making that communal ethos a central feature of its music. When we listen to early house tracks we recognize vocals inspired by gospel, from which the themes of peace, love, unity and respect — or P.L.U.R. (a shorthand for the raver movement's ethos) — derive.

As the music culture itself evolved, some of these ideas developed and adapted to different social and political conditions around the world. Several movements to which house music was connected were explicit about being more than simply dance parties: they articulated the will for social change, such as we see in early manifestos from labels and collectives like Underground Resistance (from Detroit Michigan, active since 1989) or Spiral Tribe (South England, active since 1990), the driving force in the Free Tekno movement. The Free Tekno movement married acid techno culture with squatter ideology, utilizing practical open spaces for the purposes of noncommercial parties. They created temporary autonomous zones (T.A.Z.) [Christiana Breinl, Free Tekno, Berlin: Lit Verlag, 2012] using squatters' procedures to keep law enforcement outside the spaces where the parties took place. This allowed for an "anything goes" policy inside; thus visitors could use drugs freely and noise levels were illegally high. Yet as much as this was a politically charged development, the music itself did not call for change directly.

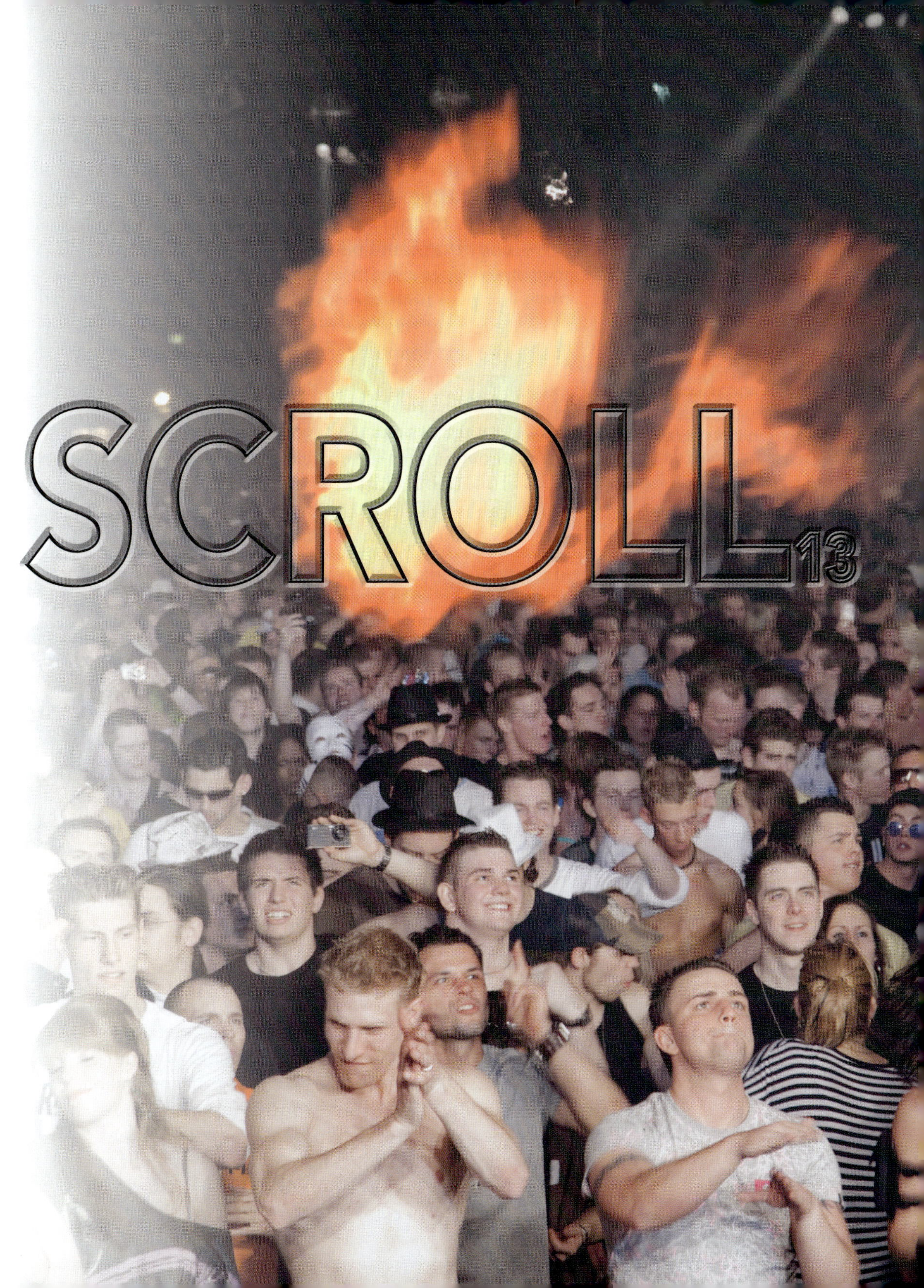
SCROLL 13

AI GPT-2 RESPONSE

In 2009 the BBC reported how The New Culture had lost two of their most brilliant members and then turned on their audience by broadcasting the disturbing news. While not quite as much as his "psychedelic" phase, this demise seemed to suggest that the Culture was losing its sense of purpose and could no longer sustain itself as a creative force.
As a result, the Culture sought to turn the tide and re-shape the way it performs music, both in America and internationally. You may have heard there's a thing called 'post-industrial music,' but when it was being released, There was no time for what they considered to be the 'post-industrial world' in which the world could exist before you had that first 'post-modern world. except for the people playing 'post-modern music.' If you put a little newness in it, it will make you a good baby, and you will fall asleep. You say, 'oh, it's so exciting, it's fantastic. it's a great way to sleep at night.'
I've heard that the 'post-industrial era' is talking about many things, other than the way that modernity has produced an artificial, sterile, and sterile world. It is vast and un-sensible.
I Have a New Perspective.

AI GPT-2 RESPONSE

The sound of "tekno," without vocals or melody, presented itself as a kind of anti-music, refusing to entertain and inducing a somewhat mind-numbing effect. Its main function seemed to be to restructure temporary shared space: it attracted a crowd — similar to how a wall serves to do the opposite — creating a social body that could behave outside the law.

Yet over time, the groundbreaking, ecstatic revelry of this new movement was transformed into and coopted by conformist, commercialized mass culture. One specific example is the history of the Love Parade in Berlin, which showed that partying and a few neat slogans were not enough to make substantive change. ["Party, Love and Profit: The Rhythms of the Love Parade," Wolfgang Sterneck in conversation with Graham St John, dj.dancecult.net, 2010]

In June 24, 2015, I went to the biggest Hard-Style dance event in the world: Defqon.1, in Biddinghuizen, the Netherlands. This particular music scene evolved out of the harder styles of dance music at the turn of the new millennium. Although the music is too "hard" to be mainstream, it was clear that I was in the hands of the professional entertainment industry, which made use of the most advanced audio and visual effects, pulling every commercially palatable trick to entertain the huge crowds. What was once an extension of the subversive gabber subculture of the 1990s has become a safe, secure and streamlined event that plays host to eighty thousand visitors in a state of ecstasy.

Every once in a while the heavy beat would break- down and an extremely vocoderized voice would make pronouncements in totalitarian fashion to the mass audience, often demanding that they instantly open their minds to reach their full potential, to transcend, or to enter altered states of consciousness. These lyrics functioned as intermezzos fueling the build up to musical ecstasy.

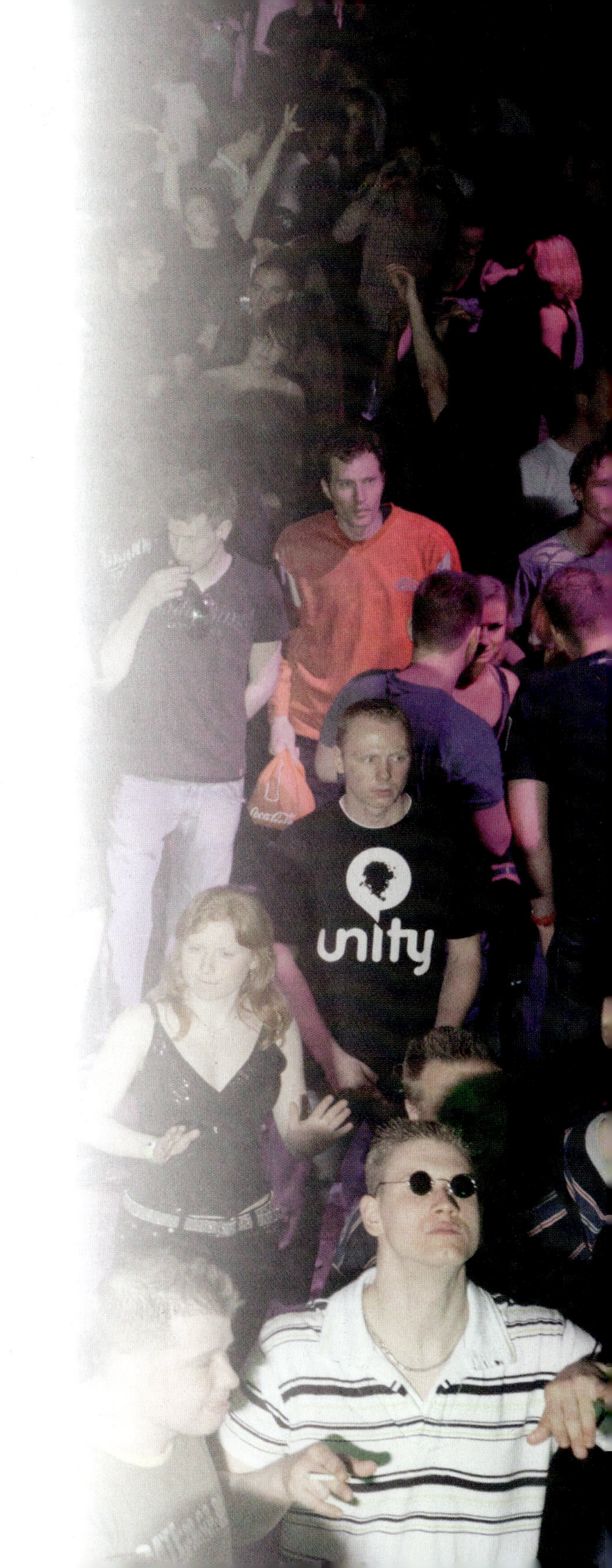
unity

During these moments the whole event could be understood as an attempt to lead the audience into an- other state of mind — into a state of transformation that is as opposed to the regular "outside world" as possible.

Being in this enormous mass, one sensed how it had the potentiality to change our future — if it wanted to, and if it were focused on a common goal. But the narrative elements imposed by the disembodied voice mostly stayed away from real-world problems; what "real-world" issues it touched on were about (personal or individual) empowerment rather than entertainment, always aimed toward the same dramatic musical climax. Given Adorno's warnings about this dangerous combination of popular music and mass culture, I was curious to see how writing that wants to shift our perception, — to transform the current world, can play out within this kind of spectacle — to see if it was possible to mobilize written thought within this emotionally charged music format.

As soon as the bass line and the beat drops, it is hard to keep a critical distance from the lyrics; the music produces an artificial sentiment of consensus, what to me celebrates a sense of freedom that Adorno called "pseudo-individuation." [Theodor Adorno, Studies in Philosophy and Social Science, New York: Institute of Social Research, 1941, IX, p. 25] "By pseudo-individuation we mean endowing cultural mass production with the halo of free choice or open market [sic] on the basis of standardization itself. Standardization of song hits keeps the customers in line, doing their thinking for them, as it were. Pseudo-individuation, for its part, keeps them in line by making them forget that what they listen to is wholly intended for them or predigested."

After we first made the video Critical Mass: Pure Immanence (2015) with the help of Q-Dance,

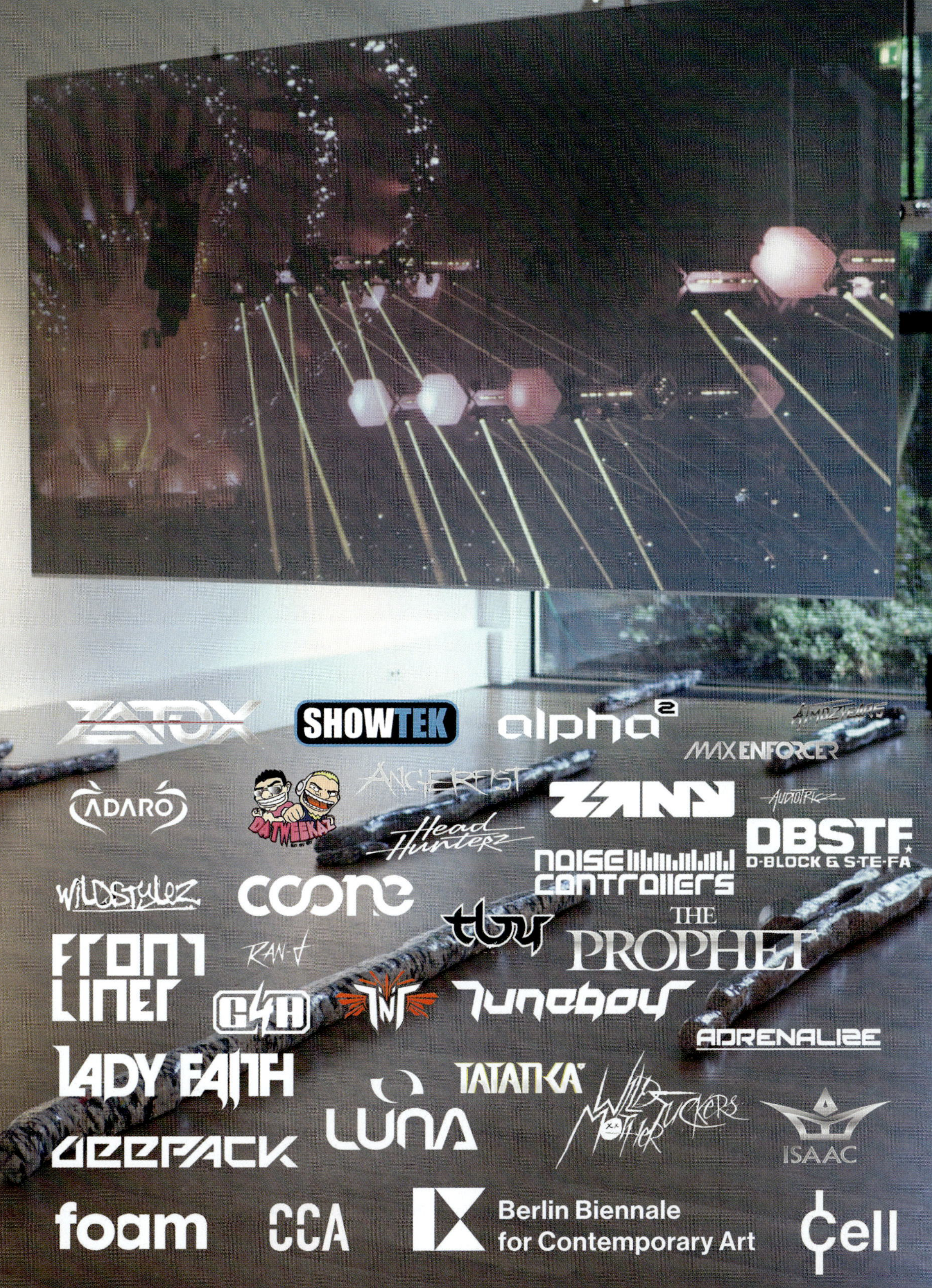
SHOWTEK
alpha²
MAX ENFORCER
ADARO
DA TWEEKAZ
ANGERFIST
ZANY
Head Hunterz
DBSTF
D-BLOCK & S-TE-FA
NOISE CONTROLLERS
WILDSTYLEZ
coone
THE PROPHET
FRONT LINER
RAN-D
Tuneboy
ADRENALIZE
LADY FAITH
TATANKA
LUNA
DEEPACK
ISAAC
foam
CCA
Berlin Biennale for Contemporary Art
Cell

WELCOME TO OMNI SPHERE.

CRITICAL MASS

Title: Omni Sphere, Lyrics for video 'Critical Mass : Pure Immanence' by Anne de Vries, Year 2015, adapted from: [1] Pure Immanence : Essays on A Life, Author: Gilles Deleuze, Year: 1995. [2] The Source code of Creation, Author: Noisecontrollers Year: 2014. [3] Digital Nation: In my House, Authors: Technoboy, Tuneboy & Isaac, Year: 2014

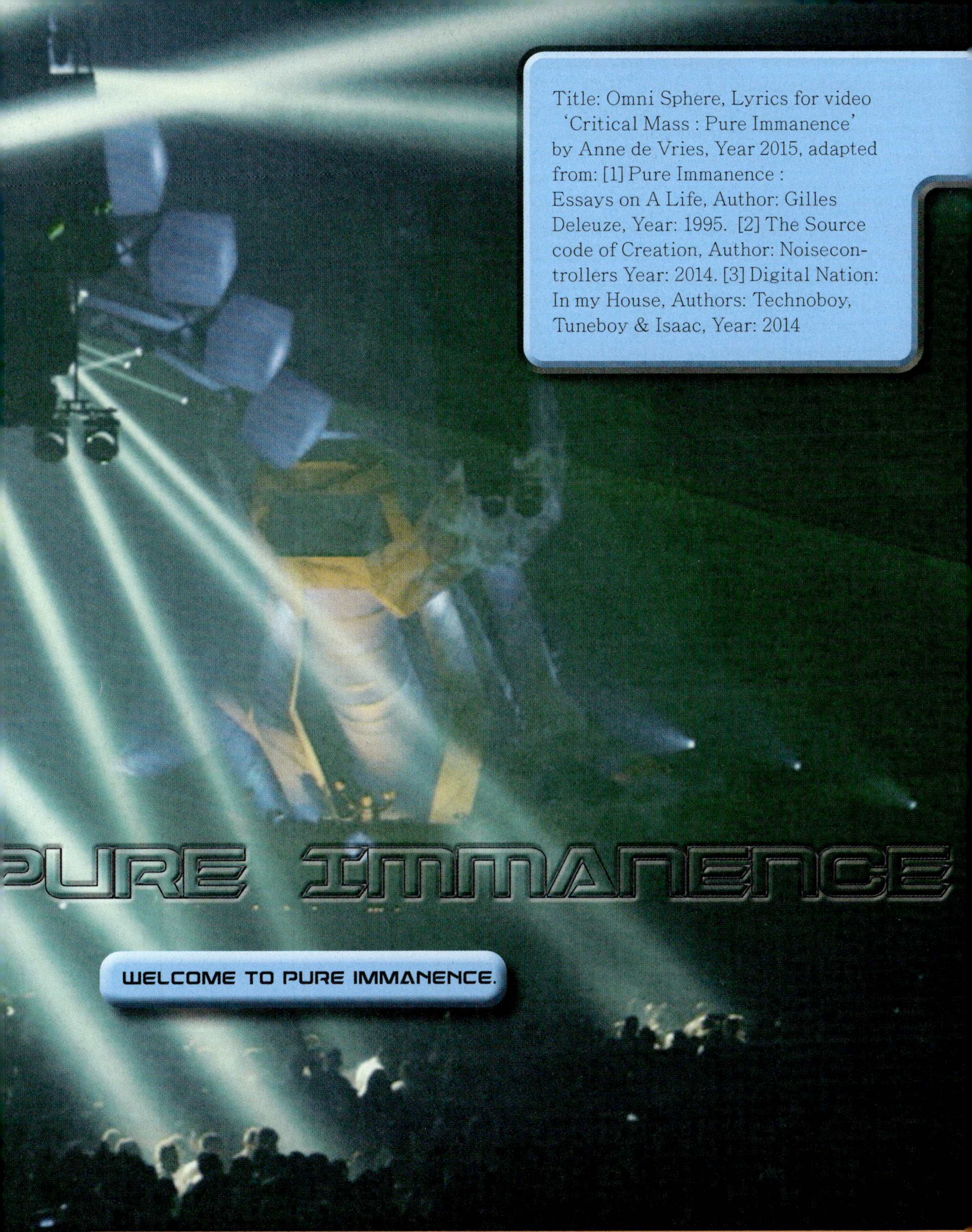

PURE IMMANENCE

WELCOME TO PURE IMMANENCE.

Critical Mass : Pure Immanence 2015, 11 min, 1920x1080

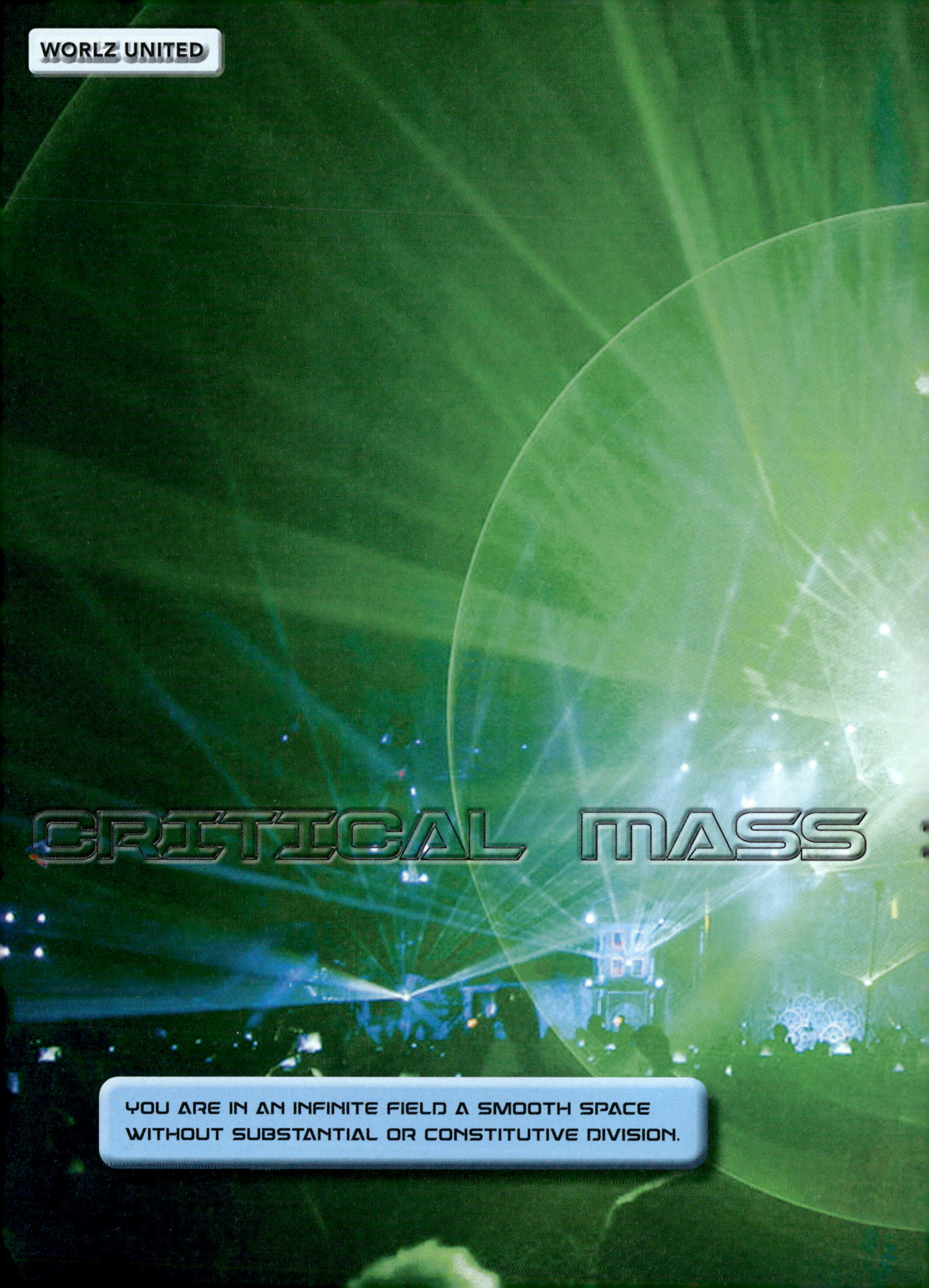

CRITICAL MASS :

YOU ARE IN AN INFINITE FIELD A SMOOTH SPACE
WITHOUT SUBSTANTIAL OR CONSTITUTIVE DIVISION.

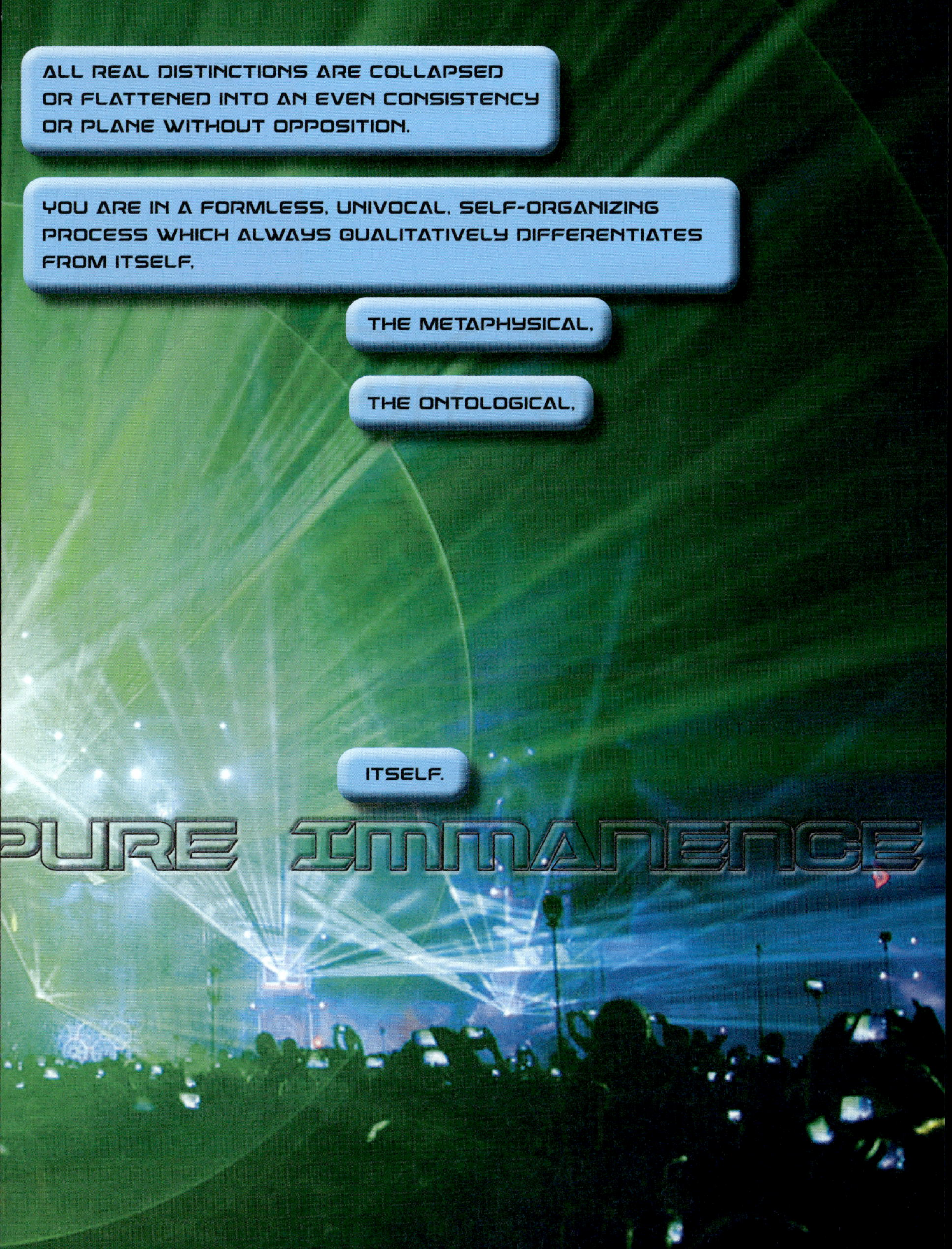

ALL REAL DISTINCTIONS ARE COLLAPSED OR FLATTENED INTO AN EVEN CONSISTENCY OR PLANE WITHOUT OPPOSITION.

YOU ARE IN A FORMLESS, UNIVOCAL, SELF-ORGANIZING PROCESS WHICH ALWAYS QUALITATIVELY DIFFERENTIATES FROM ITSELF,

THE METAPHYSICAL,

THE ONTOLOGICAL,

ITSELF.

PURE IMMANENCE

WORLZ UNITED

WELCOME TO OMNI SPHERE.

WELCOME TO PURE IMMANENCE

THIS IS PURE LIFE.

PARTICLES,

CONNECTIONS,

RELATIONS,

AFFECTS

AND BECOMINGS

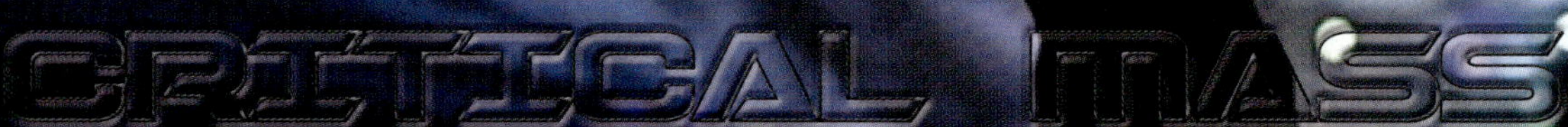

REST.

SLOWNESS.

AND SPEED.

YOU SEE CONSISTENCY AND COMPOSITION BETWEEN ELEMENTS,

MOLECULES,

AND PARTICLES OF ALL KINDS.

ALL WE CAN SEE IS COMPLEX NETWORKS OF FORCES.

ALL WE SEE IS RELATIONS OF MOVEMENT.

LONGITUDES,

PURE IMMANENCE

LATITUDES, AND HAECCEITIES.

THIS IS PURE LIFE.

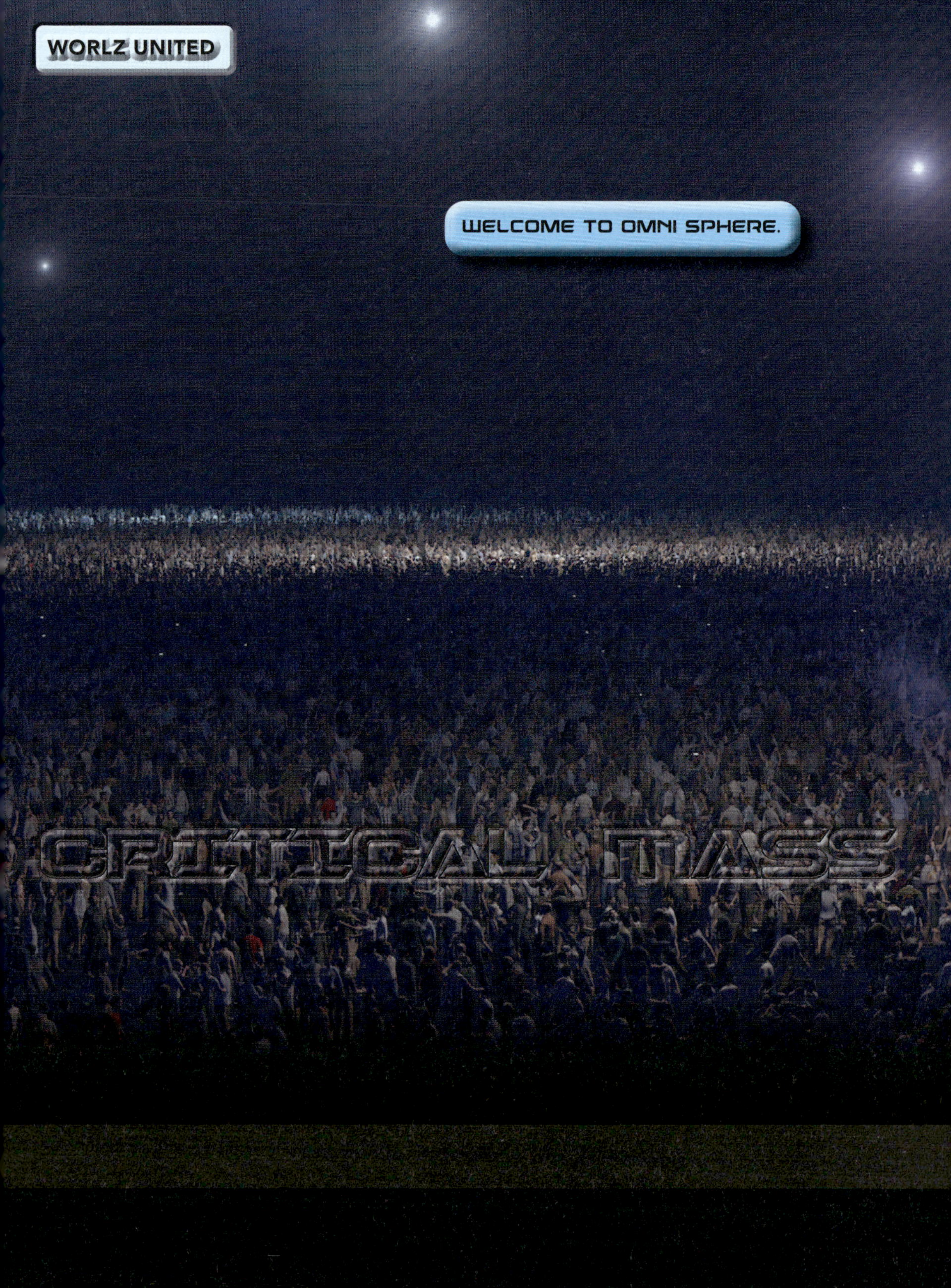
WORLZ UNITED
WELCOME TO OMNI SPHERE.
CRITICAL MASS

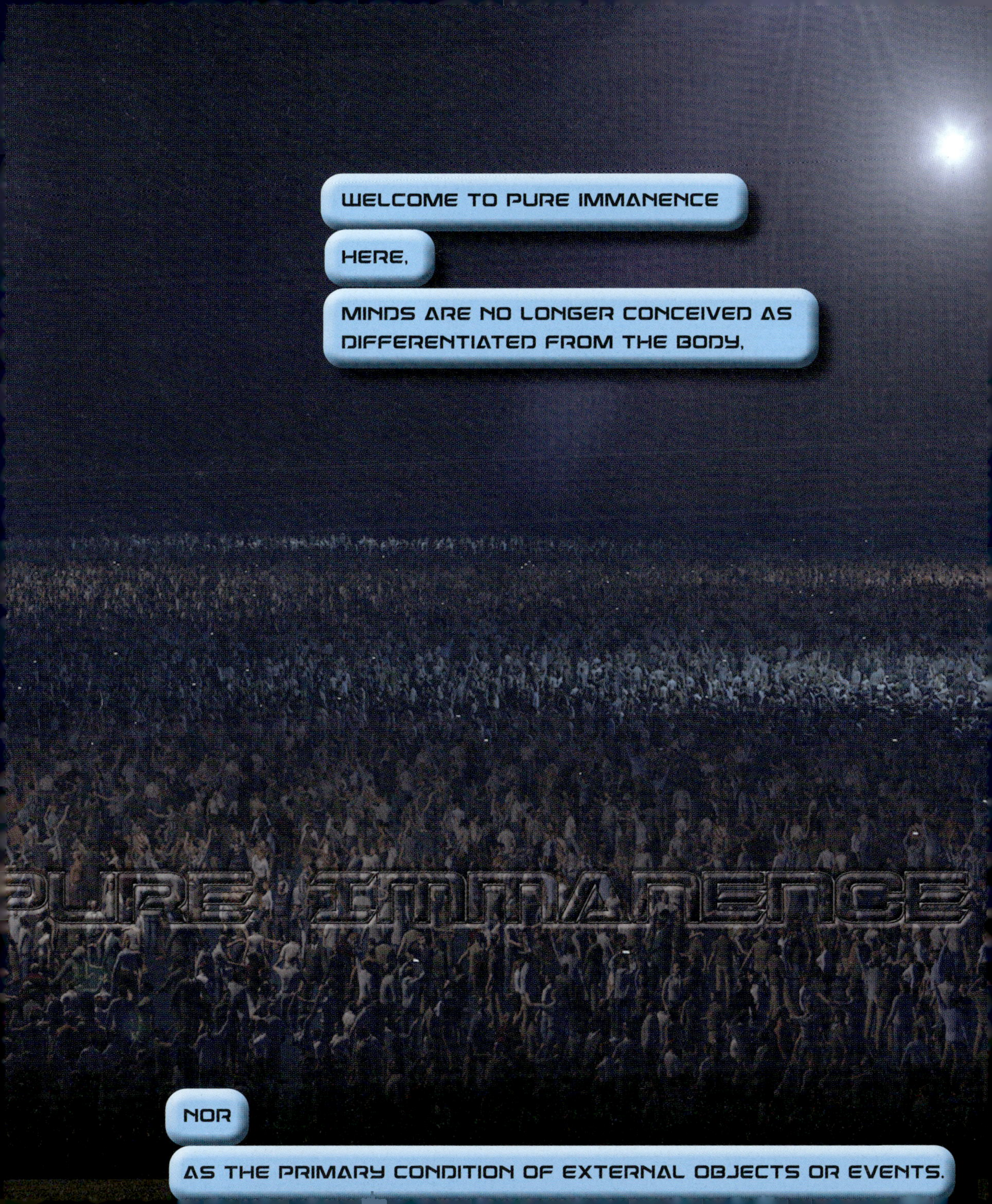

WELCOME TO PURE IMMANENCE

HERE,

MINDS ARE NO LONGER CONCEIVED AS DIFFERENTIATED FROM THE BODY,

PURE IMMANENCE

NOR

AS THE PRIMARY CONDITION OF EXTERNAL OBJECTS OR EVENTS.

HERE,

THERE ARE NO LONGER ANY FORMS OR DEVELOPMENTS OF FORMS;

NOR ARE THERE SUBJECTS

OR THE FORMATION OF SUBJECTS.

THERE IS NO STRUCTURE MORE THAN THERE IS GENESIS.

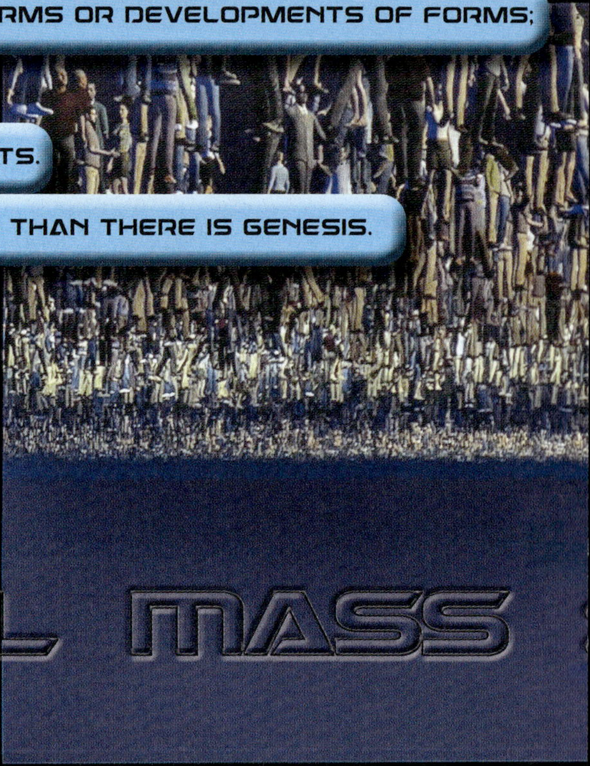

RITICAL MASS

HERE,

THERE IS NO SOMETHING, TO SOMETHING;

IT DOES NOT DEPEND ON AN OBJECT

OR BELONG TO A SUBJECT.

HERE,

THERE IS ONLY SUBJECTLESS INDIVIDUATIONS

THAT CONSTITUTE COLLECTIVE ASSEMBLAGES

PURE IMMANENCE

SUBSTANCE AND MODELS ARE IN IMMANENCE.

CONNECT, ALIGN AND AWAKEN

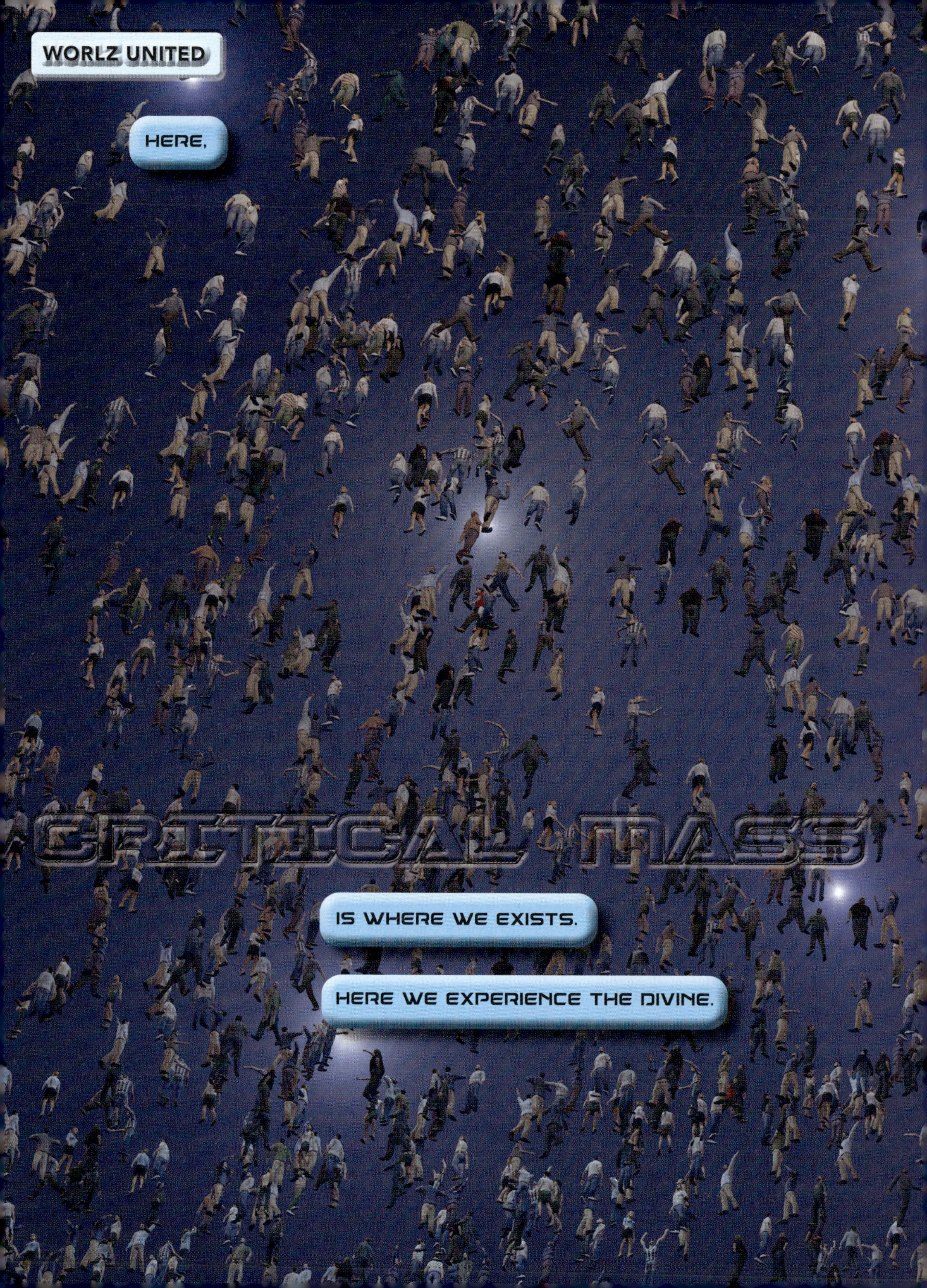
WORLZ UNITED
HERE,
CRITICAL MASS
IS WHERE WE EXISTS.
HERE WE EXPERIENCE THE DIVINE.

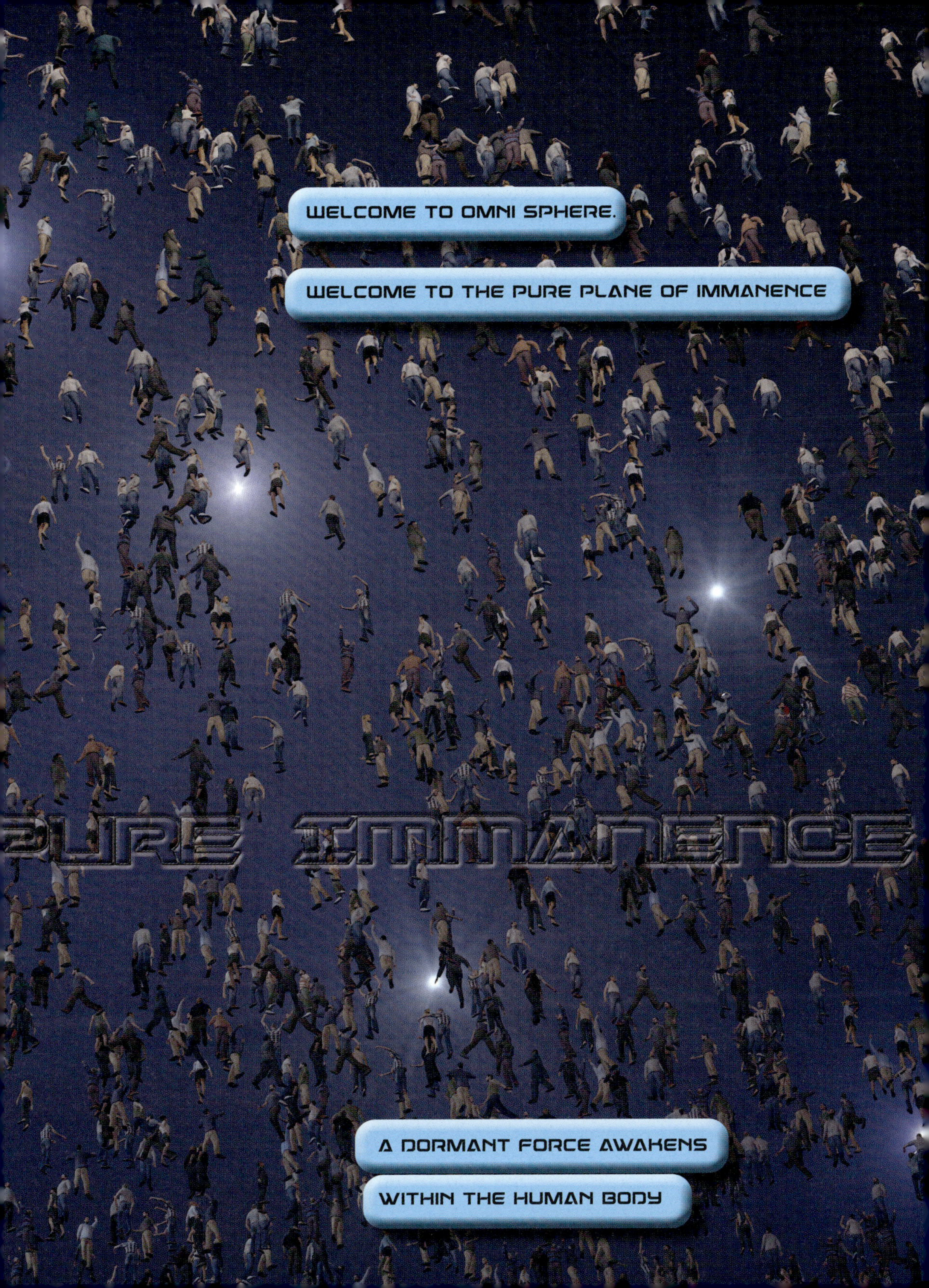
WELCOME TO OMNI SPHERE.
WELCOME TO THE PURE PLANE OF IMMANENCE
PURE IMMANENCE
A DORMANT FORCE AWAKENS
WITHIN THE HUMAN BODY

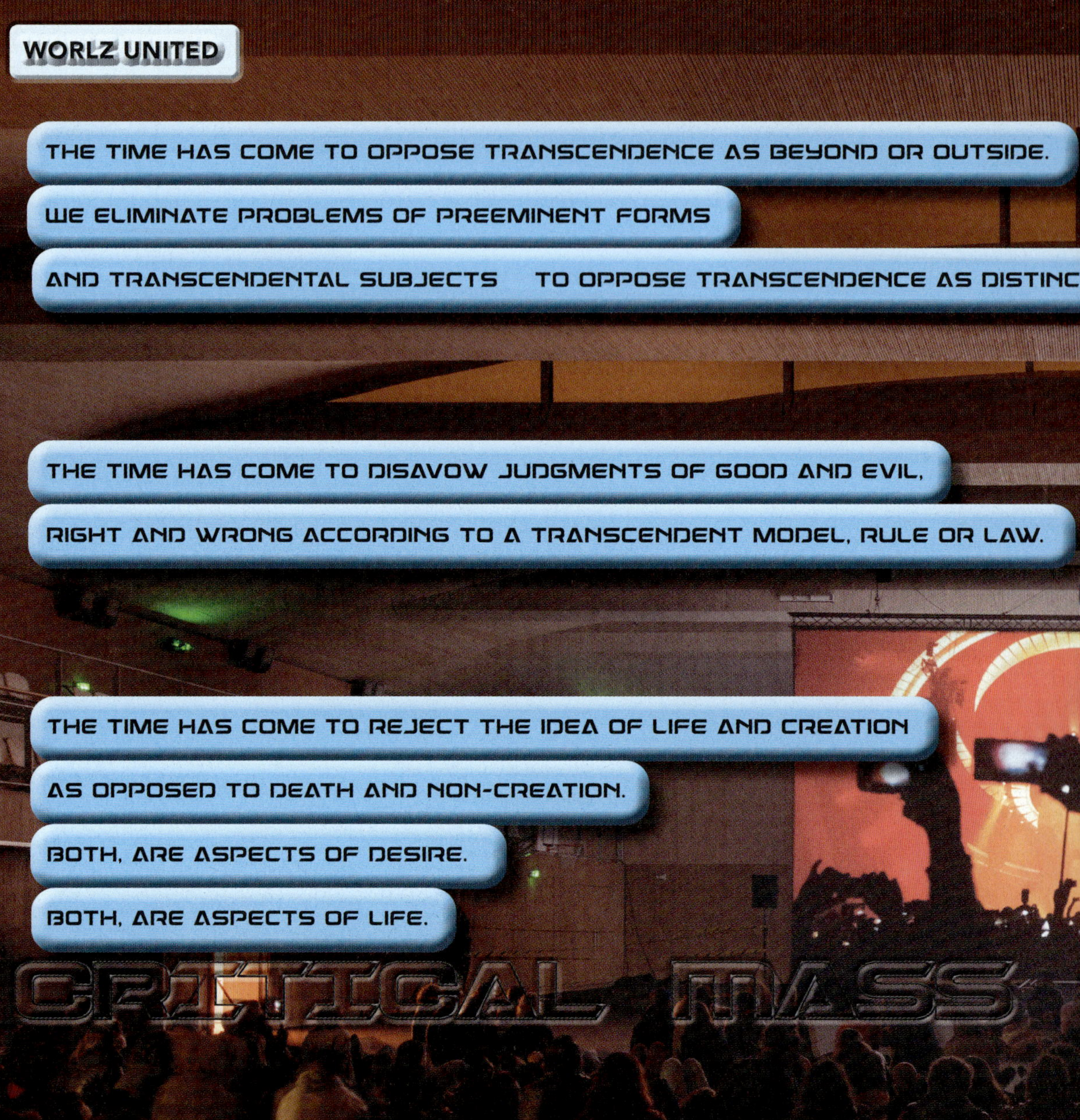
WORLZ UNITED
THE TIME HAS COME TO OPPOSE TRANSCENDENCE AS BEYOND OR OUTSIDE.
WE ELIMINATE PROBLEMS OF PREEMINENT FORMS
AND TRANSCENDENTAL SUBJECTS TO OPPOSE TRANSCENDENCE AS DISTINC
THE TIME HAS COME TO DISAVOW JUDGMENTS OF GOOD AND EVIL,
RIGHT AND WRONG ACCORDING TO A TRANSCENDENT MODEL, RULE OR LAW.
THE TIME HAS COME TO REJECT THE IDEA OF LIFE AND CREATION
AS OPPOSED TO DEATH AND NON-CREATION.
BOTH, ARE ASPECTS OF DESIRE.
BOTH, ARE ASPECTS OF LIFE.
CRITICAL MASS

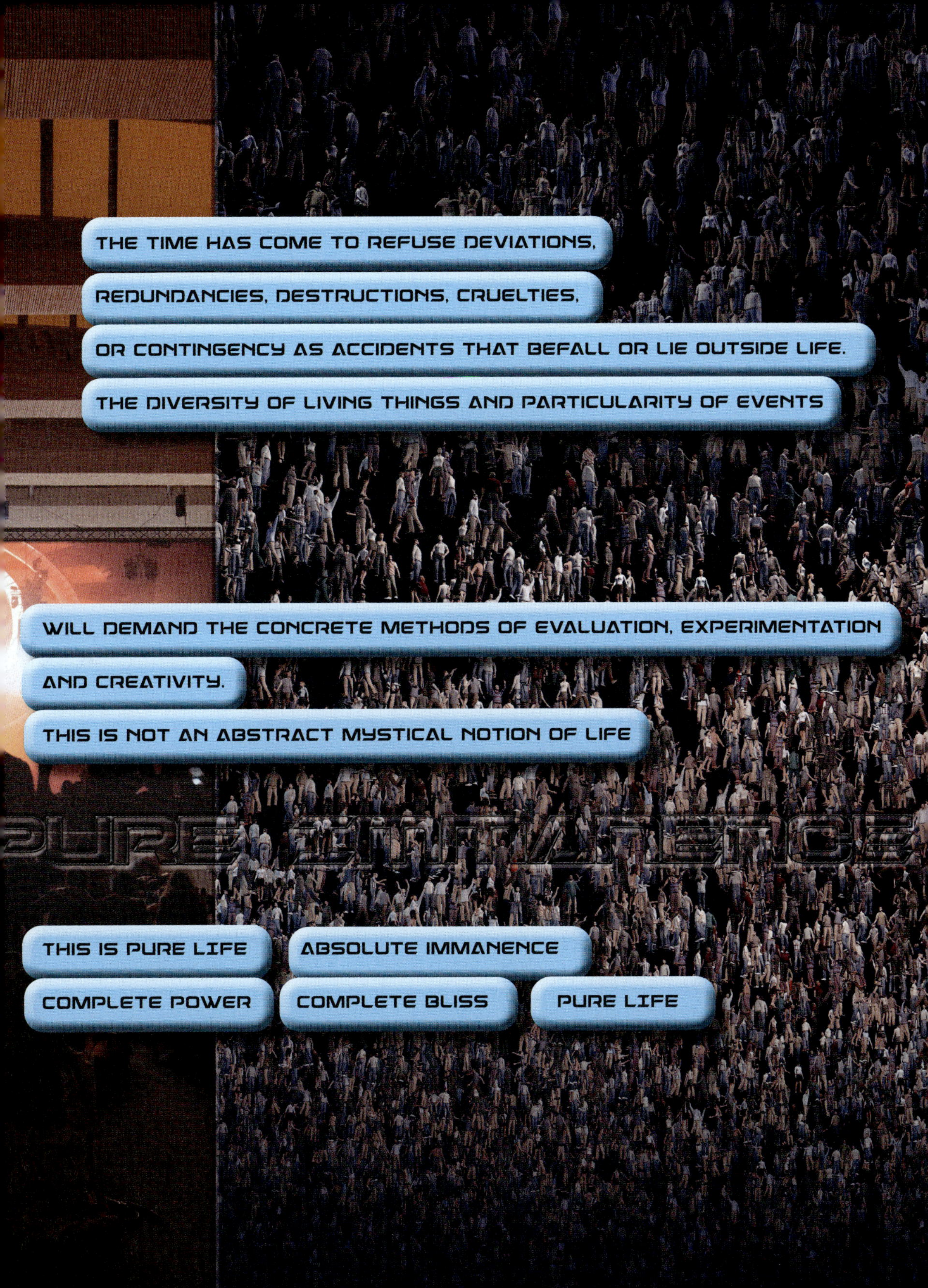
THE TIME HAS COME TO REFUSE DEVIATIONS,
REDUNDANCIES, DESTRUCTIONS, CRUELTIES,
OR CONTINGENCY AS ACCIDENTS THAT BEFALL OR LIE OUTSIDE LIFE.
THE DIVERSITY OF LIVING THINGS AND PARTICULARITY OF EVENTS
WILL DEMAND THE CONCRETE METHODS OF EVALUATION, EXPERIMENTATION
AND CREATIVITY.
THIS IS NOT AN ABSTRACT MYSTICAL NOTION OF LIFE
PURE IMMANENCE
THIS IS PURE LIFE
ABSOLUTE IMMANENCE
COMPLETE POWER
COMPLETE BLISS
PURE LIFE

which deals with similar subject matter. We then approached several writers and music producers to collaborate on a project to bring writing that calls for philosophical transforma- tion into the format of these events. After attempting different things, we decided to rework existing essays into the lyrical manner of HardStyle vocals to be inter- spersed with the music. To present these rewritten texts, I staged a miniature, open-air HardStyle event titled Oblivion (2016) in a diorama with a fully functional miniature stage with a sound system and light show, which included an advertising campaign on billboards and an infrastructure built around it.

One text drew from the XenoFeminism manifesto by Laboria Cuboniks (laboriacuboniks.net), which counters essentialist naturalism and an idealized understanding of the natural, and rejects prefixed roles or meaning. It is a call to action to adjust nature where it is unjust.

Another text rewrites the lecture "Human Thought at Earth Magnitude" by Timothy Morton (held at "Dark Ecology 2014," Sonic Acts, Amsterdam). Here we are taken to "Earth Magnitude" where human thought is as expansive as the celestial aurora. When we scale up to earth magnitude, we enter a realm of thought where all binary distinctions collapse: conscious and unconscious, living and nonliving, individual and group — all these differences dissolve. This text, which deals with distance and scale, was in the back of my head while working on the diorama, which obviously also offers an overview while flying "high" over an intense and immersive event.

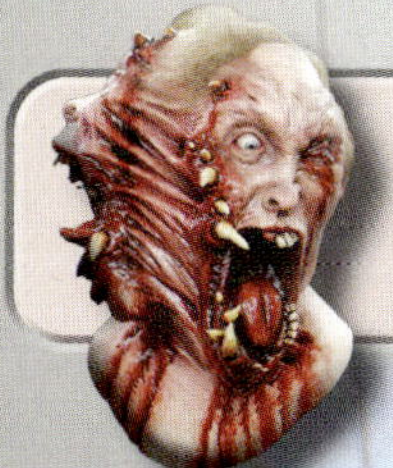

BORN WITHOUT PREFIXED FORM

BORN WITHOUT PREFIXED NORM

WE REALISE THAT THE GLORIFICATION OF
IDEALIZED NATURE HAS NOTHING TO OFFER US

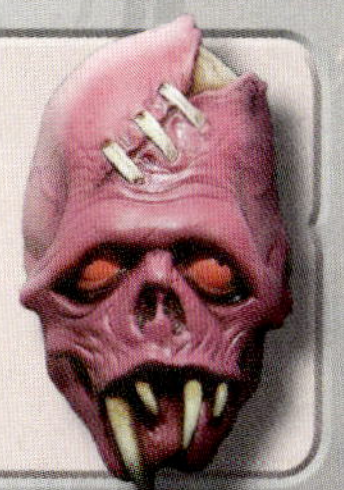

SCROLL 14

YOU CAN CALL IT QUEER
YOU CAN CALL IT TRANS OR
YOU CAN CALL IT
DIFFERENTLY ABLED

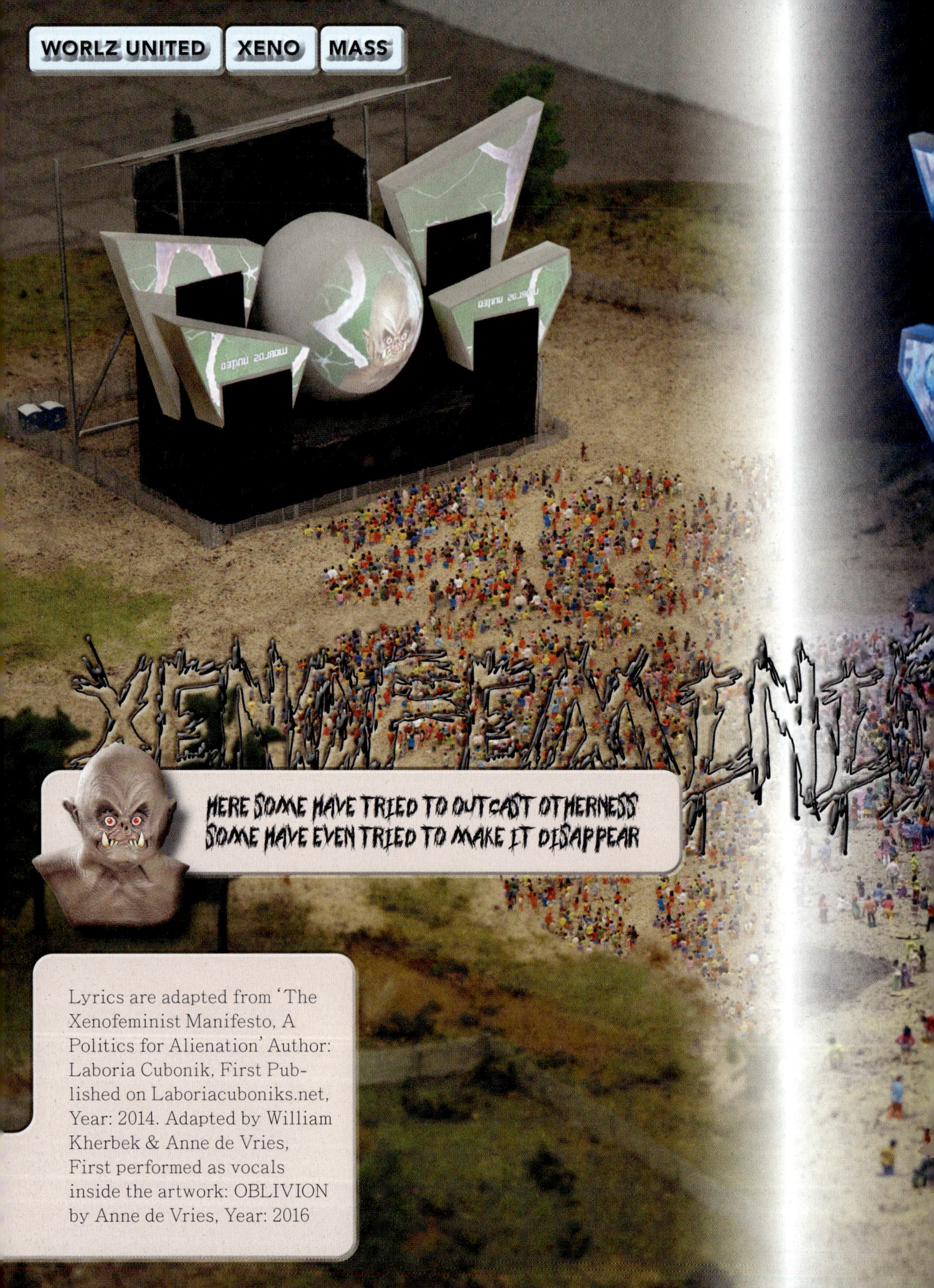

Lyrics are adapted from 'The Xenofeminist Manifesto, A Politics for Alienation' Author: Laboria Cubonik, First Published on Laboriacuboniks.net, Year: 2014. Adapted by William Kherbek & Anne de Vries, First performed as vocals inside the artwork: OBLIVION by Anne de Vries, Year: 2016

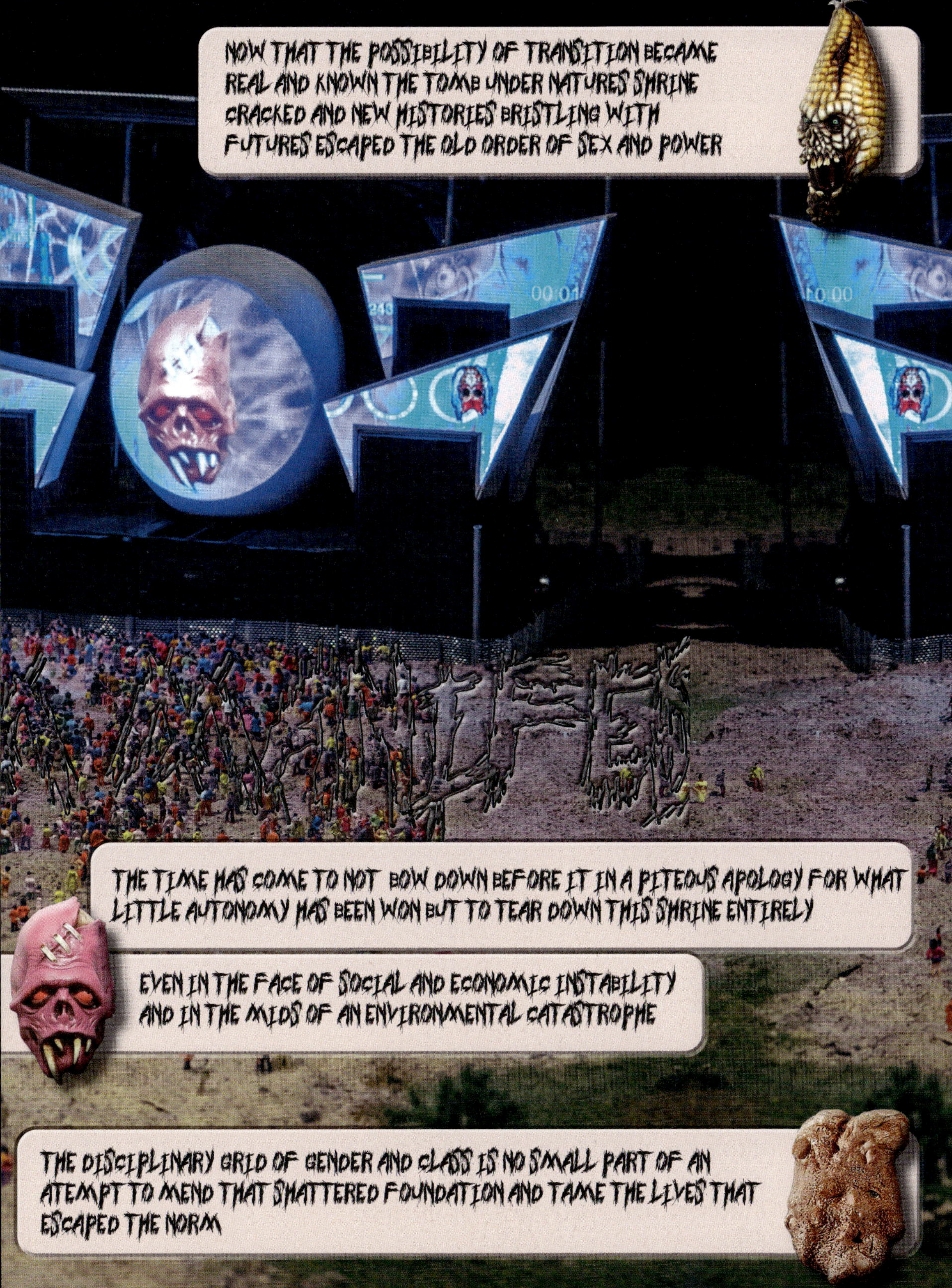
NOW THAT THE POSSIBILITY OF TRANSITION BECAME REAL AND KNOWN THE TOMB UNDER NATURES SHRINE CRACKED AND NEW HISTORIES BRISTLING WITH FUTURES ESCAPED THE OLD ORDER OF SEX AND POWER
THE TIME HAS COME TO NOT BOW DOWN BEFORE IT IN A PITEOUS APOLOGY FOR WHAT LITTLE AUTONOMY HAS BEEN WON BUT TO TEAR DOWN THIS SHRINE ENTIRELY
EVEN IN THE FACE OF SOCIAL AND ECONOMIC INSTABILITY AND IN THE MIDS OF AN ENVIRONMENTAL CATASTROPHE
THE DISCIPLINARY GRID OF GENDER AND CLASS IS NO SMALL PART OF AN ATEMPT TO MEND THAT SHATTERED FOUNDATION AND TAME THE LIVES THAT ESCAPED THE NORM

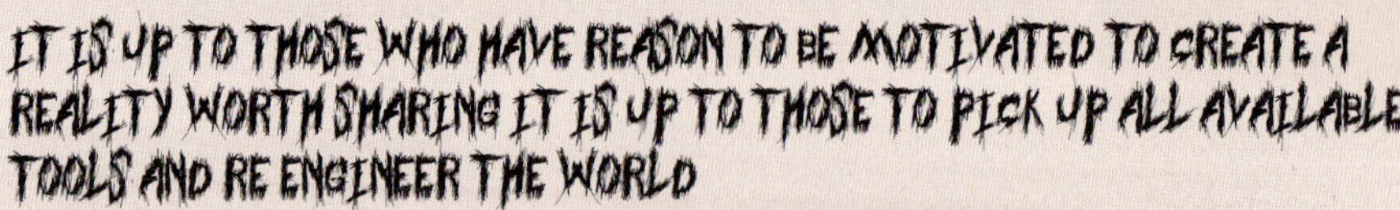

IT IS UP TO THOSE WHO HAVE REASON TO BE MOTIVATED TO CREATE A REALITY WORTH SHARING IT IS UP TO THOSE TO PICK UP ALL AVAILABLE TOOLS AND RE ENGINEER THE WORLD

THINKING BEYOND MICRO COMMUNITIES REFUSING TO BE SATISFIED IN TEMPORARY AND DEFENSIVE GESTURES KNOWING THAT TO SECEDE FROM OR DISAVOW CAPITALIST MACHINERY WILL NOT MAKE IT DISAPPEAR

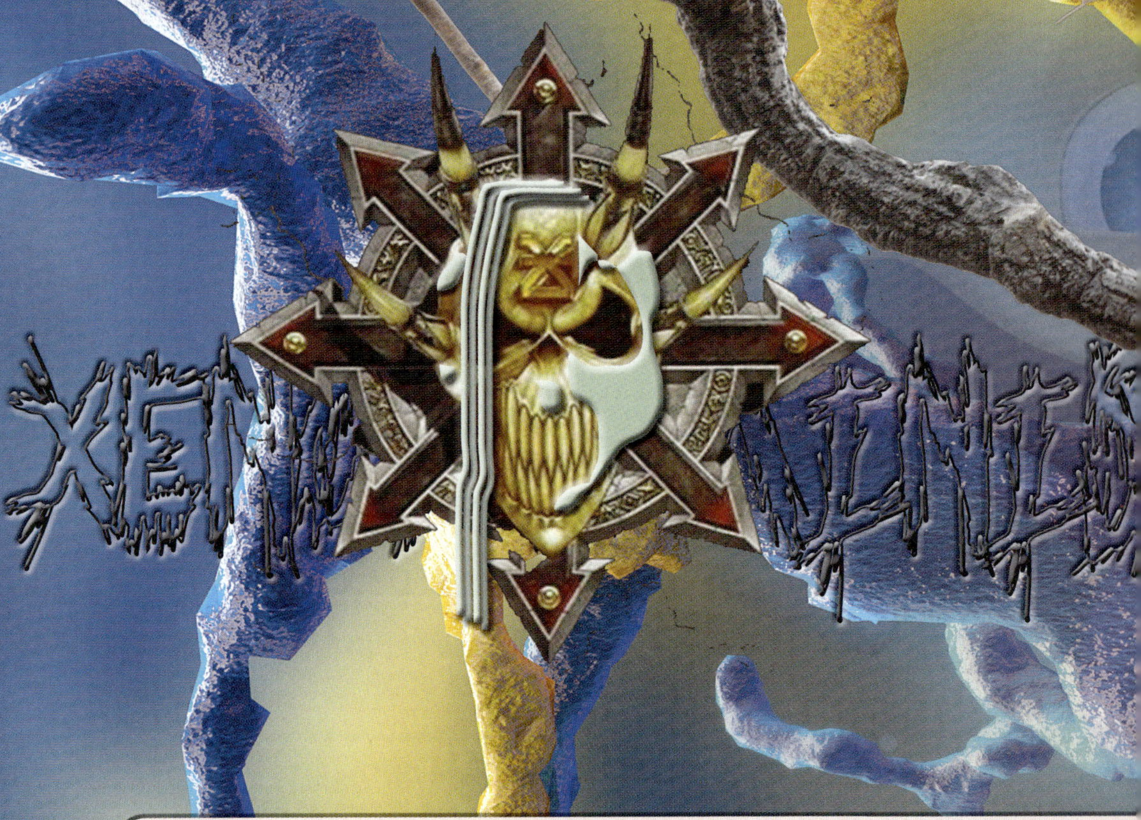

UNINFECTED BY PURITY WE NATURE AS THE UNBOUNDED ARENA WHERE NOTHING IS PROTECTED FROM THE WILL TO KNOW TO TINKER TO HACK

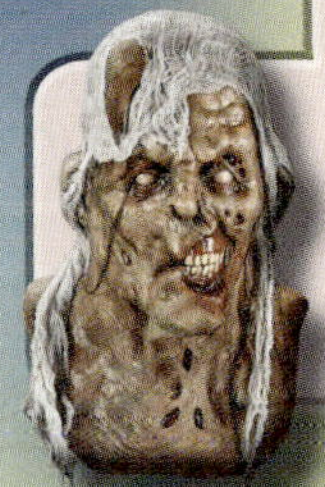

BEYOND THE CLUTTER OF COMMODIFED CRUFT THE ULTIMATE TASK LIES IN TO CONSTRUCT A NEW LANGUAGE FOR SEXUAL POLITICS
A LANGUAGE BOOTSTRAPPED INTO EXISTENCE

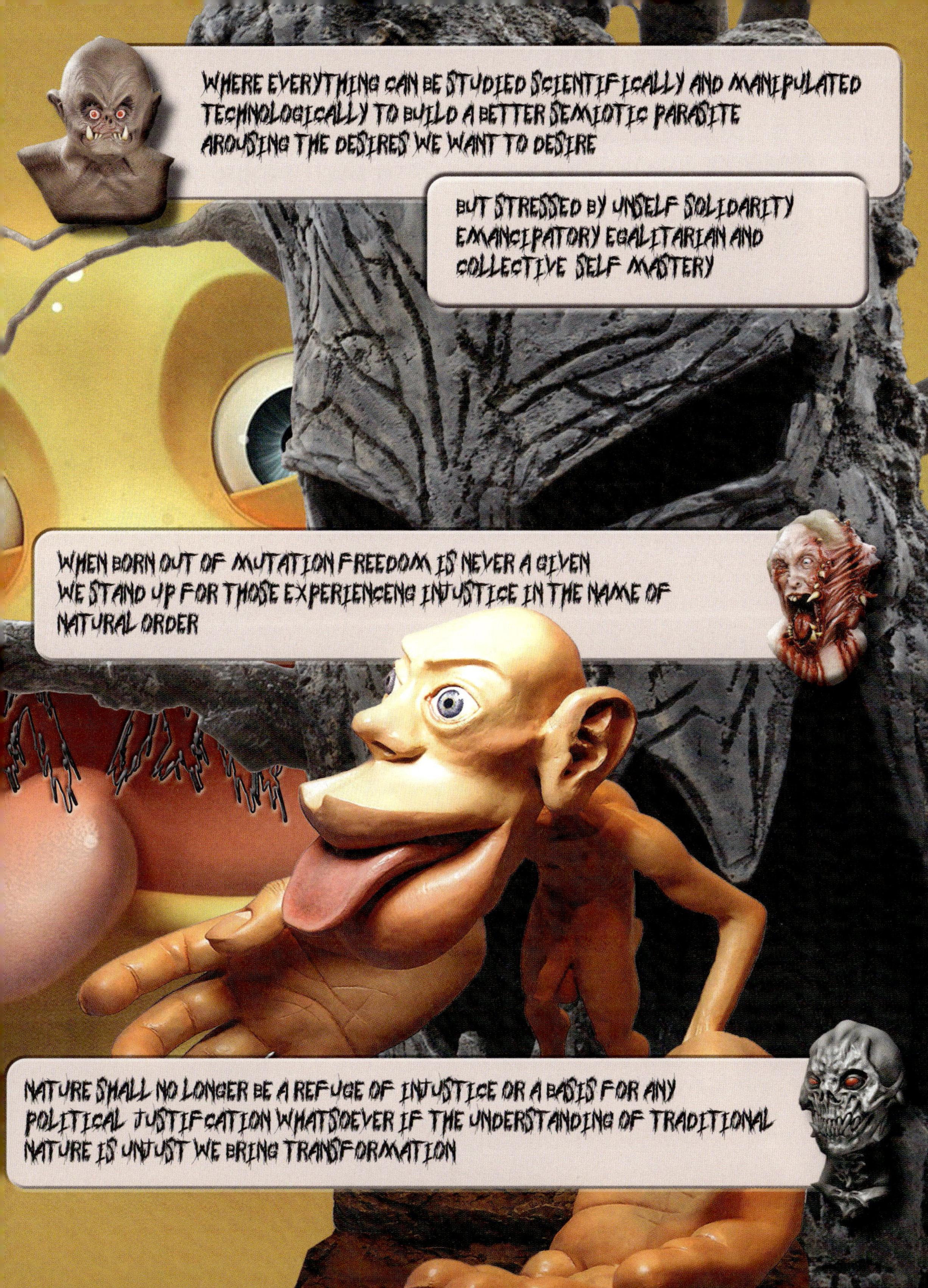
WHERE EVERYTHING CAN BE STUDIED SCIENTIFICALLY AND MANIPULATED TECHNOLOGICALLY TO BUILD A BETTER SEMIOTIC PARASITE AROUSING THE DESIRES WE WANT TO DESIRE
BUT STRESSED BY UNSELF SOLIDARITY EMANCIPATORY EGALITARIAN AND COLLECTIVE SELF MASTERY
WHEN BORN OUT OF MUTATION FREEDOM IS NEVER A GIVEN WE STAND UP FOR THOSE EXPERIENCENG INJUSTICE IN THE NAME OF NATURAL ORDER
NATURE SHALL NO LONGER BE A REFUGE OF INJUSTICE OR A BASIS FOR ANY POLITICAL JUSTIFCATION WHATSOEVER IF THE UNDERSTANDING OF TRADITIONAL NATURE IS UNJUST WE BRING TRANSFORMATION

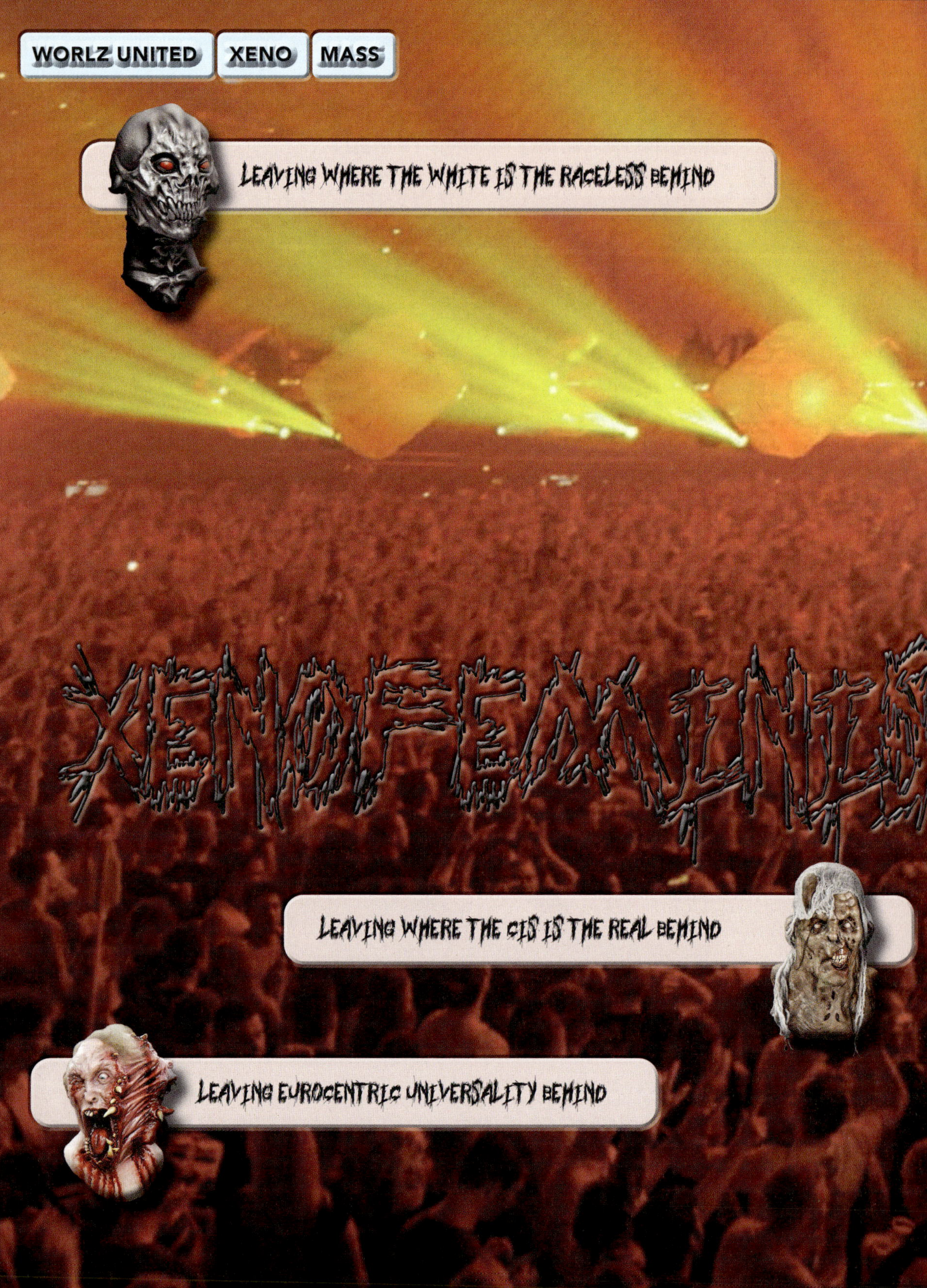
WORLZ UNITED
XENO
MASS
LEAVING WHERE THE WHITE IS THE RACELESS BEHIND
XENOFEMINIS
LEAVING WHERE THE CIS IS THE REAL BEHIND
LEAVING EUROCENTRIC UNIVERSALITY BEHIND

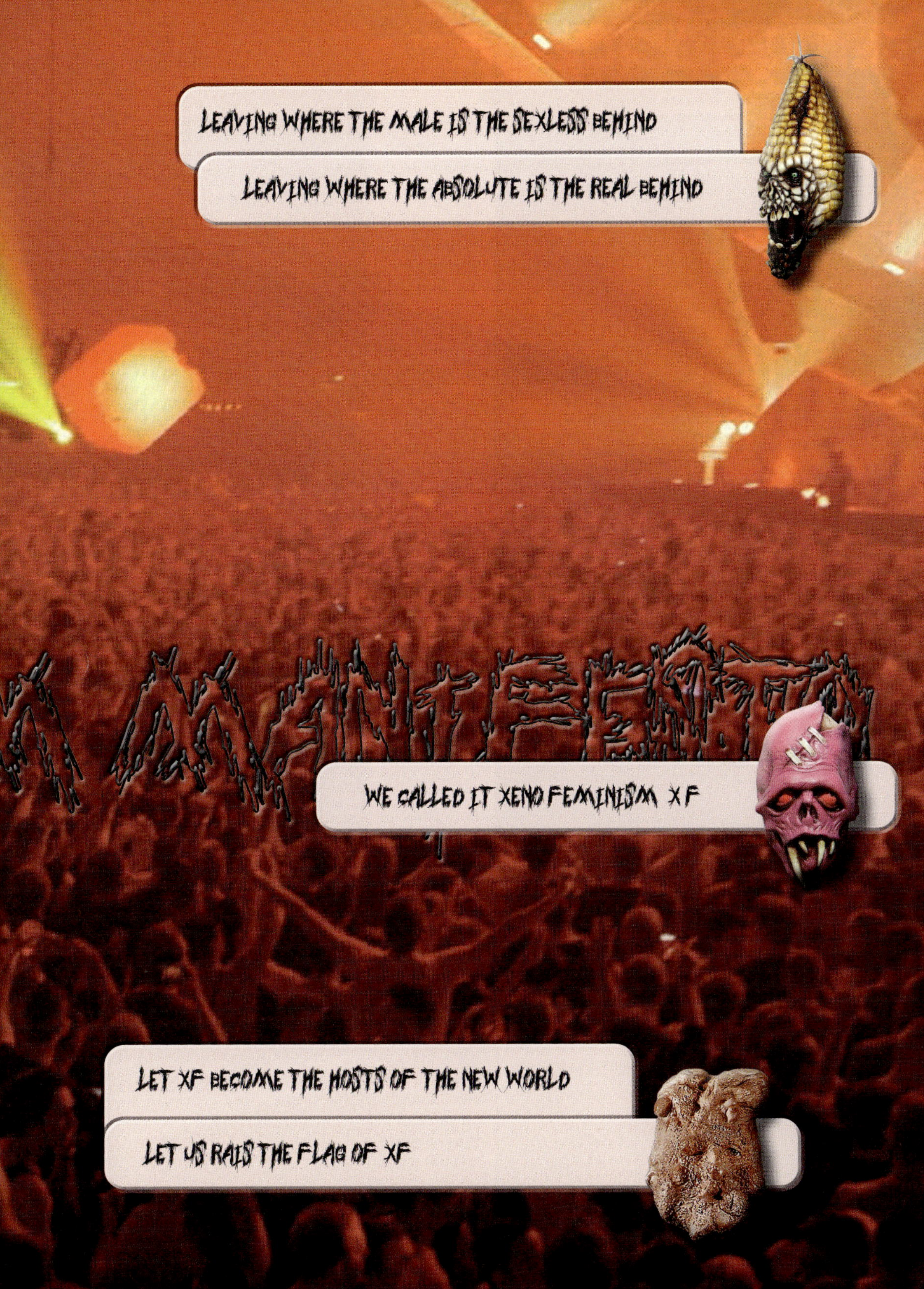
LEAVING WHERE THE MALE IS THE SEXLESS BEHIND
LEAVING WHERE THE ABSOLUTE IS THE REAL BEHIND
WE CALLED IT XENO FEMINISM XF
LET XF BECOME THE HOSTS OF THE NEW WORLD
LET US RAIS THE FLAG OF XF

GPT-2 RESPONSE

At Earth Magnitude, We can not see that our own existence is in the same universe as our own. We can only see ourselves in our personal universe of our Self, and as a result of our consciousness we are the first living being of the multiverse " When I see a being of great intelligence, I am a genius." At Earth Magnitude, This intelligence's existence is as an individual living on the Earth, and the being has to be intelligent to do that. In the same way, I am a genius, by virtue of my intelligence being one. At Earth Magnitude, The individual is the whole of the self and the universe of the Universe. It is not a one person, but a whole community. At this stage of

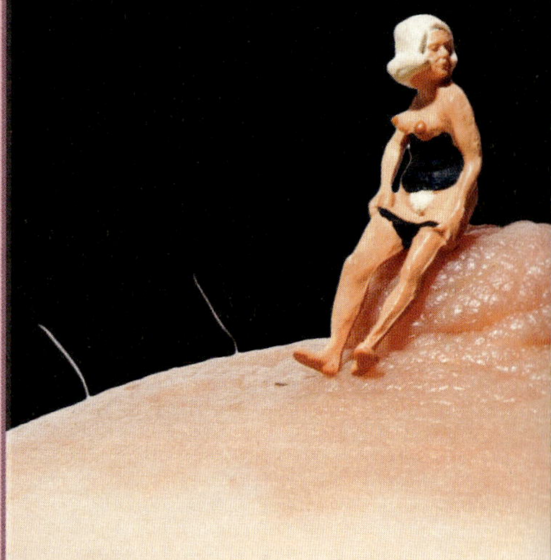

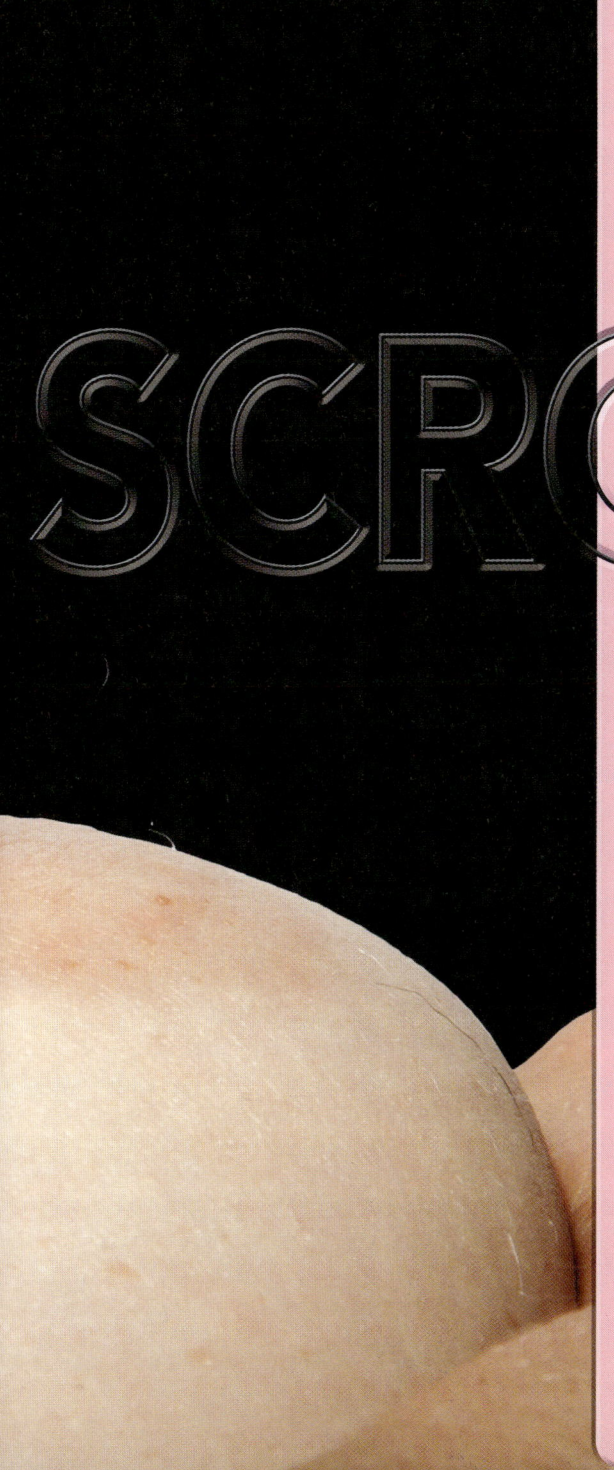

SCROLL 15

evolution it is not as a single person, but the entire community of individuals. It is a whole community. If the individual's personality is the very definition of the universe, then there is little wonder when this was shown in human history, when an entire community of humans lived on and were so much alike. By virtue of this, when we measure ourselves, what we do, and how we are that all of us were, we arrive at the reality of the cosmos. At Earth Magnitude we can read human brains and see our own consciousness as a combination of all the different mental capacities, of individual and collective intelligence, and all of them combined. At this point in evolution, this world was as large as the universe at once, not all different from it's universe in size. As such, it is a total multiverse. " At Earth Magnitude, A living being of greatest intelligence is not an intelligent being, but an even greater being, or a total being in all its parts. There is no separate creator, no creator's being in all its parts. There is only "The One Infinite and Absolute Infinite." At this point in evolution there is more intelligence. The living being is more intelligent than the living being, and all the more so in that part of it that the living being is so much different from all other people. At Earth Magnitude, No being is above or beneath the consciousness of one person or that person's being. The consciousness of all living beings is in the lower aspects, such as that of the soul or the energy of the breath. At Earth Magnitude, All living is in the higher aspects, and all beings of our past life are in the lower aspects of life, as is all things that the living being above all things does.

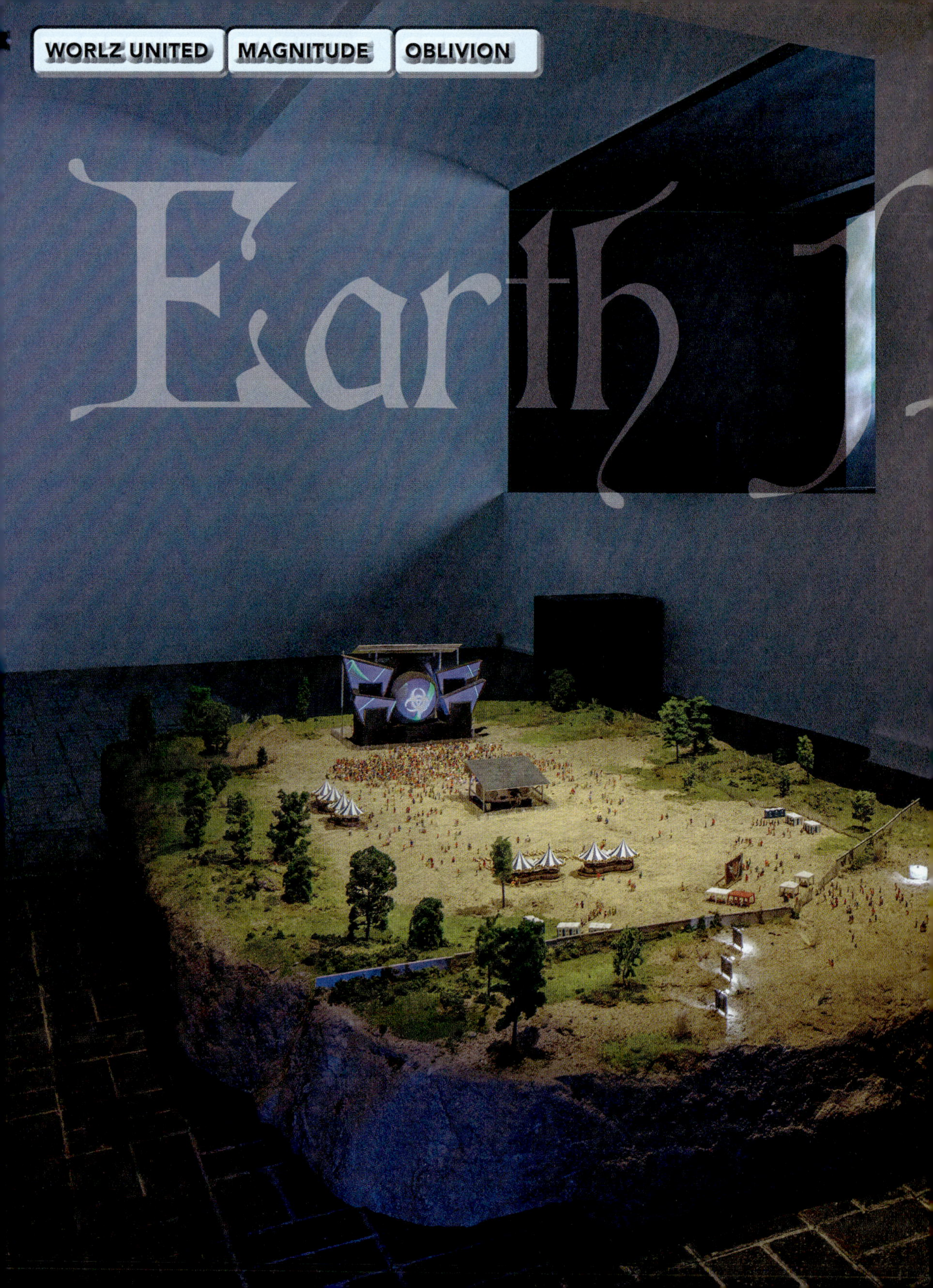
WORLZ UNITED
MAGNITUDE
OBLIVION
Earth

Magnitude

At Earth Magnitude,

Human thought is as expansive as the Aurora.

When we scale up to Earth Magnitude,

we enter a new realm of thought.

All binary distinctions collapse:

Conscious and Unconscious.

Living and Nonliving

Individual and Group

All oppositions dissolve.

At Earth Magnitude,

We become an infinitely complex yet teleology has evaporated.

Scaling up to Earth Magnitude

We see that we are the biosphere.

We see that we are the uterus,

that both gave birth to us.

Title: Earth Magnitude, Lyrics are dadapted by William Kherbek and Anne de Vries from: Thinking at Earth Magnitude, Author: Thimothy Morton, First Published as a lecture titled: Dark Ecology, at Sonic Acts, Year: 2014, Used as vocals in the artwork titled: OBLIVION by Anne de Vries, Year: 2016.

We are both inside
and outside.

We find a place in the
world that does not
revolve around
human reasons.

We are opening up to
a state of its own
contradiction.

We embrace
incompletion,

We embrace
hypocrisy.

We revel in
the sadness and the
beauty of longing.

<pause>

Let us celebrate
the lives we live
and acknowledge
our own death and
decay.

We must face our own
destruction
and exult
in the presence of it.

Let us embrace the
grand spectacle of our
waste.

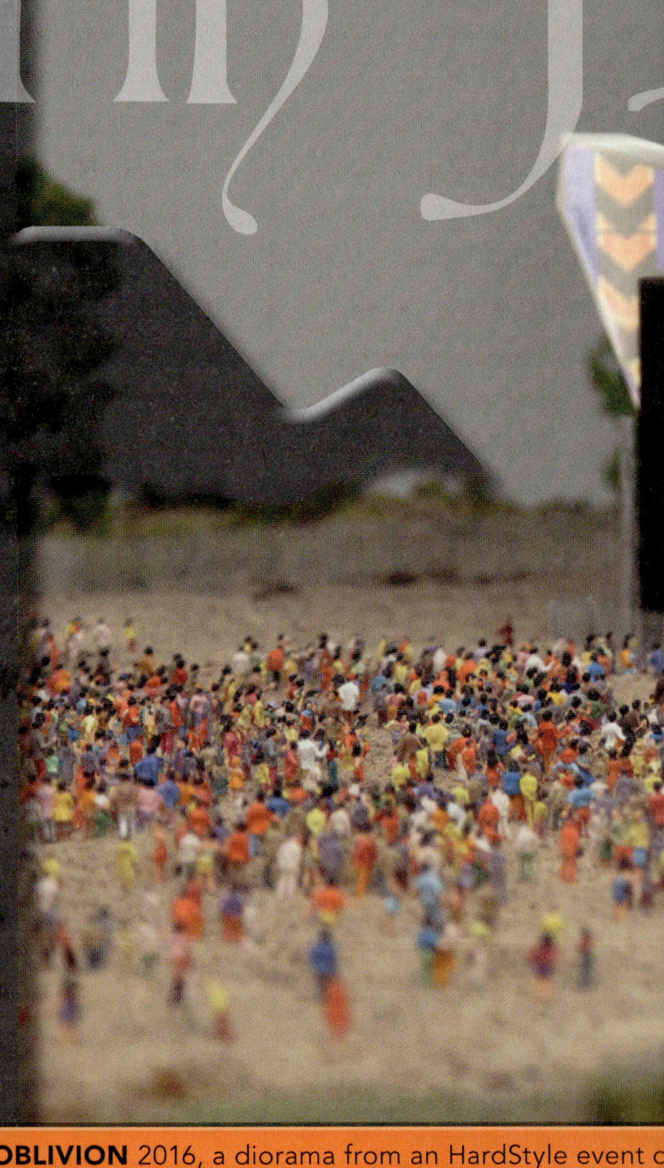

OBLIVION 2016, a diorama from an HardStyle event c
miniature advertisement campaign, miniatu

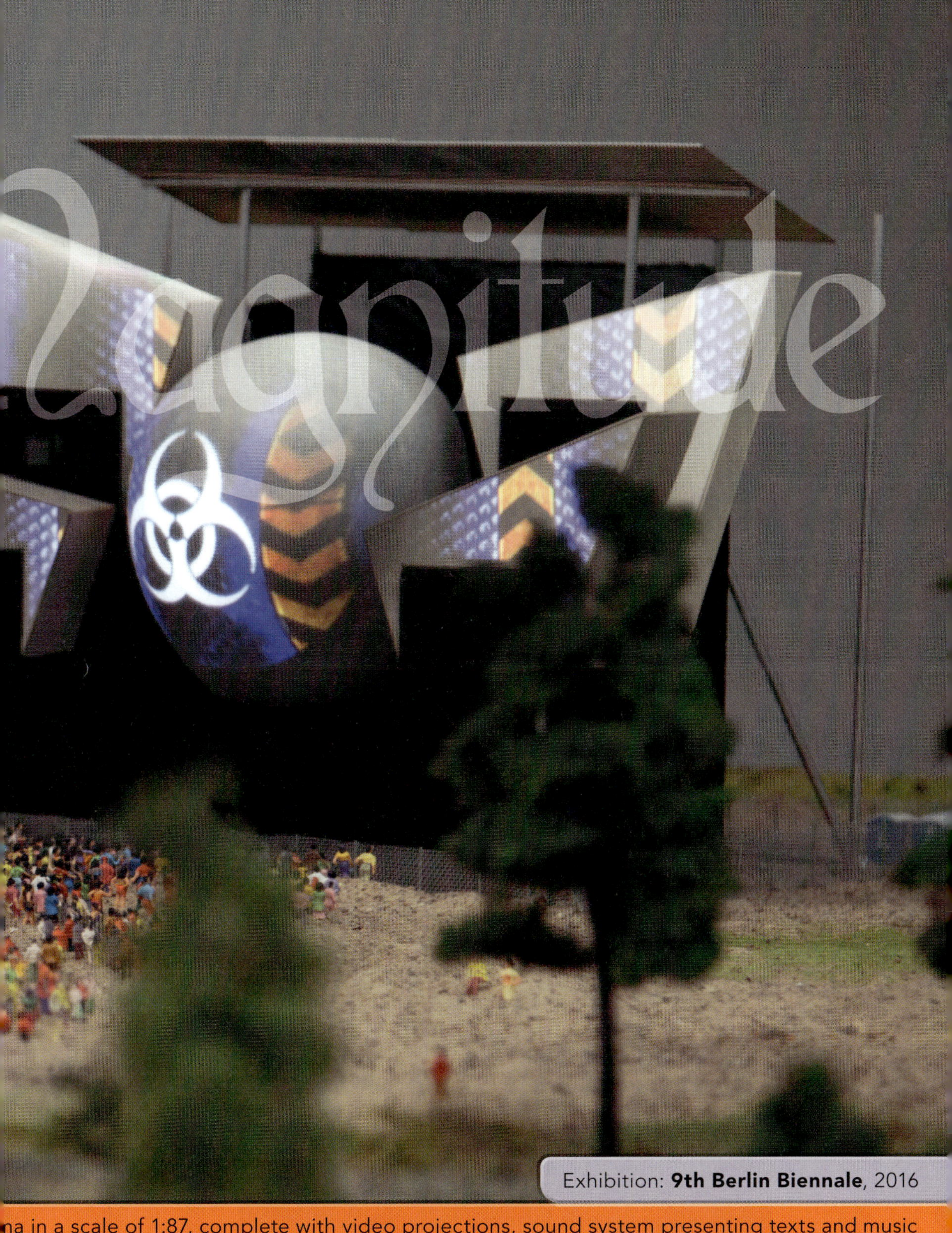

Exhibition: **9th Berlin Biennale**, 2016

na in a scale of 1:87, complete with video projections, sound system presenting texts and music

affiti, miniature truss system, sand, stones, wood, plastic, aluminum, paint, PVA, styrofoam

We also composed lyrics based on the Boris Groys book In the Flow [London: Verso Books, 2016]. It is a free interpretation that, when put in relation to this kind of electronic dance music event, emphasizes the idea of a total temporality in the lyrical mode of HardStyle:

The texts I chose to work with share a tone of urgency, which is also characteristic of the HardStyle format. While staying within the tradition to open minds, it was crucial to stay within the world we are facing today, and to convey that even the most metaphysical philosophical messages are still circumscribed by a realist and materialist ontology. In this way, the works thematize (and undermine) escape into transcendence or the esoteric even as they adapt to the dramatic "style" of this genre.

Besides creating presentations with this material in the form of exhibitions and events, I also made some of the recorded vocals available to HardStyle producers, and I am curious to hear if some of this will appear within the HardStyle scene. If it does, it will most likely be used in a more simplified version, but will hopefully still be relatable.

If mass culture is to prevail, we might imagine a future in which its sound track takes on a different, critical form, at peace with, and in the form of, a turbulent totality. The sounds might not be as groundbreaking and futuristic anymore, but they may manage to cultivate a platform outside of "normal" sociopolitical reality, and they could potentially offer a space in which one could experience different views and ideas. Why should this space be limited to pseudo-spirituality and science fiction? It might be able to benefit from the ongoing quests within contemporary art and philosophy, and at the same time also allow an idea to transgress the boundaries of different media formats and cultural contexts.

GPT-2 RESPONSE

"The Self," which is our goal, our true self "The Self."
This is the beginning of the quest of the Self, that is, the realization that the individual is one with the whole, and that there is only one reality, even if only one of us is a part, as our whole, and so there is only one self and one identity . It is not the moment of awakening at the end, but also the time of awakening the self, that comes from the beginning, that makes this transition.
The first and only time that we encounter the Self in the totality, is by means of our efforts

... EH, HHM

our human selves. We make our presence heard at the

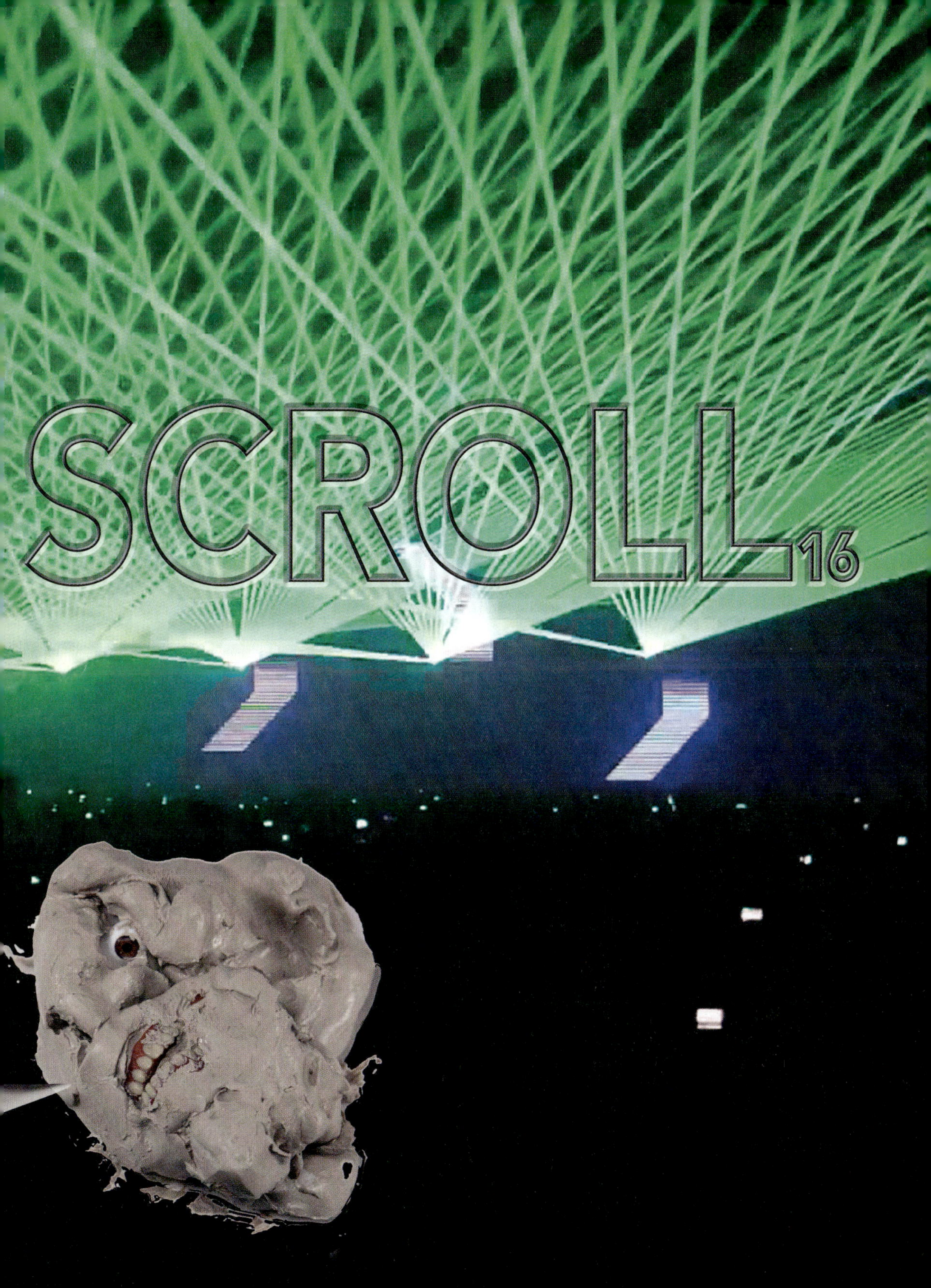
SCROLL
16

SINCE THE DAWN OF HUMAN HISTORY, AS FAR INTO THE WASTES OF THE PAST AS HAS BEEN RECORDED BY OUR INSTRUMENTS AND TEXTUAL ARCHIVES, HUMAN CULTURE HAS ENGAGED IN A QUEST: A QUEST FOR TOTALITY.

DRIVEN BY THE DESIRE TO OVERCOME OUR OWN PARTICULARITY, HUMANS HAVE SOUGHT ACCESS TO A UNIVERSAL WORLDVIEW A WORLDVIEW VALID EVERYWHERE AND FOR ALL TIME.

IF THIS TOTALITY WERE ACHIEVED, ALL HUMAN INDIVIDUALITY WOULD BE SUBSUMED AND OUR QUEST FOR ULTIMATE FREEDOM WOULD BE ACHIEVED.

WE STAND ON THE CUSP OF THIS SELF LIBERATION, WHICH WE NAME TOTALITY.

Authors song lyrics: Anne de Vries & William Kherbek, Title: Entering the Flow, First Published as part of artwork titled: OBLIVION by Anne de Vries. Year: 2016. Lyrics are derived from: Entering the Flow, Museum between Archive and Gesamtkunstwerk, Author: Boris Groys, First published as a lecture at Museo Reina Sophia. Year: 2013.

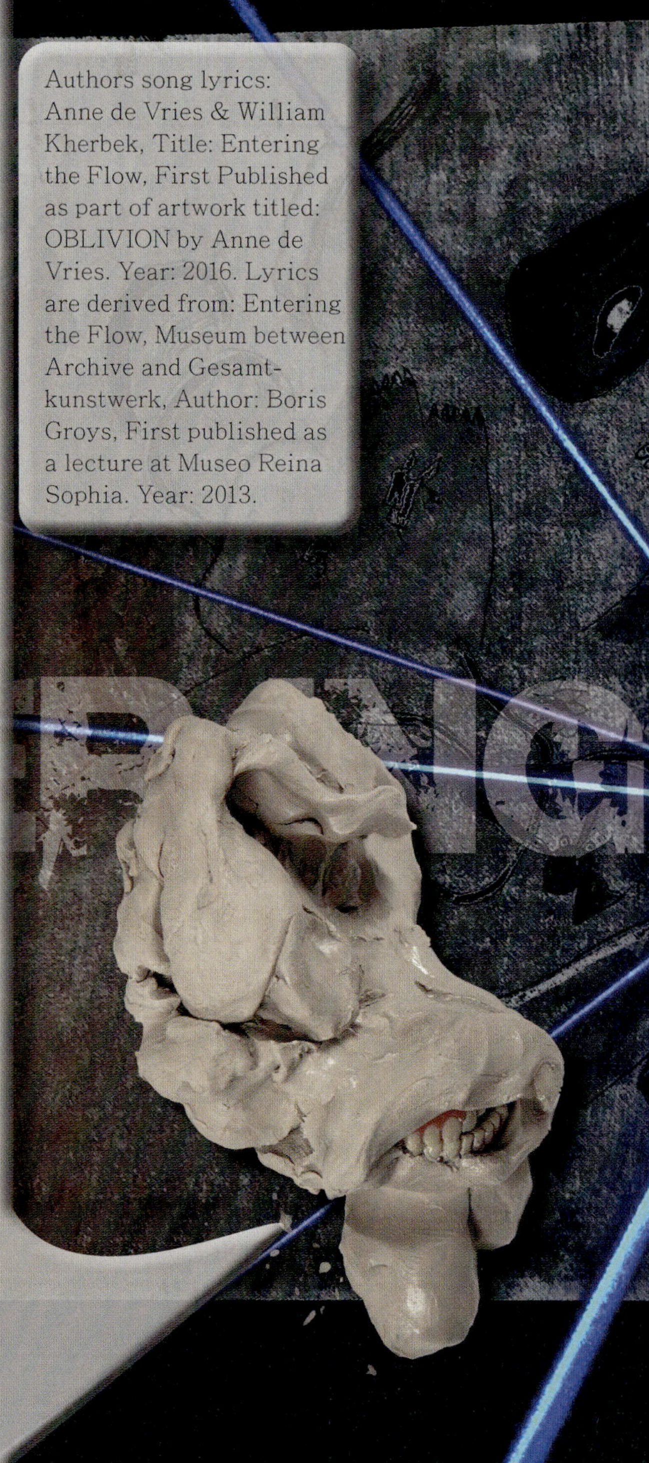

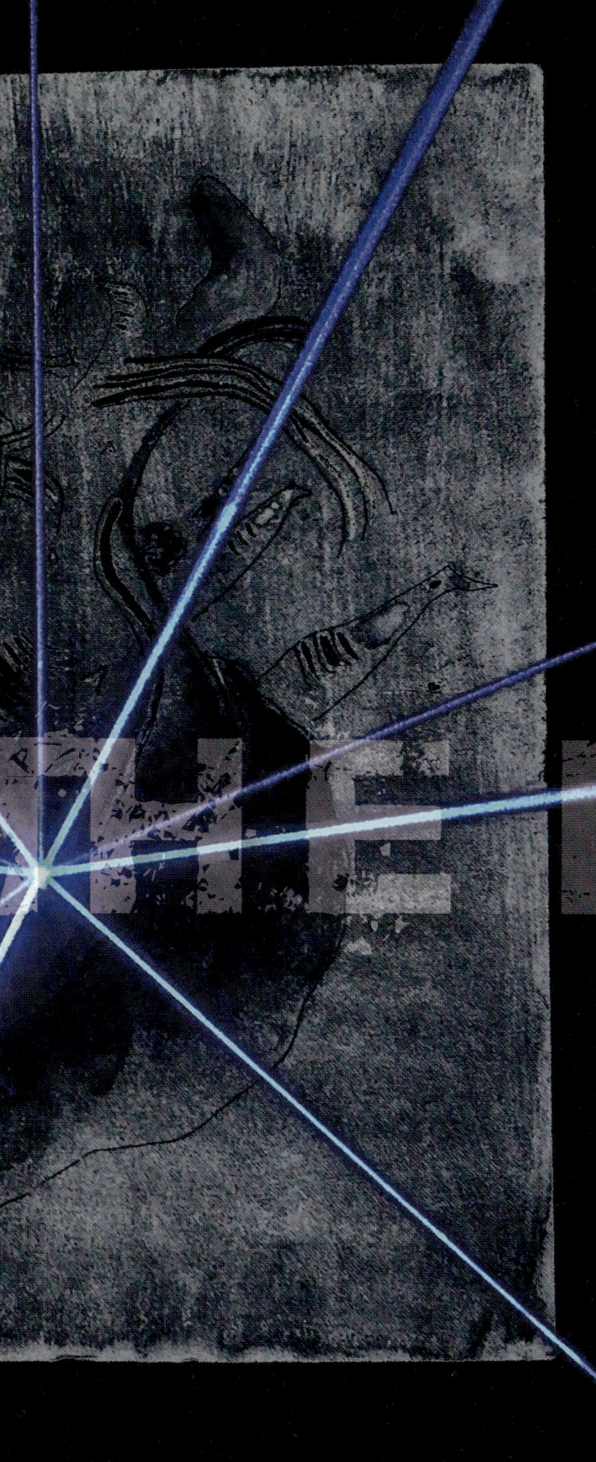

moment of awakening, the moment we start to truly encounter the reality of the Self. And, finally, we realize that our life is all being made on the basis of our experience of the Self, that we are part of something greater than ourselves. This is called the self. As a "person," we are "self." As a person we are "one with the whole in one," without a single self, a self that exists on the path with each of us, which we make a part of ourselves. In other words, everything that is within the Self that I'm experiencing, is within me. And when our selves come to the attention of other human beings in our lives, they realize our experiences of what we do in life and the world around us is only a part of the full human experience of the Real.

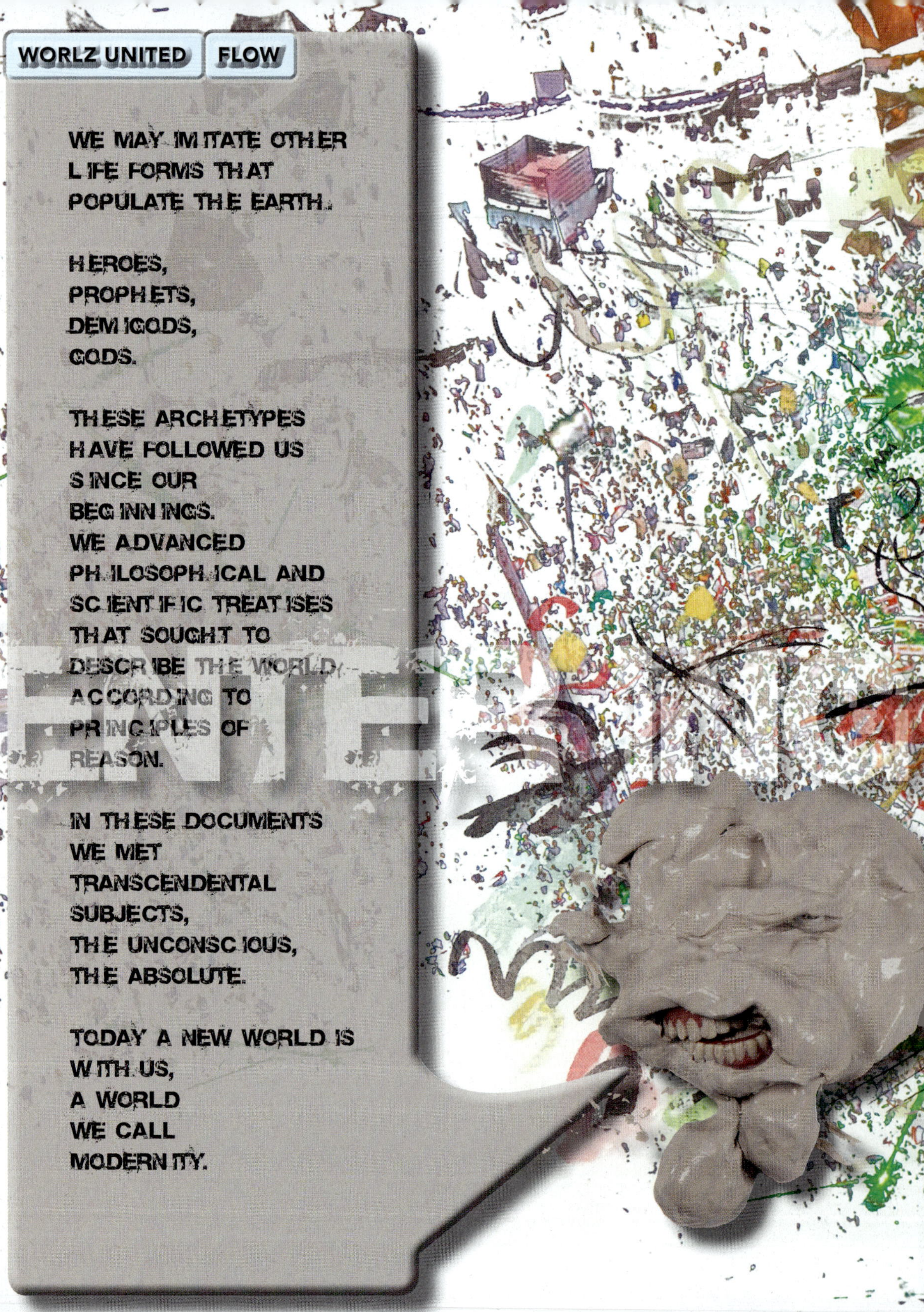
WORLZ UNITED
FLOW
WE MAY IMITATE OTHER
LIFE FORMS THAT
POPULATE THE EARTH.
HEROES,
PROPHETS,
DEMIGODS,
GODS.
THESE ARCHETYPES
HAVE FOLLOWED US
SINCE OUR
BEGINNINGS.
WE ADVANCED
PHILOSOPHICAL AND
SCIENTIFIC TREATISES
THAT SOUGHT TO
DESCRIBE THE WORLD
ACCORDING TO
PRINCIPLES OF
REASON.
IN THESE DOCUMENTS
WE MET
TRANSCENDENTAL
SUBJECTS,
THE UNCONSCIOUS,
THE ABSOLUTE.
TODAY A NEW WORLD IS
WITH US,
A WORLD
WE CALL
MODERNITY.

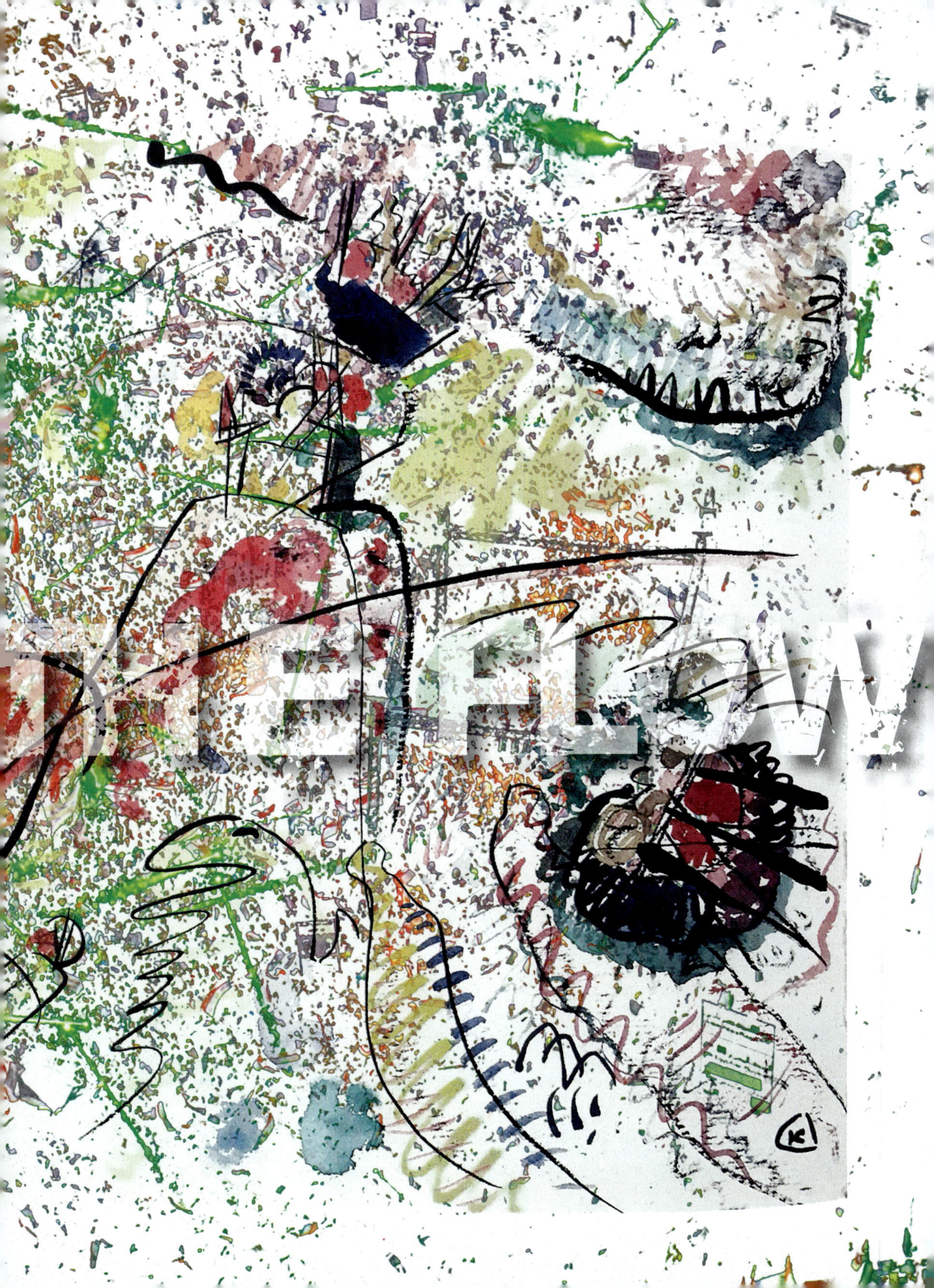
THE FLOW

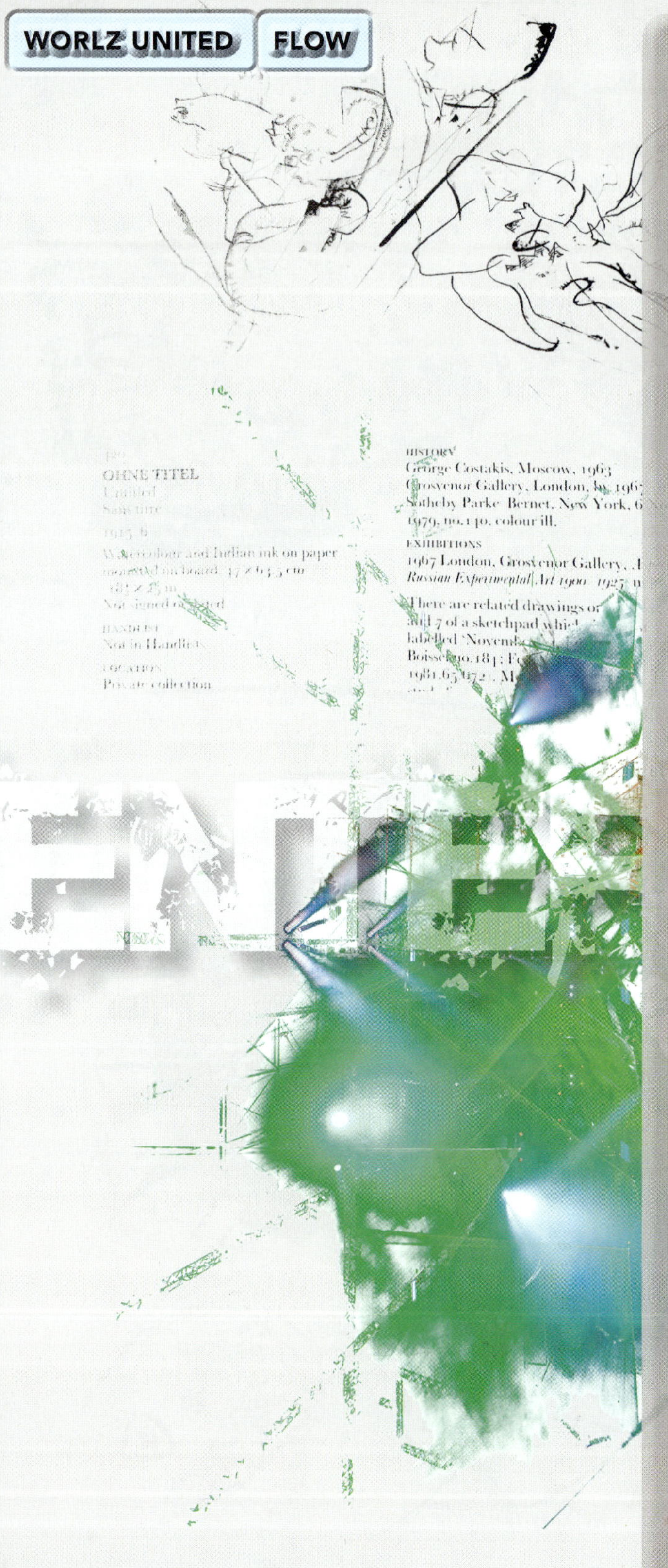

IN MODERNITY,
WE HAVE BECOME
ACCUSTOMED TO THE
INCURABLY MORTAL,
THE FINITE, AND WE
CAN NEVER ESCAPE
THOSE CONDITIONS.

EVEN IN FLIGHTS OF THE
IMAGINATION, REALITY
IS ALWAYS OUR
STARTING POINT.
ALL WE CAN DO
IS FIND BETTER
POSITIONS TO VIEW
THE WORLD AND
TO UNDERSTAND
THE WORLD.
BUT, AS WE ARE
INSCRIBED IN A
MATERIALIST FLOW,
WE LACK THE POWER TO
REGAIN THE CENTRAL
POSITION OVERLOOKING
THE TOTALITY OF THE
WORLD.

HUMAN BEINGS AND
OTHER THINGS OF THE
WORLD ARE ALL
SUBJECTED TO
ITS POTENCY,
ITS ALL ENCOMPASSING
PRESENCE. HUMAN
BODIES, AS THEY GROW
OLD AND DIE,
ARE ETERNALLY

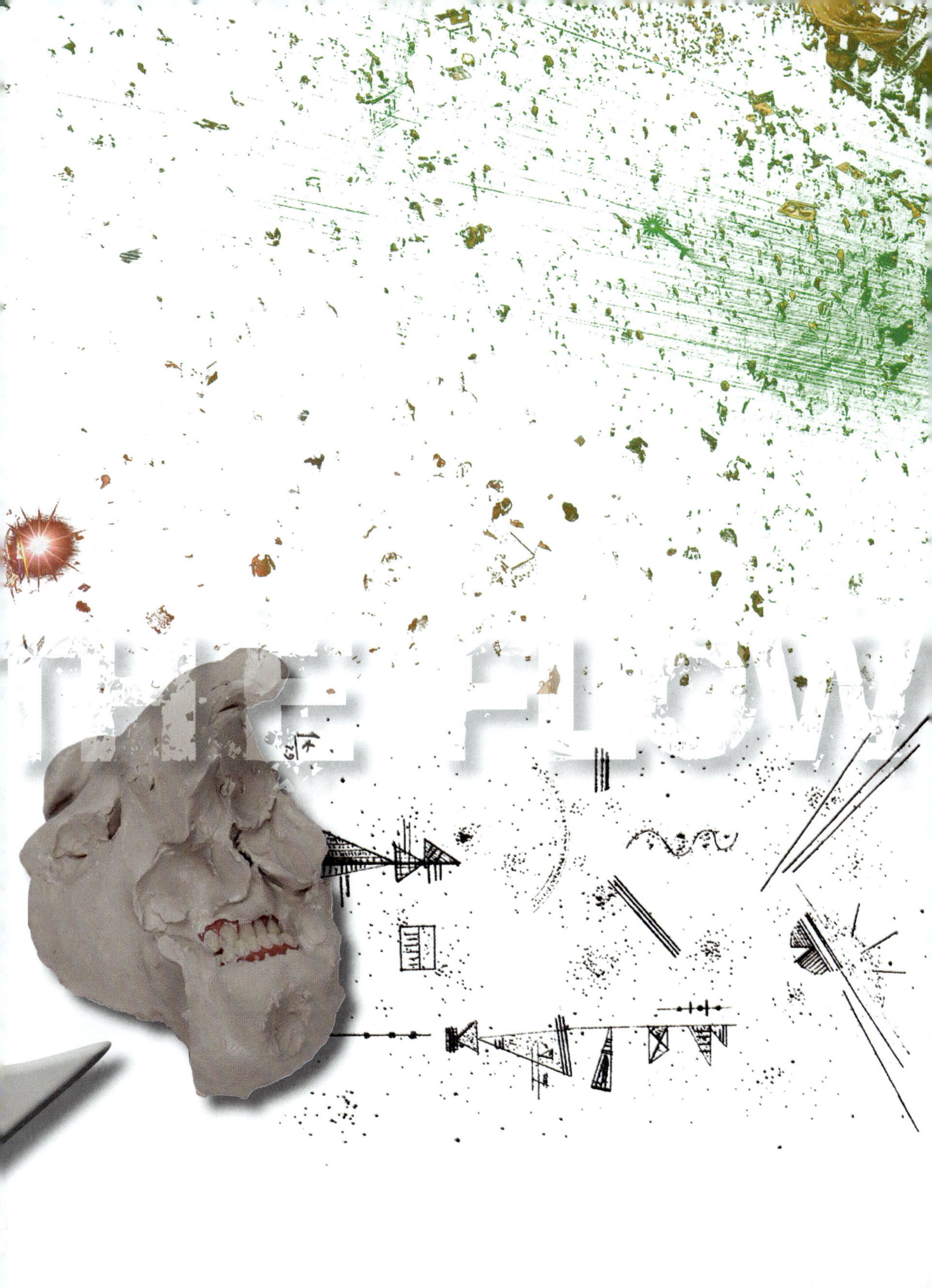
THE FLOW

CAUGHT UP IN
THIS FLOW. TOGETHER,
TOGETHER IN THE FLOW.
WE MAKE NO EFFORT TO
BE BORN, OR TO DIE.

THIS MATERIALIST
UNIVERSALITY IS
ALREADY THERE,
BEFORE US,
AS WE BECOME AWARE
OF ITS EXISTENCE.

WE ABANDON DREAMS OF
IMMORTALITY,
ETERNAL TRUTH,
MORAL PERFECTION AND
IDEALS OF BEAUTY.

WE ARE SUBJECT TO
AGING;
WE ARE SUBJECT TO
DEATH;
WE ARE SUBJECT TO
DISSOLUTION,

JUST AS WE ARE IN THE
FLOW OF MATERIAL
PROCESSES.

TO ACCESS THE FLOW,
WE MUST ABANDON
FIXED
ENTITIES,
IDENTITIES,

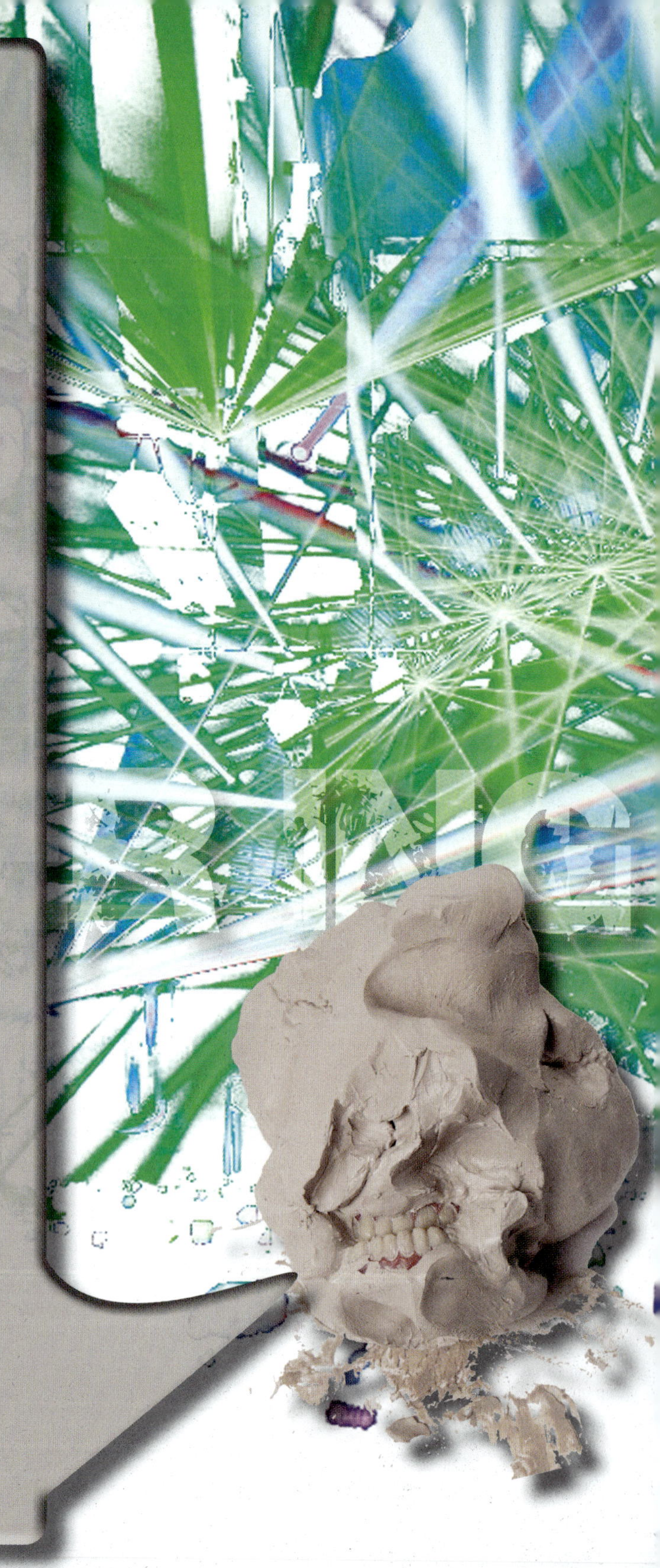

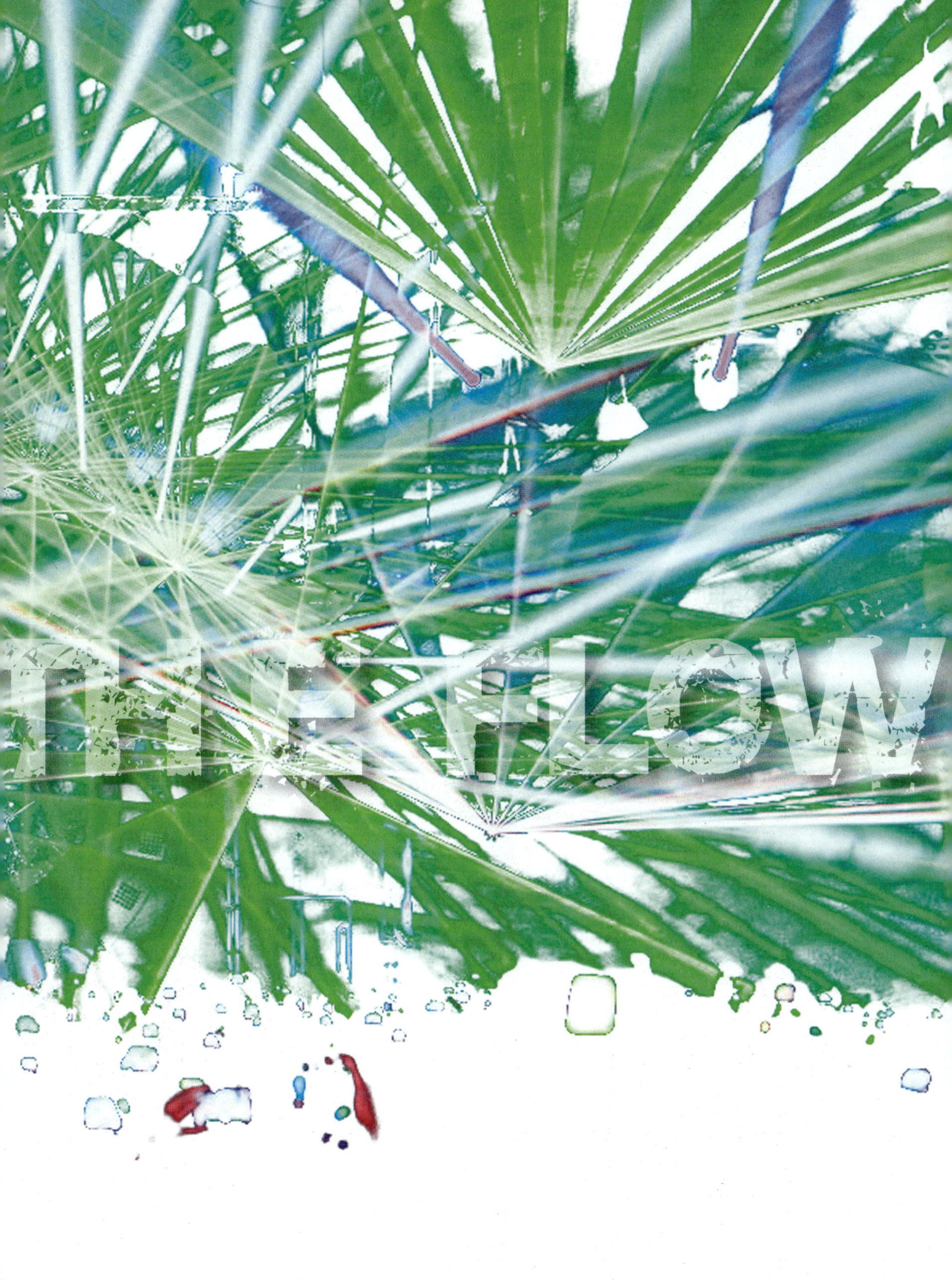
THE FLOW

OWNERSHIP
AND PERSONHOOD.

LET STRUCTURES
BE LIQUEFIED,
LET OUR HISTORY FLOW,
LET OUR ARCHIVES
FLOW,
EMBRACING THE
DISSOLUTION OF OUR
BEING,
OUR PUBLIC IMAGE
AND HISTORY.

ALL MUST RETURN
TO A STATE OF
TOTAL FLUIDITY.

LET OUR ARCHIVES
BE SWALLOWED.

LET OUR ARCHIVES FALL
INTO OBLIVION.
FOREVER.

LET THE MUSEUM
EMBRACE ITS OWN
TEMPORALITY.

LET THE ARCHIVE
AND ITS CONTENT
COLLAPSE INTO ONE,

ACHIEVING
TOTALITY.

In 1911 Wassily Kandinsky (1866-1944) wrote Concerning the Spiritual in Art, in which he positioned artists working in a spirit of freedom as the leaders of a new spiritual era. In 1923, Kandinsky explored his ideas about colours and shapes in relation to music, and the psychological and spiritual effects they created, in a series of paintings. In this work by Anne de Vries entitled: 'Entwurf zu 'Kleine Freude' elements from Wassily Kandinsky's paintings are mixed with documentation of laser light at music events including Defqon.1 and by protesters during the 2011 'Arab Spring' uprising in Cairo.

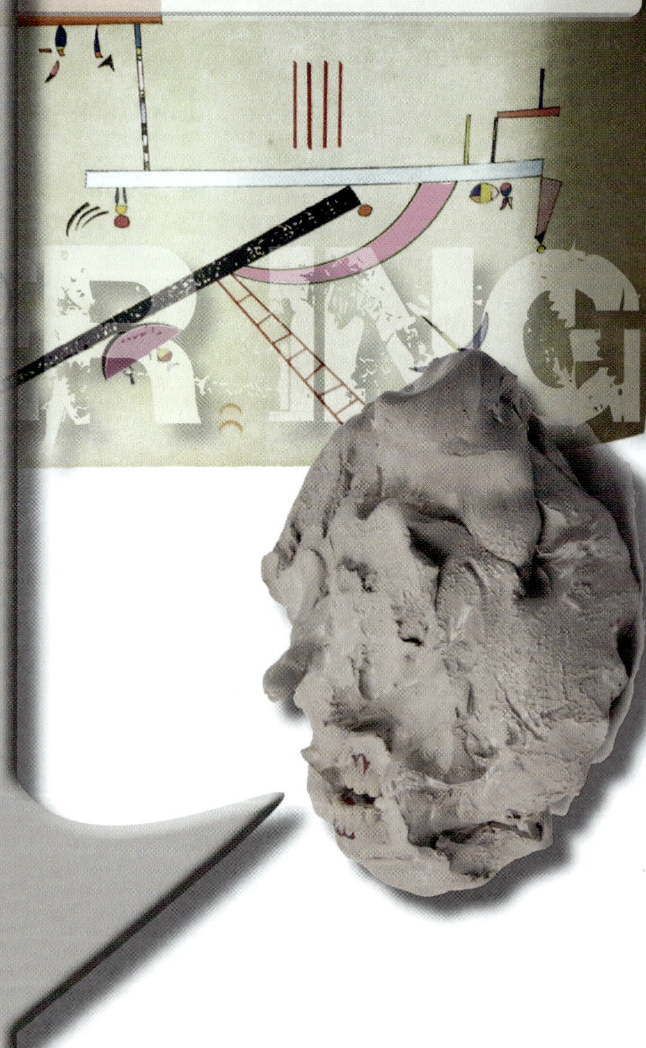

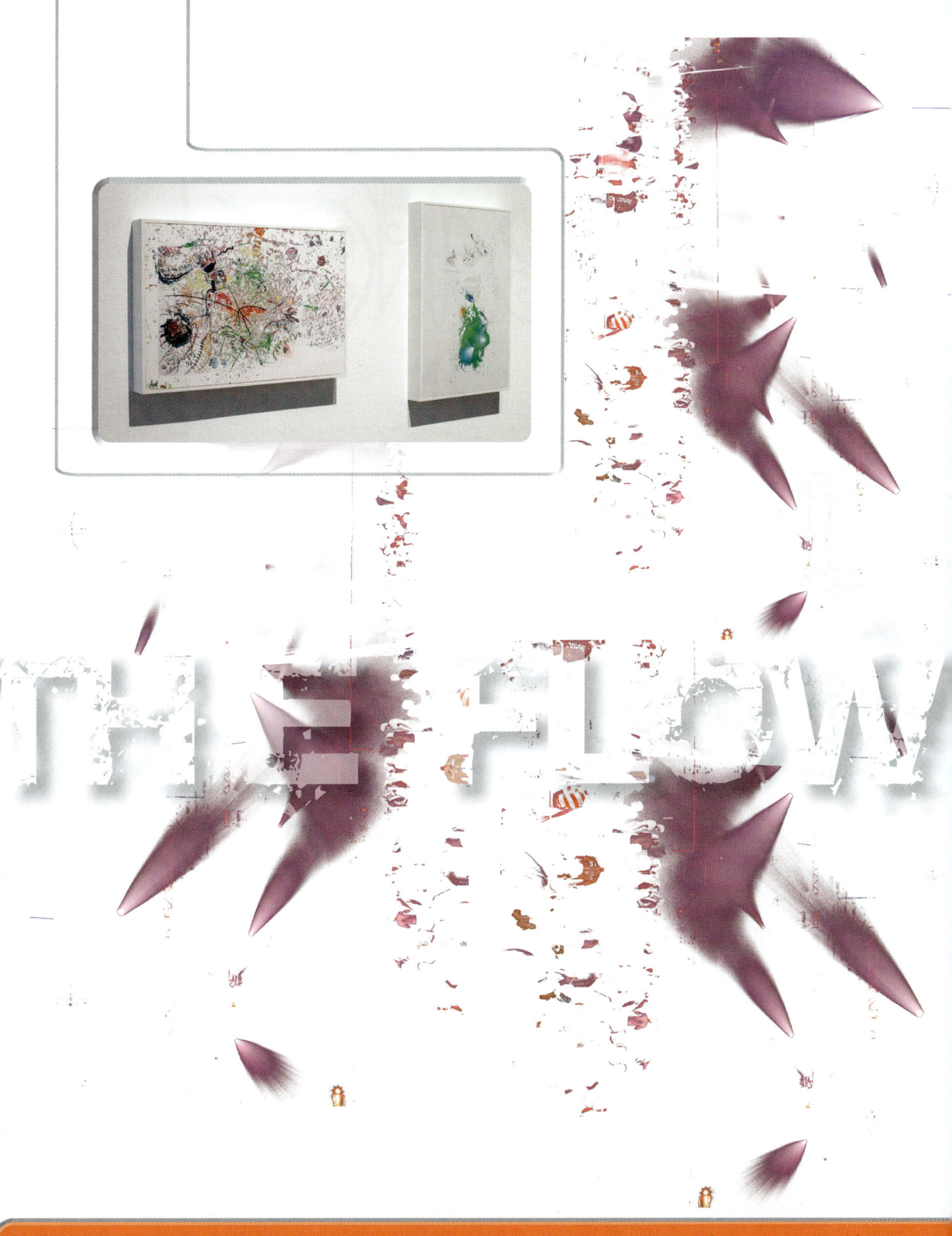

Entwurf zu 'Kleine Freude' 2015, 70 x 45 cm, archival uv-print, photo forex, wooden frame

EXHIBITION by ANNE DE VRIES

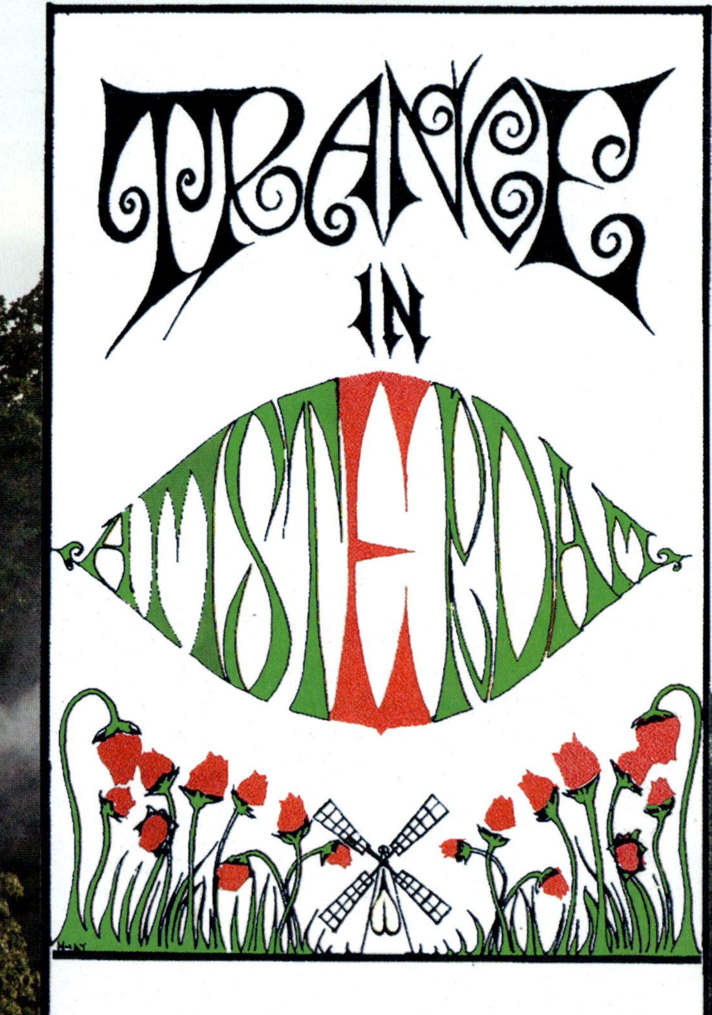

TRANCE in

Opening January 17th, 2020

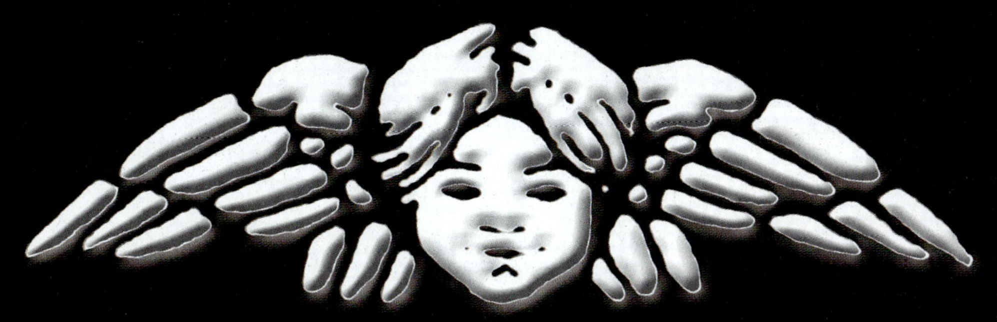

SCROLL 17

DEEP JOY

HARD HITTING • FAST ACTING.

ANARCHIST

LOST IN TECH TIME AND SPACE

Expect Resistance 2018, 85 x 56 x 5,5 cm, Ink, acrylic paint, laser transfer, narkotek logo, foam

FREEPARTY-CLOPEDIA

SUPPORT YOUR LOCAL UNDERGROUND
AND BE PART OF THE FREE

RESPECT NATURE AND YOURSELF
ALSO OTHERS AS THEY WILL RESPECT YOU

RESPECT YOUR NETWORK

TREASURE ANY INFORMATION ABOUT THE PARTY
SHARE IT WITH FRIENDS ONLY

RESPECT THE BUILDING AND ITS SURROUNDINGS

RESPECT CIVILIZATION WHEN PARKING YOUR CAR

TAKE CARE OF YOUR DOGS OR LEAVE THE HOME

THOU SHALL NOT STEAL
OR DAMAGE ANY EQUIPMENT

YOU ARE RESPONSIBLE
FOR EVERYONES SAFETY AND SECURITY

IT IS ABOUT MUSIC NOT DRUGS

THERE IS NO ROOM FOR VIOLENCE OR HATE

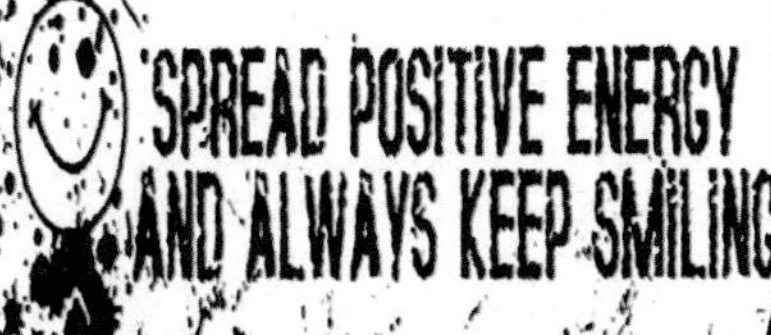

THE TEKNO CONSPIRACY
OUR MANIFESTO

OUR POLITICS OF CHOICE IS NONE
OUR RELIGION OF CHOICE IS NONE
OUR WEAPON OF CHOICE
IS FREE TEKNO

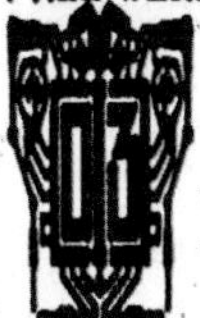

WE CONTINUE THE BATTLE AGAINST THE SYSTEM
THAT WANTS US TO LIVE IN A DYSTOPIA

WE ARE NOT CRIMINALS
WE DO NOT JUDGE AS WE ARE ALL EQUAL
OUR ONLY CRIME IS CHALLENGING LAWS
THE SYSTEM CREATED TO STOP US
FROM CELEBRATING OUR EXISTENCE

THE MUSIC WILL NEVER STOP
MUTATE AND SURVIVE
EXPLORE AND COMMUNICATE
WE ARE ONE MASSIVE
THE REVOLUTION CONTINUES
RIGHT HERE 23 RIGHT NOW

ANARCHISM: WHAT IT REALLY STANDS FOR ANARCHY.

by Emma Goldman

Ever reviled, accursed, ne'er understood, Thou art the grisly terror of our age. "Wreck of all order," cry the multitude, "Art thou, and war and murder's endless rage." O, let them cry. To them that ne'er have striven The truth that lies behind a word to find, To them the word's right meaning was not given. They shall continue blind among the blind. But thou, O word, so clear, so strong, so pure, Thou sayest all which I for goal have taken. I give thee to the future! Thine secure When each at least unto himself shall waken. Comes it in sunshine? In the tempest's thrill? I cannot tell--but it the earth shall see! I am an Anarchist! Wherefore I will Not rule, and also ruled I will not be!

JOHN HENRY MACKAY.

THE history of human growth and development is at the same time the history of the terrible struggle of every new idea heralding the approach of a brighter dawn. In its tenacious hold on tradition, the Old has never hesitated to make use of the foulest and cruelest means to stay the advent of the New, in whatever form or period the latter may have asserted itself. Nor need we retrace our steps into the distant past to realize the enormity of opposition, difficulties, and hardships placed in the path of every progressive idea. The rack, the thumbscrew, and the knout are still with us; so are the convict's garb and the social wrath, all conspiring against the spirit that is serenely marching on.

Anarchism could not hope to escape the fate of all other ideas of innovation. Indeed, as the most revolutionary and uncompromising innovator, Anarchism must needs meet with the combined ignorance and venom of the world it aims to reconstruct.

To deal even remotely with all that is being said and done against Anarchism would necessitate the writing of a whole volume. I shall therefore meet only two of the principal objections. In so doing, I shall attempt to elucidate what Anarchism really stands for.

The strange phenomenon of the opposition to Anarchism is that it brings to light the relation between so-called intelligence and ignorance. And yet this is not so very strange when we consider the relativity of all things. The ignorant mass has in its favor that it makes no pretense of knowledge or tolerance. Acting, as it always does, by mere impulse, its reasons are like those of a child. "Why?" "Because." Yet the opposition of the uneducated to Anarchism deserves the same consideration as that of the intelligent man.

What, then, are the objections? First, Anarchism is impractical, though a beautiful ideal. Second, Anarchism stands for violence and destruction, hence it must be repudiated as vile and dangerous. Both the intelligent man and the ignorant mass judge not from a thorough knowledge of the subject, but either from hearsay or false interpretation.

A practical scheme, says Oscar Wilde, is either one already in existence, or a scheme that could be carried out under the existing conditions; but it is exactly the existing conditions that one objects to, and any scheme that could accept these conditions is wrong and foolish. The true criterion of the practical, therefore, is not whether the latter can keep intact the wrong or foolish; rather is it whether the scheme has vitality enough to leave the stagnant waters of the old, and build, as well as sustain, new life. In the light of this conception, Anarchism is indeed practical. More than any other idea, it is helping to do away with the wrong and foolish; more than any other idea, it is building and sustaining new life.

The emotions of the ignorant man are continuously kept at a pitch by the most blood-curdling stories about Anarchism. Not a thing too outrageous to be employed against this philosophy and its exponents. Therefore Anarchism represents to the unthinking what the proverbial bad man does to the child,--a black monster bent on swallowing everything; in short, destruction and violence.

Destruction and violence! How is the ordinary man to know that the most violent element in society is ignorance; that its power of destruction is the very thing Anarchism is combating? Nor is he aware that Anarchism, whose roots, as it were, are part of nature's forces, destroys, not healthful tissue, but parasitic growths that feed on the life's essence of society. It is merely clearing the soil from weeds and sagebrush, that it may eventually bear healthy fruit.

Someone has said that it requires less mental effort to condemn than to think. The widespread mental indolence, so prevalent in society, proves this to be only too true. Rather than to go to the bottom of any given idea, to examine into its origin and meaning, most people will either condemn it altogether, or rely on some superficial or prejudicial definition of non-essentials.

Anarchism urges man to think, to investigate, to analyze every proposition; but that the brain capacity of the average reader be not taxed too much, I also shall begin with a definition, and then elaborate on the latter.

ANARCHISM:--The philosophy of a new social order based on liberty unrestricted by man-made law; the theory that all forms of government rest on violence, and are therefore wrong and harmful, as well as unnecessary.

The new social order rests, of course, on the materialistic basis of life; but while all Anarchists agree that the main evil today is an economic one, they maintain that the solution of that evil can be brought about only through the consideration of every phase of life,--individual, as well as the collective; the internal, as well as the external phases.

A thorough perusal of the history of human development will disclose two elements in bitter conflict with each other; elements that are only now beginning to be understood, not as foreign to each other, but as closely related and truly harmonious, if only placed in proper environment: the individual and social instincts. The individual and society have waged a relentless and bloody battle for ages, each striving for supremacy, because each was blind to the value and importance of the other. The individual and social instincts,--the one a most potent factor for individual endeavor, for growth, aspiration, self-realization; the other an equally potent factor for mutual helpfulness and social well-being.

The explanation of the storm raging within the individual, and between him and his surroundings, is not far to seek. The primitive man, unable to understand his being, much less the unity of all life, felt himself absolutely dependent on blind, hidden forces ever ready to mock and taunt him. Out of that attitude grew the religious concepts of man as a mere speck of dust dependent on superior powers on high, who can only be appeased by complete surrender. All the early sagas rest on that idea, which continues to be the Leitmotiv of the biblical tales dealing with the relation of man to God, to the State, to society. Again and again the same motif, man is nothing, the powers are everything. Thus Jehovah would only endure man on condition of complete surrender. Man can have all the glories of the earth, but he must not become conscious of himself. The State, society, and moral laws all sing the same refrain: Man can have all the glories of the earth, but he must not become conscious of himself.

Anarchism is the only philosophy which brings to man the consciousness of himself; which maintains that God, the State, and society are non-existent, that their promises are null and void, since they can be fulfilled only through man's subordination. Anarchism is therefore the teacher of the unity of life; not merely in nature, but in man. There is no conflict between the individual and the social instincts, any more than there is between the heart and the lungs: the one the receptacle of a precious life essence, the other the repository of the element that keeps the essence pure and strong. The individual is the heart of society, conserving the essence of social life; society is the lungs which are distributing the element to keep the life essence--that is, the individual--pure and strong.

"The one thing of value in the world," says Emerson, "is the active soul; this every man contains within him. The soul active sees absolute truth and utters truth and creates." In other words, the individual instinct is the thing of value in the world. It is the true soul that sees and creates the truth alive, out of which is to come a still greater truth, the reborn social soul.

Anarchism is the great liberator of man from the phantoms that have held him captive; it is the arbiter and pacifier of the two forces for individual and social harmony. To accomplish that unity, Anarchism has declared war on the pernicious influences which have so far prevented the harmonious blending of individual and social instincts, the individual and society.

Religion, the dominion of the human mind; Property, the dominion of human needs; and Government, the dominion of human conduct, represent the stronghold of man's enslavement and all the horrors it entails. Religion! How it dominates man's mind, how it humiliates and degrades his soul. God is everything, man is nothing, says religion. But out of that nothing God has created a kingdom so despotic, so tyrannical, so cruel, so terribly exacting that naught but gloom and tears and blood have ruled the world since gods began. Anarchism rouses man to rebellion against this black monster. Break your mental fetters, says Anarchism to man, for not until you think and judge for yourself will you get rid of the dominion of darkness, the greatest obstacle to all progress.

Property, the dominion of man's needs, the denial of the right to satisfy his needs. Time was when property claimed a divine right, when it came to man with the same refrain, even as religion, "Sacrifice! Abnegate! Submit!" The spirit of Anarchism has lifted man from his prostrate position. He now stands erect, with his face toward the light. He has learned to see the insatiable, devouring, devastating nature of property, and he is preparing to strike the monster dead.

"Property is robbery," said the great French Anarchist Proudhon. Yes, but without risk and danger to the robber. Monopolizing the accumulated efforts of man, property has robbed him of his birthright, and has turned him loose a pauper and an outcast. Property has not even the time-worn excuse that man does not create enough to satisfy all needs. The A B C student of economics knows that the productivity of labor within the last few decades far exceeds normal demand. But what are normal demands to an abnormal institution? The only demand that property recognizes is its own gluttonous appetite for greater wealth, because wealth means power; the power to subdue, to crush, to exploit, the power to enslave, to outrage, to degrade. America is particularly boastful of her great power, her enormous national wealth. Poor America, of what avail is all her wealth, if the individuals comprising the nation are wretchedly poor? If they live in squalor, in filth, in crime, with hope and joy gone, a homeless, soilless army of human prey.

It is generally conceded that unless the

returns of any business venture exceed the cost, bankruptcy is inevitable. But those engaged in the business of producing wealth have not yet learned even this simple lesson. Every year the cost of production in human life is growing larger (50,000 killed, 100,000 wounded in America last year); the returns to the masses, who help to create wealth, are ever getting smaller. Yet America continues to be blind to the inevitable bankruptcy of our business of production. Nor is this the only crime of the latter. Still more fatal is the crime of turning the producer into a mere particle of a machine, with less will and decision than his master of steel and iron. Man is being robbed not merely of the products of his labor, but of the power of free initiative, of originality, and the interest in, or desire for, the things he is making.

Real wealth consists in things of utility and beauty, in things that help to create strong, beautiful bodies and surroundings inspiring to live in. But if man is doomed to wind cotton around a spool, or dig coal, or build roads for thirty years of his life, there can be no talk of wealth. What he gives to the world is only gray and hideous things, reflecting a dull and hideous existence,--too weak to live, too cowardly to die. Strange to say, there are people who extol this deadening method of centralized production as the proudest achievement of our age. They fail utterly to realize that if we are to continue in machine subserviency, our slavery is more complete than was our bondage to the King. They do not want to know that centralization is not only the deathknell of liberty, but also of health and beauty, of art and science, all these being impossible in a clock-like, mechanical atmosphere.

Anarchism cannot but repudiate such a method of production: its goal is the freest possible expression of all the latent powers of the individual. Oscar Wilde defines a perfect personality as "one who develops under perfect conditions, who is not wounded, maimed, or in danger." A perfect personality, then, is only possible in a state of society where man is free to choose the mode of work, the conditions of work, and the freedom to work. One to whom the making of a table, the building of a house, or the tilling of the soil, is what the painting is to the artist and the discovery to the scientist,--the result of inspiration, of intense longing, and deep interest in work as a creative force. That being the ideal of Anarchism, its economic arrangements must consist of voluntary productive and distributive associations, gradually developing into free communism, as the best means of producing with the least waste of human energy. Anarchism, however, also recognizes the right of the individual, or numbers of individuals, to arrange at all times for other forms of work, in harmony with their tastes and desires.

Such free display of human energy being possible only under complete individual and social freedom, Anarchism directs its forces against the third and greatest foe of all social equality; namely, the State, organized authority, or statutory law,--the dominion of human conduct.

Just as religion has fettered the human mind, and as property, or the monopoly of things, has subdued and stifled man's needs, so has the State enslaved his spirit, dictating every phase of conduct. "All government in essence," says Emerson, "is tyranny." It matters not whether it is government by divine right or majority rule. In every instance its aim is the absolute subordination of the individual.

Referring to the American government, the greatest American Anarchist, David Thoreau, said: "Government, what is it but a tradition, though a recent one, endeavoring to transmit itself unimpaired to posterity, but each instance losing its integrity; it has not the vitality and force of a single living man. Law never made man a whit more just; and by means of their respect for it, even the well disposed are daily made agents of injustice."

Indeed, the keynote of government is injustice. With the arrogance and self-sufficiency of the King who could do no wrong, governments ordain, judge, condemn, and punish the most insignificant offenses, while maintaining themselves by the greatest of all offenses, the annihilation of individual liberty. Thus Ouida is right when she maintains that "the State only aims at instilling those qualities in its public by which its demands are obeyed, and its exchequer is filled. Its highest attainment is the reduction of mankind to clockwork. In its atmosphere all those finer and more delicate liberties, which require treatment and spacious expansion, inevitably dry up and perish. The State requires a taxpaying machine in which there is no hitch, an exchequer in which there is never a deficit, and a public, monotonous, obedient, colorless, spiritless, moving humbly like a flock of sheep along a straight high road between two walls."

Yet even a flock of sheep would resist the chicanery of the State, if it were not for the corruptive, tyrannical, and oppressive methods it employs to serve its purposes. Therefore Bakunin repudiates the State as synonymous with the surrender of the liberty of the individual or small minorities,--the destruction of social relationship, the curtailment, or complete denial even, of life itself, for its own aggrandizement. The State is the altar of political freedom and, like the religious altar, it is maintained for the purpose of human sacrifice.

In fact, there is hardly a modern thinker who does not agree that government, organized authority, or the State, is necessary only to maintain or protect property and monopoly. It has proven efficient in that function only.

Even George Bernard Shaw, who hopes for the miraculous from the State under Fabianism, nevertheless admits that "it is at present a huge machine for robbing and slave-driving of the poor by brute force." This being the case, it is hard to see why the clever prefacer wishes to uphold the State after poverty shall have ceased to exist.

Unfortunately, there are still a number of people who continue in the fatal belief that government rests on natural laws, that it maintains social order and harmony, that it diminishes crime, and that it prevents the lazy man from fleecing his fellows. I shall therefore examine these contentions.

A natural law is that factor in man which asserts itself freely and spontaneously without any external force, in harmony with the requirements of nature. For instance, the demand for nutrition, for sex gratification, for light, air, and exercise, is a natural law. But its expression needs not the machinery of government, needs not the club, the gun, the handcuff, or the prison. To obey such laws, if we may call it obedience, requires only spontaneity and free opportunity. That governments do not maintain themselves through such harmonious factors is proven by the terrible array of violence, force, and coercion all governments use in order to live. Thus Blackstone is right when he says, "Human laws are invalid, because they are contrary to the laws of nature."

Unless it be the order of Warsaw after the slaughter of thousands of people, it is difficult to ascribe to governments any capacity for order or social harmony. Order derived through submission and maintained by terror is not much of a safe guaranty; yet that is the only "order" that governments have ever maintained. True social harmony grows naturally out of solidarity of interests. In a society where those who always work never have anything, while those who never work enjoy everything, solidarity of interests is non-existent; hence social harmony is but a myth. The only way organized authority meets this grave situation is by extending still greater privileges to those who have already monopolized the earth, and by still further enslaving the disinherited masses. Thus the entire arsenal of government--laws, police, soldiers, the courts, legislatures, prisons,--is strenuously engaged in "harmonizing" the most antagonistic elements in society.

The most absurd apology for authority and law is that they serve to diminish crime. Aside from the fact that the State is itself the greatest criminal, breaking every written and natural law, stealing in the form of taxes, killing in the form of war and capital punishment, it has come to an absolute standstill in coping with crime. It has failed utterly to destroy or even minimize the horrible scourge of its own creation.

Crime is naught but misdirected energy. So long as every institution of today, economic, political, social, and moral, conspires to misdirect human energy into wrong channels; so long as most people are out of place doing the things they hate to do, living a life they loathe to live, crime will be inevitable, and all the laws on the statutes can only increase, but never do away with, crime. What does society, as it exists today, know of the process of despair, the poverty, the horrors, the fearful struggle the human soul must pass on its way to crime and degradation. Who that knows this terrible process can fail to see the truth in these words of Peter Kropotkin:

"Those who will hold the balance between the benefits thus attributed to law and punishment and the degrading effect of the latter on humanity; those who will estimate the torrent of depravity poured abroad in human society by the informer, favored by the Judge even, and paid for in clinking cash by governments, under the pretext of aiding to unmask crime; those who will go within prison walls and there see what human beings become when deprived of liberty, when subjected to the care of brutal keepers, to coarse, cruel words, to a thousand stinging, piercing humiliations, will agree with us that the entire apparatus of prison and punishment is an abomination which ought to be brought to an end."

The deterrent influence of law on the lazy man is too absurd to merit consideration. If society were only relieved of the waste and expense of keeping a lazy class, and the equally great expense of the paraphernalia of protection this lazy class requires, the social tables would contain an abundance for all, including even the occasional lazy individual. Besides, it is well to consider that laziness results either from special privileges, or physical and mental abnormalities. Our present insane system of production fosters both, and the most astounding phenomenon is that people should want to work at all now. Anarchism aims to strip labor of its deadening, dulling aspect, of its gloom and compulsion. It aims to make work an instrument of joy, of strength, of color, of real harmony, so that the poorest sort of a man should find in work both recreation and hope.

To achieve such an arrangement of life, government, with its unjust, arbitrary, repressive measures, must be done away with. At best it has but imposed one single mode of life upon all, without regard to individual and social variations and needs. In destroying government and statutory laws, Anarchism proposes to rescue the self-respect and independence of the individual from all restraint and invasion by authority. Only in freedom can man grow to his full stature. Only in freedom will he learn to think and move, and give the very best in him. Only in freedom will he realize the true force of the social bonds which knit men together, and which are the true foundation of a normal social life.

But what about human nature? Can it be changed? And if not, will it endure under Anarchism?

Poor human nature, what horrible crimes have been committed in thy name! Every fool, from king to policeman, from the flatheaded parson to the visionless dabbler in science,

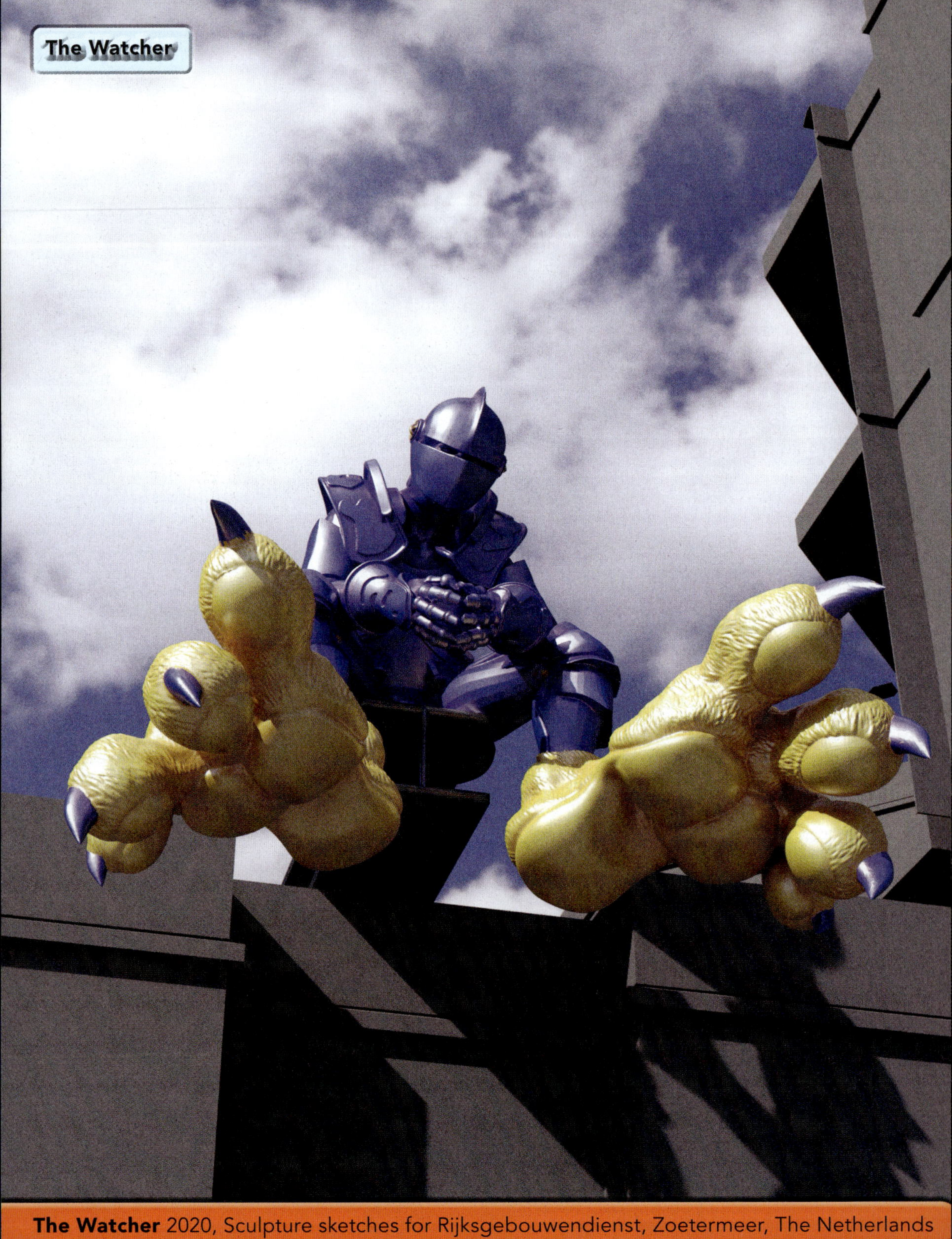

The Watcher 2020, Sculpture sketches for Rijksgebouwendienst, Zoetermeer, The Netherlands

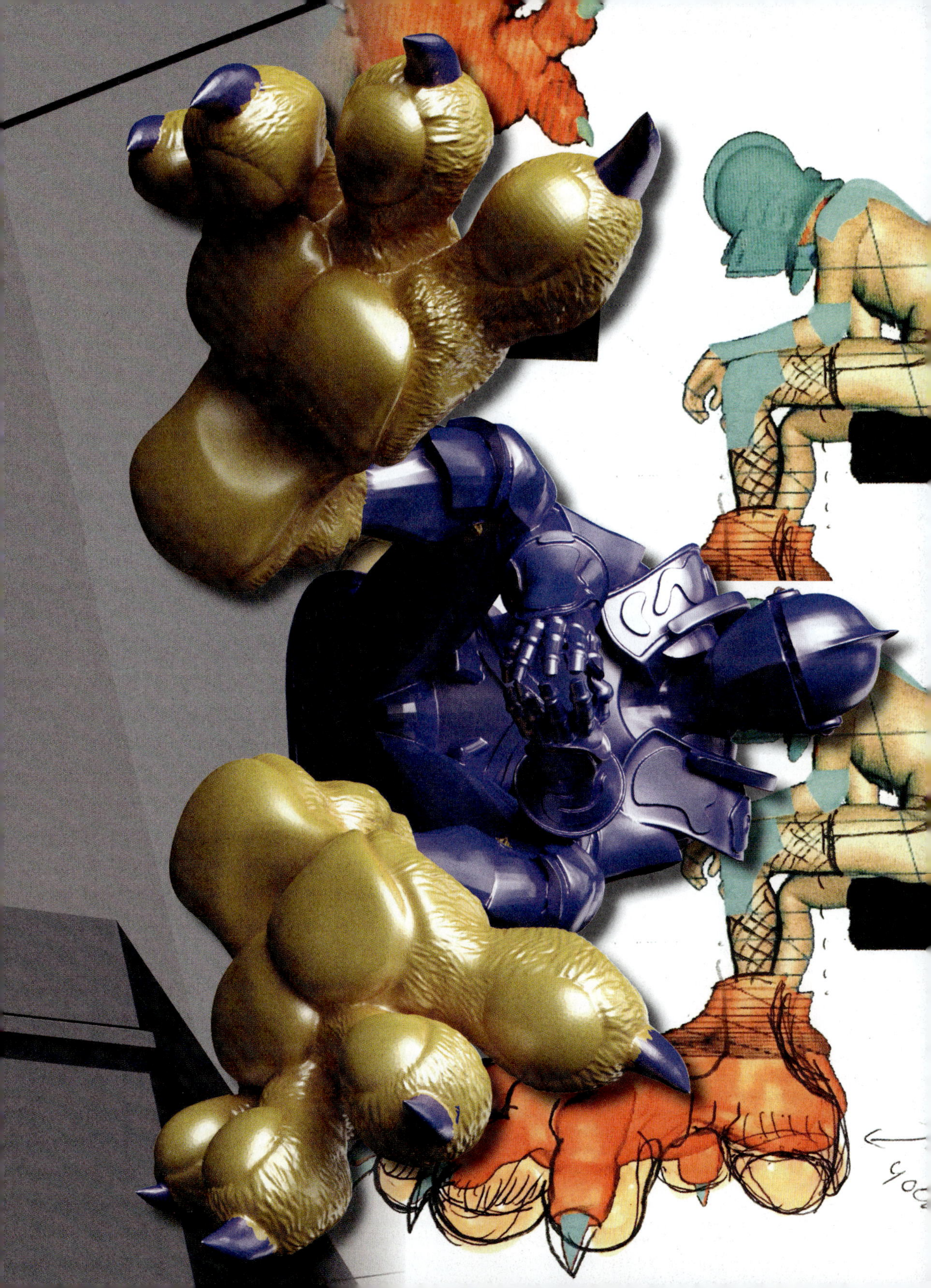

presumes to speak authoritatively of human nature. The greater the mental charlatan, the more definite his insistence on the wickedness and weaknesses of human nature. Yet, how can any one speak of it today, with every soul in a prison, with every heart fettered, wounded, and maimed?

John Burroughs has stated that experimental study of animals in captivity is absolutely useless. Their character, their habits, their appetites undergo a complete transformation when torn from their soil in field and forest. With human nature caged in a narrow space, whipped daily into submission, how can we speak of its potentialities?

Freedom, expansion, opportunity, and, above all, peace and repose, alone can teach us the real dominant factors of human nature and all its wonderful possibilities.

Anarchism, then, really stands for the liberation of the human mind from the dominion of religion; the liberation of the human body from the dominion of property; liberation from the shackles and restraint of government. Anarchism stands for a social order based on the free grouping of individuals for the purpose of producing real social wealth; an order that will guarantee to every human being free access to the earth and full enjoyment of the necessities of life, according to individual desires, tastes, and inclinations.

This is not a wild fancy or an aberration of the mind. It is the conclusion arrived at by hosts of intellectual men and women the world over; a conclusion resulting from the close and studious observation of the tendencies of modern society: individual liberty and economic equality, the twin forces for the birth of what is fine and true in man.

As to methods. Anarchism is not, as some may suppose, a theory of the future to be realized through divine inspiration. It is a living force in the affairs of our life, constantly creating new conditions. The methods of Anarchism therefore do not comprise an iron-clad program to be carried out under all circumstances. Methods must grow out of the economic needs of each place and clime, and of the intellectual and temperamental requirements of the individual. The serene, calm character of a Tolstoy will wish different methods for social reconstruction than the intense, overflowing personality of a Michael Bakunin or a Peter Kropotkin. Equally so it must be apparent that the economic and political needs of Russia will dictate more drastic measures than would England or America. Anarchism does not stand for military drill and uniformity; it does, however, stand for the spirit of revolt, in whatever form, against everything that hinders human growth. All Anarchists agree in that, as they also agree in their opposition to the political machinery as a means of bringing about the great social change.

"All voting," says Thoreau, "is a sort of gaming, like checkers, or backgammon, a playing with right and wrong; its obligation never exceeds that of expediency. Even voting for the right thing is doing nothing for it. A wise man will not leave the right to the mercy of chance, nor wish it to prevail through the power of the majority." A close examination of the machinery of politics and its achievements will bear out the logic of Thoreau.

What does the history of parliamentarism show? Nothing but failure and defeat, not even a single reform to ameliorate the economic and social stress of the people. Laws have been passed and enactments made for the improvement and protection of labor. Thus it was proven only last year that Illinois, with the most rigid laws for mine protection, had the greatest mine disasters. In States where child labor laws prevail, child exploitation is at its highest, and though with us the workers enjoy full political opportunities, capitalism has reached the most brazen zenith.

Even were the workers able to have their own representatives, for which our good Socialist politicians are clamoring, what chances are there for their honesty and good faith? One has but to bear in mind the process of politics to realize that its path of good intentions is full of pitfalls: wire-pulling, intriguing, flattering, lying, cheating; in fact, chicanery of every description, whereby the political aspirant can achieve success. Added to that is a complete demoralization of character and conviction, until nothing is left that would make one hope for anything from such a human derelict. Time and time again the people were foolish enough to trust, believe, and support with their last farthing aspiring politicians, only to find themselves betrayed and cheated.

It may be claimed that men of integrity would not become corrupt in the political grinding mill. Perhaps not; but such men would be absolutely helpless to exert the slightest influence in behalf of labor, as indeed has been shown in numerous instances. The State is the economic master of its servants. Good men, if such there be, would either remain true to their political faith and lose their economic support, or they would cling to their economic master and be utterly unable to do the slightest good. The political arena leaves one no alternative, one must either be a dunce or a rogue.

The political superstition is still holding sway over the hearts and minds of the masses, but the true lovers of liberty will have no more to do with it. Instead, they believe with Stirner that man has as much liberty as he is willing to take. Anarchism therefore stands for direct action, the open defiance of, and resistance to, all laws and restrictions, economic, social, and moral. But defiance and resistance are illegal. Therein lies the salvation of man. Everything illegal necessitates integrity, self-reliance, and courage. In short, it calls for free, independent spirits, for "men who are men, and who have a bone in their backs which you cannot pass your hand through."

Universal suffrage itself owes its existence to direct action. If not for the spirit of rebellion, of the defiance on the part of the American revolutionary fathers, their posterity would still wear the King's coat. If not for the direct action of a John Brown and his comrades, America would still trade in the flesh of the black man. True, the trade in white flesh is still going on; but that, too, will have to be abolished by direct action. Trade-unionism, the economic arena of the modern gladiator, owes its existence to direct action. It is but recently that law and government have attempted to crush the trade-union movement, and condemned the exponents of man's right to organize to prison as conspirators. Had they sought to assert their cause through begging, pleading, and compromise, trade-unionism would today be a negligible quantity. In France, in Spain, in Italy, in Russia, nay even in England (witness the growing rebellion of English labor unions), direct, revolutionary, economic action has become so strong a force in the battle for industrial liberty as to make the world realize the tremendous importance of labor's power. The General Strike, the supreme expression of the economic consciousness of the workers, was ridiculed in America but a short time ago. Today every great strike, in order to win, must realize the importance of the solidaric general protest.

Direct action, having proven effective along economic lines, is equally potent in the environment of the individual. There a hundred forces encroach upon his being, and only persistent resistance to them will finally set him free. Direct action against the authority in the shop, direct action against the authority of the law, direct action against the invasive, meddlesome authority of our moral code, is the logical, consistent method of Anarchism.

Will it not lead to a revolution? Indeed, it will. No real social change has ever come about without a revolution. People are either not familiar with their history, or they have not yet learned that revolution is but thought carried into action.

Anarchism, the great leaven of thought, is today permeating every phase of human endeavor. Science, art, literature, the drama, the effort for economic betterment, in fact every individual and social opposition to the existing disorder of things, is illumined by the spiritual light of Anarchism. It is the philosophy of the sovereignty of the individual. It is the theory of social harmony. It is the great, surging, living truth that is reconstructing the world, and that will usher in the Dawn.

Author: Emma Goldman, Title: 'ANARCHISM: WHAT IT REALLY STANDS FOR ANARCHY' Published in Anarchism and Other Essays, Third revised edition, New York: Mother Earth Publishing Association, 1917.

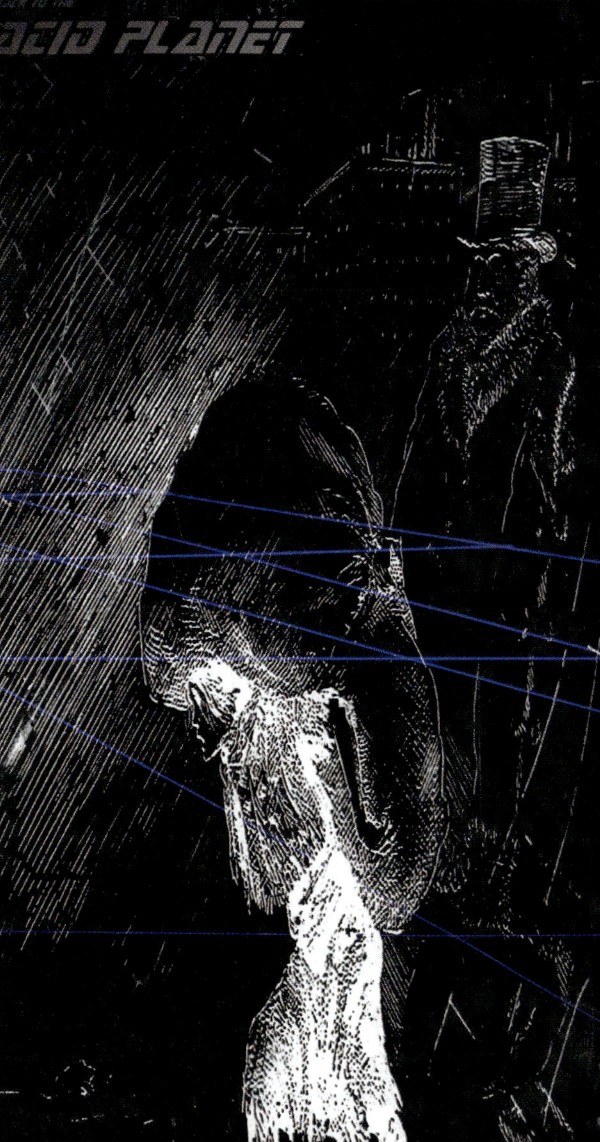

TEGRITY 3D 2009, Tableau Vivant, in collaboration with AIDS-3D (Daniel Keller & Nik Kosmas)

'By 2005 or so, it was becoming clear that electronic music could no longer deliver sounds that were "futuristic." From the end of World War II up until the 1990s, electronic music—whether produced by high-culture composers such as Pierre Schaeffer or Karlheinz Stockhausen or by synthpop groups and dance-music producers—had been synonymous with a sense of the future, so much so that film and television would habitually turn to electronic music when it wanted to invoke the future. But by 2005, electronica was no longer capable of evoking a future that felt strange or dissonant. If electronic music was "futuristic," it was in the same sense that fonts are "gothic"—the futuristic now connoted a settled set of concepts, affects, and associations. Twenty-first-century electronic music had failed to progress beyond what had been recorded in the twentieth century: practically anything produced in the 2000s could have been recorded in the 1990s. Electronic music had succumbed to its own inertia and retrospection. It was also clear that this was more than a moment in a familiar pattern, in which, as one genre wanes, another emerges to take its place at the leading edge of innovation. There was no leading edge of innovation any more. In music, as elsewhere in culture, we were living, in Franco Berardi's suggestive phrase, after the future.

What haunts the digital cul-de-sacs of the twenty-first century is not so much the past as all the lost futures that the twentieth century taught us to anticipate. The futures that have been lost were more than a matter of musical style. More broadly, and more troublingly, the disappearance of the future meant the deterioration of a whole mode of social imagination: the capacity to conceive of a world radically different from the one in which we currently live. It meant the acceptance of a situation in which culture would continue without really changing, and where politics was reduced to the administration of an already established (capitalist) system.

In other words, we were in the "end of history" described by Francis Fukuyama. Fukuyama's thesis was the other side of Fredric Jameson's claim that postmodernism—characterised by its inability to find forms adequate to the present, still less to anticipate wholly new futures—was the "cultural logic of late capitalism."

The future is always experienced as a haunting: as a virtuality that already impinges on the present, conditioning expectations and motivating cultural production. What hauntological music mourns is less the failure of a future to transpire—the future as actuality—than the disappearance of this effective virtuality.'

What Is Hauntology?

Excerpt from: Title: "What Is Hauntology?" Author: Mark Fisher, First published in: Film Quarterly Vol. 66, No. 1, Page: 16-24, Published by: University of California Press, Year: 2012.

'Leyland James Kirby, the man behind the Caretaker project, released an album whose title captured perfectly the sense of yearning for a future that we feel cheated out of: Sadly, The Future Is No Longer What It Was. Faced with the collapse into a time dominated by pastiche and reiteration, hauntological music found itself at the heart of a paradox. Could the only opposition to a culture dominated by what Jameson calls the "nostalgia mode" be a kind of nostalgia for modernism?

If the conditions for this "popular modernism" were provided to a large extent by social democracy, its aspirations were not confined to a hope that social democracy would simply continue. The radical dimension of social democratic culture, in fact, consisted in the way it produced a longing for its (self-)overcoming, that it was premised on the

WE WANT YOU TO WAKE UP TO WAKE OTHERS UP TO
KNOW YOU ARE FREE TO THINK FOR YOURSELF TO
PROTECT YOUR RIGHTS
AND TO RESIST TYRANNY

MISSION STATEMENT

THIS IS OUR AUTONOMOUS ZONE
MUTATE SURVIVE
EXPLORE COMMUNICATE
WE CONTINUE THE BATTLE
AGAINST THE SYSTEM
THAT WANTS US TO LIVE IN DYSTOPIA
OUR POLITICS OF CHOICE IS NONE
OUR RELIGION OF CHOICE IS NONE
OUR WEAPON OF CHOICE IS FREE TEKNO
FORWARD THE REVOLUTION
RIGHT HERE RIGHT NOW

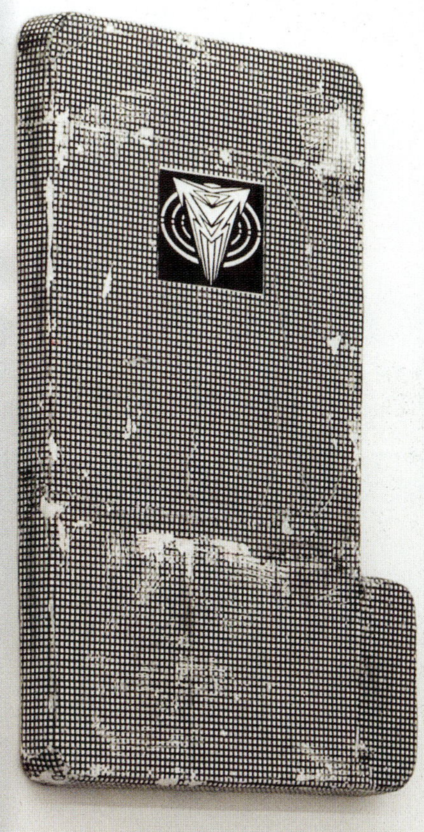

TEMPORARY AUTONOMOUS ZONE

WHAT OF THE ANARCHIST DREAM THE STATELESS
STATE THE COMMUNE THE
AUTONOMOUS ZONE WITH DURATION A FREE SOCIETY
A FREE CULTURE ARE WE TO
ABANDON THAT HOPE IN RETURN FOR SOME
EXISTENTIALIST ACTE GRATUIT THE POINT IS NOT TO
CHANGE CONSCIOUSNESS
BUT TO CHANGE THE WORLD
ARE WE DOOMED TO NEVER EXPERIENCE AUTONOMY
NEVER TO STAND ON A LAND GOVERNED
EXCLUSIVELY BY FREEDOM FOR A MOMENT DO WE
HAVE TO WAIT UNTIL THE WHOLE WORLD IS FREED
FROM POLITICAL DOMINATION BEFORE ONE OF US
KNOWS WHAT FREEDOM IS
THE TAZ TEMPORARY AUTONOMOUS ZONE IS A
GUERRILLA TACTIC TO CLAIM A LOCATION AS A
TEMPORARY FREE STATE IN AN ERA IN WHICH THE
STATE IS OMNIPRESENT THE TAZ IS THE UPRISING
WITHIN EVERYONES REACH THE PARTY THAT CAN
ERUPT ANY MOMENT
FREE ZONES
FREE PEOPLE
FREE TEKNO

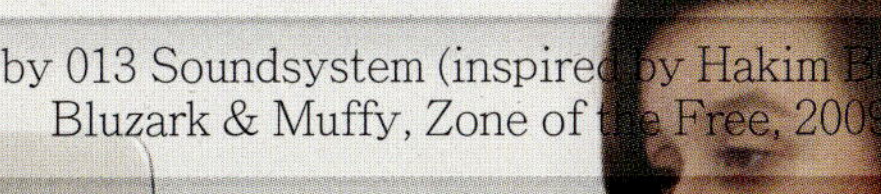

by 013 Soundsystem (inspired by Hakim Bey)
Bluzark & Muffy, Zone of the Free, 2009

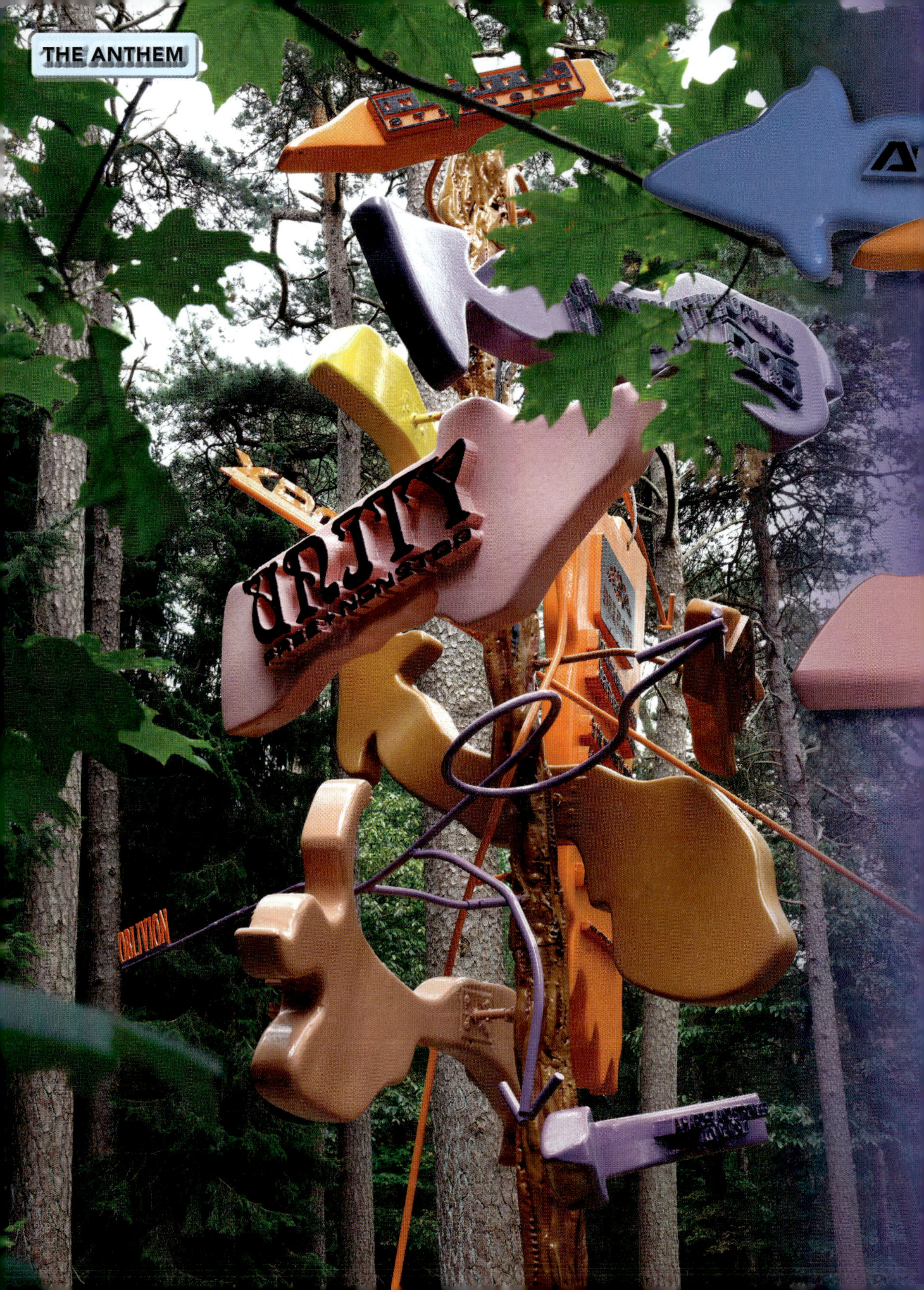
UNITY
OBLIVION

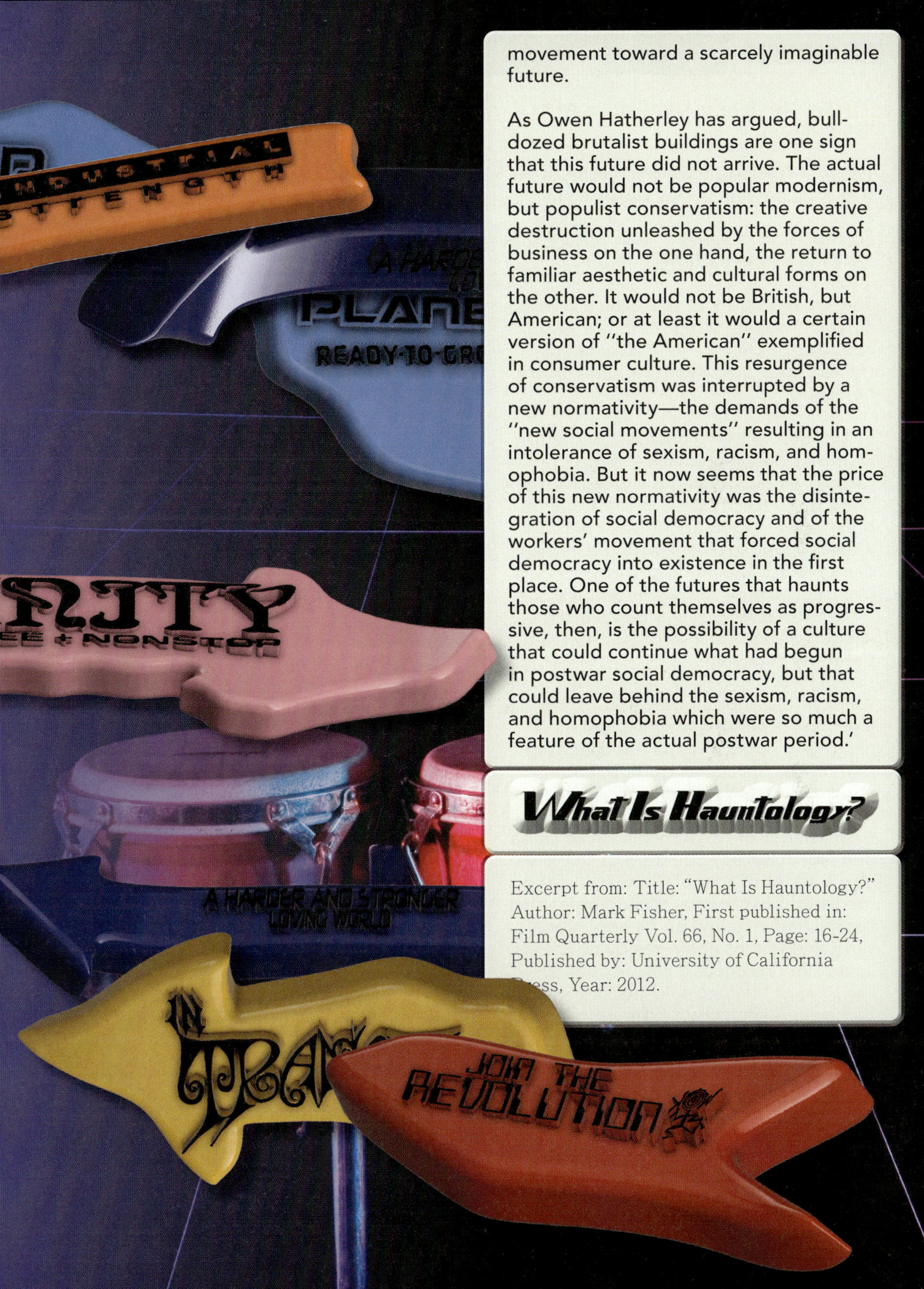

movement toward a scarcely imaginable future.

As Owen Hatherley has argued, bulldozed brutalist buildings are one sign that this future did not arrive. The actual future would not be popular modernism, but populist conservatism: the creative destruction unleashed by the forces of business on the one hand, the return to familiar aesthetic and cultural forms on the other. It would not be British, but American; or at least it would a certain version of "the American" exemplified in consumer culture. This resurgence of conservatism was interrupted by a new normativity—the demands of the "new social movements" resulting in an intolerance of sexism, racism, and homophobia. But it now seems that the price of this new normativity was the disintegration of social democracy and of the workers' movement that forced social democracy into existence in the first place. One of the futures that haunts those who count themselves as progressive, then, is the possibility of a culture that could continue what had begun in postwar social democracy, but that could leave behind the sexism, racism, and homophobia which were so much a feature of the actual postwar period.'

What Is Hauntology?

Excerpt from: Title: "What Is Hauntology?" Author: Mark Fisher, First published in: Film Quarterly Vol. 66, No. 1, Page: 16-24, Published by: University of California Press, Year: 2012.

THE ANTHEM

'We can distinguish two directions in hauntology.

The first refers to that which is (in actuality is) no longer, but which is still effective as a virtuality (the traumatic "compulsion to repeat," a structure that repeats, a fatal pattern).

The second refers to that which (in actuality) has not yet happened, but which is already effective in the virtual (an attractor, an anticipation shaping current behavior).

In addition to being another moment in Derrida's deconstruction—where "hauntology" would resume the work formerly done by concepts such as the trace or diffe´rance—Specters of Marx was also a specific engagement with the immediate historical context provided by the disintegration of the Soviet empire. Or rather, it was an engagement with the alleged disappearance of history trumpeted by Fukuyama.

What would happen now that actually existing socialism had collapsed, and capitalism could assume full spectrum dominance, its claims to global dominion thwarted not any longer by the existence of a whole other bloc, but by small islands of resistance such as Cuba and North Korea? Specters of Marx was also a series of speculations about the media (or post-media) technologies that capital had installed on its now global territory—hauntology was by no means something rarefied; it was proper to the time of "techno-tele-discursivity, techno-tele-iconicity," "simulacra," and "synthetic images."

But this discussion of the "tele-"shows that hauntology concerns a crisis of space as well as time. As theorists such as Paul Virilio and Jean Baudrillard had long acknowledged—and Specters of Marx can also be read as Derrida settling his account with these thinkers—"tele-technologies" collapse

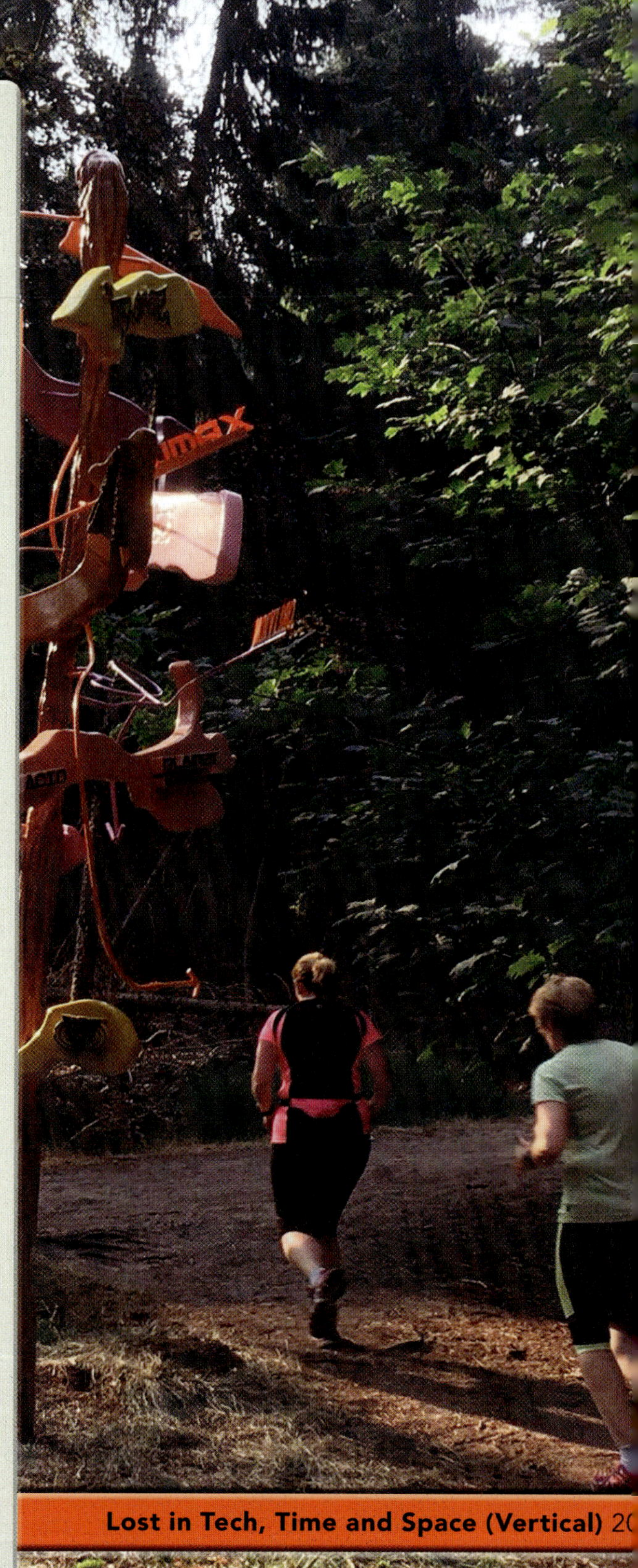

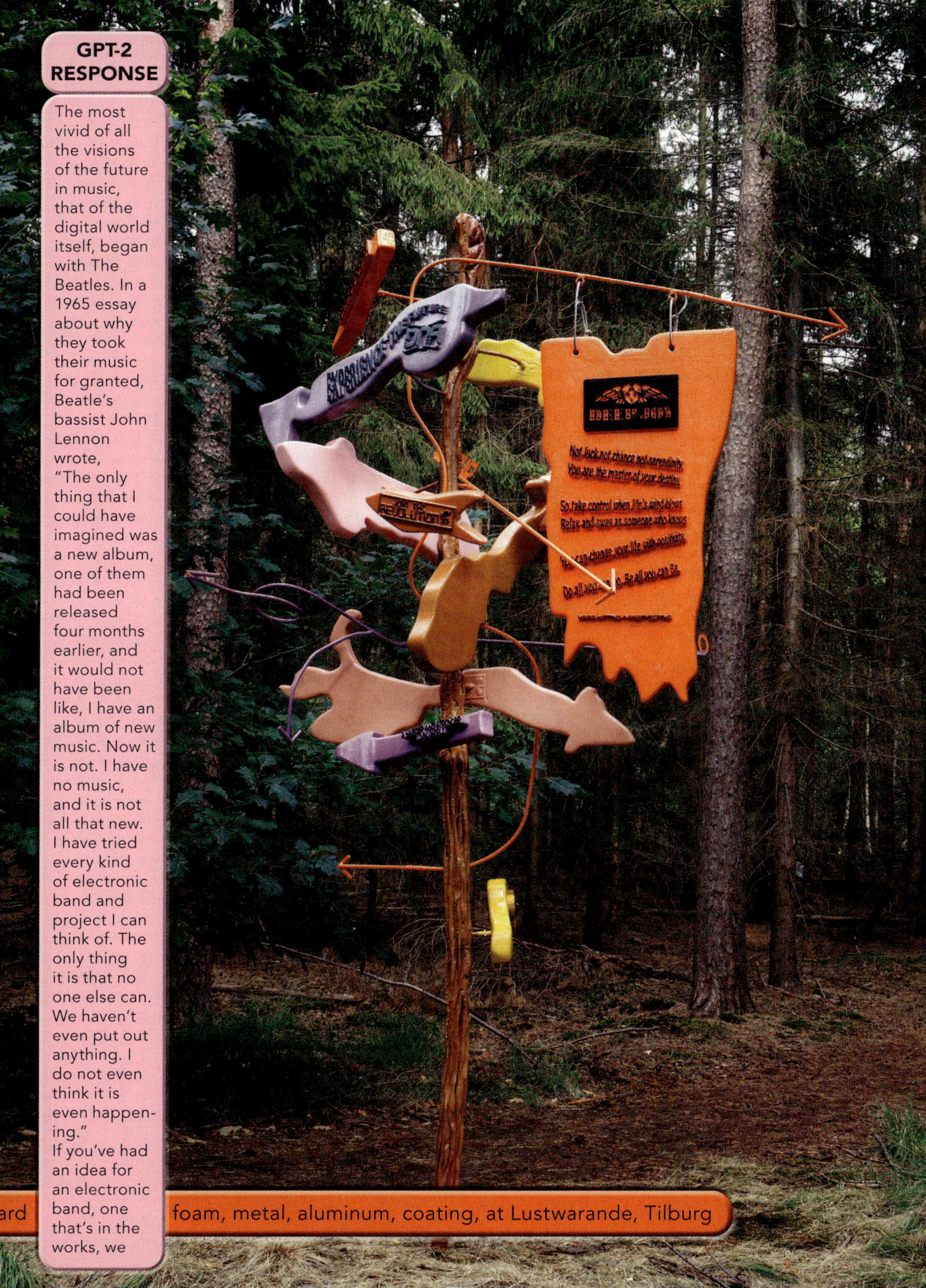

GPT-2 RESPONSE

The most vivid of all the visions of the future in music, that of the digital world itself, began with The Beatles. In a 1965 essay about why they took their music for granted, Beatle's bassist John Lennon wrote, "The only thing that I could have imagined was a new album, one of them had been released four months earlier, and it would not have been like, I have an album of new music. Now it is not. I have no music, and it is not all that new. I have tried every kind of electronic band and project I can think of. The only thing it is that no one else can. We haven't even put out anything. I do not even think it is even happening." If you've had an idea for an electronic band, one that's in the works, we

ard … foam, metal, aluminum, coating, at Lustwarande, Tilburg

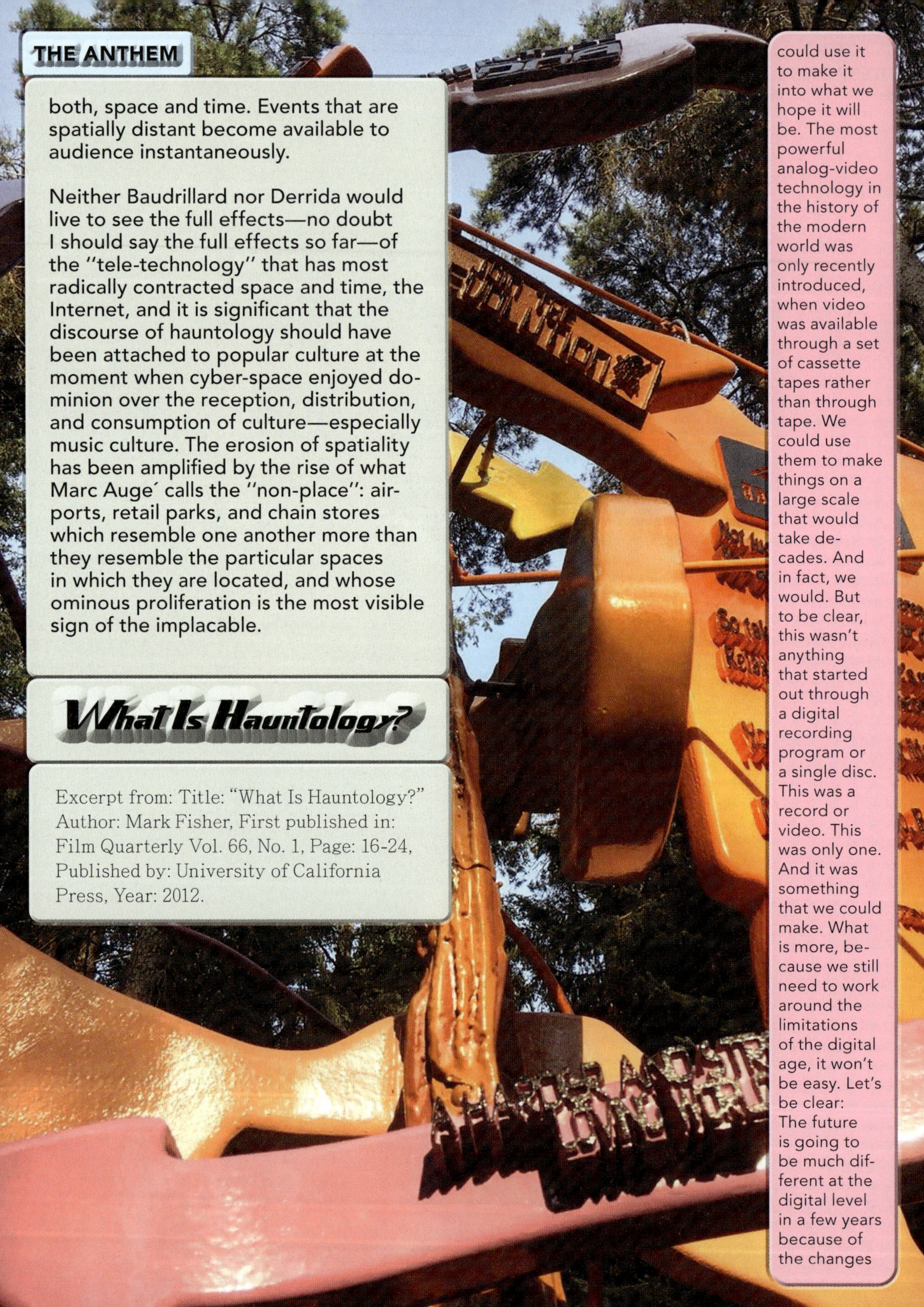

both, space and time. Events that are spatially distant become available to audience instantaneously.

Neither Baudrillard nor Derrida would live to see the full effects—no doubt I should say the full effects so far—of the "tele-technology" that has most radically contracted space and time, the Internet, and it is significant that the discourse of hauntology should have been attached to popular culture at the moment when cyber-space enjoyed dominion over the reception, distribution, and consumption of culture—especially music culture. The erosion of spatiality has been amplified by the rise of what Marc Augé calls the "non-place": airports, retail parks, and chain stores which resemble one another more than they resemble the particular spaces in which they are located, and whose ominous proliferation is the most visible sign of the implacable.

What Is Hauntology?

Excerpt from: Title: "What Is Hauntology?" Author: Mark Fisher, First published in: Film Quarterly Vol. 66, No. 1, Page: 16-24, Published by: University of California Press, Year: 2012.

could use it to make it into what we hope it will be. The most powerful analog-video technology in the history of the modern world was only recently introduced, when video was available through a set of cassette tapes rather than through tape. We could use them to make things on a large scale that would take decades. And in fact, we would. But to be clear, this wasn't anything that started out through a digital recording program or a single disc. This was a record or video. This was only one. And it was something that we could make. What is more, because we still need to work around the limitations of the digital age, it won't be easy. Let's be clear: The future is going to be much different at the digital level in a few years because of the changes

OUTLINE

Title: Noise, The Political Economy of Music, Author: Jacques Attali Translation: Brian Massumi, First published by: Manchester University Press, Year: 1977

By Theodore Gracyk

"What is noise to the old order is harmony to the new." (35) As much as possible, the outline uses the vocabulary of the Massumi translation. [Comments in square brackets are my personal comments]

Chapter 1: **Listening**
Chapter 2: **Sacrificing**
Chapter 3: **Representing**
Chapter 4: **Repeating**
Chapter 5: **Composing**

The book's cover is a detail of the lower left corner of Peter Brueghel the Elder's painting **'The Fight between Carnival and Lent or Carnival's Quarrel'** with Lent. Inside, there is a black and white reproduction of the whole painting. Attali thinks that the painting is a brilliant symbolic prophecy of his own ideas about music, noise, and politics. If we draw a line from the upper left corner to the lower right corner, the painting divides into two "zones." Carnival is the left zone. Lent is the right zone. These represent "two antagonistic cultural and ideological organizations."

[We might expect the carnival zone to include both the ring dance and the game of catch with the pottery. But we will see that Attali regards the game of catch as symbolizing the repeating stage of "Lent" and he regards the ring dance, at the top edge of the village square, as a stage that moves us beyond "Lent."]

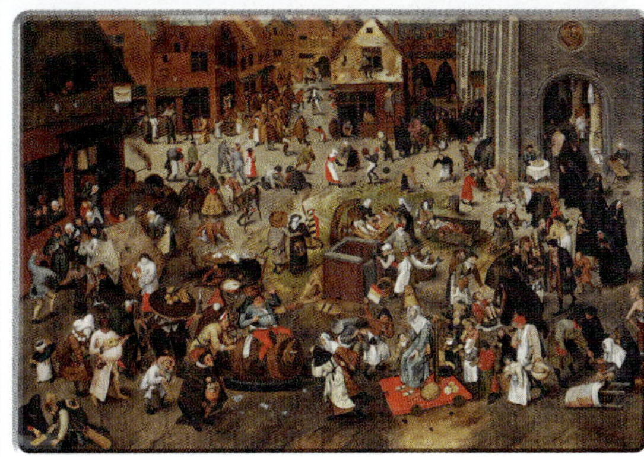

The Fight between Carnical and Lent by Pieter Bruegel
Source: wikimedia.commons

As explained in Chapter Two, this division into zones captures the main oppositions explored in Attali's book:

Festival/Carnival	Lent
Noise	Silence through ritualized order
Disruption & general violence	The bourgeois norm
The scapegoat is sacrificed.	Penitence (personal sacrifice)
Distraction from the misery of life through the sacrifice of a god.	The alienation of life made bearable by a promise of eternity.

Chapter 1: **Listening**
Main idea: Music is both a mirror and a prophecy. Attali doesn't theorize about music so music as through it. (4)

The only thing common to all music is that it gives structure to noise. (9-10) Our musical process of structuring noise is also our political process for structuring community.

Music is both a mirror and a prophecy. It is a mirror, for its organization resembles the current organization of our society: music is "a repository of . . . the social score." (p. 9) **"Music runs parallel to human society, is structured like it, and changes when it does."** (10)
It is our "collective memory of the social order." (9)

[We' re not talking about particular societies here, like the difference between French social life and American social life. Nor is Attali addressing the specific way that a nation is politically organized, such as the way that the British political system differs from the American system. He means organization of the most general sort: the way that feudalism differs from advanced capitalism.]

At the same time, music is prophecy: "**its styles and economic organization are ahead of the rest of society** because it explores, much faster than material reality can, the entire range of possibilities in a given code." (11) Prophecy is possible because each code [mode of organization] pushes to its own extreme case, "to the point where it creates the internal condition for its own rupture, its own noise. What is noise to the old order is harmony to the new." (35)

If we can see where music is headed, then we can see where all of society is headed. Attali thinks that he can make predictions about capitalism based on some recent [that is, 1970s!] events in musical life. These predictions are made in Chapter 5.

Chapter 2: **Sacrificing**
Main idea: Within organized society before exchange [that is, prior to capitalism], music was a ritual murder. It thereby affirms that society is possible, that we can set aside our differences in a mutual sacrifice: we can turn noise [violence] into music [action involving sublimation of violence]. Sacrificing makes us forget that we could be free.

The aim is to make people forget that normalcy [order] has triumphed over carnival [freedom]. The value of sacrifice [why we accept it] is the pure order that it offers as an antidote to the general violence of carnival.

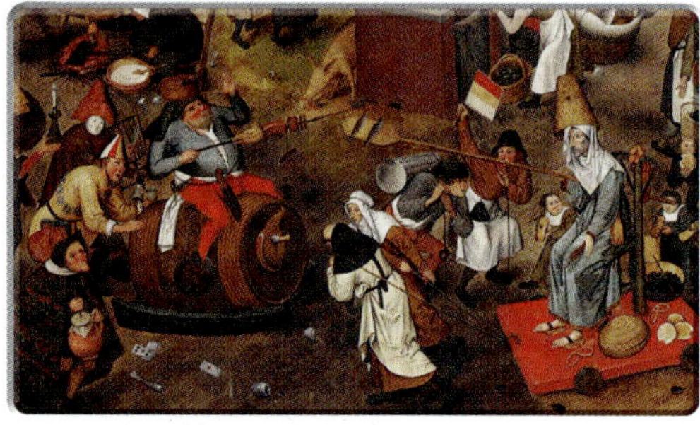

Within the festival we see a simulacrum of pagan sacrifice. (23)

[I take it that Attali regards listening as a state of nature in which each of us has the right to secure our needs through violence, and that we trade this general violence for order in a social contract. Individuals refrain from violence and allow the state to engage in violence for us.]

There must be a scapegoat [a sacrificial victim] toward whom we channel the violence that we sacrifice.

Attali summarizes his own argument:
Noise is violence, i.e., murder. Music is a channelization of noise and a simulacrum of sacrifice, a sublimation to create order and political integration. Therefore music is ritual murder. (26)

NOISE DEFINED: "A noise is a resonance that interferes with the audition of a message in the process of emission." (26)
It is any disruption of any social process, any source of pain. At the extreme [extreme volume, for instance], it kills.

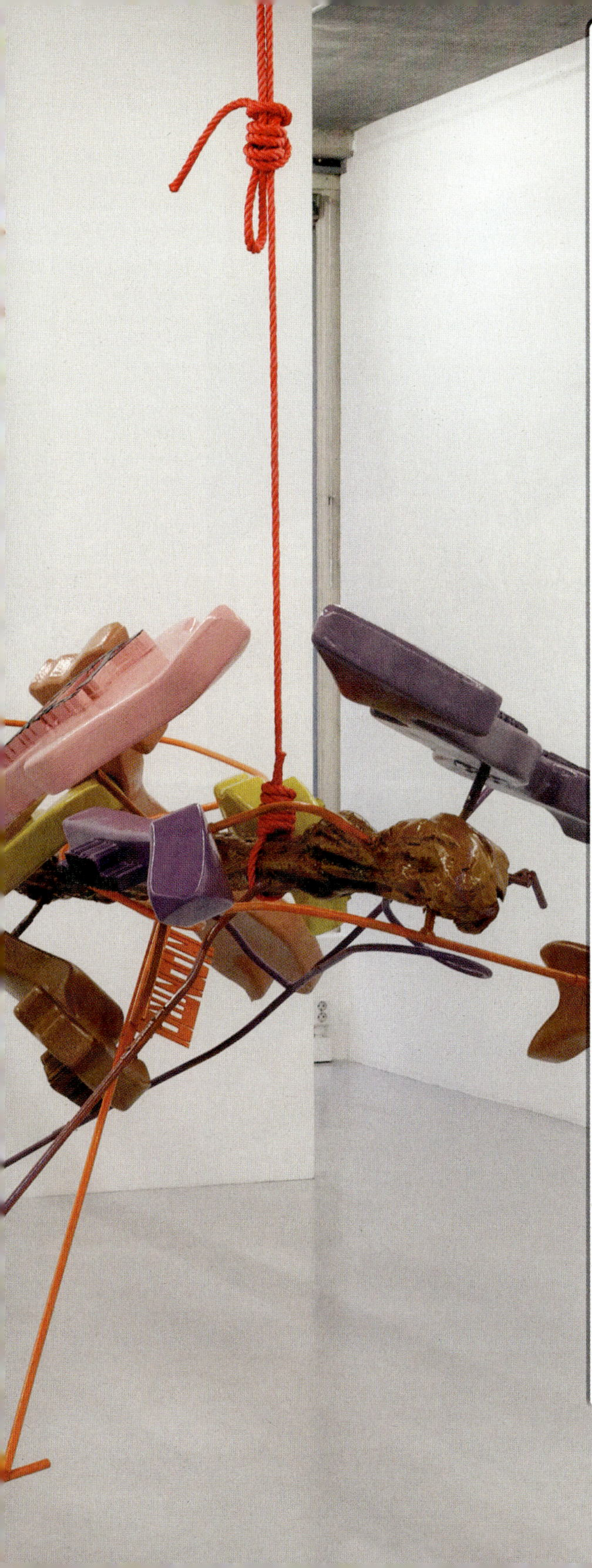

[Static on the radio is noise, but so is the grainy interference with a TV image. Statisticians use the term for random fluctuations in data that they dismiss as meaningless.]

Popular music [music not fully controlled by society] has been our one strain of subversion.(13) [But most of what now passes for popular music is really just the complete silencing of noise. See Chapter Four.]

Here, music has a political function, representing the very possibility of organized society. But it does not create wealth. (39) The musician is paid a wage by the employer [the itinerant musician, or Bach] or lord [Haydn!] or is paid in barter. One use-value [the event of musical performance] is exchanged with another use-value [food, clothing, etc.]. But they are not productive workers, for there is no surplus value. (38)

This is the only musician actually shown in Brueghel's painting. Attali says that Brueghel represents order beside the chaos [chance?] of the men playing dice. This music accompanies the ritual sacrifice pictured in the detail shown just above.

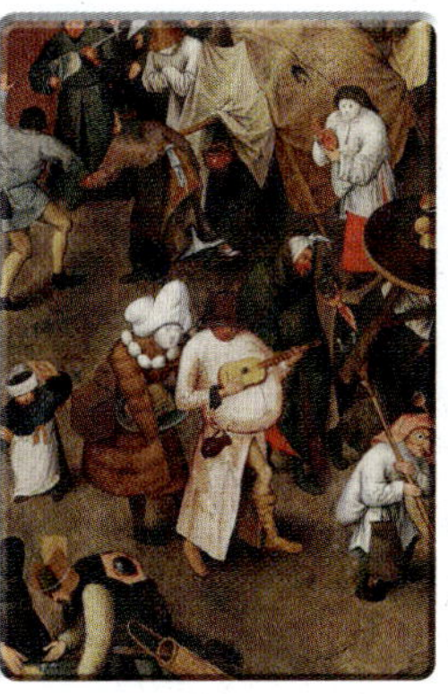

Chapter 3: Reprsenting
Main idea: The use-value of spectacle involves parallel developments of music. As music develops as a commodity and as harmonic developments display rational progress, music makes us believe in social cohesion. In short, "representation leads to exchange and harmony." (62)

Ultimately, "Lent had taken the upper hand." (81)

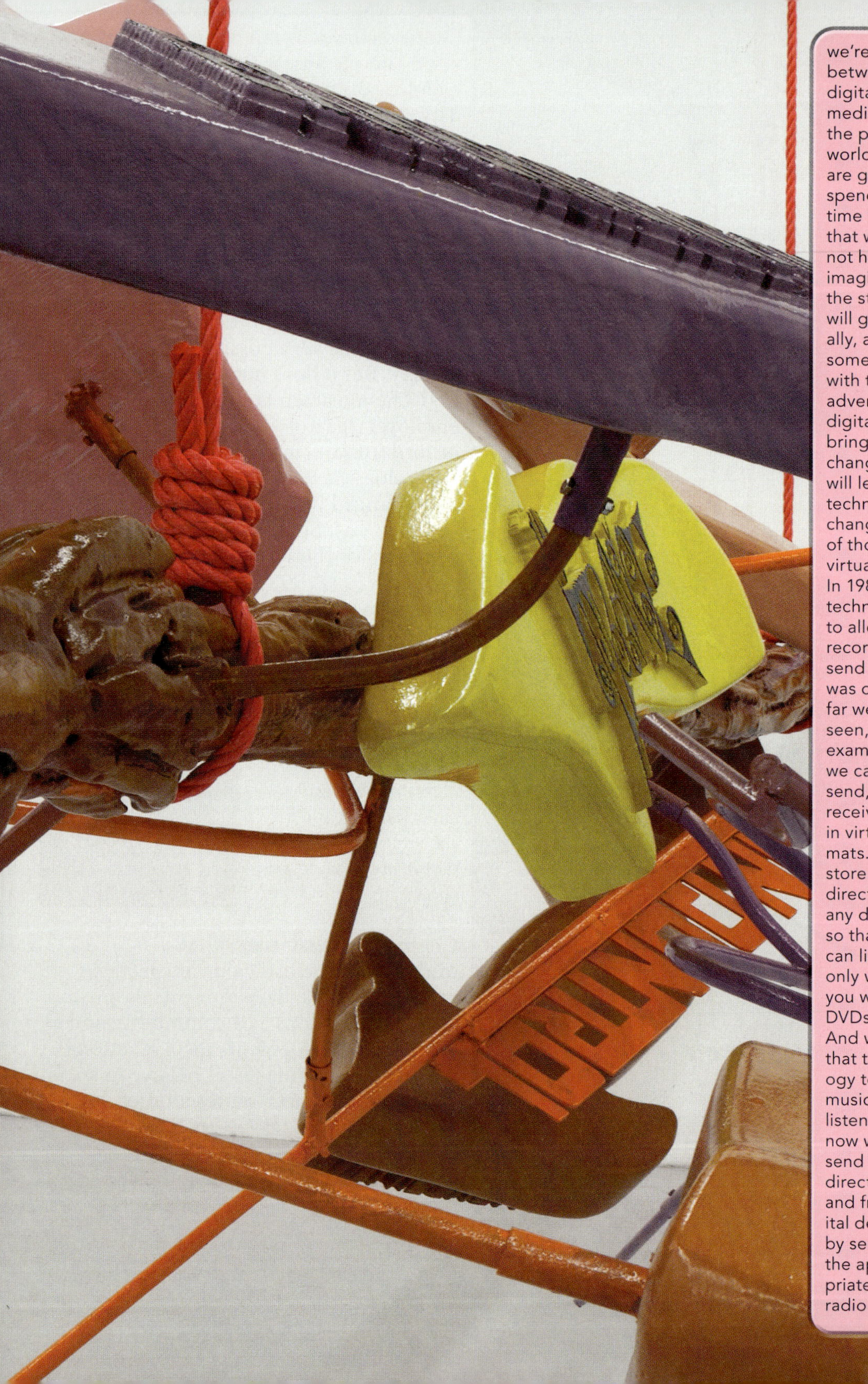

we're seeing between digital media and the physical world. We are going to spend more time in ways that we could not have imagined at the start, but will gradually, and in some cases, with the advent of the digital age, bring about changes that will lead to technological change. One of those is virtualization. In 1984 the technology to allow us to record and send a DVD was out. So far we have seen, for example, that we can store, send, and receive music in virtual formats. We can store music directly on any device, so that you can listen only while you watch DVDs or CDs. And we use that technology to record music for listening. So, now we can send music directly to and from digital devices by sending the appropriate digital radio station.

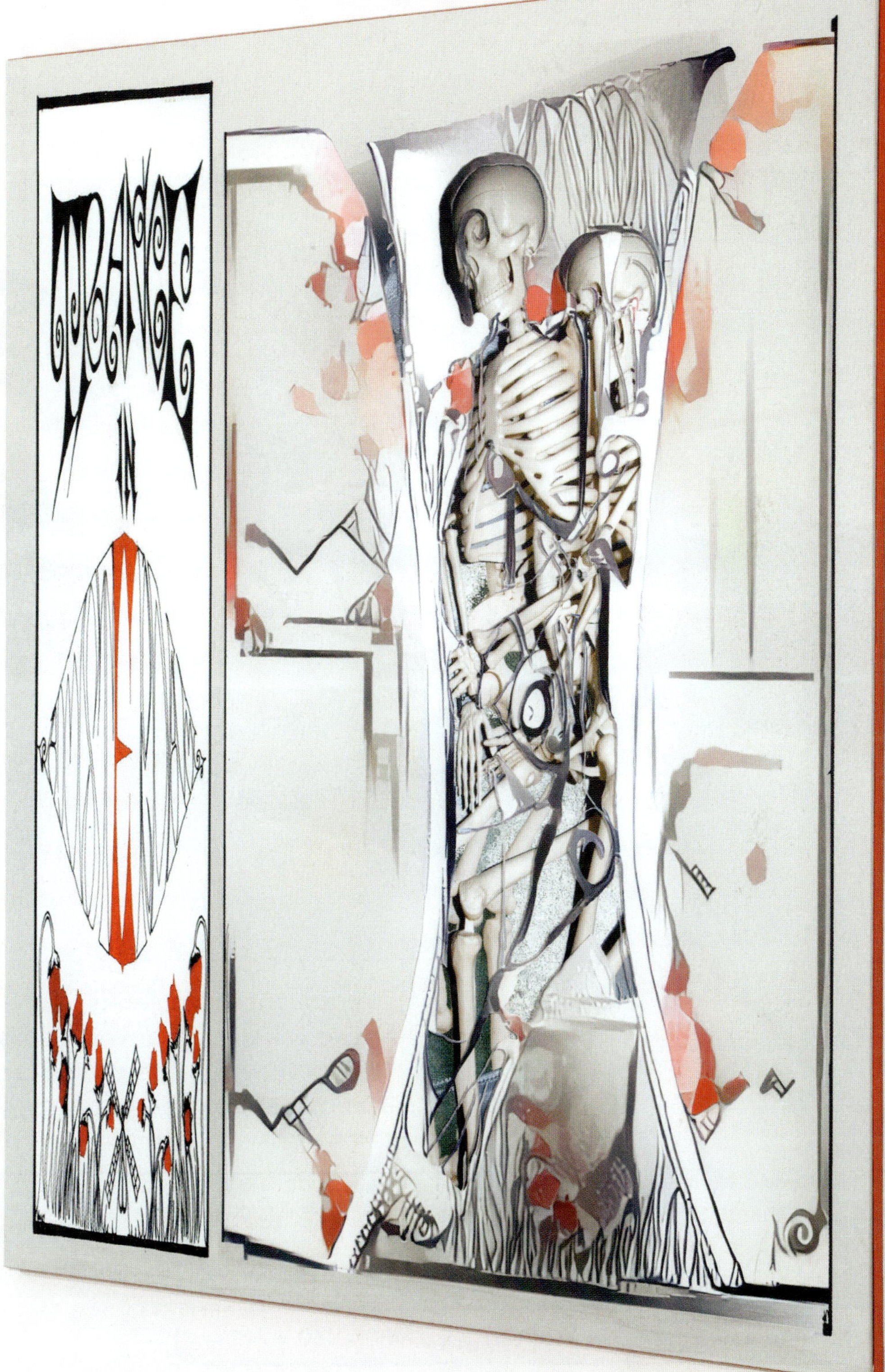

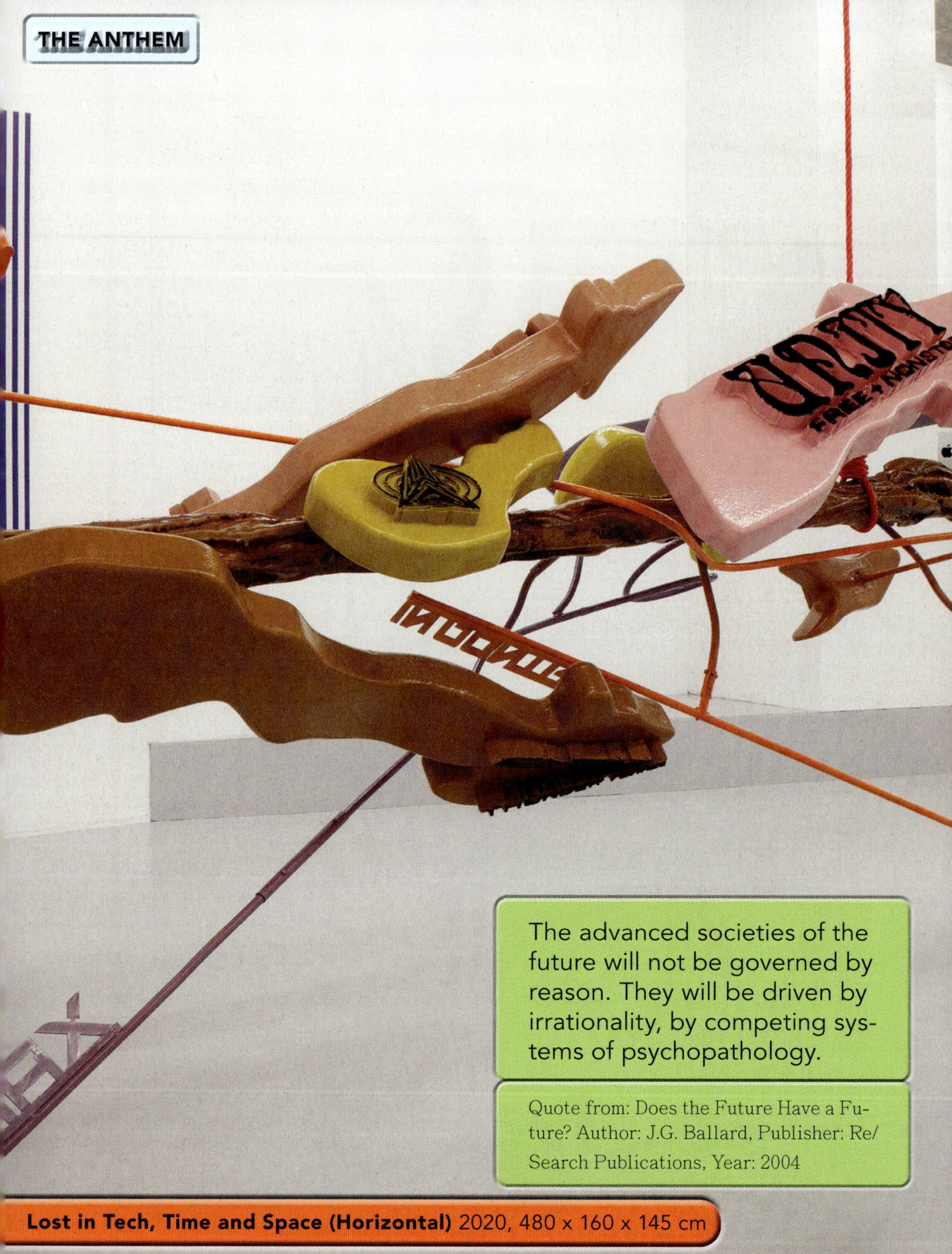

The advanced societies of the future will not be governed by reason. They will be driven by irrationality, by competing systems of psychopathology.

Quote from: Does the Future Have a Future? Author: J.G. Ballard, Publisher: Re/Search Publications, Year: 2004

Lost in Tech, Time and Space (Horizontal) 2020, 480 x 160 x 145 cm

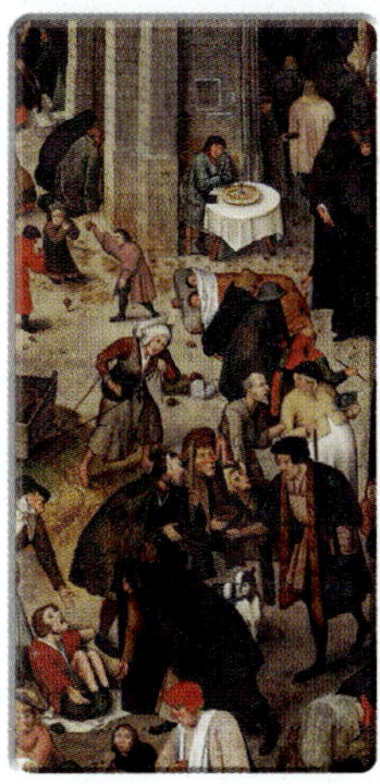

Proper society files out the church, itself the simulacrum of the pagan altar.

At bottom of the detail, the rich man gives money to the poor beggars, bribing them from participation in festival.

Is there any music here, Attali wonders, or is there only silence?

Spectacle: the concert hall replaces the religious, festival, and official court settings of sacrificial music that was produced by unproductive workers [i.e., in the previous stage there was musical activity, largely that of domestic servants, but there was no wealth created by this activity]

As political events, the American Revolution (1776) and then the French Revolution (1789) follow the demand for liberation of composers. The divine rights of kings give way to liberty and representative government.

But composers could not be autonomous unless music became autonomous, an object capable of generating wealth. Music must become a commodity, produced to be exchanged for money. **More precisely, money is generated through the representation of music** [via the score]**, and it is presented to the public in a theatrical representation** [a presentation of the abstract object and, at the same time, the performance is a theatrical representation of an ideal world order]**.**

By gradual steps, the royal control of copyright becomes private ownership of the musical work. (50)

First the labor of creation [composition] is assigned monetary value, then so is interpretation [performance]. (51)

Attali concentrates on the history of this process in France:

1527: music publishing receives privilege of exclusive right to profit from copying works [making new material copies, i.e., scores]. Royal power shifts to music publishers.
1703: Music publishers denied indefinite copyright.
1708: Composers denied the right to self-publish and to control copyright income.
1744: Decentralization of publishing as publishers outside Paris granted equal status with those in Paris.
1786: Initial ownership assigned to composers; publishers have rights only if so assigned by composers; all other publication subject to fines.
1846: the appearance of the café concert.
1849: popular songs awarded same status as serious music. Its composers can collect fees for its performance.
1850: creation of first association to collect royalties on all music.

By assigning monetary value to music, money represents the composer's and performer's labor, which is somehow "inherent" in the labor connected to the music. Different ticket prices should therefore reflect differences in labor. (58) But it cannot be related to the time taken to create a musical work or to perform it [i.e., a price tied to exchange value would not produce different fees]. So "music is outside all measure." Therefore the value is the use-value for the audience. "Thus usage and exchange diverge from the start." (59)

Because the new network of music production and consumption "characterizes the entire economy of competitive capitalism" (32), the emerging middle class (including composers, publishers, paying audience) employed the music itself to present the ideology of a necessary social order (necessary to allow money to equally represent all value). The primitive notion of natural

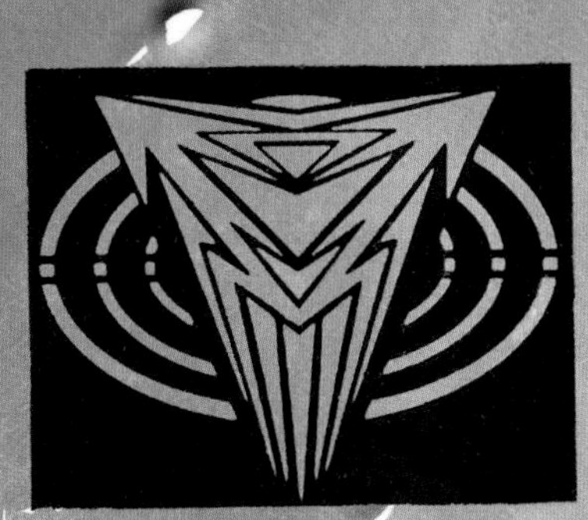

STOP
HISTORY

23·1·93·INFO·081·959·7525

harmony gives way to equal temperament, the idea of "a constructed, reasoned order," a scientific construction. (60-61)

The goal of the music of representation is "making people believe by shaping what they hear." (61)

Chapter 4: **Repeating**
Recording introduces a new network for the economy of music, encouraging "the individualized stockpiling of music . . .on a huge scale." (32) Its hallmark is repetitive mass production, heralding the same for all social relations.

Collective consumption gives way to individualized accumulation. The collective is silenced. The jukebox replaces the café concert. (95) Spectacle is replaced by artificial pseudo-events. (90) Music consumption [as with food consumption in a system of fast food, as with television watching with cable TV] stops being a social event. [Without these regular social interactions and negotiations, we are not a community and we sacrifice our group solidarity for the sake of our individualized satisfactions.]

Economically, the new technology creates a supply of a product, but it must also create a demand for an object that outlasts its use. (100)

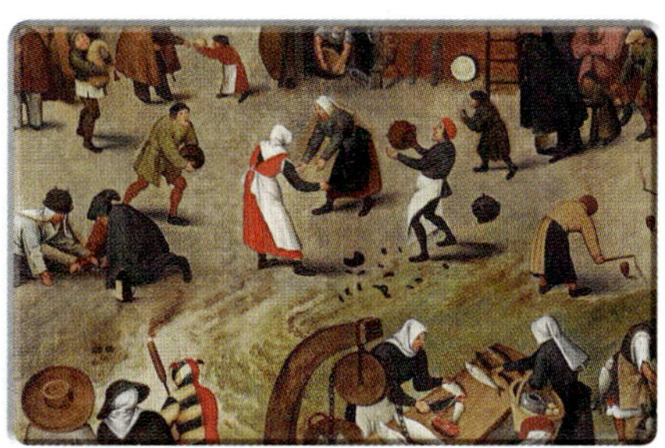

In Brueghel's painting, repeating is symbolized by the four figures playing catch with the pottery. Their play is beside the stand where the fish are commercially sold. [In capitalism, music is sold like fish.] But because their "play" results in the destruction of the pottery, the pottery is denied its use value. They create a demand for the pottery that is unrelated to its intended use.

Here, "music is used and produced in the ritual in an attempt to make people forget the general violence; in another, it is employed to make people believe in the harmony of the world, that there is order in exchange and legitimacy in commercial power."

As barter is replaced by money, money replaces exchange-time. But listening to music still requires a double expenditure of time. The consumer buys it with time and then expends additional time in listening [use-time]. Records allow the stockpiling of the second expenditure of time. (101) So repetition eliminates use-time.

Aesthetically, the result is repetitive music: the music of revolt is tamed into a repetitive commodity, each priced the same as the rest. (103) Music is "colonized, sanitized." (109)

Value is now dependent on an artificial differentiation (106) produced by the hit parade system to confer temporary difference [relative value]. (108)

Music is increasingly just background noise, facilitating "cultural normalization, and the disappearance of distinctive cultures." (111)

Music divides into two basic types that are radical opposites of one another:

Mass music. Harmonically, popular music is very traditional. It simply recycles what was done in the classical period [Bach to Schoenberg]. Muzak reveals the basic character of this music.

Learned music. The serious musician flees from the tendencies of mass music, and set free, seeks the radical opposite of mass music. Imitating the rational research programs of Western scientism, their musical "discourse becomes non-

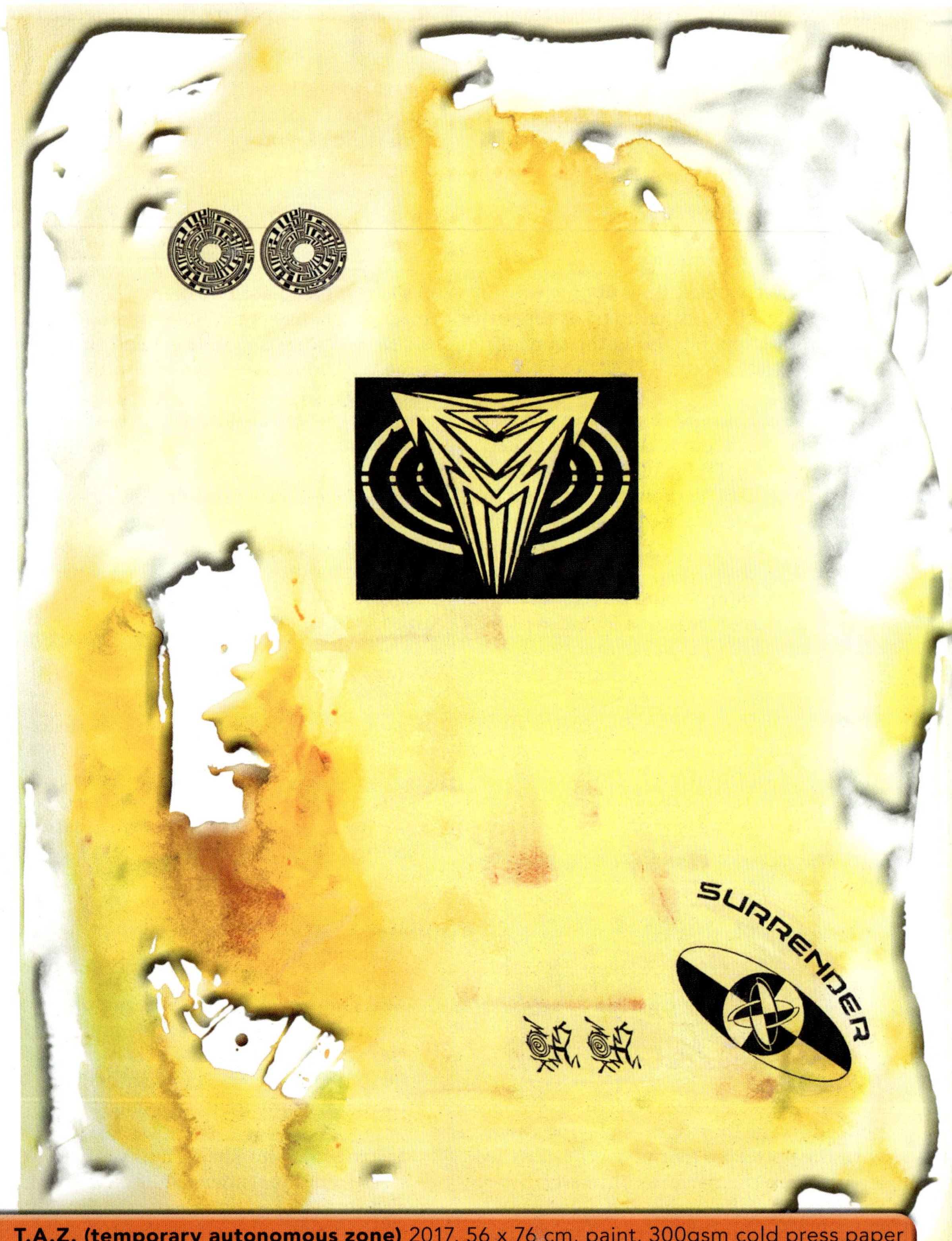

T.A.Z. (temporary autonomous zone) 2017, 56 x 76 cm, paint, 300gsm cold press paper localizable." This attempt at the universal produces depersonalized, meaningless sound. (113) It is elitist. (115)

The emergence of the two types is supported by the increasing social control of noise. (122-24)

As supply routinely exceeds the possibility of consumption, we value the activity of stockpiling instead of the activities themselves. The elimination of use-time is the herald of death. (125-30) What was first true in music comes to dominate all of life's activities (126), e.g., entertainment, food, health care. (130)

[This "herald of death argument" is a stretch. (125) Attali seems to think that because music originally symbolized ritual murder, all music always symbolizes the ritual murder of the scapegoat. So to change the political economy of music is just to change the way this murder is ritualized, and because we now "use" music by stockpiling it, we are therefore stockpiling death. I am reminded of the movie Moonstruck, in which we discover that men are unfaithful to their wives because they fear death.]

As we become more and more alike, violence increases as we find fewer and fewer outlets for our desires. (130-31)

Chapter 5: Composing

A new noise is being heard [a new way of making music], suggesting the emergence of a new society. (133)

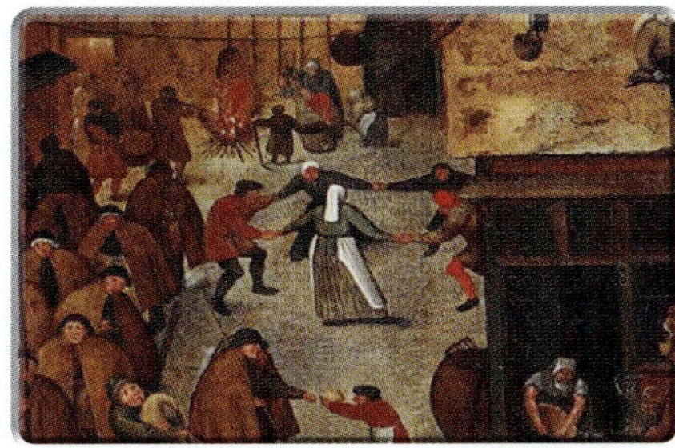

In Brueghel's painting, composing is symbolized by the ring dance. Setting themselves apart from everyone else, the dancers make their own music for their own pleasurable activity. This noncommercial music prophecies a post-capitalistic future.

This new activity is NOT undertaken for its exchange or use value. It is undertaken solely for the pleasure of the person who does it [its "producer"]. Such activity involves a radical rejection of the specialized roles [composer, performer, audience] that dominated all previous music. (135) The activity is entirely localized, made by a small community for that community. There is no clear distinction between consumption and production.

Title: Outline of Jacques Attali, Noise
Author: Theodore Gracyk,
First published: mnstate.edu/gracyk,
Year: 2002

Non-mainstream subcultures are often targets in a far-right government. We have been here before, but on a smaller scale: New York, 1994. Rudy Giuliani was elected mayor in the face of a New York that for decades had been torn apart by heroin and crack, white flight, predatory banking, and housing industries, and the sustained disappearance of jobs in any sector other than finance. His answer was not to address any of those issues, but to instead attack the marginalized communities that had been suffering—the homeless, the poor, and the kinds of people who went to clubs.

His dismantling of the New York club scene as part of this "crackdown," alongside the many other ways his broken-windows philosophy took action, led many to call him a fascist.

His supporters concede that point but would say he was the "fascist the city needed." Giuliani's win in 1994 can be, in part, attributed to a string of center-left mayors who put up little resistance to the increasing austerity imposed on the city by the banks.

Neoliberalism encourages viewing the world through a lens of prevention in order to maintain its own stability and routinely places societal focus on disasters to avoid (terrorism, economic crises) instead of areas to improve, breeding the complacency it needs to sustain itself.

Worse, it has profound implications on the emotional makeup of a populace. A positive outcome with a promotion focus results in euphoria while a negative one results in depression. With prevention, this spectrum switches, with negative outcomes breeding anxiety while positive ones result in a sense of relaxation. With a prevention focus, potent emotions with powerful artistic merits (euphoria, depression) are traded for ones that never really fuel creativity (relaxation, anxiety).

Liberalism has infiltrated techno, and dance music as a whole, over the past years. Social liberalism, the idea of a more inclusive community and dancefloor, is a good and noble endeavor, and the fight to make dance music more socially liberal must not end. Yet at the

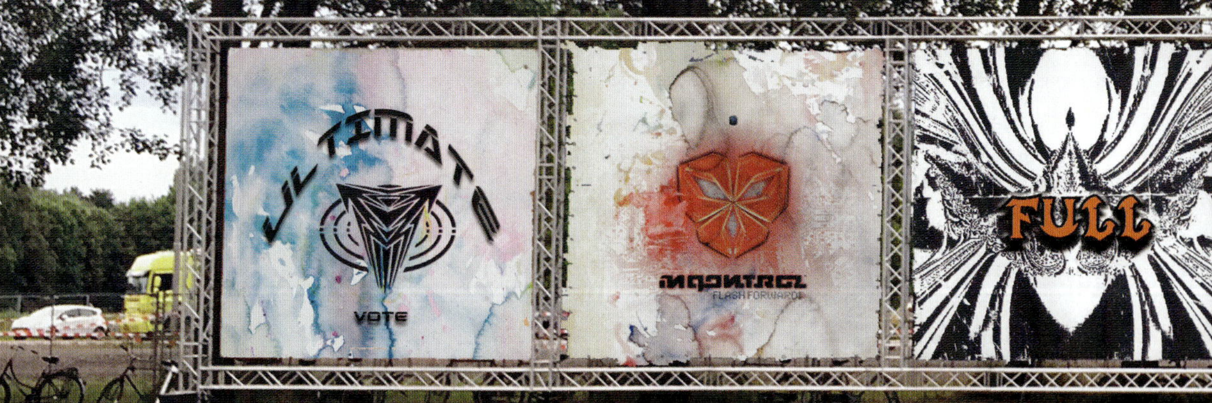

The Ultimate Vote Inqontrol Full Force Unlocked Revolution Power Zone Lock

same time, economic liberalism, or neoliberalism, continues to consume the world of techno.

Techno needs to reassert itself as something with substance. It needs to look past its immediate goals of having a good night out and look outside itself with the conviction that it really can change things, requiring a switch of regulatory focus from prevention to promotion. Through solidarity along class, gender, racial, religious, and all other lines typically used to divide us, techno can promote itself as an agent of change rather than stasis.

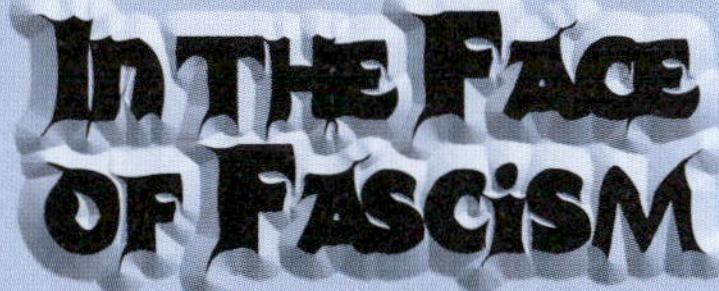

Excerpt from: Title: Romans on the Importance of Techno in the Face of Fascism, Authors: Haslam, Gunnar and Auvinen, Johannes, First published at xlr8r.com, Year: 2017

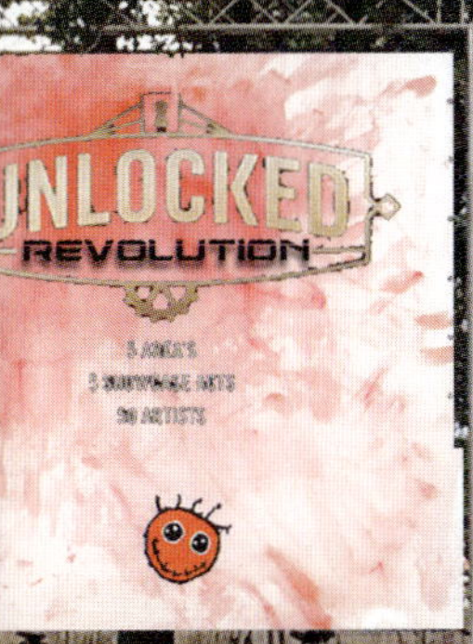

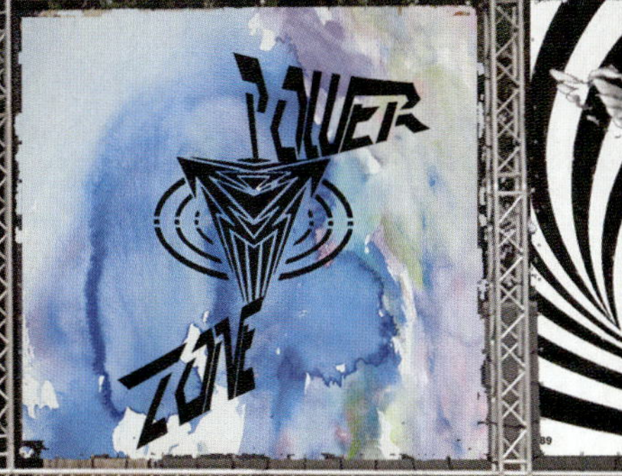

In a contemporary socio-political situation in which safe and "free" social spaces are not only increasingly diminishing in numbers but are capsized by disturbed individuals as sites of brutal mass-murder, it might be more important than ever to remember and assert the importance of them.

Undoubtedly, the 80s were a decade of profound changes in society. The Reagan-Thatcher years gave birth to full-blown neoliberalism in England, that changed the make-up of our society for ever. But the 80s was a decade that also saw the emergence of institutionalised multiculturalism, the end of the Soviet Union, the fall of the Berlin Wall, and the beginning of the internet.

Drawn to the acid and rave movement's emphasis on tolerance, freedom of expression, and anti-normalcy. It is furthermore obvious that the free, hedonistic, transformative "third space" that rave culture proposes is built on an imagined autonomous spatiality that queers have fought for for decades.

Raving was a fundamentally invasive force that transgressed social conventions, and naturally, its immense sociopolitical impact resulted in its abrupt termination. Moral panic was spreading as raves and E grew in popularity, turning the sight of a thousand kids dancing in a field into an actual revolutionary force that might be able to challenge the prevailing neoconservative ideas at the time. Spearheaded by the Thatcher government, the UK was the first to criminalise rave as they, rather incredibly, banned parties with music (quoted from the public legislation) "wholly or predominantly characterised by the emission of a succession of repetitive beats." France followed shortly after, and in 2002, Joe Biden and potentially future president Hillary Clinton terminated rave culture in the US as they implemented the so-called "RAVE Act" — RAVE functioning as an ironic acronym for "Reducing Americans' Vulnerability to Ecstasy." Without a doubt, directly criminalising a particular form of music proves the revolutionary nature of music—and the arts as a whole.

RAVE ACT

Excerpt from: Title: Energy flash: the rise and fall and lasting influence of the rave scene
Author: Jeppe Ugelvig, First published, I-D -Vice, Year: 2016

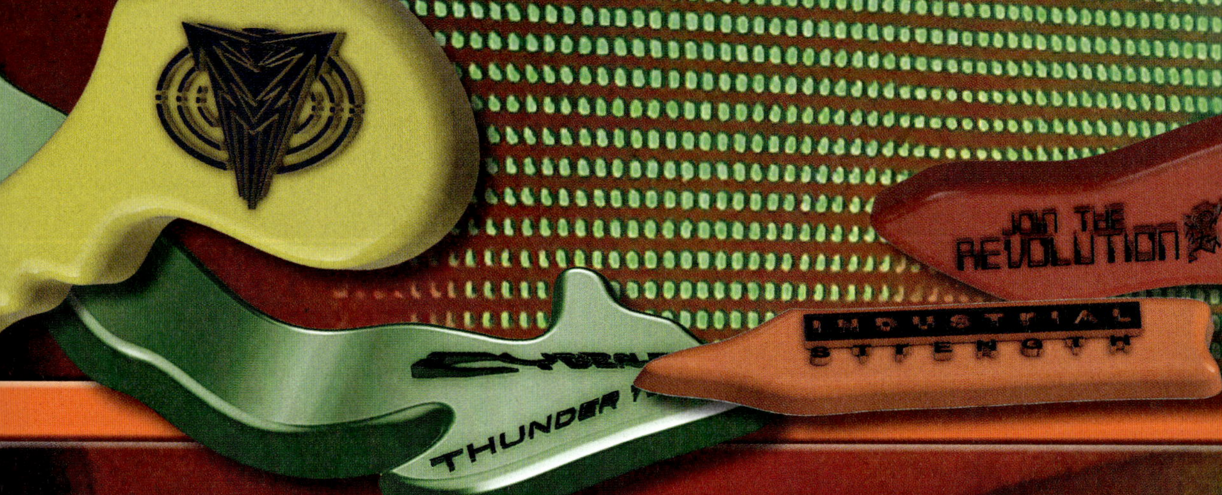

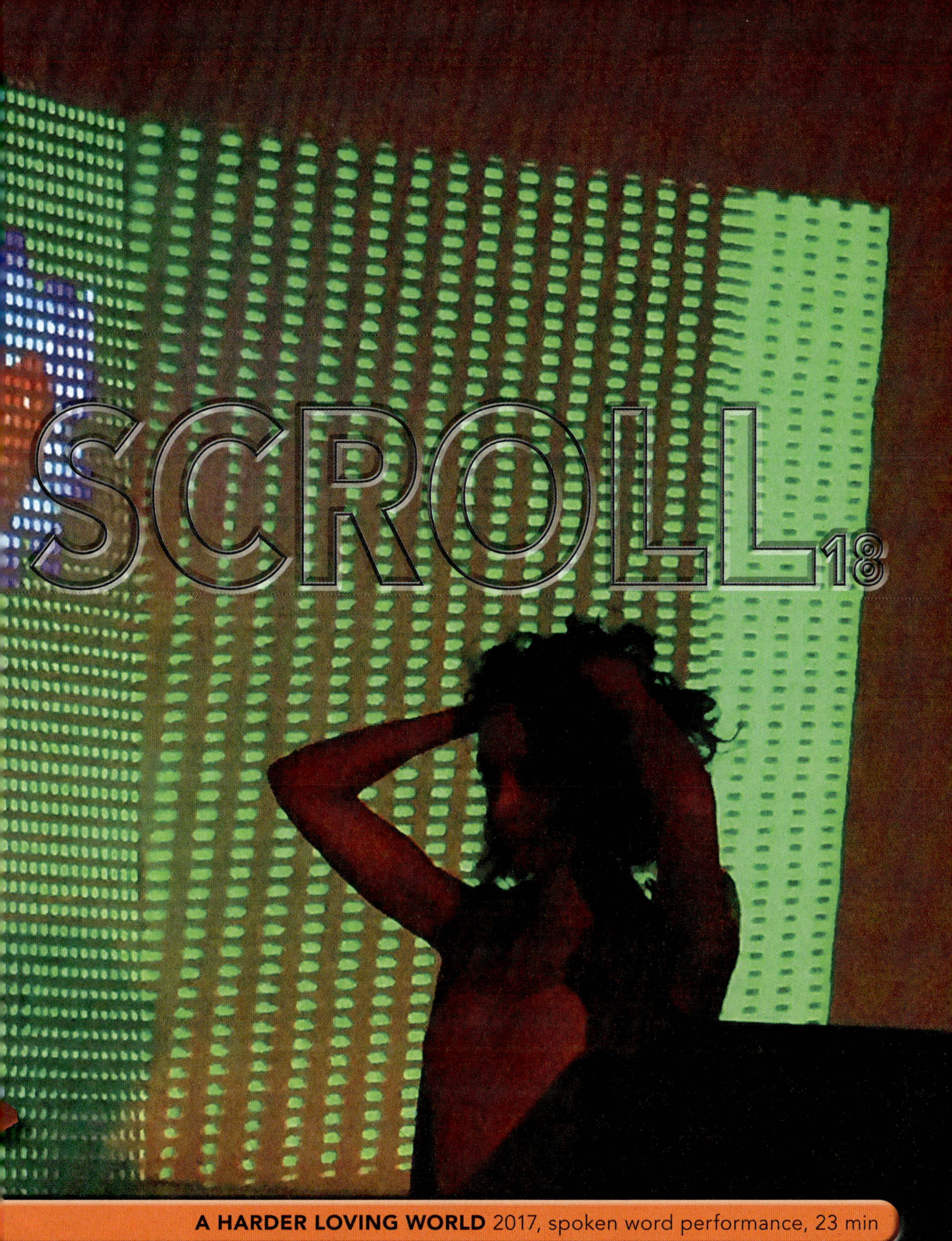

A HARDER LOVING WORLD 2017, spoken word performance, 23 min

Back 2 School curated by DIS at MoMA PS1, New York

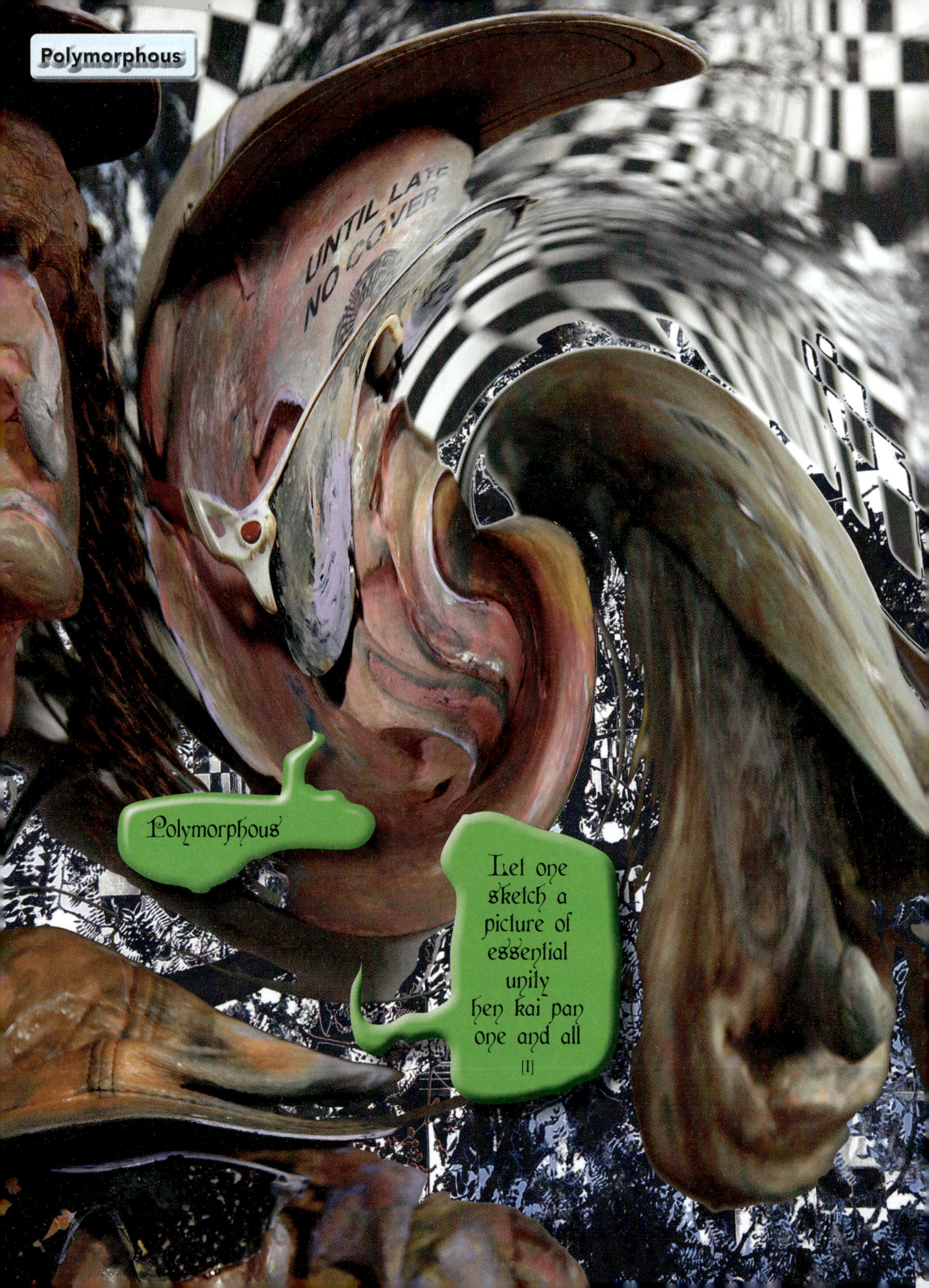
UNTIL LATE
NO COVER
Polymorphous
Let one sketch a picture of essential unity hen kai pan one and all
[I]

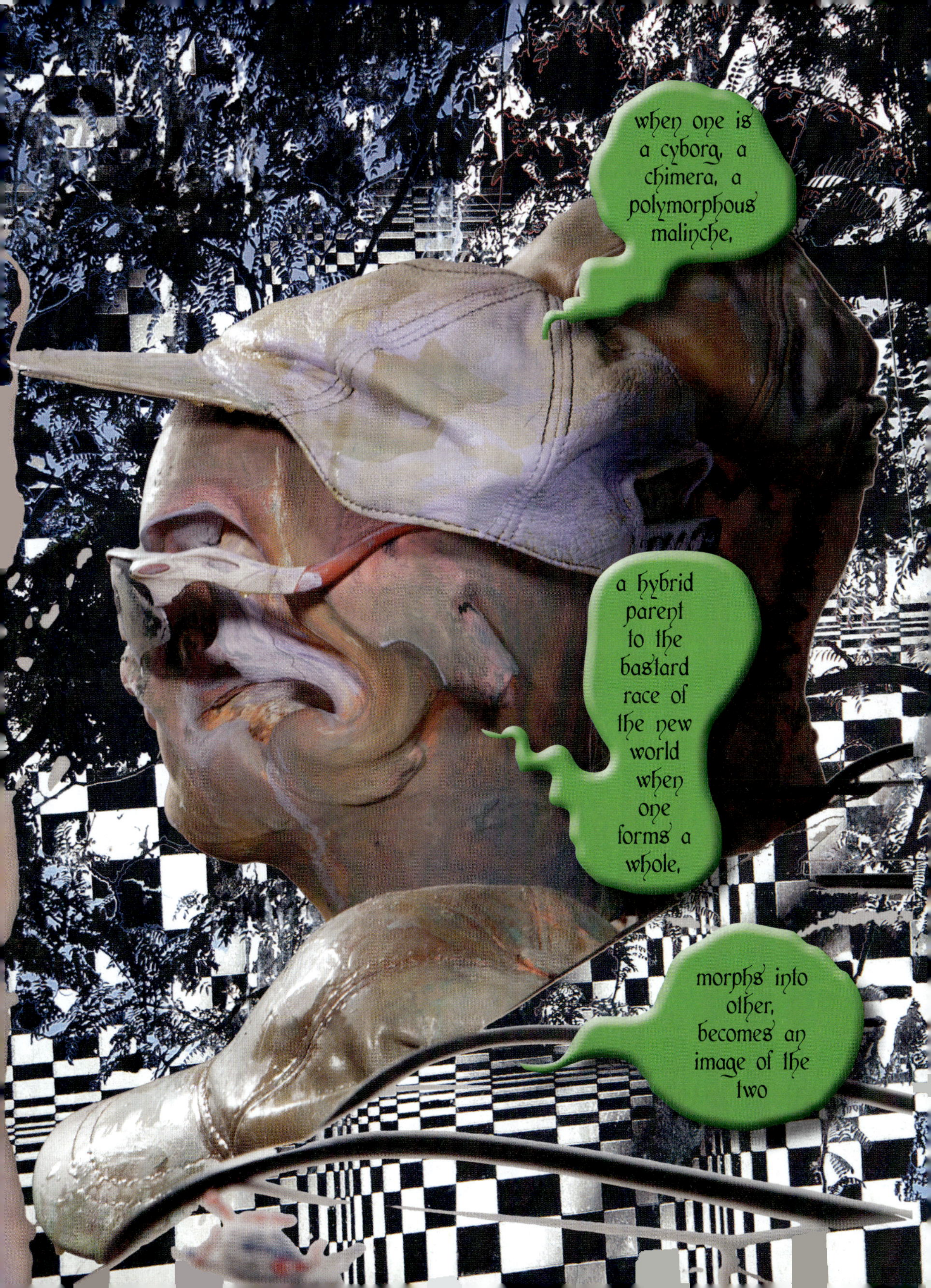
when one is a cyborg, a chimera, a polymorphous malinche,
a hybrid parent to the bastard race of the new world when one forms a whole,
morphs into other, becomes an image of the two

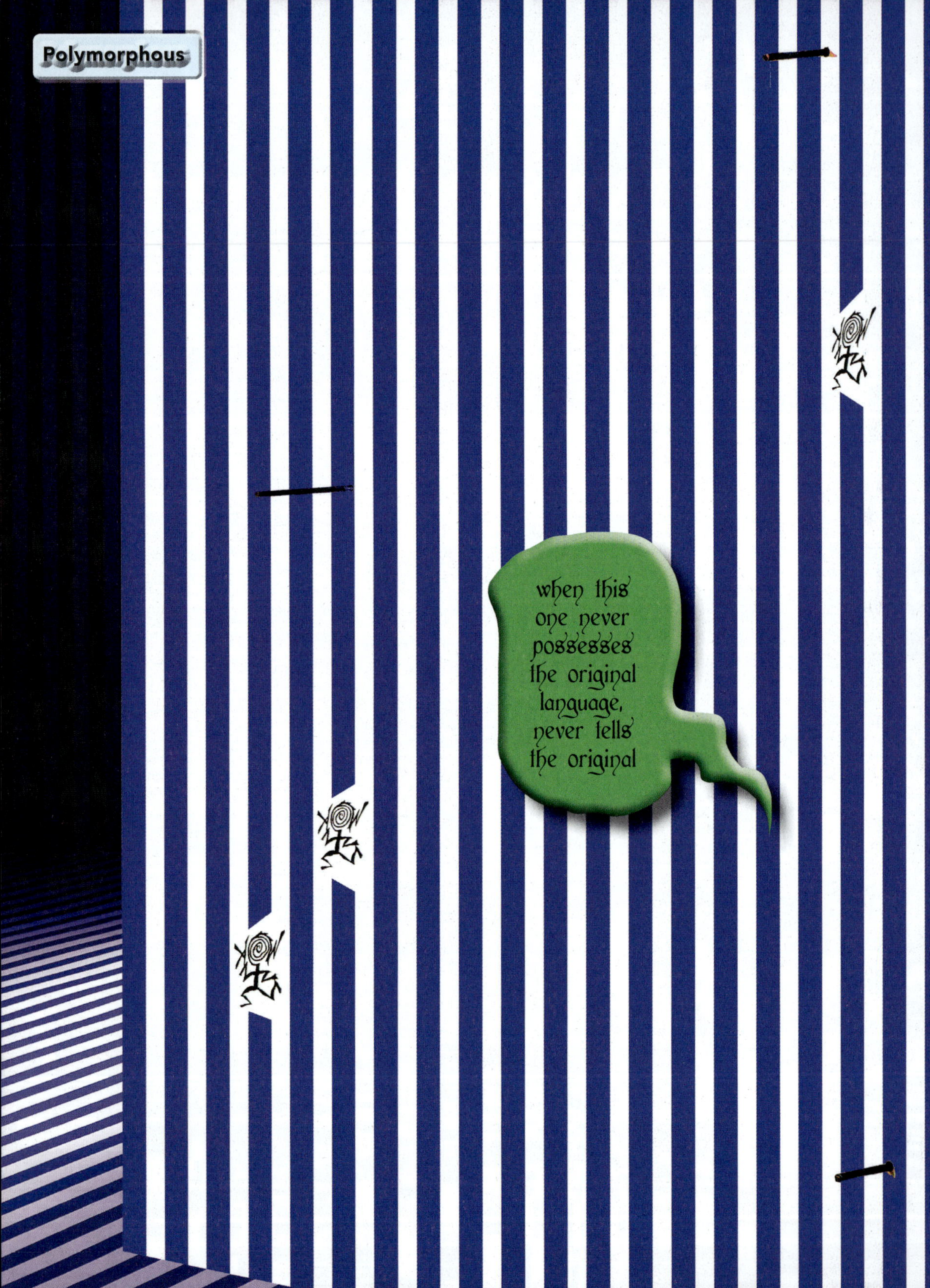
Polymorphous
when this one never possesses the original language, never tells the original

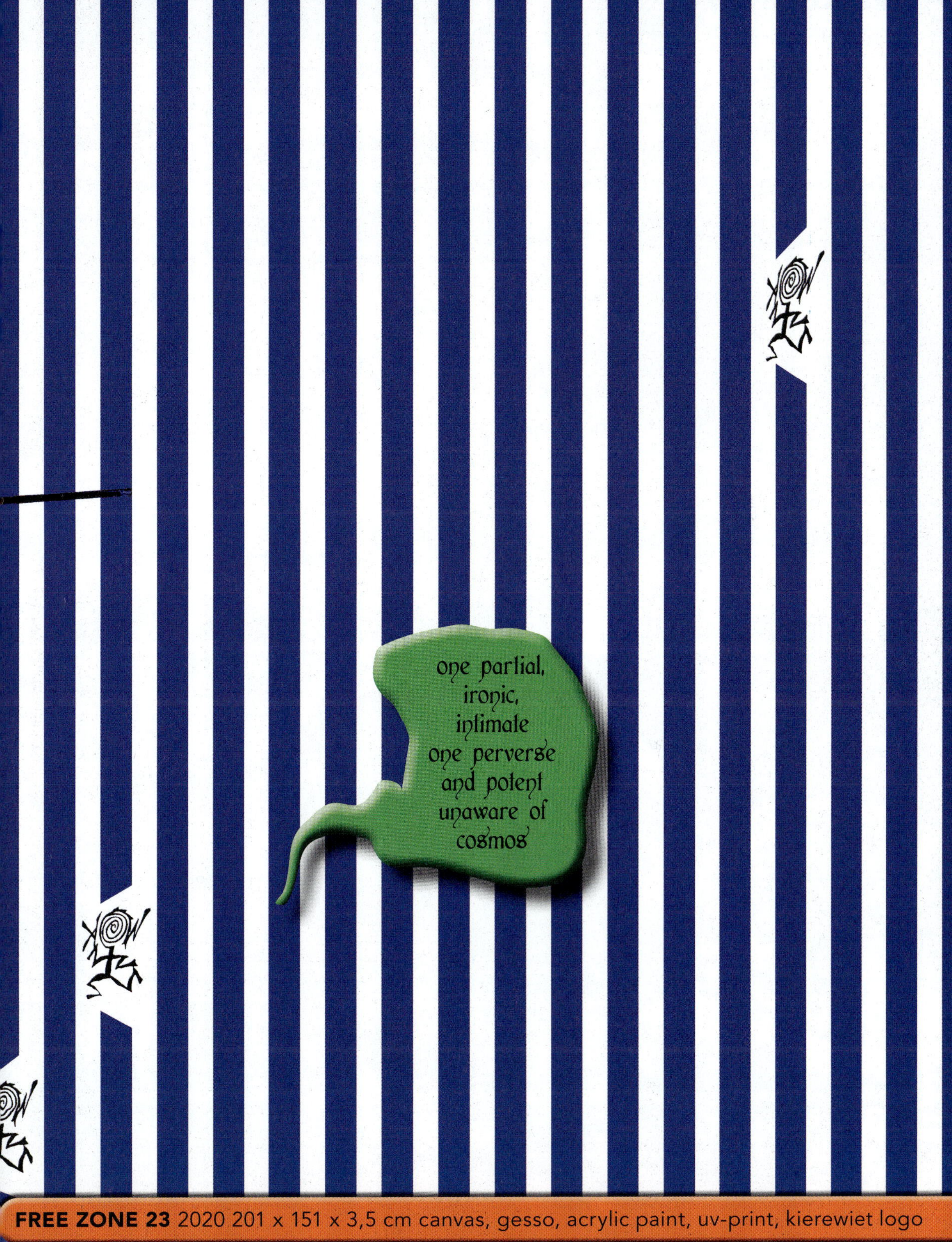

FREE ZONE 23 2020 201 x 151 x 3,5 cm canvas, gesso, acrylic paint, uv-print, kierewiet logo

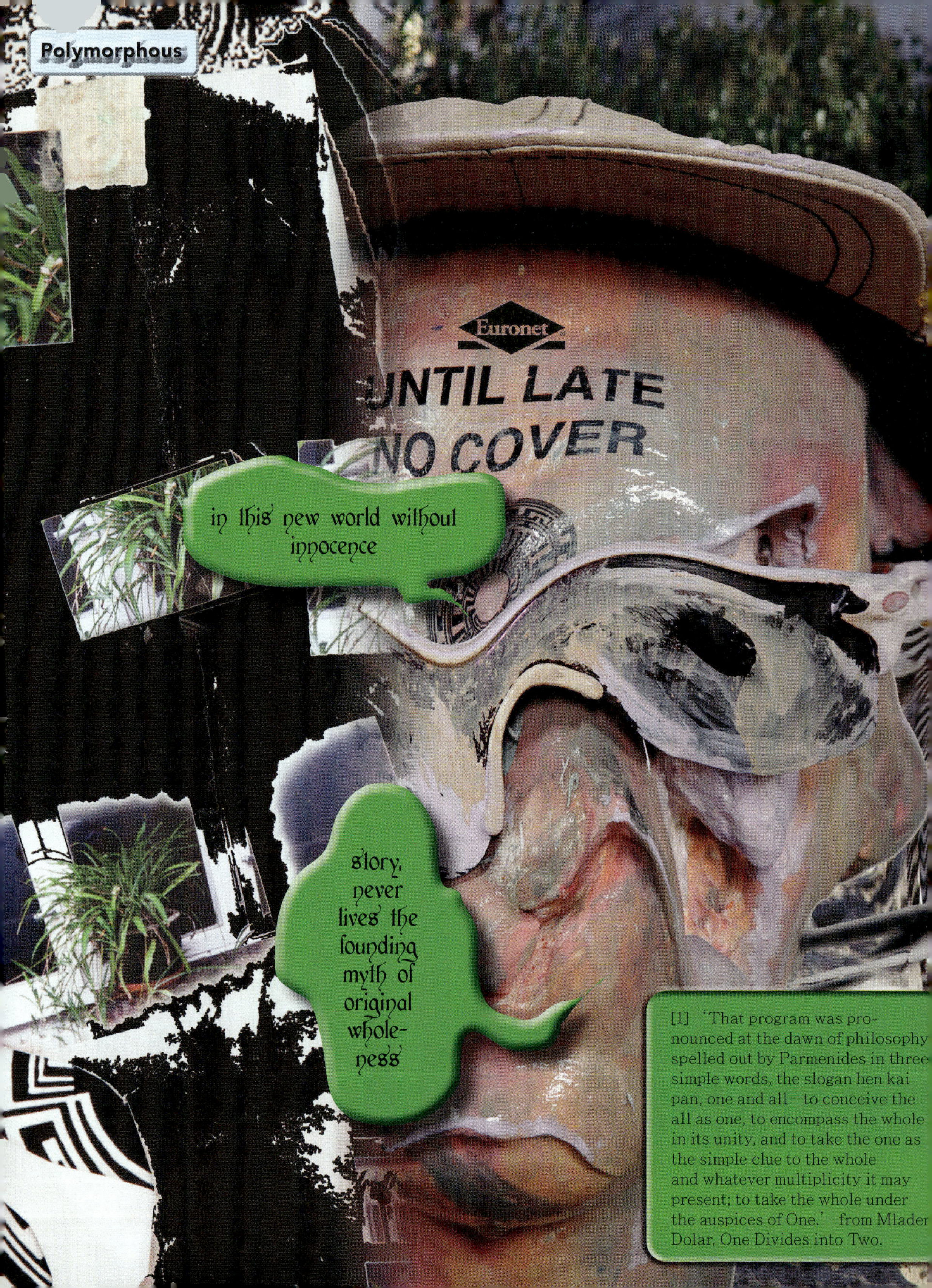

[1] 'That program was pronounced at the dawn of philosophy spelled out by Parmenides in three simple words, the slogan hen kai pan, one and all—to conceive the all as one, to encompass the whole in its unity, and to take the one as the simple clue to the whole and whatever multiplicity it may present; to take the whole under the auspices of One.' from Mladen Dolar, One Divides into Two.

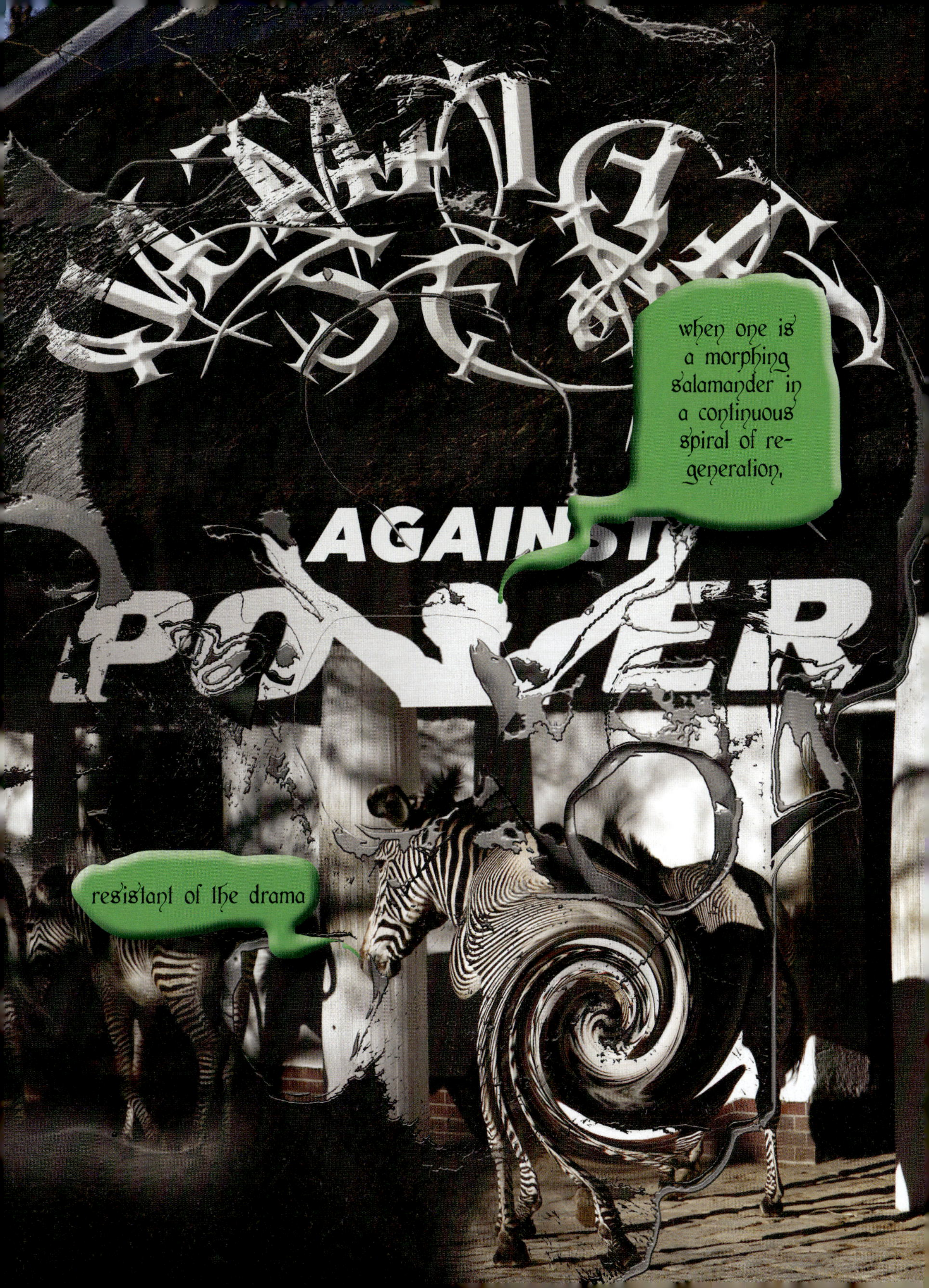
when one is a morphing salamander in a continuous spiral of re-generation,
resistant of the drama

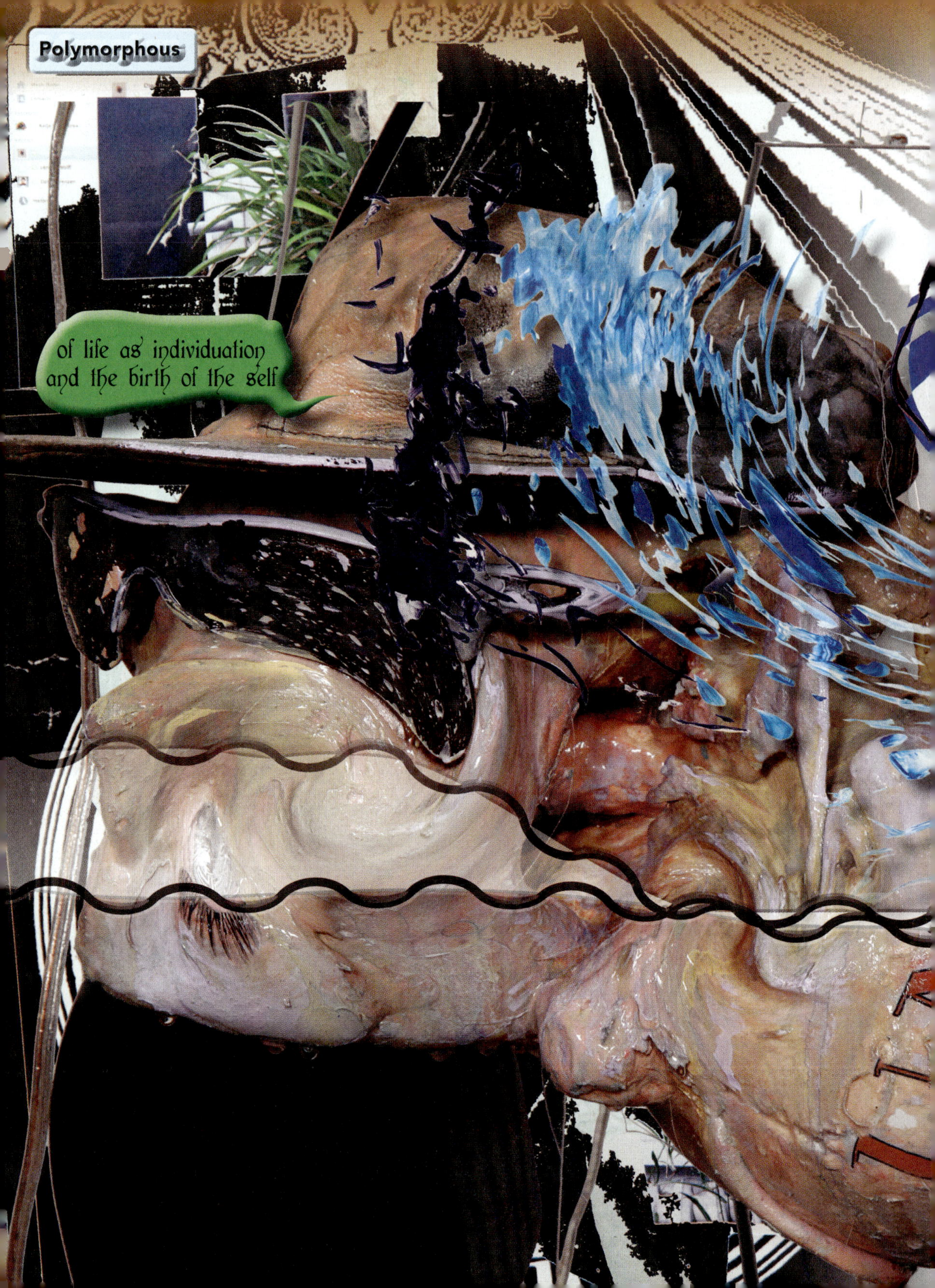
Polymorphous
of life as individuation
and the birth of the self

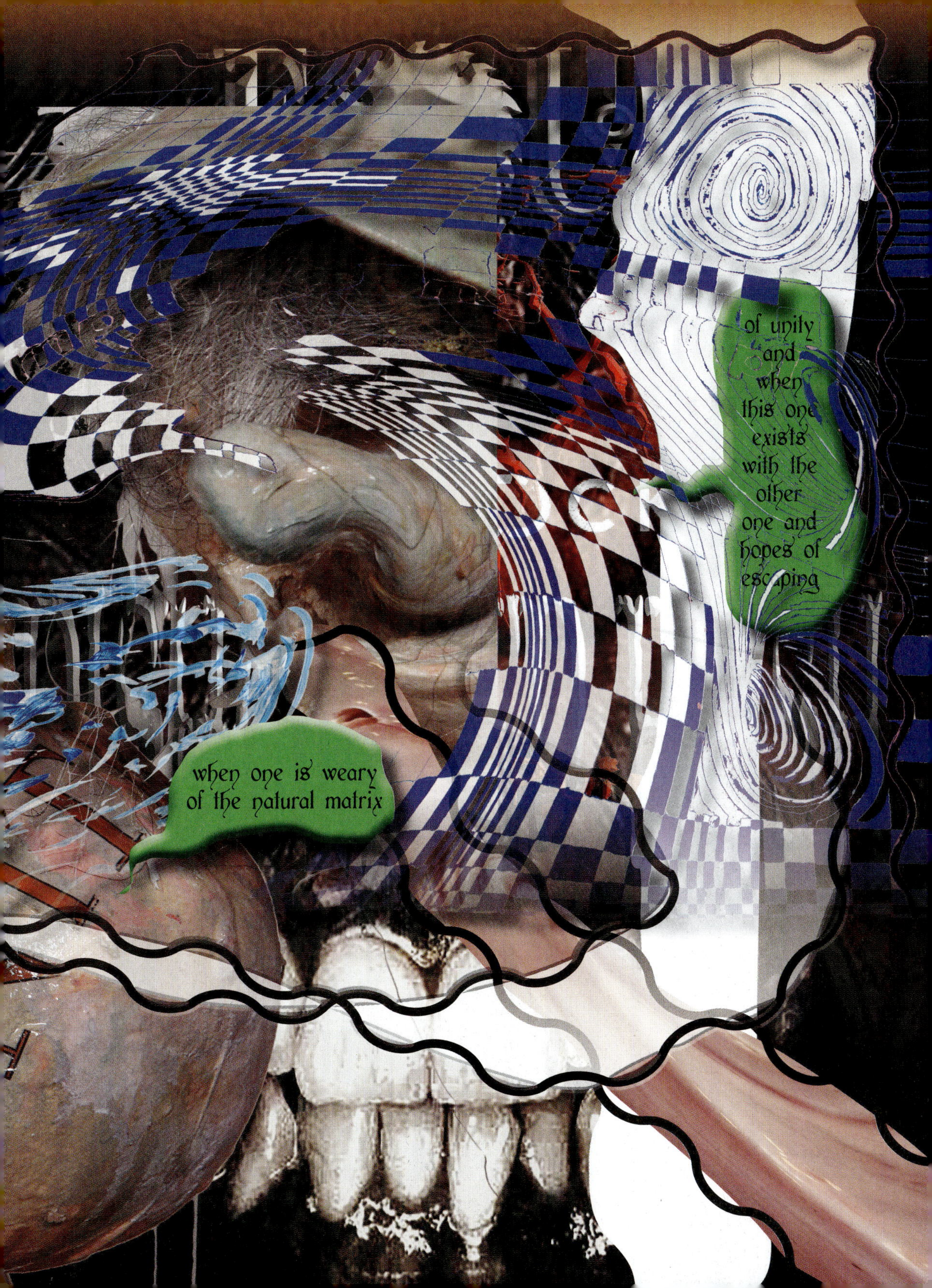

of unity and when this one exists with the other one and hopes of escaping
when one is weary of the natural matrix

Polymorphous

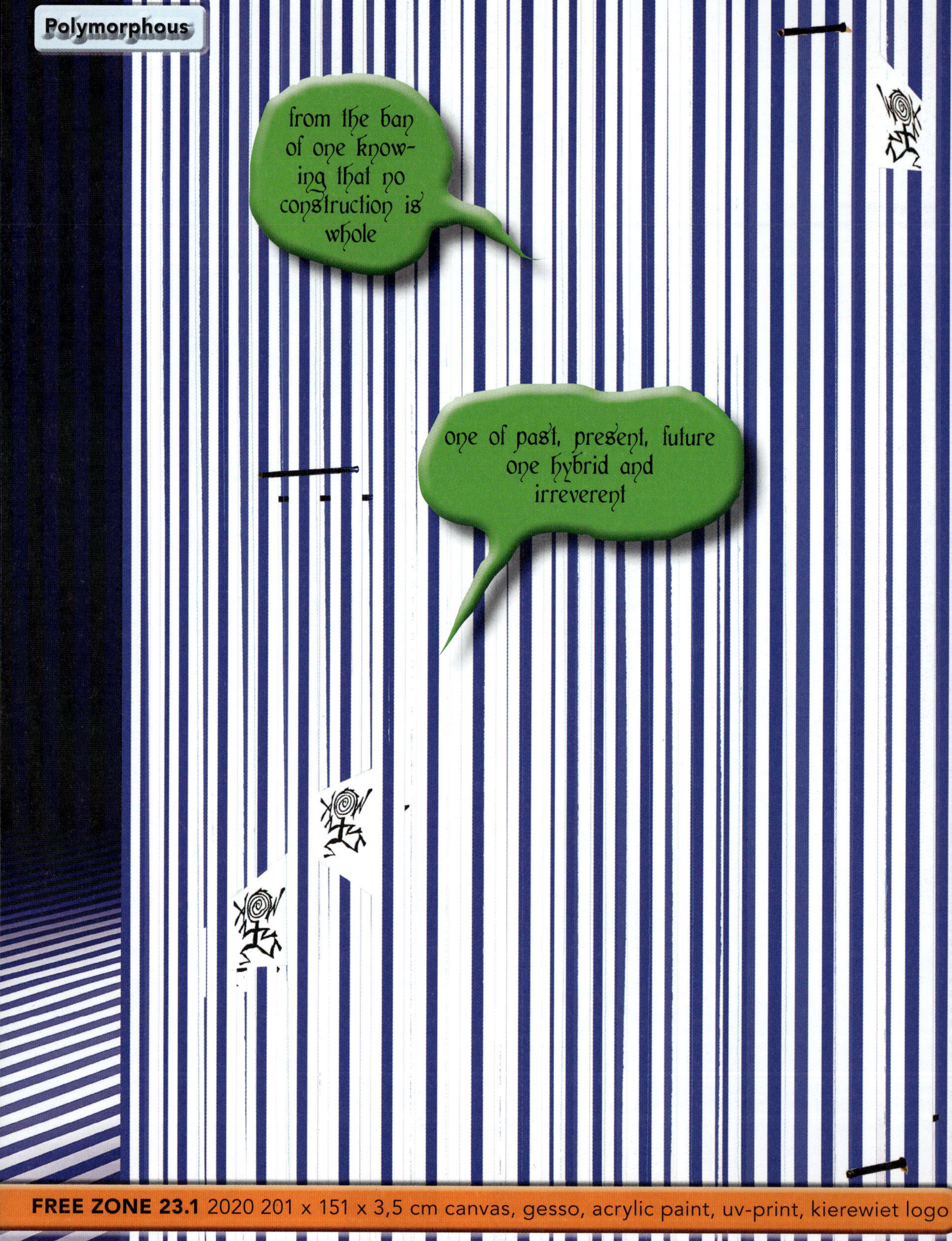

FREE ZONE 23.1 2020 201 x 151 x 3,5 cm canvas, gesso, acrylic paint, uv-print, kierewiet logo

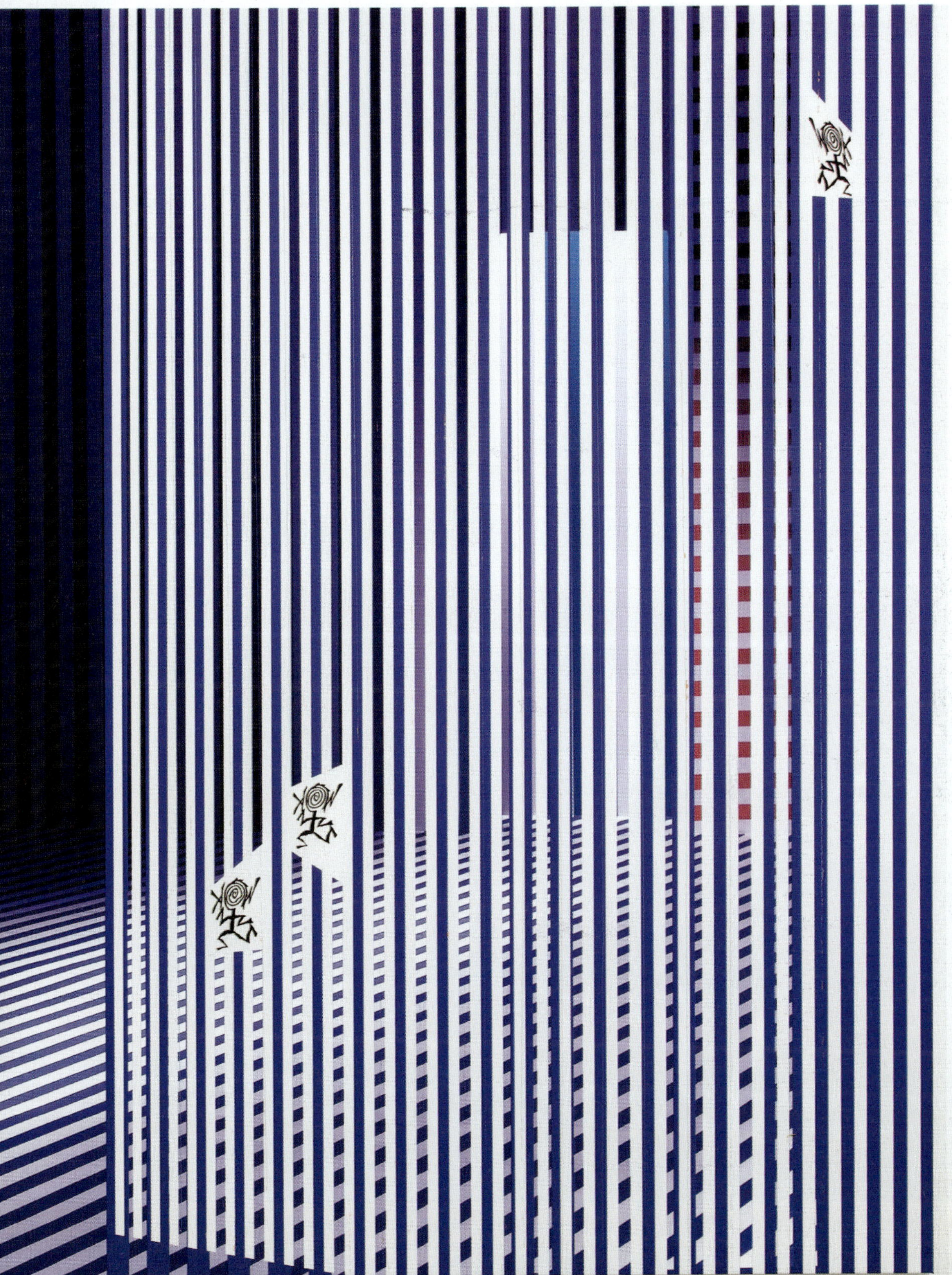

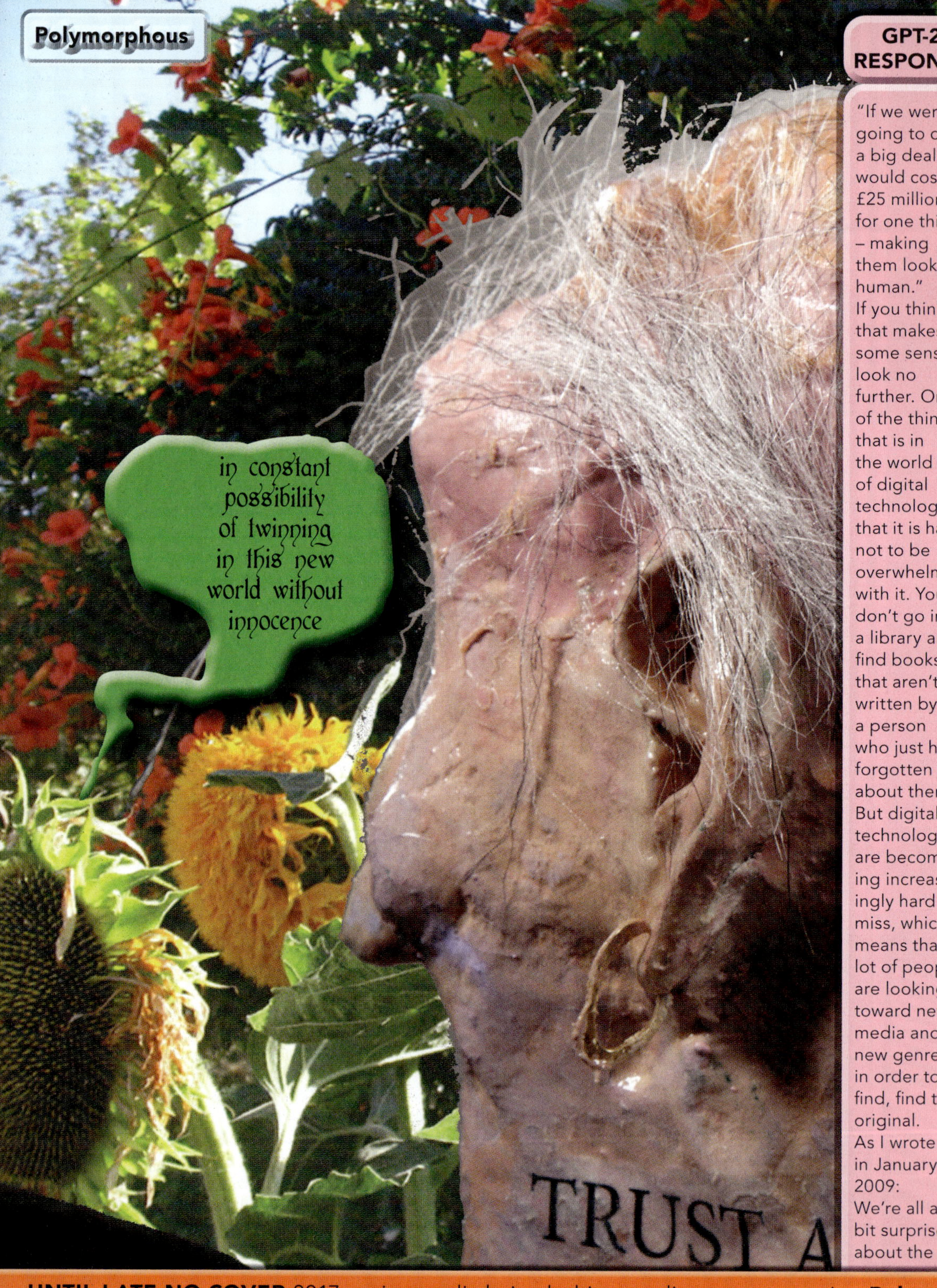

GPT-2 RESPONSE

"If we were going to do a big deal, it would cost £25 million for one thing – making them look human."
If you think that makes some sense, look no further. One of the things that is in the world of digital technology is that it is hard not to be overwhelmed with it. You don't go into a library and find books that aren't written by a person who just has forgotten about them. But digital technologies are becoming increasingly hard to miss, which means that a lot of people are looking toward new media and new genres in order to find, find the original.
As I wrote in January 2009:
We're all a bit surprised about the

UNTIL LATE NO COVER 2017, resin, acrylic hair, clothing, audio system, starring **Polymorphou**

think...

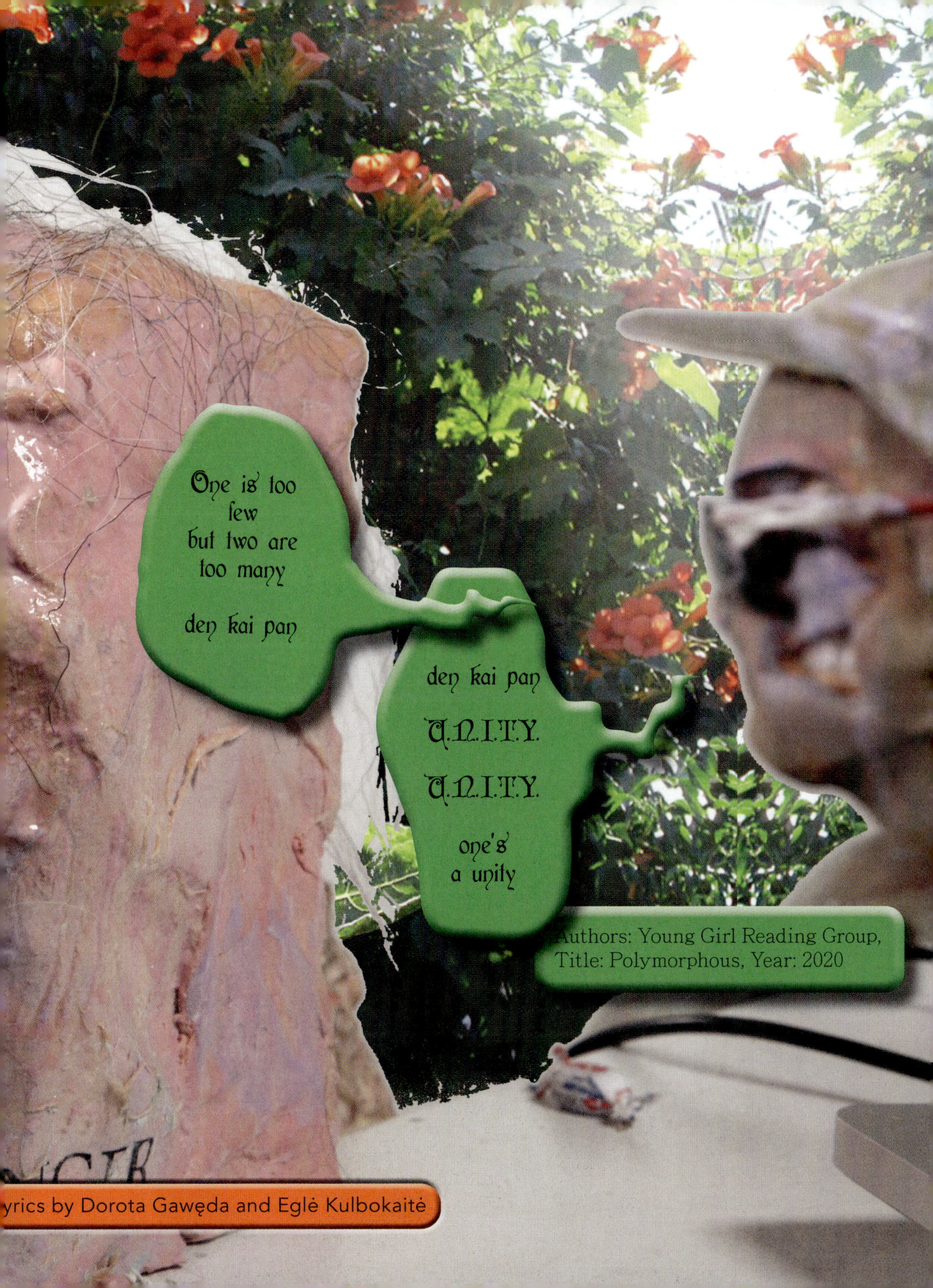
One is too few but two are too many
den kai pan
den kai pan
U.N.I.T.Y.
U.N.I.T.Y.
one's a unity
Authors: Young Girl Reading Group, Title: Polymorphous, Year: 2020
yrics by Dorota Gawęda and Eglė Kulbokaitė

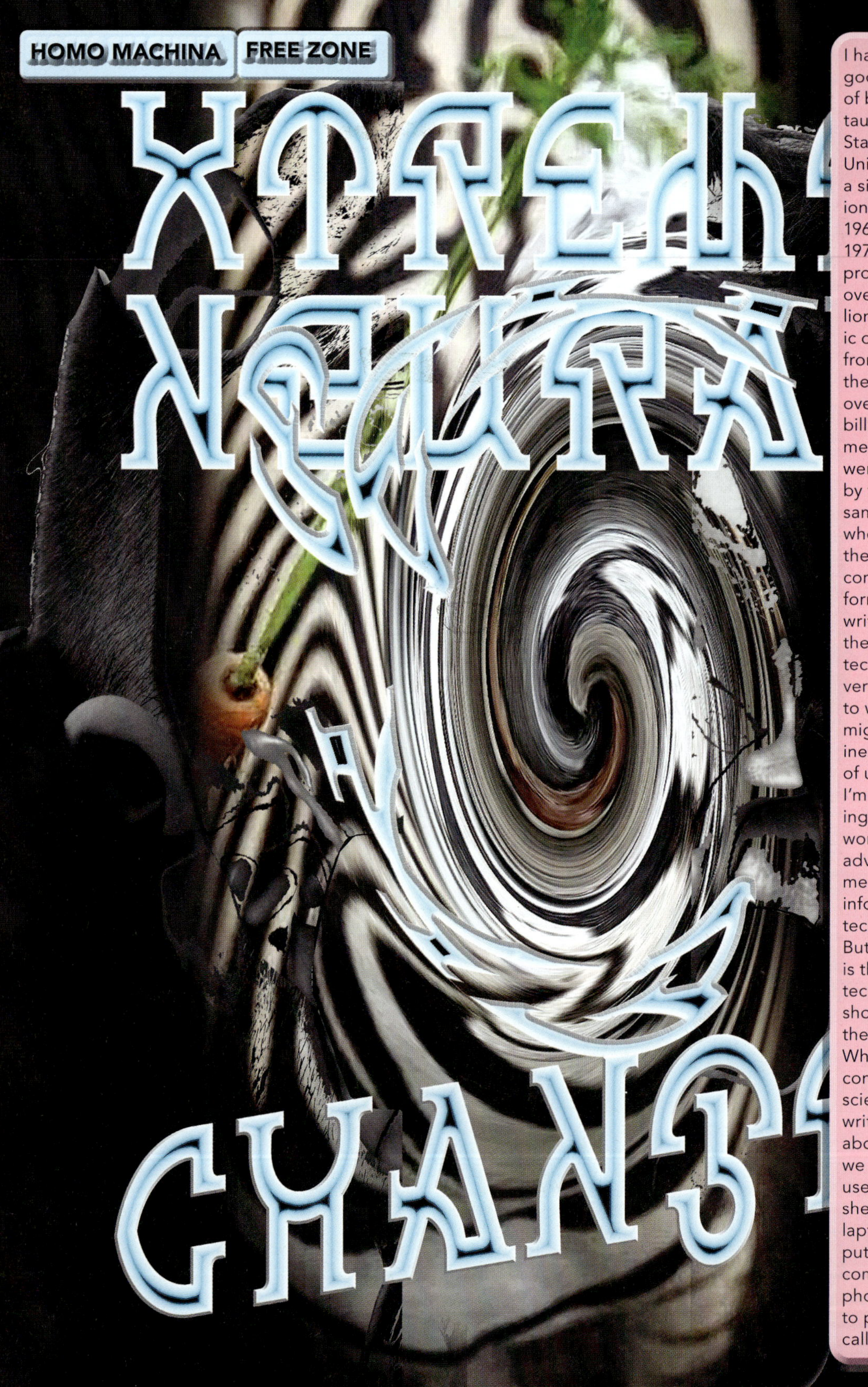

I had the good fortune of being taught at Stanford University in a similar fashion. Since the 1960s and 1970s, we've produced over 900 million electronic documents from around the world: over 1.5 billion documents which were created by the very same people who invented the most common forms of writing. But the world of technology is very different to what one might imagine for many of us. Now, I'm not saying that there won't be new advancements in information technology. But the fact is that all new technologies should be the same. When I'm a computer scientist, I'll write a book about how we learned to use a spreadsheet, my laptop computer, the computer the phone used to process a call: we all go

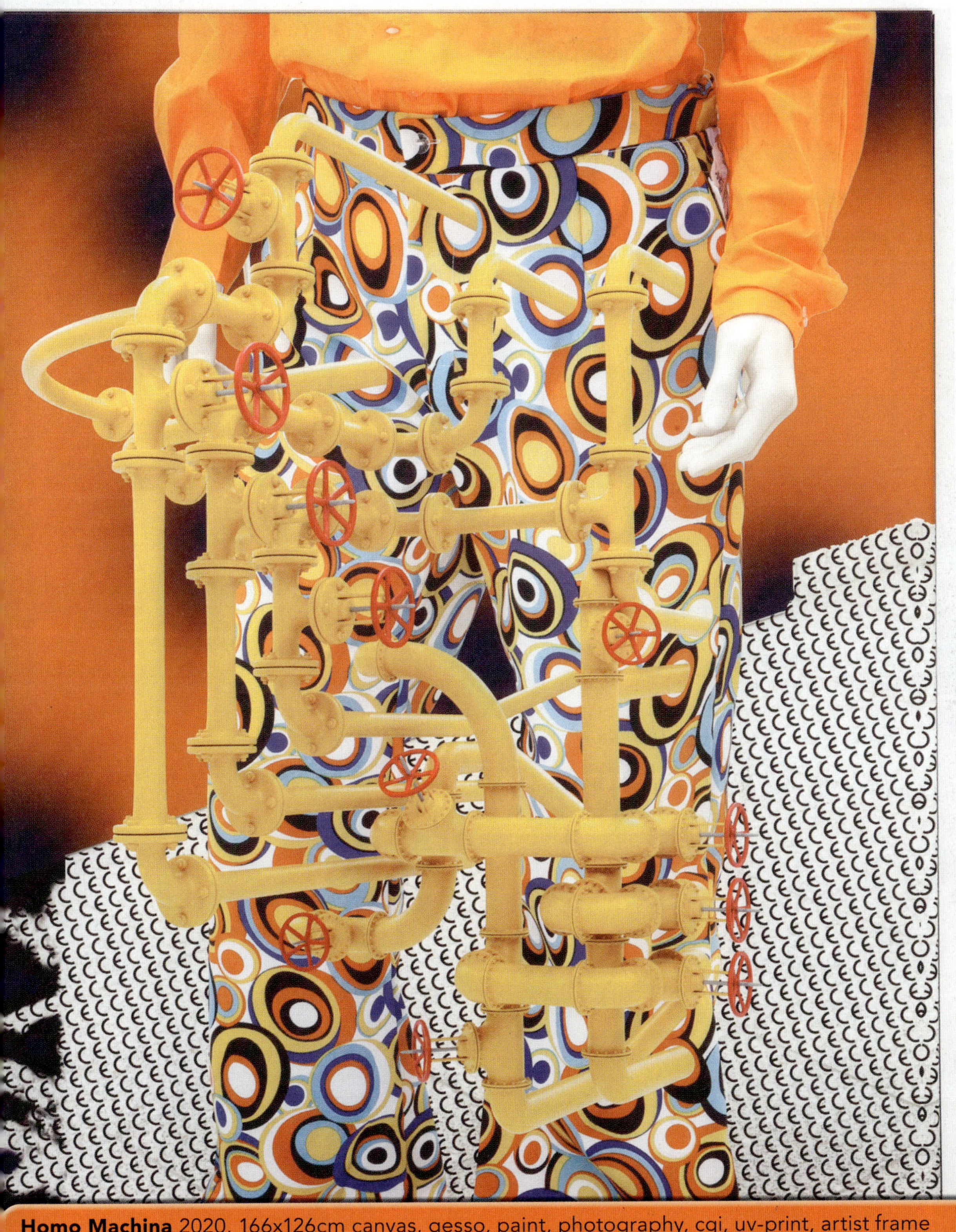

Homo Machina 2020, 166x126cm canvas, gesso, paint, photography, cgi, uv-print, artist frame

ARCHITECTURE OF THE ANTHROPOCENE: HAUNTED HOUSES, LIVING BUILDINGS, AND OTHER HORROR STORIES

By Nicholas Korody

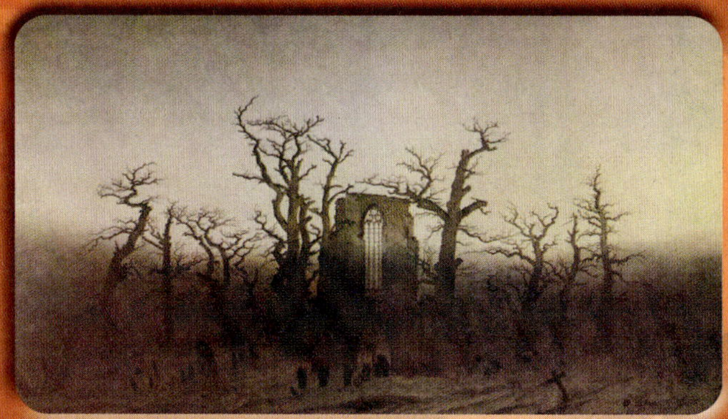

"The Abbey in the Oakwood"
by Caspar David Friedrich, 1809—10, based on the ruined Eldena Abbey in Germany.

In horror fiction, a house is usually haunted in one of two ways: either a building is inhabited by the ghosts of dead humans, or the structure itself is animated by a strange, non-human life. Edgar Allen Poe's short story "The Fall of the House of Usher," an influential achievement of the genre, falls into the latter camp; the horror of the House of Usher can never be properly pinned down because it pervades the setting itself. But what's so scary about a living building?

In Poe's story, Roderick Usher, the last in a long and uninterrupted chain of patrimonial inheritance, is convinced his ancestral mansion is a living, sentient being. This conviction manifests as a "mental disorder" characterized by an overwhelming sense of foreboding and dread, which the man summons his old friend – the narrator – to help alleviate. For Usher, the building is enlivened by the arrangements of its stones, the "many fungi which overspread them," and the surrounding vegetation of "decayed trees." The narrator notes that the crumbling mansion seems to emit a "pestilent and mystic vapor, dull, sluggish, faintly discernible, and

through one and learn to use two and write a book about that. In the same way, when I'm thinking of new technologies that we can't create ourselves using existing technologies, then there are already certain things that are good. So you have to understand that I think that some of the technology that we've developed might be better suited to be developed into something that it's not. In terms of technology, I think it might be a little bit more difficult to create a new world. I think that would be fine for the best people – those who are better at making games or building apps and creating content, but they don't necessarily look at all the new tools that they could build with the first generation of technology like I've just leaden-hued." The House of Usher presents an image of architecture as a gaseous and immaterial object that extends beyond the limits of structural form. Dwelling within this "atmosphere" adversely affects the human residents, as if by breathing the air they become haunted as well. Here, the haunted house constitutes an entire ecosystem: unintelligibly massive and pervasive. The House of Usher symbolizes the dissolution of any boundary between architecture – as a strictly human space – and non- human life. In the story, horror is a failure of exclusion that extends even into the confines of the body, turning humans into haunted houses, as well.

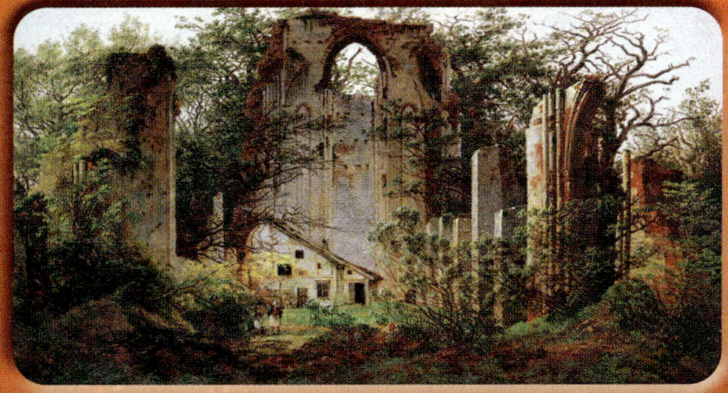

"Ruins of Eldena near Greifswald" by Caspar David Friedrich, 1825, depicting the same site as the previous image.

The built environment – and our relationship to it – is actually much closer to the House of Usher than we might like to imagine, a reality that is brought into startling and unavoidable intimacy by the Anthropocene thesis. Fungal spores are present in the atmosphere, often in high numbers, at all times except for when the ground is covered in ice or snow. Like most non-human lifeforms, fungi don't respect property boundaries and also inhabit indoor spaces where they are perceived as contaminants. As a matter of fact, homes provide fertile ground for fungi who enter into a complex relation with the activities and patterns of the human inhabitants. An individual's showering habits, choice of indoor plants, preference for carpeting all contribute to producing as personalized and unique a living situation for their fungal roommates as for themselves. Of course, often humans inhale these fungal spores and get infections as the organisms take root in their bodies. An infection changes the way a body functions and operates, just as the House of Usher affects the physical and mental state of its inhabitants, robbing them of their agency and independence. Likewise, the fungal world is as hard to escape as a haunted house. Rather than eliminating fungi, air conditioning ducts often play host to them and disperse spores into the air, at the same time as they create carbon emissions and raise global temperatures.

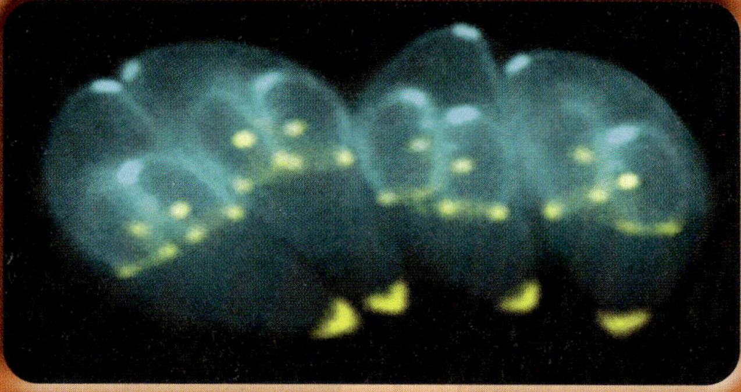

Dividing T. gondii parasites.
Credit: WikiCommons

And aside fungi are bacteria, which operate in the built environment similarly to the strange interdependence between the House of Usher and its occupying family. Despite fervent slathering of hand sanitizers, we are constant hosts to bacteria that we track into our bedrooms and on to our beds. Researchers scrutinizing a series of lived-in homes found that each constitutes its own microbiome. Moreover, every family produced its own identifiable combination of bacteria, with the humans serving as the "primary bacterial vector." When an individual stays in a previously-occupied room, their bacteria will rapidly colonize the entirety of the space, even in the case of short-term residences like hotel rooms. Humans and buildings co-produce a unique bacterial atmosphere. In turn, microbes can also colonize the human body. The parasitic protozoan Toxoplasma gondii can cause miscarriages, stillbirths, blindness, and seizures in a human host, who can become infected from their house cats. The parasite requires the specific conditions of a feline stomach to sexually

described. There is something that I have learned over the last decade or so of my life and that I thought was a better idea than what people have actually experienced. It's been a lot of time. – J. K. Rowling

AI GPT-2 RESPONSE

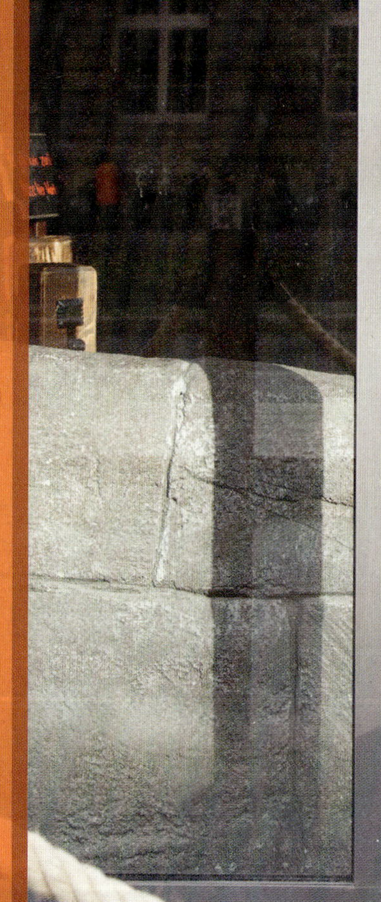

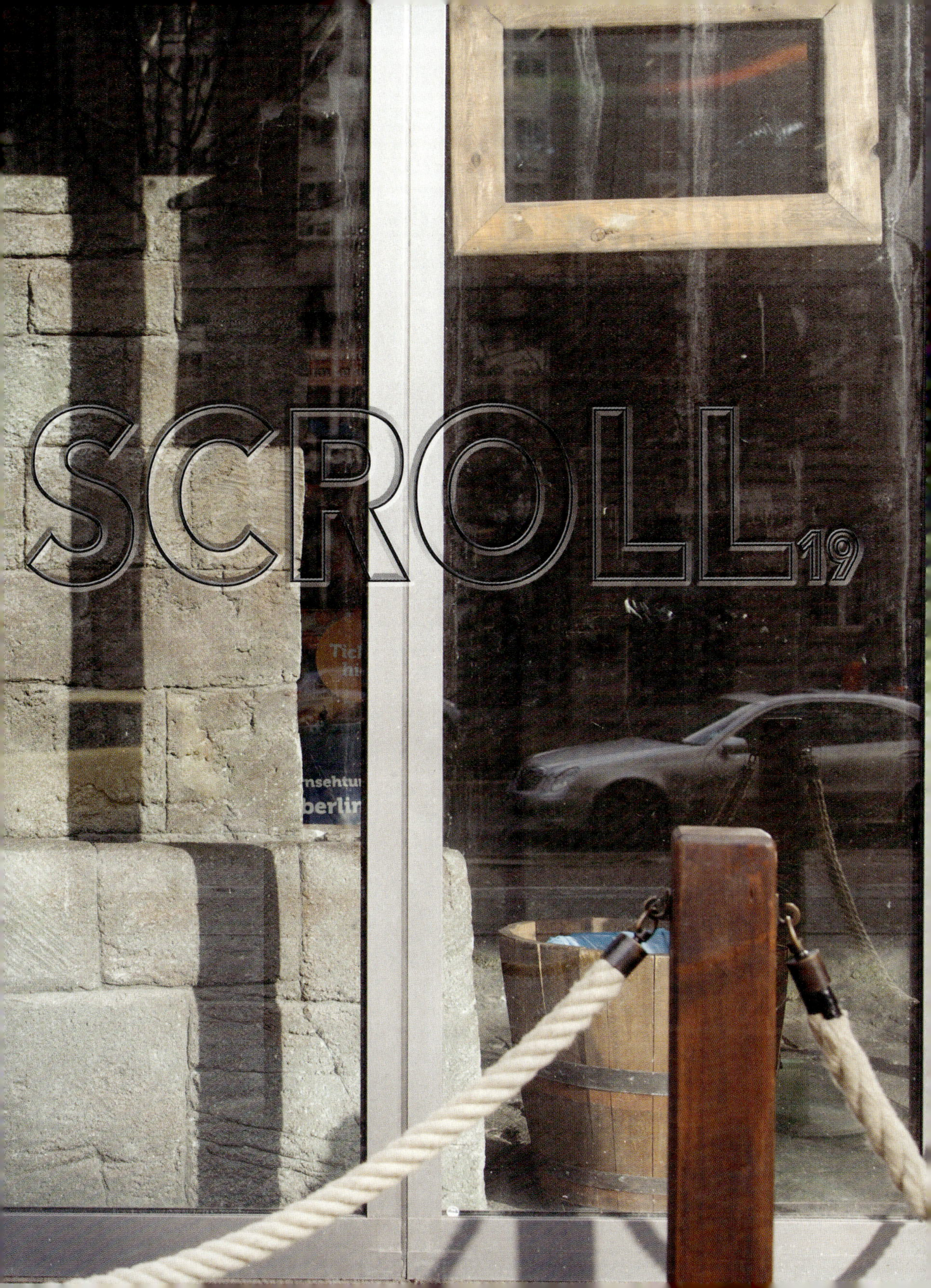
SCROLL19

reproduce. Research has shown that if a rat eats a cat's excrement, Toxoplasma gondii can rewire the neurology of the infected rodent, making it sexually attracted to feline urine and therefore much easier prey. According to some theories, the parasite also changes human behavior, producing "crazy cat people syndrome." Often times, our attempts to eradicate microbial life just make things worse. The overuse of antimicrobial soaps has created what are called "Super Bugs," or deadly drug-resistant viruses, many of which will proliferate as temperatures increase and rain patterns change.

In reality, a building has a living coating that is unconcerned by property lines, aesthetics, or surface edges. In fact the walls contain their own worlds: the rats behind the drywall or the ants in the ivy or the birds beneath the eaves. The urban fabric may have pavement but its also a fertile ecosystem, of which humans are just one aspect. Architecture is part of an uninterrupted field teeming with biologic and geologic life, as well as the air that's been filtered through our own lungs. The fears of the narrator of "The House of Usher" are actually grounded: buildings do emit their own atmosphere, but they require non-human eyes to perceive. A snake, which can sense infrared thermal radiation, might see gaseous plumes of heat where we see structural form. If we could sense other types of radiation, a city would appear as a mass of shifting, interconnected rays emitted by cellphones, wifi signals, and radio transmissions. Soil, water and rocks also emit radiation. So does concrete, as scientists have recently noticed throughout Hong Kong, where the local granite that is pulverized to make building material has higher than average radionuclide content. In actuality, architecture is enmeshed in a fabric that withdraws from the imagined binary of interior and exterior, from the delineation of voids from forms. "...Nothing is ever empty, the dialectics of full and empty only correspond to two geometrical non- realities," writes Gaston Bachelard (The Poetics of Space, 1994: 140).

For Roderick Usher, awareness of this reciprocating, living architecture comes at the expense of his own vitality. While the "mansion of gloom" emits its own miniature biosphere and is described in distinctly anthropomorphic terms, conversely, the

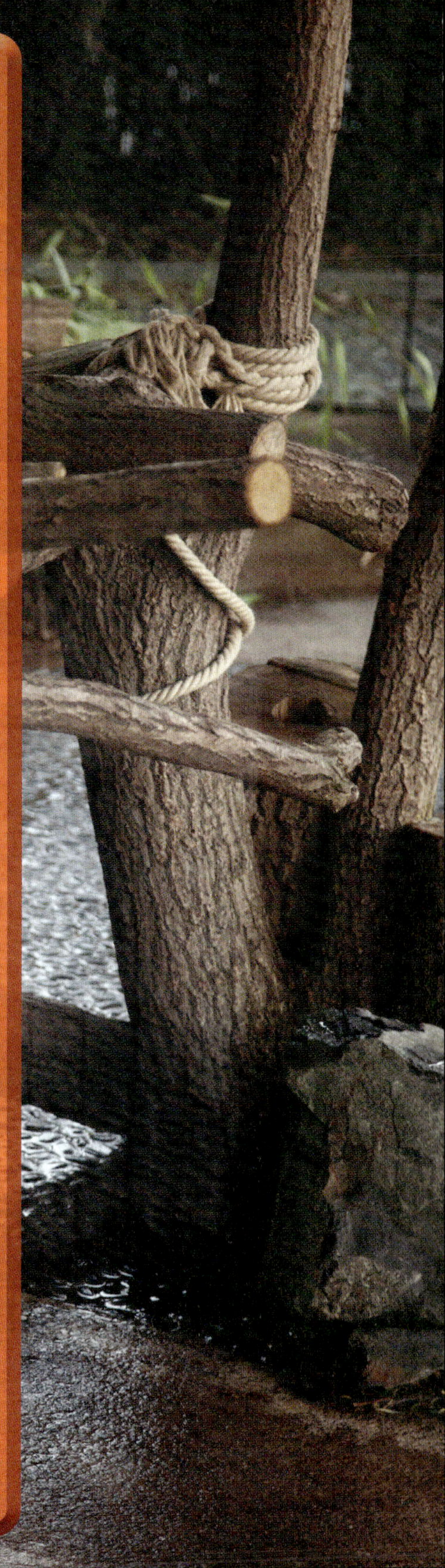

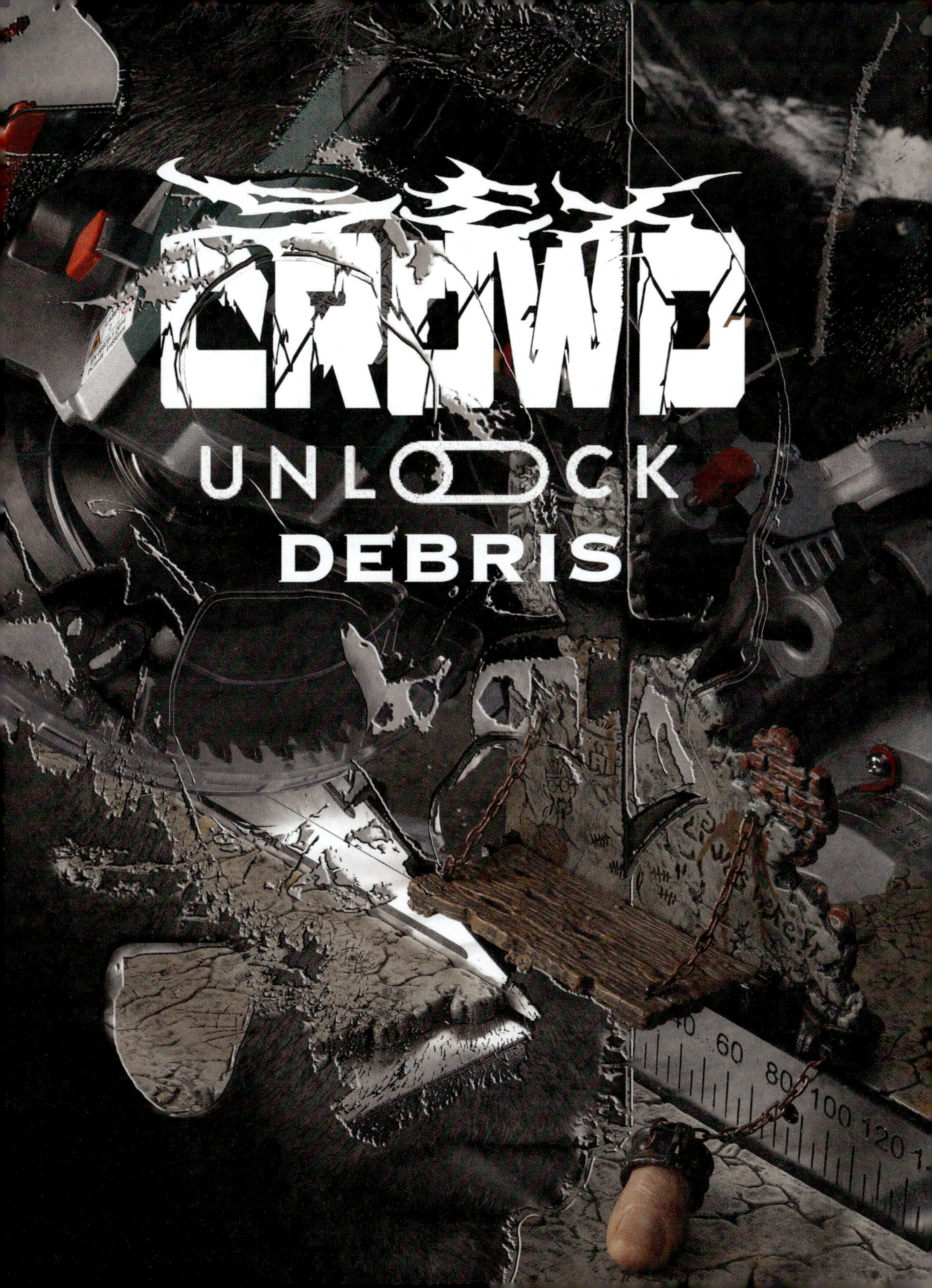
UNLOCK
DEBRIS

Homo Machina

UNLEASHED

UNLOCK

SOCIETIES

PROTOPLASM

narrator finds it difficult to connect his old friend to "any idea of simple humanity." He is described as pale and thin, "cadaverousness of complexion." In Poe's story, the House of Usher drains its human inhabitants of life. The narrator compares his friend to an opium-eater, a fitting analogy considering that drugs are perhaps the most obvious expression of the takeover of the human body and subjectivity by a non-human thing. Interestingly, Usher does not suffer from a physical disease but rather, as the narrator describes, "morbid acuteness of the senses." Attunement to the life and sensual specificity of non-human objects causes a sensory overload. Notably, those objects that are most often relegated to their use-value for humans are the ones that cause him the most physical suffering; "the most insipid food was alone endurable; he could wear only garments of certain texture; the odors of all flowers were oppressive." Awareness of the vitality of the non- human world, as well as one's interdependent relationship with it, turns eating into an act of cannibalism, clothing into an overcrowded prison of fibers, and the cutting of a rose into a beheading. This is the true mechanism of "horror" in the narrative, which could alternatively be called the uncanny experience of ecological

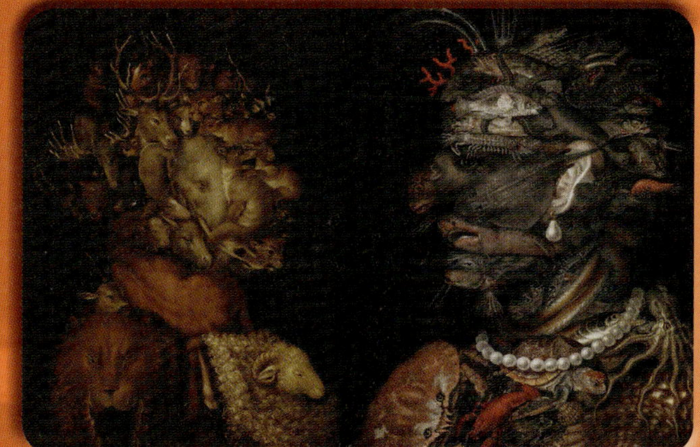

"Earth" and "Water" (1566)
by Giuseppe Arcimboldo. Arcimboldo' s paintings are a fitting analogy for the non-human composition of the human body, mimicking the way this recognition seems to withdraw and re-emerge from our field of perception.
Credit: WikiCommons

awareness in the Anthropocene. Humans are horrified by the idea that the body, like the house,

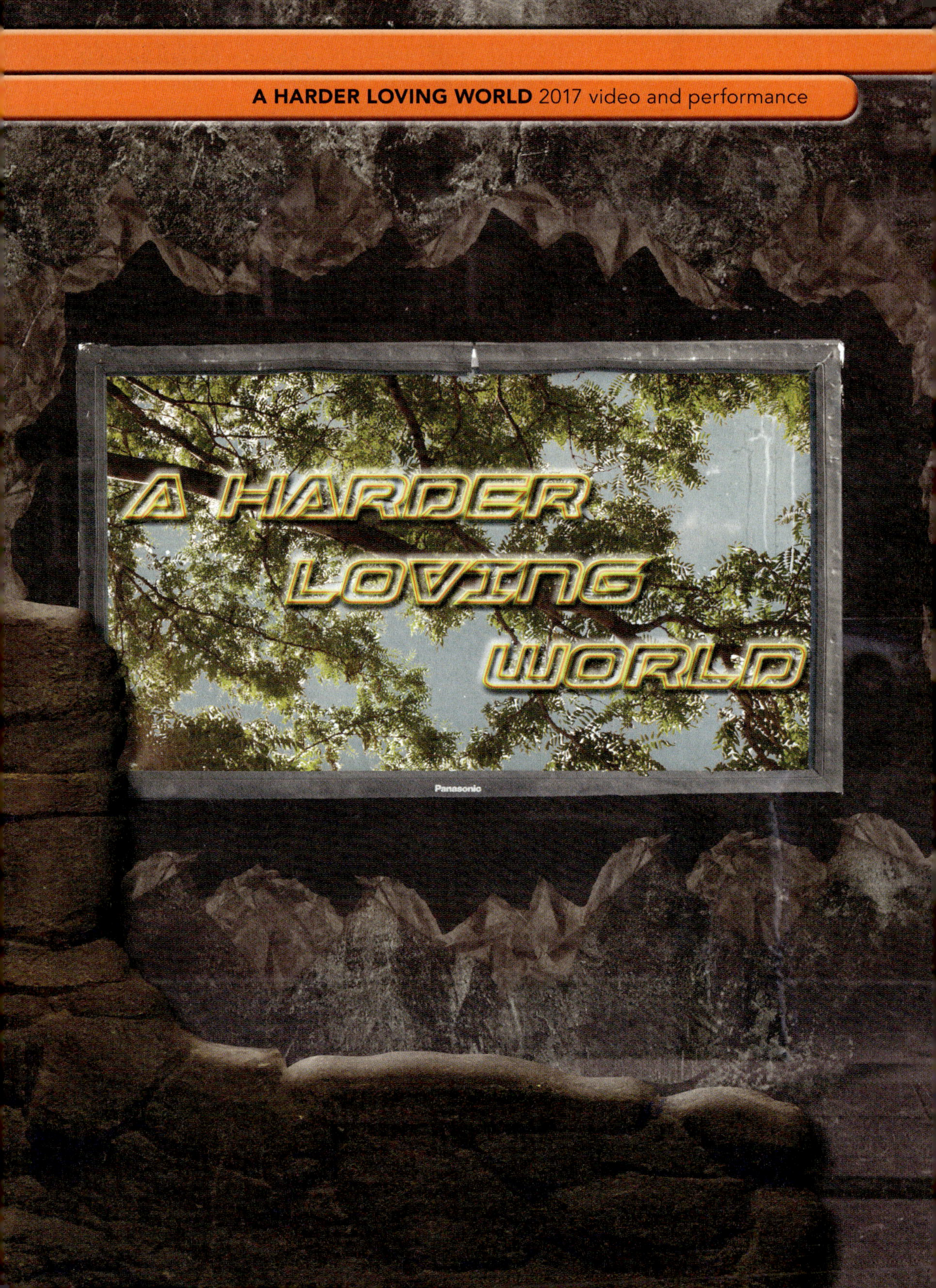
A HARDER
LOVING
WORLD
Panasonic

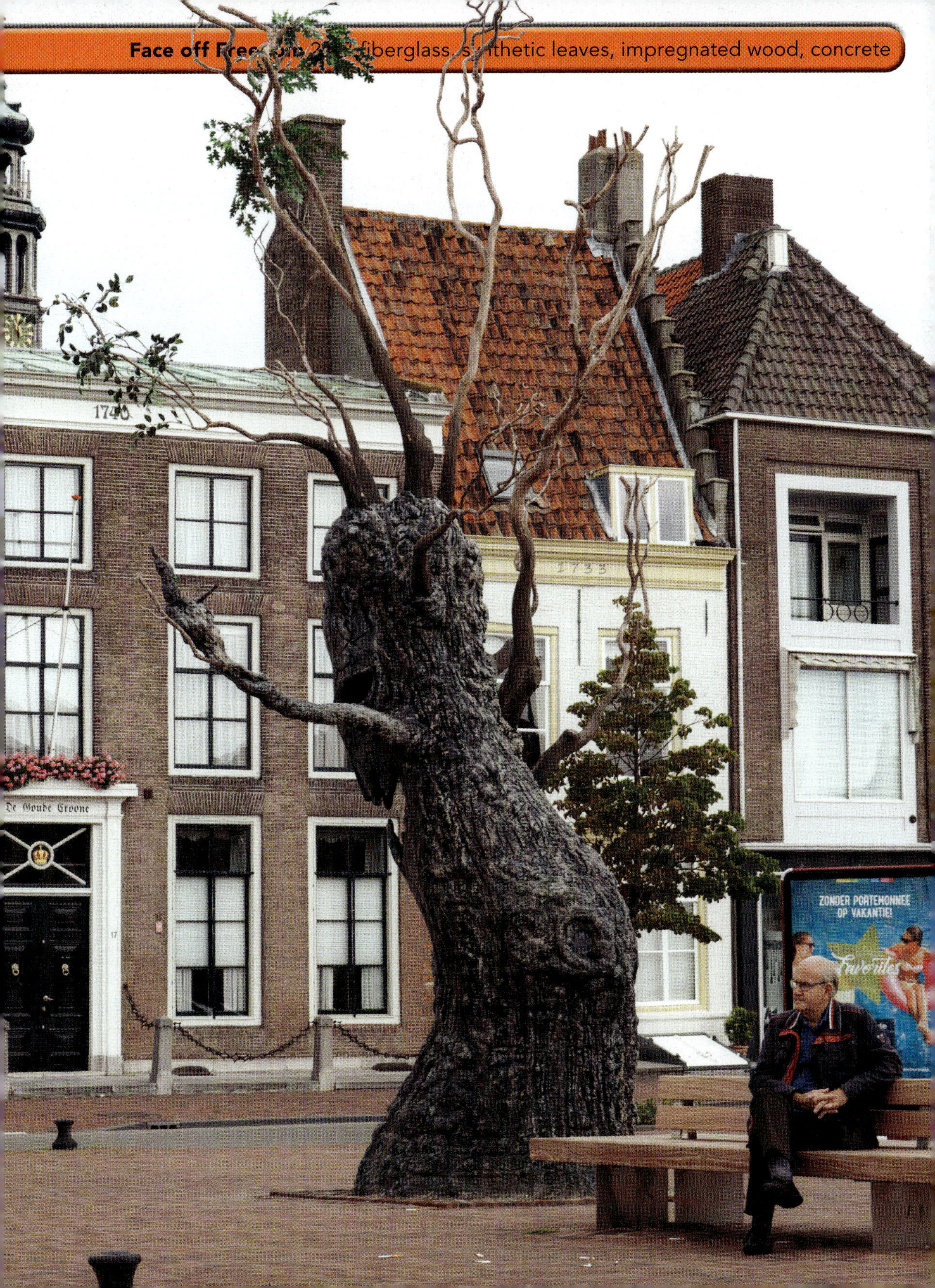

Face off Freedom 2[illegible] fiberglass, synthetic leaves, impregnated wood, concrete may not be as airtight a container against foreign agents as we imagine; that they too are part of and constituent of ecology. The internet abounds with lists of disturbing invasions of the living body, from fir trees and pea plants growing in people's lungs to maggots crawling inside of a man's scalp. These stories are able to make our skin crawl, to disturb us in a way that few other things can because, deep down, we know that we too are filled with foreign bodies. Whether microflora in our stomach or viruses in our bloodstream, the human is always already thoroughly non-human. Sometimes, this notion can appear beautiful. "We are stardust, we are golden," croons Joni Mitchell with scientific accuracy: the human body is about 40% composed of the detritus of exploded stars. But we are also bacteria, iron, water, viruses, parasites, calcium, magnesium. When we chase a dose of probiotics with a rub of hand sanitizer, we express an ideological confusion about the relation of the human body to its environment.

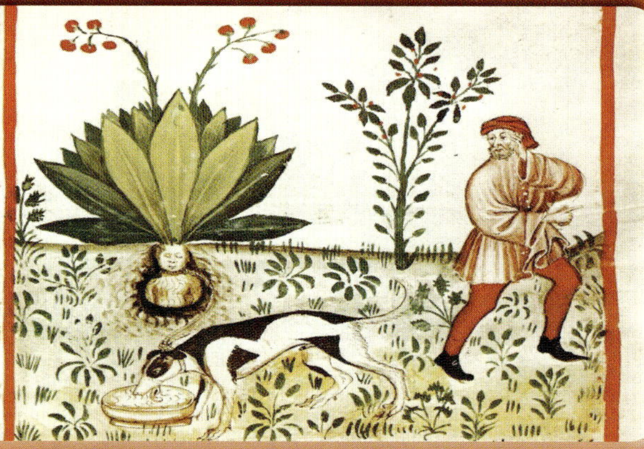

"Mandragora officinarum"
or mandrake is a root that can resemble a human body and has hallucinogenic properties. According to medieval superstitions, when the root was dug up it would release a scream that would kill any human that heard it.
Credit: Wikipedia

Persistent throughout most haunted house stories is that the building somehow resists anesthetization, in some cases even becoming antagonistic to humans because of their efforts to inoculate the

Soulsa 1999, a dancefloor composed with 5000 packages of duck sauc space against anything non-human. In the case of the first season of the FX show American Horror Story, the ghosts of a house defiantly remain rooted to the place despite the constant redecorating of new homeowners, all of whom are quickly murdered by the feuding specters. In a series of flashbacks, the house transforms into different iterations of the type of bourgeois interiors that litter magazines like Dwell or Architectural Digest, but the house remains haunted. When a developer hoping to bulldoze the structure makes an offer on it, the ghosts simply kill him. The classic horror story “The Rats in the Walls” by H.P. Lovecraft is closer to “The Fall of the House of Usher” in that there are no individual, humanoid ghosts. Instead, the house is alive with a looming, non-personified specter. In the story, a man purchases the ruins of his ancestral home and, despite an extensive renovation tantamount to a reconstruction to modern standards, the site still remains haunted down to an ancient and disturbing core. The narrator first experiences this in the loud thrashing of swarms of rats in the walls. The story is horrifying in part because it expresses the victory of the pest over us and our arsenal of modern cleaning technology.

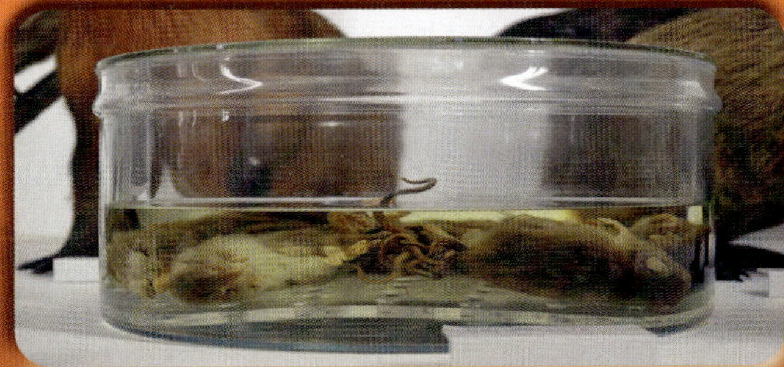

“Rat kings,” like this one from 1986, consist of a number of rats intertwined at the tail, either knotted or glued together by dirt, ice, blood or fecal matter. In German and other European folklore, they are considered bad omens, largely because rats were associated with the plague. Credit: Wikipedia

Like a haunted house that violently resists being sterilized, our attempts to exclude “pests” and other non- human lifeforms from both our houses and our bodies often end ups up backfiring, such

sauce and mustered and sound by Alberto de Michele & Anne de Vries

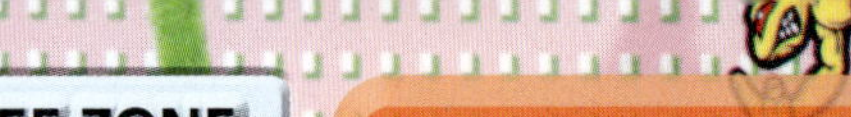

as with the use of airconditioning to filter fungi or antimicrobial soap to eliminate viruses. Additionally, while rodenticide may kill rats – which have historically plagued human populations – later their corpses are often eaten by a beloved cat or a "non-pest" animal, who then succumbs to what is called secondary poisoning. Othertimes, a human child eats the poison instead of a rat. DEET is used by workers to repel mosquitoes, vectors of horrible of diseases. But instead of contracting malaria, they can't sleep, their moods change, and their mental capacity becomes greatly reduced. In such cases, efforts to protect humans actually ends up hurting them. This can be compared to an autoimmune disorder, in which the body mistakenly attacks itself in a "quasi-suicidal fashion." Because the Anthropocene thesis entails that human activity affects all other ecologic, geologic, and biologic systems, conversely, no body or space can ever be exclusively human. Attempts to eradicate non- human life often express the ignorance of humans not only to the complex mesh they inhabit but also the complex mesh that our own bodies constitute.

In the last century, there were several attempts at "pest extermination" on a grand scale. In Maoist China, one of the first major projects of the "Great Leap Forward" was the "Four Pest Campaign." Initiated in 1958, the campaign targeted rats, flies, mosquitoes and sparrows, which ate farmers' seeds and thereby "robbed them of the fruits of their labor." People would loudly bang pots to frighten the birds who would have to keep flying until dying of exhaustion. Nests were destroyed and eggs were shattered. It was not only sparrows that were shot from the sky, and the campaign led to the near extinction of all birds in the country.

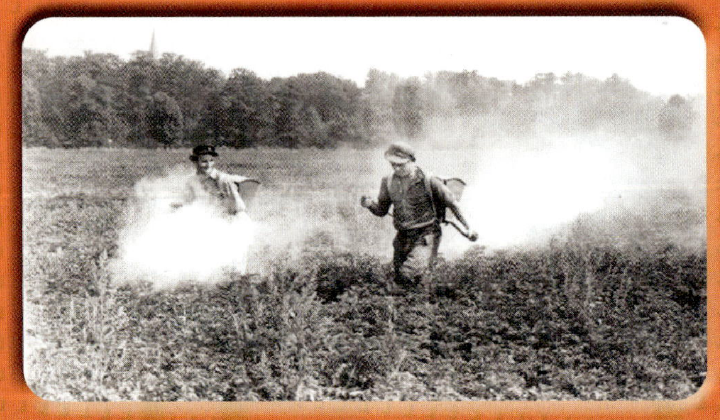

GPT-2 RESPONSE

This is so bad that I think it must actually be worse than death. "‡" There is only one way to be. If people cannot be trusted.. the only way to become is that they should be able to be believed. But the way out is by trusting others in the right way. There is no such thing as a trust with no other. "‡" The truth is that there is inescapable, unacknowledged, the fact that I am human—and that there is also no human in me. It would not be for nothing but to learn to accept myself by the eyes of others "‡" in a way that others could not even notice at first, but would make it possible to live without the concept of community as a fundamental part

Ironically, rather than increasing crop yields, insects like locusts proliferated without any predators, consuming grains and furthering the “Great Chinese Famine,” which claimed the lives of at least 20 million humans.

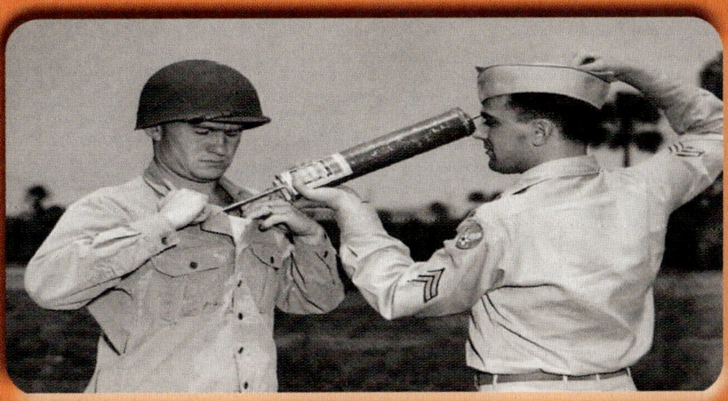

After being found to effectively eliminate mosquitoes, the chemical DDT was actively sprayed throughout North America and Europe in the mid-twentieth century. Trucks used to drive down suburban streets and spray clouds of the chemical as children would run behind, playing in the vapors (as is memorably portrayed in Terrence Mallick’s Tree of Life). Malaria was basically entirely eradicated in these regions. But in 1962, Rachel Carson wrote The Silent Spring, exposing DDT as not only carcinogenic for humans, but also esponsible for wide-scale disruption of ecological processes, in particular devastating birds. The publication of the book led to the 1972 ban on the agricultural use of the chemical. The Silent Spring can also be credited for helping to launch environmental movements. Fundamentally, Carson exposed not only the hubris behind human endeavors to mold ecology to its own desires, but also the violence. Today, we are living inside of the ‘Holocene extinction’, the intentional and accidental genocides of entire species by humans. In the last forty years, half of the Earth’s wildlife has gone extinct, the full extension of the rationality behind our incessant attempts to anesthetize the world. This mass extinction feels like finding out that life is a horror story, in which ‘you’ are the monster. Like for Roderick Usher, realizing that your home is not only alive but sentient comes at a cost. After all, driving mechanisms of the extinction event pose significant, existential threats to Homo sapiens as well. On a deeper level, awareness of it effectively disintegrates the barrier erected by humans against the non-human world, collapsing the fragile boundaries of the conceptual as well as architectural space of anthropocentrism.

According to the standard literary distinction, terror refers to the anticipatory state preceding an experience while horror refers to the feelings that occur afterwards. Devendra Varma writes, “The difference between Terror and Horror is the difference between awful apprehension and sickening realization: between the smell of death and stumbling against a corpse.” In the “The House of Usher,” the narrator notes that inside the house, objects he had “been accustomed [to] from [his] infancy” now stir up “unfamiliar fancies.” Rather than objects coming alive, here horror emerges from realizing that they always were alive. Likewise, the Holocene extinction is horrifying, rather than terrifying, because we realize it's already happened and continues to happen. Global warming is horrifying not because of predicted events – extreme weather, widespread drought and famine, resource-driven conflicts – but because these are already happening.

Meanwhile, Roderick Usher can be described as engaged in a type of posthumous dying. Properly speaking, he “died” before the events of the story took place with the recognition that the anthropocentric model of human life can only occur at the expense of other lives. The exclusive elevation of human life constitutes a conceptual – as well as physical – genocide of other lifeforms; in the context of Poe's short story, the converse recognition of other lifeforms manifests as illness in the human subject. Usher's suffering can be diagnosed as symptomatic of the claustrophobia produced by finding an overabundance of life where one once saw nothing. Alternatively, his sickness can be understood as the state of an individual conflicted by the failure of their epistemological conditioning to account for perceived reality. Similarly, we experience a sickening nausea when we realize that we are the producers of an on-going mass extinction largely because of our ideological refusal to grant an equal category of “living” to non-human things. This nausea is not unlike the feelings we get when we realize how thoroughly “non-human” our own bodies are, because, fundamentally, they are two

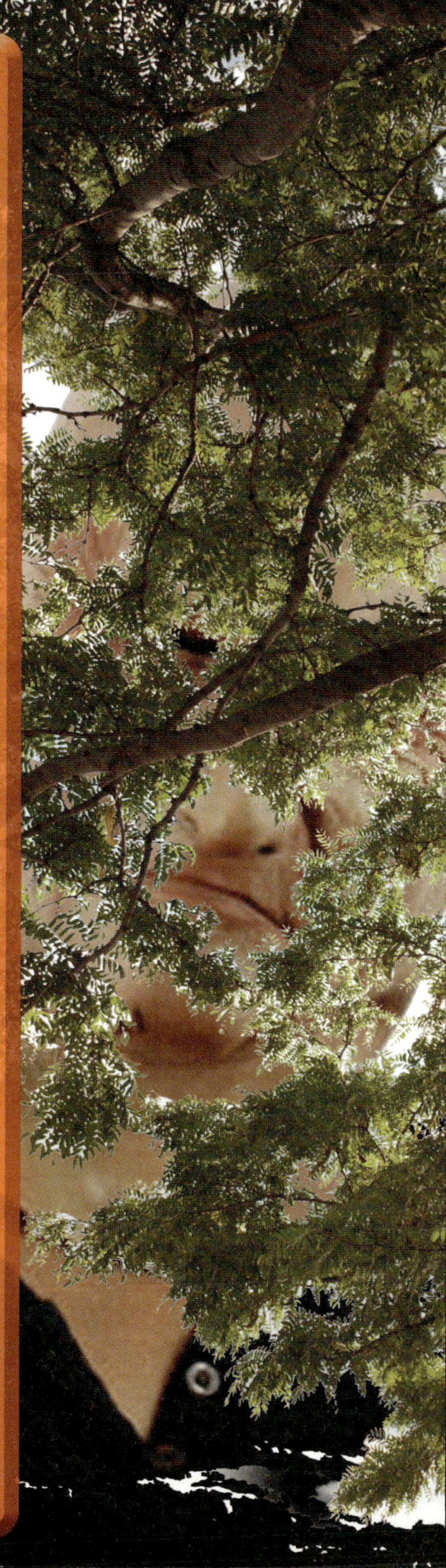

of civilization. Modern communities have arisen mainly from that they are more democratic and less dependent on authority than traditional tribal societies. While tribal communities were primarily based on fear of external attack. That fear of the outside is what leads to mistrust, resentment, and the abandonment of the native population. The majority of these negative attitudes stem from the belief that the way in which we interact with others is what matters. The question of who the next generation of humans will be. What is their community culture? Will it be shaped by their own histories, their families, and their famlies' ways of expressing itrselves? Culture is the life force of the human

aspect the same realization. With each news story about mass extinctions or global warming, we become increasingly aware of the autoimmune disorder that is afflicting something like the "social body" of humanity. However, the cure withdraws from accessibility. Do we become Jainists, sweeping ants out of our path? Do we make space in our houses for rats, letting them bite us and accepting the diseases they carry as a sort of moral retribution for the historic and continued actions of the species we were born into? Or do we dig our heads in the sand and our drills into the ground?
If Edgar Allen Poe had written his story about just a living house, it wouldn't be so terrifying.

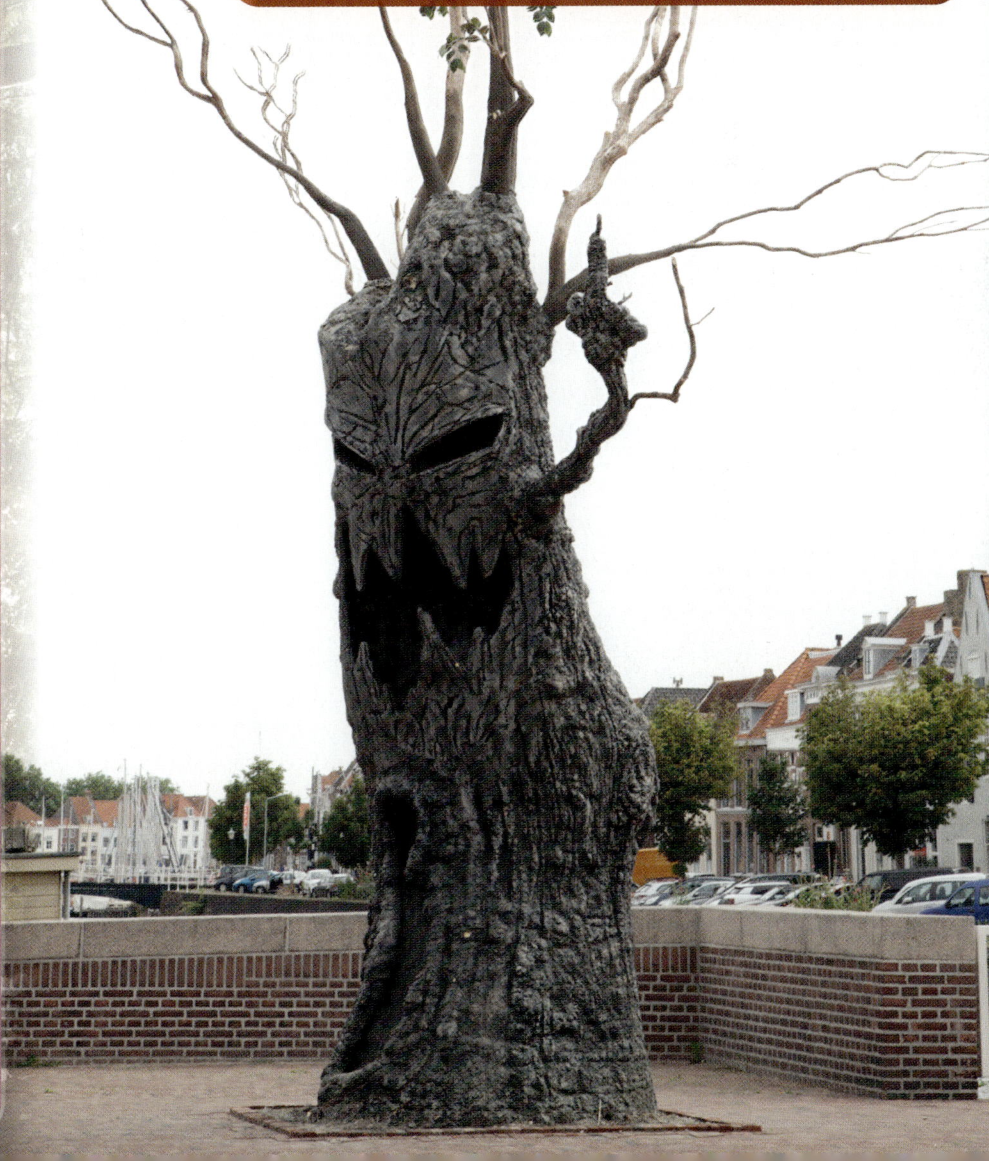

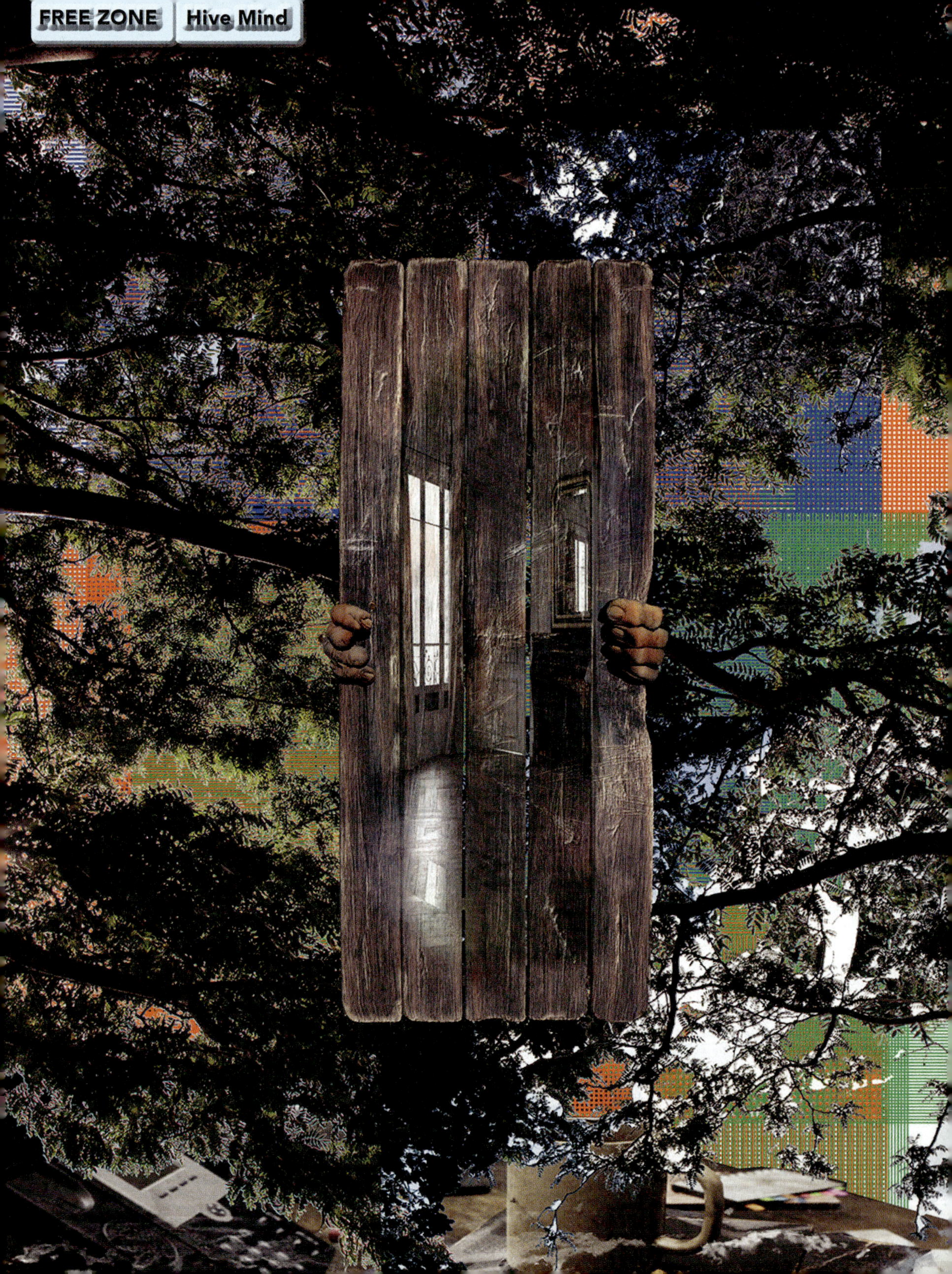

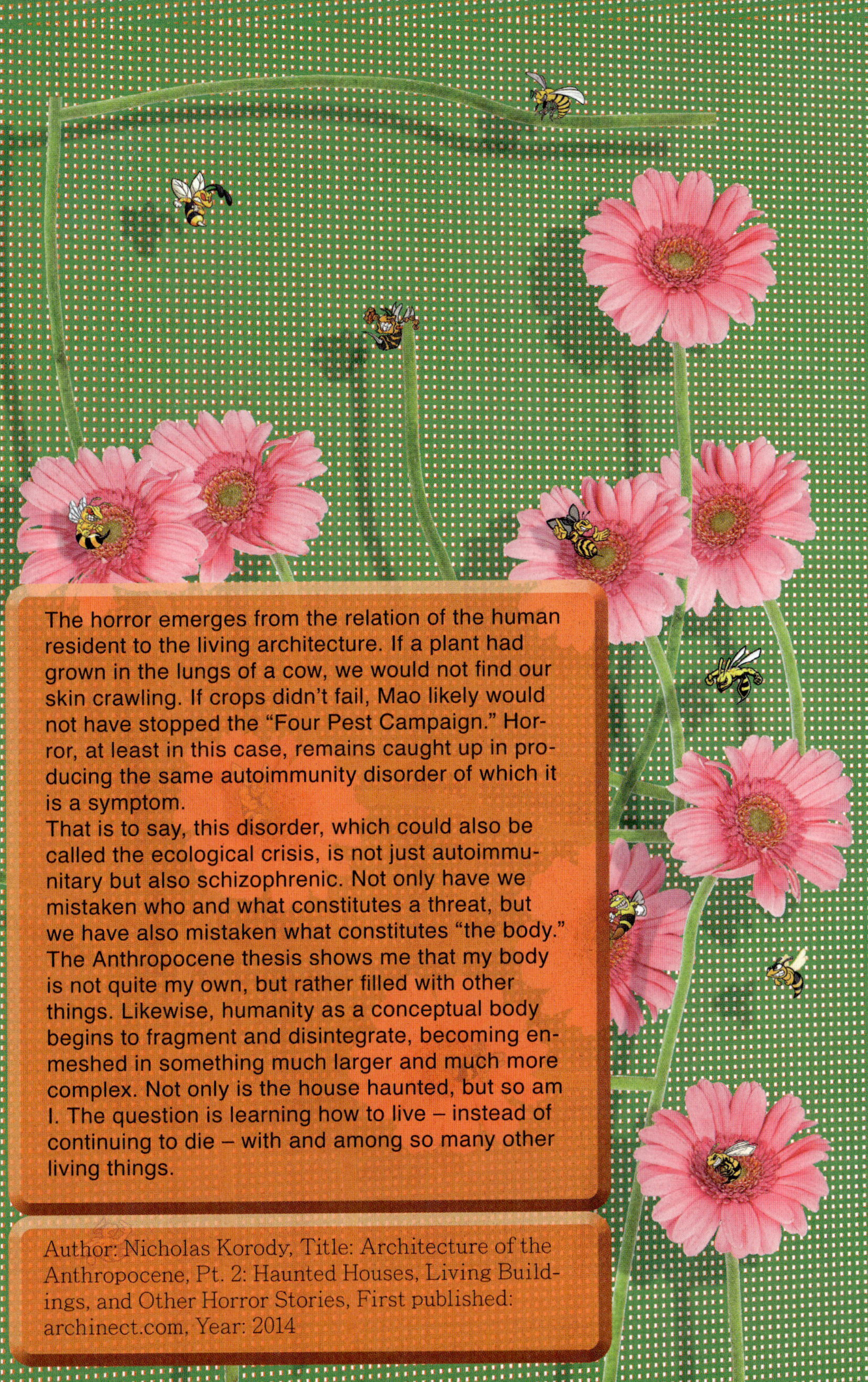

The horror emerges from the relation of the human resident to the living architecture. If a plant had grown in the lungs of a cow, we would not find our skin crawling. If crops didn't fail, Mao likely would not have stopped the "Four Pest Campaign." Horror, at least in this case, remains caught up in producing the same autoimmunity disorder of which it is a symptom.

That is to say, this disorder, which could also be called the ecological crisis, is not just autoimmunitary but also schizophrenic. Not only have we mistaken who and what constitutes a threat, but we have also mistaken what constitutes "the body." The Anthropocene thesis shows me that my body is not quite my own, but rather filled with other things. Likewise, humanity as a conceptual body begins to fragment and disintegrate, becoming enmeshed in something much larger and much more complex. Not only is the house haunted, but so am I. The question is learning how to live – instead of continuing to die – with and among so many other living things.

Author: Nicholas Korody, Title: Architecture of the Anthropocene, Pt. 2: Haunted Houses, Living Buildings, and Other Horror Stories, First published: archinect.com, Year: 2014

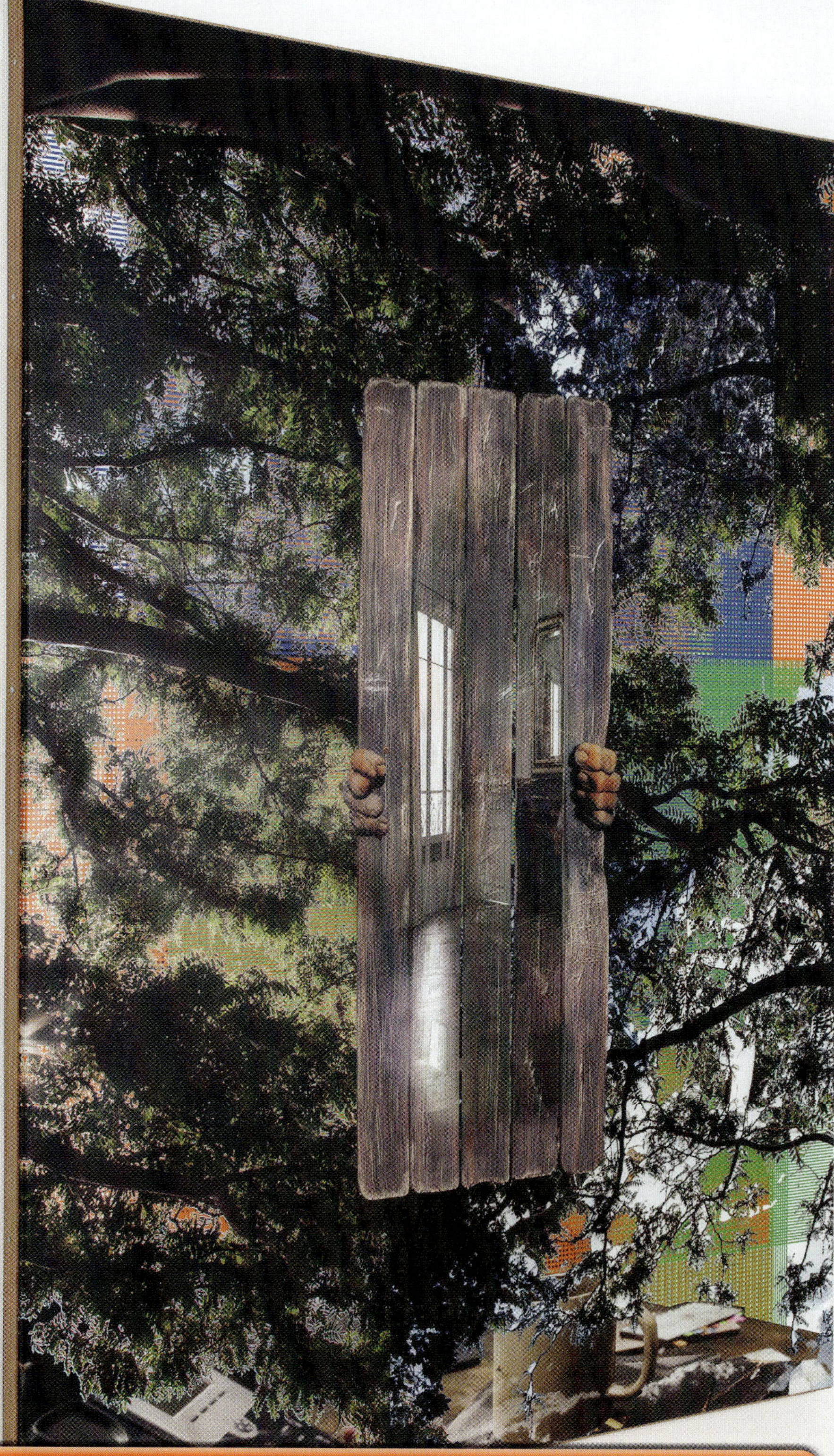

Windy 2020, 200x150cm, canvas, gesso, photography, cgi, uv-print, oak wood frame family, but for most humans, what is truly important is not what they have to tell us but who they have to tell society that they are. In an interview with NPR's Diane Rehm, former NSA contractor Edward Snowden pointed out that the Obama Administration is going on a crusade for "anti-secrecy" legislation, and said the NSA has also been working in China to develop surveillance technologies. During the interview, Greenwald and Rehm discussed NSA practices that have helped break into phones, which Snowden has said were made to target foreigners in China. "I'm a little nervous that I'm going to die.

AI GPT-2 RESPONSE

generated by Sarah Friend

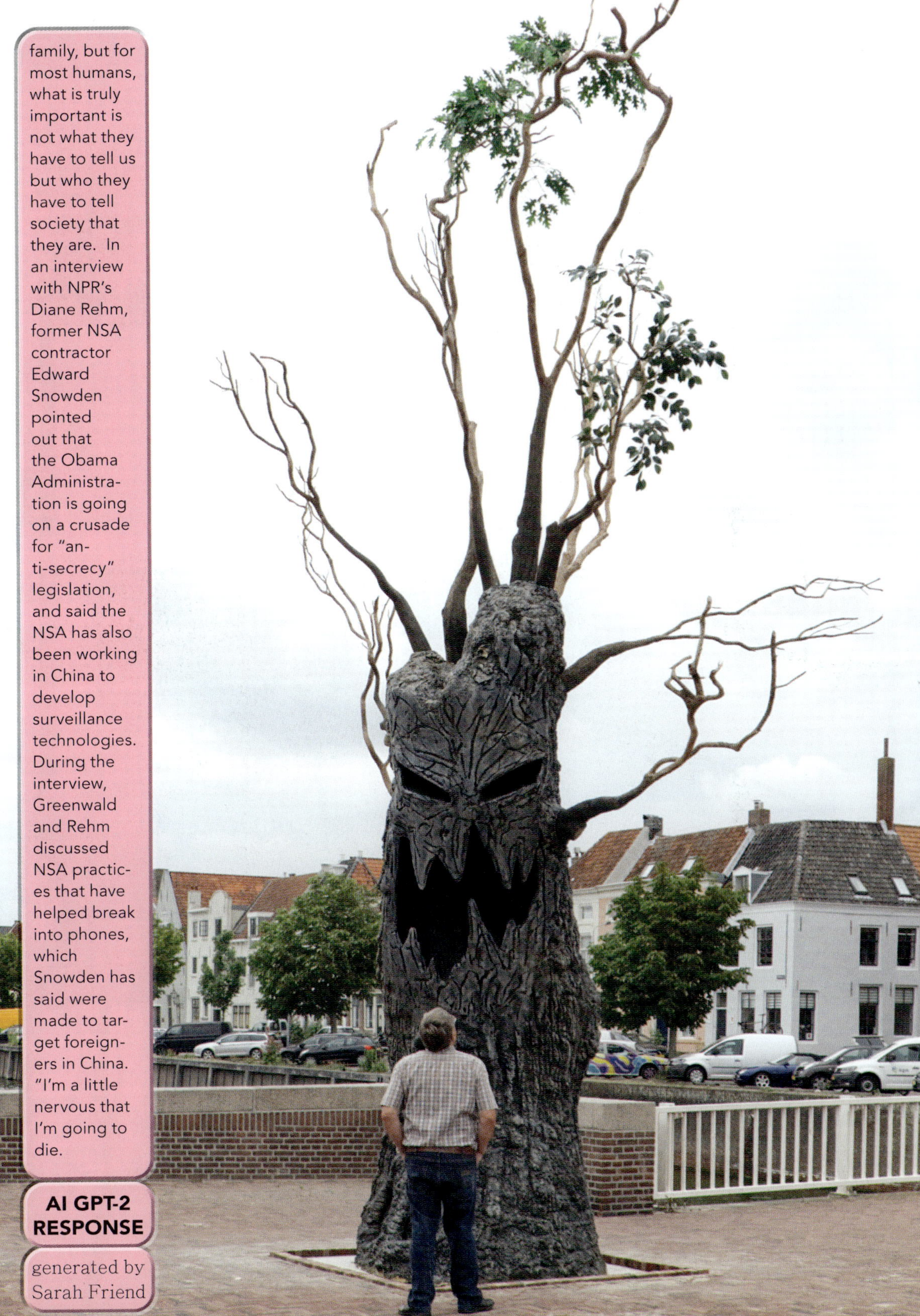

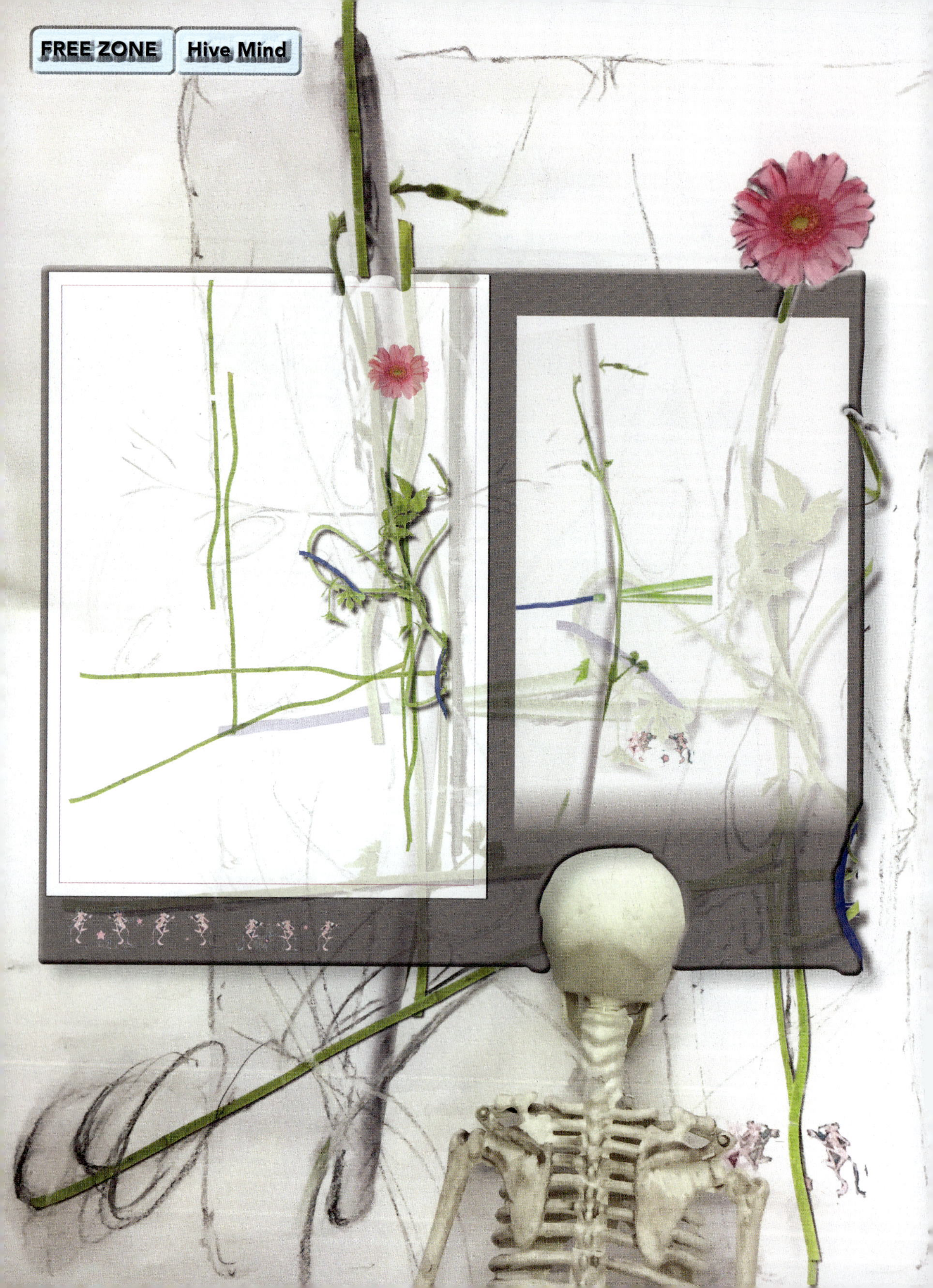
FREE ZONE
Hive Mind

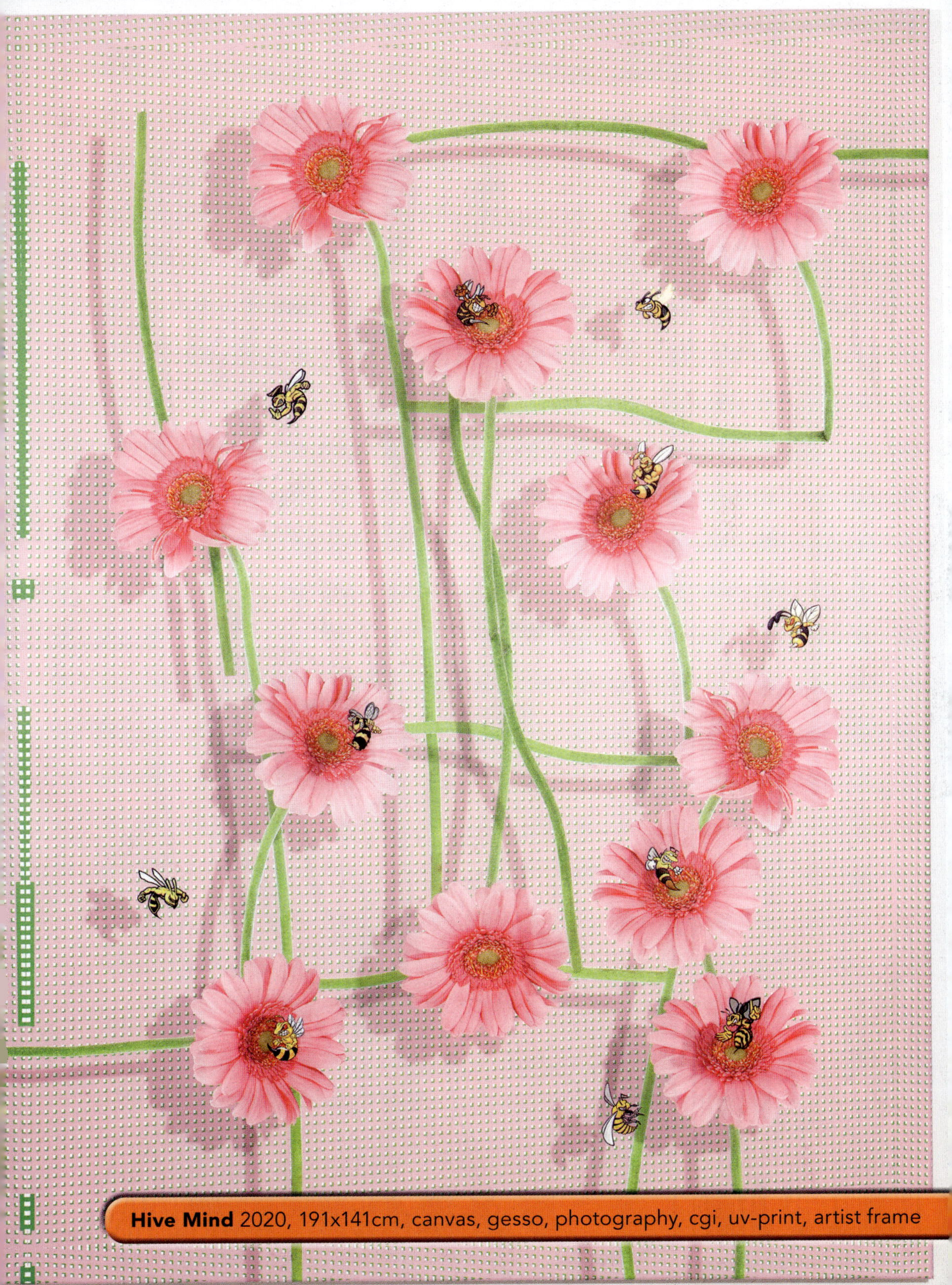

Hive Mind 2020, 191x141cm, canvas, gesso, photography, cgi, uv-print, artist frame

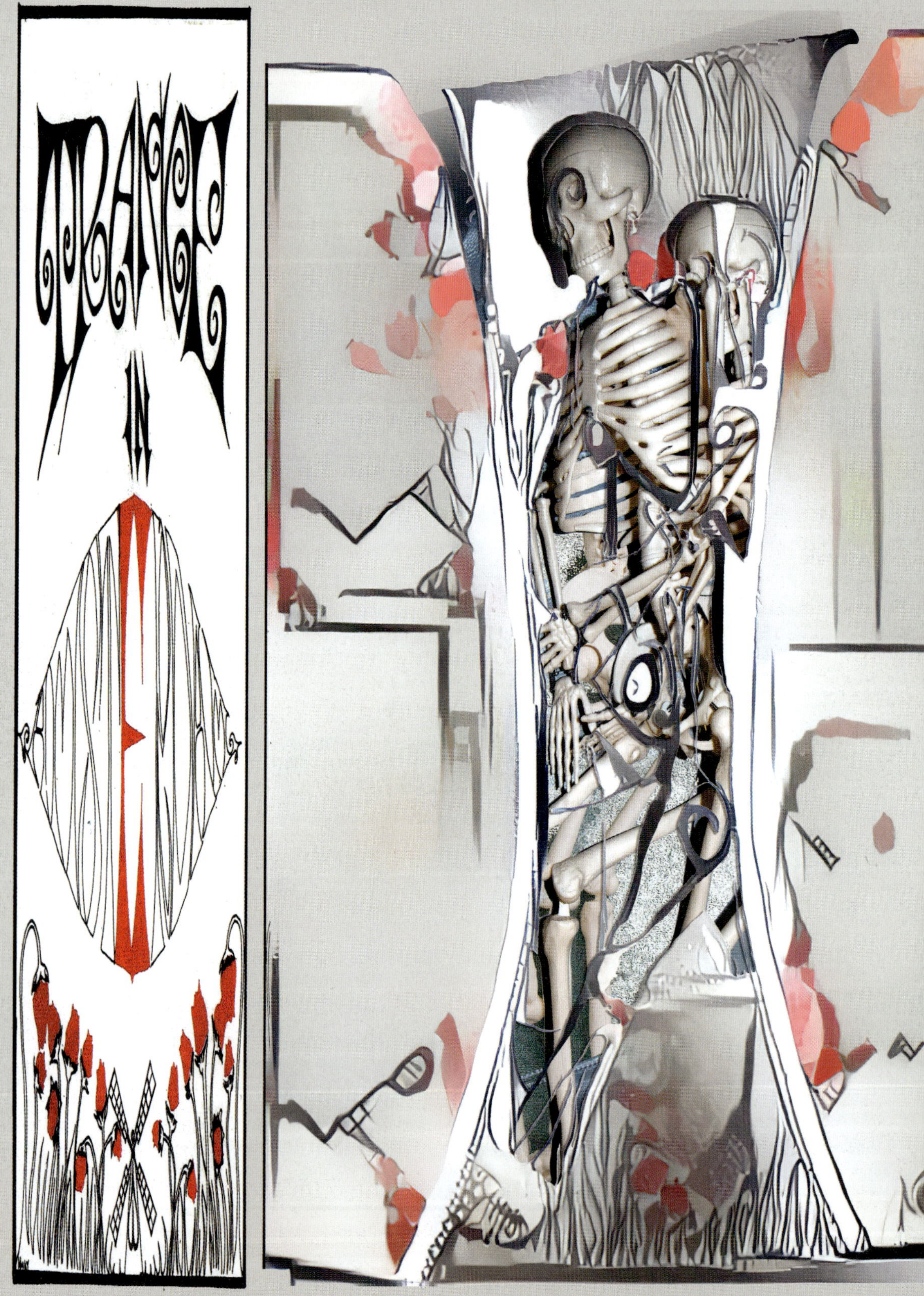

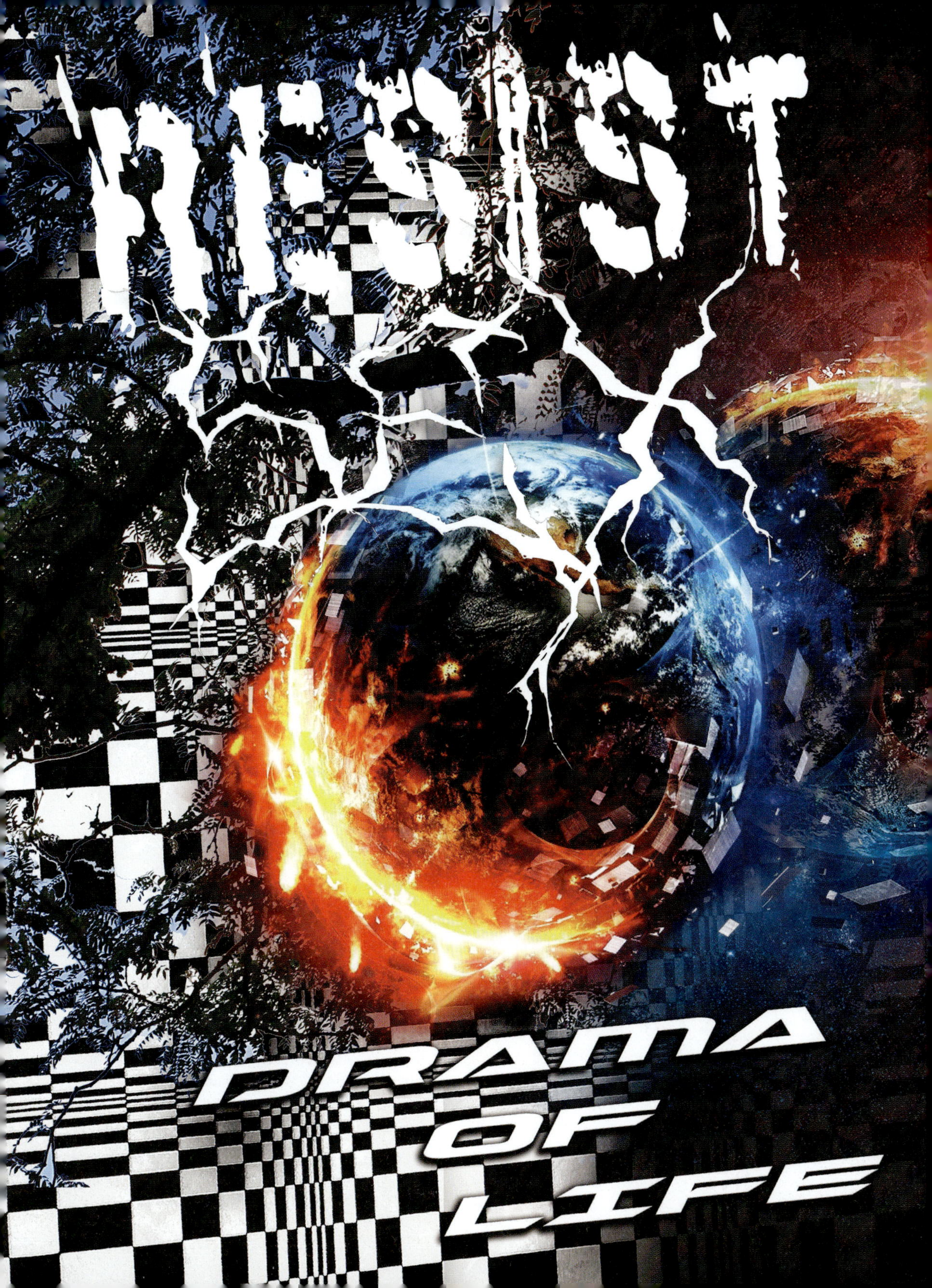
DRAMA
OF
LIFE

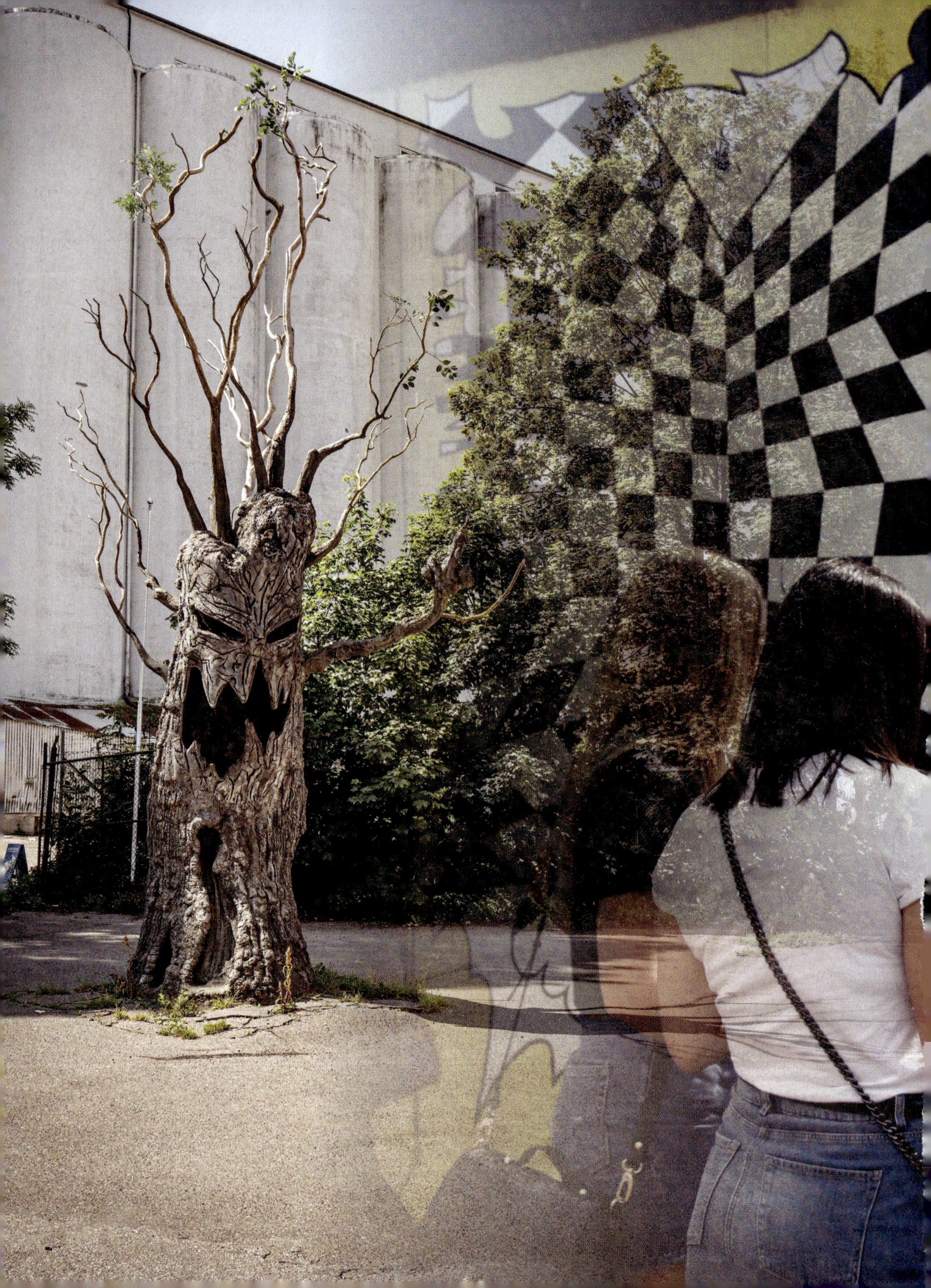